Megrahi

YOU ARE MY JURY

———

THE
LOCKERBIE
EVIDENCE

John Ashton is a writer, researcher and TV producer. He has studied the Lockerbie case for 18 years and from 2006 to 2009 was a researcher with Megrahi's legal team. His other books include *What Everyone in Britain Should Know about Crime and Punishment* (with David Wilson) and *What Everyone in Britain Should Know about the Police* (with David Wilson and Douglas Sharp), both published by Blackstone Press.

Megrahi

YOU ARE MY JURY

THE LOCKERBIE EVIDENCE

JOHN ASHTON

BIRLINN

First published in 2012 by
Birlinn Limited
West Newington House
10 Newington Road
Edinburgh
EH9 1QS

www.birlinn.co.uk

Reprinted in 2012

ISBN-13: 978 1 78027 015 9

British Library Cataloguing-in-Publication Data
A catalogue record for this book is available from the British
Library

Set in Sabon at Birlinn

Printed and bound in Great Britain by
Clays Ltd, St Ives PLC

Contents

List of plates   vi
Preface   vii
Acknowledgements   xi

1   The World's Most Wanted Man   1
2   Before the Nightmare   13
3   Pan Am 103   38
4   The Double Agent   59
5   The Shopkeeper   83
6   The Suitcase   104
7   The Fantasist   128
8   The Experts   143
9   Target Libya   174
10   HMP Zeist   196
11   Trial and Error   225
12   The Bar-L   272
13   The Truth Emerges   303
14   A Death Sentence   346
15   The Real Story of Lockerbie   366

Appendix 1   Gauci's Police Statements   379
Appendix 2   Primary Suitcase Forensic Evidence   395
Appendix 3   The Frankfurt Documents   412
Appendix 4   Justice Delayed   420
Afterword   427
Notes on the Text   437
Glossary and Abbreviations   472
People Mentioned in the Text   476
Index   479

Plates

The wrecked cockpit of Pan Am 103, *Maid of the Seas*

Luggage container from Pan Am 103

How the primary suitcase may have been loaded

Toshiba RT-SF16 radio-cassette player

Mock-up radio-cassette bomb

MST-13 timer

Circuit-board fragment PT/35B

PT/35B matched to control sample

Abdelbaset's student identity card

The photospread shown to Tony Gauci more than two years after Lockerbie

Telexes sent to and from Abdelbaset when with ABH

US government reward poster

Extracts from Tony Gauci's first statement to police

Edwin Bollier in the early 1970s

Extract from a CIA cable concerning Majid Giaka

Hafez Dalkamoni, leader of the PFLP-GC's West German cell

PFLP-GC bomb-maker Marwan Khreesat

Mohamed Abu Talb, the Swedish-based terrorist

Abdelbaset and John Ashton

Abdelbaset and Nelson Mandela

Inscription written by Mandela in Abdelbaset's copy of *Long Walk to Freedom*

Preface

'We all know he didn't do it.'

The words of one of the friendly prison officers who, every few weeks, would usher me into a tiny room at Greenock prison, where I would meet Britain's supposed worst mass murderer. We knew him as Baset; to the uninformed he was the Lockerbie Bomber.

A few minutes later I would hear a door unlock and the familiar quiet voice greet the officers with, 'Good morning gentlemen'. Then Baset would enter the room, shake my hand and sit down facing me across a small table. Invariably he would have with him a bundle of papers, the very same documents that, a few years earlier, had been used to convict him.

He had employed me as a researcher to work alongside the lawyers who were battling to overturn that conviction. He would take me through fine points of detail and I would update him on my work. He was demanding, but unfailingly polite, his frustration at his plight never sublimated into anger. He had scoured every last page. He felt he had no option. Why, after all, should he trust us when we were part of a justice system that had failed so catastrophically?

We were allowed two and a half hours together. Once we'd talked detail, the conversation usually turned to the injustice itself. The same questions always recurred. Why had certain witnesses changed their stories? How could the Crown justify withholding vital evidence? And, most importantly, how could three learned judges have reached such a perverse verdict? We had no answers.

When our time was up, Baset was escorted to his wing to resume prison life. Walking back to the railway station, it was almost impossible to imagine his daily reality. It was rather easier to daydream. I fantasised, childishly, about the day he would walk free from court and be reunited with his family. We had a strong case – the most spectacular appeal victory in memory was within our reach. And yet, after two years of visits, we were still having the same conversations and were still nowhere close to starting the appeal. The system had failed him again, this time through inertia, rather than misjudgement.

In September 2008 came the terrible news that Baset had aggressive and incurable cancer. The psychological pain which, for years, had consumed him now had a physical manifestation. Those who had called for the death penalty had got their way.

A couple of weeks later he asked to see me again. He told me he wanted to tell his story in a book and needed me to write it. He knew he would never live to see the conviction overturned, but he wanted the public to know he was innocent. I wanted to make a start immediately, but he was, understandably, too distracted by his plight to help me.

It was not until almost a year later that I got under way. By then his dream of freedom had finally been realised. In other ways, though, he remained trapped in a nightmare. Not only was he terminally ill, but in the eyes of the law, he remained guilty of one of the worst acts of terrorism ever committed. In order to secure his release he had abandoned his appeal against that guilty verdict. It was a terrible choice to have to make, as he never doubted that, if they considered the evidence objectively, the appeal judges would overturn the conviction. From the moment he made that decision, he was determined that, if he could not be judged in a court of law, then he should be judged in the court of public opinion.

I had to make numerous trips to Tripoli, where I visited him at his suburban home. Although now free, he was no less eager to set the record straight and ensure that I had every fact correct. Once again my visiting hours were restricted, not by prison rules this time, but by his pain and tiredness. Back among his beloved family, he no longer wore the strained look I had witnessed in Scotland, but our conversation was, nevertheless, punctuated by the savage symptoms of his illness.

The book tells two stories. The first is Abdelbaset's: of his life before 14 November 1991, when, out of the blue, he was charged with the bombing; and of the 20 years of suffering that he and his family have endured since then. The account is based on the numerous interviews that I conducted in Tripoli and on our informal prison conversations. With his agreement, I wove them together with his previous legal interviews to create a first-hand account, which appears in italics. It is by no means complete; in particular it contains little about his emotional state at key moments in the drama of the last two decades. He has always focused on facts rather than feelings, and, perhaps typically for his generation, he is not at ease with public expression of private emotion.

The second story is that of the bombing itself and the subsequent international investigation. It also recounts the evidence that would have been heard at Abdelbaset's appeal. It argues that Abdelbaset and the Libyan people suffered a grave injustice. The Gadafy regime was responsible for many appalling crimes, its brutal response to the February 2011 uprising only the latest. Lockerbie, however, was almost certainly not among them. There is no more reliable evidence of its involvement than there is of Saddam Hussein's involvement in the 9/11 attacks. No one will shed a tear that Gadafy was wrongly accused; what made this miscarriage of justice so uniquely appalling was that it was suffered by an entire nation. Libya endured 12 years of UN sanctions, predicated on paper-thin evidence, some of it concocted. By surrendering themselves for trial, Abdelbaset and his co-accused, Lamin Fhimah, removed the country from that headlock. Small wonder that each received a hero's welcome on his return to Tripoli.

Both stories are, at times, complicated and involve a large cast of players. To help readers navigate, I have provided a glossary and notes on some of the more important people and organisations at the back of the book (see pp. 472 and 476).

Abdelbaset insisted on checking the manuscript for accuracy, but gave me the final say on its contents. He did, however, demand that I make three things clear. The first was that he wished me to present the cases for both the prosecution and the defence, and report all the important available facts. Some of these facts are common knowledge, others have never been told before. Many of the latter concern his activities in the years before the bombing. While he swears that he is entirely innocent, he accepts that his account of those days may appear suspicious to some, especially those unfamiliar with the Libyan way of life at the time. On the advice of his lawyers, he opted not to give evidence at his trial, in part because it was clear that, in the hands of a skilful cross-examiner, some of the details could be made to appear damning. We could easily have avoided those subjects in this book, but it is important that readers know all the available facts, not only those that are most favourable to him. He provides explanations for them all and leaves it to you judge those explanations.

Secondly, he does not accuse anyone else of the bombing; all he knows is that neither he, nor Libya, was involved. As the book explains, the international investigation by the police and Western intelligence services initially suggested that other individuals, groups and nations were responsible. This information is included in order to provide you with a full picture; however, the case against those others may be as flawed as the one against him.

The past few years have seen the Western powers wage a disastrous 'War on Terror' in the Middle East and on the basis of false evidence. As the drums of war continue to roll, he is concerned that, even so long after Lockerbie, the old evidence will be resurrected and used as a pretext for new battles against the West's enemies. He therefore says, loud and clear, that he holds no other individual, group or nation responsible for the bombing, and Lockerbie should never become an excuse for further bloodshed.

Finally, we are both painfully aware that publication of this book will upset the many relatives of the Lockerbie dead who believe him to be guilty. They continue to have our utmost sympathy for their terrible loss.

Abdelbaset said to me many times, 'I understand that the public will judge me with their hearts, but I ask them to please also judge me with their heads.' To make that judgement, you need the facts. This book presents many that were previously hidden. Please consider them all – you are now his jury.

I'm often asked, 'What's he like?' I answer that he is a normal man who dealt with his appalling circumstances with remarkable patience and good grace. He is intelligent, a little shy, often humorous and quietly generous. His family and his Muslim faith are the twin pillars of his life and mean everything to him. For me, as for the prison officers, one characteristic stands out above all others – he is innocent.

Acknowledgements

Although this book bears my name, it draws heavily on the work of Abdelbaset's legal team, with whom I had the pleasure of working for three years: solicitors Tony Kelly, John Scott, Laura Morton and Jennifer Blair; advocates Maggie Scott QC, Jamie Gilchrist QC, Martin Richardson and Shelagh McCall; investigator George Thomson and research assistants Paul Scullion and Aileen Wright. Our expert witnesses, Dr Jess Cawley, Dr Roger King and Dr Chris McArdle, helped me get to grips with the forensic evidence by patiently answering my non-expert questions in plain English. Numerous other witnesses have been kind enough to speak to me, including many who searched the Lockerbie crash site. I'm also grateful to Gunther Latsch of *Der Spiegel* for helping me to unravel events in Germany.

My agent David Godwin took on the book in the knowledge that it would yield more headaches than revenue. Hugh Andrew at Birlinn recognised the story's importance and bravely opted to put principle before profit. His colleague Tom Johnstone then brought the book smoothly and skilfully to fruition, with the help of Andrew Simmons, Jan Rutherford and Jim Hutcheson. Susan Milligan provided sharp-eyed proofreading and Roger Smith produced a very thorough index.

My friends in Glasgow fed me, lent me their spare rooms and were wonderful company during my times in the city. My family has been constantly supportive of my unusual mission, especially Anja, without whose care and soothing words I would certainly now be grey.

My heartfelt thanks to you all.

Greatest thanks are due to my friend Abdelbaset for choosing me to tell his story. It's been an honour. Time will prove you innocent.

The World's Most Wanted Man   1

Alan Topp was the first person on the ground to know something was wrong. An air traffic controller based at Prestwick Airport, he was monitoring Pan Am flight PA103 as it cruised over the Scottish border at 31,000 feet. The Boeing 747 Clipper *Maid of the Seas* was about to head west over the North Atlantic on its way from London Heathrow to New York JFK. Everything seemed normal. Then, suddenly, the radar image on his screen fragmented and the altitude data disappeared. PA103 was no more.[1]

It was 19.03 on Wednesday 21 December 1988. He didn't yet know it, but Topp had witnessed Britain's worst ever aviation disaster. Within minutes, the flight's 259 passengers and crew were dead. Something had torn through the fuselage, opening the mighty aircraft like a tin can.

Until that night, the small Scottish border community of Lockerbie was unknown to most outsiders, but by morning it was known across the world. By a wretched twist of fate, much of the aircraft had fallen on the town. At Sherwood Crescent, close to the main A74 road, the fuel-laden wings had exploded, leaving a crater where houses once stood. Eleven residents were killed, bringing the death-toll to 270. A few hundred yards away, the Rosebank estate was hit by a large section of fuselage. Incredibly, no one was killed, but the locals faced the twin horrors of destroyed homes and a neighbour-hood that had become a charnel ground. Three miles to the east the aircraft's decapitated cockpit came to rest in a field, providing the tragedy with its defining image.

Twenty-one nationalities were among the dead. The great ma-jority were Americans returning home for Christmas, including US Army personnel stationed in West Germany and 35 Syracuse Univer-sity students who had been studying abroad.

Many of the victims' families learned of the disaster through the newsflashes that punctuated the Christmas TV schedules. As the terrible realisation dawned that their loved ones were on the flight, some congregated at Heathrow and JFK, desperately seeking news. Eventually it became clear there were no survivors, and they were left to cope with the searing pain of sudden bereavement.

The trauma was not confined to the relatives. Everyone who attended the scene was affected. For the police, military and civilians tasked with combing the scene for bodies it was especially distressing. One of the officers later recalled: 'They were in all sorts of states: some were intact, others weren't, a lot of them had their clothes completely ripped off them. I remember every single one of them, every single one. I mean most of us were family men and you're looking at all these kids – what on earth do you say to your kid when the plane's falling apart?'[2]

As dawn broke on 22 December, Lockerbie's full horror was revealed. Not since the Second World War had the UK witnessed such devastation. For miles east of the town the landscape was peppered with debris. The bodies were removed within a few days, but for weeks searchers came across shattering reminders of the human catastrophe.

Scattered among these Christmas presents, photographs and personal mementos lay clues to the disaster's cause. Within a week there were sufficient to sustain a shocking conclusion: PA103 had been downed, not by an accident or an act of God, but by callous and calculating humans intent on murder. It sparked the biggest criminal inquiry in UK history. By its end just one man had been convicted. The wrong man.

Plane crashes hold a particular terror for anyone who has worked in the airline industry; we all secretly fear that it will one day happen to us. Whenever I learned of one I felt a shudder of dread and my stomach knotted. Lockerbie was no different. I remember seeing the unearthly scenes from the crashsite and the raw grief of the newly bereaved. Their torment seemed unimaginable and, as with all decent people, my heart went out to them. As an airline man I also had great sympathy for the staff of Pan Am, who I knew would be deeply affected.

It was not until at least a day later that I learned of the disaster. As the horror was unfolding on the Scottish hillsides, I was at a family gathering to mark the birth of my niece a week earlier. It was the only landmark in an otherwise ordinary day. That morning I had flown back to Tripoli after an overnight stay in Malta and, as far as I recall, I then went to my office and spent the afternoon meeting the partners in my latest business venture.

Like most people, once the immediate shock of the disaster had faded, I didn't follow the story closely in the media. It was not until spring 1991 that I received the first inkling that my fate would be inextricably coupled to the bombing. Out of the blue, a Libyan Arab Airlines (LAA) colleague in Zurich called me at work. He said he was checking that I was there and would call back, which I thought odd. A few minutes later he rang back from a pay phone. He said the FBI and the Scottish and Swiss police had just paid him a visit and were asking questions about me. I asked why. He said they seemed to be investigating the Lockerbie attack and were interested in my background and my activities. He told them all he knew: that I was a normal, decent man who, when in Zurich, would buy presents for his wife and children. He advised me against travelling to Switzerland, but I said that, if the police wanted me, then I would go.

I called my relative Abdulla Senoussi, who had a senior position in the Libyan intelligence service, the JSO, to see if he knew what was going on. He didn't and he advised me not to travel until we had a clearer picture. I repeated that I was happy to speak to the Swiss police. He could have issued an order preventing me travelling, but he merely repeated his advice and promised to let me know if he learned anything more.

Not long afterwards I received a call from a Maltese man called Vincent Vassallo, who ran a travel agency in Malta with my former LAA colleague, Lamin Fhimah. He said he was trying to get hold of Lamin as the Scottish police and FBI had been to the office and were asking questions about us. They were especially interested in Lamin's desk diary for 1988. I called Lamin, who was as puzzled as I was. He was happy for Vassallo to hand over the diary and was prepared to go to Malta to answer questions, but he too was advised against it. I didn't give the matter too much thought over the coming months.

3

We were curious to know why the police were interested in us, but assumed they considered us as potential witnesses.

Nothing, then, could prepare us for the shock to come. On Thursday 14 November 1991, American and Scottish prosecutors simultaneously announced that they were charging us with the Lockerbie murders. I heard the news on the BBC's Arabic radio service. At first I assumed it was referring to some unknown namesakes, but, as the details were described, I realised with horror that we were the wanted men. In an instant I was plunged into a nightmare from which there seemed no escape. Amid the mental firestorm, all I could think was, 'Why us?' We were loving family men, who respected all human beings regardless of their nationality, religion or colour.

As I began to compose myself, it struck me that we had become pawns in the long-running power game waged against Libya by the US government. My next thought was that I did not want my family to hear the news, especially my wife Aisha, as she was five months pregnant with our third child. They had always believed me to be gentle and honest, but what if they thought I was guilty? The shame would be too much to bear.

On Thursdays, I used to go home early for my lunch and then in the afternoon drive around Tripoli with Aisha and our two small children.* Aisha would usually listen to a BBC music programme, but I was anxious because it was always followed by a news bulletin, so I persuaded her to listen to a Libyan station instead. She didn't comment, but I'm sure she noticed that I was behaving oddly.

On Fridays we always went to lunch either to my parents or hers. When Aisha said she wanted to go to hers, I pretended to be unwell and she agreed that I should stay at home.

The next day the story was being reported across the world. The time had come to break the news; if Aisha didn't hear it from me, she was bound to find out from others very soon. Naturally she was horrified, although she'd guessed by her family's rather strange behaviour at lunch that something was wrong. I swore to her that I was entirely innocent, but she knew very well that I was incapable of harming anyone. The news soon spread to my whole family. Everyone was

---

* In Muslim countries the weekend begins on Thursday.

4

shocked and upset, especially my mother. Thankfully, no one for a minute believed I was guilty – 'Anyone but Abdelbaset' was the universal refrain.

Lamin had been in Tunisia when the indictments were announced, and had not returned until the following day. His face was on every news bulletin and newspaper in the world, yet no move was made to arrest him. This was perhaps the first indication that some of our enemies had no desire for the accusations to be tested in court.

What, then, was the case against Abdelbaset Ali Mohmed al-Megrahi and Lamin Khalifa Fhimah? Under normal Scottish criminal procedure, it would not have been made public until the men reached court. But this was no ordinary case. The Scots and American prosecutors each set out the basis of the charges in detailed indictments, which were announced to the media at simultaneous press conferences in Edinburgh and Washington DC.

Both men were alleged to be undercover agents of the Libyan intelligence service the Jamahiriya Security Organisation (JSO). It was claimed that on the morning of 21 December 1988, the day of the Lockerbie bombing, they put an unaccompanied brown Samsonite suitcase containing an improvised explosive device (IED) on board Air Malta flight KM180 from Malta to Frankfurt. This so-called primary suitcase was tagged for New York on Pan Am flight PA103, causing it to be transferred at Frankfurt to Pan Am feeder flight PA103A to London Heathrow, and at Heathrow to Pan Am flight PA103.

The device incorporated an explosive, which Lamin was alleged to have stored at his office in Malta, where he had been the Station Manager for the state-owned Libyan Arab Airlines. It was built into a Toshiba RT-SF16 radio-cassette player, a large number of which had been bought by the General Electronics Company of Libya. More importantly, it was activated by an unusual timer, made by a Swiss company called Mebo, that was allegedly one of unique batch of 20 supplied exclusively to the JSO.

The two men were said to have packed the device into the suitcase along with clothes and an umbrella, which Abdelbaset had allegedly bought in Malta two weeks before the bombing, on 7 December 1988. They supposedly took the case to Malta on 20 December, with Abdelbaset travelling on a coded passport under the name of Ahmed Khalifa Abdusamad. The following morning he flew back to Libya on an LAA flight, which checked in shortly before KM180. It was alleged that, prior to departure, with the help of luggage tags illegally obtained from Air Malta, they were able to subvert the baggage system of Malta's Luqa Airport to get the suitcase onto KM180. They were alleged to have used a number of JSO front companies in the course of the conspiracy, most importantly ABH, which shared Mebo's premises in Zurich, and Medtours, the travel agency run by Lamin and his friend Vincent Vassallo in the Maltese town of Mosta.

Although no one else was charged, various other alleged JSO members were mentioned in the indictment. Among them were two good friends of Abdelbaset, Said Rashid (to whom he was also related) and Ezzadin Hinshiri, both of whom were fairly senior JSO officials, and who were said to have procured the timers from Mebo in 1985. Among the others were Badri Hassan, who was said to be ABH's man in Zurich, and another of Abdelbaset's acquaintances, Nassr Ashur. Shortly before the bombing, Hinshiri and Hassan had allegedly attempted to obtain 40 more of the timers from Mebo.

Taken at face value, the evidence against the two men appeared to be strong. Again, in a normal Scottish criminal case it would be closely guarded, but that was of no concern to the US government, who issued a summary of it in a 'fact sheet' accompanying their indictment. Even without the sheet, sufficient details of the evidence had been leaked out over the years to paint a fairly detailed picture of the prosecution case well before it was presented to the Court nine years later.

The first reported breakthrough was the discovery that a number of blast-damaged garments in the primary suitcase were made in Malta. Enquiries on the island linked the clothes to a small family-run shop in Sliema called Mary's House. Miraculously, the shopkeeper, Tony Gauci, remembered selling the clothes to an oddly-behaved man shortly before Lockerbie. Later to become the star witness against Abdelbaset, he said the mystery customer was Libyan and had little regard for the clothes' sizes.

The Malta link was confirmed by baggage records unearthed from Frankfurt Airport. These appeared to show that a suitcase from an

Air Malta Flight, KM180, had been transferred to the Frankfurt to Heathrow feeder flight, Pan Am 103A. There was no record of anyone having transferred from KM180 to flights PA103A and PA103, and none of the victims were known to own a brown Samsonite suitcase like the primary case. The police inferred from all this that the suitcase contained clothes from Mary's House, and was placed unaccompanied on KM180. They believed that it must have been labelled for automatic onward transfer at Frankfurt and had somehow evaded Pan Am's security checks prior to being loaded onto PA103A.

The third key plank of the case was a fragment of electronic circuit board, which a British forensic expert found embedded within a piece of blast-damaged shirt, of a type sold at Mary's House. In 1990 American investigators matched the fragment with a timer, known as an MST-13, which was eventually linked to the Swiss company Mebo. The company's co-owner, Edwin Bollier, said that the timers were designed and made to order for the Libyan intelligence service and that only 20 were produced, which he personally delivered to Libyan officials. He also told the police that the firm shared its offices with ABH. This company had been established by Badri Hassan and Abdelbaset was one of five partners, all of whom were Libyan. Bollier said that he had attended tests in the Libyan Desert, near the town of Sabha, in which the timers were used to detonate explosives. Then, in December 1988, Hassan had asked him to produce 40 more devices. His account appeared to be borne out by the fact that, a few months prior to Lockerbie, one of the timers was reportedly seized, along with explosives, from two Libyans who were attempting to enter the West African state of Senegal.

Abdelbaset was the common link between Bollier and Malta. He had left Malta on the morning of the disaster and had visited the island two weeks earlier, at approximately the time that Gauci said he sold the clothes. It was speculated that, as former Head of Security for LAA, he knew how to best get a bomb onto an aircraft undetected and, as LAA's Malta Station Chief, Lamin was ideally placed to help him.

In February 1991 the police appeared to have scored a bull's eye when Gauci picked out a photograph of Abdelbaset as resembling the clothes buyer. Three months later, with Lamin's consent, they obtained his Medtours diary. There were two suspicious entries for 15 December 1988. The first was preceded by an asterisk and read 'Take taggs from Air Malta.' The word 'taggs' [sic] was in English and the remainder in Arabic, and the letters 'OK' had been added at the end in a different coloured ink. The second entry, which was in Arabic, said 'Abdelbaset arriving from Zurich'. A further note at the back of the diary read 'Take/collect tags from the airport (Abdelbaset/Abdusalam)'. Again, the word 'tags' was written in English and the remainder in Arabic. The entries supposedly demonstrated that Lamin had obtained the Air Malta baggage tag required to smuggle the bomb onto KM180.

The case against the two men appeared to be sealed when a Maltese-based employee of Libyan Arab Airlines, Majid Giaka, told the FBI that, at around the time of the disaster, Abdelbaset had arrived in Malta with a brown hard-sided suitcase similar to the Samsonite one that contained the bomb, and that Lamin carried the case through Customs. He also said that Lamin had stored explosives in his office desk.

The media was briefed that Lockerbie was Libya's revenge for the US's 1986 air raids on Tripoli and Benghazi. There was no evidence to implicate any other country, the prosecutors made clear; this was 'a Libyan job from start to finish'.[3]

Under the 1971 Montreal Convention, those accused of aviation terrorism are entitled to be tried in their own country, but, having issued the indictments, the US and UK governments tore up the rule book, demanding that Libya hand the two men over for trial in Scotland or the US.[4] Incredibly, despite the charges being unproven, they also demanded that the country admit responsibility and pay compensation for the bombing. When the Libyan government refused to buckle, the two countries successfully sponsored two UN Security Council resolutions, 731 and 748, which echoed the demands.* Libya again refused, and in 1992 the UN announced sanctions against the country.

In March 1992 the Libyan government launched legal actions against the United States and UK at the UN's judicial body, the

---

* In November 1993 the Security Council passed a further resolution, number 883, which tightened the sanctions.

International Court of Justice, alleging a breach of the Convention. The application stated: 'Whereas Libya has repeatedly indicated that it is fulfilling its obligations under the Convention, the United States has made it clear that it is not interested in proceeding within the framework established by the Convention, but is rather intent on compelling the surrender of the accused in violation of the provisions of the Convention. Moreover, by refusing to furnish the details of its investigation to the competent authorities in Libya or to cooperate with them, the United States has also failed to afford the proper measure of assistance to Libya required by Article 11 (1) of the Montreal Convention.'[5]

Lamin and I, of course, denied that we had been involved in any way in the bombing. It was clear, however, that the Libyan authorities were not prepared to accept our denials. We were ordered to attend JSO's offices, where we were grilled for hours. Lamin faced tougher questioning than me because he had been based in Malta. They asked if we might have been duped into putting a bomb on an aircraft and we were adamant that we had not. Lamin had a relative in America who was known to be an opponent of the Libyan government, so I suspect that the JSO believed that we might have been put up to the bombing in order to cause trouble for Libya. Most of the questions were asked by a man called Abdusalam Zadma, who had a fearsome reputation in Libya. Lamin became very upset, which, to our great relief, eventually helped convince Zadma that we were innocent and should be released.

Nevertheless, a judge was appointed to investigate the case. He confiscated our passports, identity cards and driving licences and placed us under house arrest. We were ordered to report weekly to a police station and not to leave Tripoli without the Court's permission. The investigation got nowhere, because it proved impossible to obtain further details of the evidence from the Scottish and American authorities, but, despite my objections, the restrictions remained.

We were advised to take legal advice, so a few days later met with two well-known Tripoli lawyers, Dr Ibrahim Legwell and Kamal Maghour. It was decided that Legwell would represent me and Maghour, Lamin. We saw them a few times over the next week or so. There were never any government people at the meetings, but on one occasion Maghour introduced us to a British lawyer, who explained English, rather than Scottish, criminal law.

No Arabic translation of the indictment was available, so we had only a limited understanding of the charges. The lawyers set out what they saw as the key allegations: that the JSO had procured bomb timers from Mebo; that on 7 December 1988 I had bought the clothing in Malta; that we had travelled together to Malta the day before the bombing; that I had travelled under a false name; and that we had taken with us a brown Samsonite suitcase.

I told the lawyers the truth: Lamin and I did fly to Malta on 20 December and I travelled under a different name, but neither of us took a suitcase; I was connected to Mebo, via the company ABH, in which I was a partner, but I knew nothing about timers; I was in Malta from 7 to 9 December, but I didn't buy clothes there. Most importantly, we both made clear that we had nothing whatsoever to do with Lockerbie.

Twelve days after the indictments were issued, Legwell called to tell me that the government had requested that we do a TV interview with the American channel ABC. He explained that the American media had reported that we had been executed, and it was feared that the US government would believe Libya was trying to evade justice and might therefore attack the country, as it had in 1986. He said that the purpose of the interview was simply to demonstrate that we were still alive, but, to my horror, added that the TV crew would be arriving at my house at lunchtime. He reassured me that the interviewer, Pierre Salinger, knew our Foreign Minister, Ibrahim Bishari, and that the questions would focus on the impact of the indictments upon us and our families. He said that Lamin and I would be interviewed separately, and further reassured me that one of our legal representatives would be present, along with an interpreter. Just in case the interview strayed outside the agreed areas, he advised me strongly against discussing any of the specific allegations.

At 13.00 two government cars pulled up outside our house, each with an official driver. Salinger got out, along with a cameraman, a soundman and a producer. Accompanying them were Bishari's secretary and another Arab man, whose role was unclear to me, but there was no sign of a lawyer or interpreter. While the crew set up their equipment, Aisha and I organised refreshments. Bishari's secretary told me that Salinger was a good friend of the Minister and promised me that the interview would be very easy and would cover only family matters.

We made small talk while waiting for the lawyer and interpreter to arrive. Salinger asked if I was really a flight dispatcher for Libyan Arab Airlines. I told him I was and that I had a licence from the United States, which surprised him.

After half an hour neither the lawyer nor the interpreter had appeared. I asked Salinger if we could delay the interview, but he said he was working on a tight deadline and had another assignment to fulfil while in Libya. He reassured me that the interview wouldn't be challenging and said my English was good enough to cope without an interpreter. I agreed that the interview could go ahead, but remained concerned by the lawyer's absence.

Unfortunately Salinger failed to keep his promise and repeatedly asked me about the indictment. Had a lawyer been present, he could have intervened to stop the questions, but, with no one to guide me through the minefield, the interview was a disaster. I knew I should avoid discussing the allegations, but refusing to answer these direct questions would inevitably fuel suspicions that I had something to hide. However, if I told the truth, it was inevitable that the US government would reject my claims of innocence and seize upon the admissions that tallied with the allegations. Caught in the headlights, I did what I thought best, which was to lie.

His questions about my movements on 20 and 21 December 1988 were especially awkward, as I had not only used my Abdusamad coded passport, but had done so behind Aisha's back. Although she by then knew about the coded passport, she wasn't aware of all my travels and would have been upset by the deception. I flatly denied making the trip, claiming that I was at home in Tripoli, and said I'd never heard of Abdusamad. I also denied any connection to Mebo, although I told him truthfully that I knew nothing about timers. I admitted that I was in Malta from 7 to 9 December and asked Aisha to bring my passport so I could show him the entry and exit stamps. I couldn't recall why I'd been there, but was certain that I'd never bought clothes. On the *most important issue I also told the truth – I was innocent. I added that if British and American investigators wished to come to Libya I was prepared to answer their questions. Salinger subsequently became convinced I was innocent, but, by lying to him, I'd badly undermined my chances of proving that innocence in court. If I were ever to take the witness stand, the prosecution would make hay branding me a liar.*

In 1992 our lawyer Dr Legwell instructed Scottish lawyer Alastair Duff, of the Edinburgh firm McCourts. Shortly afterwards he was invited to Tripoli and we met him at Legwell's office. I asked him directly: 'If we went to Scotland to appear before the court there, would we receive a fair trial?' His answer was immediate and unequivocal: 'No.' In his view it would be impossible to find a jury which would not have been swayed by the media coverage of the case since the indictments, almost all of which assumed we were guilty. I greatly respected him for his honesty, as he could easily have given an answer that was good for his career and bank balance.

When, years later, we agreed to be tried by judges rather than a jury, Duff again warned us that we were unlikely to receive a fair trial. If only I had heeded his words.

Before the Nightmare 2

I was born on 1 April 1952 in Tripoli, the third of eight siblings. It was my father who chose my name. He worked for the Libyan Customs service and my mother looked after the home and supplemented the family income by sewing for neighbours. Libya at the time was a poor country, and for most people everyday life was a struggle. Until I was nine we shared our house with two other families. We then moved to our own house, which my father had built.

As a young child I was sick for several months with a chest infection and for two months had to endure twice daily injections. My school was supervised by the United Nations Educational Scientific and Cultural Organisation, UNESCO, which ensured that we received daily vitamin supplements.

After primary school I attended intermediate school for three years, followed by three years at secondary school. By the standards of the time, I had a fairly normal childhood and teenage years, and had the usual range of interests. My passion was football and, when we could afford it, I liked the cinema.

Like most people in Libya, I was brought up a faithful Muslim. Islam was, and remains, the binding force of our society; but, although we're a devout country, we have never been an extremist one. Sadly, that is a distinction that has been obscured by the hysterical rhetoric of the War on Terror. To me, and every Libyan I know, Islam is a religion of peace and charity, which can never be twisted to justify violence.

Shortly after finishing school in 1970, I read an advertisement by the Libyan Commercial Marine Organisation, which was recruiting students to study marine engineering in the UK. I applied and was one of 55 candidates accepted onto the five-year course at Rumney Technical College in Cardiff.

In truth marine engineering held no great appeal for me, as I really wanted to be a ship's captain or navigator. Unfortunately, I subsequently discovered that my eyesight was not good enough. My hopes dashed, I decided to abandon my course and return home.

Back in Libya I was torn between getting a job or going to university. My father had retired, leaving the family short of money, so I opted to find work. I answered an advert for the job of flight dispatcher with Libyan Arab Airlines. I was one of 12 of the 30 applicants who were accepted. A flight dispatcher is responsible for preparing a so-called flight plan for each flight, which contains details of the route, meteorological information, the time of entry to each country, the flight level, the arrival time and an alternative airport in case there are problems. The plan is given to the pilot and representative of the aviation authority at the airport of departure, each of whom have to sign and keep a copy.

Most of our training took place in Libya, but at one point we were sent to Pakistan to obtain a Flight Operations Officers Licence. This didn't go well, so we returned home and were subsequently sent to complete the training in the United States. I returned to the country twice for refresher courses in 1977 and 1981.

After four years in the job, I had risen through the ranks to become the airline's Chief Flight Dispatcher and then Controller of Operations at Tripoli Airport. I was next appointed Head of Training, but by then I had grown restless. I wanted to improve my education, so in 1975 I entered the University of Benghazi as an external student to study geography. I came top of my class every year, and on graduating in 1979 accepted an invitation to join the staff as a teaching assistant in climatology, on the promise that I would be sent to the United States to do a Master's Degree or a PhD in climatology. The Chairman of LAA at the time, Badri Hassan, wanted me to stay with the airline and said it could sponsor my studies in America, but the University was having none of it, so I had to resign from LAA.

Despite my obtaining an offer from the University of Pennsylvania, my own university's promise never materialised, as various academics had persuaded the government that there was no need to send students abroad to study. It was a ridiculous notion, especially in relation to my chosen field, which was reliant upon comprehensive meteorological records of the kind that were simply not available in Libya. There was no point holding on to a dead-end academic job, which paid less than half of what I was earning when I left LAA. Disillusioned, I resigned at the end of 1979 and returned to work for the airline. I was immediately sent to Toulouse in France to attend a course organised by the Airbus company, as LAA had recently signed contracts to purchase a number of Airbus aircraft.

As I approached my 30th birthday, I knew it was time to think about marriage and settling down into family life. My parents and older sisters suggested that I should consider a girl called Aisha, one of ten siblings from a neighbouring family who had lived in our area of Bab Akarah for a long time. I was attracted by the fact that her parents were modest, yet highly respected among local people. Her father Al Haj Ali was a medical assistant in a local hospital and her mother Salma was the head of a primary school.

My eldest sister Zeinab took the lead, and along with other family members visited Aisha's family to discuss the matter. The discussions went well, and after a few weeks the engagement was completed. At this point I had still not set eyes on my bride-to-be. Western readers might find this strange, but the arrangement was in accordance with Libyan community and family traditions. In contrast to Western convention, an engagement marks the beginning rather than the end of the courtship process, and allows a couple to get to know each other and establish whether they are compatible.

I met Aisha for the first time shortly after the engagement was agreed. We chatted and got on well. I visited her a few more times, and eventually it was decided that we should go ahead and get married. We tied the knot on 18 March 1982, around nine months after our first meeting.

Our first home was a flat on the fourth floor of an apartment block in the Bab Bengashir area of Tripoli. In 1983 we were blessed with the birth of our first child, a baby girl, who, at my mother's suggestion, we called Ghada. She was followed three years later by our first son, Khaled, whose name I chose. We were very happy, but the flat wasn't suitable for raising a family, as it was fairly small *and the lift was usually out of order. I could see the physical and psychological toll that it was taking on Aisha and I feared for the children's health. We decided that the best and most affordable solution was to build our own house. I bought a plot of land in Ben Ashour from the Tripoli municipal authority and took out a bank loan to pay for the construction, but progress was to be painfully slow.*

By the time I returned to LAA after working at the University of Benghazi, Badri Hassan had been ousted as Chairman of LAA as he had been caught receiving illegal commission payments. He was subsequently convicted, and for a few years was forbidden to leave Libya. His replacement, Captain Ali Hannushi, created a lot of petty problems for me. The Minister of Transport didn't like him and wanted to get rid of him, so decreed that the airline should be run by a committee, rather than a chairman. Six or seven people were selected to serve on the committee, four of whom were from within LAA and the others from outside, including a military man who was appointed as Chair. When I was subsequently promoted by LAA to the position of Tripoli Station Manager, I became one of the four LAA representatives.

It was during this period that I first got to know Lamin Fhimah. He had joined LAA in 1975, three years after me, and, like me, was originally trained as a flight dispatcher and based at Tripoli Airport. He was later selected to work in operations control at LAA's head office and was appointed Malta Station Manager in 1982. In 1984, Aisha and I stopped over on the island for a few hours on our way back to Tripoli. On learning of our arrival, Lamin invited us to lunch with his family. Until that day I had never got to know him socially. His family were very welcoming and kind. When his wife learned that we had had a daughter a few months earlier, she gave Aisha as a gift a small bag for carrying baby items.

After that I would make a point of seeing Lamin whenever I travelled through Malta. We would often go shopping together, as he knew the best places to buy essentials and gifts that I wanted for my family. We were never close friends and didn't socialise much together, but he was a nice man and good at his job. After the indict-

ments were issued against us, one newspaper quoted an anonymous source who claimed he was a religious fanatic committed to destroying America.[1] This was a total fabrication. Lamin loved life in Malta and the Western-style freedoms on offer there, including the chance to drink. He was popular and considerate, in short the last person who would commit mass murder in the name of Islam, or any other cause.

In 1985, after I had served on LAA's committee for around two-and-a-half years, the Minister decided to reinstate Captain Hannushi and disband the committee. Although I continued to receive a salary I was, effectively, out of a job.

At that time LAA's security was provided by the JSO. It was JSO personnel who searched passengers and travelled on flights to prevent hijackings, which were quite common at that time. Relations between the regular airline staff and the security people were often strained, especially over the issue of firearms on aircraft. The JSO routinely carried their guns on flights and made it quite clear that they would use them against hijackers. The crews were very concerned, as a misplaced bullet could easily endanger the whole plane. In order to resolve such conflicts it was decided that the security officers should become full-time LAA employees. It was expected that the change-over would take around a year to enact. To accelerate the process, Abdullah Senoussi, who was then a departmental head in the JSO, and my friend Said Rashid, who was one of his deputies, asked if I would help to train the JSO staff who were to be transferred in all the relevant aspects of the airline's operations. I agreed, and soon after was appointed LAA's Head of Airline Security for the transition period. I remained in the position from the start of 1986 until the end of November that year. Officially I was on secondment to the JSO, but my salary continued to be paid by LAA.

In addition to the training, my primary responsibility was to ensure the safety of all flights and passengers. Ironically, given the false accusations that were later made against me, I had to keep abreast of warnings about potential terrorist threats, which I received from the JSO and the International Air Transport Association (IATA). I remember in particular receiving warnings about the

17

Lebanese Shia faction Amal, which at one point was alleged to be threatening Libya.*

At a more mundane level, I was also required to resolve any residual conflicts between security staff and flight crews. The crews liked to deal with me because they viewed me as one of their own, but the ex-JSO people were mistrustful, considering me to be an airline man with little understanding of intelligence and security matters.

During my tenure as Head of Security, it was decided that every LAA Assistant Station Manager would be chosen from among the former JSO employees. All were required to submit security reports to me. Among them was Lamin's Deputy, Majid Giaka, whose name would return to haunt me. It was agreed with the JSO that LAA would continue to pay the Assistant Station Managers' salaries and would recover the money from the JSO. I was different, however, as officially I was an LAA staff member who was on secondment to the JSO. I continued to receive my salary from LAA and was never paid by the JSO. It was the only time I ever worked for the JSO, yet the US and Scottish prosecutors branded me a senior intelligence agent, a claim slavishly parroted by the world's media ever since.

My interim post finished at the end of 1986. In January 1987 I was again co-opted by Abdullah Senoussi, this time to become the coordinator of the Centre for Strategic Studies in Tripoli. The Centre, which was the brainchild of the former Foreign Minister and JSO chief, Ibrahim Bishari, was intended to ensure that the government was better informed about world events. It was one of six centres in Libya operating on similar lines, the others being for African studies, Libyan history, oil studies, industrial research and marine biology.

There was no money in the Foreign Ministry budget to establish the Centre, so funding was found from the JSO's. Senoussi oversaw its creation and maintained a close interest in its work; however, it was not, as some have portrayed it, a sinister wing of the JSO. Its annual budget was only the equivalent of around £30,000, some

* Amal was the armed wing of the Lebanese Movement of the Disinherited, which was founded by Imam Moussa al-Sadr in 1974. Four years later al-Sadr disappeared while visiting Libya. It's widely believed that he was killed on Gadafy's orders, which probably accounts for Amal's hostility towards Libya.

of which came from other government departments. It was never headed by a military or JSO officer – indeed, only three employees belonged to the JSO: an administrative and financial supervisor, a typist and a driver.

More importantly, its work was straightforwardly academic; its research was based almost entirely on publicly available sources and its reports were distributed to all its sponsoring departments. With one exception, the research studies were wholly unrelated to security or intelligence matters. Subject areas ranged from water resources in Africa, to strategies for developing the desert region, and the economy of the Soviet Union. The exception was a study of Islamic fundamentalism among young people in Libya. There had been an upsurge of the phenomenon resulting in some violent disturbances, which had generated serious security concerns. The Centre was called upon to help the JSO, and the government as a whole, to understand the problem. I met with some of the professors to discuss how they might best research the issue. It was agreed that we should gather as much international literature as possible on the subject. They also wanted to interview fundamentalists who had been jailed following the disturbances, but permission was refused, probably because the JSO didn't trust the Centre to do its spying.

The Centre was not at all secretive. Academics would come and go freely, and on one occasion a French TV company, Channel 5, filmed the outside of the building for a feature on the Paris to Dakar car rally, the Libyan stage of which I was involved in organising. This would never have been allowed at a JSO facility. I often met friends there and held business meetings unconnected with my job as coordinator, as it had fairly advanced facilities by Libyan standards, such as telex machines and reliable phone lines. I enjoyed working with the professors and found the academic atmosphere very stimulating. I was able to put to use the organisational skills that I'd learned at LAA. My proudest achievement was organising the construction of an extra storey for the building, which meant the professors no longer had to share rooms.

Given the Centre's very limited budget, it was decided that my salary should continue to be paid by LAA, so officially I was only ever on secondment from the airline. I knew there was a good chance

19

that I would one day return to LAA and therefore took care to maintain my flight dispatcher's licence. This required me every six months to undertake a so-called route check, which involved flying with LAA as a dispatcher.

In truth, my job at the Centre was rarely taxing and was effectively only part-time. It meant I had plenty of time for other, more lucrative ventures. In 1986 my former LAA boss Badri Hassan told me that he had established a Liechtenstein-registered business in Zurich called ABH, which was acting as a mediator in the sale of an ex-LAA aircraft to a Swiss company. He chose the name ABH after the initials of his son Ali Badri Hassan, although the company letterhead said Aviation Business Holding Company. He explained that there was considerable commercial potential in supplying equipment and replacement parts to LAA and other state enterprises. Libya was subject to strict US sanctions, which banned the sale of many industrial and technical goods. Since many of its aircraft were made by the American company Boeing, the impact on the airline was especially severe. The only way in which LAA and government departments could source such equipment was via third parties, which were often small companies. As these firms were uneasy about dealing directly with Libyan state bodies, the government slightly eased its tight restrictions on private enterprise, enabling Libyan entrepreneurs to make deals on behalf of LAA and other organisations affected by the sanctions. Hassan asked me if I'd like to become a partner in ABH. I agreed, and thus began my career as a sanctions-buster.

While the work might have been out of the ordinary, there was nothing unusual in me combining my work for the Centre with business activities. Many state employees became small-time entrepreneurs in order to supplement their meagre wages. The government generally tolerated this moonlighting, especially after the tightening of sanctions in 1986.

Soon after taking up Hassan's offer we were joined by one of my friends, Mohamed Dazza. Hassan suggested bringing in two other people: Nun Seraj, his former LAA secretary, and Abdelmajid Arebi, who was commercial manager of African Airlines, for which Hassan was an advisor. Hassan told me that he had earned $70,000 from the aircraft deal and that this would serve as working capital for the

*company. I opened an account at the Zurich Airport branch of the
Credit Suisse bank, for which I needed only my passport and $100.
I didn't have to invest any more of my own money, as Hassan was
instead relying on my experience in the aviation world and my good
relationships with a number of state organisations, in particular LAA
and the Civil Aviation Department.*

*There can be no doubt that my connection to such organisations
was one of the reasons that I became a target of the police investigation. I could easily have lied and denied any close connection to
state bodies and to the JSO officials named in the indictment, such
as Abdullah Senoussi, Said Rashid* and Ezzadin Hinshiri, but it's
important that readers know the truth. They are all known to many
other entirely innocent people. Libya's professional class is small and
its members often have a number of diverse jobs over the course of
their careers, so intermingle professionally and socially more than
they might in a larger country.*

*Unfortunately, my contacts within government departments
were not sufficient to guarantee ABH's success. The $70,000 injec-
tion proved to be insufficient seed funding. We realised that, if the
company was to develop as we hoped, we required a commercial
loan. We knew this would be very difficult if ABH was perceived
to be Hassan's company, as his corruption conviction was common
knowledge in Libya. I offered to approach a personal acquaintance
who was the head of one of the country's commercial banks. As the
application was to be in my name, it was decided to assign 90 per*

---

* Sennousi was reputedly one of the most feared members of the Libyan
government. In June 2011 the International Criminal Court indicted him
for war crimes, along with Gadafy and Gadafy's son Saif al-Islam, over alleged armed attacks on civilians in anti-Gadafy regions of Libya. He was
captured in November 2011. In 2001 a French court convicted him *in absentia* for the 1989 bombing of a UTA passenger plane over Niger, which
killed 170 people. He denied involvement in the attack.

Rashid was wanted in Italy for the alleged assassination of a Libyan exile in 1983. He was arrested in France, but freed, supposedly because the
Italian arrest warrant did not arrive in time. An Italian court subsequently
convicted him *in absentia*. He was also the alleged mastermind of the 1986
La Belle disco bomb attack in Berlin (which is discussed in Chapter 9). He
denied the allegations.

cent of the company's shares to me as a default guarantee and to divide the remaining 10 per cent between the other partners. I only subsequently discovered that the bank required me to put up my property as security. Since my house was still under construction and was fully mortgaged, this was a non-starter. Without the loan we were heavily reliant upon our personal efforts and connections within Libyan companies and public authorities. I retained my 90 per cent stake in the company, but we agreed to split the profits equally between us.

Hassan had rented office space for ABH in Zurich from the small electronics company Mebo, which did a lot of business with Libyan state bodies. He agreed to use our connections to help the company's owners, Erwin Meister and Edwin Bollier, to retrieve substantial sums they were owed by some of these organisations. In return ABH would receive a percentage of the recovered debt and an opportunity to participate in some of Mebo's business activities. A memorandum was prepared to this effect, but our failure to secure a loan meant it remained unsigned.

In the event we only did two deals with Mebo, both of whch were in 1987. One was for a satellite receiver, for use by the JSO, and the other for 50 field communication radios required for military and civil aviation purposes. ABH's many other commercial activities were wholly unconnected to the Swiss firm, and I conducted almost all of my ABH business a thousand miles away from Zurich in my office at the Centre for Strategic Studies.

Initially most of ABH's business was within the aviation sector. Many of the deals were for spare parts, but, among other things, we organised the retreading of 600 LAA aircraft tyres by a Swiss company, and the servicing of aircraft engines in Ethiopia. Some deals did not breach US sanctions: for example, we arranged for LAA pilots to be trained in Switzerland using a flight simulator belonging to the national airline Swissair. At one point we tried to obtain a Fokker 27 aircraft from a Canadian company, Aero Leasing and Sales, whose boss, Victor Pappalardo, we met at the Savoy Hotel in Zurich. *

---

* In 1996 Pappalardo was charged with 35 counts of illegally exporting goods to Libya and 26 of making false or deceptive claims under the Canada Customs Act.

Given that Libya was then the US and UK governments' public enemy number one, the frequent foreign travel was potentially risky for me, but more so for our US suppliers, some of whom faced long prison terms if caught.

My numerous absences created difficulties at home. Like most Libyan marriages at the time, ours was very traditional. Aisha's life was focused on the home and family, and she rarely questioned me about my work. Nevertheless, she was understandably unhappy about my frequent foreign trips and would often become very upset on learning that one was imminent. I therefore fell into the habit, on the shorter trips, of telling her that I was visiting people elsewhere in Libya. I disliked deceiving her in this way, but neither did I wish to see her upset, so I considered it the lesser of two evils. At the time the Libyan telephone system was fairly poor and no one had mobile phones, so, even if she wanted to, it would have been difficult to check up on me.

The Libyan government had by then introduced a policy of issuing those involved in the importation of embargoed goods with so-called coded passports, which concealed their real names and their connections to state bodies. These passports were in no sense forgeries, but were rather official documents issued by the Secretary of Transport and tightly regulated.

In autumn 1987 I was due to travel to Nigeria to finalise a deal for aircraft spares. A senior Nigerian official had indicated that he could broker a deal for Airbus spares via British and American contacts. Although Airbus was a European company, many of the components were American, so the suppliers would be breaching US sanctions. The Nigerian said he was concerned that they would get cold feet if they knew I worked for LAA and therefore suggested that I conceal my connection to the airline. Since my regular passport stated that I was a flight dispatcher, anyone studying it might have correctly inferred my connection to LAA. I approached Hinshiri, who then had a senior position within the JSO, to ask if he could instruct the immigration department to provide me with a coded passport. He agreed and the department duly issued one in the name of Ahmed Khalifa Abdusamad, and recorded my occupation only as 'Employee'. In the event the deal did not go ahead, as I didn't trust the Nigerian, but I

23

was allowed to retain the passport, in case similar situations arose in future. A further advantage was that it enabled me to leave my normal passport at home, which made it easier to travel abroad without Aisha knowing.

ABH soon branched out from aviation. In 1987 we imported a million disposable cigarette lighters from South Korea, and at the end of the year we travelled to Brazil, Argentina and Uruguay with representatives of the Libyan Arab Foreign Investment Company, Lafico, in an effort to source supplies of meat. In 1988 we purchased Audi and Opel cars, uniforms and other equipment for the Libyan police. One of the companies that offered to supply these items was a West German firm called Chemical Marketing. It is possible that this gave rise to the claim, which appeared in a US State Department 'fact sheet' handed out to the press the day after we were indicted for the Lockerbie bombing, that 'An Al Megrahi subordinate operating in Germany in 1988 played an important role in acquiring and shipping chemical weapons precursors to Libya.'[2]* *If this had been so, the CIA would perhaps have difficulty explaining the numerous telexes that we received from a company executive named Trinckert. A typical example, dated 27 January 1988, read:*

'ACC[ORDING] TO YOUR INQUIRY FOR OPEL ASCO-
NA, 4-DOOR, LS, 1,6 L EURONORM MOTOR, 55 KW
(88E) (75 HP) NORMAL STANDARD.
WE CAN OFFER TO YOU AS FOLLOWS:

ASCONA , 4-DOORS, LS
COLOUR GREEN AND WHITE
WITH ANTENNA
RED LIGHT ON THE TOP
POLICE SIGNAL
CANDF TRIPOLI DM 21.675,--
DELIVERY TIME: PART SHIPMENT 3 WEEKS AFTER

---

* This story was rehashed by the *Sunday Times* newspaper on 29 November 2009. The paper failed to acknowledge that its scoop not only lacked hard evidential support, but was also based on an 18-year-old press release.

RECEIVING THE LETTER OF CREDIT

WE HOPE TO HEAR FROM YOU SOON'[3]

Chemical Marketing also provided quotes for the supply of washing machine powder, and tallow and coconut oil for use in soap, as at one stage we were looking to broker a contract with the Libyan National Soap Company.[4] The deal never came off, as we found the soap company very difficult to deal with. If 'Opel Ascona', 'machine powder' and 'coconut' were merely our code for chemical weapons precursor chemicals, then Trinckert would surely have been arrested and his firm closed down.

In late 1988, when I was supposedly using ABH as cover for the bomb plot, the company was in fact finalising the police equipment deal. It was also negotiating with a Swiss aviation company for the supply of aerial crop-spraying equipment and pilot and engineer training programmes, and was looking to purchase satellite TV equipment from a Swiss electronics firm.[5]

If ABH had been a JSO front company, we wouldn't have needed to fight for government contracts. Although at times we did quite well, in the case of the soap contract and other ventures we lost out because we didn't know the right people in the relevant departments. On other occasions we fell victim to changes in Government policy; for example, we were hoping to broker a deal with a Brazilian company to build and supply schools in Libya, but when negotiations had reached an advanced stage we were told by the Libyan authorities that we should only deal with European firms.

As time passed, the other partners and I suspected that Hassan was concealing financial information from us. It was clear that ABH was not doing well and, following meetings in November and early December 1988, we decided to order him to liquidate the company. At that point my involvement with ABH came to an end.

By then I was immersed in a new business venture with my ABH colleagues Mohamed Dazza and Abdelmajid Arebi. We had secured the rights to run the Libyan leg of the following year's Paris to Dakar car rally, which involved organising accommodation, fuel and other services to the competitors and their backup teams. Since it was one of the very few globally prestigious events to involve Libya, it was being overseen by the Ministry of Justice, which added to the already considerable pressure we were under.

Arebi had by then begun his own venture, a Prague-based travel agency called Al-Khadra. According to the indictment, both it and Lamin's travel agency, Medtours, were merely fronts for the JSO, but, like almost everything else in the indictment, this was total nonsense. Arebi established the company purely because he identified a gap in a potentially lucrative market. In those days many Libyans travelled to Czechoslovakia for medical treatment and to buy consumer goods, which by our standards were relatively plentiful there. Although the official exchange rate was not especially favourable, it was easy to get much better rates on the black market. Travel arrangements were overseen by the Libyan Embassy* in Prague, which had previously used a Kuwaiti travel agency. Arebi knew that he could offer a cheaper service, better tailored to Libyans' requirements, especially to those travelling for medical reasons. He approached the Ambassador, who said he'd be happy to put business his way. So too did the head of the Embassy's military procurement section, which separately organised travel and medical care for military personnel, many of whom were veterans of Libya's war with Chad.

At the time foreigners could only establish businesses in Czechoslovakia as branches of foreign companies. Arebi therefore asked Lamin if he could use the Medtours name in return for a commission. Lamin agreed, and Arebi had a shop sign and stationery printed in the name of Al-Khadra Medtours. The law then changed, allowing foreigners to set up companies in partnership with Czech citizens, so he dropped the Medtours partnership and set up the company with his Czech secretary.[6]

Although I had only known Arebi since 1986, I considered him a close friend, and in October 1988 I decided to pay him a visit in Prague. I had a good time there, as he was great company and laid on lots of entertainment. The city's hotels were quite expensive, but the Embassy could obtain substantial discounts, so through him I was able to get the military procurement section to book me a room at

---

* Embassies were known formally as People's Bureaux, as they existed primarily to assist Libyans abroad, rather than for diplomatic purposes.

the Intercontinental. The Scottish and US prosecutors viewed this as evidence that I was in Prague on government business, but the truth is that it was commonplace for Libyan tourists to use their connections in this way and I settled the bill privately. While I was in Prague, Arebi asked me if I could loan him $50,000 to help get his company off the ground, offering me a partnership in the business in return. I thought better of becoming a partner, but on leaving Prague I immediately transferred the money from my Credit Suisse account during a stopover in Zurich Airport. While the police may have viewed this as sinister, helping out friends in this way is normal in my culture.

The following day I flew to Belgrade to see a doctor who'd been recommended by an acquaintance who worked for the Yugoslavian state airline JAT. My two-year-old son Khaled had a medical problem which we thought might require surgery and I wanted the doctor's advice. He reassured me that the problem was not urgent, and that we should wait a further year before considering surgery. He said that, in the meantime, we might be able to solve the problem with a particular type of medication. As far as I recall, while I was in the city I arranged to meet up with another good friend, Mohamed Ben Rabha, who was LAA Station Manager in Sofia. After an enjoyable three-day stay, I returned to Tripoli on 22 October.

Apart from my job and my business ventures, my major preoccupation at the time was our new family home. Almost three years had passed since work had commenced, but the house was yet to be completed. Libya had been subject to sanctions since 1981, which tightened considerably following the US air raids on the country in April 1986. As a consequence, building materials and interior fittings were hard to come by, and I often had to source them outside Libya. In early December I decided to return to Czechoslovakia, primarily for this purpose. We particularly wanted some crystal chandeliers, and knew there was little chance of finding them for a reasonable price in Tripoli. In the run-up to Christmas consumer goods were relatively plentiful in Eastern Bloc countries and a fair selection of chandeliers was available in Prague. Apart from the shopping, I looked forward to another chance to sample the city's manifold attractions.

I booked to fly from Tripoli to Malta on 7 December and planned to travel on to Prague, via Zurich, the following day. It was one of two trips to Malta in December that became central to the case against me. On 7 December, I supposedly bought the clothes from Tony Gauci at his Mary's House shop, and on the second, between 20 and 21 December, Lamin and I allegedly prepared and executed the bombing. As later chapters explain, both visits were entirely innocent.

As I jetted around Europe I was unaware that elsewhere events were unfolding that many believe were a prelude to Lockerbie. The remainder of this chapter describes those events. I had no idea about any of them until I was indicted for the bombing, and it was not until my trial that I became aware of much of the detail. The facts and allegations were all uncovered by the international investigation. I have made it clear that I do not wish to blame anyone for the bombing. The information is set out here simply to give readers a full picture of the investigation.

For the Western intelligence services in late 1988, the news that a terrorist attack was imminent came as no surprise. The writing had been on the wall since 3 July 1988, when an aviation catastrophe equal to Lockerbie briefly stunned the world. The cursed flight was Iran Air flight 655 from Bandar Abbas to Dubai, which was shot down over the Persian Gulf by an American battle cruiser, the USS *Vincennes*. A total of 290 people were killed, most of whom were travelling to Mecca on the annual Hajj pilgrimage.

The Pentagon immediately shrouded the massacre in a fog of disinformation. It claimed that the *Vincennes* had believed itself to be under attack from an Iranian F-14 jet fighter descending rapidly towards it, and in the short time before the attack had issued ten radio warnings, but received no response. Vice-President George Bush Snr later claimed that the ship had gone to the aid of a neutral vessel and was under attack from an Iranian gunboat.

It eventually emerged that the airliner had not been descending, but was, in fact, still climbing after take-off. Seven of the ten messages were broadcast on a frequency that was unavailable to civilian aircraft, and the other three were unlikely to have been received. A message might well have got through from a neighbouring US Navy frigate, the *Sides*, but this was sent just 39 seconds before the attack. The Commander of the *Sides*, David Carlson, was so perturbed by

28

the affair that he undertook his own investigation. By interviewing members of the *Vincennes*'s crew and studying its data tapes and video footage shot by a TV crew, who happened to be on board at the time of the attack, he eventually discovered that the gunboat did not initiate the attack, but merely returned fire after the *Vincennes* attacked it. In 1992 the former Chair of the Joint Chiefs of Staff, Admiral William Crowe, admitted that, at the time of the incident, the ship had illegally entered Iranian territorial waters. Carlson established that it had chased the gunboat inside the waters and continued to fire. Small wonder that the *Vincennes* was known to Carlson and other commanders by the nickname 'Robo Cruiser'.[7]

US President Ronald Reagan offered neither apology nor compensation for the mistake and, in a staggering act of insensitivity, the *Vincennes*'s entire crew received the Combat Action Ribbon. In 1990 the ship's Commander, William Rogers, received the Legion of Merit decoration from George Bush Snr, who was by then President. The citation said the reward was for 'exceptionally meritorious conduct in the performance of outstanding service as commanding officer'.[8]

The Iranian government was, unsurprisingly, enraged by the slaughter. State radio warned that the deaths would be avenged 'in blood-spattered skies' and President Ali Khamenei promised that the country would employ 'all our might . . . wherever and whenever we decide'.[9]

The threats were taken very seriously. Two days after the shoot-down, the US Air Force's Military Airlift Command warned its civilian contractors, 'We believe Iran will strike back in a tit for tat fashion – mass casualties for mass casualties . . . We believe Europe is a likely target for a retaliatory attack. This is due primarily to the large concentration of Americans and the established terrorist infrastructures in place throughout Europe.'[10] Within a couple of days the US State Department disseminated the warning to its own staff.

Later in July, the West German foreign intelligence service, the Bundesnachrichtendienst (BND), passed on a number of more specific warnings to the country's Federal Police, the Bundeskriminalamt (BKA). They concerned a radical Palestinian splinter group, the Popular Front for the Liberation of Palestine – General Command (PFLP-GC), which was suspected to be planning attacks in the country. The group was formed in 1968 by Ahmed Jibril, who broke away from the Popular Front for the Liberation of Palestine (PFLP), which had been created the previous year by George Habbash. While Habbash's group was the larger and better-known of the two, Jibril's was the more violent. In 1974 both factions withdrew from the Palestine Liberation Organisation's executive committee following the Arab League Summit in Rabat. Together with a number of smaller groups, they formed an alternative coalition known as the Rejection Front, which in April 1987 was re-formed as the Salvation Front.

Based in the Syrian capital Damascus, the PFLP-GC was closely connected to the country's intelligence services. It also developed close ties to Iran following the Revolution of 1979. During the 1970s it was among a number of Palestinian groups that trained Iranian radicals who were later at the forefront of the Revolution. The group subsequently built a strong relationship with the Iranian Revolutionary Guards and their Lebanese Shi'ite proxies Hezbollah, who were especially active in the Syrian-controlled Bekaa Valley. It also received financial support from Libya in the 1980s.*

The BND was probably warned about the PFLP-GC by the Israeli intelligence service, Mossad, as one of the warnings suggested it might target Israeli football and handball teams that were touring West Germany. Another claimed that 'a joint commando' of the PFLP-GC and Hezbollah could be about to attack American installations in West Germany.[11] In fact the PFLP-GC had already launched bomb attacks against American targets in West Germany in August 1987 and April 1988. Remarkably, on both occasions the group had targeted US military trains as they passed close to the town of Hedemünden. No one was killed in either blast.

The group's West German cell was led by Hafez Kassem Dalkamoni, a 43-year-old Palestinian, who in 1969 lost part of his right leg during a botched bomb attack on an Israeli power line. In January 1988 he moved to the town of Neuss near Düsseldorf, where he stayed in a flat at 16 Isarstrasse owned and occupied by his brother-in-law, Hashem Abassi, who ran a nearby greengrocery.

* It has variously been reported that Libya's support ended after the US air raids on Libya in 1986 and in 1989, when Colonel Gadafy publicly renounced terrorism.

When, six months later, Iran was looking to avenge the downing of Flight 655, its trusted friend the PFLP-GC was the obvious choice to do its dirty work. Not only did it have a well-developed European infrastructure, but, more importantly, it also had a specific expertise in targeting civilian aircraft. In February 1970 it successfully smuggled a bomb on board a Swissair flight from Zurich to Tel Aviv. The device, which was thought to have been built into a transistor radio, exploded when the plane reached 14,000 feet. The resulting crash killed all 47 on board. On the same day the group also targeted an Austria Airlines flight from Frankfurt to Vienna. The bomb detonated at 10,000 feet, blowing a hole in the fuselage, but this time the pilot was able to navigate safely back to Frankfurt. Investigators established that the device was in a mailbag that was due to be transferred to a flight to Israel, and that it too was housed within a transistor radio. Two years later the group struck again, this time targeting an El Al flight from Rome to Tel Aviv. The explosion occurred at 15,000 feet, but again the pilot was able to land safely at the originating airport without any casualties. It was discovered that the bomb had been built into a record player, which had been given to two unwitting British women by an Arab man who had befriended them in Rome.

All of the bombs were thought to have used barometric switches, which were activated by the drop in pressure in the baggage holds as the aircraft gained altitude. They were believed to be the handiwork of a young Jordanian PFLP-GC technician called Marwan Khreesat.

Imagine, then, the BKA's alarm when, on 13 October 1988, Khreesat arrived at Dalkamoni's flat in Neuss. Dalkamoni had been under 24-hour surveillance since at least as early as 5 October, when he arrived back in West Germany following a trip to Cyprus. So too had been another senior group member, Abdel Fattah Ghadanfar, who rented a flat at 28 Sandweg in Frankfurt. For three weeks the BKA followed Dalkamoni as he met with various Arab associates around the country. The operation was code-named *Herbstlaub*, meaning Autumn Leaves.

Khreesat was less visible, spending most of his time in the Isarstrasse apartment. On 20 October he received a call from Dalkamoni, who told him that he was about to receive 'three black tins with lids', 'gloves' and 'paste' from Ghadanfar, whom he referred to by the cover name Masoud. Dalkamoni said he would personally also bring 'at least seven white pointed buttons, four of which would be electric'. Khreesat subsequently made a call to Jordan to someone called Abed, telling him, 'I've made some changes to the medication. It is better and stronger than before.' Two days later, Khreesat emerged from the flat and drove with Dalkamoni to Frankfurt, where they were observed visiting two electrical shops. On 24 October they again went shopping, this time to the Huma-Markt store in Neuss, where they bought alarm clocks, and a local shopping centre, where they bought batteries, electric switches, screws and glue. Later the same day, in a telephone call to Jordan, Khreesat said he had started work the previous day and would be finished in a further two to three days.[12]

It was clear that whatever the group was planning might be imminent. On 26 October Dalkamoni and Khreesat again left the Isarstrasse flat together and drove away in Dalkamoni's Ford Taunus car. A short distance away they stopped, and Khreesat went to make a call from a telephone box. As he emerged, the BKA struck, arresting both men and simultaneously swooping on Ghadanfar and fourteen others, most of whom had been visited by Dalkamoni that month. In Ghadanfar's Frankfurt apartment they found an extraordinary terrorist arsenal, which included 5 kilos of Semtex, 6 kilos of TNT, 14 sticks of dynamite, 30 hand-grenades, mortars and 6 automatic rifles. Also recovered were a number of Lufthansa luggage stickers and 14 airline timetables, including ones for Lufthansa, Air France, Iberia and British Airways.[13,14] The BKA found far fewer weapons in Neuss; however, in view of Iran's threat to avenge Flight 655, an item recovered from the boot of the Ford Taunus was much more significant than the weaponry. It appeared to be an ordinary single-speaker Toshiba radio-cassette player, model type BomBeat RT-F453D. When BKA technicians dismantled it, they discovered that the device lived up to its name, because concealed within was a sophisticated bomb incorporating 300 grams of Semtex and a time-delay mechanism. More significantly, there was a barometric pressure switch. In other words, the bomb had been designed to detonate on board an aircraft. It seemed that the PFLP-GC had been at it again. And it seemed that they had no intention of stopping at one bomb, because in the Isarstrasse flat they found more barometric switches, soldering irons and a detonator.

In November there was a further raid on another PFLP-GC safe house in the Yugoslavian town of Krusevac, which was kept by senior group member Mobdi Goben. Among the items seized were detonators, fuse-wire and seven-and-a-half kilos of Semtex. Goben managed to evade detection[15] and fled to Syria. Dalkamoni's passport contained an entry stamp for Yugoslavia dated 16 September 1988, and Khreesat's had one dated 21 September.[16] According to Khreesat, while there he met Dalkamoni and Goben, whom he knew as Abu Fouad.[17] Ghadanfar met Goben and Dalkamoni in the Yugoslav capital Belgrade in the middle of October.[18] Another of Dalkamoni's associates to visit Goben in Yugoslavia was Martin Kadorah, who, like Ghadanfar, lived in Frankfurt.[19] He travelled there by bus on 24 October, arriving the following day,[20] and did not return until 28 November, when he was arrested and held in custody before being released without charge on 17 January 1989.[21] Dalkamoni admitted that he had ordered Kadorah to make the trip.[22]

Within days of the 26 October raids, most of the suspects had been released owing to lack of evidence. There was apparently no shortage of evidence against Khreesat, Dalkamoni and Ghadanfar, all of whom had been caught red-handed with weaponry capable of killing hundreds of people. Remarkably, however, Dalkamoni and Ghadanfar were only charged with the 1987 and 1988 troop train bombings. It was three years before they were convicted, with Dalkamoni sentenced to 15 years in prison and Ghadanfar 12.

Khreesat's fate was stranger still. Interviewed by the BKA the day after his arrest, he volunteered a few details about the PFLP-GC's structure, but said he knew neither of a European cell, nor of a plan to target airlines. Interestingly, he said that there were two PFLP-GC members in West Germany to whom Dalkamoni was subordinate. Khreesat said he had not met them and did not know their names, but thought that one of them lived in Frankfurt.[23]

On 5 November he reportedly asked to make a phone call to Amman.[24] Later that month the BKA applied to the Federal High Court in Karlsruhe for the bomb-maker to be kept in custody. To

MEGRAHI: YOU ARE MY JURY

their amazement, Judge Christian Rinne refused the application and allowed Khreesat to go free on the grounds that 'the strong suspicion of crime necessary for warrant of arrest is . . . lacking.' He went on: 'It is not possible to prove at present a connection between the residence at 28 Sandweg in Frankfurt, in which weapons of warfare and explosives have been secured, and the accused. No weapons, or similar, were found in the residence at 16 Isarstrasse in Neuss, where he stayed. It has not been possible to discover a target or location for a crime of explosion. Also, the involvement of the accused as regards the purpose of his stay in the Federal Republic, the nature of his relationship with the other accused parties and his ignorance of the preparations for the crime, have not been so clearly refuted that a strong suspicion of crime can be confirmed.'[25]

The explanation for this extraordinary leniency, it later emerged, was that Khreesat was a mole, who was reporting back to the Jordanian intelligence service, the Mukhabarat, and their West German counterparts, the BND. Both services have historically been very close to the CIA. Interviewed a few months later back home in Jordan, Khreesat said that, on the day of his arrest, a German officer told him, 'Don't say anything. You will get a call from your case officer in Jordan.' The case officer subsequently called and assured him that he was coming to West Germany immediately. Khreesat added that, following his release, a BND officer thanked him in the name of the West German authorities for the important role he had played in avoiding a massacre.[26] With hindsight, the Khreesat story was the first indicator that the Lockerbie bombing was far more complex and murky than it first appeared.

Although they had disrupted the PFLP-GC's plans, the BKA knew that other members and bombs might be at large. On 9 November 1988 it issued a warning through Interpol, which gave details of Khreesat's Toshiba bomb. Over the next couple of weeks it was disseminated to government authorities worldwide, including the UK Department of Transport and the US Federal Aviation Authority (FAA), which in turn forwarded it to the world's airlines.

The last few weeks of 1988 brought further indications that an airline attack might still be imminent. The best known of these warnings was received by the US Embassy in Helsinki on 5 December, when a man called to say that during the next fortnight there would be a strike on a Pan Am flight from Frankfurt to America. Three people were named, an Arab man living in Finland called Yassan Garadat, a Frankfurt resident referred to only as Abdullah, and a Mr Soloranta. The caller said that Garadat and Abdullah were members of the Abu Nidal Organisation (ANO) the well-known Palestinian faction, also known as the Fatah Revolutionary Council, which carried out a string of high-profile terrorist attacks against Western targets during the 1980s. He claimed that Abdullah would give Garadat a bomb, which he would in turn plant on an unwitting and unidentified Finnish woman.

When the Finnish police investigated the warning they discovered that Garadat had nothing to do with the ANO, or any terrorist group, and concluded that the call had been made by a Palestinian student living in Helsinki called Samra Mahayoun, who harboured a grudge against him. The reference to Mr Soloranta, however, was intriguing, because the ANO's most notorious commander, Samir Kadar, was married to a Finnish woman called Soloranta.[27] Kadar had supposedly been killed in Athens in July 1988 when a car carrying explosives blew up a few hours before an attack on a tourist ship, the *City of Poros*, in which nine people were killed and 90 injured. However, the body was too badly damaged to identify, and some believed it unlikely that such a senior figure would be involved in high-risk, frontline operations.[28]

Two days after the call was received, the FAA circulated a security bulletin to all US airlines and embassies. On 9 December, Pan Am's European Corporate Security Manager Jim Berwick flew to Helsinki to check out the warning with US Embassy officials. They told him that it had been thoroughly checked and was found to be a hoax. Berwick nevertheless ordered that all Finnish women transferring to transatlantic flights in Frankfurt should be specially screened.[29]

Another who took the warning very seriously was William Kelly, an administrative counsellor at the US Embassy in Moscow. On 13 December he produced a memo summarising the warning, which was marked for the attention of all embassy staff and posted on the staff noticeboard. Despite the Helsinki Embassy's dismissal of the warning, the memo stated: 'The FAA reports that the reliability of the information cannot be assessed at this point, but the appropriate police authorities have been notified and are pursuing the matter. Pan Am also has been notified.' It went on, 'In view of the lack of confirmation of this information, post leaves to the discretion of individual travellers any decisions on altering personal travel plans or changing to another American carrier.' Kelly's actions were in breach of the FAA's guidelines on the dissemination of warnings; however, embassy staff claimed that, prior to posting the warning, the FAA had failed to respond to a request for clarification.[30] It is not known how many embassy staff changed their Christmas travel plans as a result of the warning, but a consular official later revealed that there was 'a real push in the Embassy community to make sure that everybody was aware that there had been a terrorist threat made, and that people flying Western carriers going through such points as Frankfurt should change their tickets'.[31]

Whether or not the warning was a hoax, the US intelligence community knew that the Autumn Leaves raids had not eliminated the Iranian threat. On 1 December, the US Defence Intelligence Agency (DIA) issued an intelligence summary, which stated: 'Although there have been no recent publicised threats of retaliation against the US for the 3 July Iranian airbus shootdown, Tehran's general intent to conduct terrorist attacks against the US continues . . . Some Middle Eastern terrorist groups have conducted assassinations and bombings in West Germany and have the infrastructure to conduct both bombings and assassinations.'[32]

Incredibly, the intelligence community also had information suggesting that a radical Palestinian group, matching the description of the PFLP-GC, was planning to attack Pan Am in Europe. The warning was received by the US State Department's Office of Diplomatic Security. A departmental digest of it reported: 'Team of Palestinians not assoc[iated] with Palestinian Liberation Organisation (PLO) intends to atk [attack] US tgts [targets] in Europe. Time frame is present. [Targets] specified are Pan Am airlines and US mil[itary] bases.'[33] The warning was dated 2 December 1988 and was therefore entirely unrelated to the supposedly hoax Helsinki phone call, which was not made until three days later. It was not made public until seven years after the Lockerbie bombing.[34]

Unlike the Helsinki warning, it received hardly any media attention, yet, unlike the Helsinki warning, the US government never claimed it was a hoax.

Could it have been referring to the PFLP-GC? It was certainly one of the Palestinian factions hostile to the PLO, it had a recent track record of attacking the US military in West Germany, and it was clearly planning to target airlines. However, the Autumn Leaves raids had destroyed the group's European infrastructure six weeks before the warning, and there was no evidence to suggest it was specifically targeting Pan Am. Or so it seemed. But evidence would eventually emerge that cast grave doubt on both of these supposed facts.

As they stumbled across the fields on the dark night of 21 December 1988, the shell-shocked police had no idea what had caused the carnage around them. Nevertheless, they knew the crash-site must be treated as a potential crime scene. Once it was apparent that there were no survivors, their priority was to locate the victims' bodies and begin the search for clues to the disaster's cause.

By chance the plane had fallen on the patch of Britain's smallest police force. The Dumfries and Galloway Constabulary had only around 400 officers, yet was faced with a crash-site that covered 845 square miles, fanning out eastwards from Lockerbie to the North Sea coast 70 miles away. Within hours hundreds of officers were drafted in from forces across Scotland and Northern England. They were joined by military personnel, some of them still teenagers. Mountain rescue volunteers and search dog-handlers from across Britain also became essential to the recovery effort, many of them dedicating hundreds of hours to the task.

Constables David Connel and Alisdair Campbell found the first vital clue. On 24 December the two British Transport Police dog-handlers were searching a field near Carruthers Farm, a few miles east of Lockerbie, when they recovered a small piece of twisted and blackened aluminium.[1] The following day, detective constables from the Lothian and Borders Police found another nearby.[2] On 26 December, the items were sent to the Ministry of Defence's Royal Armaments Research and Development Establishment (RARDE), at Fort Halstead in Kent.[3] Although primarily a weapons research and development facility, its forensic division had responsibility for investigating most British terrorist bombings committed outside Northern Ireland. Chemical residue tests were conducted on the two items. The results were consistent with plastic explosives.[4] The next day it was publicly announced that PA103 had been destroyed by a bomb. Lockerbie was now officially a criminal inquiry.

The crash-site was divided into 11 areas, designated A to K, with a senior officer placed in charge of each. Search teams combed each sector, collecting the debris in plastic sacks. Aircraft fragments and items belonging to passengers were separated out. The police set up two main storage centres in Lockerbie: the Blue Band Motors garage was used for the aircraft debris, while personal belongings were stored in a disused warehouse belonging to a company called Dexstar. It was soon obvious that the Blue Band garage was too small, so the aircraft debris was moved to a Ministry of Defence ammunition depot at Longtown in Cumbria.

Both stores were divided into areas corresponding with the alphabetical search sectors. Every item that arrived at the stores was labelled by the police and given a reference number comprising a two-letter alphabetical prefix and a sequential number. The first of the two letters was either A or P, depending on whether the object was aircraft debris or a personal item, while the second denoted the search sector in which it was found. Thus the 200th personal item from sector F would be labelled PF/200. Each sector had its own log, in which all the items were documented. The logs and labels were supposed to record details of exactly where each item was found, when and by whom; however, the volume of debris was so overwhelming that the task became impossible. For the most part, therefore, the person recorded as having 'found' an object was not the person who actually found it at the crash-site, but rather the officer who labelled it in the store. The original locations and dates of recovery of many items therefore remained unknown.

The police investigation was conducted in tandem with the Department of Transport's Air Accidents Investigation Branch (AAIB). Despite the massive challenge of the evidence-gathering operation, the early months of 1989 saw them make good progress. The two pieces of blast-damaged aluminium proved to be struts of one of the luggage containers that had been loaded into the 747's belly at Heathrow. These containers were approximately five-feet-square cubes, with an extended section incorporating a 45-degree angled floor to accommodate the curvature of the fuselage. All the surfaces were thin aluminium, and one of the sides was open to allow bags to be loaded. Once loading was complete, a curtain was pulled across this aperture and secured.

PP8932 TSH-363 CONTAINER

Further pieces of the container were recovered, which revealed that it had the serial number AVE4041. When investigators checked Pan Am's load plan for Flight 103, they discovered that it had been loaded into the aircraft's front left hold. The AAIB was able to reconstruct the container and much of the front of the aircraft. The results appeared to be consistent, enabling the AAIB to conclude: 'The in-flight disintegration of the aircraft was caused by the detonation of an improvised explosive device located in a baggage container positioned on the left side of the forward cargo hold.' They calculated that that the centre of the explosion was within the angled section of the container, only around 25 inches from the fuselage skin.[5]

In the early months of 1989 the police and volunteer searchers found a number of fragments of reddish-brown suitcase shell. Forensic analysis by RARDE's lead examiner, Dr Thomas Hayes, suggested that the inner surface of some were blast-damaged, which was a strong indicator that they originated from the primary suitcase, as the case containing the bomb was by then known.

Attached to one of the fragments was piece of lining bearing a pattern, which the police recognised to be the logo of the American luggage manufacturer Samsonite. On 3 March, Detective Inspector Donald MacNeil, accompanied by an FBI agent, took a piece of the lining and a shell fragment to the company's headquarters in Denver, Colorado. Technical manager Owen Schneider confirmed that they originated from a Samsonite suitcase, and was able to narrow it down to their System 4 luggage range.[6] The cases were available in a number of colours, this one being known as Antique Copper.

More fragments were found over the next few months, including, most significantly, on 16 May, a suitcase locking mechanism. On 22 May DS Macleod, again accompanied by an FBI agent, paid a further visit to Samsonite, taking with him photos of the lock. Noting that it had a gold square painted on it and an embossed number 351, Owen said that it originated not from the System 4 range, but from a very similar one known as Silhouette 4000. The System 4 was produced primarily for the US domestic market and the Silhouette 4000 for the company's international division. He handed Macleod export sales figures for both ranges,[7] which showed that a large proportion of the Silhouette 4000 range were sold to the Middle East.[8] The range was available in different sizes. On the basis of some fragments of its outer trim and inner frame, the police were eventually able to determine that the primary suitcase was the 26-inch model.

The discovery was potentially highly significant, not least because of information gleaned by the BKA from the Neuss shopkeeper, Hashem Abassi. Questioned about the October 1988 visit of his brother-in-law, the PFLP-GC commandant Hafez Dalkamoni, and the bomb-maker Marwan Khreesat, Abassi told the BKA: 'I think I can remember that on his visit Khreesat had a rigid dark-coloured Samsonite suitcase', although, when shown photos of brown Samsonites, he said, 'I have never seen before the two suitcases which are shown on the photograph. In reply to a question I also can't remember whether Dalkamoni or Khreesat had such cases with them when they were living with us.'[9] Abassi and his brother Ahmed also recalled seeing a hard-shell Samsonite suitcase in the boot of Dalkamoni's green Ford Taunus shortly before the arrests on 26 October 1988. This prompted Detective Superintendent Pat Connor to note in a June 1989 report on the PFLP-GC's West German activities: 'There is also some significance between the fact that the IED used to bring down PA 103 was carried in a hard-sided Samsonite suitcase and the evidence provided by the Abassi brothers which clearly suggests that the bomb radio recovered from the boot of the Ford Taunus motor vehicle on 26 October 1988 was also being carried in a "brown or dark coloured suitcase." This is denied by the BKA although they do agree that a bomb radio as previously described was found in the cardboard carton for a radio within the boot of the vehicle previously referred to. However to date photographs showing the contents of the boot of the car when it was first opened by the BKA and which would support their denial, have not been made available to the [Senior Investigating Officer] at Lockerbie.'[10] The police eventually accepted that there was no hard evidence that there was a brown Samsonite in the car boot, but it was never disproved that the suitcase Khreesat brought to Neuss was a dark Samsonite one. A number of suitcases were recovered from the PFLP-GC's apartment in Sandweg, Frankfurt, one of which was described by the BKA as grey plastic. This almost certainly meant that it was hard-sided, although the make was not recorded.[11]

What of the bomb itself? Within a day or so of the incident the police were told of the Autumn Leaves raids in West Germany and of Marwan Khreesat's barometric Toshiba radio-cassette bomb. Although the raids had supposedly disrupted the PFLP-GC's plans, the group was, inevitably, the prime suspect. On 15 January 1989, evidence emerged that confirmed the link. While examining the remains of AVE4041, senior AAIB inspector Peter Claiden found a small mass of carbonised material trapped within the fold of a small aluminium identification plate, which was originally attached to the container.[12] On close inspection, the debris was found to contain a number of tiny fragments of electronic circuit board which were given the reference number AG/145.

It was one of the police's most promising leads. On 17 January the fragments were delivered to RARDE, where they were examined by

Allen Feraday, an expert in the electronic aspects of terrorist improvised explosive devices (IEDs), who, along with Hayes, had primary responsibility for the Lockerbie forensic investigation. He was certain that they were explosively damaged and thought it more than likely that they originated from the bomb. On 23 January he visited the BKA's forensic laboratory in Wiesbaden to compare them with Khreesat's device, but they did not match.[13] Undeterred, Feraday continued to pursue the Toshiba connection and eventually was able to match the fragments with a circuit board that was used in five similar models of stereo radio-cassette players, plus close variants of two of them manufactured outside Japan. Although all seven models had two speakers, and looked rather different to the mono BomBeat RT-F453D model used by Khreesat, the Toshiba connection was surely no coincidence.

On 5 May the police discovered a crucial item, which for months had languished at the Dexstar property. Given the reference number PK/689, it consisted of two stuck-together pages of what appeared to be a radio-cassette instruction manual. Although badly damaged, the letters 'IBA' of Toshiba were clearly visible; more importantly, so too were the words BomBeat SF-16.[14] It was obviously the manual of a Toshiba BomBeat RT-SF16 radio-cassette player, which, critically, was one of the seven models containing the particular circuit board from which AG/145 had originated. Furthermore, the BomBeat prefix was a yet another firm circumstantial link to Marwan Khreesat and the PFLP-GC.

On 14 July DCI Harry Bell sent a lengthy memo to SIO John Orr, spelling out why he believed the bomb had come from Frankfurt. Under the subheading 'I.E.D. Radio-cassette Player' he wrote: 'It is some what of a coincidence that the "SF16" has a model name of "Bombeat" the same as the "Bombeat" radio-cassette player recovered in Frankfurt [sic]. It is appreciated that the Frankfurt radio is a different model namely the "453" but the significance of the "Bombeat" name cannot be underestimated in the contexts of the circumstantial evidence.'

Over in West Germany, April 1989 saw a dramatic development. The BKA raided the Neuss greengrocery owned by Dalkamoni's brother-in-law Hashem Abassi, and in the basement found two radio tuners and a Sanyo monitor, which, unbeknown to Abassi, also contained barometric bombs. To the BKA's embarrassment, Abassi said that all three devices had been in the Isarstrasse apartment when it was raided as part of Operation Autumn Leaves the previous October.[15] Tragically, when two BKA technicians attempted to examine one of the tuners it exploded, killing one and badly injuring the other. The second tuner was disabled with a water cannon, leaving only the Sanyo monitor intact.

The BKA appeared to have missed the three devices during the Autumn Leaves raids. Could they also have missed one built into a Toshiba RT-SF16? Of the four devices recovered in total, none were contained in anything resembling an RT-SF16; however, when the police originally raided the Isarstrasse apartment, they found three other radio-cassette players, one of which, like the RT-SF16, was a stereo model.[16] Since it is unlikely that temporary residents of a small flat would need three such machines purely for entertainment purposes, they may have been an indication that Dalkamoni and Khreesat were planning more bombs.

Khreesat was obviously the person the Scottish police most wanted to interview, but, to their intense frustration, they were unable to get access to him. The FBI had better luck. In November 1989, Special Agents Edward Marshman and William Chornyak questioned him for two days at the headquarters of the Jordanian intelligence service in Amman. He claimed that he was first ordered to make barometric bombs in 1985 by PFLP-GC leader Ahmed Jibril. He bought five Toshiba BomBeat RT-F453D radio-cassette players and partially constructed the bombs, but said he subsequently dismantled them. He claimed the bomb components were returned to the group's office and he stored the radio-cassette players at his cousin's house. His wife took one of the machines with her when they travelled to West Germany in October 1988.

He confirmed that, prior to that trip, in September 1988, he had met Dalkamoni and Mobdi Goben, a.k.a. Abu Fouad, in Yugoslavia. Goben had avoided arrest during the Yugoslavian police raid on his house in Krusevac in November 1988. They were later joined by a young man who was introduced as 'Salah', whom Khreesat recognised as a Salah Kwekes, a.k.a. Ramzi Diab, one of those arrested during the Autumn Leaves raids. Dalkamoni said that they would also be joined by an individual called Abu Elias, but he did not arrive. Elias was to prove the most intriguing and elusive of all the suspects. Seemingly always one step ahead of the authorities, his name was to crop up time and again, but his identity remained one of Lockerbie's enduring mysteries.

Khreesat said he was subsequently ordered to travel to Neuss by Dalkamoni, who said he would meet him there. He confirmed that while in the town he made all four of the barometric bombs later recovered by the BKA. More importantly, he said he had made a fifth device, using another radio-cassette player, which Dalkamoni gave him on 22 October. He said it was larger than the Toshiba RT-F453D, but, unlike the RT-SF16, it also had only one speaker. Khreesat insisted he had designed all the devices so they would not explode. Earlier on the 22nd, he and Dalkamoni had driven Khreesat's wife to Frankfurt Airport, as she was returning to Jordan. Khreesat recalled that, while there, Dalkamoni had said something about Pan Am, but couldn't recall what. He did, however, remember that Dalkamoni had also commented that many people were flying to the USA and that some airlines flew there twice a day. Dalkamoni later mentioned that Abu Elias had just arrived in West Germany, adding that Elias was an expert in airport security. Khreesat told Marshman and Chornyak that he was concerned because he thought that Elias might spot that the bombs had been designed not to work.

Two days later, Dalkamoni told Khreesat that he was going to Frankfurt. Later that day Khreesat noticed that the fifth bomb was missing. The following day, 25 October, the two men drove to Düsseldorf airport, where Dalkamoni picked up several airline timetables. Among them was one for Pan Am. Dalkamoni said he was keen to target a flight during the next week and had settled on Iberia Flight 888 from Madrid to Tel Aviv, via Barcelona. The plan was for a courier to fly with the Toshiba bomb from Madrid to Barcelona, where he would arm the bomb and leave it on the plane. An Iberia timetable was among the 14 recovered from the Sandweg apartment in Frankfurt.[17] The next day Dalkamoni took the Toshiba bomb and placed it in the boot of his car before they drove off. He said they were going to Frankfurt, and Khreesat was under the firm impression that they would be meeting Abu Elias, but within minutes the pair had been arrested.

Khreesat's two surviving bombs had been thoroughly analysed by BKA technician Rainer Gobel. He established that the Toshiba radio-cassette device had to be primed by inserting a mini jack plug into a corresponding socket. Once activated in this way, the barometric mechanism would trigger the time-delay switch when the atmospheric pressure had dropped to around 950 millibars, which would be approximately seven minutes after take-off. The time-delay switch would then detonate the bomb approximately 40 to 45 minutes later, i.e. between 47 and 52 minutes after take-off. The time-delay in the Sanyo monitor bomb was shorter, at around 30 to 35 minutes.

PA103 took off at 18.25 and was destroyed at 17.03, 38 minutes later. Again, this seemed to be further evidence that one of Khreesat's devices had destroyed the aircraft. However, Gobel poured cold water on the suggestion, pointing out that such a bomb would have detonated on the 78-minute flight PA103A from Frankfurt to Heathrow. There was no question of Khreesat having circumvented the problem by using a longer time-delay, Gobel said, because the time-delay switch would have reset itself as the aircraft plane reduced its altitude. He concluded, 'If we assume that an explosive of similar design was used for the attack, it must have been put on board in London, or primed there by plugging in the main switch.'[18]

The Scottish police could be forgiven for believing that the BKA was trying to put them off the scent of the PFLP-GC's West German cell. After all, the BKA had failed to discover three of Khreesat's bombs until after Lockerbie, at least one other radio-cassette bomb was missing, and a key PFLP-GC operative, Abu Elias, remained at large. If the Scots could prove that the Lockerbie plot was launched from West Germany, the organisation would have some very awkward questions to answer.

The police asked RARDE's Allen Feraday to consider Gobel's calculations. On 23 June 1989 he sent DCI Bell a four-page handwritten memo headed, 'Some comments concerning the BKA analysis of possible flight durations'. It concluded: 'In view of the aforementioned 9 points, it is apparent that for a variety of reasons it would be perfectly feasible for any unknown improvised explosive device not to function aboard PA103A yet to subsequently function aboard PA103.'[19]

The mass of circumstantial evidence against the PFLP-GC and Iran was bolstered by leaks from within the Western intelligence services. Detailed reports appeared in the media, alleging that negotiations between the group's leader Ahmed Jibril and hardliners in the Iranian government had begun shortly after the downing of Iran Air Flight 655. It was claimed that the Israeli intelligence service, Mossad, intercepted messages between Iranian Revolutionary Guards in Lebanon's Bekaa Valley and the PFLP-GC's Damascus Headquarters, shortly after which Jibril travelled to Tehran. US intelligence sources claimed that the US National Security Agency had eavesdropped on a telephone call between the Iranian Interior Minister, Ali Akbar Mohtashemi, and Jibril, in which the Palestinian offered to attack a number of unnamed European targets in return for an appropriate fee.[20] One report suggested the fee was $1.3 million,[21] while another put it as high as $10 million.[22]

On 11 September 1989, the FBI's Associate Deputy Director responsible for anti-terrorism, Oliver 'Buck' Revell, told a US congressional committee that the Bureau believed it had identified the organisation responsible for Lockerbie.[23] He did not mention any names, but it was obvious to anyone who had followed the case that he meant the PFLP-GC. It was the closest that any official figure had come to an on-the-record statement of blame.

As the first anniversary of the bombing approached, a new prime suspect emerged. Mohamed Abu Talb, an Egyptian, was based in the Swedish university town of Uppsala, near Stockholm, and was a member of the PFLP-GC's fellow Salvation Front group, the Palestinian Popular Struggle Front (PPSF).

Born in Port Said in 1952, Talb joined the Egyptian army as soon as he left school at 16. Soon afterwards he was sent to Armenia on a six-month commando course, and in 1969 spent 18 months in the Soviet Union, where he learned how to use SAM 3 surface-to-air missiles. He returned to the Egyptian army in 1970, but at the end of 1970 escaped to Jordan, where he joined the military wing of the PLO. He then went to Lebanon before returning to Egypt, where he again worked for the PLO, this time on political matters. He was arrested in 1972 and was imprisoned until the end of 1973, when he fled to Lebanon and joined the PPSF. Five years later, he became the personal bodyguard of the group's leader, Samir Gousha. While in Lebanon, he met and married another PPSF member, Jamila Mougrabi, who was from a well-known family of violent activists. Her sister Rashida was jailed for 12 years in the UK for her part in an attack on the Iraqi Ambassador in London in 1978, and another sister, Dalal, was killed during an attack on an Israeli bus. Talb and Jamila moved from Lebanon to Uppsala in February 1983. He claimed to have given up on the armed struggle, but this proved to be a lie.

On 13 October 1988, the BKA had observed a white Volvo with Swedish number plates arrive at Hashem Abassi's apartment in Neuss, where Dalkamoni and Khreesat would arrive later the same day. The car belonged to a close associate of Talb's called Martin Imandi, a.k.a. Imad Chabaan, and the driver was Talb's brother-in-law Mohamed Mougrabi, who, like the other two, lived in Uppsala. His brother, Mahmoud, shared an apartment in Uppsala with Abassi's brother Ahmed, who himself travelled to Neuss on 22 October and was later observed visiting electrical shops in Neuss with Dalkamoni and Khreesat.

Mohamed Mougrabi had been asked to drive to West Germany by Imandi to collect his brother Jehad Chabaan and cousin Samir Ourfali, who were staying with Hashem Abassi. Mougrabi stayed overnight, and the three of them left together the following day.

Jehad Chabaan and Ourfali subsequently travelled to Sweden separately on the Kiel to Gothenburg ferry.[24] It was their second attempt to get to Sweden. They had arrived in East Germany from Damascus on 5 September, along with a third Chabaan brother, Ziad. In September Imandi himself had tried to drive them to Sweden, via Denmark, but they were apprehended at the Danish border town of Rødbyhavn on suspicion of having false identity papers. Jehad and Ziad Chabaan and Ourfali were refused entry to Denmark, following which Ziad flew back to Damascus, while Jehad and Ourfali remained in West Germany. Imandi was allowed to travel on to Sweden alone, but only after spending two days in custody, during which he was fingerprinted. By chance the Danish police discovered that his prints matched one found in June 1985 on a piece of paper wrapped around an unexploded bomb that was intended for the Copenhagen offices of the Israeli airline El Al. The same day there were two other bomb attacks in the city, one at a synagogue and the other at the offices of Northwest Orient airline. One person was killed and 22 injured. It was thought that the same gang was responsible for a similar bomb attack on El Al's Amsterdam office later that year, and one on the Stockholm office of Northwest Airlines in April 1986. Imandi had been under surveillance ever since the Rødbyhavn incident.

Shortly after the Autumn Leaves raids, the BKA told the Swedish Security Police, the Säkerhetspolisen (SAPO), what they had observed. On 1 November the SAPO swooped, arresting Talb, Imandi, Mougrabi and several of their associates. All were released without charge, but the investigations into the airline office and synagogue bombings continued, and on 18 May 1989 Talb, Imandi, Mohamed and Mahmoud Mougrabi, their brother Mustafa and 11 others were arrested.[25] Among the items seized during the raids were four false passports belonging to Talb, one of which was very burnt, and two other burnt ones, the names of which were obscured.[26] The SAPO also found a calendar belonging to Talb's wife, Jamila. Someone had put a small mark next to the '21' of 21 December 1988,[27] although Talb denied that it was him.[28]*

Talb and his wife had little visible means of support other than a small café and video rental business in Uppsala, yet the SAPO discovered that in 1988 a total of 86,000 Swedish kronor was paid into his bank account in five instalments, one of which was of 45,000. He claimed that the 45,000 was a bank loan for the business, and that another deposit of 20,000 kronor was the repayment of a loan he had made to another Arab man. He could not explain the origin of two 10,000 kronor deposits, but speculated that they were from the café. He claimed that 16,000 kronor in cash found at his home during the first raid belonged to his wife.[29, 30]

More intriguingly, the SAPO found stored under a bed 14 wristwatches, some of which were also missing parts, plus a barometer, which was missing its barometric mechanism, and electrical components. Talb said the watches were intended as gifts for his family in

* It has been widely misreported that the date was circled.

Egypt, and that he was not aware that anything was missing from the barometer.[31]

Mahmoud Mougrabi confessed to his involvement and implicated Talb, Imandi and his brother Mohamed. He claimed that in 1985, at Talb's behest, he had travelled to Lebanon to learn bomb-making under the tutelage of a man called Abu Hassan and a close relative of Imandi's, called Sultan, who was responsible for the PPSF's terrorist operations abroad. He said that, among other things, Hassan taught him to adapt wristwatches as bomb timers. At the end of his training he was given $4,000 to $5,000 for him, Talb and Imandi to launch attacks against Jewish targets in Scandinavia and elsewhere. He was also given a bag to take back to Sweden, plus a letter, which he was told not to open until he was home. On reading it, he learned that four detonators had been concealed within the handle. They had been wrapped in carbon paper in order to avoid X-ray detection.[32]

Imandi also confessed that he and Mahmoud had accompanied Talb to Copenhagen when the bombs were planted. All three were convicted, along with Mohamed Mougrabi, on 21 December 1989, the first anniversary of the Lockerbie bombing. Talb and Imandi were each given life sentences while Mahmoud and Mustafa were sentenced to six and one year respectively.[33] By that time it was being reported virtually as fact that Talb was a lynchpin of the Lockerbie plot. This was, in large measure, because evidence had emerged to link him to Malta, which by the autumn of 1989 had become a focal point for the investigation.*

For the couple of weeks after Lockerbie our Paris to Dakar Rally business venture held most of my attention. The rally took place in January and went very well, netting the six partners around $200,000 in total. Our confidence riding high, we went along with Mohamed Dazza's suggestion that we should reinvest the money in another commercial venture.

At the time the Libyan government had introduced a policy to encourage small trading with neighbouring countries, which amounted to a system of barter. It didn't want people to sell goods abroad for hard currency, so the theory was that small businessmen would take

* See Chapter 5.

Libyan produce abroad and exchange it for goods that could be sold in Libya.

The reality turned out to be rather different, as the traders took with them hard currency and then sold the Libyan goods and used the money raised, plus the hard currency, to buy much more than they could have hoped to barter for. As far as the government was aware, however, Libyan produce was being exported and foreign goods imported.

Our plan was to import foods that are popular during the festival of Eid, which marks the end of the holy month of Ramadan, such as bananas, nuts and dried apricots. We knew that pistachio nuts were available cheaply in Dubai, so decided to mainly import those. Our chief export products were to be potatoes and garlic, which were particularly expensive in Dubai, and we also planned to take lemons, oranges, tomatoes and tuna.

Through our LAA connections we were able to lease a Boeing 707 for 22,000 dinars, which at the official exchange rate was $66,000, but at black market rates amounted to only $10,000.

Dazza travelled out to Dubai with hard currency and Lamin followed shortly after with the cargo and more hard currency. They successfully sold the cargo, then visited various traders buying goods to bring home, eventually managing to buy 13 tonnes of pistachios, plus bananas, dried apricots and children's toys. Bananas were particularly expensive in Tripoli at the time and we were able to sell them at a good price. The apricots and toys also sold well, but the pistachios were a disaster. We had hoped that they would fetch 11 dinars per kilo, but by the time we returned the price had plummeted to just 3 dinars. We decided to store them in a warehouse and wait for the price to rise, but a couple of weeks later we found that some of the sacks had become infested with insects. We then discovered that one of them contained a severed cow's head. We had hoped that the venture would set us up for life, but ultimately it brought us only a small profit and badly burned fingers. By the end of the episode it was time to start preparation for the 1990 Paris to Dakar Rally, but my appetite for the project had diminished and there was a lot of quarrelling between the various official bodies involved, so I decided to bow out.

I continued with other business ventures. In 1989, Badri Hassan and I were asked by Ezzadin Hinshiri, who was then Minister of Justice, to source 50 cars for the government. It was initially proposed that the cars should be Spanish, and it was estimated that they would cost $20,000 each. The Libyan Embassy in Madrid therefore made an upfront payment of $972,000 into my Swiss bank account. However, Hinshiri was then advised that Spanish cars had never before been used by the government and that there might be problems obtaining spare parts, so we were asked instead to buy Peugeots. I managed to source the cars from a Cyprus-based Lebanese businessman called Hijazi for around just $11,300 each. They were delivered in two batches the following year, the first of 20, for which I paid $228,000, and the second of 30, for which I paid $336,000. It was probably my most successful business venture and netted me profit of over $400,000.

Over the years there were other fairly large payments in and out of my Swiss account, all of which were legitimate and could be verified by the payers and recipients. Nevertheless, once I fell under suspicion it was probably inevitable that the transactions would be added to the patchwork of falsehoods that was to envelop me.

In the months after Lockerbie the circumstantial case against the PFLP-GC and its Iranian and Syrian sponsors seemed overwhelming. In 1986 the US government used far flimsier evidence, which was untested by a police investigation, as a pretext for air strikes against Libya. Yet in 1989, despite being briefed regularly by their police and intelligence services, the US and British governments refused publicly to point the finger.

The only exception – and a partial one at that – was the British Transport Secretary, Paul Channon. On 16 March 1989 he gave a non-attributable briefing to five lobby journalists in which he claimed that the case was almost solved. Under banner headlines, the next day's front pages variously claimed that the bomber 'may be named within a few days [and] has been tracked down to a desert hideout';[34] that 'Detectives probing the Lockerbie jet disaster now know WHO planted the bomb, HOW he did it and WHERE he put it on the plane';[35] and even that 'the terrorist who planted the bomb was under close arrest last night.'[36]

Channon was, at the time, under huge pressure following his department's failure to circulate full details of the Khreesat's Toshiba bomb to airlines prior to the disaster. The briefing was clearly a diversionary ploy, but it was to backfire badly when the US TV network ABC named him as the leak's source. Had any of Channon's senior colleagues confirmed what he had told the press, Channon stood a slim chance of survival, but none of them did and his frontbench career was all but over. He limped on for a few months until the next ministerial reshuffle, when he was dropped from the Cabinet.

As the months passed it was increasingly obvious that there was a reluctance at the very top of government to probe too deeply into Lockerbie. This became clear to relatives of the British victims when their repeated calls for a public inquiry were rebuffed. Eventually, in September 1989, they were granted a meeting with Cecil Parkinson, who had replaced Channon as Transport Secretary. The discussion went well and Parkinson said he would recommend to the Cabinet that there should be an inquiry led by a Scottish judge. However, a few weeks later a clearly embarrassed Parkinson informed the relatives that the inquiry had been blocked by the Prime Minister, Margaret Thatcher. Thatcher's reluctance was perhaps explained by an article that appeared a few months later in the *Washington Post*, claiming that during a telephone conversation in March 1989, Thatcher and President George Bush Snr agreed that the Lockerbie investigation should be toned down. The reporters responsible for the story were Jack Anderson and Dale Van Atta, both of whom were renowned investigators known to have very good government sources. Anderson, indeed, was a former Pulitzer Prize winner, who in 1972 was the target of an unsuccessful assassination plot by two of the conspirators in the Watergate scandal.[37] Among the reasons behind the leaders' pact, the article said, was the need to avoid upsetting negotiations with Iranian and Syrian-backed groups holding Western hostages in Lebanon.[38]

One of the British relatives, Martin Cadman, who lost his son Bill in the bombing, received further evidence of the American government's apparent allergy to the truth. In February 1990 he was invited to the US Embassy in London to meet the members of a Presidential Commission, which had been established to examine aviation security policy with particular reference to Lockerbie. At the end of the meeting, Cadman was taken aside by one of the Commission's seven members, who told him to 'keep up the fight', before adding, 'Your government and ours know exactly what happened but they are never going to tell.'[39]

We may never know what influence Thatcher and Bush brought to bear on the Lockerbie investigation, but over the course of three years its focus shifted away from the PFLP-GC, Iran and Syria, and towards Libya. It is also clear that, from the night of the bombing, successive governments have denied some inconvenient truths.

One of these is that within two hours of the bombing, American officials were present at the scene. Among those to notice them were members of a mountain rescue team from the south of Scotland, who had arrived in Lockerbie under police escort at approximately 21.00. They immediately reported to the police station, but were unable to find anyone in the reception area, so one of the members looked through the door of an adjoining room. Inside were a number of men wearing trench coats, who spoke with American accents and were looking at maps. They made it clear that he was not welcome and told him to leave. The team commented at the time that it was strange that Americans had reached the town so quickly, and ever since remained adamant that they had not imagined the episode.[40] The US government later publicly denied that any of its officials had reached Lockerbie before 23.00.[41]

Later that night a member of the same mountain rescue team found a passenger's bag full of US dollars.[42] Over the next few days mountain rescue teams made three similar finds, one of which was nearby and the other many miles away in Northumbria.[43] Teesdale Mountain Rescue Team leader David Thomson, who witnessed one of the Northumbrian finds, later recalled passing to the police two or three paper packages, each of which contained a great many new, large-denomination US dollar bills.[44] When this matter was later raised in Parliament by the Labour MP Dr Norman Godman, he was told that nothing had been found other than 'what might ordinarily be regarded as personal money'.[45]

The Government was equally adamant that no drugs were found

at the crash-site, despite persuasive evidence to the contrary. An officer involved in the recovery of debris from search Sector D was briefed to be on the lookout for heroin, which a young male Arab passenger was suspected of carrying. There was only one such passenger on the plane, a 20-year-old Lebanese-American called Khaled Jaafar.[46] On the night of the crash a mountain rescue volunteer found an unmarked cellophane package containing white powder, which had drawn the attention of a search dog. The volunteer was quite certain that the powder was some type of drug.[47] A couple of days later there was another substantial drug find at a farm in Sector D. The farmer noticed that the police had overlooked a suitcase that had landed in one of his fields, so phoned them to come and collect it. When the officer arrived, they noticed that the case contained a wide belt incorporating large pouches, in which were visible clear plastic packages of white powder. The officer said something like, 'Uh oh, I know what we've got here'[48] and contacted headquarters. Rather than taking the suitcase to the Dexstar store, he waited until some Americans arrived, who took it away in their four-wheel-drive vehicle.[49] When Labour MP Tam Dalyell raised the matter with successive governments, he was told that no drugs were found, other than a small personal quantity of cannabis.[50]

Dalyell's interest in Lockerbie began on New Year's Eve 1988, when an officer from his local police force, the Lothian and Borders Constabulary, arrived at his house unannounced and asked to speak with him in confidence. The officer said he had been at the crash-site since 22 December and had become increasingly concerned by the presence of Americans who were roaming the crash-site, apparently conducting their own searches, unsupervised by the police. He did not pretend to know that they belonged to any particular US organisation and was simply concerned that they were not abiding by the Scottish police's strict investigative procedures, which required all finds to be corroborated by two police officers and properly recorded.[51]

It was clear that the police had been ordered to make a priority of recovering certain items belonging to the US government and its employees. A few days after the crash a member of the Scottish mountain rescue team found a silver-grey padded pouch, resembling an anti-static envelope, attached to which was a label of a US government department (he subsequently could not recall which). The envelope was passed down the line to the police, who shortly afterwards called off the search. The team thought this a little odd, as searches usually continued until dusk, yet there was around an hour of daylight left and they had not covered all of that day's target area.[52]

On the afternoon of 22 December a military helicopter involved in the search effort picked up two Americans, who the crew members were led to believe were 'CIA men'. Dressed incongruously in suits and light-coloured raincoats, they asked to be flown to a particular area, which they searched while the crew waited in the aircraft. Having apparently not found what they were after, they asked to be taken to another location. This time they returned with sacks, the contents of which were not discussed. Later that day the men were flown to Glasgow Airport so they could return to the US.[53]

There were at least two temporary no-go areas, from which volunteer searchers were barred.[54] One of them was a few miles east of Lockerbie, in a field just north of the B7068 road at approximate grid reference 293 817. When a mountain rescue team tried to enter the field to search for debris, their leader was approached by a police officer, who said they must keep away. The team assumed that the order had something to do with a large object which lay a few hundred yards away, concealed by a red or orange tarpaulin. The team leader was curious and, since no one would tell him what the object was, decided to have a look for himself at night. However, before he got a chance, he learned that whatever it was had been removed from the field by a mechanical digger and taken away on a low-loader.[55] The helicopter crew member also recalled seeing the tarpaulin and suggested that the concealed object was slightly smaller than a car.[56]

The other no-go area was on Carruthers Farm, about six miles to the south-west. Farmer Innes Graham was on one occasion ordered by two plain-clothed Americans to stay away from a low hill just east of the farm.[57] A couple of nights earlier a volunteer searcher had found a bundle of US State Department papers there, which were marked 'sensitive'.[58]

The incident probably related to Charles McKee, a Major in the US Defence Intelligence Agency, who, at the time of his death, was returning from Lebanon, where he and two fellow passengers, Matthew

Gannon and Ronald Lariviere, had been engaged in a highly sensitive hostage rescue mission. Unlikely as it may seem, papers apparently containing details of the hostages' locations were found by searchers near the English border, in the Newcastleton Forest. A policeman who saw the documents at a temporary storeroom near the forest later recalled that they included detailed maps.[59]

One of McKee's suitcases was found on a ridge near to Graham's farm by a dog-handler. Like the drugs found on the neighbouring farm, it was removed from the scene by Americans, who ignored the standard procedures for the recovery and recording of debris. The case was then cleansed of any sensitive contents and placed back on Graham's land.[60] A day or so later, on 24 December, CID officers were instructed by senior officers to search for McKee's luggage. They were introduced to plain-clothed Americans, whom they were told worked for Pan Am and would be accompanying them on the search. They were ordered to follow the Americans' instructions. The officers suspected that the men were in fact intelligence agents, and feared that they would be required to do something that contravened the strict rules of evidence-gathering. Using the excuse of deteriorating weather, the officers eventually insisted on heading back to base.[61] Later the same day, McKee's case was 'found' by a Dumfries and Galloway Police dog-handler and a British Transport Police officer, who were unaware that anything was amiss.[62]

On 11 January, SIO John Orr ordered two senior officers, Detective Chief Inspector Jack Baird and Detective Inspector William Williamson, to examine McKee's cases and relay to him any items considered to be of 'potential relevance to intelligence matters'.[63] Among the items they found were photos of what appeared to be a Middle Eastern building.[64]

At 08.00 on 1 February 1989, the Edinburgh radio station, Radio Forth, broadcast a news story which revealed the presence of McKee's team on the flight and claimed that the bomb had been planted in their luggage. The reporter behind the story was David Johnston, who had very good sources in the Lothian and Borders Police. Although his voice and name were not used in the report, within an hour he was visited by two senior Lothian and Borders officers, who demanded that he divulge the source of the story. When he refused, the police made an extraordinary offer: they said they could take him immediately to see Prime Minister Margaret Thatcher and that he could reveal the source to her in private. When he again refused, he was warned that he could be jailed for contempt, and, in a highly unusual move, the case was sent directly to Scotland's head prosecutor, the Lord Advocate, Lord Fraser of Carmyllie. Unfortunately for the police, Johnston's plight began to be reported elsewhere in the media, and on 3 February Fraser announced that the case had been dropped.[65]

Many years later, Orr's distant successor as SIO, DCI Michael Dalgleish, made the following admission about McKee in a letter to the Scottish Criminal Cases Review Commission (SCCRC): 'the presence of Mr McKee on PA103, along with certain others, appears to have been the focus of high level discussions between Senior Police, Security Service and American officials. It is clear that the American authorities were keen to recover any items that may have belonged to McKee in particular, which could be linked to their duties. It may well have been the case that certain items were not recorded in the normal manner to protect American interests but this is purely speculation on my part.'

Early on in the investigation, the Dumfries and Galloway Police formed a Joint Intelligence Group (JIG), which acted as the interface between the police inquiry and the intelligence services. The SCCRC established that the JIG kept a file, known as File X, which recorded details of McKee's possessions. The Commission inspected the file and satisfied itself that it contained nothing of relevance to the destruction of PA103.[66] Twenty-one years after the event its contents remain unknown, but, to borrow a phrase from the fictional *X-Files*, the truth probably remains 'out there'.

The Double Agent 4

Of the legion of characters in the Lockerbie saga, Edwin Bollier is undoubtedly the most colourful. He was also one of the few whom I ever met.

Bollier and his partner Erwin Meister were owners of Mebo, the tiny Zurich-based electronics firm, from which ABH rented office space. It was in this office that ABH's founder, Badri Hassan, first introduced me to the two men. It struck me as a strange place. In one of the rooms there was a young woman with a small dog, which made me wonder whether we weren't in fact in someone's home. Much of the discussion focused on whether we could help them to retrieve money owed by various Libyan state authorities, including the JSO, which Mebo had supplied with two-way radios, antennae and amplifiers. Although these deals had nothing to do with ABH, we promised to do what we could. We also discussed the possibility of ABH lending Mebo $500,000 in return for a share of its business, but this came to nothing.

On returning to Libya, we contacted the officials who controlled the relevant purse-strings and kept Mebo informed of our progress by telex. I recall at one point notifying them that some of the money was available for collection. Meister then travelled to Tripoli to collect it, but, to my embarrassment, left empty-handed. I also recall Hassan travelling to Zurich on behalf of the JSO with $100,000 in cash, to cover part of its debt.

On the only other occasion on which I met Bollier in Zurich, he came alone to meet Hassan and me at our hotel. We had brought some jewellery with us from Libya, hoping, with Bollier's help, to sell it for a good price. He accompanied us to various jewellers, but their offers were all disappointing.

My third and final meeting with him was in Tripoli in 1989, the year after Lockerbie, by which time ABH had been dissolved. He was

*still owed money and came to my office to enlist my help once more.
I called my friend Ezzadin Hinshiri, who was then the Minister for
Justice, and he in turn contacted the JSO's finance department.*

*During the two years in which I was involved with ABH we only
did the two business deals with Mebo, for the satellite receiver and
the 50 field communication radios.* *

By the middle of 1989 the police investigation was well on course.
They knew the explosion had occurred low down within container AVE4041, and were confident that the bomb was housed in a
Toshiba BomBeat RT-SF16 radio-cassette player, which had been
placed within an antique copper-coloured Samsonite Silhouette
4000 suitcase. The Toshiba BomBeat brand provided a clear link
to the PFLP-GC's West German cell, part of which was based in
PA103A's originating city, Frankfurt. There was clear intelligence
suggesting that the Iranian government had hired the group to
avenge the shoot-down of Iran Air flight 655. Although the cell's
leader, Hafez Dalkamoni, was in custody and bomb-maker Marwan
Khreesat was back in Jordan, other group members had evaded arrest, including, most notably, the mysterious Abu Elias. Over the
next two years, however, the entire focus of the investigation would
shift from the PFLP-GC and Iran to Libya and its two citizens Abdelbaset al-Megrahi and Lamin Fhimah.

The trail that led to the men was in places tenuous and in others
highly dubious. With hindsight it began to be laid within days of the
bombing. On 8 January 1989 the *Sunday Telegraph* reported that
an unnamed US intelligence official had claimed that the bombers,
although from Iran, had been aided by Libya, adding that there was
a suspicion that the Libyans acted as 'a conduit' for the explosives
and provided intelligence for the Iranian team. Less than three weeks
later Bollier put down the first solid marker. On 24 January 1989[1]
he delivered an anonymous letter to the CIA, which he handed in in
person to the American Embassy in Vienna. Written on the headed
notepaper of Tripoli's Al Kabir Hotel, it was marked for the attention of 'CIA to the chief USA'. In it he posed as a Libyan radio operator belonging to the 'signals corps', who gave himself the code-name

* See Chapter 2.

AGA. He claimed that, together with 'two Europeans', he had been observing the Abu Nidal terrorist group and 'Mr Ibrahim Zennousi', which was probably a reference to the chief of the Tripoli broadcasting station, Ibrahim Bishari, who later became the Chairman of the JSO, rather than Abdullah Senoussi (Bollier had dealt regularly with Bishari, but could not recall meeting Senoussi[2]). Under the heading of 'PAN AM flight 103', it claimed that on 8 December 1988 the Libyan leader Colonel Muammar Gadafy had called a meeting of 'Zennousi' and Abu Achmed, who was described as the right-hand man of both Abu Nidal and 'Shebrill SYRIA'. The latter was obviously a reference to Ahmed Jibril, leader of the Syrian-based PFLP-GC, who was at the time widely believed to have been behind the attack. Colonel Gadafy was said to have ordered that something be done to undermine the PLO leader Yasser Arafat, who the previous month had announced the termination of his organisation's military campaign against Israel. The letter then briefly described how a bomb plot was hatched, which involved a suitcase containing military explosives being taken on a Swissair flight from Tripoli to Zurich by a German called 'Mr Karlheinz', who also had a Pan Am ticket.

AGA suggested a radio frequency by which he could communicate with the CIA, and asked them to be on standby to receive his messages every Friday at 15.00, 16.00 and 17.00 Greenwich Mean Time. He said that it was his group's intention 'to eliminate this group of criminals terrorists [sic]'.[3]

Years later it emerged that the CIA had made radio contact in response to the letter. The Agency claimed that the contact had proved useless,[4] but the exact nature of the discussions and the resulting actions remain a mystery. What did become clear, however, was that Bollier was no ordinary businessman. Like a spy novel caricature, beneath his respectable business suit lay a Cold War profiteer who vigorously exercised his Swiss neutrality by skipping across the Iron Curtain, buying from the West and selling to the East.

By the time he wrote the letter, Bollier had been on the radar of the Western intelligence services for almost two decades. Their interest was first triggered by the launch by him and Meister in 1970 of Radio Nordsee International (RNI), a pirate radio station operating from the *Mebo II*, a converted Dutch-built coaster anchored in international waters off the Dutch coast. In the run-up to the British General Election in June 1970, RNI found itself jammed by Harold Wilson's Labour government. The station's extraordinary response was to broadcast anti-Labour and pro-Conservative propaganda. Labour narrowly and unexpectedly lost the election. Although RNI's role in the defeat was probably negligible, what appeared to most as a simple act of revenge was seen by some as more sinister. In 1971 a young British journalist called Paul Harris was paid a visit by a Special Branch officer and a retired Detective Chief Superintendent, whom he described as MI6's 'Man in Scotland'. Harris had written two books about pirate radio and was involved in the funding and running of a rival pirate station, Capital Radio. He was therefore both hugely knowledgeable on the subject and vulnerable to prosecution under the Marine Broadcasting Offences Act 1967. His visitors made clear that he would be granted immunity from prosecution if he was prepared to cooperate with MI6 by sharing what he knew about RNI and helping to bring down the station.

As Harris revealed in his 2009 memoir, *More Thrills than Skills*, MI6 was especially concerned about RNI's relationship with the East German intelligence service, known as the Stasi, and suspected that the *Mebo II* was carrying spying equipment. Harris was able to infiltrate RNI's office, which was located in a hotel suite in the Dutch coastal resort of Scheveningen. Although Bollier and Meister gave little away, with the help of a little subterfuge he established that the company was shipping US-made radio transmitter parts to the Stasi's Scientific and Technical Institute in Bernau, near Berlin, despite such exports being banned under American Federal law. At around the same time as MI6's approach, a Dutch newspaper published a leaked CIA report which claimed that ten pirate radio ships, based on RNI, were being built by East Germany's close Warsaw Pact ally, Poland.

RNI was eventually closed down by the Dutch government in 1974, and in 1977 Bollier and Meister sold *Mebo II* to the Libyan government. It was initially used for broadcasting, but was later used by the Air Force for target practice.[5]

Shortly after Bollier delivered his letter to the CIA, a chain of physical evidence began to unfold, which, 18 months later, would take the police to his doorstep. On 13 January 1989, Detective Constables Thomas Gilchrist and Thomas McColm were sifting through the myriad scraps of debris stored at the Dexstar warehouse in Lockerbie when they found a piece of charred grey cloth. It was a fairly routine discovery. It was allocated the reference number PI/995 and, in common with the other recovered debris, a police label was attached and signed by the two officers. Four days later, on 17 January, it was recorded in the register of recovered items known as the Dexstar log.[6]

The police recognised that the charring might be an indication of blast damage, so on 8 February they sent it, along with scores of other debris items, for further examination by the scientists at RARDE.[7] A week later it underwent initial examination by Dr Thomas Hayes, who considered it worthy of further scrutiny.[8] RARDE was inundated with work, so it was not until 12 May 1989 that Hayes could conduct a more detailed examination, during which he produced a detailed sketch and notes. He confirmed that the cloth was blast-damaged and noted that it appeared to be possibly the collar of a shirt. More importantly, he extracted from it a number of tiny debris fragments, which clearly did not originate from the shirt. Among these were a scrap of paper, fragments of black plastic, and, most significantly, a fragment of green electronic circuit board just a few millimetres in size. The items were allocated the reference number PT/35, with each given an alphabetic suffix. The circuit board fragment was PT/35b.[9] It was to become the most significant forensic item in the entire case.

Four months later, on 15 September 1989, Hayes's colleague Allen Feraday notified the police of the find. In a handwritten memo, addressed to Detective Inspector William Williamson, he wrote, 'I feel that this fragment could be potentially most important so any light your lads/lassies can shed upon the problem of identifying it would be most welcome.'[10] Feraday enclosed four Polaroid photos of the fragment, which showed it to have two rough edges, two straight ones and one that formed a concave curve. A circuit pattern was clearly visible, which consisted of a broad elongated area – known as a pad, or land – which was shaped like a figure 1, and two separate thin parallel tracks with angled bends.[11] The police then sifted items of electronic debris held at the Dexstar store to see if anything matched the fragment, but nothing did.[12]

In January 1990 the police visited RARDE to discuss the fragment, and later that month Feraday and Williamson travelled to Germany to see if it matched any of the items recovered from the PFLP-GC suspects, in particular Marwan Khreesat's barometric bombs. Again they drew a blank.[13]

The police then turned to the printed circuit board industry for help. Over the next five months Williamson took the fragment to various specialist firms in the UK and to Siemens in Germany. All of PT/35b's constituent elements were examined using standard analytical methods, such as scanning electron microscopy and infrared spectrometry. In the process a number of tiny slivers were removed, which left the fragment looking rather different to when it was first found, but still clearly recognisable.[14]

No one could identify the source of the fragment, but the test results enabled the police to build a fairly comprehensive profile. The board itself was of a standard glass fibre and resin construction, which was very common within the PCB industry. The circuitry comprised a layer of copper 35 microns thick, coated with a thin layer of tin. Again, this was a fairly standard form of construction; copper conducts the electrical charge and the tin coating enables components to be attached. Towards the top of the '1' shaped area was a blob of solder, which appeared to bear the imprint of fine strands of wire. This was a strong indication that an electronic component had been attached and been ripped away by the bomb blast. Finally, it was determined that the reverse side of the board was coated with a compound known as solder mask.[15] Some experts considered this rather strange, as solder mask is designed to protect the circuitry from hot solder and is therefore generally applied to all areas of the circuitry except those where components were supposed to be attached. Why, they wondered, had it only been applied to the side without circuitry? Eventually, however, there would be a straightforward explanation for this curiosity.

The Scottish police decided to enlist the help of the FBI. Detective Superintendent Stuart Henderson, who had by then succeeded John Orr as SIO, authorised a photograph of the fragment to be passed on to the Bureau's lead forensic investigator, James 'Tom' Thurman.[16] The move paid off. On 15 June 1990 Thurman scored a direct hit, matching the photograph to a circuit board contained in an electronic timing device shown to him by a CIA technical analyst, John Orkin,* to whom he had turned for help.[†] The timer had been recovered from the West African state of Togo in 1986 by the US Bureau of Alcohol Firearms and Tobacco (BATF).

The timer measured 71 × 66 × 21 millimetres and was open-sided, making it possible to see the wiring and components. The only outwardly visible clue as to its origin was the text 'MST-13' which appeared on its upper surface. It had been part of an arms cache that had been seized in Togo during an abortive coup attempt against the pro-Western government by left-wing exiles based in Ghana. The country's President, Gnassingbe Eyadema, invited the US government to send representatives to inspect the weapons. BATF agents Richard Sherrow and Edward Owens were despatched to the capital city Lomé in September 1986. Having been given, in Sherrow's words, 'the run around' for a couple of days, they were eventually given access to the cache, which included explosives, machine-guns, shoulder-launched weapons, thousands of rounds of ammunition and two electronic timers. They returned to Washington DC around a week later, Sherrow taking with him one of the timers and some samples of explosive.[17] The other timer eventually found its way into the hands of the French intelligence service.[18]

Within a couple of days of hearing of Thurman's breakthrough, Henderson, Williamson and Feraday flew to Washington to view the timer for themselves.[19] The match was obvious. The only notable difference was that the timer's circuit board did not have any curved edges. There was, however, a curved mark in a position that corresponded exactly with PT/35b's curve.

* John Orkin was an assumed name.
† Curiously, when he was interviewed by the Crown prior to Abdelbaset's trial, Orkin recalled that Thurman had first shown him a photograph of the circuit-board fragment in March, rather than June, 1990. At the end of the statement a Crown official noted: 'More detailed questioning revealed that this date may have been based on his recollection of the prevailing weather conditions at the time. He could not recall whether this date could be established by documentation.'

The police and FBI received further vital information from the CIA. The Agency reported that another MST-13 timer had been seized in the Senegalese capital Dakar on 20 February 1988 from two Libyans who had arrived on a flight from Benin. The men, Mohamed El-Marzouk and Mansour El-Saber, were also reported to have been carrying explosives and weapons. They were charged, along with a Senegalese accomplice Ahmed Khalifa Niasse, with conspiring to attack French military bases in Senegal in retaliation for France's support for Chad in the war against Libya. The charges were eventually dropped and the Libyans allowed to go home, but the Senegalese authorities held on to the weaponry and allowed two CIA officers, Kenneth Steiner and Warren Clemens,* to take photos of the timer. The MST-13 marking was clearly visible on the photographs, but, unlike the device recovered from Togo, it was housed in a grey plastic box measuring approximately 80 × 75 × 52 mm. The corners of the box were reinforced to accommodate the screws, so in order to fit in the box, a concave curved section of each corner of the main circuit board had been cut away, just like PT/35b.[20]

The challenge now was to identify the timers. Initially the police and the FBI only had the letters 'MST-13' to go on, but when the investigators dismantled the Togo timer there was a further clue. Below the main green circuit board was a smaller white circuit board. On close examination they noticed a short word, which had been partially scratched out. It appeared that it might be 'MEBQ' or 'M580', but they eventually worked out that it was 'MEBO'. The name meant nothing to the Scottish police, but three months later they were to learn that it was the electronics company owned by Bollier and Meister.[21]

Formal permission was obtained from the Swiss government to question the pair and Mebo's technician, Ulrich Lumpert. Over the next few months they were each interviewed by the Swiss police, Scottish police and the FBI. They were happy to cooperate and appeared to be telling the police all they knew.

In the course of those interviews a fairly consistent narrative emerged. It began in the summer of 1985, when, during a visit to Tripoli, Bollier received a request from Abdelbaset's friend Ezzadin

* Kenneth Steiner and Warren Clemens were both assumed names.

Hinshiri, who was then a departmental head in the JSO, to supply some electronic timing devices for the Libyan army. *(The JSO was often asked to procure equipment on the army's behalf, as it had far better connections to international suppliers.)* Bollier was led to understand that, if the initial timers fitted the bill, five to ten thousand of the devices would be required. On returning to Zurich he ordered Lumpert to design a timer, which became known as the MST-13.[22]

Once Lumpert had done so, Mebo ordered the necessary components from their suppliers. Most of these items were off-the-shelf, but the timer's two circuit boards had been designed by Lumpert and therefore had to be specially ordered. The main one, which like the timer was called MST-13, measured approximately 70 × 65 mm, while the smaller one, known as a UZ4, was approximately 32 × 30 mm. The boards were ordered from a Swiss company called Thüring, which was one of Mebo's regular suppliers. The initial order, which was placed on 13 August 1985, was for 20 boards of each type.[23]

Owing to the urgency of the order, Mebo specified that the MST-13 boards should be solder-masked only on the opposite side to the circuitry. Solder-masking required Thüring to create a special template, and would also have made it more difficult for Lumpert to iron out any design glitches when making the timers. Masking the reverse side of the board was far easier, as no template was required, and was done purely for cosmetic purposes.

In the event Thüring delivered 24, rather than 20, of the boards.[24] Two months later, Mebo placed a further order with Thüring, for 35 of each type of circuit board. This time the MST-13 boards were to be solder-masked on both sides. They were delivered to Mebo on 5 November 1985.[25]

The Mebo witnesses were clear that only 20 MST-13 timers were made and that the circuit boards were not used in any other device. All of the MST-13 boards used were green, with some solder-masked on one side only and some on both sides. The UZ4 boards were all semi-translucent off-white. Some of the timers, like the Senegal device, were housed in grey plastic boxes, while the others, like the one examined in Washington DC, had open sides and no box.

The time was set by means of so-called decade wheels, which were small rotary switches bearing the digits 0 to 9, and a simple slide switch that enabled the user to choose between hours and minutes. The Washington timer had two decade wheels and the Senegal one had four. Thus, it was possible to set the Washington timer to activate from anything between one minute, or hour, and 99minutes, or hours; and for the Senegal device the upper limit was 9,999 minutes, or 166 hours 39 minutes.

Crucially, Bollier confirmed that he personally gave all 20 of the devices to Libyan officials. He said that he had handed them over in three batches. The first batch, which was of five, he delivered in person to Hinshiri's office in Tripoli; the second, also of five, he took to the Libyan Embassy in East Berlin during a business trip to the city; and the remaining ten he again delivered to Hinshiri's office.[26]

It was crystal clear to the investigators that the Lockerbie fragment PT/35b originated from one of the boxed MST-13 timers containing a board with single-sided solder masking. Bollier was a godsend. And he had much more to tell.

He said that, some time after he delivered the last batch of timers, he was asked to attend military tests in the Sahara desert, in which the timers were used to activate airborne explosives. Here, apparently, was proof that the MST-13s were intended for use in bombs. He claimed that the devices were brought to the test site by a military colonel who was also in the JSO, Nassr Ashur. Ashur was head of security for LAA before the airline security personnel were transferred from the JSO to LAA (a transition which Abdelbaset oversaw).

Bollier said he heard nothing more about the timers until around three weeks before Lockerbie, when Abdelbaset's ABH partner Badri Hassan visited Mebo's offices and told him that 40 further MST-13s were required urgently by the Libyan army. Bollier checked with Lumpert whether they had enough components in stock and Lumpert advised that they did not. Concerned not to lose the order, Bollier bought 40 off-the-shelf Olympus-brand timers from an electronics supplier, and on 18 December 1988 flew to Tripoli to deliver them to Hinshiri. The following day he met Hinshiri, who told him that the Olympus timers were too expensive and that he wanted MST-13s. According to Bollier, Hinshiri nevertheless retained the timers and told him to go to Abdelbaset's office that evening, where he would be paid for them. Bollier said that at 8 p.m. he was driven to Abdelbaset's house and waited for two hours outside an office adjoining the house. He said that he neither saw Abdelbaset nor got paid, but while waiting saw that there was a meeting going on in the office.* The only person he recognised in the room was Ashur.

The following day, he claimed, he again saw Hinshiri, who said he wanted to keep the timers and pay for them later. Bollier insisted on having the devices back and said he would be taking the next flight back to Zurich. He waited for about an hour until Hinshiri's chauffeur brought him the timers. He was sure that, during that hour, the timers had been taken somewhere.[27]

He said that after Lockerbie he had a 'bad feeling' about the incident.[28] He tried to call Hinsihri about the payment for his expenses, but couldn't reach anyone. His suspicion that Libya was behind the bombing was heightened when he noticed that one of the Olympus timers had been set to activate on a Wednesday at 19.30. The Lockerbie bombing had occurred on a Wednesday at 19.03. He suspected that this was no coincidence, and that someone had set the time when the timers were out of his possession, perhaps as a rehearsal for Lockerbie.

He also claimed that in January 1989, while in East Berlin, he was visited in his hotel by the Libyan official to whom he had passed five MST-13 timers in 1985. The man, whom he knew only as 'Mustafa', was accompanied by a German man, who asked Bollier if he had noticed that the Olympus timers had been tampered with. From that point, Bollier said, it was 'absolutely clear' that Libya had something to do with the bombing.[29]

Bollier's evidence gave the police one of their greatest breakthroughs and appeared to pin responsibility for the bombing very firmly on Libya. It was clear from their line of questioning that Abdelbaset had become the prime suspect. However, despite implicating Libya, he was sure that Abdelbaset had nothing to do with either the MST-13 timers or the bombing.[30] The investigation of the circuit board fragment was, nevertheless, heralded as a triumph of international cooperation and straightforward, old-fashioned police work. As the

* This could not have been true, because I did not have an office at the house.

years passed, however, it became clear that the timer saga was anything but straightforward, and, from the outset, was riddled with oddities and inconsistencies, which cast a cloud of doubt over this crucial element of the prosecution case.

Some of these concerned the MST-13 timers that were supposedly retrieved during the abortive September 1986 coup in Togo and the February 1988 arrests in Senegal. It was originally suggested that the Togo coup attempt was Libyan-backed, but no evidence could be produced to substantiate the claim. Moreover, there was some doubt as to whether the two MST-13 timers were ever part of the arms cache. Richard Sherrow, the BATF agent who retrieved one of the timers shortly after the coup attempt, suspected they were not and may have been planted. He also reported that they 'had been handled and manipulated by unknown parties'.[31] In September 1990, Detective Inspector Watson McAteer and Detective Sergeant Peter Avent travelled to Togo, with FBI agent Craig Bates, in order to investigate the devices. President Gnassingbe Eyadema and his Chief of Police Colonel Walla showed one of the timers that had been seized, which was strange because both the timers had supposedly been taken from Togo long ago; one by Sherrow and the other, it later emerged, by the French intelligence service.[32] Stranger still, it bore the name 'Flash', and was very different to the MST-13s. When the officers subsequently inspected the arms cache they found the weapons laid out in exactly the same position in which Sherrow and his BATF colleague Owens had found them in 1986,[33] and the only timer present was another Flash device.[34] When McAteer showed a photo of Sherrow's timer to the President Eyadema, Colonel Walla and another officer, Colonel Assih, who had been involved in the coup investigation, all said that they had never seen such a device before.[35] Furthermore, Assih told McAteer that the timer that was taken by the Americans in 1986 was of the same Flash type that they had been shown.[36] The police then interviewed the officer who had headed the coup investigation, Colonel Meneme. He too was shown a photo of Sherrow's MST-13 timer and a statement was taken from him. That statement has never been disclosed and his response was not recorded in the police officers' corresponding statements; however, what he told them was of sufficient interest for them to request Colonel Walla to re-interview Assih. Walla agreed, and also said he would make further enquiries to establish whether there were ever MST-13 timers in Togo, but the police heard nothing more.[37] They returned to the UK and no further investigations were conducted.

The mystery was further deepened by FBI agent Bates, who later told Abdelbaset's defence team that he had been told that the original timers had been given to 'an unfriendly government, i.e. not the US or the UK'. When pressed to reveal which government, he was advised by an FBI attorney, who was present during the interview, not to do so 'on national security grounds'.[38] The claim was remarkable, for the obvious reason that the BATF was part of the American government and the French government could hardly be described as unfriendly.

The experiences of Sherrow, McAteer and Avent in Togo all suggested that the two MST-13 devices 'found' in 1986 were never part of the arms cache, and rather had been planted, with the likely purpose of implicating Libya in the coup attempt. At the time Libya had powerful enemies, not least the US government, which, a few months earlier, had ordered air strikes against against the capital, Tripoli, and the second city, Benghazi. Under its director William Casey, the CIA had, for years, been been engaged in a major disinformation campaign against the country and its leader Colonel Gadafy.* This was stepped up in August 1986, a month before the coup attempt, when President Ronald Reagan signed a secret National Security Decision Directive, which, according to a press leak, ordered 'covert, diplomatic and economic steps designed to . . . bring about a change of leadership in Libya'.[39] Part of the strategy involved feeding false stories to the media about Libya. The same month it was reported that the Togolese authorities had foiled a Libyan-backed plot to 'blow up the United States diplomatic mission' in the capital city Lomé. Two suitcases packed with explosives, three grenades and an automatic pistol were alleged to have been smuggled from Libya via the Libyan embassy in Contonou, capital of Togo's eastern neighbour, Benin. The United States and Togo's close ally France were reported to have 'helped Togo with its inquiries'. The country's Interior Minister would

* The US government's covert campaign against Libya is detailed in Chapter 9.

71

not say how the authorities had learned that the Embassy was the target of the attack.[40]

France had a motive to implicate Libya in the attack, as the two countries were, at the time, effectively at war in Chad. Its forces provided substantial military support for the government of President Hissen Habré, including air strikes against Libyan bases. The CIA also gave covert assistance to Habré as part of its wider campaign against Libya.[41] As the former colonial power, France had a significant presence in Togo and it is quite possible that its foreign intelligence service, the DGSE, made common cause with the CIA to falsely implicate Libya.

If either was aware that MST-13 timers were produced exclusively for Libya by Mebo, then the devices were the perfect Libyan 'signature' to plant in Togo. So could they have known? Many years later, John Orkin, the CIA technician who helped the FBI's Tom Thurman to identify the circuit board fragment, revealed that he had known about Mebo since 1985, when he had examined a radio-controlled device that had been seized in Chad. The device incorporated radio receivers manufactured by Motorola. On checking their serial numbers against Motorola's delivery records, the CIA established that they had been purchased by Mebo. At Orkin's behest, a CIA station officer in Switzerland asked the Swiss authorities to question Mebo about the radio-controlled devices. The company produced records indicating that it had sold 16 of them to the Libyan Office of Military Security.[42] Orkin's subsequent report on the Chad device named Mebo as the manufacturer.[43]

If Orkin, as a mere technical expert, was able to find out so much about Mebo, simply by relaying a request to the Swiss authorities, how much easier would it have been for the CIA's intelligence officers to find out exactly what the company was supplying to Libya? It is quite likely that the Agency knew all along that Bollier was supplying MST-13s to Libya, because, as the journalist Paul Harris revealed, Mebo had been monitored by the Western intelligence services since the early 1970s. Thanks to Harris, MI6, and presumably also the CIA, were aware that Bollier was selling Western technology to the Stasi. It is inconceivable that Mebo would have been allowed to get away with this trade unless he could be of use to the Western intelligence services.

Bollier has never admitted that he was a CIA asset, but he was certainly reporting back to the Swiss Federal Police from as early 1970, when, following his second visit to the Stasi's Scientific and Technical Institute, he was contacted by a Commissioner Leuenberger of the Federal Police who asked him detailed questions about the trip.[44] So, even if he was not strictly speaking a double agent, the CIA could certainly keep tabs on exactly what he was up to and, given who he was selling to, it is certain they would have done so. It is therefore quite possible that the CIA had MST-13 timers before the Togo coup attempt.

We might never know whether or not the Togo timers were planted. Nevertheless, despite the arrest of many of the alleged plotters in both of the Togo incidents, Libyan involvement was never proved.

The story of the Senegal timer also raised suspicions of DGSE and CIA interference. The two Libyans arrested in Senegal in February 1988, Mohamed El-Marzouk and Mansour El-Saber, and their Senegalese accomplice, Ahmed Khalifa Niasse, were alleged to be involved in a straightforward plot to target French military installations in retaliation for France's role in the Chad war. (Although a ceasefire had been agreed five months earlier, Franco-Libyan relations had remained hostile.)* According to the CIA's Kenneth Steiner, however, Niasse, a Muslim religious leader, was reporting back to the Senegalese President's Secretary-General, Jean Collin, and had been issued with a false passport under an assumed name 'in order to demonstrate to the Libyans that he had influence in Senegal'.[45] Steiner said that Collin tipped him off a month prior to the arrests, and he in turn informed CIA Headquarters. Collin subsequently became upset, as he believed that the US government had tried to persuade the government of the Ivory Coast to arrest the three men when their flight from Benin to the Senegalese capital Dakar stopped in the Ivorian capital Abidjan.

Steiner later recalled: 'I suggested to Collin that the French Service, the DGSE, be brought in on the operation, because my initial impression was that this was entirely a Senegalese operation being run by Collin. Later it became clear to me that the French Service, whose representative had his office next to Collin's, had been involved in the

---

* No formal peace agreement was signed in the Chad conflict until 1994.

73

operation from the outset.'[46] This was hardly surprising, as Senegal, like Togo, was a former French colony, and Collin was an ex-colonial administrator.[47†]

Steiner and Collin were both present at Dakar Airport when the flight arrived and the arrests were made.[48] Later, questioned by the police, El-Marzouk admitted that he had carried a suitcase containing the weapons and the timer, but claimed he thought it belonged to Niasse, and he and El-Saber each denied knowledge of its contents.[49] It was clear from their custody photos that the two Libyans had been beaten up,[50] yet neither confessed to plotting an attack, and four months later the charges against them were dropped on the grounds of insufficient evidence.[51] Many years later, at Abdelbaset's trial, the judges concluded that the evidence did not establish any connection between the two men and the timer.[52]

In July 1990, Detective Inspector Williamson and Detective Sergeant Michael Langford-Johnson travelled to Senegal to investigate the 1988 arrests.[53] Among the documents obtained from the Senegalese authorities was an official order, signed by Collin and dated 17 January 1989, commanding the police and army to destroy all the items seized, with the exception of an automatic pistol and some ammunition.[54] It appeared that the order had been carried out, because also handed over was a report confirming the destruction, which was signed by the Head of the Army's Equipment Establishment and dated 8 September 1989. The report precisely listed all of the destroyed items, but missing from the list was the timer.[55] What, then, had become of it?

In January 1991, Williamson and Langford-Johnson conducted a decidedly frosty interview with Collin, who had by then retired. When asked if he knew where the timer was and whether any 'foreign services' had had access to it, he replied only, 'I don't know.' They then enquired whether, given his senior position, he would expect to be informed of what had happened to it. He replied contemptuously, 'I

† The extent of the DGSE's role in the affair remains unknown. It is nevertheless noteworthy that it was a French magazine, *L'Express*, which first broke news of the discovery of the timer fragment, PT/35b. Published on 4 October 1990, the article also detailed the Senegal connection. The journalist responsible, Xavier Raufer, was known for his good contacts within the intelligence services.

would answer that question if it were put to me by my superior at the time.' Asked whether the two Libyans had taken the timer to Libya following their release, he retorted, 'That supposition is straight out of a serialised novel!' Collin was right, it was ludicrous to suggest that his government would have given the timer to suspected terrorists. Curiously, he later added, 'I am convinced that the timer discovered in Senegal could not have been used for terrorist purposes.'[56] Collin, it seemed, knew more than he was saying, while the officers remained in the dark.

Being in the dark was, by then, a familiar experience for the Scottish police. It was not until September 1990 that they had finally learned of the existence of Mebo, having once again been spoon-fed information by the intelligence services. According to the Deputy SIO Detective Chief Superintendent James Gilchrist, they were advised to inquire about the company by 'one of the "technical boffins" at the Security Service.'[57]* SIO Stuart Henderson also later recalled being tipped off by the security services, but, to the best of his recollection, he had first heard of Mebo from the FBI, who were 'probably acting on information from the CIA'.[58] Henderson travelled to Zurich with members of the Security Service to meet with the Swiss police. Prior to their departure, the CIA requested the Security Service to defer or delay the trip, but the request was refused. However, the day before the visit, CIA officers met with the Swiss police and intelligence service.[59] Once again, the Americans were a step ahead of the Scots.

The Swiss police gave Henderson the impression that they knew about Mebo and its supply of electronic equipment to various countries. On his return to Scotland he arranged for a formal request for legal assistance – known as a *Commission Rogatoire* – to be sent to the Swiss government, but, prior to the Swiss acting on the request, he learned that the FBI's legal attaché in Switzerland had already made contact with Mebo's Edwin Bollier. Henderson was furious and, suspecting that the attaché's approach had been prompted by the CIA, immediately wrote to his FBI opposite number, Richard

* The Security Service is the official name of MI5. It may be that the police officers used the terms Security Service and security services interchangeably, although the latter also includes MI6, a.k.a. the Secret Intelligence Service.

Marquise, to demand the contact be withdrawn.[60] Marquise later acknowledged that there were 'political difficulties' between the various countries involved and 'more importantly, political differences between the agencies within each country'. He said that it eventually became necessary to hold a meeting with the CIA to discuss these problems and that following the meeting, on 2 October 1990, the Agency 'backed off'.[61]

If the police hoped it would be plain sailing from then on, they were to be sorely disappointed, as the difficulties that they faced in getting to Bollier were as nothing compared to the headaches that the mercurial businessman would subsequently cause them. Although there was no doubt that his company had supplied 20 MST-13 timers to Libya, other important aspects of his account proved to be extremely shaky.

Especially dubious was his explanation of the anonymous letter that he sent to the CIA in January 1989. Two events, he said, had prompted him to point the Agency in Libya's direction: the first was his discovery, shortly after the bombing, that one of the Olympus timers had been set to activate on a Wednesday at 19.30 hours; and the second was the subsequent episode in East Berlin when the German man accompanying the Libyan Embassy official Mustafa had asked him if he had noticed that the timers had been tampered with.

There were two major flaws in the timer settings story. Firstly, Libya, like Malta and Switzerland, is in the Central European time zone, which is one hour ahead of the UK. So, if the Lockerbie timer had been set to explode at 07.30 Libyan time, it would have exploded at 06.30 UK time, which was only five minutes after Flight 103 took off. Secondly, and more importantly, the Olympus timers only had a 24-hour clock setting. In other words, it was not possible to set the timers for a Wednesday, or any other day of the week. As for the East Berlin episode, although he initially claimed that it took place before he wrote the letter,[62] he later told the police that he had been mistaken and that it had in fact taken place some time after.[63]

FBI agents questioned Bollier about the letter during five days of interviews at the FBI academy in Quantico, Virginia in February 1991, which were also attended by CIA and Scottish police representatives.[64] When asked why he had posed as a Libyan radio operator, he said it was partly to establish his credibility, partly to protect his and Meister's identity – presumably in case it fell into Libyan hands – and partly to establish a means of future communication. He admitted that much of what he had written was invention, including Mr Karlheinz and the Swissair flight. However, he claimed to have an informant who worked for high officials within the Libyan government and he insisted that he had met Abu Achmed – whom the letter named as the right-hand man of both Abu Nidal and, formerly at least, Ahmed Jibril – on at least two occasions, one of them being during the desert tests of the MST-13 timers.

He said that about ten to fourteen days after sending the letter he received and answered radio communications from the United States. He claimed he had subsequently tried, unsuccessfully, to send the CIA a taped high-speed message in Morse code. He then called a contact number in Washington DC and attempted to relay the message verbally, but the person who answered did not understand what was happening, so he sent the CIA a tape recording of the message. The tape obviously found its way into the right hands, because the FBI was able to show Bollier a transcript of the message, which, to the best of his recollection, was accurate. He said that some weeks later, on 14 April 1989, he faxed the CIA to tell them his informant had stated that Colonel Gadafy believed the Americans were angry about terrorist attacks and had ordered that Libyans should cease operations against US targets.[65]

When interviewed by the Crown prior to Abdelbaset's trial, the FBI's Richard Marquise said that the CIA had told him about the December 1988 letter soon after receiving it.[66] He added that the FBI had checked out all the names it mentioned, but the inquiries came to nothing. When, two years later, Bollier confessed to having sent the letter,[67] Marquise realised its potential importance, so sent Special Agent Hal Hendershot to retrieve the original from the US Embassy in Vienna. The CIA told Marquise that the contact with the letter's author had proved useless and had ended in June 1989;[68] however, details of that contact, such as the tape transcript, have never been made public.

Bollier tried to give the impression that he had written to the CIA purely out of concern to put the Lockerbie investigation on the right track, but his motivation was plainly far less altruistic. The letter made clear that he was hoping to gain from the tip-off, stating, 'We've heard that you will pay for classified information,' adding, 'We are willing to work for the CIA USA under the conditions of the highest degree of security possible.'[69]

It was a theme that Bollier pursued unashamedly during his FBI interview, the report of which noted, 'BOLLIER is still interested in the reward . . . BOLLIER sees three (3) possibilities for BOLLIER to receive money from the United States government. The first is by Mebo entering into commercial agreements with the United States to supply electronic equipment. The second is for BOLLIER to enter into an agreement where he works for the United States as a covert operative. The third is for BOLLIER to receive part of the reward money for providing information about the Pan Am Flight 103 bombing.' Bollier emphasised that he and Meister were ideally placed to be covert operatives: 'as Swiss nationals they are neutral so they are well trusted by the Arabs. Both BOLLIER and MEISTER have many contacts and could be very useful to the American authorities. Many of their contacts are in the military, police and security services.'[70]

While discussing rewards with the FBI, Bollier was simultaneously trying to take advantage of Libya. On 6 February 1991 he wrote to Ezzadin Hinshiri to inform him that he had been interviewed by the police, who had told him that a Mebo timer had been used in the Lockerbie bomb. He added, 'I have been asked to whom such timers had been delivered to, and I could proove them that in 1985 they have been sold to a Mr Khoury in Beyrut, Lebanon [sic].' He added as a PS: 'I heard you are now minister of Communications, are there any new projects we could participate?' Bollier told the FBI that he wrote the letter as protection in case the Libyans were considering silencing him, but it could also be read as a none-too-subtle offer to divert the police away from Libya in return for some government contracts.[71]

Despite the letter, for two years Bollier's position remained that only 20 MST-13 timers were made and that they were all supplied to Libya. In 1993 that position changed dramatically. Bollier declared that his earlier statements were mistaken and that he had in fact supplied two of the timers to the East German security service, the Stasi.

The revelation appeared to deal a major blow to the official account of Lockerbie, as the Stasi was known to be very close to the original suspects in the bombing, Ahmed Jibril's PFLP-GC. Interviewed by the BKA in October 1993, Bollier claimed he had been reminded about the Stasi timers by Mebo's technician Ulrich Lumpert.[72] Lumpert subsequently recalled that he'd had to work on a Saturday in order to complete the timers in time for Bollier to deliver them to East Germany.[73] Bollier was in fact not the first person to confirm the supply of MST-13s to the Stasi. During a later interview the BKA informed him that an unnamed former Stasi officer had first confessed 18 months earlier to receiving at least one MST-13 from him.[74] Perhaps Bollier got wind of the confession and chose to admit the error in his previous accounts, rather than later be accused of concealing the facts.

When questioned about the new information, Bollier freely admitted that he was motivated 'first and foremost by financial interest and gain', and that he was particularly concerned to fend off a $32 million civil action that had been launched against Mebo by Pan Am. Nevertheless, he insisted, he was telling the truth and that 'perjury in return for payment is out of the question'.[75] He appeared to have some success in turning the situation to his financial advantage. He told the Swiss Federal Police that in March 1993 Abdelbaset and Lamin's Libyan lawyer Ibrahim Legwell had assured him that there was a possibility of organising a $1.8 million loan at a favourable rate of interest. Although the loan did not materialise, Bollier admitted that Mebo received $120,000 from Legwell to cover 'expenses'.[76] In December 1993 he offered to hold a press conference in Geneva to publicise his claims, for which he submitted 'an estimate of probable costs' of $300,000.[77] Small wonder that one close observer of the Lockerbie case commented that Bollier was the Swiss equivalent of a 'wee Glasgow chancer'. Any payments were unfortunate and unwise, and gave the impression of witness tampering.

Ever since his admission about the Stasi timers, Bollier consistently sought to undermine the case against Abdelbaset and Libya, but for the most part his claims ranged from the eccentric to the outright unhelpful. In early 1994 he claimed to have found an invoice that indicated that he sold seven, rather than two, MST-13s to the

Stasi, although he suggested that it might have been planted during a break-in at Mebo's office.[78] Stranger still, he claimed that the CIA letter, rather than being written at his own and Meister's initiative, was produced on the orders of a mysterious man who turned up at the office on 30 December 1988. He claimed the man was obviously from the security services and had said to him, 'Mr Bollier, you were in Libya. You delivered 40 MST timers. You returned via Malta to Zurich. And I can tell you that the Libyans are connected with this attack.' He said the man instructed him to produce the letter on a typewriter with Spanish characters and warned that if he failed to comply he would 'suffer the consequences'.[79] As for the January 1989 encounter in East Berlin, Bollier resiled from his earlier account, saying he was fairly sure that neither of the men who approached him about the Olympus timers was the Libyan Mustafa and that they both appeared to be Stasi officers.[80]

His most persistent claim was that the circuit-board fragment PT/35b depicted in the photographs originally shown to him by the police was from a greyish-brown prototype MST-13 board, rather than from one of the green boards manufactured by Thüring. This was of the utmost significance, he said, because the prototype boards were used only in the Stasi timers. The fact that all the photographs of PT/35b subsequently disclosed by the police showed it to be green was, according to Bollier, because the original fragment had been substituted. The green fragment in these photos, he insisted, had not been involved in an explosion.[81] In the absence of any supporting evidence, the assertion that the Stasi timers did not contain green boards undermined the subsequent submission by Abdelbaset's defence team that PT/35b could have originated from a Stasi device.

Bollier was far quieter on the subject of his relationship with both Eastern and Western intelligence services, but, as the layers of his career were unpeeled, an ugly core was exposed. In 1992, well before he revealed that he had supplied MST-13 timers to East Germany, he confirmed to the Swiss police that his relationship with the Stasi's Scientific and Technical Institute in Bernau dated back to 1970. This was confirmation of what, thanks to the journalist Paul Harris, had been known to MI6 since 1971. Bollier said that he was introduced to the Institute by a Swiss intermediary, who had enquired whether he would be interested in building a business relationship with East Germany. He subsequently travelled to East Berlin and met with a Dr Steinberger, who asked him to procure electronic equipment, including telephone monitoring devices and other bugging technology. Bollier estimated that the total value of sales to East Germany during the 1970s was around one million Swiss francs, and admitted that the goods he supplied included radio-controlled devices for triggering explosives.[82]

A fuller picture of Bollier's relationship with the Stasi was provided by five of his former handlers. Known by the code names Steiner, Arnold, Wenzel, Gardener and Gerber, they confirmed that he had been classified as an 'unofficial employee' and given a code name of his own, Rubin. They also revealed that Mebo was paid in advance for its equipment and consequently was, for long periods, heavily in debt to the Stasi. Herein, perhaps, lay the reason for Bollier's initial failure to reveal anything that might implicate the Stasi in the bombing.

Among the equipment he supplied, they said, were special radio receivers, sophisticated encryption and deciphering devices, and military night vision equipment.[83] In the early 1980s he attempted to procure a West German encryption and encoding device via West German intermediaries, but the plan was thwarted by the West German authorities and the intermediaries were convicted.[84] Bollier, however, was never arrested.

The handlers correctly assumed that Bollier was under surveillance by Western intelligence because he had been working for the Stasi for so long.[85] They also believed he was, in fact, a double agent. 'We assumed that Bollier was working for several secret services. This suspicion was based on an estimate of his personality. His character was governed by turning everything into money and exploiting the needs of governments,' Gardener told the BKA.[86] Among those he was thought to be working for were, unsurprisingly, the CIA and the West German Federal Intelligence Service, the BND.[87]

Such was the Stasi's concern that in 1987 Gerber was asked to consider how best to terminate the relationship. He produced a 13-page report on agent Rubin, dated 29 July 1987, which was forwarded to the Deputy Minister of State Security, Lieutenant General

Wolfgang Schwanitz. Gerber subsequently received the order that contact should be 'terminated in a gradual and systematic manner'. In late 1989 Bollier was informed by telephone that his services were no longer required.[88] The news coincided with the fall of the Berlin Wall and the collapse of East Germany's Communist dictatorship. Freedom was bad for business. Small wonder that he was keen to profit from the Lockerbie bombing.

The Shopkeeper 5

Malta, and its smaller sister islands Gozo and Comino, lie 200 miles north of the Libyan coast. These tiny specks in the Mediterranean are home to around 350,000 people, although the Maltese diaspora is far larger. During the late 1980s the country was of great importance to my country. Relations with our immediate Arab neighbours, Egypt and Tunisia, were bad and we were at war with our southern neighbour, Chad. The Libyan government was beginning to embrace private enterprise as a means of boosting the economy, but strict US trade sanctions, which included a total ban on direct imports and exports, ensured that many goods remained scarce. Malta was our main gateway to the world. Libyans were able to travel there without visas and with conventional ID cards, rather than passports. Once there, communication was relatively easy, because Maltese is based in part on Arabic and Italian.*

For these reasons, there were plenty of LAA and Air Malta flights between Tripoli and Malta's Luqa Airport. There were more Libyans on the island than any other foreign nationality, around 15,000 at any one time. They tended not to stay long; some would visit for the day, while most of the rest stayed only for a day or two. There were other Arabs present too, in particular Egyptians, Tunisians and Palestinians, but the Maltese frequently called all Arabs 'Libyano'.

Libyans tended to like Malta. Compared to home there was more entertainment to be had and many more goods in the shops. I first visited in 1972, but didn't return until 1984, when I first met Lamin and he invited my wife and me to eat with his family. After the birth of our son in 1986 I travelled there a lot. He was born prematurely and suffered digestive and liver problems, which required us to take great care with his diet. He needed clean water and a lot of fresh

* Since Libya is a former Italian colony, our dialect contains many Italian words.

83

fruit, both of which could be hard to obtain in Tripoli. I therefore brought back bottled water, fruit and other scarce goods, such as disposable nappies. I also passed through the island on business trips, and on these occasions generally made a point of staying over for a night or two. I would often return with gifts for the family and items for the home, as well as the essentials for my son.

The Lockerbie investigation first tilted towards Malta on 22 May 1989, when RARDE forensic scientist Dr Thomas Hayes examined a small blue and white mass of fabric labelled PK/669, which had been found in Northumbria a week after the bombing.[1] On untangling it, he discovered that it consisted mainly of a clothing label, which read 'Age 12-18 months . . . Height 86 cm . . . 75% modacrylic . . . 25% polyester . . . Rib 100% acrylic . . . Keep away from fire . . . Made in Malta.' Two facts were clear: the item was heavily blast-damaged and it originated from a child's garment. There was also a plastic tag in the label, suggesting it had never been worn.[2]

The damage suggested that the garment was very close to the bomb, and quite possibly in the primary suitcase. So, if the police could establish its origin, it might lead them to the bomber. On 2 June, Detective Inspector George Brown began investigating the item. Malta was the obvious starting point. He soon established that its main exporter of children's wear was PVC Plastics Ltd, which had a sister company in Leicestershire called Hellane. With the help of Hellane's commercial director, he confirmed that the garment was a Capri blue babygro, which PVC Plastics had produced for the retailer Primark. Further inquiries established that 552 of the babygros had been made for the 12 to 18-month age range and that, of those, 410 were sent to Ireland, 125 were sold as surplus stock to a Maltese wholesale company called Big Ben, and 17 were used as samples and for display purposes. Further inquiries were undertaken in Ireland, and on 5 July Brown and a police colleague visited Big Ben and interviewed its co-directors.[3] Frustratingly, the company did not keep distribution records, so they could not say which retailers had bought the surplus stock.[4] The Malta link appeared to be a dead end.

However, it was soon to be dramatically revived. In August 1989, the BKA informed the police that there was documentary evidence

from Frankfurt Airport that the primary suitcase had begun its journey in Malta.* The police looked again at other blast-damaged clothing fragments to see if any could be linked to the island. Among them
was item PT/28, which was one of four fragments of a pair of dark-
brown checked trousers. Attached to it was a label marked 'Yorkie
Clothing', and stamped on a pocket lining was the number '1705'.[5]
Inquiries on Malta established that there was a clothing manufacturer called Yorkie Clothing, which was based at the San Gwann
Industrial Estate in Birkikara.

On 30 August 1989, DCI Harry Bell and Detective Sergeant William Armstrong travelled to Malta, taking with them an album of
photographs of PT/28 and other heavily blast-damaged clothing. The
following day they met with the Maltese police to explain the nature
of their inquiries and on 1 September they visited Yorkie Clothing,
where they interviewed Alexander Calleja, the son of the company's
founder and owner. On being shown the photographs, he confirmed
that the company had made the trousers. More importantly, he explained that the '1705' stamp was the order number, and that this
would allow him to pinpoint the retailer to whom the trousers were
supplied. Now the police were getting somewhere. On checking the
company's order book, he established that the purchaser was someone called Gauci of Mary's House shop, at 63 Tower Road in the
Maltese town of Sliema. The delivery book indicated that the order
was delivered on 18 November 1988 and signed for by a Mr Tony
Gauci. There were five pairs of dark-brown checked trousers in the
order: 1 × 32-inch waist, 2 × 34-inch and 2 × 36-inch. One of the
other trouser fragments had a paper label attached, on which was
printed the number '340001'. Calleja explained that this meant that
they were the first of the 34-inch pairs to be made.

The police wasted no time in visiting Mary's House. In the shop
they found the owner, Edward Gauci, who was elderly and obviously in poor health, and his 44-year-old son, Tony. When asked
about the 1705 order, Tony said they still had two of the pairs of
dark-brown checked trousers in stock. He fetched them and handed them over to the police. Both were size 36. When the police
asked if there was any way that he could recall to whom the other

* This evidence is described in Chapter 6.

85

three pairs had been sold, Edward became very excitable and upset. Tony called his younger brother Paul, who shortly after arrived at the shop. While Tony looked after Edward, the police asked Paul whether he recognised any of the other blast-damaged garments in their photo album. He quickly spotted that two fragments of a pair of pyjamas matched ones they stocked, and immediately brought over a pair.

Then came the police's big break. Overhearing the conversation, Tony interjected to say that he could recall selling a pair of dark-brown checked Yorkie trousers and three pairs of pyjamas, plus other clothing, to a man.[6] It had stuck in his memory because the man had behaved rather strangely, not caring about what he bought: 'It was as if anything I suggested he buy he would take it.' The police asked if he could recall what other clothes the man had bought. He could, and reeled off a list. There was a second pair of Yorkie trousers, this one a light brown herringbone pattern, a 42-inch imitation Harris tweed jacket, a woollen tartan cardigan, a black umbrella and . . . a blue babygro! The police showed him photos of two fragments of light-brown herringbone material, which he confirmed matched the second pair of trousers. Tony gave the police a pair of these trousers, plus a tweed jacket like the one he had sold.

So, the brothers had confirmed that three of the garments sold to the man matched ones that were close to the Lockerbie bomb, and Tony had also confirmed that the man had bought a blue babygro. But who was the man and what did he look like? The shopkeeper was able to provide a full description:

'He was about six feet or more in height. He had a big chest and a large head. He was well-built but he was not fat or with a big stomach. His hair was very black. He was speaking Libyan to me. He was clearly from Libya. He had an Arab appearance and I would say he was in fact a Libyan, I can tell the difference between Libyans and Tunisians when I speak to them for a while. Tunisians often start speaking French if you talk to them for a while. He was clean shaven with no facial hair. He had dark-coloured skin. He was wearing a dark-coloured two piece suit. I think it may have been blue-coloured. His overall appearance was smart. I will think things over tonight and try to recall anything else about the man.'

Middle-aged and single, Tony was a solitary and rather simple character, devoted to little other than the shop, the care of his father and his racing pigeons. But, to the police, he was gold dust. And he could recall more. The purchase had taken place during the winter of 1988. It happened not long before the shop's closing time of 19.00, so probably around 18.30. Tony was alone in the shop, because Paul had gone home to watch a football match. The bill came to 76.50 Maltese pounds and the customer paid in cash with ten pound notes. He told Tony that he had other shops to visit and that he would return for the clothes. As the man left the shop they noticed that it had begun raining, so he bought an umbrella, which he opened as he went out on to the street. Tony parcelled up the clothes with brown paper and string, and about 15 minutes later the man returned. Tony asked if he could carry the parcels for him, assuming that he had a car. The man said that he had a taxi waiting for him. He took the parcels and Tony followed him to the door. Once on the street he turned left. Tony looked up the road and noticed that there was a white Mercedes taxi parked on the next corner. He assumed it was the one to which the man had referred, but did not see him actually get into it. The man had not been in the shop before or since.[7]

The police asked Paul if he could remember a day in November or December 1988 when he had taken the afternoon off work to watch football on TV. He could, but he couldn't remember the date or the match. He said that it most probably featured Italy in the European Nations Cup, or an Italian club side in a European competition, and would have been on one of the Italian RAI channels.[8]

Over the next five weeks the police visited Tony a further nine times, taking ten further statements. They also took four more from Paul.

The FBI and BKA were soon invited to join the Gauci investigation. On 13 September Tony helped a photofit specialist from the BKA to create a photofit image, which he said was as close as he could get to the man. Although the eyes and eyebrows were smaller than the man's, most other features were similar, including his age, which, crucially, he described as around about 50.[9] Later the same day an FBI artist, George Noble, produced a drawing under Tony's direction, which Tony said bore 'a very close resemblance' to the man.[10]

The same day Tony had some important news to impart. He'd remembered that about a month earlier he had seen a man resembling the customer sitting on the Strand in Sliema outside a place called Tony's Bar. It was about 19.00 and the man was with three others, one of whom was about 60 and the other two around 55 to 60. Tony repeated that the man himself was about 50. They asked for Pepsi, but the waiter told them none was available, so two of them ordered orange juice, one lemonade and the other nothing. They sat at a table four to six feet away from Tony, conversing in their own language in a friendly manner, before leaving together.[11] The following day Tony was asked to look at sets of photos of Arab men which had been supplied by the Maltese police, but none resembled the man.[12]

On 26 September there was still more dramatic news. Tony believed that the mystery clothes buyer had returned to the shop at 11.30 the previous day. He was able to give a clear description: '[He] had the same hairstyle, black hair, no hair on his face, dark skin, he was around 6 feet or just under that in height. He was about 50 years of age, he was broad built, not fat and I would say he had a 36-inch waist . . . the man spoke English when he came into my shop yesterday. He had a Libyan accent and I am convinced that he is a Libyan.' The man bought four children's dresses at a cost of eight Maltese pounds, and on leaving the shop turned right. Tony said he hadn't notified the police at the time because his father and brother had told him to have nothing more to do with them, for fear of 'something bad' happening.[13]

At around this time the police were pursuing a vital new lead concerning Mohamed Abu Talb, the Swedish-based PPSF member, who for the previous five months had been in prison awaiting trial for the 1985 and 1986 bombings in Copenhagen, Amsterdam and Stockholm. It emerged that Talb had travelled to Malta on 19 October 1988 and remained there until 26 October, the day of the Autumn Leaves raids in West Germany, in which the PFLP-GC's Hafez Dalkamoni and Marwan Khreesat were arrested. Shortly before Khreesat's arrival in West Germany, Talb's brother-in-law, Mohamed Mougrabi, had visited the Neuss apartment flat in which Dalkamoni was staying. Talb had called Mohamed after returning from Malta. It also emerged that Talb's stay on the island came immediately after a two-week visit to Cyprus, the first three days of which overlapped with Dalkamoni's presence there. Furthermore, when he returned from Malta to Sweden, he took with him some Maltese clothes.[14]

Could Talb be Tony Gauci's mystery clothes buyer? If he was, then he certainly could not have made the purchase during that particular stay in Malta, as the Yorkie trousers 1705 order was not delivered to the Gaucis' shop until 18 November 1988, almost a month after his return to Sweden. A week after the Autumn Leaves arrests Talb was himself arrested, along with his brother-in-law and several of their associates. Although released shortly afterwards, they were re-arrested in May 1989 and charged with the 1985 and 1986 bombings. Among the items seized from his house were false passports, one of which was burnt, and the unused return half of the airline ticket that he bought in Malta, which was dated 26 November. It must have crossed the police's minds that he had returned to Malta under a false name to buy more clothes, or had, at least, intended to.

Talb's account of the Malta trip further fuelled suspicions. His journey there from Cyprus was via Athens and Rome. He claimed that he missed his original connecting flight from Rome and decided instead to fly to Libya, as he wanted to travel on from there to visit his mother in Egypt. He said he was able to buy a ticket for Libya, with the help of a Libyan man he befriended at Rome airport called Fawzi Mehedwi, who lent him the $20 that he needed to make up the fare. He claimed that, when he attempted to board the flight, he was refused access by Libyan security officials and therefore reverted to his original plan. He said he went to Malta to do business with an old Palestinian acquaintance, Abdelsalem Abu Nada, and his brother Hashem. He explained that Hashem exported Maltese clothes to Egypt and the United Arab Emirates, and that he wished to discuss with him importing them to Sweden.

He later amended his story, saying the original purpose of the trip was to take a boat from the island to visit his parents in Egypt, yet there were no passenger ferries from Malta to Egypt. His account of his relationship with Abdelsalem contained further contradictions. He initially described him as a friend, but later said he was not a friend and that he had got to know him in the early 1980s through his (Abdelsalem's) wife. He said he had called Abdelsalem from Cyprus to tell him that he would be visiting, and claimed that Abdelsalem had met him on his arrival at Luqa Airport. He also claimed that Abdelsalem had paid for both his accommodation in Malta and his flight back to Sweden.[15]

When interviewed by the police in July 1990, Abdelsalem gave a very different account. He denied that Talb had called him from Cyprus and, stranger still, stated they met for the first time by chance on the street in the Maltese capital Valletta. He said that Hashem dealt in cereals and fruit, rather than clothes, and denied having paid Talb's hotel and flight home. One fact upon which he and Talb agreed was that, not long after his return to Sweden, Talb had sent him a parcel containing videos to a PO box.[16]

Abdelsalem was part-owner of a bakery called Miska, which he had established with four other Palestinians: Alaa Shurrab, Dr Khaled Nahhal, Imad Hazzouri and Magdy Moussa. Talb said he helped out in the bakery, but claimed to know neither its name nor the identity of those four; however, the police had earlier found a list of the directors in his possession, which they believed he had prior to his trip to Malta. He also denied knowledge of another Palestinian, Jamal Haider, who took joint control of the company with Abdelsalem, following the resignation of Shurrab, Nahhal, Hazzouri and Moussa at the end of October 1988. According to the police, Haider was an intelligence officer for the main PLO grouping, Fatah.[17] The police also discovered that Hazzouri's girlfriend, Gaetana Borg, worked at Yorkie Clothing, and that she often obtained suits and trousers for him from the firm at a substantial discount.[18]

Talb maintained that, despite his discussions about clothes importation, the only Maltese garments that he took back to Sweden were a sample pair of black jeans given to him by Hashem, two sweaters from Abdelsalem's wife, one of which was emblazoned with the word 'Malta', and two shirts, which a female acquaintance of the brothers' family had asked him to deliver to her brother in Sweden.[19] However, when SAPO officers searched his house as part of the Lockerbie investigation in November 1989, they discovered two Maltese-manufactured T-shirts, one of which bore the word 'Malta'.[20]

Talb said the garments were samples, which he intended to show shop-owners in Sweden in order to gauge the commercial potential of importing Hashem's clothing. As a Scottish police report noted, 'This story appears to be a pack of lies, first of all there is no trace of Hashem Salem being involved in any clothing business in Malta or elsewhere and secondly the clothing brought back to Sweden by Talb is not of a quality that would make any shop owner in Sweden interested in importing it.'[21] If Talb's role in the Lockerbie bombing was to obtain Maltese clothes in order to lay a false trail to Libya, then he may have originally intended to use ones, such as the T-shirts, which were unambiguously Maltese.

It is possible that further garments were hidden elsewhere, or were disposed of. Shortly after the searches the SAPO eavesdropped on a telephone call in which Jamila Mougrabi urged her brother Mohamed's wife, Wafa Toska, to get rid of the 'red pyjamas'.* She later admitted that she was aware that the police might be listening and that 'pyjamas' was code for a red travel bag that Toska had at her house. Both claimed they were concerned that the bag was of the type used in the Copenhagen bombing and that Toska might therefore be viewed as guilty by association.[22] However, this begged the question: why hadn't they disposed of it when their husbands were arrested for the Copenhagen bombing six months earlier?

On 2 October 1989, the police showed Tony Gauci a freeze-frame image of Talb taken from a BBC *Panorama* programme. He noted that the customer had a fuller, more rounded hairstyle, which did not recede at the temples, and that his face was broader, but, encouragingly, told them, 'I can state that the photograph I was shown is similar to the man that came in to my shop, although I am unable to say that it is definitely the same person.'[23] However, on 6 December, Gauci failed to pick out an image of Talb from a photospread.[24] This was, perhaps, hardly surprising, as he had consistently described the customer as around 50 years old, about 6 feet tall and well built. Talb, by contrast, was 36 and more slightly built. Furthermore, owing to a battle injury sustained in Lebanon in 1976, he had an unusual way of walking, which Gauci was likely to have noticed.[25]

There was, however, further intriguing evidence to suggest that Talb had been in the vicinity of Gauci's Mary's House shop

* It has been frequently misreported that Jamila Mougrabi told Wafa Toska to 'Get rid of the clothes'.

at around the time of the clothes purchase. A few days after the freeze-frame was shown to Gauci, it was shown to another Tower Road shopkeeper, Alfred Frendo. He told the police in a statement: 'I immediately recognised the photograph of the man as an Arab who had been in my shop last year before Christmas 1988. I told the officers that I could remember faces and I would say it was the same man.' He was sure that the date was before 6 December, as that was the day he had put up the Christmas decorations. He described the man as approximately 27 to 30 years old and around 5 feet 8 to 5 feet 9 inches tall. He could not remember which language he spoke, but thought he was a Libyan, although he might not have been able to distinguish the various Arab nationalities.

Frustratingly for the police, there was no hard evidence that Talb was in Malta after 26 October 1988.

They appeared to make better progress in establishing the date of the purchase. They discovered that the only afternoon football matches played during the relevant period were UEFA Cup third round matches. Each tie had a home and away leg, which were played on Wednesday 23 November and Wednesday 7 December 1988.

On 19 October 1989, hoping to jog his memory, the police showed Paul Gauci fixture lists for the two dates. The matches involving Italian clubs were Dynamo Dresden v Roma, Standard Liège v Juventus, Bayern Munich v Inter Milan and Bordeaux v Napoli. In a statement taken at the time, Paul said that he watched matches on both the dates. On 23 November he had watched Dynamo Dresden v Roma, and on 7 December the return fixture. However, he implied that he had watched two games on the afternoon in question, and concluded, 'On the basis that there were two games played during the afternoon of 23 November 1988 and only one game on the afternoon of 7.12.88 I would say that 23 November 1988 was the date in question.' But the statement was rather confusing. He said that, if he watched the game after the Roma v Dynamo Dresden match on 7 December, then he would have only watched the early stage of the second half, adding, 'then as far as I recall I went to Tower Road but not necessarily to my shop. I would visit shopkeepers in the street.' This perhaps suggested that Paul was not altogether ruling out 7 December, and that visiting Tower Road after the football was something that he did habitually,

92

rather than on that particular occasion. Furthermore, he considered 7 December less likely on the grounds that all the other games that day were played in the evening, yet he told the police that it would help if they could confirm the kick-off times, which implied that the list may not have included the times and that he may therefore have been relying on his memory.[26]*

On 14 December, in Bell's presence, Detective Constable John Crawford showed Paul the *Times of Malta's Soccer on TV* listings for the two dates. These showed that the first live televised game on 23 November 1988 was Dynamo Dresden v Roma, which began at 17.00, and on 7 December it was the reverse fixture, which began at 13.00, followed by Juventus v Standard Liège at 16.45. For reasons that were not explained, Paul refused to give a statement, but Crawford's corresponding one noted, 'Paul Gauci stated in his previous statement that he had watched a football match in the afternoon and then saw part of another match before he returned to Tower Road, Sliema, although he did not go to the shop St. Mary's House [sic], right away. He agreed that the probable date was therefore the 7th December, 1988.'[27] This date was to become critical to Abdelbaset's conviction, yet the police were unable to verify it with the crucial witness, Paul.

They had more success on the clothing front. RARDE's lead forensic examiner, Dr Thomas Hayes, was able to confirm a match between the remains of eight garments, plus an umbrella, and control samples obtained from the Gaucis and their suppliers. In addition to the two pairs of Yorkie trousers, the pyjamas, jacket, babygro and umbrella, there was a beige cardigan and two Slalom-brand shirts, one grey and the other pinstriped.[28] The grey shirt was particularly important, because it was in one of its fragments, PI/995, that the tiny piece of circuit board PT/35b was found, which was linked to Mebo's MST-13 timers.

In December 1991 Hayes and his colleague Allen Feraday signed off on the final RARDE forensic report. It concluded that the eight garments and the umbrella were not only blast-damaged, but were very likely to have been in the primary suitcase. There were four other such items: a part of a training shoe, a piece of blue cloth, the remains of a sweatshirt and a T-shirt. The training shoes and blue

* The fixture list was not disclosed to Abdelbaset's defence team.

cloth were each too damaged to be identifiable. The sweatshirt and T-shirt were of a type sometimes stocked at Mary's House,[29] but were not among the items that Tony Gauci recalled selling.

Plenty of other blast-damaged garments were, of course, recovered from the crash site, but, according to the forensic report, these were more likely to have been in the surrounding suitcases. It made this distinction on the basis of the presence, or absence, within the garments of tiny fragments of the bomb and/or suitcase shell. Those containing bomb fragments, such as black plastic from the casing of the Toshiba radio-cassette player, but no suitcase fragments, were considered most likely to have been in the primary suitcase and were designated Category 1. Those containing no fragments, or fragments that included ones from a suitcase, which were designated Category 2, were thought more likely to have been in the other luggage.[30] The underlying logic appeared simple: the explosion caused fragments of the bomb and the shell of the primary suitcase and other nearby luggage to travel outward, away from the bomb. Therefore all clothing that was close to the bomb in surrounding suitcases could potentially trap these fragments. However, since no suitcase shells lay between the primary suitcase clothes, they should only have trapped bomb fragments. That, at least, appeared to be the theory.

Secrets are difficult to keep in Malta. Despite the police's best efforts, within two months of them finding Tony Gauci, news of their inquiries leaked out. On 20 October 1989 a local newspaper, *Il-Helsien*, revealed that the investigators had traced the primary suitcase clothing to a shop in Sliema.[31] Over the next two months the British *Sunday Times* published five more stories, all of which reported that the clothes had been bought in Malta. Some repeated that the shop was in Sliema, with one claiming: 'the boutique owner is reportedly under 24-hour armed police protection.'[32] Worse still, in November the shop was identified in news items broadcast by the BBC and the American ABC channel.[33]

The *Sunday Times* consistently named Abu Talb and the PFLP-GC as the prime suspects, but on 29 October it revealed that the shopkeeper recalled selling the clothes to 'a man he believed was a Libyan'.[34] It was the first time that Libya had been publicly linked to

Lockerbie and, unsurprisingly, this set nerves jangling in Tripoli. Just three years earlier, the country had suffered US air strikes, and its government remained paranoid about further attacks.* On 30 January 1990, Gauci told the police he believed he was being watched by a man from the nearby Libyan Cultural Centre.[35] On 31 August he reported that, for the previous two months, more men from the building had been standing outside the shop. He said they walked in but, 'They never buy anything. They just look at me.'[36] Ten days later he picked out photos of some of the men he believed were involved.[37]

Unfortunately for the police, their success in identifying the clothes was not matched by progress in identifying the purchaser. During the first year of their Maltese investigation, they showed Gauci photospreads on five separate occasions, but he was unable to make a positive identification. In late 1990, however, their efforts dramatically regained momentum, thanks to their investigation of the timer fragment, PT/35b. Not only did it convince them of the Libyan link, but the interviews of Mebo's Edwin Bollier also yielded a new prime suspect – Abdelbaset.

In February 1991 they decided to show Gauci a further selection of twelve photos, including four provided by the FBI, one of which was of Abdelbaset. At 1.10 p.m. on 15 February, Gauci attended the headquarters of the Maltese Police in Floriana, where he met DCI Bell, DC Crawford, FBI agent Philip Reid and a Maltese officer, Inspector Godfrey Scicluna. Bell explained the by now familiar procedure, then Crawford handed over a card containing the photos, which Bell removed from its brown paper covering and placed on the table at which Gauci was seated. Abdelbaset's photo was number 8. Bell asked Gauci to look at each one carefully and to take as much time as he wanted. He advised him that the selection might not include the clothes buyer.

Gauci studied all the photos, then told Bell, 'They are all younger than the man who bought the clothes.' Bell asked him to try to allow for any age difference and to judge which most closely resembled the man. Gauci looked again, at one point picking up the card. He studied Abdelbaset's photo three times.[38] Crawford subsequently described thinking to himself, 'He's gonna pick him.'[39] And sure enough, Gauci

---

* The air strikes, and the reasons behind them, are detailed in Chapter 9.

did. 'I would say that the photograph at No. 8 is similar to the man who bought the clothing,' he said, adding, 'the hair is perhaps a bit long. The eyebrows are the same. The nose is the same and his chin and shape of face are the same. The man in the photograph No. 8 is in my opinion in his thirty years. He would perhaps have to look about ten years or more older and he would look like the man who bought the clothes. It's been a long time now and I can only say that this photograph No. 8 resembles the man who bought the clothing, but it is younger.' At the end of the statement he added, 'I can only say that of all the photographs I have been shown this photograph No. 8 is the only one really similar to the man who bought the clothing . . . other than the one my brother showed me.'[40] This was a reference to a photograph of Mohamed Abu Talb in an article, which he had been shown by Paul. The comment appeared to be of little significance. What mattered was that Gauci had picked out the police's prime suspect.

The Scottish officers were euphoric, but did their best not to show it.[41] Gauci, by contrast, was visibly upset, telling Bell that he was worried he would become a 'target', and that every time he heard a bang, he thought that 'they' had come to get him. His role in the investigation had already been widely reported, and he was worried that there might be further publicity.[42]

Bell broke the good news to SIO Stuart Henderson by telephone from the British High Commission. Henderson asked him to call him back from the hotel, so he could thank each officer in turn for his hard work. According to Crawford, the officers then marked their success by getting 'very pissed'.[43]

It was the crowning glory of the police investigation. But the crown proved to have many thorns. Compared to the police's other star witnesses, Edwin Bollier and Majid Giaka,* Gauci was a fairly straightforward character, but, like the other two, his evidence was anything but straightforward. In all he gave the police 19 statements, covering all the subjects they wished to pursue. On many subjects his accounts were so erratic that it beggars belief he became the lynchpin of Abdelbaset's conviction.†

---

* Giaka's evidence is detailed in Chapter 7.
† The fluctuations in Gauci's statements are described in greater detail in Appendix 1.

Perhaps the most alarming example concerned the grey Slalom shirt, which was, of course, critical to the case, because it was within one of its fragments, PI/995, that the MST-13 timer fragment PT/35b was found. In his original account he never mentioned selling shirts.[44] In January 1990, when the fragment had become the focus of their investigation, the police went back to him and showed him PK/1978, a section of the shirt including the Slalom label. He confirmed that he stocked such shirts, but added, 'I am sure that I did not sell him a shirt . . . That man didn't buy any shirts for sure.'[45] But nine months later, almost two years after the event in question, he demonstrated his uncanny knack for changing his story in a way that fitted snugly with the police case. He remembered that he had, after all, sold two Slalom shirts.

He gave fluctuating descriptions of three of the other items sold: the babygro, the jacket and, most notably, the cardigan. He originally described it as red and black tartan,[46] but the only one found at Lockerbie was plain beige. When shown a photograph of it by the police he agreed that the one he sold was identical.[47]

There were also substantial U-turns in his account of various sightings of the mystery customer. His first statement made it clear that he had never previously seen the man in Mary's House,[48] but a few months later he said that in May or June 1987, someone resembling him had bought blankets from the shop and asked him to deliver them to him in Room 113 of the Hilton Hotel.[49] The police later discovered that Abdelbaset stayed at the Hilton Hotel in late March and early April 1987, but may have been disappointed to learn that he was not in Room 113.[50] Furthermore, according to an extract from Bell's diary, which was disclosed to Abdelbaset's lawyers shortly before his return to Libya, Inspector Scicluna and his boss, Assistant Commissioner George Grech, 'found it difficult to believe Tony's story about the Hilton Hotel and were of the opinion he had become confused about things.'[51]

As for the later possible sighting in the shop, in his statement of 26 September 1989 Gauci said it had happened the day before, i.e. on 25 September.[52] The police subsequently learned that Abdelbaset visited Malta between 21 and 24 September, fuelling their belief that he was the mystery customer. On 4 November 1991, more than two years after the incident, they went back to Gauci to ask again about the date. They informed him that, despite what appeared in his statement, he had originally told them the date was the 21st or the 22nd, rather than the 25th. It was, to say the least, odd that anyone would say that a memorable event had occurred the day before when it had in fact been four or five days earlier, yet Gauci duly gave a statement confirming that he had mixed up the dates.[53]

There is no suggestion that Gauci lied, or that the police told him what to say, but the numerous fluctuations and U-turns in his accounts call into question at the very least the reliability of his evidence and indicate a degree of suggestibility. As Crawford later recalled, the police saw it as vital to keep him onside: 'Harry [Bell] told me to sit in with Tony . . . to see if anything could be learned and to build up some sort of relationship with the shopkeeper. It was imperative that this man, our sole witness, be kept absolutely on our side and continued to co-operate with us as far as possible. This association was emphasised by Harry. He could not personally be with Tony each and every time he was with us, but Harry took the sensible step of ensuring that wee Tony was happy with his situation.'[54]

Given the number of times that they visited him, and his centrality to the case, it was perhaps inevitable that the police and 'wee Tony' would develop a close rapport. In such circumstances there is a significant risk that a witness will develop a loyalty to the officers and that he might then subconsciously tailor elements of his account to fit the police case.

A cornerstone of the case against Abdelbaset was that he was in Malta on 7 December 1988. On the basis that Paul Gauci was at home watching football on the afternoon of the clothes purchase, the date had been narrowed down to either 23 November or 7 December. Crawford's interview of Paul on 14 December 1989, in which he was shown details of the televised games on those dates, appeared overwhelmingly to favour 7 December.[55] However, the football evidence was far less clear-cut than first appeared. The first difficulty was that Paul would not give a statement to Crawford. In the most detailed statement that he gave on the subject, he had earlier told the police that he watched both legs of the Dynamo Dresden v Roma fixture. The first leg, on 23 November, kicked off at 17.00 and ended at 18.45, whereas the second, on 7 December, kicked off at 13.00 and ended at 14.45.[56] The shop's afternoon opening hours were 16.00 to 19.00,[57] so Paul could easily have watched the whole of the match on 7 December and made it back to work the afternoon shift in the shop. The second game on 7 December, Standard Liège v Juventus, did not start until 16.45, which meant Paul would have had two hours without football. It finished at 18.30, so he could easily have watched the whole game and made it to Tower Road in good time to visit his fellow shopkeepers, or Mary's House, before closing time. The second match on 23 November began straight after the first one ended at 18.45.[58] Paul could have watched the early part of the first half and made it back to Tower Road shortly after closing time. His 19 October 1989 statement was unclear on whether, on the date in question, he watched two whole games or only a part of the second one,[59] but Crawford seemed clear it was the latter,[60] which meant 23 November was the more likely date. In his first statement Paul referred only to a football 'match', which suggested that he only watched one game. If that was the case, given that he was fairly sure he had watched both legs of Dynamo Dresden v Roma, then 23 November was almost certainly the date.

Tony had no precise memory of the date. He originally told the police that it was during the winter of 1988,[61] and in seven subsequent statements he said November or December.[62] Finally, on 10 September 1990, he said that it was in late November.[63]

Two elements of Gauci's account gave clues as to the date. The first was that it was sometime before the Christmas decorations were erected, which generally happened around 15 days before Christmas,[64] and the second was that shortly before the man first left the shop, a light rain shower had begun.[65] The police were unable to establish the dates on which the decorations were erected and illuminated, but detailed weather data was available from the Maltese Civil Aviation Authority's Meteorological Office. On 14 September 1989 the Chief Meteorological Officer, Major Joseph Mifsud, handed over two sets of data. The first was a summary of the daily weather conditions on the island between 17 November and 21 December 1988, which was based on figures recorded at the Meteorological Office at Luqa Airport. The second was the daily rainfall totals for November and December 1988 recorded at 20 locations across the island.[66] Of these, 19 were police stations, including the one in Sliema, and the other was the Luqa Meteorological Office. The daily totals were for the 24 hours up to midday on the date in question, thus the period when the man bought the clothes from Mary's House would be covered by the next day's figure. The Sliema police station total for 24 November, which covered the evening of 23 November, was 5.2 millimetres,[67] while the one for 8 December, which covered the evening of 7 December, was 3.3 millimetres.[68] However, it appeared from the daily weather summaries that, whereas there was sporadic light rain on 23 November, with the exception of a slight shower at 08.40, 7 December was dry.[69] Since Luqa is only a few kilometres away from Sliema, there was no reason to believe that the weather there was substantially different; indeed, there were no 24-hour periods in November and December when rain was recorded at Sliema police station and none was recorded at the Meteorological Office.

The two sets of data were analysed by DC Crawford, who reached a similar conclusion.[70] The police subsequently obtained more detailed rainfall figures for Luqa, which recorded light showers at the relevant time on 23 November and no rain after 09.00 on 7 December.[71] Assuming Gauci's recollection of the rain shower was correct, this meant that the purchase almost certainly took place on 23 November, when Abdelbaset was not in Malta.

There was, of course, an even bigger flaw in the case against him. One of the few consistent elements of Gauci's account was his description of the clothes buyer. He was, Gauci maintained, around 50 years old, heavily built, 6 feet tall, dark-skinned and with a full head of hair. At the time Abdelbaset was 36, 5 feet 8 inches tall, fairly slender, light-skinned and with a receding hairline. Gauci was eight years his senior and around six years younger than the customer. It would be very surprising if he confused someone so many years younger with someone considerably older. He had also spent most of his working life selling clothes, so was far better equipped than most to judge a customer's size.

Setting that aside, the fact remained that on 15 February 1991, despite picking out Abdelbaset's photo, Tony did not identify him as the clothes buyer. Rather, he stated categorically that to look like the man he would have to be at least ten years older. Official guidelines on the conduct of ID parades, which were issued to the Scottish police in 1982, recommended that photo line-ups should comprise people 'of similar age and appearance', yet most of those in the photospread were younger than Abdelbaset, half of them considerably so and the only one older than him was Chilean, rather than an Arab.* Furthermore, Gauci only picked the photo having been told by Bell to ignore any age difference. There was no record of receiving such instructions during any of the previous photoshows. The guidelines also said, 'The photographs should bear no marks which would enable the witness to identify the suspect's photograph.'[72] Before the photoshow, DCI Bell had noted that Abdelbaset's picture was of poor quality, dull grey colour, and therefore asked a Maltese police photographer to re-photograph the other 11 to ensure they were of the same general quality.[73] However, despite the photographer's best efforts, the photo was of markedly different quality to the others. As well as being pale and grainy, it had two white parallel horizontal lines and a series of white dots down the left-hand side. Although the marks did not directly identify him, they certainly made the photograph stand out.

Another questionable aspect of the episode was the police's apparent failure to record all their conversations with Gauci. This was revealed in the statement by DC Crawford, which reported a discussion he had had with the shopkeeper that same day. It said: 'During breaks in the procedure I spoke to Tony Gauci about a number of things. Among these were the cardigans sold to him by an "ex-policeman who lives in Msida", I went over this with Tony and he now realises that the Puccini cardigan was bought from Eagle Knitwear and not from this ex-policeman.' Given the importance of the occasion, everything that occurred should have been recorded, yet this was the only statement by those present to refer to breaks in the procedure and to additional discussions within those breaks; furthermore, there was no clue as to the other matters that Crawford discussed with Gauci.

* The dates of birth of nine of the twelve people were given. Only one of the three whose dates of birth were not given appeared to be anything like Abdelbaset's age.

It was not until the indictments were issued against us in November 1991 that I learned of my alleged visit to Mary's House almost three years earlier. I did my best to recall what had happened on the 7 December trip and the one a fortnight later when we allegedly planted the bomb. However, the truth was that both trips were fairly routine and therefore largely unmemorable.

On 7 December, as far as I remember, when I landed in Malta I dropped in on Mustafa Shebani, who had replaced Lamin as LAA Station Manager three months earlier. He told me that Lamin had taken a year's leave from LAA in order to set up the Medtours travel agency with his Maltese friend Vincent Vassallo. This came as news to me, although I was aware that the Libyan government now offered support to anyone who invested in Malta, providing them with financial services and easing money transfer restrictions.

Shebani asked me if I could help Lamin, so we arranged to meet him. Lamin spoke about the state-owned Arab Drilling and Workover Company (ADWOC), which provides rigs and drilling services to the Libyan oil industry and whose foreign personnel – mainly engineers and technicians from Britain, the USA and Canada – travelled to Libya, via Malta, to work two-week shifts. At the time, most of their travel arrangements were handled by a Maltese company, but Lamin was convinced he could provide a superior service and better value. I told him I would have a word with my wife's brother-in-law, who worked in the legal department of the National Oil Company.

At some point that day I checked into the Holiday Inn in Sliema, which is just a few minutes' walk away from Tony Gauci's shop. I liked to stay there as it had good facilities, although I didn't particularly like Sliema, which I found rather downmarket. I can't remember what I did for the remainder of the day, but I know for sure that I did not buy clothes in Tony Gauci's shop. The following day Mustafa drove me to the airport and I checked in and boarded the flight to Zurich. Had I taken with me a lot of newly-purchased clothing, I would have needed a check-in-sized suitcase, yet as the Swissair flight manifest demonstrated, I did not check in any luggage.[74] Our take-off was delayed by bad weather and eventually the flight was cancelled, so the airline arranged for the passengers to overnight at the Holiday Inn, and put us on a flight the following morning.

102

More than that I cannot remember. The memory can, of course, play tricks, so it may be that some of the details are inaccurate, but any such mistakes are, like that visit, entirely innocent.

The Suitcase 6

The case against Abdelbaset had three golden threads. The first was the MST-13 timer circuit-board fragment PT/35b, which linked him to the bomb. The second was Tony Gauci, who linked him to the primary suitcase clothing. The third was evidence from Frankfurt Airport, which linked the suitcase with Malta and the Frankfurt feeder flight PA103A. Until learning of the Frankfurt evidence in August 1989, the police believed the suitcase originated with the PFLP-GC's West German cell, part of which was based in the city. Bomb-maker Marwan Khreesat had made at least five barometric bombs, one of which was built into a Toshiba BomBeat radio cassette player. Although the cell's plans had been disrupted by the Autumn Leaves raids, at least one other bomb and one other senior group member, Abu Elias, had evaded detection.

In order to prove the German connection, the police needed to demonstrate that the primary suitcase had travelled on PA103A. Their investigation at Heathrow appeared to support this suggestion. Naturally, it was largely focused on the baggage-loading procedures for PA103 and, in particular, the container AVE4041, in which the blast had occurred.

There were three distinct groups of luggage on the flight. The first and largest comprised items checked in by passengers who had commenced their journey at Heathrow. The second were those that had arrived at Heathrow from Frankfurt on PA103A. The third, and smallest, were those belonging to so-called interline passengers, who had arrived at Heathrow on other flights.

Inquiries at the airport established that AVE4041 contained none of the first group, because luggage checked in at Heathrow had been loaded into containers within Terminal 3, in what was known as the baggage build-up area. AVE4041, on the other hand, had been used to load luggage from the third group and had therefore been located in the interline shed, which was a few hundred yards from the terminal.[1] During the afternoon and early evening the interline bags arrived at the shed sporadically and were loaded into the container. By the time PA103A arrived from Frankfurt it was less than a quarter full, so it was taken out onto the tarmac and filled up with bags belonging to USA-bound passengers, which were being unloaded from the hold of that flight. It was then taken directly to the hold of the Boeing 747.

This of course meant that the primary suitcase must either have been transferred from PA103A, or it was one of the interline bags loaded into AVE4041 prior to PA103A's arrival. Loaders John Bedford, Amarjit Singh Sidhu and Tarlochan Singh Sahota all said that, when they last saw the container, prior to its being taken to PA103A, a number of suitcases were standing upright in a row at the back and a couple of others were lying flat towards the front. They confirmed that this was how they usually loaded containers. Crucially, they were fairly sure that the entire floor area of the container was covered, and that none of the items had any other luggage loaded on top.[2] This indicated to the police that the Frankfurt baggage must have been in the second layer of luggage and above. So, if they could reliably determine where the explosion had occurred, then they might be able to establish whether or not the primary suitcase had arrived on PA103A.

In April and July 1989 nine explosive tests were conducted, the first seven of which aimed to resolve this issue. The five April tests were devised by RARDE's Allen Feraday, in conjunction with the FAA and FBI, and took place at the US Naval Explosive Ordnance Disposal Technology Center at Indian Head, Maryland. The first two July tests were conducted at the initiative of the FAA's lead forensic examiner, Walter Korsgaard, and took place at the FAA's Headquarters in Atlantic City, New Jersey. Feraday was present, along with DCI Harry Bell, Korsgaard and James 'Tom' Thurman, who led the FBI's forensic investigations, plus a variety of other US personnel. In all seven tests a replica Toshiba bomb was packed, along with clothes, into a hard-sided suitcase, which was in turn placed within a luggage container like AVE4041 and surrounded with other luggage.* In the July tests the container was placed, along with another, into a section

---

* Two further tests were conducted in July 1989 at Indian Head, but these used only one suitcase and did not involve luggage containers.

of fuselage of a DC10 aircraft. Varying amounts of plastic explosive were used in the seven tests, ranging from 360 to 680 grams. In each instance the primary suitcase was positioned close to the surfaces of the container that would have been adjacent to the aircraft's skin. In Tests 1, 2, 3 and 5, the suitcase was in the second layer of luggage and in Test 4 in the bottom layer.

Following the April tests DCI Bell produced a report, which set out the investigators' preliminary conclusions about the Lockerbie bomb. It stated that the 'IED configuration and location' used in Test 5 were 'the most consistent of the five tests conducted compared to the actual damage indicated by the recovered components of AVE4041'. Test 5 had used 460 grams of Semtex and the primary suitcase overhung the one below it by 6.5 inches (16 cm). The centre of the charge was 10.5 inches (26 cm) from the floor of the container. More importantly, he reported that the results of Test 4 'clearly indicate that the case containing the IED was not in direct contact with the container floor. That is that the device was not in a suitcase directly in the bottom layer of the passenger baggage.'

The conclusion was subsequently supported by separate investigations by the AAIB and the Royal Aeronautical Establishment (RAE) at Farnborough. The AAIB concluded that the centre of the explosion was around 10 inches (25.5 cm) above the container's base and around 25 inches (64 cm) from the aircraft's skin. The RAE was concerned only with the latter measurement – known as the standoff distance – which it calculated to be 24 inches (62 cm).[3]

So it seemed clear that the primary suitcase was in the second layer of baggage, which meant that it must have been among the baggage that was loaded into AVE4041 from PA103A. Or did it? In fact, even if the primary suitcase was in the second layer, this by no means ruled out the Heathrow interline bags. It was quite possible that, when loading the bags from PA103A into AVE4041, the loaders had rearranged some of the Heathrow interline bags such that they ended up in the second layer.

The police were, nevertheless, convinced that the bomb had come from Frankfurt. Their next challenge was to establish how the bombers had got it onto the feeder flight PA103A. Frankfurt Airport was the busiest in mainland Europe. In order to cope with the huge volume of luggage, the Frankfurt Airport Company Ltd, known as FAG, had some years earlier installed a sophisticated computerised baggage transit system. The computer, which was known as KIK, kept a record of all transactions involving the system for every departing flight. Unfortunately for the police, however, the computer's memory was routinely wiped every few days, and no one had thought to preserve the records for 21 December 1988. At least, that's what they were told. But it turned out they had been misinformed, because a forward-thinking KIK operator, Bogomira Erac, had printed off a copy of the records for PA103A. She had then stored it in her locker and, on returning from her Christmas holidays, had given it to her supervisor, who passed it on to the BKA.[4] The job of analysing the printout fell to Inspector Jürgen Fuhl, who had been tasked with a wider inquiry into PA103A's luggage. His conclusions transformed the investigation, shifting its focus from Germany to Malta.

The document recorded that 111 bags were dispatched by the baggage transit system to PA103A. Fuhl established that 86 were probably checked in by the flight's passengers at Frankfurt, and the remaining 25 were transferred from other flights. Most transfer bags were taken from their incoming flights to one of two reception areas, known as V3 and Halle Mitte. Within each area were a number of so-called coding stations where individual bags were entered into the baggage system and dispatched to their outgoing flights. Of the 25 transfer bags, six were unaccompanied by a passenger. Four of the six could be traced to individuals, but two could not. One appeared to have arrived on Lufthansa flight LH1071 from Warsaw and was coded in at station HM3 at 15.44. The other one proved to be of far greater interest. It appeared on the printout as follows:

'B8849 F1042 S0009+Z1307 TO HS33+Z1517 BO44+Z1523'[5]

'B8849' was the bag itself, or, rather, the tray into which it was placed for transit through the baggage system, and 'F1042' was the computer system's code number for flight PA103A. 'TO HS33+Z1517 BO44+Z1523' indicated the route that the bag took through the baggage transit system and recorded that the bag exited the system at Gate 44, from which PA103A departed, at 15:23. The crucial entry was 'S0009+Z1307', which showed that the bag entered into the baggage system at point S0009 at 13.07. S0009 denoted coding station 206, which was one of seven stations in the V3 reception area. On checking the worksheet for station 206, Fuhl discovered that between 13.04 and either 13.10 or 13.16 (depending on whether the last digit was a 0 or a 6) the coders were processing bags from Air Malta flight KM180,[6] which had flown from Malta's Luqa airport. It therefore appeared that B8849 had arrived on that flight. As Fuhl noted in a subsequent report, 'This conclusion receives considerable significance from the findings of RARDE according to which the bomb case contained textiles which had been purchased in a shop on Malta.'[7]

Evidence from Frankfurt Airport suggested that the interline bags would have been among the last to be loaded onto PA103A.[8] They were therefore likely to have been among the first unloaded at Heathrow, which meant that those labelled for onward travel to the United States could well have been among the first Frankfurt bags to be placed in the container AVE4041. Given that the bottom of the container was covered with a single layer of luggage before PA103A arrived, this meant they were likely to have ended up in the second layer of luggage. However, since there were no rules governing the sequence of loading and unloading, it was not possible to say with certainty that this had indeed happened.

Neither the computer list, nor the worksheet, were revealed to the Scottish police until August 1989. The Scottish police were furious that the BKA had sat on this vital lead for seven months. Nevertheless, they could console themselves that the documents appeared to settle the issue of the primary suitcase's origin.

All the passengers on Air Malta KM180 were interviewed. All could account for their baggage, none possessed a brown Samsonite that matched the primary suitcase and none owned clothes matching those sold by Gauci. It was clear to the police that the suitcase was unaccompanied and had an interline tag marked for PA103, which meant that it would have been automatically transferred at Frankfurt and Heathrow. Since Air Malta had no record of any unaccompanied bags being loaded onto KM180, the police concluded that someone had managed to get the case into the plane's hold undetected. That someone, they believed, was Abdelbaset, or rather him and Lamin Fhimah. Their conclusion was largely based upon the pair's presence in Malta on 20 and 21 December 1988 and upon Abdelbaset's use on that occasion of the false name of Ahmed Khalifa Abdusamad.

Exactly how the police made the Abdusamad link was revealed many years later by the FBI's lead investigator, Richard Marquise, in his book *Scotbom*. It describes how, on 25 February 1991, he received a phone call from 'an analyst from an American intelligence agency near Washington . . . [which] did not deal in live sources and investigations'. Although not named, this was almost certainly the US National Security Agency, which specialises in electronic eavesdropping. According to Marquise, the analyst 'said his analysis concerning Megrahi showed connections to a man named Ahmed Khalifa Abdusamad'. Marquise had never heard the name before, but when he asked it to be checked in the database of people who had passed through Maltese immigration, he soon discovered that someone of that name had visited the island on those dates.[9]* Given that Abdelbaset never used the Abdusamad passport after 21 December, Marquise's revelation strongly suggested that the NSA, or one of its feeder agencies, was monitoring his movements prior to Lockerbie.

Although the police could not be certain how the men had got the bomb onto the flight, they figured that it could not have been a coincidence that, shortly before KM180's departure, Abdelbaset had returned to Tripoli on LAA flight LN147, whose check-in times overlapped with KM180's. Lamin's 15 December 1988 diary, which read, 'Take taggs from Air Malta. OK' and 'Abdelbaset arriving from Zurich', and the note at the back, which read, 'Take/collect tags from the airport (Abdelbaset/Abdusalam)', convinced the police that Lamin had obtained the necessary Air Malta interline tag.

That is what the police believed. Here is what really happened.

When I returned to Tripoli from Czechoslovakia on 17 December, I had a two-hour stopover in Malta, during which I met briefly

---

* It was not until after Abdelbaset surrendered for trial 1999, when the Libyan authorities handed over documents relating to the coded passport and he handed over the passport itself, that the police could prove that he was Abdusamad – see Chapter 10.

with the new LAA Station Manager Mustafa Shebani. In the course of our conversation he again asked if I could help Lamin with his Medtours travel agency venture. My partners in the Paris to Dakar Rally project and I had decided that we needed someone based in either Tunisia or Malta to organise the paperwork required to get the participants in and out of Libya. When Mustafa reminded me about Lamin, I realised that he would be the ideal man for the job, as he was familiar with Libyan bureaucracy and had good contacts both there and in Malta.

Lamin had finished as Malta Station Manager in September 1988 and was living back in Tripoli temporarily while Medtours was getting off the ground. On my return I took the opportunity to tell him of our plans for the rally, and how there was a role for him and the new company. He told me he was thinking of travelling to Malta on 20 December to finalise the company paperwork and invited me over to see its offices and meet his business partner Vincent Vassallo. I accepted the invitation, partly because I also wanted to buy some more things for the house, in particular carpets.

On 20 December Lamin called me at my office to tell me he was definitely travelling to Malta that afternoon. We arranged to meet at Tripoli Airport and take an Air Malta flight, which departed at around 16.30, and I booked to fly home on the first LAA flight the following morning. I didn't want to be away for more than a night, because there was work to do on the Paris to Dakar Rally, and on the evening of the 21st my sister was having a party to celebrate the birth of her daughter a week earlier.

Rather than travelling on my own passport, I used the coded one in the name Khalifa Abdusamad. I honestly can't remember the precise reason for doing so, as it wasn't of great importance at the time, but the most likely one is that I didn't want my wife to know I was in Malta. Although it was only an overnight trip, I knew she wouldn't be happy, as I'd just been away for ten days and, more importantly, Malta had a bad reputation among Libyan wives as a place of low moral standards, where men were easily led astray. I may therefore have told her that I was visiting a friend on the other side of Tripoli and intended to spend the night there. If so, then to prevent her suspecting my true destination, I would have left my regular passport at

110

home. She had no idea about the coded passport, which I always kept at my office. I was supposed to use it only for business purposes, but I had occasionally taken it on my personal travels, for example when I went to Mecca for the Umrah pilgrimage, for no other reason than that it was the closest to hand.

Another possibility is that my regular passport was with my Libyan bank. At the time Libyans were allowed to take only 500 US dollars out of the country annually, and any remaining amount could not be carried over to the following year. It may be that, since returning from Prague, I had lodged the passport with my bank in order to guarantee my remaining allocation before the year end.

It was also possible that I chose my coded passport in order to secure hard currency, as it contained a stamp, dated 22 June 1988, that entitled me to an additional allowance of $1,000, providing I could demonstrate that I had travelled abroad before the year end. Libyans often made short trips to neighbouring countries in order to get the necessary foreign entry stamp in their passports.

While on the Air Malta flight I filled in a disembarkation card in the name of Abdusamad. We touched down at Luqa Airport at around 17.30, and as I passed through immigration control I handed in the card.

Since we had no check-in luggage, we left the airport immediately via the Customs area to the car park. Thanks to Mustafa Shebani, Lamin had the use of an LAA Volvo and, as far as I recall, this was the car in which he drove me to meet his business partner Vincent Vassallo. Vassallo welcomed us into the living room of his house, and we drank tea and chatted, mainly about the Paris to Dakar Rally and their plans for Medtours. Libyans and Maltese tend to be mutually suspicious, with the Maltese having a reputation among Libyans as being difficult, but Vassallo didn't come over that way and struck me as a very kind person.

I noticed that the house had a nice wooden staircase and mentioned that I was after something similar for our new family home. He and Lamin said that they knew of a Maltese workshop that could build one for me. I asked if they would contact the company on my behalf so I could inspect their work in person. After about an hour we thanked Vincent for his hospitality and left.

111

Lamin then showed me the building in which Medtours was based. He had a flat nearby, but he said it was virtually empty and that he preferred to stay at a small local hotel called the Central. We passed by the hotel so he could pick up his keys, as the family who ran it tended to lock up and go to bed early and, since he was something of a night owl, he had on at least one occasion found himself locked out. He asked me if I also wanted a room, but I preferred the more upmarket Holiday Inn.

I'd hoped to drop by at the carpentry workshop, but time was getting tight and my priority was to buy some carpets. Lamin took me to a carpet-dealer who operated out of a lock-up garage, rather than a shop, and I eventually bought two at $100 each. By then it was too late to visit the carpenters, so we agreed to pass by there in the morning on our way to the airport. Lamin drove me to the Holiday Inn and accompanied me to the front desk, where I was checked in by receptionist Doreen Caruana, whom Lamin recognised as a former LAA stewardess. The hotel offered a commercial discount to LAA staff, so as I began filling out the registration card, Lamin asked her to give me this cheaper rate. It was only when she asked for identification that he became aware that I had a coded passport, which, unlike my regular one, did not give my profession as flight dispatcher. As far as I recall, he asked to speak to the duty manager, whom he also knew, in order to vouch for me. Although I have no clear memory of being given the discount, when the police later retrieved the registration card they found that it had 'Libyan Arab Airlines' written across the top. It confirmed that I was charged 26.55 Maltese pounds and gave the tariff code as 'B2',[10] which, as Caruana confirmed at my trial, was the commercial rate.[11]

Once I'd checked in, Lamin said he would collect me in the morning. I recall him saying that he had decided to stay in the flat after all and giving me his telephone number there. I presumed he'd decided against the Central Hotel because he wished to save money. I took the carpets with me, as I feared they might be stolen from the car, or, more likely, that Lamin would stay out late and oversleep.

My suspicion was well founded, as the next morning there was no sign of him. I called the flat, but someone else answered. I couldn't understand exactly what he was saying, but my impression at the time *was that Lamin had inadvertently given me the wrong number, or there was a crossed line. I wasn't very pleased and decided I would order a taxi, rather than wait any longer. Once at the airport I dropped by Mustafa Shebani's office. While we were talking, Lamin phoned to apologise. As predicted, he had stayed out late and overslept. I told him not to worry and asked him to visit the carpenters on my behalf. (He was as good as his word. On 29 December he brought two of the carpenters, Tony Camilleri and Joseph Mercieca, over to Tripoli to size up the job, although their subsequent estimate was very high and I eventually managed to get the work done in a Libyan workshop.)*

It is likely that I stayed with Shebani until he gave his orders to commence the check-in of LAA flight LN147, which I was taking back to Tripoli. Before giving the order, he had to wait for a so-called movement message from LAA, which confirmed that the in-bound flight would be arriving on time. As check-in commenced, he would hand over to the check-in staff the same number of boarding passes as there were passengers booked to fly. Normally when I flew with LAA I didn't have to check in with the rest of the passengers, as the Station Manager would take my ticket directly to the check-in staff and obtain a boarding pass for me. I assume that's what happened on this occasion, as I've no memory of anything out of the ordinary occurring. I would have waited in Shebani's office until it was time to board the flight.

According to the prosecution, at some point during the check-in period Lamin and I conspired to divert the brown Samsonite suitcase containing the bomb on to KM180. The truth is that LAA flights were checked in by Air Malta staff; moreover, neither of us had a brown Samsonite suitcase and, since he was no longer LAA Station Manager, Lamin was not even present. I boarded the flight as normal and it left on time. On landing I went straight to my office and re-sumed work on the Paris to Dakar Rally preparations.

It turned out to be the last time that I used the coded passport, as early in 1989 Aisha discovered it my jacket pocket. She was, under-standably, very upset and I promised her I would never use it again. To prove it I crossed out the pages that included my photograph and personal details, but, since it was government property, I stopped short of destroying it.

When viewed logically, the claim that I had visited Malta secretly on a false passport, in order to enact the final stage of the bomb plot, is reduced to nonsense. Had I wished to enter Malta without a written record of my visit, I would not have bothered with a passport, as my flight dispatcher's identification was still valid. This would have enabled me to travel as part of an LAA flight crew and thus bypass Passport Control and avoid having to fill out a disembarkation card. As it was, we flew by Air Malta, rather than LAA. In reality, even if there was no paper record of my entry, I couldn't hope to enter Malta anonymously, as I had spent a lot of time at the airport over the previous four years and was therefore known by sight to plenty of Air Malta staff. And, if we were on an undercover mission, then surely we would not have visited Vassallo, whom I'd never before met. Vassallo wrote in his diary 'Lamin & Baset returned from Tripoli. Mr Baset first visit to our house',[12] which proved that I was introduced to him by my real name, rather than the one on my coded passport.

If, as the Crown and Court asserted, I was really a JSO agent, the organisation would surely have ordered me to stay at Lamin's flat, or at one of the Maltese hotels owned by Libya's foreign investment company Lafico. As it was, I stayed at the Holiday Inn, where the receptionist was known to Lamin, and checked in using the coded passport only two weeks after staying there under my real name. Not only that, but Lamin successfully negotiated an LAA staff discount for me, thereby increasing the likelihood of my dual identity being exposed.

The suggestion that Lamin recorded his plans in his 1988 diary is also absurd. The truth is that all the supposedly incriminating entries were wholly innocuous. The references to obtaining Air Malta tags reflected a continuing problem that LAA's Malta station was having at the time of his handover to Shebani in obtaining sufficient tags from LAA in Tripoli. The shortfall had for some time been made up by using Air Malta tags, and Shebani had asked Lamin to talk to someone at Air Malta to secure a further supply. Air Malta tags and boarding passes were routinely used for LAA flights between Malta and Libya, and some other airlines used them too. The reference to me arriving from Zurich on 15 December was probably because I returned from Prague via Zurich. I often called in to the Malta station to inform them of my arrival and it's likely that on this occasion I left a message for Lamin, possibly because I wanted to speak to him before returning to Tripoli about buying a carpet in Malta. In the event, of course, I did not return from Zurich until the 17th. According to Lamin, the undated entry, 'Take/collect tags from the airport (Abdelbaset/Abdusalam)' was a reference to him collecting LAA tags from Tripoli Airport for use by the Malta station. He thought this probably happened in early 1989, which perhaps explains why it was at the back of the diary. 'Abdelbaset' and 'Abdusalam' were two different people, both LAA colleagues based at Tripoli Airport.[13] He recalled that the former was probably Abdelbaset Shukri and the latter was definitely Abdusalam El-Ghawi.[14]

Had Lamin documented our terrorist plans in the diary, then surely he would have destroyed it, or taken it back to Libya. As it was, he left it in the Medtours office for more than two years until April 1991, when, with his consent, Vincent Vassallo handed it over to the police. It's hard to imagine petty fraudsters acting so recklessly, let alone calculating terrorists.

Setting aside Abdelbaset's story, the Maltese suitcase theory was riddled with holes. No one witnessed either him or Lamin on Luqa Airport's airside at the time they were supposed to have planted the bomb. Furthermore, the airport presented potential terrorists with an unusually stiff challenge. The Maltese authorities had been acutely sensitive to the terrorist threat since 1985, when ANO hijackers forced an Air Egypt flight to land at the airport. In a subsequent botched raid by Egyptian commandos, 58 passengers and crew were killed. Since then the airport had been guarded by the Maltese military, and approximately once a month security staff underwent an exercise in which people unknown to them would attempt to smuggle in weapons.[15] In August 1987 the airport was inspected by the FAA, which found that it provided effective security measures in line with international standards. In a letter to Malta's Director of Civil Aviation, the FAA's Director for Europe, Africa and the Middle East, Benjamin Demps, said that the airport officials with whom his inspectors dealt 'displayed an excellent attitude towards security and appeared dedicated to accomplishing security needs for Luqa airport'.[16]

Crucially, one of the measures that had been put in place made it virtually impossible to put a rogue bag on an Air Malta flight. This was the requirement for baggage loaders physically to count every bag that was loaded into the aircraft to ensure that the number tallied with the check-in records. The check-in staff would inform the flight dispatcher of the total and he would then ask the loader for his figure, without revealing to him the one obtained from the check-in staff. If the figures tallied, the hold would be closed and the flight allowed to depart. If they did not, the aircraft would be held on the tarmac until the discrepancy was resolved and the numbers reconciled. No such measures were in place at Frankfurt and Heathrow airports.

The total was recorded by the loader and the dispatcher respectively in documents known as the load plan and the ramp progress sheet. The police obtained copies of the ones that were completed for KM180 on the day of the bombing. Each noted the figure as 55, which was exactly the number checked in and subsequently accounted for by the police.[17]

The dispatcher responsible for the flight was Gerald Camilleri. In a statement, he told the police, 'I can assure you that 55 was the figure I was given by check-in and 55 was the figure given by the head loader. They reconciled without doubt.'[18] The loader, Michael Darmanin, was the head one on duty that day. He was equally adamant that the figures reconciled and stressed that it would have been impossible for an extra bag to be put on the flight during loading.[19]

If it was impossible for an extra suitcase to have been placed on KM180, then the Frankfurt Airport documents were irrelevant; but, even if there was a theoretical possibility, the Frankfurt evidence was very shaky. The documents provided no proof that bag B8849 was loaded onto PA103A, let alone that it was from Malta. If it had been loaded onto the flight, then it would have been X-rayed prior to loading. An FAA review of Pan Am's Frankfurt security procedures, conducted after Lockerbie, found that the standard of the X-ray operators' training was poor. Nevertheless, both the Helsinki and Toshiba warnings had been circulated to staff, so the

116

operator on duty that day, Kurt Maier, knew that a bomb attack had been threatened and to be especially vigilant for radio-cassette players. He also told the FAA investigators that he was able to spot explosives.[20]

The Maltese bag theory depended on the accuracy of the timings recorded on the two key documents. The KIK printout stated that the bag had been coded in at 13.07 and the coders' worksheet suggested that they were processing bags from KM180 between 13.04 and 13.10, or 13.16 (depending on whether the last digit was 0 or 6). So, if either timing was out by a few minutes, the theory collapsed. The coders filled in the times by hand, and were reliant upon their own watches, or a nearby clock. The computer's timings were, of course, automated, but the time had to be re-entered each day by FAG employees, who again relied on their watches, or the clock. Furthermore, small fluctuations in the electrical circuit by which the system was powered would sometimes cause deviations of up to a few minutes.

In 1992, the Frankfurt evidence was tested by two of the UK's leading airline security experts, Denis Phipps and Nan McCreadie, who were instructed by lawyers representing Air Malta. The airline was suing the British TV company Granada over a drama-documentary *Why Lockerbie?*, which, like Abdelbaset's prosecutors, alleged that the bomb had begun its journey in Malta and had reached Heathrow via Frankfurt. Like the prosecution, Granada was reliant on the Frankfurt documents.

Eventually, Granada opted to settle the case before it reached court, without admitting liability. In a statement read to the court and approved by the judge, counsel for Air Malta said the result achieved, 'in substance, its purpose in bringing the action'. Granada's decision to settle no doubt had much to do with the numerous flaws that Phipps and McCreadie had uncovered in the documents.

Unlike Luqa, Frankfurt was a huge airport within which anyone with a security pass could move around anonymously. It was clear from the pair's observations that it would be possible for anyone to add a stray bag to a wagon or to process it at one of the coding stations, without its being recorded.[21] Precisely this scenario was witnessed on 22 September 1989 by Detective Inspector Watson

McAteer and FBI agent Lawrence Whittaker. McAteer's corresponding statement recalled how the two officers observed a pair of operators process a wagonload of luggage at coding station 206. What happened next severely undermined the claim that B8849 must have originated from KM180. The operators went from the coding station, leaving it unattended, but with the computer still on and operable. Within a minute another worker arrived with a single suitcase, which he had carried from a batch about about 50 yards away. He then coded in the case at station 206 and walked away without noting the transaction on the station's worksheet. When McAteer questioned an FAG supervisor about this practice, he reluctantly agreed that it was not unusual. The statement concluded: 'Bearing in mind that KM180's luggage input was the last entry recorded on the work sheet, by Koca, and the relatively short time taken to input a single piece of luggage into the system, it is feasible that items attributed to KM180 from Gate 206 on 21.12.88, may well have been input after that aircraft's luggage had been disposed of.'[22]

The airport documentation indicated that more wagonloads of baggage were sent for processing at certain coding stations than were recorded on the coders' worksheets. The clearest example was of four wagonloads that arrived on Lufthansa flight LH669 from the Syrian capital Damascus. The worksheets only recorded the processing of two and a half wagonloads, one and a half of which was at station 202 and one at 207. So, one and a half wagonloads remained unaccounted for. Clearly this baggage had not disappeared, so what had happened to it? One credible explanation was that it was coded in at less busy neighbouring stations without being recorded. The coding in at stations 202 and 207 coincided almost exactly with that of the KM180 luggage at station 206. Given that 206 was immediately adjacent to 207, it raised the possibility that some or all of the 'missing' Damascus bags were processed at station 206 without being recorded. Intriguingly, the airport's incident log for 21 December recorded that at 13.01 a person called 'Graf' reported that smoke was seen coming from a suitcase.[23] The worksheet for coding station 207 recorded that, at the time of the incident, it was being manned by an employee called Axel Graf, which strongly suggests that the smoking suitcase was discovered at that station. If that were so, then it is quite possible that the incident delayed the processing of one of the wagons from LH669 and that operators of station 206 therefore transferred it to their own station.

Setting aside all the anomalies in the Frankfurt documents, even if they proved that B8849 was from KM180 and made it onto PA103, neither the police nor the Crown ever demonstrated that the primary suitcase was the only unidentified bag recovered from the crash site. If there were other unidentified bags, then in theory any one of them might have been B8849. A review of all the recovered baggage was carried out by Detective Constable Derek Henderson and Detective Sergeant James Russell.[24] Whether that review established the ownership of all the bags is not known, as it was never disclosed to Abdelbaset's lawyers.

Not everyone involved in the official investigation shared the police's conviction that the primary suitcase was transferred from KM180 to PA103A. Perhaps the most prominent sceptic was the Frankfurt Public Prosecutor Volker Rath, who had been duty-bound to conduct his own investigation of the Frankfurt Airport evidence. No doubt to the discomfort of British and American prosecutors, in 1994 he stated publicly that there was no proof that the bomb had passed through the airport and commented, 'No German judge could, with the present evidence, put the two suspects in jail.'[25]

None of the Frankfurt Airport baggage workers could recall seeing a brown Samsonite suitcase. This was perhaps unsurprising, given the volume of luggage they would have to deal with on any given day. However, one of Pan Am's Heathrow loaders, John Bedford, did recall seeing just such a suitcase; moreover he saw it in AVE4041, the container in which the bomb was later to explode. He originally mentioned the item to the police on 3 January 1989,[26] but was not asked to describe it until 9 January 1989. He said it was hard-shelled, 'the type "Samsonite" make' and 'brown in colour'.[27] He first noticed the case when he returned from a tea break at around 16.40. He said that it was lying on the floor of the container in front next to another one, which had also appeared while he was on his break. The handles of both cases were facing inwards. He said that he asked his colleague Sulkash Kamboj who had loaded the items, and Kamboj said that he had,[28] although Kamboj later disputed this.[29] The two suitcases could not have reached Heathrow on PA103A from Frankfurt, because that flight did not touch down until 17.36, well after Bedford went off duty.[30] It is possible that they were the two hard-sided cases belonging to Major Charles Mc-Kee, one of which was a Samsonite. These were almost certainly loaded into AVE4041 at some point after the arrival of his flight from Cyprus; however, both were dark grey. Furthermore, the Cyprus flight arrived at 14.34, which was at least an hour and a half before Bedford went on his tea break.[31]

There were eleven Heathrow interline bags on Fight 103, but only six of these would have been loaded into AVE4041, as the others arrived after it had been taken from the interline shed, so were instead placed in the cargo hold.[32] In his police statements Bedford consistently said there were more than six cases in the container when he took it from the shed prior to going off duty at around 17.00.[33] His colleagues were less consistent in their recollections and Kamboj initially put the figure at four or five; however, since it was he who took the container out of the shed, Bedford would have seen it for longer than the others. Furthermore, Bedford and fellow loaders Amarjit Singh Sidhu and Tarlochan Singh Sahota each said that the base of the container was covered when Bedford took it from the shed.[34]

On 9 January, at the request of the police, he loaded a luggage container in the way AVE4041 had been loaded on 21 December. He placed five suitcases in a row along the back and two flat at the front.[35]* Sidhu and Sahota undertook a similar exercise, with each also loading seven cases.[36] It was clear from these trial loadings that six suitcases would probably not have covered the container's floor.

The Bedford suitcase was ruled out as the primary case because it was lying on the base of the container. The Indian Head and Atlantic City explosive tests in April and July 1989 supposedly established

* Bedford also placed two soft holdalls in the angled section to the left of the row of suitcases, to illustrate what was the normal practice, but he could not recall whether any were packed this way on 21 December 1988, and none of the six legitimate items of interline luggage that were in the container that day were of this type.

that the explosion occurred in the second layer of luggage and must therefore have been in a bag that was transferred from PA103A. However, the tests were far from conclusive.[†] Even if the explosion *was* in the second layer, it was quite possible that the Bedford case ended up there if the bags were rearranged during the subsequent loading of luggae from PA103A.[37]

Bedford revealed that, prior to going off duty at around 17.00, he left AVE4041 by the baggage build-up area. It would have remained there unsupervised for around 45 minutes until PA103A arrived.[38] So, regardless of whether the brown case he saw was the primary suitcase, it was possible that someone placed the primary case into the container during this interval. Although no one reported any suspicious activity, Heathrow, like Frankfurt, was a huge airport, which afforded anonymity to anyone with a security pass. The month after the bombing it was calculated that 779 passes issued by Heathrow Airports Ltd had been reported lost or destroyed. A further 900 British Airways staff passes were unaccounted for as of June 1988.[39] At the time Terminal 3 was being redeveloped, which meant there were many construction workers on-site.[40]

It was in the build-up area that the Heathrow check-in bags were loaded. Although they were all supposed to have been in other containers, there was forensic evidence to suggest that at least one of them, a purple holdall numbered PH/137, may not have been. There were small slits in the bag, around which were sooty deposits and singed fibres,[41] and inside were found two small fragments of the primary suitcase. If this bag had been in AVE4041, it suggested that the loading was less orderly than the police believed, in which case a stray bag might have ended up in the container.

The Bedford bag was not the only reason for suspecting that the bomb had been loaded at Heathrow. The AAIB's calculations suggested that the centre of the explosion was within the angled section of AVE4041, only around 25 inches from the fuselage skin.[42] It was implicit that, had the distance been significantly greater, then the skin would not have been punctured and the aircraft would have survived. If the bombers had sent the primary suitcase from Malta or

† The flaws in the explosive tests evidence are explored in further detail in Chapter 8 and Appendix 2.

Frankfurt, then they were reliant on the unwitting Heathrow loaders placing it where it was likely to do most damage. They would have known that they stood a much greater chance of success if they could somehow place it themselves at Heathrow.

A greater mystery than the Bedford suitcase was that surrounding Khaled Jaafar, the 20-year-old Lebanese-American who, according to an internal police briefing, was suspected of carrying drugs.* At the time of his death he was flying home to Dearborn, Michigan, after spending six weeks in West Germany. Prior to that he had stayed with family members in Lebanon's Bekaa Valley, in order to be near his fiancée. The Bekaa was notorious at the time as the centre of Middle Eastern drug production and a stronghold of fiercely anti-Western armed groups, most notably Hezbollah and Amal. On 30 and 31 December 1988 the *Washington Times* and the *Daily Express* newspapers respectively alleged that the terrorists had planted the bomb in his luggage.[43] The *Express* claimed to have sources within both the Metropolitan Police and the FBI.† On 16 April 1989, the *Sunday Times*'s Washington correspondent, Mark Hosenball, who was known for his good contacts within the US intelligence services, reported a leak from 'Washington sources' that traces of heroin had been found in the debris and that the terrorists may have duped a drug smuggler into carrying the bomb.[44]

Jaafar's father, Nazir, denied that his son had anything to do with terrorism and claimed that he was wholly westernised.[45] However, two months after the bombing a cousin of Khaled's approached the FBI, through an intermediary, with information that he thought might be of relevance to the inquiry. Although he did not think that Khaled would have carried drugs, he believed he would be easy prey to terrorists requiring a dupe to take something onto an aircraft.[46] Shortly afterwards, another cousin came forward, who claimed to know Khaled much better and to have seen him during his visit to the Bekaa the previous autumn. He too said that Khaled was malleable, all the more so because he was head over heels in love with his fiancée, whose

* See Chapter 3.
† Although the Lockerbie investigation was led by the Scottish police, they were assisted by the Metropolitan Police Anti-Terrorist Branch.

brother was a Hezbollah captain. He alleged that Khaled had been persuaded to carry drugs and was given a radio-cassette player as a gift, unaware that it contained a bomb.[47]*

One of the passengers on PA103A also volunteered information about Jaafar. Yasmin Siddique was standing directly behind him in the passport control queue at Frankfurt Airport. As his American passport was inspected she noticed that he was 'very agitated and nervous'. She thought he was not carrying any hand luggage,[48] which meant that he must have checked in all his bags. However, his father initially claimed that he did not check in any bags and only had two items of hand luggage.[49] Pan Am's check-in records subsequently demonstrated that he had in fact checked in two items. Two of his bags were recovered from the crash site. The Crown claimed that these were the two checked-in bags, and, since they displayed no sign of blast-damage, did not contain the bomb. However, the lack of explosive damage was not proof that the bags had been checked in; indeed, blast-damage would have proved they *were* checked in. Neither of the bags had check-in labels attached and, although the fall from 31,000 feet may have detached them, none were found loose at the crash site.

Crucially, both bags were much smaller than normal check-in bags, with the largest measuring only 60 x 30 x 20 centimetres and the other just 40 x 30 x 20.[50] A Pan Am leaflet found in one of them gave the airline's hand luggage limit as 22 x 14 x 9 inches, which equates to 55.88 x 35.56 x 22.86 centimetres.[51] So, the smaller bag was easily within the limit and, given that the other one was less than 5 cm too long, it would be unusual if the airline insisted that it be checked in.

Jaafar's journey from Frankfurt to the United States would have taken at least ten hours, so it would be surprising if he had no hand luggage. Some of the bags' contents certainly suggested that he had

---

* The relative did not hide the fact that he was a cannabis producer and that in return for information he wished to be allowed to import a consignment of the drug into the United States. This probably accounts for why nothing came of the lead. Nevertheless, it was clear that the relative had a mole within Hezbollah, as a few years later he was able to obtain video footage of a Hezbollah meeting at which PFLP-GC leader Ahmed Jibril was present. The footage subsequently featured in the documentary *The Maltese Double Cross*.

them with him in the cabin. These included two small document pouches and paperwork relating to his various journeys. Furthermore, the bags did not contain items such as towels and toiletries, which travellers would normally have in their luggage when away from home for two months.[52]

Both the bags were recovered from search Sector D. Quite separately, in Sector H, the police found a piece of brown material, allocated reference number PH/695, within which there were a number of additional papers belonging to Jaafar. The initial police description suggested the material was part of a suitcase-lining, which, if true, would indicate that he had an additional suitcase and that at least one of the small bags was therefore hand luggage. Unusually, on 21 February 1989, the items were flown down especially to RARDE for forensic examination.[53] No contemporaneous record of that examination was disclosed to Abdelbaset's legal team and no statements were taken by the police from RARDE personnel. The only reference to the items within the RARDE scientists' examination notes is a list produced by Feraday, over a year later on 29 March 1990, in which each item is followed by the abbreviation 'N.P.E.S', standing for 'no particular explosive sign'.[54] The material and papers were returned to Nazir Jaafar in 1992, by which time the police described it as a pocket.[55] One of the officers who accompanied the pieces to RARDE, Detective Inspector William Williamson, later said he understood the material to be a pocket from one of Jaafar's garments.[56] Since no evidence to support this claim has ever been disclosed, the material's origin remains a mystery. In 2007 it emerged that, on 8 April 1989, numerous other items belonging to Jaafar were tested for fingerprints at the Metropolitan Police forensic laboratory.* According to the officer who undertook the tests, a total of 41 sets of marks were recovered,[57] but what the Scottish police did with them – for example, whether or not they attempted to compare them with the prints of the Autumn Leaves suspects – was never revealed.

While in West Germany, Jaafar stayed with Lebanese brothers Hassan and Souheil El-Salheli, in their apartment at 16 Mozartstrasse

---

* This was revealed by the Scottish Criminal Cases Review Commission in its Statement of Reasons on Abdelbaset's case.

in Dortmund. His father Nazir said the brothers were childhood friends of Khaled's,[58] yet Hassan claimed never to have met Khaled before his arrival in Dortmund.[59] When first interviewed by the BKA in April 1989, he refused to answer any questions, but then relented. Although four months had passed since the bombing, he gave an unusually precise description of Khaled's luggage and possessions, claiming there were only the two small bags and that he had watched Khaled pack them.[60] Souheil also said Khaled had only two bags, as did their cousin, Hussein Ali Allam. Allam had an apartment at 16 Mozartstrasse, but his registered address was a refugee hostel, 47 Klosterstrasse in Pfullingen.

The brothers said that on 21 December they and Allam took Khaled to Dortmund railway station, from where he caught the train to Frankfurt. However, they failed to mention that they were accompanied by a fourth man, Abdel Salame. Also strange was that Allam told the BKA that he had no idea how Khaled had got to the airport.

Salame brought Hassan El-Salheli's camera and said that he or Hassan took some photos of Khaled at the station.[61] Hassan said he sent all the pictures to Nazir Jaafar and that all the other photos on the film were taken later in his flat and sent to his family in Lebanon. None of the railway station photos showed Khaled's bags. One of them was clearly of Khaled with someone else, but the photo had been cropped so the other person, or people, were no longer present. Stranger still, Hassan said that he threw away the negatives.

There were also peculiarities surrounding Jaafar's air ticket. On 14 December he booked and paid for a flight from Düsseldorf to Detroit on 19 December at the Ali Reisburo travel agency in Iserlohn, near Dortmund. He was accompanied there by Hassan and an acquaintance of the brothers called Naim Ali Ghannam, who knew the agency's owner Ali Jadallah. Later the same day he was told that the flight was fully booked, so the ticket was changed to 21 December and Ghannam collected the ticket from Jadallah at Dortmund railway station. Hassan denied accompanying Jaafar and Ghannam to the travel agency on 14 December,[62] but later claimed that he was there and that they visited the agency two or three times in all.[63] Jadallah, however, said he never met Hassan until after Jaafar's ticket was booked.[64]

Hassan said he first met Ghannam by chance on the street in Dortmund a few weeks before Jaafar's arrival,[65] but Ghannam claimed to have known the brothers for two years.[66] Ghannam had been in the Lebanese army, and for about three years had fought with Palestinian groups against the Israeli forces.[67] Not long after the street meeting, he travelled to Lebanon to attend his brother's funeral, returning shortly before Jaafar's arrival. Hassan thought the brother had drowned at sea,[68] but Ghannam presumed he had been shot because he had been recruited by Hezbollah.[69]

Allam apparently had more direct connections to a radical Shi'ite group. A fellow inhabitant of 16 Mozartstrasse, Bilal Dib, one of the residents of the Pfullingen hostel Charif Makke and a third acquaintance, Yassar Hamdan, each independently told the BKA that Allam was a member of Amal.[70]

Another of Jaafar's contacts, Abdallah Morue, was also a member of Amal and had fought with the group during the Lebanese Civil War. He said that he met Jaafar for the first time when he sat next to him on the flight from Beirut to Frankfurt on 8 November.[71] On arrival, he asked Jaafar and a fellow passenger, Adnan Assaf, to help him find somewhere to stay. Assaf called a Lebanese man, Khaled Graupnerspath, on Morue's behalf, then passed the phone to Jaafar. Graupnerspath's number was found among Jaafar's possessions at Lockerbie,[72] and he later told the BKA that he had been to school with Jaafar in Lebanon and that he recognised him by his voice when he called. Strangely, however, when shown a photograph of Jaafar, he said that it was not the person he knew from school.[73] Morue also claimed not to recognise the photograph, but admitted that he was on the same flight and that a fellow passenger had made a call for him.[74] So, either Graupnerspath and Morue were wrong, or there were two people using the name Khaled Jaafar, one of whom was impersonating the other.

Assaf was never traced by the BKA; however, early on in the investigation, they conducted inquiries into a Lebanese man called Ali Nasri Assaf, who, according to a BKA memo dated 15 February 1989, 'is possibly implicated in the bombing of the airliner'. It stated that he had travelled from Beirut to Belgium on 13 or 14 December 1988 and had travelled on from there to West Germany and the UK.

It went on, 'it is known that he was in contact with Lebanese groups of terrorists for the Hizbollah . . . and acting as drugs dealer.'[75] There was no evidence that Ali Nasri Assaf was Adnan Assaf.

It also seemed that there was nothing to connect Jaafar's associates to the men arrested during the October 1988 Autumn Leaves raids, but eventually a rather different picture emerged.

The Fantasist 7

On 10 August 1988, a 28-year-old Libyan man entered the American Embassy in Malta and asked to talk to a CIA officer. Speaking through an interpreter, he made a simple offer: if the Agency would relocate him to the USA, he would provide them with sensitive information about Libya. The man was Majid Giaka, a lowly JSO officer, who for the previous two years had been on secondment as LAA's Assistant Station Chief. By the time he entered the lives of the Scottish police three years later, he had directly linked Abdelbaset and Lamin to terrorist activities and, more importantly, to a brown Samsonite suitcase. Giaka seemed too good to be true. And, as events proved, he was.

In their first meeting Giaka assured the CIA man that, although no longer active in security work, he maintained regular contact with Libyan security officials. He was making the offer, he said, because he feared being relocated back to Libya following a complaint against him by an LAA passenger. He said he was a trained mechanical engineer and had joined the JSO in 1984. He claimed that his first job was in the secret files section and that he was then moved to the security collection department, where he compiled reports on dissident activities and handled domestic informants who worked within government ministries. He explained that, during this period, due to his mechanical abilities, he was also assigned to the motor pool. He also claimed to have received training from KGB instructors in Tripoli and boasted that he was very close to Abdelbaset's friends Ezzadin Hinshiri and Said Rashid,[1] and well acquainted with Abdullah Sennousi. The CIA gave Giaka the code-name P/1. They interviewed him again over the next two days, during which he relayed details of the JSO's structure and some of its members.

All the meetings were summarised in secret telex cables to CIA headquarters in Langley, Virginia. When, many years later, heavily redacted copies of the telexes were released to Abdelbaset's lawyers, they revealed very little about the JSO, but a great deal about the absurd *folie à deux* into which the CIA and its new recruit had become locked.

With hindsight, the harbingers of a dysfunctional union were present as early as the second meeting. By then Giaka had changed his mind about relocating to America, as he feared the consequences for his family. Rather, he said, he wished to remain on the island, marry his Maltese girlfriend and start a car rental business.[2]

On 14 September he agreed to meet on a 'regular and clandestine basis'. His CIA handlers offered him a salary of approximately $1,000 per month.[3] He eventually accepted,[4] but had a more immediate and bizarre demand. He said he wanted the Agency to pay for sham surgery on his arm in order to manufacture a disability that would exempt him from further government service. The handlers expressed a willingness to help, and agreed that the best way forward was for him to identify a Maltese doctor who could perform the operation. In the corresponding cable the CIA officers expressed themselves pleased with their new recruit, noting that he had 'demonstrated that he is currently able to obtain valuable information'. It also recorded that they hoped to persuade him to rejoin the JSO by offering him 'generous rewards', and that, in the meantime, they would demonstrate their willingness to meet his needs.[5]

On 5 October the officers held a 'productive four hour rapport building and assessment meeting' with Giaka. They noted that he 'lives in dread of reassignment' to JSO Headquarters and that his demand for sham surgery was a 'non-negotiable'. Significantly, Giaka went on, for the first time, to implicate Abdelbaset in terrorist activities. Asked what he knew about weapons caches on the island, he stated, 'that he was personally aware of one cache of eight kilos of orange coloured explosive that had been stored for many months at the LAA office'. He added that he understood 'that these explosives first arrived circa 1985 when Abd-Al-Basit (Magrahi) [sic] was in Malta'. He pleaded for permission to leave the JSO and for funds to establish his car-hire business, but was told very firmly that the Agency wished him to remain *in situ* and make himself as useful as possible to the JSO in order to expand his access to useful information.[6]

On 7 October the officers discussed P/1 with a senior colleague. It was agreed that he would be introduced to Giaka so they could discuss the available medical options. That day's cable reassured Headquarters that 'P/1 is strategically placed in the Valletta [LAA office] which he himself describes as "a primary launching point" for Libyan intelligence and terrorist teams en route to/from Europe'. The senior officer's initial reactions were reported as positive, and he believed that 'we should be able to accommodate the essence of P/1's requirements with medical evidence that can not be easily disputed or disproved by routine medical examination.' The cable noted that Giaka 'will need to be carefully coached on normal symptoms of the selected complaint'.[7]

The report of the next meeting, dated 11 October, continued the upbeat tone, claiming it had demonstrated Giaka's 'commitment and ability to pass terrorist type intelligence on a timely basis'. More importantly, he fleshed out the story of the explosive, claiming explicitly that Abdelbaset had smuggled it into Malta and that it was stored at the LAA's office in Valletta 'until recently'.[8] The following day his handlers reported a further crucial Giaka allegation, namely that Lamin had set up a business in Malta 'as an ESO front company'.[9] Although the business was not named, it was cleary a reference to the Medtours travel agency.

I had no idea that Giaka was telling lies about Lamin and me, but with hindsight it was hardly surprising. From the outset there was something in his demeanour that I neither liked nor trusted. He would be perfectly pleasant to me, carrying my bag and helping me with administrative formalities, but I never took to him and suspected that he was merely trying to curry favour. He knew that I was related to Abdullah Sanoussi and Said Rashid and was a friend of Ezzadin Hinshiri, so probably regarded me as someone worth knowing.

It was Hinshiri who recommended him for the post of Malta Assistant Station Manager. He said he was a good worker, whose vigilance was reflected in the fact that he had once submitted a report on his own father. Although I respected Hinshiri, I was aghast that anyone could behave in such a way. Within three or four months of his arrival in Malta, I heard reports that Giaka was causing problems for Lamin and LAA crews. He was typical of the worst type of security officer, whose JSO membership granted them a status way beyond their actual abilities and fertilised an insufferable self-importance. His security reports sometimes used vile language about LAA personnel and made allegations that were often ill-based and occasionally fanciful. For example, he once reported that certain crew members had been making frequent telephone calls to London and the USA, implying that they were spies. I ignored him, as it was well known that the people in question had girlfriends in those places.

Ironically, given his subsequent actions, he was also given to ostentatious displays of patriotism. Following the US raids on Libya in 1986, he claimed he was prepared to do anything to avenge our country's loss, and spoke of targeting US and British tourists. I told him very firmly that his sole focus should be the security of LAA passengers and crews. He seemed confused by the put-down and looked awkward, though I suspected that, beneath the surface, I had angered him. From then on he did his best to avoid me, and we barely spoke until I stepped down as LAA's Head of Security at the end of that year.

It was claimed that he was stealing from passengers. He certainly stole from me at least once and possibly twice. On the first occasion he took a carved cane, which I had brought back from Nigeria for my grandfather. It went missing as I transited through Malta, and Lamin told me that he subsequently saw Giaka with it. On the other occasion my mother and father were in Malta and asked me to forward them some money. I sent them cash in an envelope via LAA and asked Giaka to pass it on. When I later checked with my father, he was adamant that the envelope never contained the amount I'd sent.

Giaka claimed that I somehow delayed his posting to Malta, but in fact it was Nassr Ashur who objected to the posting, as he favoured another JSO officer for the role, and it was I who insisted that he be allowed to go. It was nevertheless true that on a subsequent occasion when he was visiting Tripoli I tried to block his return, as he had by then begun to create problems, but Said Rashid intervened and allowed him to resume his position.

On 5 November 1988, Giaka was introduced to a doctor who examined him and discussed the options for his fake disability, which included the CIA's suggestion of a lower back problem, such as a ruptured disc. The report of the meeting noted that he appeared to be a hypochondriac and was 'beginning to convince himself that he already suffered from the aches and pains described to him as symptomatic of a slipped disc'. The following day, his handlers discussed how he might improve his access to the JSO. Giaka said he had given the matter a lot of thought and accepted that he should stay with the organisation. He acknowledged that while in Malta he had been a 'shirker', had generally dodged JSO assignments and 'that he must make up for his previously marginal performance'. The best way to do this, he believed, 'would be to establish an impressive reporting record'. For this, he required the CIA's assistance to come up with credible intelligence, which he could feed back to the JSO without jeopardy to the Agency. His handlers commended his forward thinking and agreed to 'have HQ's experts work on some of these subject areas to produce "feed material"'.[10]

On 6 November Giaka made further claims about the structure and senior personnel of the JSO's external division, the ESO. Among the titbits he divulged was that since 1987 Abdelbaset's friend Said Rashid was working for the General Electronics Company of Libya, which, according to Giaka, was 'an ESO subsidiary'.[11] This was of interest, because the Scottish and US prosecutors later alleged that the Lockerbie bomb was housed in one of a batch of Toshiba radio-cassette players purchased by the company.

On 16 January 1989, Giaka arrived at his regular debrief in a glum mood, but, according to his handler, his spirits lifted markedly 'when it became obvious that we were beginning to respond with assistance with feed info and after detailed discussion of monthly salary escrow and ops expense remuneration'.[12] The following day he received a cash payment of 1,500 Maltese pounds for operational expenses, which was handed over in a hollowed out Arab-English dictionary.[13] During the same meeting, he claimed that Lamin was about to embark upon an unspecified intelligence mission to Europe on behalf of Senoussi.[14]

The strategy of providing Giaka with 'feed material' did little to improve the quality of the information that he fed to the CIA. For the most part he reported the comings and goings of Libyan officials to Malta and rumours about the political situation in Libya. Most strikingly, he said nothing whatsoever about 20 and 21 December, the days on which Abdelbaset and Lamin were in Malta and were supposed to have executed the bomb plot. On 20 December he reported, correctly, that Abdelbaset had been in Malta on 7 December and had flown on to Zurich with Swissair and returned to the island on 17 December. However, the account contained two glaring errors: firstly, he said the flight was on 8 December, whereas it was in fact delayed until the 9th; secondly, and more importantly, he said that Abdelbaset had remained in Zurich for the week, whereas he only stayed there for a night before flying on to Prague. He claimed that Abdelbaset was a JSO technical communications expert, and that it was likely he was carrying high-tech intelligence-gathering equipment and was involved in an intelligence operation. *(This claim was especially ludicrous, as my only fields of expertise were geography and airline operations. I was going to visit my friend Abdelmajid Arebi and was aiming for nothing more than to buy things for the house and have a good time.)*

Some of Giaka's inventions betrayed a glaring ignorance of the subject matter. For example, he claimed that an LAA flight from Tripoli to Rome had stopped to refuel in Malta, even though the flight took around one hour forty minutes, and the type of aircraft used, a Boeing 727, had sufficient fuel capacity to fly for many hours.[15]

On 11 April Giaka came with dramatic news: he had been ordered to return to Tripoli on 1 May, as he was being replaced as Assistant Station Manager. His handlers cannot have been happy to hear that he had no desire to return, or remain with the JSO, and wished only to stay in Malta and start a business. He said he had found a local doctor who was willing to attest to a sham surgical injury and that all he now needed was the CIA's assistance in finding a surgeon. In the corresponding cable the handlers reiterated their keenness for him to return to Tripoli and penetrate JSO Headquarters, and suggested that, in order to help persuade him, an Arabic-speaking CIA officer should be present at a future meeting.[16]

On 17 April Giaka reported that he had found a surgeon who was willing to perform the operation later that week for 2,000 Maltese pounds. The doctor had agreed to give him two scars, the first on his right arm, which would correspond with a genuine injury documented in his Libyan medical records, and the second on his lower back as evidence of a fictional back injury. The doctor would also recommend in writing that he should avoid strenuous physical activity, which should enable him to avoid military service once he had left the JSO.

The CIA agreed to foot the bill,[17] but, like a hopeless gambler waiting for the big win, continued to be simultaneously frustrated and fleeced. On 10 May Giaka accepted an expenses payment to cover flights for him and his wife from Tripoli to Malta, yet, as an LAA employee, they were both entitled to free tickets. There is nothing in the CIA reports to indicate that his handlers were aware of the con.[18]

However, by September 1989 they were becoming seriously concerned. On 31 August he had adamantly declared that he had no intention of returning to work for the JSO and that he was considering an offer to join the operations department of the Revolutionary Committees. The corresponding report expressed the handlers' disappointment and said they would 'consider other options for our future relationship'. Giaka nevertheless requested to be reimbursed 1,000 Maltese pounds for a second operation on his arm and for various other expenses. His handlers agreed, but assured Headquarters that at their next meeting he would be told in no uncertain terms that they would not finance further surgery. The report added, 'If P/1 is not able to demonstrate sustained and defined access to information of intelligence value by January 1990 the Agency will cease all salary and financial support until such access can be proven again.' It concluded, 'It is clear that P/1 will never be the penetration of the ESO that we had anticipated . . . Unfortunately it appears that our assisting him in scam surgery on his arm to avoid military service has had the reverse result than we had intended, it has allowed him to avoid further service with the ESO, P/1's true intention from the beginning. P/1 has never been a true staff member of the ESO and as he has stated at this meeting, he was co-opted with working [sic] with the ESO and he now wants nothing to do with them or their activities.'[19]

A week later his handlers 'strongly advised' Giaka to take the job with the Revolutionary Committees, and told him that their relationship would be reviewed on 1 January. They handed over $5,000 in back pay and 1,500 Maltese pounds for operational expenses, then asked him to sign a receipt. At this point he abruptly rose and headed for the door, complaining that receipts should not be required in their 'struggle as "brothers" against terrorism'. After 'much back slapping and reassurances' he was persuaded to stay.[20]

At around this time his handlers began to question him indirectly about Lockerbie. On 28 August he was asked whether it was possible to insert a suitcase bomb into the luggage-handling operation at Luqa Airport. He claimed that JSO or LAA officers could recruit airport workers to help them and that explosives could be brought from Libya in diplomatic pouches, but he knew of no instances of explosives being placed aboard planes 'and does not think this type of operation could have slipped by him'.[21] However, less than a week later he said it could have happened without his knowledge.[22]

The following month the handlers asked him directly about Abdelbaset's activities in the run-up to the bombing, but he could tell them only that he had visited Malta nine months later in September 1989. The subsequent cable noted, 'P/1 had no further information regarding Al-Magrahi.'[23]

Over the next nine months the CIA's faith was pared to the bone. Giaka continued to nag his handlers to pay for an extra round of surgery, stressing the importance of a fresh wound that would provide 'shock value' with the military medical review board. On 24 October he received a strong warning that '"Washington" was becoming increasingly impatient' with his demanding nature, especially as he had failed to secure a job in either Libya or Malta. Despite this, the handlers sought the blessing of Headquarters to pay for the final round of surgery, arguing that it would be unwise to abandon him at 'this critical juncture', especially given the amount already invested. They also suggested that their stern lecture had had the desired effect.[24]

On 16 November Giaka reported that he had had the operation at a cost of $2,000 and believed that it would gain him the desired waiver from military service. He said it was likely to leave him with permanent damage to his arm, but seemed unconcerned by the prospect; indeed, he proudly told his handlers that it was already developing the symptoms of rheumatism.[25]

On 15 December 1989, he announced that he would be moving back to Libya two days later. He declared his intention to obtain a position within the Revolutionary Committees' Operations Centre and to meet his handlers every four to six months. He then asked them to increase his salary to $1,500 a month, citing an agreement dating back to the previous April. They reminded him that the offer was contingent upon his returning to Tripoli and remaining with the JSO, or working in the Operations Centre, neither of which he had so far achieved. The Agency nevertheless planned to award him a $1,000 bonus as an incentive to return.[26]

One can only imagine the handlers' frustration when, at their next meeting, on 13 February 1990, they learned that he had not returned to Libya after all. He explained that he'd decided to remain in Malta and obtain a certificate from his doctor indicating that he was receiving therapy for his mock disability. He claimed that he had attempted to relay this news in late December, but they were sceptical. He once more expressed his commitment to find work with the Revolutionary Committees, but the subsequent CIA cable noted that his financial position seemed to be his primary motivation for meeting. $4,000 in back pay, given to him in December, had been spent on surgery, car hire and hotel expenses, and he also had to pay damages in connection with a recent car accident. The cable ended: 'P/1's procrastination beyond reasonable limits is testing patience.'[27]

A further meeting was scheduled for later in February, but Giaka failed to attend and there were no further meetings until 7 June. A week or so earlier, the interpreter had bumped into him and suggested he should see his handlers, but he said he was on his way to Libya and asked her not to mention their encounter. When asked to explain his long silence, he told the handlers it was simply because he'd had nothing to report. As for his broken promise to find work with the Revolutionary Committees, he explained that such matters took time, but failed to elaborate. The handlers informed him that Headquarters had ended his salary payments, but he appeared unperturbed. He said he had married his Maltese girlfriend, who was currently living with him in Libya, and that they would probably return to Malta in one to three months once he had secured his exemption from military service. Asked about his current priorities, he said his car-hire business was number one and obtaining a job with the Revolutionary Committees was now low on the list. The handlers gave vent to their despair in the corresponding cable: 'It is clear to us that P/1 resigned from the ESO shortly before he walked into the US Embassy and met with [CIA] officers. Since then, he has steadily attempted to wean himself away from involvement in Libyan security and intelligence matters, opting to build a personal business instead.' They considered him to be, at best, a cooperative contact, but clung to the hope that he might yet 'develop information of operational or intelligence interest'.[28]

Under normal circumstances the story might have ended there, and Giaka faded back into obscurity, but over the next six months everything changed. By December 1990 the Lockerbie investigation was firmly focused on Abdelbaset and Libya. It was time for the CIA to dust off its useless informant. By then things were not going nearly so well for Giaka. He had yet to be formally signed off by the JSO, and in the meantime was living at home, unsalaried, and 'somewhat at a loss for his lot in life'. His handlers asked if he would be prepared to meet with 'experts from Washington' who wished to discuss his role at Luqa Airport around the time of the bombing. He said he could not see them immediately, as he was returning to Tripoli the following day, but might be able to in a couple of months, once he had obtained his formal discharge from the JSO. Asked if he had ever personally placed a suitcase on a flight from Luqa Airport, or arranged for someone else to do it, he replied with a firm no, adding that no one had ever approached him about such a plan and that 'he had no further information in this regard'. However, when asked who would have been in a position to undertake such an operation, he suggested Abdelbaset and Lamin, although he did not elaborate. At the end of the hour-long meeting he asked if his CIA salary would be resumed. He was told no, but was given 200 Maltese pounds (approximately $700) for his troubles. He then wondered aloud if it would be possible to obtain $2,000 as he wished to purchase bananas in Malta and import them to Libya, where they fetched three or four times the price. He was told that 'Washington' was unsure of his commitment to fighting terrorism, and 'would not approve such money without more detailed information'. His chief handler then added that he would raise the issue with the proper authorities 'who might recompense him if he would be willing to be completely debriefed'. The handlers reported, 'We believe P/1 is becoming desperate as he searches for his role in life in his post ESO world . . . and is certainly milking all of his contacts, including us, for whatever he can get during this transition period.' Tellingly, they then added, 'This does not rule out however that P/1 was ideally positioned in December 1988 to witness individuals passing through Malta and ESO/LAA care at LIA [Luqa International Airport].' Giaka had been told loud and clear that if he delivered the goods on Lockerbie he'd be back on the payroll, while CIA Headquarters now knew that the habitual milker was ready to milked.[29]

It would be a further seven months before Giaka was back in touch. On 7 July 1991 he and his wife slipped out of Libya into Tunisia, from where they flew to Malta. He had passed the point of no return and was now at the CIA's mercy. On 10 July he explained to his handlers that a few weeks earlier he had approached Lamin to enlist Abdelbaset's help in obtaining his JSO release papers. Lamin told him that Abdullah Senoussi had ordered that neither of them were permitted to leave the country due to 'problems' relating to Lockerbie. Lamin added that his Maltese business partner, Vincent Vassallo, had told him that the CIA had thick files on him and Abdelbaset. Giaka decided it was time to flee the country, but was also afraid to linger in Malta, believing the Maltese government might hand him back to the Libyans. He was scared to leave via Luqa Airport and asked to depart by sea if possible. The CIA therefore made plans to evacuate him in the next day or two.[30]

The following day Giaka was told that officials from the US Department of Justice wished to meet with him somewhere away from the island. It was made clear to him that they would be assessing his value as a witness and that they would accept or reject him on the basis of the answers that he gave. He was warned that if they rejected him he might be returned to Malta and, although the US government would consider continuing the relationship, there was no guarantee that it would.[31]

Late the following evening Giaka contacted his handlers to request an emergency meeting. They noted that 'he did not sound good'. During an emotional discussion he revealed that his wife was four months pregnant and pleaded to know how their safety would be guaranteed. They reported that he was 'a shattered person' and believed his life to be in danger in Malta. He concluded that, although the path offered by the US Government was no guarantee of security, it was the only one open to him.[32] In short, he knew they had him over a barrel. A few hours later he was spirited out of Malta and taken to the USS *Butte*, a US Navy auxiliary vessel anchored 27 miles off the coast in international waters. The following day he was interviewed by two FBI officers, Philip Reid and Hal Hendershot, in the presence of two officials from the US Attorney General's office.

For the most part the interview concentrated on his background and on various people he alleged were members of the JSO; however, he reported details that tallied neatly with the case that was being built against his two LAA colleagues. Elaborating on the explosives story, he said Lamin had shown them to him in March 1985 and had explained that Abdelbaset had smuggled them into Malta. He added that Abdelbaset later told him that he should take responsibility for the explosive in the event of Lamin being transferred from the airport, and that between May and July 1988 he delivered it to the Libyan Embassy. Previously, he said, it had been stored at the LAA office at Luqa Airport, perhaps forgetting that three years earlier he had stated that it was held at the Valletta office.*

He also claimed that towards the end of 1988 he saw Abdelbaset and Lamin in the Luqa Airport Customs area with one or two unidentified people who appeared to have arrived on a flight from Tripoli. He said he was not sure whether Abdelbaset also arrived with the two men at the airport or had just met them at the airport, but he was sure that Lamin was not on the flight. Crucially, he claimed that Abdelbaset and Lamin removed a large, brown, hard-sided Samsonite suitcase from the baggage reclaim carousel and exited the airport without its being inspected.[33]

Giaka had given the FBI the last piece of the jigsaw – first-hand witness testimony that shortly before the bombing the two suspects

* *The Luqa 'office' was in fact a partitioned-off area of an open plan area shared with other companies. Since people were constantly coming and going, it offered absolutely no privacy.*

had a brown Samsonite case in Malta. The obvious question was why Giaka had failed to mention this vital detail to the CIA either at the time, or when later asked about Abdelbaset's activities in the run-up to the bombing? The obvious answer was that he was lying through his teeth in order to avoid being sent back to Malta.

The tactic worked. Within a week he was in the USA undergoing a week-long debrief by the same FBI officers at the Bureau's Tyson's Corner office in Northern Virginia. He gave further details of the suitcase episode, claiming that one of the previously unidentified men was Libyan Abougela Masoud and that Abdelbaset had arrived on the same flight from Tripoli. He also said that the men all drove off in Lamin's new Hyundai Stellar car. The police established that Lamin took delivery of the car on 14 December 1988,[34] which further convinced them that the episode had occurred on 20 December.

Giaka threw in some fresh allegations. One was that in June 1986, two months after the US raids on Libya, Said Rashid had asked him to produce a report on whether it was possible to send a suitcase on a British flight from Luqa. Another was that Abdelbaset's activities in Malta increased between October and December and were 'of an intelligence nature' related to Lamin's company Medtours, which, he said, Abdelbaset had funded.[35] Remarkably, he claimed that Colonel Gadafy, the Foreign Minister Ibrahim Bishari and the Maltese President Guido de Marco were all masons.[36]

The CIA did not want the Scottish police to know about Giaka, but, at the insistence of the FBI's lead investigator, Richard Marquise, the Agency relented.[37] In early August 1991 the Libyan was interviewed by SIO Detective Superintendent Stuart Henderson and repeated his claims about the brown Samsonite, the explosive, which he named as TNT, and Medtours.[38] A Department of Justice official oversaw the interview 'to ensure Giaka did not contradict himself', as Marquise later put it.[39] In October, about three weeks before the two Libyans were indicted, Giaka testified before the Federal Grand Jury that delivered the US indictment.

Setting aside the fact that he had recovered his memory over two and a half years after the alleged event, there were a number of major problems with Giaka's account. His claim that Abdelbaset had brought explosives to Malta in 1985 was rather undermined by the fact that there was no evidence that Abdelbaset set foot on the island that year. There were at least three significant flaws in his account of the brown suitcase episode. Firstly, with the exception of his Grand Jury evidence, which was ambiguous on the subject, he consistently stated that Lamin was waiting at Luqa Airport and did not arrive on the flight, whereas he and Abdelbaset in fact flew together. Secondly, there was no evidence that they travelled with two other Libyans. Thirdly, in his second FBI interview he said that when he saw them together at Luqa, Lamin had had the Hyundai for a few weeks. If that was the case, then the incident cannot have occurred on 20 December, as by then Lamin had only owned the car for six days. Furthermore, the insurance records recovered by the police show that the car was insured from 1 January onwards.[40]*

Neither the FBI and police interviews, nor the Grand Jury testimony, referred to the fact that Giaka was a paid CIA informant, and that the CIA considered that he had taken them for a ride. No one thought to tell the US State Department either. Michael Scharf worked in the Department's Office of the Legal Adviser for Law Enforcement and Intelligence and was responsible for drafting the UN Security Council resolutions that were passed against Libya in 1992. In 2006 he angrily recalled, 'The CIA and the FBI kept the State Department in the dark. It worked for them for us to be fully committed to the theory that Libya was responsible. I helped the counterterrorism bureau draft documents that described why we thought Libya was responsible, but these were not based on seeing a lot of evidence, but rather on representations from the CIA and FBI and the Department of Justice about what the case would prove and did prove. It was largely based on this inside guy [Giaka]. It wasn't until the trial that I learned this guy was a nut-job and that the CIA had absolutely no confidence in him and that they knew he was a liar.'[42]

---

* As far as I could recall, we drove to Vassallo's house in the LAA Volvo, but in any case Lamin had the use of his brother's car, which had been in Malta for maintenance work and was about to be shipped back to Libya.[41] A further reason to disbelieve the story is that Giaka, the self-confessed shirker, only usually went to the airport when he absolutely had to, which was generally when LAA flights arrived or departed. He tended to show up just a few minutes before the landing or departure and left again as soon as he could.

141

The FBI may well themselves have been in the dark. Marquise came to know Giaka well, dining with him once a month,[43] and believed him to be credible. Remarkably, he never asked for nor received copies of the CIA cables, or any other relevant documentation held by the Agency.[44]

The FBI reports and police statements contain no records of Giaka being offered a reward for information about Lockerbie, but it is unlikely to have escaped his notice that money was on offer. In 1989 the US government announced a $2 million reward scheme,[45] which in May 1990 was augmented by a further $1 million from the airline industry.[46] Later that year the US State Department relaunched the reward programme, which was now worth $4 million, as *Heroes*. Adverts featuring US movie stars Charlton Heston, Charlie Sheen and Charles Bronson, urging people to provide information, were translated into five languages, including Arabic.[47]

Giaka was to get rich from the rewards programme, but proved very poor value for money.

The Experts 8

Lockerbie presented the investigators with an unprecedented challenge. The Boeing 747 was one of the largest aircraft then in production, and its remains, and those of its passengers and their belongings, were scattered across 845 square miles, much of it impenetrable forest. While a small army of police officers, military personnel and search volunteers were on hand to recover the debris, the task of analysing it fell principally to just two men, the Royal Armament Research and Development Establishment (RARDE) scientists Dr Thomas Hayes and Allen Feraday.

Their investigation took almost three years and culminated in a joint report, which they signed in December 1991. The report provided the forensic scaffolding around which the prosecution case was built. Crucially, it confirmed that the bomb contained a Mebo MST-13 timer of the type supplied to Libya, that it was surrounded by clothes linked to Tony Gauci's shop and that it was located in the second layer of luggage of container AVE4041.

With a lineage dating back to the Gunpowder Plot of 1605, RARDE had a reputation as one of the world's leading centres for terrorist forensics. The true picture, however, was far less happy, as the Establishment was central to a string of appalling miscarriages of justice, of which Abdelbaset's was only the latest.

In 1974 its scientists helped convict a young woman called Judith Ward for three IRA bombings, including the M62 coach blast, which killed twelve soldiers. At her trial the head of the forensic explosive laboratory, Douglas Higgs, claimed that chemical residue tests conclusively demonstrated that she had handled the explosive nitro-glycerine (NG). In 1992, having spent 17 years in prison for a crime that she did not commit, Ward's conviction was overturned. Her appeal team not only demolished the credibility of the tests, but, more worryingly, discovered that, at the time they gave evidence, the

RARDE team were well aware that a wide range of entirely innocent substances could produce the same results as NG. In an unusually strong judgment, the Appeal Court said that the RARDE team 'took the law into their own hands' and 'knowingly placed a false and distorted scientific picture before the jury'. It concluded, 'Forensic scientists employed by the Government may come to see their function as helping the police. They may lose their objectivity. That is what must have happened in this case.'[1]

The year after the Ward case, Higgs was again involved in a high-profile IRA case, this time with four of his RARDE colleagues, among them the Lockerbie scientist Hayes. The defendants were seven members of a London-based Irish family called Maguire, who were accused of preparing bombs for the IRA. The family were implicated by false confessions made by a relative, Gerard Conlon, and his friend Paul Hill. The pair were part of the so-called Guildford Four, who were themselves wrongly convicted of pub bombings in Guildford and Woolwich. The Maguire Seven made no such confessions and were convicted solely on the basis of swabs taken from their hands and fingernails. As in the Ward case, the RARDE scientists claimed that the results of thin layer chromatography (TLC) tests conducted on the swabs indicated that the defendants had knowingly handled NG. This became known as the kneading hypothesis.

Following the overturning of the Guildford Four's convictions, the UK government ordered an official inquiry into both cases, which was led by Sir John May. During the course of the inquiry the Maguires' lawyers gained access to the RARDE scientists' notebooks. These revealed they had conducted further tests that proved that TLC tests were not specific for NG and that similar results could be obtained for another explosive, PETN. This was significant, because PETN was chemically very different to NG, which meant the tests might not be capable of distinguishing between many other chemicals. This evidence contradicted what they had told the Court and, had it been known to the defence, might well have resulted in acquittals. May regarded the failure to mention PETN at the trial, for which Higgs and his colleague Walter Elliot were largely responsible, as 'wholly misleading'.

Hayes did not escape criticism. May's interim report commented: 'It is clear from the notebooks that when hand kits were tested

RARDE was not looking for PETN. The explanation advanced to me for this exclusion of PETN by Mr Higgs and Dr Hayes that in the context of IRA terrorism they believed it to be irrelevant, I accept as genuine. It was nonetheless improper for the scientists to presume in that way to exclude it.' More damningly, the report continued: 'At the time the material tests were carried out and reported on the failure to report the confusion of NG with PETN was honest but mistaken. However, before long an element of calculation crept into the continuing failure. When Mr Higgs prepared a list for the consultation on 15th January 1976 which purported to exclude /all substances which NG might mimic by reference to three criteria, he deliberately left out PETN which could not be so excluded.'

The notebooks revealed that further tests had been conducted, which demonstrated that the original results may have arisen from innocent or laboratory contamination, rather than deliberate kneading of explosive. Higgs and Hayes told the Inquiry that they had not advanced the kneading hypothesis during their trial evidence in absolute terms. May disagreed, saying it was 'wholly at variance with the evidence given at the Maguires' trial and elsewhere'. He added that, 'had this been the scientists' opinion, they should have made it clear to counsel. They did not.'[2]

Although only 27 at the time of the trial, Hayes was the only member of the RARDE team to have a PhD in Chemistry, so probably should have known that the team's evidence was nonsense.

Feraday was far less academically qualified, his only formal qualification being a Higher National Certificate in applied physics, which he achieved in 1962.[3] He too was involved in a miscarriage of justice arising from a notorious IRA bombing. The victim was Gilbert 'Danny' McNamee, who was convicted in 1987 for being the bombmaker behind the 1982 Hyde Park bombing, which killed four members of the Household Cavalry. The case against him rested on fingerprints found on the battery of an unexploded bomb and on masking tape in two IRA arms caches. As with the Lockerbie case, a small piece of circuit board was found at the crash site, and, as with Lockerbie, Feraday testified that it precisely matched a control sample board, which, in this case, had been recovered from one of the caches. He made two other crucial assertions: the first was that the board had been specifically designed for use in a radio-controlled bomb; and the second was that the same person had made both boards.

Subsequent to McNamee's conviction, Feraday's evidence was reviewed by electronics expert Dr Michael Scott of Dublin City University. He condemned the key claims as technical and logical nonsense. In his view the boards were of quite a general design, which could have been used for a variety of purposes besides terrorism. Furthermore, the two boards could have been made by different people using the same circuit pattern, just as two identical garments could be made by different people using the same pattern.[4] McNamee's conviction was overturned in 1998, largely on the grounds of fingerprint evidence, with the judgment making no criticism of Feraday.[5]

But a lesser-known judgment five years earlier singled out Feraday for strong criticism. The case was that of John Berry, a former Marine, who was convicted in 1982 on terrorist conspiracy charges and sentenced to eight years in prison. It revolved around electronic timers, which he had supplied to a Syrian client. The prosecution claimed the devices were specifically designed for terrorist purposes and supplied in the knowledge that they would be used by terrorists. The Crown case relied largely on Feraday, who told the Court: 'As a result of an examination of the timing device I came to the conclusion that it was specifically designed and constructed for a terrorist purpose, that is to say to be attached to an explosive device.'[6]

In fighting the appeal, Berry's lawyers lined up four experts, including Scott, all of whom described Feraday's contention as nonsense. Their views were summed up by Dr John Wyatt, a 23-year veteran of the Royal Engineers, who had spent much of his career in bomb disposal and counter-terrorist operations, rising to the rank of Lieutenant Colonel. He said, 'As far as I am concerned this is only a timer, nothing else.'[7]

In overturning Berry's conviction, England's most senior judge, the Lord Chief Justice Lord Taylor of Gosforth, commented that, although Feraday's views were 'no doubt honestly held', his evidence had been expressed in terms that were 'extremely dogmatic' and his conclusions were 'uncompromising and incriminating'.[8]

In 1985 Feraday played a remarkably similar role in the conviction of Libyan-born Palestinian Hassan Assali, who ran a successful electronics company in Hertfordshire. In 1984 a disgruntled ex-employee told the police that Assali was making and supplying timers to an Arab diplomat for use in bombs. The police subsequently raided Assali's premises and recovered a number of timers. In an echo of his evidence in the Berry trial, Feraday later testified: 'After due consideration, I am unable to envisage any lawful domestic or military purpose for which these timer units have been prepared. I am of the opinion that they have been specifically designed and constructed for terrorist use. I am unable to contemplate their use in other than bombs.'[9] Having failed in his initial appeal against conviction, in 1997 Assali's case was referred to the Criminal Cases Review Commission (CCRC), the statutory body that reviews alleged miscarriages of justice in England, Wales and Northern Ireland. His application was supported by a similar array of experts to those who appeared at Berry's appeal, and who were again unanimous in their view that Feraday's central claim was nonsense. One of them was retired RAF Squadron Leader Michael Moyes, a qualified electronics engineer, whose report concluded: 'There is no evidence that we are aware of that timers of this type have ever been found to be used for terrorist purposes. Moreover the design is not suited to that application.'[10] In 2005 the CCRC announced that Assali should be granted a second appeal. In doing so it said that the strong criticism made of Feraday in the Berry judgment 'applies equally to the expert evidence he provided in Mr Assali's case'.[11] In July 2005 Assali's twenty year quest for justice ended when the Crown informed the High Court that it would not contest the appeal.

The FBI's lead forensic investigator, Tom Thurman, also had a far from spotless record. In 1995 a colleague in the Bureau's forensic lab, Fred Whitehurst, made a formal complaint that Thurman had altered technical reports in a manner that significantly changed their meaning. The matter was investigated by the US Department of Justice's Inspector General, who found that 30 of the 52 reports that they examined had been altered by Thurman and that in 13 cases the alterations had resulted in a bias towards the prosecution. A confidential internal memo was subsequently uncovered that stated: 'It is clear that SSA Thurman does not understand the scientific issues involved with the interpretation and significance of explosives and explosive residue compositions. He therefore should realise this deficiency and differentiate between his personal opinions and scientific fact . . . SSA Thurman acted irresponsibly. He should be held accountable. He should be disciplined accordingly.'[12] Thurman retired from the FBI in January 1998, shortly after the publication of the Inspector General's report.

According to his FBI colleague Hal Hendershot, Thurman had a laboratory in Lockerbie within days of the bombing.[13] Apart from his involvement with explosive tests that took place in the United States in 1989 and in the identification of the circuit-board fragment PT/35b in 1990, almost nothing has been disclosed of his forensic investigation. However, it is clear from documents found after Abdelbaset's conviction, tucked away in files obtained from the BKA, that the FBI were aware of the significance of certain forensic items before RARDE.

One of the documents was an FBI memo of a telephone conversation on 8 May 1989 with Hendershot, who was stationed at Lockerbie. It concerned the Toshiba RT-SF16 radio-cassette manual fragment PK/689, which comprised two pieces of paper stuck together. Hendershot reported that the inside pages contained instructions, which appeared to be in Arabic.[14] The item was not transported to RARDE until three days later and not examined by Hayes until 16 May.[15] The RARDE joint forensic report noted 'Detailed examination revealed the fragment to consist of two overlaid sheets lightly adhering together.'[16] Clearly someone had pulled the pages apart and examined the fragment prior to it being sent to RARDE.

The second document was a letter sent by the FBI's Legal Attaché in Bonn, David Keyes, to the BKA on 17 July 1989 concerning debris item PI/1389, which was a blue T-shirt. Keyes explained that the garment 'shows blast damage and the imprint of the grills of two radio speakers which could mean that the shirt could have been in the suitcase containing the IED device'. Significantly, the letter revealed that inquiries had been conducted with the T-shirt's American manufacturer on 1 May 1989.[17] Hayes's laboratory notes record that he examined it on 17 August 1989, which indicated that someone had examined it before him and realised that it was potentially of great importance. Strangely, whereas Keyes's letter referred only to speaker imprints, Hayes's notes described circular cuts in the fabric, which perhaps suggests that someone had made the cuts prior to his examination.[18]

The FBI was not the only agency whose forensic work remains a mystery. Scientists at the Lothian and Borders Police forensic laboratory conducted fibre analysis on the Category 1 clothing,[19] which was supposedly in the primary suitcase, but results of those tests were never disclosed. Hayes's examination notes revealed that PK/689 underwent fingerprint examination at the Metropolitan Police forensic laboratory.[20] The result of that test was not disclosed until 2007* – it was negative.[21] A police memo, found within previously undisclosed RARDE files released to Abdelbaset's legal team in October 2009, two months after his return to Libya, revealed that a number of the alleged primary suitcase fragments had also been sent to the lab for fingerprinting.[22] Had either of the two accused's fingerprints been found on either the manual or the suitcase fragments, it would have been a very important element of the Crown case, but obviously they were not.

The RARDE documents also revealed that the Scottish police and Feraday did not entirely trust Thurman. In April 1991 Thurman requested that he be present during Feraday's examination of a number of items, including the control sample MST-13 timer, which was supposedly recovered from Togo in 1986. In a subsequent fax to the Deputy SIO James Gilchrist, Feraday made clear that he did not want Thurman present, adding, 'I also can see no advantage for Thurman if I only examine [the timer] in his presence, because he has already done that himself. Clearly he is seeking entry to all the other exhibits and examination notes, which I am unwilling to supply him. If he comes . . . I will have to watch him 100% of the time.'[23]

The FBI subsequently made a formal request that Thurman be allowed to visit RARDE, and the US Department of Justice made a similar request to Scotland's prosecuting authority, the Crown Office.

* The disclosure came in the Scottish Criminal Cases Review Commission's Statement of Reasons on Abdelbaset's case.

On 11 November 1991, SIO Stuart Henderson wrote to Feraday's boss, Dr Maurice Marshall, to register his opposition to the requests. He did not mince his words: 'The excuse used by the Americans is that Thurman requires to visit RARDE in order to get access to two electronic components, which would then enable him to furnish his report in the USA. That excuse is not accurate, because it is not necessary for Mr Thurman to examine any components at RARDE to complete his report. This charade is an attempt by Thurman to gain access to RARDE and all the forensic evidence held by Mr Feraday, in order to return to America with the "poached" information and include it in a report he would submit on behalf of the FBI. In all probability he would then claim that the information contained in that report was in fact the result of his own efforts.'[24]

From time to time there was also tension between the police and the RARDE scientists. In March 1990 Henderson wrote to Hayes and Feraday to propose a meeting, at which AAIB investigators would also be present. He wrote, 'I am aware, that you, like myself, feel there may be some breakdown in communications amongst ourselves, and I would like that rectified before the submission of any final reports.'[25]

Feraday was placed under considerable pressure to deliver the final forensic report. The job of leaning on him often fell to DC Callum Entwistle, who was the Scottish police officer assigned to liaise with the RARDE scientists. He later told the Scottish Criminal Cases Review Commission: 'I was often asked to tell Feraday . . . where is this report, we need it yesterday.' Feraday had a huge workload at the time and Entwistle felt a good deal of sympathy for him, but suggested that Henderson and Gilchrist were not always so understanding. He recalled: 'At one stage I went in in front of Jimmy Gilchrist and Stuart Henderson and they were asking me why, what about this, tell Feraday that, and I said I was trying to explain to them that Allen Feraday had problems and responsibilities outwith the Lockerbie case and I was accused of going native . . . Looking back now what I should have done when that comment was made was say goodbye, and turned and walked out that office, and told them to get somebody else to carry on with Feraday because I don't think they could have said a more hurtful thing because . . . I was extremely loyal to this enquiry.'[26]

In July 1991 Feraday and Henderson had an angry spat over over a tiny sliver of circuit board, DP/11, which was originally part of the alleged MST-13 timer fragment, PT/35b. The previous year it had been removed from PT/35b, with the police's blessing, by a company called New England Laminates, to which they had turned for help when trying to identify the fragment.[27] Unbeknown to Feraday, three of DP/11's nine layers of glass fibre were subsequently ground away by another expert whom the police consulted, Allan Worroll of the electronics company Ferranti.[28] Having noted the difference, Feraday wrote to Henderson early on 8 July 1991, stating, 'It is clearly obvious to me that it does NOT originate from PT/35(b) . . . I am therefore puzzled as to where DP/11 really originated from.' Later that morning DI William Williamson called Feraday to assure him that DP/11 was indeed part of the fragment. Feraday, however, was having none of it. Shortly afterwards he wrote again to Henderson, telling him, 'I have to say to you, despite what DI Williamson has suggested to me this morning, is that DP/11 does not match the rest of PT/35. The DP/11 fragment is six layers of glass cloth, contrary to the nine layers of glass cloth in the rest of PT/35. Which, in fact means that DP/11 is a rogue production. I am not suggesting that your officers have done anything wrong, but I am suggesting that when DI Williamson was given the fragment back from the Company (New Zealand Laminate Company) [sic] they did not supply the original fragment, but handed over something else. DI Williamson has suggested that this is not the case, however I have reminded him that I am the forensic scientist and I do know what I am talking about. If you believe that I am not capable of doing this work and making such identifications and observations, then perhaps I should not be continuing on the case.' Henderson hit back, 'I do not think such attitudes will be of any benefit to any of us. I am not in a position to question your knowledge at this stage, but I will not accept any question of the integrity of any of my officers.'[29] Feraday did not repeat his claim about DP/11 in the final forensic report, presumably because he realised he had been wrong.

Despite the various tensions, the police, the FBI and RARDE were able to bury their differences and present a united front, with the police and the FBI heaping praise on Hayes and Feraday's final forensic report. Known as the joint report, as they were joint signatories, it was completed a month after the indictments were issued against the two Libyans. Its conclusions fitted the indictments like a glove. But how well founded were they?

The most basic one – that the aircraft had been destroyed by an explosion – appeared beyond doubt, but the conclusion that the bomb contained a Semtex-type explosive was rather less solid. The primary ingredients of Semtex and similar explosives are the compounds pentaerythritol tetranitrate (PETN) and cyclotrimethylene-trinitramine (RDX). The claim that this type of explosive was used was based on tests performed on just two items, PSI/1 and PSI/4, which were aluminium struts thought to have been part of the luggage container AVE4041. The items were swabbed by Hayes and Feraday's RARDE colleague Dr John Douse, who then used two different methods to test for PETN and RDX: gas chromatography and TLC. While the gas chromatography results indicated that both substances were present, only PETN was confirmed by TLC.[30] Furthermore, there was no indication from the disclosed RARDE paperwork that Hayes had taken precautions to ensure that his work area was free from explosive traces. The most commonplace precaution was the taking of swabs from the work area and the scientist's hands or gloves, but there was nothing to demonstrate that such swabs had been taken or tested. If there were no such precautions, there could be no guarantee that PSI/1 and PSI/4 had remained uncontaminated and not registered false positive results.

A more important conclusion concerned the position of the primary suitcase. It was, the report asserted, either lying flat in the second layer of luggage, with the part containing the bomb overhanging the 45-degree-angled floor section, or it was lying flat against the angled floor section, with its lower edge propped up by the bottom layer of luggage (see illustrations p.153).

Either way, the suitcase was in the second layer of luggage and not lying against the base of the container.[31] Given that the entire bottom layer was covered with Heathrow interline bags before the arrival of the Frankfurt feeder flight, PA103A, the finding gave strong support to the claim that the bomb had arrived on that flight.

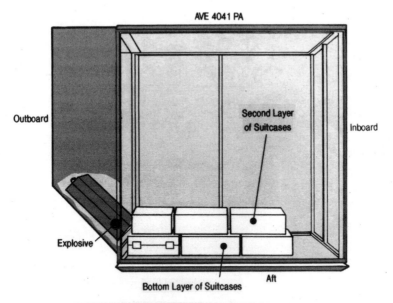

FIRST POSTULATED POSITION OF THE IED WITHIN THE CARGO CONTAINER

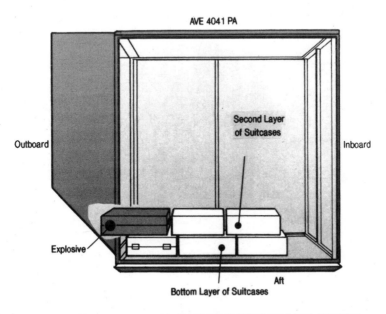

SECOND POSTULATED POSITION OF THE IED WITHIN THE CARGO CONTAINER

In reaching this conclusion, Hayes and Feraday were able to draw upon the results of the seven explosive tests conducted in the United States in April and July 1989. In each test a radio-cassette bomb had been placed within a clothes-filled suitcase and loaded, along with other baggage, into a luggage container similar to AVE4041. According to the joint report, the results 'confirmed' its assessment of the bomb's location. However, the test reports revealed that they were far from conclusive. Crucially, the bomb suitcase was positioned in the bottom layer of luggage in only one of the seven tests; furthermore, the results of that test had been rendered almost useless by a resulting fire.[32] Also, according to Dr Thomas Hayes's examination notes, the largest piece of the primary suitcase shell was damaged in a manner that suggested it was in the bottom layer.[33] This inconvenient opinion was omitted from the joint report.

Hayes also appeared to perform a U-turn in relation to PH/137, the Heathrow-originating bag, within which were found two small fragments of the primary suitcase. The side of the bag contained slits, around which were sooty deposits and singed fibres.[34] The police initially assumed that the bag had been in the fibreglass container AVN7511, which was immediately adjacent to AVE4041, and also displayed blast damage.[35] In a draft forensic report, dated 15 November 1990, Hayes and Feraday listed the bag under the heading 'Lightly explosion damaged luggage'.[36] Strangely, their final forensic report, which was completed a year later, appeared to rule out explosive damage, claiming that the slits were not penetration holes and that the two suitcase fragments had most likely been 'picked up and placed inside the plastics bag which was then itself placed inside the purple holdall for convenience of carriage.'[37] Nothing in the scientists' notes explained these changes of position.

The previously secret RARDE documents disclosed to Abdelbaset's lawyers in October 2009 revealed that the FAA's lead investigator, Walter Korsgaard, believed the Lockerbie bomb contained considerably more explosive than Feraday thought. He wished to carry out further tests, but Feraday strongly objected, complaining in an internal memo that the proposal was 'unnecessary and ill advised'. He added, 'I do urge you in the stongest possible terms that Korsgaard be stopped from carrying out any further tests in connection with the Lockerbie investigation.' More worryingly, Feraday wrote that the additional tests 'could readily be misconstrued by any defence counsel as implying some doubts concerning the results of the earlier trials, and as such could be destructively exploited by counsel'. He continued, 'It would be foolish and detrimental to the case to allow any errant defence laywer to gain succour from any future explosions tests designed purely to enhance an opinion as to the charge weight against all previous test results and the scientific findings to date.'[38] As a forensic scientist, Feraday's duty was to pursue the truth, not stifle work that might contradict his own conclusions. Still less should he have been concerned to thwart defence counsel in any future trial. Although written 15 years after Judith Ward's conviction, the memo appeared to bear out the Appeal Court's observation that 'Forensic scientists employed by the Government may come to see their function as helping the police.'

The October 2009 files contained photographs indicating that a further test *was* done, but apparently in the UK under the control of RARDE. Had the results supported the case against the Libyans it would almost certainly have been used by the Crown, but, as it was, it was not disclosed to Abdelbaset's trial defence team. Twenty years on, the results remain unclear, as the newly disclosed material contained no corresponding report.

As well as determining the size and location of the bomb, the explosive tests aimed to establish whether the contents of the primary suitcase could be distinguished from those of the surrounding luggage. The joint report suggested that they could. This was on the basis that certain garments, designated Category 1, contained fragments of the bomb, but no fragments of suitcase shell, while others, designated Category 2, contained either no bomb fragments, or bomb fragments together with suitcase shell fragments. It asserted that the Category 1 clothes were most likely from the primary suitcase and the Category 2 clothes from the others. The report gave the strong impression that this categorisation system was based on the findings of the tests, but, on close inspection, it was clear that this scientific underpinning was at best tenuous and at worst non-existent.

The test reports revealed that only two of the nine tests, numbers 6 and 7, were conducted with a view to establishing how the primary suitcase clothing might be distinguished from the rest. However, both tests were conducted at the initiative of the FAA, with RARDE's representative, Allen Feraday, taking no active role. Furthermore, whereas the Lockerbie bomb, according to the RARDE scientists, contained between 350 and 450 grams of explosive, tests 6 and 7 respectively used 680 and 570 grams. At the end of both tests the luggage was saturated to prevent the spread of fires. This might well have affected the distribution of the bomb and suitcase fragments within the clothes, which further undermined the tests' experimental value. A more fundamental problem was that they were conducted at ground level and therefore could not come close to replicating what would happen when an aircraft suffers catastrophic decompression in high winds at 31,000 ft.

Feraday's reports on the tests were very brief and, for the most part, merely descriptive. They confirmed that the debris was closely examined to determine what parts of the bomb, the primary suitcase and its contents could be recovered, and to study 'the cross-fertilisation from the IED suitcase into the adjoining baggage'. However, the disclosed RARDE material neither detailed those examinations, nor contained any kind of scientific analysis to support the clothing categorisation system.

The categorisation system not only appeared to have no reliable scientific underpinning, but was also not applied consistently. A couple of the items attributed to the luggage surrounding the primary suitcase met the Category 1 criteria (for example, PI/148, which was a pair of jogging trousers contained fragments of the bomb, but no fragments of suitcase shell). More importantly, some of the items attributed to the primary suitcase failed the Category 1 criteria as they contained no IED fragments. One such item was the cardigan PI/594 (see p.157), which was of a type stocked by the Gaucis.

A number of very much more damaged items were placed in Category 2, for example, PK/2120 (see p.157), which comprised five small scraps of blue and black material, each just a few centimetres across.[39]

Although some of the Category 2 items could be positively linked to passengers who owned luggage surrounding the primary suitcase, in the case of PK/2120, and many others, there was no obvious link.

Piece of cardigan (PI/594) placed in Category 1.

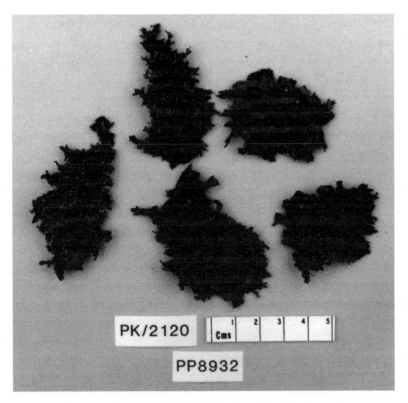

Scraps of material (PK/2120) placed in Category 2.

157

PI/594 was especially odd, because when Hayes first examined the item he noted that it displayed only 'distant explosive involvement'. Similarly, he originally noted that the largest fragment of the brown checked Yorkie trousers, PI/221, probably also originated from the surrounding baggage.[40] Yet it was the trousers that had led the police to the Gaucis' shop. If they were not in the primary suitcase, the Crown case was in tatters. However, the joint report subsequently glossed over Hayes's observations, claiming that both items were in the primary case.

Feraday also performed a notable U-turn, this one in relation to the model of Toshiba radio-cassette player that housed the bomb. The joint report stated unequivocally that the device was a black BomBeat RT-SF16. Since the PFLP-GC's bomb-maker, Marwan Khreesat, had also used a Toshiba BomBeat model (albeit a single-speaker one) the police originally considered this to be further circumstantial evidence of the group's involvement, but it later became part of the case against Abdelbaset and Lamin. In the six months from October 1988 to March 1989 almost 30,000 RT-SF16s were sold to the General Electronics Company of Libya, whose chairman was Abdelbaset's friend Said Rashid. Although this represented almost 76 per cent of world sales for the period, the figure was not as convincing as it first seemed. The model had been in production since October 1985 and in the three years from then until October 1988, sales to Libya totalled 8,000, only 11 per cent of the global total; furthermore many of the remainder were sold elsewhere in the Middle East, including Lebanon and Khreesat's home country, Jordan.[41]

The RARDE paperwork revealed that Feraday was initially convinced the bombers had used a different model. On 2 February he visited Toshiba's UK Headquarters in Surrey, in an attempt to identify the circuit-board fragments AG/145, which the AAIB's Peter Claiden had found two weeks earlier at the Longtown warehouse. The company's Technical Services Manager, Reginald Phillips, showed him an array of circuit boards used in its electronic products, one of which he was able to match with the fragments. The following day he sent a handwritten memo to SIO John Orr, stating, 'I am completely satisfied that the fragments originate from a Toshiba brand RT-8016 or RT-8026. The fragments are shattered in a manner consistent with their intimate involvement in a violent explosion and I therefore conclude that the bomb was concealed in the aforementioned Toshiba type radio/cassette player.' He added, 'The set used in the bomb possessed a white plastics case.'[42]

On 14 February Feraday met with Phillips again, this time in the presence of Detective Chief Inspector Harry Bell and Detective Constable Callum Entwistle. During the course of the meeting Phillips handed Bell a sales distribution list which he had received from Toshiba in Tokyo. It showed that the same circuit board was used in three other models besides the RT-8016 and RT-8026, namely the RT-SF12, the RT-SF16 and the RT-SF26.[43] On 20 March the police again visited Phillips, who this time gave them two RT-SF16 devices, which the officers delivered to Feraday the following day.[44] The machines were almost identical to the RT-8016. The following month, Feraday, Bell, Entwistle and the FBI's Tom Thurman visited Toshiba's Tokyo Headquarters to meet some of the company's senior managers. They confirmed that the circuit boards were used in the five devices in the sales distribution list and in two slight variants of the RT-SF16 and RT-8016, which were manufactured in South Korea and India respectively.

During their visit to Tokyo in late April 1989, Feraday and the police were told that the RT-8016 or RT-8026 models were aimed mainly at the American and European markets and the RT-SF16 and RT-SF26 at Asia and the Middle East. Two weeks later, on 5 May, the police found the RT-SF16 instruction manual fragment, PK/689, in the Dexstar store. The item was originally recovered the morning after the disaster by Gwendoline Horton, from her farm in Longhorsley, Northumbria, about 60 miles east of Lockerbie.*

* PK/689 had irregular torn edges and was around six inches across at its widest point. When the police showed it to her subsequently, Mrs Horton confirmed that it was the one she found. However, at Abdelbaset's trial she described the item as 'approximately eight inches square' and, in statements for Abdelbaset's then solicitor, Eddie MacKechnie, in 2003, she and her husband Robert both recalled it being rectangular and unfragmented. By contrast, the police officer to whom she handed it in was certain that the item he was subsequently shown was exactly the one handed in. Nevertheless it was, perhaps, surprising that neither of the Hortons' fingerprints were found on the manual.

Given that the letters 'iba' of Toshiba and the words 'Cassette re-corder SF16 BomBeat SF16' were clearly visible on the front, it was rather surprising that it then languished in the store for four months, apparently unnoticed. Between 5 May and 1 June five much smaller paper fragments were recovered by Hayes from items of clothing,[45] all of which, he and Feraday concluded, were from the manual.

The discovery of these items caused Feraday to conclude that the bomb was contained in a black RT-SF16, rather than a white RT-8016. The joint report played down the volte-face, claiming the original identification of an RT-8016 was merely 'tentative'. It implied that the authors were unaware that the circuit boards were used in models other than the RT-8016 and RT-8026 until the Tokyo meetings.[46*] This was odd, because, on 14 February, more than two months prior to the Tokyo trip, Phillips had given Bell the sales distribution list, which detailed five of the models that incorporated the identical circuit boards, including the RT-SF16. The report also stated that control samples of the RT-SF16 and the other models were not obtained by RARDE until after the Tokyo visit, whereas Feraday had in fact taken delivery of two RT-SF16s a month earlier.

It is not clear why Feraday was initially insistent that the radio-cassette player had a white case. RT-8016s were available in white, black and red, yet nothing in the disclosed RARDE paperwork suggested that he had sufficient white plastic fragments to sustain his conclusion.

There was also a question mark over the provenance of the circuit-board fragments AG/145, although this one was unrelated to the RARDE investigation. Claiden had found them trapped within a fold of the AVE4041 detached and contorted aluminium identity

---

* The joint report stated, 'After a search of over 130 different data sheets, the particular small diamond-shaped tracking pattern noted upon one of the Lockerbie circuitboard fragments was tentatively identified as originating from a Toshiba brand portable radio-cassette player model No RT-8016. A detailed examination of an unserviceable RT-8016 radio provided by the Toshiba Company that same day (2 February 1989) confirmed this similarity. Subsequently a visit was made to the HQ of the Toshiba Company in Japan between 23 April 1989 and 1 May 1989, where it was learned that similar circuitboards to that noted in the model RT-8016, were in fact installed into seven different models of portable radio-cassette players manufactured by the Toshiba Company or assembled by their subsidiaries or agents.'

plate. When he gave evidence at Abdelbaset's trial, he could not suggest a route by which the explosion could have blasted the fragments within the plate; indeed, he was adamant that the fold did not occur at the same time as the explosion. Exactly how they got into the fold remained a mystery, but, if Claiden was correct, it could not be ruled out that someone had deliberately placed them there.

The single most important forensic item was, of course, the circuit-board fragment PT/35b, which was supposedly recovered from the piece of grey shirt PI/995. Here too there were striking anomalies. The first of these dated back to the recovery of PI/995 by police officers Gilchrist and McColm, on 13 January 1989. Gilchrist described the item on its label as 'Cloth (charred)'; however, this was later changed to 'Debris (charred)'. There is nothing wrong *per se* with making such alterations, but under the standard Scottish police procedure the officer responsible should have struck through the original word 'Cloth' and initialled the change. In this case, however, 'Cloth' had been carefully overwritten with 'Debris', so the alteration was only detectable through close inspection.[47]

The next anomaly concerned Dr Thomas Hayes's examination notes. PI/995 appeared on page 51 of the notes; however, the next page was also numbered 51, but had been overwritten by Hayes to become page 52. The next four pages, which were originally numbered 52 to 55, were similarly amended to become pages 53 to 56.[48] When asked about these alterations during his trial evidence, Hayes was unable to recall why he had made them, but conjectured that he had accidentally numbered two of the pages 51 and only realised the mistake after numbering the next few pages.[49] During the preparations for Abdelbaset's second appeal, the notes were examined by a specialist document examiner. He established that, although page 51 bore indentations of the previous page – which is what one would expect if they had been written in sequence - there were no indentations of page 51 on page 52.[50] Although this far was from proof that page 51 had been inserted, it heightened suspicions that something was amiss.

The reference number PT/35 was definitely an insertion. The 'PT' prefix was given to all fragments that were recovered from other items by the RARDE scientists during the course of their examinations. However, unlike the items catalogued by the police at the Dexstar and Longtown stores, the PT items were allocated numbers retrospectively. As a consequence, the items were not numbered in chronological order; for example, while the PT/35 fragments were supposedly recovered on 12 May 1989, PT/30, which was a fragment of circuit board from the radio-cassette player, was not recovered until 8 June 1989.[51]

Hayes and Feraday were very well aware that any explosively damaged electronic fragments were potentially of the utmost importance, as they may well have originated from the bomb. The recovery of PT/35b should therefore have been very carefully recorded; however, Hayes noted it only with the single line 'a fragment of a green coloured circuit board'. And, whereas he produced a detailed sketch of the fragment of paper he removed from PI/995, there was no such sketch of PT/35b. This was in marked contrast to PT/30, which Hayes sketched and described in some detail.[52] The casual approach to PT/35b was particularly surprising because, according to Feraday, Hayes called him over to look as he extracted the fragment from PI/995[53] and they knew immediately that it must be significant.[54]

Hayes and Feraday's subsequent joint report, which was the cornerstone of the Crown's forensic case, contained two photographs of PI/995. One of them, photo 116, showed PI/995 along with three other fragments of grey cloth, which were alleged to have originated from the same Maltese-made Slalom-brand shirt. The largest piece, PK/1978, which contained a Slalom label sewn into a breast pocket, was the one shown to Tony Gauci on 30 January 1990. The other, photo 117, was a close-up, which showed the item after it had been dissected, along with PT/35b and the other items that Hayes had extracted on 12 May 1989. According to the report,[55] and Hayes's sworn testimony at Abdelbaset's trial,[56] photo 116 was taken prior to PI/995's dissection, which must have been on or before 12 May 1989. However, some of the other shirt fragments that featured in the photograph were not received at RARDE and examined by Hayes until well after that date; indeed PK/1978 was not examined until 10 October 1989.[57] There were two possible explanations for this anomaly; either the dissection of PI/995 and the extraction of PT/35b did not happen until after 12 May 1989, which meant Hayes had produced and dated the notes retrospectively, or photo 117 showed PI/995 after dissection, rather than before, in which case the forensic report was wrong and Hayes gave false evidence at trial. The matter was subsequently investigated by the Scottish Criminal Cases Review Commission (SCCRC), which unearthed RARDE records indicating that that photo 117 showed PI/995 after dissection. The Commission therefore concluded that Hayes had made an honest mistake. If nothing else, this cast doubt on the overall reliability of the forensic report and Hayes's trial evidence.

A further anomaly concerned PK/1978. The item was obviously the breast pocket and surrounding fabric of a shirt, yet when it was sent for analysis at RARDE the accompanying Dumfries & Galloway Police form described it as 'Piece of Fragmented Charred Material (Trousers?)'.[58] The form was completed by the police officer who was in day-to-day charge of the Dexstar store, Detective Constable Brian McManus, who was clearly selected for the task because he was meticulous and thorough. It is therefore a little surprising that he might have confused a piece of a shirt with a piece of trousers.

Although Hayes found PT/35b, unlike Feraday, he was not an electronics specialist, so he left it to his colleague to investigate the fragment. Feraday said that he knew from the outset that it was potentially of great significance,[59] yet he did not inform the police of the find until four months later, in September 1989.[60] When he sent Polaroid photos of the fragment to Detective Inspector Williamson on 15 September the accompanying memo said, 'Sorry about the quality [of the photos] but it is the best I can do in such a short time.'[61] RARDE in fact had a dedicated police photographer, Detective Constable Stephen Haynes, who had been taking high-quality, large-format photographs of the Lockerbie debris throughout 1989. It has never been explained why he was not assigned to take proper photographs of the fragment back in May 1989.

Stranger still, given the urgency of the investigation, PT/35b was not actually handed over to the police until January 1990, a full seven months after its discovery, and it was not until the same month that the police began to investigate whether Slalom shirts were supplied to Gauci's Mary's House and sold to the mystery clothes-buyer.

What happened to PT/35b between 12 May 1989 and January 1990 remains unclear. Feraday certainly compared it with electronic items recovered from the Lockerbie crash-site and with a database of explosive devices, dating back to 1968, which he kept at RARDE;[62] however, no paperwork relating to those comparisons was ever disclosed.

Apart from its appearance, the most obvious means of determining whether the fragment was close to the explosion was to test it for explosive residues. At trial Hayes said that such tests were not done and were not necessary, because he could tell by looking at it that the fragment was explosively damaged and the additional work would therefore have been unjustified. Furthermore, he said, the chances of finding explosive residues were 'vanishingly small'.[63]

Six years after Hayes testified, a previously secret police memo came to light that contradicted his evidence and stated that a residue test had, in fact, been conducted. Written by Detective Constable Callum Entwistle, on 3 April 1990, it reported on a visit by a delegation of French police officers who were investigating the 1989 bombing of UTA flight 772 in Niger.* It contained the following passage: 'Mr [Stuart] Henderson explained [to the delegation] that the piece of PCB from the Toshiba RT-SF16 bore no trace of explosive contamination and that this was due to the total consummation of the explosive material. Similarly with PT/35, the item was negative in regard to explosive traces.'[64]

Some of those closely involved in the investigation were under the impression that the fragment had been found by Feraday, rather than Hayes, among them Detective Inspector Williamson,[65] who led the investigation of the fragment, and Richard Marquise who headed the FBI's Lockerbie investigation. Marquise also believed that the fragment had been found in January 1990, rather than May 1989.[66] So too did the Germans. In a memo dated 14 May 1990, BKA officer

---

* The UTA bombing took place on 19 September 1989, claiming the lives of 170 people. Four days earlier a Lebanese magazine, *Ash-Shirra*, had reported that Iranian-backed Islamic militants were planning to attack French interests in Africa. They were quoted as accusing France of reneging on a 1988 deal that resulted in the release of French hostages in Lebanon. However, as with Lockerbie, Libya was eventually blamed for the bombing.

Helge Tepp reported to his superiors on a conversation he had had with Detective Superintendent Gordon Ferrie of the Scottish police. The memo included the following line: 'When questioned, H. Ferrie also said that this fragment of a circuit board had been found in the cuff of a "Slalom shirt" in January 1990.'[67] In October 1990 the assertion was repeated by the US Department of Justice, when it issued a formal request to the Swiss government for assistance in investigating the Mebo connection.[68]

In his 2006 memoir *Scotbom: Evidence and the Lockerbie Investigation*, Marquise said that he first learned of PT/35b in January 1990, when the Scottish SIO Stuart Henderson took him aside during a conference of senior investigators. The book revealed that it crossed their minds that the fragment could have been a CIA plant. 'Neither of us believed the CIA or any government official would do such a thing,' Marquise wrote, adding that Henderson was convinced of its veracity. The fact that the two heads of the transatlantic inquiry could even contemplate the CIA planting evidence was, nevertheless, notable and suggested that they were sometimes in the dark about the Agency's role in the investigation.[69]

Both men said it was not until June of that year that Henderson passed on a photograph of the fragment to the FBI.[70] However, the Bureau's forensic examiner, Tom Thurman, claimed to have received the photograph from an FBI liaison officer 'several months' before June 1990. He said it was handed over subject to a caveat imposed by Henderson, 'that it was not to be shown to any other agencies outside the FBI'.[71]

There was a further strange aspect to Marquise's account. When interviewed for a Dutch TV documentary in 2009 he insisted that PT/35b had never been taken to the US. This claim was echoed by the former Lord Advocate, Lord Fraser of Carmyllie, and by Henderson. Henderson then amended his position, saying that the fragment had never been in 'the control' of the US investigators.[72] He had chosen his words carefully, because the truth, as he must have known, was that PT/35b was taken to the FBI forensic lab in Washington DC on 22 June 1990, in order to compare it with the MST-13 timer held by the FBI's Tom Thurman; indeed, Henderson was one of the officers who took it there.[73] It was strange that this fact could have slipped the minds of both the head of the FBI investigation and the chief prosecutor responsible for the Lockerbie indictments.

The Washington visit was crucial, as it enabled Allen Feraday and the Scottish police to confirm that PT/35b matched the MST-13 timer, but here too the accounts of the key players were contradictory. According to Feraday, when he saw the partially scratched out word 'Mebo' on the smaller of its two circuit boards, he thought it read 'MEBQ'. He said that the letters meant nothing to him and that he was not aware that it actually read 'Mebo' until Henderson told him, a short while after his return to the UK.[74] However, according to Detective Inspector Williamson, Feraday told him in Washington that he had seen the word Mebo or MEBQ before, and that on his return 'Feraday went straight to his office explaining that he was looking for the record which he had referred to in Washington.'[75]

One of those present on 22 June who certainly already knew about Mebo was Thurman, because when first shown the Togo timer by the CIA's John Orkin a week earlier, Orkin advised him to 'look at Mebo'.[76] Orkin had, of course, known about Mebo since 1985, when he examined one of the country's radio-controlled devices, which had been seized in Chad.[77]* More significantly, when interviewed by the Crown a few months before Abdelbaset's trial, he revealed that he also knew well before Lockerbie that the MST-13 timers were made by Mebo. This was because in March 1988 he had received photos of the timer that had been seized in Senegal the previous month, and soon noticed that the timer's wire terminals and LED light were identical to those on the Chad device.[78]

As Thurman was a member of the interagency Technical Threat Countermeasures Committee, he should, according to Orkin, have been in possession of Orkin's reports on the Chad device and the MST-13 timer well before he approached Orkin for help in June 1990.[79] If that was the case – and Thurman never denied that it was – then he had sufficient information to put him on the trail of MST-13 timers and Mebo without Orkin's help. Even assuming that Thurman had no knowledge of Mebo prior to meeting Orkin, the fact that Orkin advised him to 'look at Mebo' begs the question of why he never mentioned the company to the Scottish police and Feraday when he

* See Chapter 4.

166

showed them the MST-13 timer on 22 June 1990. As it was the police were not told about Mebo until September 1990.[80]

This was not the only information that was withheld by Thurman. After the indictments were issued against the two Libyans, he claimed in a TV interview that he had identified the circuit board fragment, but it was later revealed that it was, in fact, Orkin who noticed the similarity with the MST-13 timer, and he who brought it to Thurman's attention.[81] More seriously, when testifying during the US Grand Jury hearing that preceded the indictments, Thurman said that the timer had been made available to him by the US Bureau of Alcohol Tobacco and Firearms, and made no mention of either the CIA or Orkin.[82]

When interviewed prior to the Lockerbie trial by members of the prosecution team, Thurman said that the crucial breakthrough came only after he had successfully pleaded with Henderson to allow him to share the photo of PT/35b with other agencies. He also admitted that he was told to conceal the CIA's role. 'As far as the CIA was concerned it was not to be involved in the chain of custody and that the timing device was to be regarded as having come directly from the Bureau of Alcohol, Tobacco and Firearms,' he explained, adding, 'for public consumption, the Bureau of Alcohol, Tobacco and Firearms had provided the timer.' In other words, the CIA had encouraged him deliberately to mislead both the public and the Grand Jury, by concealing the fact that it had had possession of the timer and that one of its officers had matched it with the Lockerbie fragment. Thurman added that this was the first occasion on which he had 'fronted' for the CIA.[83]

Most of these contradictory accounts about how PT/35b was linked to the MST-13 timer were only revealed seven years later, when the Crown's precognition statements of Feraday, Williamson, Thurman and Orkin were released by the SCCRC. Had the defence known about them at trial, they would have provided the basis for vigorous cross-examinations of the relevant witnesses.

Viewed in isolation, the individual anomalies surrounding the fragment may have appeared trivial, but together they formed a shroud of suspicion that could not be dislodged. Had they concerned a less important item, they could, perhaps, have been overlooked, but the fragment was easily the most crucial physical evidence in the entire case – the golden thread that linked Abdelbaset to the bomb.

A further peculiarity concerned the most important clothing item, PT/28, which was the fragment of brown checked trousers containing the Yorkie label and the stamped order number 1705. These were the vital clues that led the police to Tony Gauci and enabled them to determine that the clothes purchase took place after 18 November 1988. Hayes first examined the item on 14 March 1989. His notes of the examination stated: 'One severely damaged pair of trousers – a small portion including the seat area and right hip pocket. Dark brown patterned. Dark brown tartan patterned. Relatively close explosives involvement.' There was no mention of either the Yorkie label or the number 1705 until further down the page, where he wrote: 'N.B . . . Fragment of damaged "Yorkie" brand label sewn into a seam, also the number "1705" printed in black ink on underside of hip pocket lining.' It appeared that this sentence might have been added some time after the first note.

On 21 March the Scottish officer assigned to liaise with RARDE, DC Callum Entwistle, requested to see the item along with the much larger brown checked trouser fragment PI/221. According to his corresponding statement, it was clear that the two items originated from the same garment, yet according to Hayes's examination notes he did not examine PI/221 until almost two months later, on 16 May 1989, and it was not until that date that he formally noted the two items' common origin.[84] Stranger still, according to Entwistle, Hayes showed him the number 1705, but the statement made no mention of the Yorkie label; indeed Entwistle later squeezed in the words: 'there were no other apparent marks of identification visible on either piece at this time.' This was surprising, because the label was on a seam adjacent to a white pocket and the number stamp was close by on the pocket itself. Entwistle asked Hayes to remove a sample of the cloth in order to help the police identify the trousers' origin. Then, on 30 March, Entwistle and DI George Brown began making inquiries and in the process visited several textile outlets.[85] Neither of these steps should have been necessary had the police been aware of the label.

Brown's statement added to the confusion, stating that the Yorkie label was on PI/221, rather than PT/28.[86] Subsequent statements by his colleagues DCI Harry Bell and DS William Armstrong also stated that the Yorkie label and the 1705 stamp were each on different fragments.[87]*

Many years later the anomaly was investigated by the Scottish Criminal Cases Review Commission, who concluded that it resulted from a simple mix up and that the Yorkie label was, after all, on PT/28 along with the 1705 stamp. But this still begged the questions, why was there no mention of the Yorkie label in the relevant statements of Entwistle and Brown, and why did the police find it necessary to establish the trousers' origin when the label offered such an obvious clue?

When questioned by the SCCRC, neither of the officers could explain why their statements made no mention of the label. Entwistle still had a clear memory of suggesting to Hayes that he open out the pocket and of then seeing the number 1705. The Commission pointed out that the number and the label were very close together and Entwistle initially insisted it was impossible that the label could have been missed 'because I know how thorough I was in my investigation and I know how thorough the other officers and how thorough RARDE were'. When shown his statement he could offer no explanation for the apparent inconsistency.[88]

Hayes told the Commission that he had little or no memory of the events. When presented with his notes and Entwistle's statement he expressed bemusement. Having shown him photos of PT/28, the Commission asked: 'Can you envisage a situation whereby the 1705 might have been discovered by you but that the label was not, at the same time at least, discovered by you?' He replied, 'Not really, no.'[89]

So, either something very strange had gone on with the two trouser fragments, or Hayes had missed a very obvious clue to their origin. Whichever was true, it thickened the cloud of doubt that loomed over the forensic investigation.

---

* In their original form, neither Bell's nor Armstrong's statements specified which of the two productions, PT/28 and PI/221, the label and number 1705 appeared on. This was due to the fact that that the early versions of statements tended to leave gaps where the production numbers were supposed to be, as these numbers were sometimes not confirmed until later. The final version of the statements on the HOLMES computer included the production numbers, but the references to the label and 1705 had been removed.

There were further revelations in the RARDE paperwork disclosed in October 2009. Among the most remarkable was that Hayes believed he would not have to sign the joint report and that, as far as he was concerned, the report was Feraday's work. He was even reluctant to review the final draft. In a letter to the head of RARDE's explosive forensics division, Dr Maurice Marshall, dated 13 September 1990, he wrote: 'I have reflected carefully on our discussions the other day but can now see no useful purpose that will be achieved in your suggestion that I might return to RARDE for 2-3 days to review the final report with Allen in say six months time. Not only will the report's contents then be even further from my immediate thoughts but, as a non-signatory, my opinions will not I believe have much relevance in any subsequent court proceedings alongside Allen's own "reported" conclusions and those of the scientist appointed to corroborate his findings.'[90]

Hayes had resigned from RARDE in 1989 in order to retrain as a chiropodist, but was persuaded to continue working on the case on a part-time consultancy contract. In August 1990 he formally notified Marshall that he was terminating the contract. He explained, 'Because of these continuing unpredictable delays and the apparent absence of any clearly foreseeable endpoint to the investigation, I have now a year on very reluctantly decided to adjust my own priorities in favour of my new career aspirations in order to complete my studies by the end of September – the course's 3-year study deadline.' Having spent much of the previous year tied up with the May Inquiry into the Maguires and Guildford Four cases, he pointedly referred to 'the apparent reluctance of RARDE to offer me an active supportive involvement rather than seemingly give priority to self-preservation and damage limitation'.[91]

There is no doubt that Hayes and Feraday were acutely overstretched. At the time of the bombing, Hayes was working on around 12 animal-rights cases and Feraday had 'approximately 56 other bombings to work on' during the investigation.[92] This may explain why Feraday's examination notes ran to just 116 pages covering two and a half years. None of them contained sketches of the items he had examined and most were simply a draft of the final report.[93] To be fair to Feraday, most of the objects described in the joint report were examined by Hayes. Hayes's notes were much more detailed and contained neat sketches of many of the things he examined. They ran to 177 pages spanning an 18-month period from late December 1988, and detailed a total of 256 debris items. Given the scale of the disaster and the length of the inquiry, this was a surprisingly small number. It seems that some of Hayes's work was not recorded, at least not within the RARDE material later disclosed to Abdelbaset's lawyers. A BKA memo dated 24 April 1989 revealed that, three days earlier, he had visited the BKA in Wiesbaden, where he had been handed 'a small piece of circuit board' from the time-delay mechanism of the Toshiba radio-cassette bomb found in the boot of Hafez Dalkamoni's car during the Autumn Leaves raids.[94]* The RARDE paperwork made no mention of the visit and neither Hayes's nor Feraday's notes referred to the examination of this potentially important fragment.

Many more debris items were sent by the police to RARDE than those detailed in the scientists' notes. The majority were judged, on preliminary examination, to be of no forensic significance and were returned to Lockerbie. For the most part this filtering exercise was conducted by Hayes. He later described the process as 'rather crude to say the least', and acknowledged that significant items therefore may well have been missed.[95]

One such may have been PF/546, which was found on 25 December 1988 by Detective Constables James Barclay and William Grant in a field near to Carruthers Farm, a few miles east of Lockerbie. Grant's notebook described it as 'Piece of yellow wire soldered to +ve of a Duracell 1.5V battery'[96] and in his corresponding statement Barclay said it 'appeared to be an American battery'.[97] The statement did not specify the size, but he later recalled it was AA.[98] The fact that the wire was soldered on suggested that the item did not originate from a standard commercial battery-powered appliance and was, rather, part of an improvised construction. It was potentially of great significance, because BKA photographs of Khreesat's Toshiba radio-cassette bomb showed clearly that the detonator was powered by four 1.5-volt AA-sized batteries, the terminals of which

* The memo was contained within the voluminous BKA files disclosed to Abdelbaset's defence lawyers.

were connected by pieces of wire, which had been attached with solder.[99] The battery was one of the first batch of items sent to RARDE for forensic analysis;[100] however, it was not referred to in any of the subsequently disclosed RARDE paperwork. On 8 February 1989 it was moved to the Longtown warehouse.[101] What happened to it after that remains a mystery.

Likewise PH/930, which the Dexstar log described as 'Pieces and fragments of black plastic casing broken circuit board and wiring.'[102] On 28 February 1989 it was one of a number of items examined by Hayes and Feraday at the Dexstar store. They presumably considered it worthy of further examination, because on 9 March it was sent to RARDE, but neither scientist's examination notes described it.[103] It appeared in Feraday's notes in a list headed 'Electronic items'. Next to the list was a note by him dated 6 October 1989, which read, 'None of the items possess any explosive significance.'[104]

There were other intriguing discoveries at the crash site, none of which were explained in the disclosed RARDE paperwork. The only documents in which any of them featured were lists compiled by Hayes of the objects that underwent preliminary examination. In each case they are marked with a 'G', to denote green, which meant they were considered to be of no forensic significance. Two of the items, PF/1138 and PH/780, clearly originated from a Toshiba device. The former was described on the police's laboratory examination request form as 'Broken piece of grey plastic casing 12" × 7" with electrical wiring and circuitry therein, bearing "Toshiba" brand name.' It was not clear whether the fragment was from a radio-cassette player, but PH/780 clearly was, as its laboratory request form described it as 'Front Piece of "Toshiba" Radio/Cassette Player 7" × 3.5, black in colour.' This was not the only item originating from a radio-cassette player, for example, PI/1117 was described as 'control section (red plastic) from a radio or cassette player', PH/717 as 'grey coloured plastic battery cover from radio/cassette player 9" × 1.75"' and PH762 as '2 × pieces of grey plastic casing from a radio-cassette or cassette player'. Two items included cassette tapes: AI/189 was noted to be 'polythene bag containing aircraft lining with cassette tape intertwined' and PF/1117 as 'piece of black plastic, 2 blue wires & strands of cassette tape attached'. There were other items that, from their description, may have been close to the bomb. PB/1356, for example, was described as 'lump of charred/molten material including duracell battery and piece of red wire' and PH/738 as 'piece of plastic (charred and melted) (possibly acid battery casing)'.

Two further objects, PK/1992 and PE/354, although apparently unrelated to the bomb, may have contained explosives. PK/1992 was described as 'Green box 4" × 2" × 1" with 'warning – explosive device' printed thereon. no. NSN 1370-00-617-2541. (possibly national stock number relating to a device from a US military aircraft).'[105] Unusually, Feraday's examination notes featured a sketch of the item. An accompanying note read 'Activation charge for USAF chaff distribution 0.00416 explosive black powder.'* The second, PE/354, was noted on the laboratory request form to be 'various pieces of charred material & paper marked "military explosive"'.[106]

In 2008 Abdelbaset's legal team sought access to some of the items. In a letter dated 1 September 2008, Scotland's prosecuting authority, the Crown Office, said that Dumfries and Galloway Constabulary had been unable to locate PF/546 and AI/189, and that PH/780, PI/1117, PH/717, PB/1356 and PH/738 were all destroyed by the police in 1990.[107] There may have been perfectly innocent explanations for all of the items, but, in the absence of any detailed examination records, it is impossible to rule out that they were connected to the destruction of PA103.

Given the unprecedented scale of the disaster, the fact it occurred at 31,000 ft, and the size and nature of the crash-site, the forensic investigation was never going to be perfect. When overstretched scientists and RARDE's unfortunate track record were added to the equation, the potential for error was significantly inflated. Whatever lay behind the multiple anomalies, inconsistencies and omissions, their cumulative effect was to erode the façade of forensic certainty that surrounded the Crown case. In such circumstances, how could the Crown ever claim the two Libyans were guilty beyond reasonable doubt? And, in the absence of so much potentially important evidence, how could the two men ever hope for a fair trial?

---

* Chaff is small fragments of aluminium foil, which are extruded from from military aircraft as a radar countermeasure.

At first I thought it was a thunderstorm. The regular bangs and flashes certainly sounded similar, but, the more I listened, the clearer it became that something more serious was occurring. When I looked from our apartment window I noticed that the flashes were not in the sky, but at ground level, and that the cacophony of individual explosions was woven together by the scream of low-flying jets. Down on the street people were panicking in case our neighbourhood was the next to be hit, but thankfully it was not.

It was 14 April 1986, and the United States was launching operation El Dorado Canyon, its first ever sustained air strikes on an Arab country. Forty-one people were killed in Tripoli and Benghazi, including a grandfather and his grandchildren, whose house was hit by a missile intended for the nearby JSO Headquarters.

President Ronald Reagan had been talking tough for years, but no one believed he would stoop so low as to order an attack on innocent people as they slept. Mercifully none of my family were caught up in the raids. Although shaken, I was not as panicked as others. My only fear was that the raids might be followed by an invasion. Little did I know that the US government's misplaced obsession with Libya would one day shatter my life.

The modern nation of Libya is barely 50 years old. Many of the lands within the current borders were for 360 years part of the Ottoman empire. In 1911 it became an Italian colony, and it was only in 1934 that it gained the name Libya. In 1943, following the Italians' defeat in the North African Campaign, it came under British administration, until 24 December 1951, when it gained independence under the constitutional monarchy of King Idris I. Had it not been for the discovery of massive oil reserves a few years later, the vast but sparsely populated country might have been barely noticed, but as it was it rapidly assumed global importance. Sadly, the new oil wealth was distributed only among the nation's elite, generating great resentment among ordinary Libyans and fuelling support for 'Nasserism', the socialist Pan-Arabism espoused by Egypt's President Gamal Nasser. On 1 September 1969, while King Idris was receiving medical treatment abroad, a group of young, Nasserite army officers, led by 27-year-old Muammar Gadafy, seized power in a bloodless coup.

Gadafy's government succeeded in improving the incomes and living standards of most Libyans. Unfortunately these advances were accompanied by brutal repression, which saw thousands of political opponents imprisoned and many executed. During his first decade in power Libyan–US relations steadily deteriorated, and in 1979 the government of President Jimmy Carter declared Libya a state sponsor of terrorism. Carter's animosity was, however, as nothing compared to that of his successor, Ronald Reagan. Hardliners within Reagan's inner circle, in particular the CIA Director and arch neo-conservative William Casey and Secretary of State Alexander Haig, became fixated with what Haig called 'rampant international terrorism'. It was, they claimed, a global Soviet-led conspiracy that had opened a new front in the Cold War. This came as news to the CIA's Soviet specialists and to Haig's own State Department intelligence analysts, who briefed him that there was no evidence to support the claim, but their caution was brushed aside. Remarkably, Casey and Haig took their inspiration from a book called *The Terror Network* by journalist Claire Sterling, which provided plenty of supposedly conclusive examples of the Soviet Union's role in terrorist attacks. Haig ordered his analysts to produce a Special National Intelligence Estimate on the subject. When it provided him with a far more sober assessment than Sterling's, he reportedly told them, 'Read Claire Sterling's book and forget this mush . . . I paid $13.95 for [it] and it told me more than you bastards whom I pay $50,000 a year.'[1] When the head of the CIA's Office of Soviet Affairs, Melvin Goodman, pointed out to his boss that the book was largely recycled disinformation, Casey refused to believe it. Goodman later recalled: 'When we looked through the book we found very clear episodes where CIA black propaganda, clandestine information that was designed under a covert action plan to be planted in European newspapers were picked up and put in this book . . . a lot of it was made up . . . We told them that point blank and we even had the operations people to tell Bill Casey this. I thought this might have an impact but all of us were dismissed. Casey had made up his mind. He knew that the Soviets were involved in terrorism, so there was nothing we could tell him to disabuse him. Lies became reality.'[2]

Crucially, he and Haig bought Sterling's line that Colonel Gadafy was 'the Daddy Warbucks of terrorism'.[3] Before Reagan was even inaugurated, they held a meeting of his department's most senior intelligence officials to discuss what action could be taken against Libya. Among Casey's delusions was that Libya's purchase of Soviet arms masked a strategy to create Soviet military bases in North Africa. When State Department intelligence analyst Lillian Harris presented Haig with a memo pointing out that the missiles were comparatively low calibre, and not of the quality that the Soviets would themselves use, Haig wrote in the margin, 'Oh come on, they've got 'em in droves.'

Attention to the truth was the least of the new administration's concerns. Their priority was to assert America's muscle after the humiliations of the defeat in Vietnam a few years earlier and the 1979–80 Tehran Embassy siege, in which US staff were held hostage for over a year. However, this was easier said than done. A direct showdown with the Soviet Union was out of the question given the size of the Soviet nuclear arsenal. The Tehran hostage crisis had demonstrated Iran's capacity to burn America's fingers, and Washington's other prominent Middle East enemy, Syria, could inflict similar damage via its powerful influence over radical Palestinian and Lebanese groups. Libya was far easier to deal with, as it was politically and geographically isolated, was weak militarily and had a small population. As Harris later ironically put it, 'Gadafy presented this marvellous target because you could fight the Soviets, you could fight terrorism, and you could fight the "evil Arabs".'[4] The Libyan government waged an open campaign to assassinate Libyan dissidents living abroad. In common with some Middle Eastern governments and, among others, the US government, it also supported a number of terrorist organisations. However, there was little evidence that its own agents were directly involved in terrorist attacks on Western targets and less still that it was running a Soviet-inspired international terror network.

Despite this, Casey launched a programme against Libya that was to be one of the largest in the CIA's history.[5] Within a short time intelligence information began to filter back that Colonel Gadafy was planning a huge terrorist campaign against the United States. Haig told a news conference, 'We do have repeated reports coming to us from reliable sources that Mr Gadafy has been funding, sponsoring, training, harbouring terrorist groups, who conduct activities against the lives of American diplomats.'

The rash of reports about Libyan terrorism should not have been entirely surprising, as Casey had issued a directive to all CIA station chiefs to disseminate disinformation about Libya.[6] There were additional sources of dodgy intelligence, among them a Libyan informant who claimed to have witnessed a meeting at a terrorist training camp at which the Libyan leader had approved a plot to dispatch assassins to the United States to kill Reagan and his Vice-President George Bush Snr. Despite the self-proclaimed mole failing a lie-detector test, his account prompted an outbreak of hysteria in Washington, which resulted in Reagan being ferried around in unmarked cars and decoy limousines being used to foil the non-existent gunmen. Reagan publicly endorsed the reports, insisting, 'We have the evidence and he [Colonel Gadafy] knows it.' Some of those who worked closely with Casey believed that he personally fabricated intelligence to feed the general paranoia.[7]

Another highly suspect source of Libyan intelligence to fail a lie-detector test was Iranian arms-dealer Manucher Ghorbanifar. Despite being regarded by the CIA as a fabricator, he was also used as a middleman in the notorious 'Iran-Contra' operation, in which illegal arms sales to Iran were used to fund the equally illegal support of the Contra terrorists, who throughout the 1980s waged a brutal campaign against the government of Nicaragua. It was run by the same cabal of White House intelligence staff as the campaign against Libya, including most famously the National Security Council (NSC)'s Deputy Director of Politico-Military Affairs, Lieutenant Colonel Oliver North.

The echo chambers of the US media and Capitol Hill rapidly elevated the disinformation to the status of 'irrefutable evidence'. The assassins story gave Reagan's hawks the excuse they needed to prepare for military action. Haig, Casey and the Secretary of Defense, Caspar Weinberger, ordered plans to be drafted for 'military action against Libya in self-defense following a further Libyan provocation'. All options apart from a full-scale military invasion were to be considered.[8] Despite the State Department being unable to substantiate a single example of Libyan involvement in terrorism, in 1983 a secret plan was hatched, code-named 'Early Call', which aimed to provoke Libya into attacking Sudan, in order for its forces to be ambushed by the Egyptian Air Force with the assistance of US Air Force AWACS radar aircraft. The plan fell through when a sandstorm forced the landing of the AWACS planes at Cairo's civilian airport, and news of the operation was leaked to ABC Television.

In 1984 the NSC's Director of Politico-Military Affairs, Donald Fortier, and the head of its Libya Task Force, Vincent Cannistraro, proposed two new strategies for dealing with Libya. The first, described as 'broad', proposed a variety of very public measures to increase pressure on Colonel Gadafy, including US naval exercises off the Libyan coast involving deliberate incursions into what Libya considered to be its own territorial waters. The second approach, characterised as 'bold', would employ a variety of visible and covert actions 'designed to bring significant pressure to bear upon Gadafy and possibly to cause his removal from power'. Among the covert measures suggested was the supply of arms and intelligence to opposition groups to enable them to carry out sabotage operations within Libya. Another was to encourage Egypt and Algeria 'to seek a *casus belli* for military action against Tripoli'.[9]

A more concrete plan was developed in 1985 under the code name 'Flower/Rose' by Robert Gates, who was later appointed CIA director and eventually served as Defense Secretary under Presidents George Bush Jnr and Barack Obama. This urged the planning of pre-emptive military strikes against Libyan targets, among them the military barracks in which Colonel Gadafy lived. It was as close as anyone had come to advocating the leader's assassination. Four years earlier Reagan had signed an executive order that specifically banned any US personnel from plotting or carrying out assassinations, but he made it clear to Gates that he would shoulder the responsibility were the plan to result in the leader's death.[10]

Although the plan was never enacted, the NSC continued to push for a showdown. Their cause was helped by a series of terrorist attacks on Western targets in the latter half of 1985. In June a TWA flight was hijacked on its way from Athens to Rome and the passengers, including 40 Americans, held captive for 17 days as the aircraft shuttled backwards and forwards between Beirut and Algiers. During one of the Beirut stops an American passenger, US Navy diver Robert Stethem, was killed. The two hijackers were Lebanese Shi'ite radicals aligned to Hezbollah. In October members of the Palestine Liberation Front hijacked an Italian cruise liner, the *Achille Lauro*, off the coast of Egypt and murdered an elderly, wheelchair-bound, Jewish-American passenger named Leon Klinghoffer. Frustratingly for the hawks, there was no Libyan link to either attack.

However, within weeks they claimed to have evidence of Libya's hand in three far bloodier attacks. The first was the ANO's hijacking of an Air Egypt flight from Athens to Cairo, which, following a raid by Egyptian commandos at Malta's Luqa Airport, resulted in 58 deaths.* The NSC said that intercepted communications between the Libyan Embassy in Malta and Tripoli indicated that the Libyan government was in communication with the hijackers. This came as news to the Maltese government and the Egyptian intelligence service, each of which subsequently confirmed that the operation had been masterminded in Syria.[11] The renowned Watergate journalist Bob Woodward reported that the intercepts may have been pure invention.[12]

The next two attacks occurred on 27 December, when ANO members opened fire on check-in queues at Rome and Vienna airports, killing five Americans and fourteen others. This time Reagan spoke again of 'irrefutable evidence' linking Libya to the attack, but there was none. The attackers had Tunisian passports, which the Tunisian government claimed had been confiscated from Tunisians working in Libya, but no evidence was presented to substantiate the allegations. The only attacker to survive the Rome massacre told Italian investigators that he had been trained in Lebanon's Bekaa Valley

* See Chapter 6.

by Syrian agents, who had escorted the gunmen from Damascus to Rome.[13] The Italian prosecutor in charge of the investigation eventually concluded that both attacks had been planned in Syria.[14]

The Libyan Foreign Ministry consistently denied Libyan involvement in the attacks, but the US government was not listening.

In early 1986, Donald Fortier, who was by then Deputy National Security Adviser, proposed that the US respond to any Libyan aggression with 'disproportionate' force. A Presidential aide subsequently claimed that the decision to launch a military attack was taken at a White House National Security Planning Group meeting on 6 January. The operation was planned by a small sub-committee of NSC's Crisis Pre-planning Group. Chaired by North, it included the NSC's Near East specialist Howard Teicher and US Navy Captain James Stark, who was also from the NSC's Office of Politico-Military Affairs. The Group authorised contingency military planning, including air raids using B-52 bombers from the United States and F-111 fighters from US bases in the south of England. At around the same time, a US spy satellite was moved from a position over Poland to over North Africa, enabling it to monitor Libyan communications. National Security Agency (NSA)* listening stations in the UK, Italy and Cyprus were also ordered to focus on Libya. Normally all intercepted communications would be analysed by NSA stations, but in this instance a high-priority Special Category (SPECAT) clearance was put in place, which meant the intercepts bypassed most stations and were channelled directly to the White House.

On 15 January the US Secretary of State, George Shultz, gave a speech, clearly intended to prepare the public for what was to come, which argued that America had a legal right to use military force against states supporting terrorism. He claimed that under international law 'a nation attacked by terrorists is permitted to use force to prevent or pre-empt future attacks, to seize terrorists or to rescue its citizens, when no other means is available'. January also saw the US Sixth Fleet commence exercises in the Gulf of Sidra, which were obviously intended to provoke a response, but, despite ever deeper

---

* The NSA is the US government's electronic eavesdropping agency. It is not to be confused with the National Security Council, which is the White House's principal forum for national security and foreign policy.

encroachments, Libya did not hit back. In March the US action escalated, with three aircraft carriers, 30 warships and 225 aircraft being deployed to the area in an operation code-named 'Prairie Fire'. The US Military's standard rules of engagement only permitted retaliation against a hostile act, but at the government's instigation the rules were amended to allow strikes against anyone considered to have hostile intent.

On 25 and 26 March, the Sixth Fleet destroyed two Libyan naval vessels and US Navy aircraft twice attacked a radar station on the Libyan coast, but still Libya did not respond. Within a few days, however, the White House appeared to have the pretext it needed.

In late March the NSA allegedly intercepted a message from the Libyan government ordering its agents in various European capitals, including East Berlin, to 'prepare to carry out the plan'. On 5 April a bomb exploded in *La Belle*, a West Berlin nightclub frequented by American servicemen. Three people were killed, including two US servicemen. Within a few hours the NSA had decoded, translated and forwarded to the White House a further message, purporting to be a cable sent from the Libyan Embassy in East Berlin to Tripoli, which said, 'We have something planned that will make you happy.' A few hours later the NSA forwarded a second cable, sent at almost the exact time of the bombing, which declared, 'an event occurred. You will be pleased with the result.'

By 7 April the US Ambassador to West Germany had announced on national television, 'There is very, very clear evidence that there is Libyan involvement.' Yet the West German authorities conspicuously failed to support his account. Police officials told journalists that they knew of no evidence linking Libya to the attack, and the head of the Hamburg branch of the German domestic intelligence service, the Bundesamt für Verfassungsschutz, Christian Lochte, told a TV programme the following week, 'It is a fact that we do not have any hard evidence, let alone proof, to show the blame might unequivocally be placed on Libya. True, I cannot rule out that Libya, in some way, is responsible for the attack. But I must say that such hasty blame, regarding the two dreadful attacks at the end of the year on the Vienna and Rome airports, for which Libya had immediately been made responsible, did not prove to be correct.'

German official scepticism might have abated if the White House had handed over its 'irrefutable evidence', but the intercepts remained under wraps. The Libyan SPECAT intelligence traffic was normally processed and evaluated by a group known as G-6 at the NSA's head-quarters in Maryland, before being forwarded elsewhere. Another of America's most renowned investigative journalists, Seymour Hersh, established that the La Belle intercepts were never sent to G-6. An NSA official told him, 'The G-6 section branch and division chiefs didn't know why it was taken from them. They were bureaucratically cut out and so they screamed and yelled.' Another explained, 'There is no doubt that if you send raw data to the White House, that consti-tutes misuse because there's nobody there who's capable of interpret-ing it . . . You screw it up every time when you do it – and especially when the raw traffic is translated into English from a language such as Arabic, that's not commonly known.'

The inevitable attack was launched nine days after the La Belle bombing. Despite official denials, there is no doubt that the raids were planned with the specific aim of assassinating Colonel Gadafy. The stated targets in the official bombing orders were the command-and-control centre and administrative buildings of Al-Azziziya Barracks in Tripoli, but US Air Force insiders told Hersh that the real target was the leader's house and the Bedouin tent in which he worked, both of which were within the barracks. Infrared intelligence photo-graphs taken after the raid showed that the laser-guided bombs left a line of craters skirting both the house and the tent. Although the Libyan leader escaped unscathed, his adopted daughter was killed, and his wife and all eight other children were injured.[15]

In 2001 the US attack finally appeared vindicated when a Berlin Court convicted four people of the *La Belle* bombing, all of whom were connected to Libya's East Berlin Embassy. The alleged ringleader was Yassir Chraidi, a Palestinian who was employed by the embassy as a driver. Also convicted were another employee, Lebanese-born German Ali Chanaa, Libyan official Musbah Eter, and Chanaa's wife Verana, who was said to have planted the bomb.

It was the clearest example of Libyan involvement in a major act of terrorism, but was still far from straightforward. Eter had orig-inally struck a deal with prosecutors, promising to testify against

Chraidi and implicate Libya, but he then fled to Italy, only to be recaptured and extradited to face trial. Although he was called as a prosecution witness, he withdrew his earlier statements, claiming the wrong people were on trial.[16]

The prosecution relied on material seized from the Stasi's archives following the collapse of East Germany. The documents contained apparently damning information, much of it supplied by Arab informants, yet the US and German intelligence services were curiously reluctant to hand over all of their own files. Indeed, the judge noted that the prosecution's failure to prove Colonel Gadafy's hand in the attack was partly down to this 'limited willingness' to share evidence.[17] Their reticence was no doubt because, as they knew better than anyone, the true picture was far murkier than the verdicts suggested. Cold War Berlin was a toxic soup of conflicting loyalties and double-dealing into which many of the city's Arabs were dragged by both the Eastern and Western intelligence services. Keeping both sides happy was for many a tactical necessity, and for others, perhaps, a lucrative career sideline.

Eter, for example, although named in the Stasi files as both the JSO's point man in East Berlin and a Stasi agent, was later revealed by a German TV investigation to be a long-time CIA asset who regularly visited the US Embassy. Chraidi-had been well known to the West Berlin authorities since 1984, when he became the prime suspect in the murder there of a Libyan alleged CIA informant, Mustafa El-Ashek. Despite this, he continued to travel regularly from East to West Berlin, through the heavily monitored and guarded Checkpoint Charlie. The Stasi and the PLO both believed he was working for the West Berlin police, who were ultimately controlled by the joint occupying powers, the United States, UK and France. The police chief, Lothar Jackmann, admitted in 1990 that one of the Stasi's informants, a Libyan close associate of Chraidi's, called Mohamed Ashur, was working for the police.

The defendant Ali Chanaa was himself a Stasi informant who had previously implicated Chraidi and Libya. A few years earlier he had been a witness in the aborted trial of another suspect, PFLP-GC member Imad Mahmoud, during which he admitted on oath to earlier lying. The Stasi files revealed that yet another key informant and member of Chraidi's inner circle, Mahmoud Abu Jaber, was himself, along with his brother Mohamed, the leader of a freelance Palestinian terrorist cell. Furthermore, Stasi intelligence indicated that the CIA knew that Abu Jaber and another group member, Khaled Shatta, were involved in the bombing. The Stasi also noted that the group was trusted by neither the mainstream PLO, nor the rejectionist Salvation Front.

The German TV investigation, broadcast in 1998, asked why, given all the evidence of their involvement, the Abu Jaber group were barely troubled by the German authorities. In the months prior to the attack they lived in East Berlin, meeting with the defendants almost daily, and hours before the attack they travelled to West Berlin. Their movements were monitored by both the Stasi and the Russian intelligence service, the KGB, who concluded that they were working for Western intelligence. A declassified KGB document indicated that Jaber was suspected of being an agent provocateur, who was being used by the CIA to concoct a case against Libya. The KGB reported that, two days before the bombing, he told his CIA contacts that it would cost $30,000, rather than the previously quoted amount, $80,000.

The programme makers were able to interview group member Mahmoud Amayiri, who was both Shatta's brother and Jaber's right-hand man. He had fled Germany for Norway in 1990, following the issuing of an arrest warrant, which was later dropped. When asked which secret service he was employed by, he insisted that filming stop; however, his Norwegian lawyer subsequently confirmed that Amayiri was working for the Israeli intelligence service, Mossad, which had a close relationship with the CIA.[18]

The Mossad connection was strengthened by one of its former agents, Victor Ostrovsky. In his whistle-blowing 1994 memoir, *The Other Side of Deception*, he claimed that the messages that were supposedly sent between East Berlin and Tripoli were in fact part of a Mossad disinformation operation code-named 'Trojan'. He said that in February 1986, Mossad agents secretly installed special communications equipment in an apartment near Colonel Gadafy's headquarters, which was subsequently used to broadcast phoney terrorist orders.[19]

According to Vincent Cannistraro, had it not been for Prime Minister Margaret Thatcher, the US air-strikes might never have taken place. Other European leaders refused to allow the aircraft to use their airspace, but Thatcher agreed, enabling the USAF to launch the raids from the Royal Air Force base at Lakenheath in Suffolk. A critical factor in her decision was the murder two years earlier of a British policewoman, Yvonne Fletcher, who was shot outside the Libyan Embassy in London, when someone fired a sub-machine gun at a group of anti-Gadafy demonstrators. A senior figure in the Reagan administration later privately revealed that, from the White House's perspective, the murder was 'the best thing that could have happened'.

Like the *La Belle* case, the Fletcher murder was portrayed as an act of state-sponsored terrorism, but, on close scrutiny, proved equally murky. A few months afterwards, the West German police arrested a Berlin scaffolding contractor, Hilmar Hein, and two underworld accomplices, Manfred Meyer and Helmut Nägler, in connection with the assassination of Libyan diplomats in Europe. The killings were carried out by a US-backed anti-Gadafy terrorist group called Al Burkan, which was run by Hein's friend, Libyan exile Rageb Zatout. Hein's gang purchased and delivered weapons for the group in return for cash and the promise of lucrative contracts in Libya, once Gadafy was deposed.

Hein assured Meyer that he enjoyed the protection of Oliver North and NSC Director Admiral John Poindexter, but, following the arrests, that protection evaporated. With nowhere left to turn, they opted to tell the police all they knew. Crucially, Nägler claimed that, six weeks before the shooting of Yvonne Fletcher, he smuggled into Britain three handguns, which he personally delivered to Zatout. Meyer was left in no doubt that Al-Burkan was involved in the killing. He recalled that, on hearing news of the murder, Hein was jubilant and that the gun 'was talked about quite openly as our weapon'. A 1997 Channel 4 *Dispatches* documentary uncovered forensic evidence that corroborated the claim. It suggested that WPC Fletcher could not have been killed by the sub-machine gun fire from the embassy's ground floor and rather was shot by a handgun from the top floor of a neighbouring building. The programme established that, at the time, the floor was being used by the security services and that they had advanced warning that shots would be fired from the embassy.

The German authorities naturally wished to interview Zatout, who had by then moved to America, but the US government refused their request for assistance. Despite talking tough, the Thatcher government also clearly lacked the will to solve the murder. Police officers were sent to interview Meyer and Nägler, but their information was never acted upon. The SAS was put on standby to storm the embassy, as it had the Iranian Embassy in 1980, but the operation was cancelled and the embassy staff allowed to go free. The government's explanation for this uncharacteristic leniency was that attacking the embassy would endanger British ex-pats in Libya. The real reason, *Dispatches* discovered, was that the diplomatic staff included a number of Al-Burkan moles. Meyer recalled, 'There were secret Al-Burkan members in the Libyan People's Bureau in London and they were supposed to get out [of] this operation, but without arousing suspicion or creating a stir in Tripoli.'

This, of course, raised the possibility that the machine gun was fired by one of the Al-Burkan members. If so, it was probably not the first time that the US-backed group had used an agent provocateur. Four months after the Fletcher murder, in August 1984, a Libyan called Ali El-Giahour was shot dead in a London apartment. At the time he was awaiting trial for five bomb attacks against anti-Gadafy targets in London. The murder weapon was traced to the Hein gang, suggesting it was a straightforward Al-Burkan assassination of a pro-Gadafy target. But El-Giahour was not all that he seemed. His solicitor, Anthony Elletson, recalled, 'He was quite adamant in protesting his innocence because he felt that he had been assisting the British authorities for some time in Libya. He had been providing them with what he considered to be intelligence.' Remarkably, given the seriousness of the charges, the court had granted him bail, yet he believed he had become expendable and told Elletson that he expected to be killed. 'He felt that whatever happened he was really no longer of any use to any of the people for whom he'd previously been working . . . his useful life had come to a grinding halt.'[20] MI5 was seemingly well aware of Giahour's ambiguous position. Professor Christopher

Andrew's book, *Defence of the Realm: The Authorized History of MI5*, quotes an MI5 document as saying: 'We and the Police know a great deal about Jahour [sic]. He appears to have tried unsuccessfully to keep in touch with both the pro and anti Gaddafi factions.'[21]*

Following the air raids on Libya, NSC Poindexter ordered Cannistraro, Stark and Teicher to produce a report for President Reagan summarising future options. North pushed hard for further military action, but, in the absence of a pretext, the focus shifted to psychological warfare. In October 1986 Bob Woodward was leaked a State Department memo, dated 6 August, which advised, 'The goal of our near-term strategy should be to continue Kadafi's paranoia so that he remains preoccupied, off-balance . . . [and] believes that the army and other elements in Libya are plotting against him – possibly with Soviet help. Believing that, he may increase the pressure on the [Libyan] army, which in turn may prompt a coup or assassination attempt.' The memo provided the basis of a subsequent National Security Decision Directive (NSSD) signed by Reagan, which ordered 'covert, diplomatic and economic steps designed to . . . bring about a change of leadership in Libya', although the reference to coup and assassination attempts were dropped.[22] Woodward revealed that the first victim of the disinformation strategy was the *Wall Street Journal*. On 25 August 1986 it ran a front-page story, based on anonymous official sources, which claimed, without qualification, that 'The US and Libya are on a collision course again.' The article reported as fact various other falsehoods, which the memo, and a subsequent one by Poindexter, suggested should be disseminated.[23]

Most of the proposals floated by the NSC staff were described 'Wizard of Oz' by one of their colleagues, Elaine Morton, a State Department North Africa specialist, who was on secondment to the NSC. Among them was the suggestion that Colonel Gadafy's paranoia might be increased if SR-71 reconnaissance aircraft were flown over Tripoli to create sonic booms. Replying to her criticism, Cannistraro

---

* Andrew's book makes no reference to the Giahour murder weapon being linked to the Hein gang and quotes a note found near his body that suggested the murder was carried out by pro-Gadafy forces, who suspected that he was cooperating with the British authorities.

wrote, 'Elaine, I have profound disagreements with the substance of your position . . . we have established, I think, that pressure against Qaddafi [sic] does indeed work and can serve to condition/moderate his behaviour . . . There is a psychological momentum among those opposed to Qaddafi that needs to be sustained. Sonic booms are indications that Qaddafi is not out of the woods, thus encouraging his opposition, and effecting his equilibrium. Not to say this is effective in and of itself, but as part of, albeit [an] important part, of a broader campaign, it is necessary. We should sustain pressure, not release it, and not blindly hope his economy will collapse and save our strategy.'[24]

In addition to heading the NSC's Libya Task Force, Cannistraro was deeply involved in the Iran-Contra affair.[25] In January 1987, a few months after the operation's cover was blown, he moved on to become Special Assistant for Intelligence in the office of the US Secretary of Defense. Two months before Lockerbie he returned to the CIA as the Chief of Operations and Analysis of its Counterterrorism Center.[26] In that capacity he, in his own words, 'led the intelligence side' of the Lockerbie investigation. This involved 'collect[ing] intelligence that would help the law enforcement side find the kind of evidence they would need to bring indictments in a court of law'.[27]

Exactly what information Cannistraro contributed to the Lockerbie investigation remains unknown. According to the head of the FBI investigation, Richard Marquise, he attended a few joint CIA-FBI meetings. To Marquise's fury, within no time of retiring from the Agency, in late 1990, Cannistraro began making public statements about Lockerbie.[28] On 20 November he told reporters that 'From an intelligence point of view, the case has been solved' and that the Department of Justice was 'very close' to securing indictments against the bombers.[29]

The revelation came on the heels of the first media reports that a fragment of the bomb's timer had been linked to Libya. The French magazine *L'Express* had broken the story in October 1990, and within days it was confirmed by the *New York Times*, which based its story on anonymous briefings by US government investigators. These sources emphasised that the new evidence did not clear the PFLP-GC and their Iranian and Syrian sponsors. Had they claimed the opposite, their assertions of Libyan involvement would have met with incredulity from those who had followed the case closely, in particular the relatives of the Lockerbie victims. The sources reconciled the apparently contradictory accounts by suggesting that the PFLP-GC had subcontracted the job to Libyan agents after its plans were disrupted following the Autumn Leaves raids.[30]

Cannistraro confined his remarks to alleged Iranian involvement in the bombing, saying that 'ruling members of [the Iranian] government made a conscious, joint decision' to retaliate against the United States for the downing of Iran Air Flight 655. Although he would not be drawn on the reports of Libyan involvement, for those who cared to read between the lines, his remarks were a tacit endorsement of the Libyan subcontract theory.[31]

During the following month he began openly to discuss the emerging Libyan connection with the media. On 19 December 1990 he told the *Independent* that Libya had been suspected of involvement for several months and that the circuit board discovery provided hard evidence of the link.[32] In June 1991 he publicly endorsed the subcontract theory, confirming that Libya had taken over from where the PFLP-GC had left off, but went further, adding, 'I don't think you can blame the Syrians for what Libya did.'[33] Iraq's invasion of Kuwait in August 1990 caused a dramatic realignment in US–Syrian relations. As a long-time enemy of Saddam Hussein, Syria's President Assad was brought in from the cold and was regarded as a very important strategic ally. Following the issuing of the Lockerbie indictments in November 1991, the US and British governments announced that there was no evidence to implicate any other country in the bombing, and President Bush went so far as to say that Syria had taken 'a bum rap'. The sidelining of the original suspects provoked fury among the victims' relatives. In spite of his earlier remarks, Cannistraro added his voice to the chorus of protest, saying the appeasement of Assad overlooked his government's involvement in some 'really horrible' acts.[34]

Cannistraro's divergence from the official line made him popular with journalists seeking independent comment on Lockerbie. In numerous media interviews he continued to insist that the evidence pointed both to the original suspects and Libya. This also gained him the respect of some of the victims' relatives, none more so than Daniel and Susan Cohen, from New Jersey, who lost their daughter

Theodora in the bombing. It appears that the man they called affectionately 'Vinnie the spy' fuelled their vocal advocacy of the Libya-subcontract theory. Among other things he told them how the CIA had learned that, shortly after Lockerbie, PFLP-GC leader Ahmed Jibril held a champagne party at which he boasted, 'The Americans will never, ever find out how we did it.' Cannistraro added, 'We didn't know what he meant by that at the time. Now we do.'[35]

No one in the mainstream media saw fit to ask whether a former political agent, who spent a significant part of his career plotting the downfall of Libya's leader, was the right man to lead the CIA's Lockerbie investigation. Neither, it seems, did they reflect on whether someone who had been involved in the illegal covert operations of the Reagan White House was an appropriate person from whom to seek comment.

Geopolitics may not have been the only reason for sidelining the original suspects, the PFLP-GC and Iran. Within days of the bombing, rumours began to circulate that the Lockerbie story was far murkier than was immediately obvious. Eleven months later, a sensational intelligence report was leaked to the press, which alleged CIA complicity in the bombing. It had been prepared for Pan Am's insurers, which at the time was facing a massive civil action brought on behalf of the Lockerbie victims' relatives. The author was Juval Aviv, the Israeli founder of a New York-based corporate intelligence firm called Interfor. He spent three months investigating the bombing, drawing largely on his contacts within various Western intelligence services, including Mossad. His report claimed that the bombers exploited a heroin-smuggling operation involving Khaled Jaafar. The young man's suitcase was, it said, supposed to contain a consignment of the drug, but at the last minute was switched for one containing the bomb. More controversially, he alleged that Jaafar's activities were known to a group within the CIA and that this group was allowing his Lebanese masters to ship drugs to the United States in return for help in freeing American hostages held by Syrian and Iranian-backed groups in Lebanon. According to Aviv, the suitcases containing the drugs were allowed safe passage on transatlantic flights. He claimed that the operation became known to Ahmed Jibril, who realised that it offered a fail-safe means of getting a bomb onto one of those flights. To complicate matters, Aviv claimed that the drugs-for-hostages deal also became known to Major Charles McKee, who was conducting a separate hostage rescue mission in Lebanon. Appalled by the CIA's complicity in drug dealing, at the time of his death, McKee was reportedly returning to Washington to blow the whistle on the Agency. The report's most sensational allegation was that the CIA group knew of both the bombers' and McKee's plans and, rather than jeopardise their own operation, allowed McKee and 258 others to fly to their deaths.

Aviv made it clear that the report was purely intelligence-based and that he had no hard evidence of the rogue CIA operation.[36] Nevertheless, if true, it perhaps made sense of the early press reports concerning Jaafar's involvement, and some of the events at the crash site, including those surrounding McKee's suitcase. It also possibly explained both the official denials of the drugs finds, and the bizarre and heavy-handed response to David Johnston's radio news story about McKee.*

The leak sparked a remarkable vendetta against Pan Am's insurers, their lawyer James Shaugnessy and Aviv himself. Shaugnessy filed a third party legal action against the US government for its alleged role in the bombing. In response he was threatened with prosecution for basing his case on information that he knew to be false, in particular the contents of the Interfor Report. Aviv too was threatened with indictment for conspiring to concoct a story that would exonerate the airline for its security failings and gain more work for his company. The spectre of criminal investigation hung over the two men for years, but the threatened indictments never materialised.

In the meantime, Aviv found himself under attack in the media. A number of articles and TV programmes denounced him as a serial fabricator. Among those quoted were Vincent Cannistraro and the Israeli Prime Minister's anti-terrorism advisor, Yigal Carmon, who claimed Aviv was never a senior Mossad officer and had been sacked from a junior security post with the airline El Al for being unreliable and dishonest.[37]

More seriously, Aviv endured what appeared to be a coordinated campaign to ruin him and his business. A number of his clients told

* See Chapter 3.

him they had been approached by FBI and Drug Enforcement Administration (DEA) agents, who said they were gathering evidence for Federal Grand Jury proceedings against him and others. Among the clients was a government agency, the Federal Deposit Insurance Corporation (FDIC), which had hired Interfor to help trace $35 million, which had been embezzled by a convicted banker called Jacobo Finkielstain. Aviv claimed that in 1993 an FBI and a DEA agent visited FDIC managers and told them that he was under investigation over the Lockerbie case. They showed them various articles that repeated the smears and claimed he was dishonest and unpatriotic. In 1995 Aviv's lawyer Gerald Shargel got confirmation of the story from one of the managers. This person said he would be happy to provide further details, but had to seek clearance from his superiors. He later reported that permission had been denied.[38]

Stranger still, according to Finkielstain, an FBI agent visited him in prison and alerted him to the fact that Aviv had traced some of his stolen assets to Liechtenstein and that the FDIC was trying to delay his release from prison in order to complete the recovery of the money.[39] The agent in question admitted he had visited Finkielstain, but denied relaying the information.

In May 1995 Aviv appeared in a feature-length documentary about Lockerbie, *The Maltese Double Cross*.* The film was highly contentious, not least because it was backed by Tiny Rowlands, the controversial Chief Executive of the British multinational company Lonrho, which had a number of joint commercial ventures with the Libyan government. The US and UK governments went to extraordinary lengths to discredit the film. In late 1994 it was premiered in the Houses of Parliament by another of its interviewees, Tam Dalyell MP. A few months later, shortly before its broadcast by Channel 4, Dalyell was requested to meet an official of the US Information Agency called Todd Leventhal, who went by the Orwellian title Program Officer for Countering Disinformation and Misinformation. Leventhal told the MP at the meeting and in a follow-up letter that some of the film's contributors, including Aviv, were 'known fabricators'.[40]

More was to follow. On the eve of the broadcast the Scottish Crown Office and the US London Embassy simultaneously issued

* The author John Ashton was a researcher on the film.

192

press-packs to every UK and Scottish national newspaper, which attempted to debunk the film and repeated Leventhal's smears against some of its interviewees.[41] The exercise was repeated by the British High Commission in Canberra when the documentary was shown by the Australian channel SBS the following week.[42]

The extent of the UK government's campaign was revealed in documents released under the Freedom of Information Act ten years later. Among them was a fax from a First Secretary at the High Commission to the FCO's Drugs, International Crime and Terrorism Department. A week before the SBS broadcast, the rival ABC channel ran a half-hour spoiler on its *Lateline* programme. The First Secretary revealed, 'I colluded with the producer before the "Lateline" programme . . . I later spoke to Kerry O'Brien, the interviewer, to thank him for the demolition job he had done.' The last paragraph boasted, 'I have been an information officer before, but I cannot recall such an effective hatchet job co-ordinated by the FCO. I have to thank "Lateline" (and its professionalism) for delivering the most savage blows, and you and the Information Department for providing the raw material. Please mark this up as a major success in undermining a potentially damaging programme.' He added the postscript: 'We are understaffed and overworked, or we would have blown our own trumpet before, without prompting. I'm afraid we just do the essential, which is the demolition job, not the fancy write-ups.'[43] Not everyone harboured such delusions about the two governments' efforts. As an editorial in the *Guardian* observed, the 'clumsy attempt' to discredit the film 'only invites us to pay more attention'.[44]

The campaign against the film was as nothing to that launched against Aviv. A few days before the UK broadcast, he was indicted on fraud charges, which, although ostensibly unrelated to Lockerbie, mirrored the central allegation that he had concocted intelligence findings in order to win his company more work. The allegations concerned a report he had produced for the General Electric Company a few years earlier about the security situation in the US Virgin Islands. According to an affidavit by the FBI agent who led the investigation, Aviv falsely claimed in the report to have interviewed a number of the Islands' officials. He also alleged that the investigator had falsely claimed to be a former Mossad employee. Curiously, General Electric had never complained about Aviv, so the investigation appeared to have been undertaken entirely at the FBI's initiative.

Aviv was able to disprove all the claims relating to the Virgin Islands report, and a few months later Shargel filed a motion for the case to be dismissed. In it he complained, 'In all my years of practice, I have never seen the resources of the FBI and the US Attorney's Office devoted to such an insignificant, inconsequential, isolated four-year-old contract matter . . . What in the world is the Government doing sending FBI agents to the Caribbean to interview individuals as having met with Mr Aviv four years ago for a client who paid $20,000 for the work, never complained, [and] did not challenge Mr Aviv's conclusions? . . . We believe that the evidence points to a clear relationship between Mr Aviv's authoring of the Pan Am report and this mail fraud prosecution.'

In defending the charges Aviv was able to demonstrate, through documents obtained under the US Freedom of Information Act, that he had previously been secretly employed by two Federal Agencies: the Internal Revenue Service and, embarrassingly for the prosecutors, their own employer, the Department of Justice. Moreover, the documents, which were heavily redacted, revealed that he had been thoroughly vetted by the FBI, prior to signing his agreement with the DoJ. It seemed that the FBI had been sufficiently convinced of his Mossad background that it went to some lengths to reassure itself that he was not still a Mossad agent. The vetting exercise included a lie-detector test, which Aviv passed. The agent who interviewed him observed in one of the documents that the supposed fraudster 'was professional in his manner and did not appear to be trying to impress the investigating agents'.[45] Shargel's motion was unsuccessful, but during preliminary hearings the judge described the defence presentations as 'unusually strong' and one of the prosecution submissions as 'dishonest and not helpful.'

The smears nevertheless continued. In December 1995 the *Wall Street Journal* ran a story parroting the prosecution case, which appeared to have been spoon-fed to the reporter by the FBI or prosecutors.[46] Since the newspaper was read by many of Interfor's corporate clients, the article was highly damaging. In May 1996 Aviv was forced to resign from the board of an asset claims and recovery company, which he and two partners had established a few months earlier. One of the partners, international lawyer Martin Kenney, explained that some of the company's investors had been warned by US government officials to have nothing to do with Aviv. Kenney was himself satisfied with Aviv's credentials and, in an affidavit for the fraud case, stated, 'I found the incongruity between the fact of the indictment, and the quality and content of Mr Aviv's professional background, standing, and professional and client references to be remarkable.'[47]

The case was eventually heard in December 1996. Aviv was acquitted on all charges.

Also indicted within days of the broadcast of *The Maltese Double Cross* was John Brennan, the President of Pan Am's insurers US Aviation Underwriters (USAU). Once again the charges, while not relating directly to Lockerbie, mirrored the central allegation, namely that the company had attempted to fraudulently shift the blame for an air crash away from one of its clients. As with Aviv, the alleged fraud had occurred years earlier, in this case 1987. It concerned the crash of a Pacific Southwest Airlines flight in which 43 people were killed. The case dragged on until May 1997, when Brennan was convicted and was sentenced to 57 months in prison and his company fined $20.6 million. The sentence was stayed pending an appeal, which, two-and-a-half years later, was successful.

By then Abdelbaset was awaiting his own trial. Unlike Brennan and Aviv, he was to be denied justice.

HMP Zeist 10

For eight years, Lamin and I lived in a strange and miserable limbo. Our days as international entrepreneurs were over. Shortly after the indictments were issued in November 1991, my family and I were ordered to leave our happy home and were placed in more secure accommodation, where the authorities could keep an eye on us. I was placed under house arrest and had to seek permission to leave the house. International travel was out of the question; we were not allowed to visit friends or mix with others. We felt under siege, completely isolated from the world and everyday reality.

One of the few consolations was the birth in 1992 of our second son, Mohamed, whom we named after my grandfather. His older siblings, Ghada and Khaled, who were by then nine and six, were deeply affected by the move, as they were forced to abandon their familiar bedrooms and beloved toys.

We were not the only ones who suffered. The United Nations sanctions, imposed in 1992, placed an awful burden upon the entire country. Our public infrastructure crumbled by the day, and many basic goods were scarce. There were no flights in and out of the country, so those wishing to fly had to make the gruelling overland journey to Tunisia or Egypt, or travel 200 miles by ferry to Malta. Many were forced to travel for medical reasons, as the hospitals were deprived of medicines and equipment. Those who could not afford to travel had to rely on their prayers.

In 1994 we were allowed to return to the family home, but I remained under house arrest. Although our third son, Ali, was born, life remained difficult. Aisha and I feared that the children would grow up isolated from the world, so in 1995 I contacted a manager in the Minister of Justice's office to plead that the ban on foreign travel be lifted for my family. Word came back that it was feared that, if they travelled under the family name, they might be detained and *used as a lever to force my surrender to the United States. Ghada and Khaled had set their hearts on attending an international children's festival in another Arab country. Eventually the Minister, Mohamed al-Zwai, agreed that Aisha be allowed to take them, and therefore arranged for the children to be issued with coded passports under false names.* The trip went well and when they returned we handed the passports back to the immigration authority.*

The knowledge that the case against us was weak was of some comfort during those years, but our dearest wish – to clear our names – was denied us.

Throughout the 1990s Libya was portrayed in the West as stubbornly preferring to endure the sanctions than surrender the two men for trial. The truth was very different. In 1994 relatives of some of the British Lockerbie victims asked the Scottish legal academic, Professor Robert Black QC, if he could suggest a legal mechanism that might put an end to the stalemate. His suggested solution was a trial held under Scots law in a neutral country. Libyan law did not allow its citizens to be tried outside the jurisdiction of the country's courts, but, after some discussion, the government indicated that it was prepared, in principle, to accept the proposal. It was a bold step, which matched almost all of the US and UK governments' demands, yet they flatly rejected it. It appeared that they preferred stalemate to having their fragile evidence tested in court.

But, with time, things changed.

In 1997 President Nelson Mandela of South Africa and the Saudi Arabian Ambassador to the United States, Prince Bandar bin Sultan, began lobbying the British and American governments to accept a neutral venue trial. Mandela had himself been lobbied by the British Lockerbie relatives. He also owed a debt of gratitude to the Libyan government for the support that it had given the African National Congress during its long struggle against South Africa's Apartheid regime.† The politician most receptive to their mediation efforts was

* Aisha was able to travel under her own name, as Arab women traditionally do not adopt their husband's family name after marriage.

† In October 1997 Mandela awarded Colonel Gadafy the Order of Good Hope, which is the highest honour that his country can award a foreigner.

Robin Cook, the Foreign Secretary in Tony Blair's recently elected Labour government. Cook was also very sympathetic to the British Lockerbie relatives, whom he had met while part of Blair's Shadow Cabinet and to whom he had promised a public inquiry if Labour gained power. He managed to convince Blair of the merits of a neutral venue trial and together they eventually persuaded US President Bill Clinton.

The two governments' shift in position was undoubtedly shaped by broader political interests. Since Lockerbie was a mess of their predecessors' making, they were less vulnerable to its fallout. Moreover, the world had changed and with it their geopolitical priorities. Libya's relatively secular regime – for so long a pariah – was now viewed as a buffer against radical Islam.

There were perhaps other, less obvious, reasons. In October 1997, the UN's International Court of Justice considered an objection by the UK and US governments to Libya's still outstanding claim that the parties to the Lockerbie case should be dealt with under the Montreal Convention. If the Court was to find in Libya's favour, it might pave the way for the men to be tried in Libya, and would also allow Libya to overturn the UN sanctions which had been imposed under the 1992 UK and US-sponsored Security Council resolutions 731 and 748.* The objection claimed the Court had no power to consider an issue that had been adjudicated upon by the Security Council. In February 1998, the Court rejected the objection, clearing the way for Libya's claim to be heard. The UK and US governments therefore may well have viewed a neutral venue trial as the only way to rid themselves of this millstone.

Another potential problem for the two governments was the increasing discontent that their stance had generated among African nations. In 1998 leaders attending an Organisation of African Unity summit in Ouagadougou, Burkina Faso, passed a courageous resolution threatening to defy the UN sanctions against Libya if the British and American governments failed to respond to President Mandela's mediation efforts.

* See Chapter 1.

I personally, and Libyans in general, were thrilled by these developments, and for the first time in seven years I dared to hope that our nightmare might end.

I discovered through media reports that UN-brokered negotiations had made good progress and that the Dutch government had agreed in principle to host the trial. Soon afterwards I received a call from Mr al-Zwai, who asked Lamin and me to attend his office as soon as possible. I tried to contact Lamin, but he was looking after his sick father, so I went alone. The Minister told me that the negotiations were at an advanced stage and that an agreement was imminent. It was initially suggested that the Court would comprise five international judges with a Scottish one presiding, but it was later reported that there would be only three judges, all Scottish. He explained that Libya had been advised that it would be impossible to find jurors who'd not been exposed to prejudicial media coverage, and that it was therefore considered wiser to be tried by three Scottish judges.

Shortly after our meeting, on 24 August 1998, the US and UK governments wrote to the UN Secretary General Kofi Annan, confirming that they would accept a trial before a Scottish court sitting in the Netherlands. Three days later the UN Security Council passed Resolution 1192, which established the international legal basis for the trial.

I was very heartened by the news, but remained concerned that President Clinton and Secretary of State Madeleine Albright repeatedly referred to us as terrorist murderers, rather than suspects in an unproven case. Moreover, Resolution 1192 upheld the appalling resolutions 731 and 748, which the two governments had sponsored in 1992. So Libya was still required, not only to surrender us for trial, but also to accept responsibility for the crime and compensate the victims' families. If it failed to comply, it risked a continuation of the crippling sanctions. So, if we were acquitted, Libya would be placed in the ludicrous position of having to admit to the crime and pay reparations. If the UN could succumb to a blatant subversion of natural justice, then why shouldn't a Scottish court?

Mr al-Zwai made clear that, if a deal was agreed, then it was entirely up to us whether we should attend the Court. He also revealed that Colonel Gadafy had no trust in the proposed trial process, as he felt the case was too politicised. I thanked the Minister and promised him that he would receive my answer after I'd discussed the matter with Lamin and my immediate family. We very much wanted to stand trial in order to shift the dark cloud hanging over us since 1991, but we were worried about abandoning our families to an uncertain future.

Eventually we informed the Minister that we were prepared to go to Holland. All we asked for was guaranteed access to our families. Explaining my decision to my family was not easy. Aisha and my mother were particularly concerned. I reassured them that, under Scottish law, cases generally had to be brought to court within 110 days and, since the case was predicted to last a few months, I should be home within a year.

Since it was technically illegal for us to be tried outside Libya, we had to attend a specially-convened hearing before a judge. In the presence of our lawyer, we explained that we had agreed to stand trial in a foreign jurisdiction. We were then required to sign an acknowledgement of our decision before the General Prosecutor.

In December 1998, our fifth child, Motasem Billah, was born. The joy he brought us was a welcome distraction from the months of international negotiations which thrashed out the precise detail of the trial and our handover to the Scottish authorities.

As the trial arrangements were finalised, our legal team began to take shape. For the previous few years we had been represented in Libya by Ibrahim Legwell and in Scotland by Alastair Duff. Duff was retained, but Legwell resigned, as he felt strongly that we should not surrender ourselves for trial. He was replaced by Kamal Maghour, who had represented Lamin when the indictments were first issued in 1991. In an unusual move, Maghour instructed the London-based international law firm, Eversheds, to appoint senior defence counsel. At the firm's request, Duff put forward three names, one of whom, Bill Taylor QC, was subsequently appointed by Eversheds. One of Scotland's most respected criminal advocates, Taylor had defended many major crime cases and was also a member of the English Bar. He selected as his junior a highly-regarded young advocate, John Beckett.

Taylor was invited to Tripoli to advise us on our best interests, and on the safeguards that would be in place under Scottish criminal procedure and the UN agreement, if we attended court. At the time I was unfamiliar with the concept of juries and wasn't sure whether jurors were specially qualified, or simply ordinary members of the public. We had previously been told that it would be better to have the case heard by judges, rather than a jury, but Taylor took a very different view, strongly advising us not to surrender ourselves unless we had the safeguard of a jury. With hindsight, I realised he was right.

The venue eventually chosen for the trial was Kamp Zeist, a disused former US Air Force base, close to Utrecht. Under a special bilateral treaty between the Dutch and UK governments it became, in law, a landlocked Scottish island, with its own court, prison and police station.

When all the arrangements for the trial had been agreed and signed off, it was announced that we would travel to Kamp Zeist on 5 April 1999. A week before our departure we were visited by Duff, who repeated what he had told us years earlier in Tripoli, that we would not receive a fair trial. He went further than Taylor, advising us that we should not surrender ourselves under any circumstances. Again, with hindsight, he was right, but by then there was no turning back.

On the evening before our departure I packed my suitcases, then, as usual, sat playing with the younger children. Mohamed and Ali liked to climb on my back, pretending I was a horse, while I carried them to bed. There was a lot of fun and laughter and I was happy that our last night together could be so light-hearted, but behind my smile I was tortured by the knowledge that a few hours later they would awaken to find me gone.

The following morning, Monday 5 April, I awoke early and said my morning prayers. I beseeched God to protect my family and keep them in His divine care. I persuaded Aisha not to wake the children as I wanted to avoid the heartbreak of saying goodbye, but unfortunately Ghada and Khaled were already awake. We sat together and chatted briefly as we waited for my friend, an LAA pilot, who would be driving me to the airport. I reassured them that everything would *work out fine, and I told them to look after their mother and to help her out in the home. I said to Khaled, 'You are nearly an adult and now you are the man of the house.' He was just thirteen. I lifted the four-month-old Motasem from his cot, kissed him and said a final prayer.*

My friend arrived, I embraced the family one last time, and I walked out of my home for the last time in ten years. Ghada broke down in tears and Khaled looked extremely miserable. To spare me the further agony of a prolonged goodbye my friend drove off at high speed.

At the airport I was met by the Ambassadors of all the member states of the UN Security Council, with the exception of the UK and the USA, who, since they had no diplomatic presence in Libya, were respectively represented by those of Italy and Belgium. Also present were Prince Bandar and President Mandela's Chief of Staff, Jakes Gerwel. Prince Bandar told me that, as far as he could determine, the case against us was entirely circumstantial. I assured him, as I assured everyone, that we were innocent.

Shortly afterwards an Italian Air Force airliner, displaying the UN emblem, touched down and taxied slowly towards the terminal. The first international flight to land at the airport in almost six years, it symbolised a new phase in Libya's relations with the West. Prior to boarding, we made a brief statement to the press, emphasising our innocence and that we had chosen to stand trial in order to clear our names. We left the terminal and climbed the steps to the aircraft, pausing at the top to wave goodbye to the airport staff who had gathered to see us off.

As we stepped on board, our old lives ended and a new one began. In an instant we were transformed from normal family men to international terror suspects. We were searched by UN security officers, in the presence of Italian military guards and fearsome dogs, then ushered to a rear section, which was separated from the front by a large door with a surveillance camera attached.

As we taxied down the runway and took off, I looked out of the window at Tripoli and wondered, 'Shall I ever see Libya again?' We tried to remain positive, telling ourselves that, as long as we received a fair trial, we would be fine. Every so often one of the guards would check on us. Thankfully, they were not our only company on the flight. As well as Kamal Maghour, we had with us another well-known Libyan lawyer, Mohamed al-Kirao, my brother Mohamed and one of Lamin's cousins. It was good to see these friendly faces, but all I could think about was my family. As well as Aisha and the children, I was especially worried about my elderly mother. As I performed my midday prayers I asked God to grant them the patience and strength to hold themselves together.

About three hours later the aircraft touched down at the Valkenberg airbase near The Hague. As it came to a halt I saw that a Dutch police car was waiting by the aircraft's steps. One of the security officers told me that I should disembark first. As I reached the bottom of the steps a Dutch policeman asked me, 'Are you Mr Abdelbaset al-Megrahi?' I confirmed that I was and he formally arrested me, then asked me to follow him to a nearby small building. On entering, I was led to a windowless room, where I was left to wait. Lamin was taken through a similar procedure and held in a different room. I was visited by Libya's Brussels-based Ambassador to Belgium and Holland, Dr Hamid al-Hideiry, who again briefed me on the formal legal procedures that the Dutch authorities were obliged to follow. Eventually, in his presence, a Dutch prosecutor formally asked Lamin and me, separately, if we were willing to accept extradition to Scottish soil. We each agreed and signed the necessary paperwork. The formalities took several hours to complete, far longer than anyone had anticipated.

Three helicopters landed, which were to ferry us to Kamp Zeist. Then it all became ludicrous. A number of Dutch security officers arrived, one of whom, I recall, was exceptionally tall. Rather than simply leading us on board, they handcuffed us and bound our hands and feet with chains. We were then blindfolded and each of us was shackled to an officer. The ankle chains were so short that one of the officers had to instruct us on how to move. Even then we could only shuffle slowly and had to be helped into the helicopters. We were put in separate aircraft and flanked on both sides by officers. The blindfolds were only removed when we were airborne. I noticed that the two other helicopters were in front of us, one carrying Lamin and the other one the Libyan lawyers. The blindfolds were reinstated as we began our descent towards Kamp Zeist a short while later. On landing, we were put in a police car and, still blindfolded and shackled, driven the short distance to the temporary Scottish police station. The police officer who received us, SIO Thomas McCulloch, was clearly shocked to see us in chains and blindfolded, and asked the Dutch to remove them immediately. He then formally cautioned us, and arrested us in turn. As he did so he placed his hand on my shoulder, which I read as an apology for our treatment by the Dutch. It was the first of many humane gestures by the Scottish officials whom I encountered over the next decade. An Arab interpreter was present to ensure that we understood the procedure. Next we were told we would be strip-searched. In my culture it is not acceptable for a man to be naked in front of another. Although I knew there was no way of stopping the search, I requested that the interpreter be absent. Next, the police took DNA and fingerprint samples, and measured and photographed us. We were supposed to be then formally remanded in custody by a Sheriff, but, as the Dutch procedures had taken so long, he had gone home for the day. We therefore had to spend the night in the police station's cells. Our solicitor, Alastair Duff, kindly stayed with us.

The next day the Sheriff returned and the committal formalities were completed. The specially constructed prison, HMP Zeist, was nowhere near ready, so we were placed in a temporary prison adjoining the police station. It consisted of two sections, one front and one rear, which were grandly called wings, but which in fact each consisted of just a few rooms. We were in the front wing, which had two cells. I was allocated Cell 1 and Lamin Cell 2. There were two rooms for the prison officers, one of which contained a TV, which we were allowed to watch. There was only one bathroom, which, to everyone's discomfort, we had to share with the officers.

After a few days Duff told me that on 13 April I had to take part in an identity parade, which was being organised for Tony Gauci. On the night of the 12th I was sitting at the table in my room when I noticed that the corridor light had been switched off, which was unusual, because it was always left on at night. I was aware that two or three people were looking into my cell, but I was unable to see their faces. The people were only present for a short time, and after they left the light was switched back on.

The following morning a police officer arrived to escort me to the parade. I was wearing normal casual clothes and a pair of brown shoes, but the officer handed me a tracksuit, which he said I was required to wear. I liked the blue and orange colours and jokingly asked him if I could keep it as a present. He smiled but said it wouldn't be possible. I was taken to the small room that had been chosen for the parade, where 11 stand-ins were waiting. I was immediately struck by how different they all looked to me. The majority seemed far younger, one was a white European, two were considerably taller, while another was about six inches shorter, podgy, had a moustache and was nearly bald. Only seven were required for the line-up, so I was allowed to select the four who were to be excluded. I chose the one who was obviously the youngest, who turned out to be half my age, and three others. The subsequent police report stated that I rejected all four on the grounds of age, but this was not the case, because I was never told how old they were and, with the exception of the very young one, the hierarchy of ages was not obvious. Indeed, the three other rejects were all older than some who remained in the line-up.

Duff made a vigorous formal objection to the procedure. As well as the glaring dissimilarities between me and the stand-ins, he pointed out that the alleged clothes purchase had occurred more than ten years earlier, which made a reliable identification impossible. Equally obviously, my photo had appeared repeatedly in the media for the past eight years and it was inconceivable that Gauci had not seen it on many occasions.

An issue not raised was my footwear. Although we each wore identical tracksuits, the stand-ins all had training shoes, whereas I was wearing brown shoes, which looked quite strange in combination with the tracksuit and made me stand out.

Once we were ready to go, the eight of us were required to form a line and face a one-way mirror. Gauci was led in on the other side of the mirror, accompanied by police officers, while Duff observed. Inspector Brian Wilson of the Dumfries and Galloway Police told Gauci that the man who bought the clothing may or may not be in

205

the line-up. He then invited him to view us all. On finishing, Gauci said, 'Not exactly the man I saw in the shop ten years ago. I saw him, but the man who look a little bit like exactly is the number five.'[1] Number five was me. Duff told me what Gauci had said, pointing out that it fell way short of a positive identification. In any case, as he had made clear to the police, it was a ludicrous exercise.

In 1982 the Scottish police were issued with guidelines on the conduct of ID parades. It is clear that the Kamp Zeist parade significantly breached those guidelines. For example, they stated: 'It is more important that the stand-ins should resemble the suspect or accused than that they should be like any descriptions given by witnesses.'[2] The police report of the parade subsequently revealed that only one of the men was Abdelbaset's age, the white man, who turned out to be a Dutch police officer. Only two others were in their forties, one of whom was the short balding man, and the other was much stockier than Abdelbaset and had far more hair. Of the remainder, one was nine years younger and the others at least twelve years younger. None matched Gauci's original description of a six-foot, well-built, dark-skinned man with a full head of hair. One of the officers who was present at the parade, Sergeant Mario Busuttil of the Maltese Police, later said in his defence precognition statement: 'The others at the ID parade did not look enough like Megrahi to be confused with him.'[3]

The guidelines also stated: 'The suspect or accused should be placed beside persons of similar age, height, dress and general appearance', yet Abdelbaset was next to the short bald man and the stocky one, neither of whom looked anything like him.[4]

Equally significantly, they advised: 'Care should be taken that any witness who has identified a suspected person by his photograph and who is subsequently called upon to identify that person on his apprehension is not again shown the photograph before identification proceedings.' However, it later emerged that, prior to attending the parade, one of Gauci's neighbours had shown him an article about Lockerbie, from a magazine called *Focus*, which featured a photograph of Abdelbaset. Gauci subsequently showed the picture to Inspector Godfrey Scicluna, and said in Maltese 'Dan hu', meaning, 'That's him.'[5] A 1991 amendment to the guidlelines warned: 'It is essential that the witnesses who are to view the parade do not at any time have an opportunity of seeing the suspect or accused or the other parade members.' Although concerned with the conduct of identification parades, the principle applied equally to exposure to media images. Tellingly, Busuttil's statement noted: 'I could pick out Megrahi although I had never seen him personally myself.'

The *Focus* magazine episode was doubly significant because the article contained the following lines: 'Eighteen months later, Gauci told them the shopper had actually been Al Megrahi [sic]. He even described him: 50 years old, 6ft tall and of strong build. But Al Megrahi was actually 36 when he's alleged to have met Gauci, 5ft 8in tall and not particularly strongly built. Gauci said it was raining when he met Al Megrahi and there was a European Cup football game on TV. This pins the date down to 23 November or 7 December 1988. But it wasn't raining on 7 December and there's no evidence that Al Megrahi was in Malta before then.'[6] There can be no doubt that this passage would have alerted Gauci to the weaknesses in his evidence.

The first few weeks in the prison were very hard. We had the highest security classification, Category A, which meant further strip-searches and regular searches of our cells. The guards were sometimes aggressive. On one occasion one of them took my copy of the Holy Koran and began leafing through the pages. This caused me huge stress because, according to our religion, he was not supposed to touch it.

We were not allowed to keep our luggage, which was stored in the prison's reception area. We were only permitted some clothes and a few additional items. We were forbidden from taking our shoes into the cells, as the laces were considered a security risk, probably because prisoners had used them to hang themselves.

I didn't see Aisha and the children until the start of the school holidays in late June 1999. Their visit was marred by the heavy-handed security procedures to which they were subjected. They had to pass through a cordon of ferocious police dogs and be scanned with a metal detector. Worst of all, our baby Motasem was searched, including inside his nappies. The younger children were terrified of the dogs, and to this day Ali, who was then only five, mistrusts anyone in uniform.

To my great distress, when we were finally reunited, Motasem didn't recognise me and reacted as if I were a stranger.

There were numerous other stresses. The Scottish Prison Service had a contract with a Dutch company to supply food to everyone at Kamp Zeist, including the two of us. We were supposed to receive halal food, but one day we discovered that our rations included slices of pork, which Muslims are forbidden to eat. We were very upset and angry and immediately informed the head prison officer, who in turn informed the prison's Governor, Ian Bannatyne. He promptly apologised and assured us that the error would not be repeated. When we checked our delivery the following day, we discovered that the supplier had marked bottles of water 'halal'. Either he was unaware that there is no such thing as halal water, or someone was making a sarcastic taunt. We decided not to pursue the matter further.

Eventually the main prison was completed and we were transferred across from our temporary accommodation. It consisted of two cells, a kitchenette and a small laundry room, and was separated from the guards' office by a glass barrier, to which two CCTV cameras were attached. It was more comfortable than the temporary prison, but it was still prison and we desperately missed our families and our freedom.

The number of searches had by then declined and the prison officers were generally more relaxed, obviously recognising that we were not the monsters we were supposed to be. While we waited for the trial to begin, Lamin and I fell into the routine of life in the world's smallest prison. It was a surreal existence, two innocent men in an ultra-high-security facility. It was no less strange for the warders and armed policemen, who had to remain vigilant for a security threat that, as they must have eventually realised, did not exist. During the trial there were 200 of them at the site. Fortunately they had a gym, tennis court, football pitch, and recreation room to relieve the tedium. By contrast, we had a caged outdoor exercise area measuring only about eight by five metres.

Like men the world over, we bonded with the prison officers through football. The Scottish game is dominated by the giant Glasgow rivals Celtic and Rangers, with most men in the western part of the country supporting one or the other. Lamin and I respectively supported Tripoli's equivalent Al-Ittihad and Al-Ahli. Since Celitic, like Al-Ahli, play in green, Lamin chose to support them, so, in order to add a little spice to the televised matches, I plumped for Rangers. In truth I was fairly neutral, and my favourite player was Celtic's striker Henrik Larsson.

Lamin and I tried to coincide our family visits, which generally occurred during the school holidays. Our most regular visitors were the lawyers, and we were also seen by Minister al-Zwai. UN observers, and US and UK government officials also came to inspect the prison's facilities, but, for the most part, we had only each other for company.

Lamin's presence was, nevertheless, a great comfort. I felt for him because he was not in good health. As well as having to endure twice-daily injections for diabetes, he suffered eyesight and kidney problems. He was nevertheless a naturally upbeat person, who seldom complained and did his best to make our situation bearable. He shared my strong Muslim faith, so we would pray together and celebrate important dates in the religious calendar. We continued to receive our food from the Dutch supplier, but every now and then we were allowed to cook traditional Libyan food. I had known Lamin for many years, but it was only then that I learned he was a great cook.

Our lead counsel, Bill Taylor QC, felt strongly that Lamin and I should have separate legal representation, in case there was any conflict between our respective defences. It was decided that Alastair Duff, Taylor and John Beckett would continue to represent me. The solicitor appointed to represent Lamin was Eddie MacKechnie of the Glasgow-based firm McGrigor Donald. It was, at first glance, a surprising choice, as both MacKechnie and the firm were civil litigation specialists with little experience in criminal law. What the firm did have, however, was a wealth of experience of dealing with substantial amounts of often highly technical evidence. MacKechnie chose as leading counsel Richard Keen QC, who similarly had almost no experience of criminal trials, but who was widely regarded as one of the sharpest advocates of his generation. Another able young advocate, Murdo Macleod, was selected as his junior. My team was augmented by Duff's fellow partner at McCourts, Alex Prentice.

209

Lamin's team was rather bigger. In addition to MacKechnie and the two advocates, five other McGrigor's staff were drafted in: aviation specialist Paul Phillips, who was based at the firm's London office, plus Gavin Walker, Andrea Summers, Gordon Balfour and trainee Ingrid Elliott from the Glasgow office. Eversheds oversaw the two teams and controlled the budget. Although the firm's role was largely administrative, they helped to identify expert witnesses and take statements.

The disparity in the teams' sizes was not a concern, as it was agreed that they would pool their efforts in order to handle the mountain of evidence. Everyone was given their own areas of responsibility, and all worked with barely a break until the end of the trial. A huge burden of responsibility was placed on my junior counsel John Beckett, especially in the months prior to the appointment of Lamin's team. He was tasked with reading and evaluating the evidence in relation to many crucial areas of the case, including Mebo and the timer, Heathrow Airport, my movements in the couple of years before Lockerbie and, most importantly, Tony Gauci.

Under Scottish legal procedure, defendants are provided with a list of Crown witnesses, whom their representatives are then allowed to interview. This process is known as precognition, and the resulting statements are known as precognition statements or precognitions. In this case the witness list ran to over 1,100 names, very many of whom were in Europe and the United States and some of whom were as far-flung as Japan and Uruguay. As well as interviewing the witnesses, the defence team had to read and absorb over 3,000 Crown documentary exhibits – which are referred to in Scotland as productions – some of which ran to many hundreds of pages.

The task was made all the greater when the defence managed to obtain, via the Maltese government, most of the police statements taken by the Scottish police in Malta (although it later transpired that a number were missing, including some of critical importance). The job of analysing the statements was nothing compared to the task of evaluating all the evidence from Germany. After some effort, the defence was given all the BKA's files relating to both the Autumn Leaves and the Lockerbie investigations. The latter alone ran to 169 volumes, most of which were in German and therefore required translation.

The files presented us with a very tough question: would it be part of our defence that others were responsible for the bombing? In Scots law this is known as a special defence of incrimination, and requires the defence to notify the Court in advance. The lawyers advised that we should at least keep the option open, as there was a good deal of circumstantial evidence to suggest that the PFLP-GC, Abu Talb and others were involved in a terrorist conspiracy in the months prior to Lockerbie.

I wish to stress here that neither Lamin nor I personally wished to blame others for the bombing. The evidence in question was not ours, but the police's. We were acutely aware of how flawed such evidence could be, but it was only fair that the Court should know that we were not the sole suspects.

Our lawyers visited Libya, interviewing dozens of witnesses and gathering evidence that supported our claims of innocence. They were shown the carpets that I bought in Malta on 20 December 1988 and the chandeliers, which I had bought in Prague the previous week, complete with the original Czech assembly instruction-sheet and guarantee. Fortunately, much of the paperwork relating to the company ABH had been preserved, including numerous telexes to and from foreign suppliers, including ones in the aviation sector. Many of the telexes bore the telex number of the Centre for Strategic Studies, from where I had conducted much of my ABH business. They demonstrated that, far from being a JSO front, ABH was in fact a general trading company, which for the most part purchased nothing more sinister than aircraft parts, cars and meat. The origin and content of the telexes, and the various witness statements, tallied with the stamps in my passports and the accounts that I gave my lawyers. The company paperwork also included invoices for the two deals that we did with Mebo, one for a satellite receiver for the JSO and the other for 50 mobile radio communication units.

Lamin handed over documents relating to his company Medtours, which, among other things, demonstrated its involvement in the Paris to Dakar Rally preparations. The lawyers were also given a bundle of telexes, which he had sent while LAA's Malta Station Chief, in which he repeatedly warned colleagues that he was running *out of tags and pleaded with them urgently to send him some from Tripoli. These supported his claim that the reference to tags in his diary simply reflected that ongoing issue.*

The Libyan government offered its full cooperation to Crown. A joint police and Crown Office team spent weeks in Tripoli interviewing people, including the sixty or so whom our side had identified as potential defence witnesses. In addition, the authorities handed over documents relating to the coded passport issued to me in the name of Abdusamad. I handed over the passport itself, which proved I'd travelled to Malta under that name on the day before the bombing and returned the following morning. I also surrendered the regular passport that I used in 1988, which showed that I was also on the island on 7 December. Until then the Crown had no cast-iron proof that I was Abdusamad, and neither were they aware that the Malta trip was the last time that I'd used the passport.[7] If I and the government had wished to conceal the truth, we could easily have destroyed the passport and documents. However, a fair trial required the truth to be aired, and the Malta trips and use of the coded passport were among the few important Crown allegations that happened to be true.

The only organisation actively to destroy evidence was the Dumfries and Galloway Police. A couple of months after the Libyans' arrival at Zeist, to the defence's amazement they learned through Crown sources that the police had destroyed most of the notebooks of the officers involved in the investigation.* In a subsequent letter to Conservative MP Sir Teddy Taylor, the Lord Advocate, Andrew Hardie QC, explained: 'While it is the case that some police notebooks have been destroyed in line with the ordinary police standing orders relating to destruction of police notebooks, I can assure you that the presentation of the evidence in the case will not be hampered by this, since the primary means of recording the enquiries was the police HOLMES computer system and not by reference to police notebooks.'[8] This was utter nonsense; notebooks are the primary means

---

* Since copies of certain officers' notebooks were among the Crown productions disclosed to the defence, some had obviously survived, but the exact number or proportion that had been destroyed remained unclear.

of recording evidence and are therefore the bedrock of any police inquiry. The HOLMES computer did not log the notebooks' complete contents, so without them it was impossible for the defence to get a full picture of the Lockerbie investigation. Anecdotal evidence from the crash-site suggested that certain finds, such as the packages of drugs and cash, were suppressed, which raised suspicions that some of the notebooks recorded items and events that contradicted the official version of the bombing.

More generally, despite claiming to have a liberal disclosure policy, the prosecution failed in its legal responsibility to disclose all relevant material to the defence. This duty arose under the European Convention on Human Rights, which was applicable through both the Scotland Act 1998 and Human Rights Act 1998, and had been established in case law in England since the early 1990s. Unfortunately, by the time of the Lockerbie trial, the Crown did not have appropriate disclosure procedures in place. While they may not have understood the full scope of their obligations under the Convention, they knowingly adopted a restrictive interpretation of those obligations.* Masses of documents remained withheld, among them thousands of police statements. When they were eventually released, years later, some of them proved to be of vital importance to Abdelbaset's defence.

The indictment was not formally served until October 1999. It contained three alternative charges. The first stated that between 1 January 1985 and 21 December 1988 the two accused conspired to destroy a civilian airliner. It claimed the conspiracy encompassed various foreign trips that Abdelbaset made using the Abdusamad passport and involved ABH, Lamin's Maltese company Medtours and Abdelmajid Arebi's Prague-based company Al-Khadra, all of which were alleged to be JSO front companies. The second charged them directly with murder and focused narrowly on the events of

---

* It was not until after the trial, in 2002, that a House of Lords ruling set out the 'golden rule', which obliged the Crown to disclose all material that might undermine the prosecution case or help the defence. The explicit requirement to disclose all police statements was not incorporated into Scots law until two Scottish appeal judgments in 2005.

December 1988. Charge 3 was far more brief than the other two and contained very little detail. It did not refer directly to Pan Am 103 and instead accused the two Libyans of a general plot to destroy a civilian aircraft. Significantly, all three charges alleged that both men were JSO agents.

Three senior Law Lords were appointed to hear the case. The Presiding Judge was Lord Ranald Sutherland QC, a 68-year-old, who had been an advocate since 1956 and a judge since 1985. Sitting with him were Lord Coulsfield, formerly John Taylor Cameron QC, a 66-year-old who was appointed to the bench in 1987, and Lord Ranald MacLean QC, who had ten years' experience as a judge and, at 61, was the youngest of the three. A reserve judge, Lord Abernethy, was appointed in case any of his colleagues became incapacitated.

The Crown team was led, officially at least, by the Lord Advocate. As well as being the country's chief prosecutor, the Lord Advocate is also a Scottish government minister, as is his deputy, the Solicitor General. At the time of the defendants' arrival in the Netherlands the post was held by Andrew Hardie QC; however, just two months before the trial began he unexpectedly resigned, fuelling rumours that he considered the case to be a poisoned chalice. He was replaced by the Solicitor General, Colin Boyd QC. Although the Lord Advocate was in charge of the prosecution, the responsibility for presenting the case to the Court was devolved to Advocates Depute Alastair Campbell QC and Alan Turnbull QC, who were supported by junior counsel, Jonathan Lake and Morag Armstrong. Behind the scenes, the Crown Office team of Procurators Fiscal was led by Norman McFadyen.*

At a preliminary hearing before Lord Sutherland, defence counsel challenged the indictments, arguing that Charge 1 – the conspiracy charge – was unrelated to Scotland and, since the alleged conspiracy

---

* Advocates Depute are the prosecuting counsel in High Court cases. Procurators Fiscal and Fiscal Deputes are Crown Office employees responsible for the investigation and prosecution of crimes, and also act as prosecutors in the lower courts. Although the Lord Advocate was a figurehead, Boyd himself was quite closely involved in preparing the Crown's case. In an August 2001 paper for the International Society for the Reform of Criminal Law, he wrote: 'The [Crown] team was chaired by me as Solicitor General and met on a weekly basis right through from October 1998 until near the start of the trial itself in about January 2000.'

resulted in murder, was a duplication of Charge 2. They claimed it was merely a device that would enable the Crown to introduce evidence that would otherwise be irrelevant. Lord Sutherland rejected the submissions.

Under normal circumstances the trial should have begun within 110 days, but it was soon apparent that neither side would make the deadline, so two further 110-day extensions were subsequently agreed. After a few months it was decided that both defence teams required an additional senior advocate. David Burns QC was appointed to Abdelbaset's team and Jack Davidson QC to Lamin's. Two inquiry agencies had been hired at an earlier stage to help with the precognition process: Glasgow-based ID Inquiries was instructed by McCourts, and the London firm, Network International, by Eversheds.

The investigative effort was supplemented by journalist and Middle East academic Dr Alan George, who was also instructed by Eversheds.

In addition to the thousands of documents, the Crown evidence included over 550 non-documentary exhibits – known in Scotland as label productions – most of which were debris items from the crash-site. It was obvious that this evidence, along with the forensic report and other materials produced by RARDE's Thomas Hayes and Allen Feraday, required expert analysis. Having taken soundings from various experts, the defence instructed RARDE's Northern Irish equivalent, the Forensic Science Agency of Northern Ireland (FSANI). For many years it had sole responsibility for the forensic investigation of major crimes committed in the Province, and therefore, with the possible exception of RARDE, had unrivalled experience of UK terrorist cases.

FSANI was first instructed in August 1999, and senior scientists Gordon McMillen, Dr Gerard Murray and Ian Fulton were allocated to the case. In early December they spent three days in Dumfries viewing debris and various Mebo and Toshiba control samples. On 10 December they reported their preliminary findings to Alastair Duff. Disappointingly for the defence, they agreed with most of the key findings of Hayes and Feraday's joint report: the bomb was contained in a Toshiba RT-SF16 radio-cassette player; it utilised around

400 grams of plastic explosive and a Mebo MST-13 timer; and it had been placed within a brown Samsonite suitcase along with 12 items of clothing and an umbrella.[9]

In a meeting with the defence team later that month, they reported only one point of dispute with the Crown's forensic experts. Both RARDE and the AAIB claimed that the explosion occurred within the second layer of luggage in the container AVE4041.[10] The RARDE report suggested that the distance from the centre of the explosion to the base of the container was 25 to 30 cm, while the AAIB suggested 10 inches (25.5cm).[11] Since the bottom layer was already full when the bags from the Frankfurt feeder flight PA103A were added, if these calculations were correct, unless the original layer was re-arranged during that process, the primary case must have arrived on that flight. The FSANI experts, by contrast, believed the distance to be around only 10 cm,[12] which, if true, made it very likely that the primary suitcase was in the bottom layer of luggage. This lent very strong support to the suggestion that the primary suitcase was the brown hard-sided case that the Heathrow loader John Bedford recalled seeing on the base of the container prior to the arrival of PA103A.

Soon after the meeting Gordon McMillen assumed sole responsibility for the case. In early February 2000 he spent a further three days viewing items in Dumfries, including the reconstructed luggage container AVE4041. On the basis of these examinations he revised his view, now believing the distance to be around 20 cm, which would mean it was probably in the second layer.[13] So, unless it could be demonstrated that a rearrangement may have occurred, or that the experts were wrong, it was very difficult to implicate the Bedford suitcase.

One slightly surprising aspect of the division of labour was that Paul Phillips was not assigned any direct oversight of the FSANI experts' work. Probably the most vigorous of the defence solicitors, his work on other areas of the case raised some important questions about the forensic evidence. As the trial approached, he grew increasingly concerned that the defence would not be able to mount a strong forensic challenge. In early March 2000 he warned colleagues in a memo: 'We have agreed that if this was a civil trial, we would have compendious experts' reports in our hands some time ago in relation to each of the matters in issue, and spent some considerable time with the experts going through the drafts of their reports, raising questions, challenging assumptions etc. The absence of any form of forensic report from our Northern Irish experts with 53 days to go is deeply worrying.'[14] At a team meeting two days earlier Richard Keen QC and Eddie MacKechnie also expressed their concern, and it was agreed that, if McMillen's report was of no use, then they should seek a second expert opinion.[15]

McMillen delivered a draft report around two weeks later, and his final report on 20 April. It ran to just eight pages. There were only two serious challenges to the Crown forensic case. The first concerned the lack of corroboration for the claims concerning the explosive residues. In McMillen's view, the weak positive results may have arisen from laboratory contamination. The second was his finding that the purple holdall PH/137, which had been checked in at Heathrow, exhibited explosive damage, which, in his view, meant it must have been in the container AVE4041.[16] If Heathrow check-in bags had been loaded into AVE4041, then it undermined the Crown's claim that the primary suitcase could not have originated from Heathrow.*

Five days after receiving the draft report, Eddie MacKechnie wrote, 'At the end of the day its conclusions may prove to be entirely justified but the report lacks apparent depth.'[17] It was decided to instruct a specialist forensic metallurgy firm, Capcis, which was attached to the University of Manchester Institute of Science and Technology. In his letter of introduction MacKechnie explained: 'We are concerned to test fully the Forensic and Expert evidence likely to be adduced by the Crown.'[18] In the event, however, Capcis was invited to focus mainly on the evidence concerning the explosion's location, in particular the stand-off distance (the distance between the centre of the explosion and the aircraft skin).[19] The AAIB put that figure at 25 inches (64 cm) while the RAE suggested 24 inches (62 cm). Both distances were consistent with the primary suitcase being in the second layer of luggage. When they scrutinised the complex calculations that underpinned these estimates, Capcis experts

* See Chapter 6.

Professor Salim al-Hassani, Dr Denis Ryder and Stephen Burley uncovered significant flaws, which, if rectified, reduced the stand-off distance to a figure consistent with an explosion in the bottom layer.

It was obvious to the defence team that Tony Gauci's identification evidence was highly problematic for the Crown. Not only had he consistently described the mystery customer as much older and bigger than Abdelbaset, but his identifications of 15 February 1991 and at the ID parade were only partial. The ID parade was further devalued by Gauci's previous exposure to Abdelbaset's photo in articles and TV broadcasts. The team gave consideration to leading expert evidence on the fallibility of eyewitness identification, but concluded that such opinions were unlikely to be admissible and would, in any case, be telling the judges what they already knew.[20]

Among the Crown productions were the artist's impression of the clothes buyer, which had been produced under Gauci's direction by the FBI's George Noble in September 1989. Gauci had originally described the man as dark, but it struck me that the man depicted by Noble, although he appeared to have Afro hair, was fairly light-skinned. Strangely, the Crown production was not the original drawing, but a copy. I asked the lawyers to request the original, but the Crown informed them it was not available.

In October 1999 the defence precognosced Gauci. When asked if he could recall the date of the clothes purchase, he gave a startling answer: 'I remember it was the 29th of the month. I think it was November. I am asked why it was the 29th and all I can say is that is what I think.' Since Abdelbaset was alleged to have bought the clothes on 7 December, if Gauci repeated the claim in court then Abdelbaset would have been acquitted. The statement contained other information that contradicted the Crown case. The Crown evidence suggested that he sold one grey shirt and one blue-and-white pinstriped one, but he now said that one was beige check and the other blue, and he claimed that the man bought two pullovers, rather than one cardigan.

He gave details that were completely at odds with his earlier accounts. Whereas he told the police that he saw the man walking towards a taxi, but not actually get into it, he now said that he accompanied the man to the taxi with the parcels of clothes and placed them on the front seat for him. More importantly, he claimed that his brother Paul arrived at the shop as the man was leaving. Neither Tony nor Paul had mentioned this detail in any of their police statements. If true, it meant that Paul may also have seen the man and might therefore be used by the Crown to bolster Tony's partial identification of Abdelbaset.

When asked about the man's age, Gauci said, 'He was younger than 60. It is difficult to tell age.' He was not specific about the man's height, but said, 'He was tall.' He was not sure whether he had ever seen the man before that occasion, but, when asked if he had seen him since, he replied, 'Definitely not.' This ruled out the man he had seen in the shop in September 1989, who he had claimed might be the one in question. His statement of 26 September 1989 claimed this sighting occurred the previous day, but two years later he gave the peculiar statement in which he agreed that he had originally told the police that it was in fact on 21 or 22 September.[21]* Had that been true, it was potentially a vital point for the Crown, as Abdelbaset had been in Malta between the 21st and 24th, but the point now appeared lost.

Gauci said that when he was first shown photographs he picked out two people, whom he considered 'more or less looked like the person'.[22] This was odd, because at the first photoshow of which the defence were aware – which occurred on 14 September 1989 – he'd picked out only one person, whom he'd described as 20 years younger than the clothes buyer, rather than 'more or less the same'.[23]

When the defence interviewed Paul Gauci he made no mention of having returned to the shop as the man was leaving. On the subject of football, he said, 'There was really nothing in particular that I could tell the police at all about any of these football matches because the truth which I told them was that if possible I would have watched every single football match that was on. It seemed to me that there was little point in trying to concentrate on one game rather than another game because I could not really tell any games apart.'[24] This statement was rather at odds with the one produced by DC John Crawford on 14 December 1989, which reported that Paul had agreed, on the basis of the *Times of Malta* TV listings, that the date

* See Chapter 5.

in question was 7 December. For reasons that were not explained by Crawford, Paul had on that occasion refused to give a statement.[25] Paul also told the defence team that he was often absent from the shop for reasons other than football.[26] This raised the possibility that the clothes purchase could have occurred on any day during the relevant period, rather than on one of only two dates.

The defence made a further discovery that substantially undermined the Crown's claim that the clothes purchase must have occurred on 7 December 1988. They learned that 8 December was a public holiday in Malta to mark the Feast of the Immaculate Conception, when, by tradition, all shops were closed. Had the purchase taken place on the eve of an important public holiday then it would have been all the more memorable, yet none of Gauci's 19 police statements made mention of the special occasion.

After the Gaucis, the most important Maltese witness was Lamin's former business partner Vincent Vassallo, whom Abdelbaset and Lamin had visited the evening before the bombing. He confirmed that it was his first meeting with Adelbaset, who had introduced himself by his real name, rather than the one on his coded passport. He also confirmed that neither of the Libyans was carrying a suitcase. He described Lamin's shock on learning of the police investigation and his willingness to allow them to search the Medtours office and take his diary. Once the search was finished, he said, DCI Bell reminded him that 'a big reward' was on offer for any helpful information he could provide.[27]*

---

* When asked about the conversation at Abdelbaset's trial, Vassallo said: 'What I remember is that when they came to my office, Harry Bell asked me – he said, "Try and remember well. You know there is a large reward, and if you wish to have more money, perhaps go abroad somewhere, you can do so." I am not saying, to be clear, that Harry Bell was offering me something. He was simply telling me what the conditions were: that for information that I might be able to give, there is a large reward. And I also read it, and I also heard it on the news. To be clear, he didn't say, "Here, this is the money," to give the wrong interpretation. He only said, "There is a reward, and if you for any reason wish to be more relaxed with money, we would not find any difficulty, even if you do not wish to give us information here"; that is, in Malta.'

The most difficult witness to get to was the PFLP-GC bomb-maker and double agent Marwan Khreesat. Thanks to the persistence of Kamal Maghour, the Jordanian authorities and Khreesat eventually agreed that he could be interviewed. Duff and MacKechnie travelled to Amman, where they were escorted to the meeting by the Jordanian secret police. He confirmed that the PFLP-GC's leader Ahmed Jibril had asked him to prepare bombs in 1985 and said that, at the time, he saw a number of already prepared radio-cassette bombs in one of the group's houses in Syria. He recalled that some of these had one speaker and some two, and that they definitely included Toshibas. He bought four more devices, but insisted that they were all single-speaker Toshiba RT-F453D models, like the one seized in Neuss, and were different to those he had seen in Syria.

Asked about the aim of his October 1988 mission to West Germany, Khreesat was unambiguous: 'It was made very clear to us by Ahmed Jibril that he wanted to blow up an aeroplane. This was the whole purpose of us being there and in telephone calls to Dalkamoni Jibril repeated on a number of occasions he wanted a plane blown up. In fact the day before we were arrested in a telephone call to Dalkamoni Jibril absolutely insisted that he wanted a plane blown up. Dalkamoni and I travelled to Frankfurt in order to go to the offices of Pan Am to get information about their flight schedules. We did this. There is absolutely no doubt in my mind that Jibril wanted a Pan Am flight out of Frankfurt blown up.'

He claimed Dalkamoni had brought the explosives from Yugoslavia, possibly in a car with a secret compartment. He said he too had been to Yugoslavia and had remained there for a few days before travelling on to Neuss.

Asked about the mysterious Abu Elias, he said Dalkamoni told him Elias was in Germany and wanted to see the bombs he'd made in Neuss, 'in order to check them'. He added, 'I was told that [Elias] was an expert in explosives. I was told that he understood his work.'

Although Khreesat remained adamant that his bombs were not of the twin-speaker type used for the Lockerbie bomb, he revealed that Dalkamoni had at least one other radio-cassette bomb. He recalled: 'Dalkamoni brought a cassette recorder to me. It had already been taken apart to some extent and he asked me to weld a wire to

221

a particular place in the recorder. It was not obvious to me why he was asking me to do this. This had no electronic purpose at all and I got the impression that my loyalty was being tested to see whether I would ask any questions but right after I did this I went with Dalkamoni to his car and he opened his trunk of the car and in the trunk I saw a cassette recorder. I could only see part of it. There was one end of it where there was a speaker. I also saw wires and Semtex.' Crucially he added, 'It seemed to me that the cassette recorder in the back of his car was a two-speaker cassette recorder because it was long and thin and the speaker was at one end suggesting to me that there was another speaker at the other end. I think also that it was a Toshiba make so in other words I think that the cassette recorder in his car was a Toshiba two-speaker cassette recorder. The one which he asked me to weld a wire to another part of the device was almost definitely a two-speaker cassette recorder. I could not see the make because it was lying face down but it definitely had two speakers.' If Khreesat was right, here, at last, was confirmation that the PFLP-GC had at least one twin-speaker Toshiba device in West Germany. Since no such devices were recovered by the BKA during the Autumn Leaves raids, Dalkamoni may well have passed it on to another group member prior to his arrest.

Khreesat said that he was willing to help uncover the truth. When asked if he would give evidence at the trial, he said he might be prepared to do so via a video link, or even in person if his personal security could be guaranteed, but said he would have to think about it.[28]

After months of preparations and following a few preliminary hearings, it was announced that the trial would commence on 3 May 2000. By then we had spent over a year in custody and were desperate for the case to be heard. Once the finishing touches had been completed, a few days before the trial opening, we were driven the short distance from the prison to get a preview of what was one of the most secure, hi-tech and costly courts ever built. Having never before set foot in a criminal court, I had nothing with which to compare it, but it seemed very modern and sophisticated.

Although our lawyers were fully prepared for the opening chapters of evidence, their workload remained relentless. One of the reasons was the sheer volume of evidence that was still to be anaylsed. This was due in part to the Crown's failure to disclose all the evidence when we first surrendered ourselves for trial. Almost 200 documentary productions, 65 label productions and the names of 70 witnesses were not released to the defence until the end of November 1999, by which time we had been in custody for over seven months.[29] Many more were disclosed in February and April 2000, with the last ones not reaching us until just five days before the trial opened.[30] A basic principle of natural justice is that all relevant material should be disclosed to the defence. As subsequent events proved, it was a principle that the Crown would fail to honour.

We were nevertheless keen for the trial to start on time. A particular concern for my lawyers was that the Crown was seeking access to my Credit Suisse bank account through the Swiss courts. I had no wish to block their efforts and eventually the bank released the material. Had the Crown obtained it before the trial commenced, then it might have been used as evidence against me, but in the event the Swiss didn't hand it over until two months into the trial, which meant it could only be used if I opted to testify.

Of greatest interest to the Crown was the payment of $972,000 which I received in October 1989 from the Libyan Embassy in Madrid. In a memo dated 1 July 2000, which was released by the SCCRC in 2007, Fiscal Depute Mirian Watson wrote: 'I cannot identify anything in the movements which would explain the deposit of almost a million dollars, the bulk of which remained in a personal current account for a considerable period of time. This is no doubt something that the accused will be able to explain in due course.'[31] The payment was in fact for the 50 Peugeots, which I bought on behalf of the Ministry of Justice from the Lebanese businessman Hijazi.* The bank statements also recorded the payments of $228,000 and $336,000, which I made to his company following the delivery of the cars in 1990, and copies of the corresponding cheques were among the documents handed to the Crown. There were, of course, many other payments in and out of the account, all of which I could account for. Following my return to Libya, the Sunday Times *claimed that, at the time of the trial, I had £1.8 million in the*

---

* See Chapter 3.

account.[32]† Conservative MP Ben Wallace, a member of the House of Commons Scottish Affairs Committee, told the newspaper: 'Far from being the wrong man, I think this suggests Megrahi was an international co-ordinator of terrorism for Libya.' In fact, the most recent statement that the Crown received, which I got before leaving for Zeist, showed a balance of around $23,000, a figure that had remained unchanged since 1993. I received no further statements and assumed that the bank had closed down the account. These unspectacular truths, it seemed, could never be allowed to interfere with a good story.

† The article was one of a series of wildly inaccurate stories published by the *Sunday Times* following Abdelbaset's return to Libya.

Trial and Error 11

When 3 May 2000 finally arrived, the Court was packed with the world's media, relatives of the Lockerbie victims and members of our own families. We were led into the dock and took our seats next to each other, a few yards away from where Lords Sutherland, Coulsfield and MacLean would be seated. Inevitably we were nervous; the first day of any new venture is daunting, let alone one that would determine our entire futures. Although the setting was new, the Scottish court procedures and language were archaic and only added to our disorientation.

The proceedings were monitored by a number of official observers, among them Professor Hans Köchler, who was nominated by UN Secretary General Kofi Annan, under the terms of UN Security Council Resolution 1192.

As the trial opened, Bill Taylor QC immediately notified the Court that he was lodging a special defence of incrimination, which alleged that others were responsible for the bombing. A schedule of names was read to the Court, including the PFLP-GC, Abu Talb, and his associates in Malta, Abdel and Hashem Salem Abu Nada.

In the converted sports hall that served as the international media centre, hundreds of journalists reported on the opening days, as witnesses recounted the horrors of 21 December 1988. Within a week all but a handful of reporters had left. Since few of these knew much about the case, they frequently missed the significance of what they were hearing. As a consequence, Britian's largest criminal trial became one of its worst-covered. Time and again over the following months, cross-examinations by our counsel revealed significant flaws in the Crown case, yet hardly any of these facts were reported.

One of the matters ignored by the press, but of great concern for us, was the presence on the Crown benches of US Department of Justice officials Brian Murtagh and Dana Biehl. This was a

Scottish court and a Scottish prosecution, over which the United States government had no jurisdiction. In his subsequent report, Professor Köchler described this situation as 'highly problematic', adding: 'The two state prosecutors from the US Department of Justice were seated next to the prosecution team. They were not listed in any of the official information documents about the Court's officers produced by the Scottish Court Service, yet they were seen talking to the prosecutors while the Court was in session, checking notes and passing on documents. For an independent observer watching this from the visitors' gallery, this created the impression of "supervisors" handling vital matters of the prosecution strategy and deciding, in certain cases, which documents (evidence) were to be released in open court or what parts of information contained in a certain document were to be withheld.' I raised the matter with my legal team, but was told that, if they made a formal objection to the judges, then the Crown would object to the presence of our Libyan lawyer Kamal Maghour.[1]*

Most evidence was given in English, but many of the foreign witnesses used their native language. The Scottish Courts Service therefore employed a team of interpreters whose translations were relayed via headphones. My English was of a good standard, but I often listened to the Arabic translation. The two languages are very different, making real-time interpreting very difficult, especially when the dialogue is finely nuanced or highly technical. If the interpreters were unable to keep up, they would switch on a light and the witness was asked to pause, but I nevertheless noticed frequent mistakes.

As the case gathered pace, we soon became familiar with our respective lead counsels' contrasting styles. Taylor was generally the more affable and relaxed of the two, although he could show his teeth when necessary. It was easy to see why he had a reputation as a good persuader of juries. At times he was too relaxed for my liking, as he sometimes didn't have facts and arguments at his fingertips when challenged by the judges. Keen tended to be more direct and clinical, and had a phenomenal grasp of detail. His cross-examining style generally

---

* Köchler also viewed Maghour's presence as unfortunate, but noted that, since he was not observed to interact with the defence lawyers, his presence was less problematic than Murtagh and Biehl's.

ranged between businesslike and fierce, and many observers regarded him as the trial's star performer.

To guarantee guilty verdicts the Crown had to satisfy the judges that Abdelbaset bought the clothes from Tony Gauci on 7 December 1988, that the bomb contained one of the 20 MST-13 timers supplied by Mebo to Libya, and that, on the morning of 21 December, the two men had conspired to put the primary suitcase on flight KM180 at Luqa Airport. Scores of witnesses were called, the great majority of whom added only small pieces to the jigsaw. Only five could be described as crucial: Gauci, Mebo's Edwin Bollier, the two defendants' former LAA colleague, Majid Giaka, and the RARDE experts Thomas Hayes and Allen Feraday. Similarly, although the Crown had over 1,800 documentary productions, only a handful really mattered: the computer printout and coding station worksheet from Frankfurt Airport, which supposedly demonstrated that a bag from Air Malta Flight KM180 was loaded onto PA103A; the order sheet from the Yorkie clothing company in Malta, which demonstrated that the brown checked trousers bearing the stamp '1705', was part of an order manufactured exclusively for the Gaucis' shop and delivered on 18 November 1988; Abdelbaset's passports and the immigration and hotel registration documents, which proved that he visited Malta on 7, 20 and 21 December 1988; and Lamin's diary, with its references to baggage tags and Air Malta.

Hayes and Feraday were the first of the main witnesses. Their Crown evidence was, essentially, an extended recitation of their joint report, with each speaking to his own areas of responsibility; in Hayes's case this was the luggage and clothing, and in Feraday's the bomb itself, including the timer.

During his examination of Hayes, Alastair Campbell QC anticipated potentially tricky cross-examination by raising some anomalies in the clothing evidence. The joint report suggested that it was possible to distinguish clothes that were in the primary suitcase from those in the surrounding luggage on the basis of the tiny debris fragments that were found blasted into them. Clothes containing fragments of the bomb and no fragments of suitcase shell were designated Category 1 and were thought most likely to have been in the primary case. Those containing either no fragments, or fragments including suitcase shell, were designated Category 2 and were thought most likely to be from the surrounding cases.* Campbell drew Hayes's attention to the fact that during the investigation some of the items had, in effect, migrated from the surrounding cases to the primary one. Among these was PI/221, which was the largest piece of the dark-brown checked Yorkie trousers, which had originally led the police to Malta and Mary's House. In his examination notes Hayes had judged the item to have probably originated from a suitcase close to the primary one, but in the joint report it had shifted to Category 1. Hayes said that his change of opinion came about, 'after a revision of the overall recovery, and a need to assess defined categories and the allocation of damaged clothing to those categories'.[2] Another potentially awkward Category 1 garment was the cardigan PI/594. Campbell pointed out to Hayes that, since it did not contain any fragments of the bomb, it did not meet his own Category 1 criteria. Hayes admitted that the evidence 'suggests quite strongly that it will be more correct to consider this as in the first category than in the second category', but he did not explain why he had included it in Category 1.[3]

During cross-examination by Richard Keen QC, Hayes made some important concessions about the clothing categorisation system. The first was that he was not present at the explosive tests in America, the results of which supposedly provided the theoretical basis for the system. The system was reliant to a great extent on the claim that many of the Category 1 items contained fragments of black plastic originating from the Toshiba radio-cassette player. When asked whether the fragments recovered from a particular garment had been proved to be part of the Toshiba by chemical testing, Hayes was remarkably vague:

Q. Did you carry out any chemical analysis on the fragments, Dr. Hayes?
A. Again, I'm afraid I can't help you with an answer to that question. I know chemical analysis was done on fragments. Whether it was performed on these fragments, I don't know.

* See Chapters 5 and 8, and Appendix 2.

Q. Did you carry out any chemical analysis or instruct any chemical analysis on these fragments, Dr. Hayes?

A. I did instruct chemical analysis to be done on certain fragments of plastics. Whether on these particular fragments, I can't help you.

Q. Where are the results of the chemical analysis that you instructed?

A. I would like to think they would be in an appropriate file.

Q. Where is that appropriate file, Dr. Hayes?

A. I'm afraid I can't help you with that.[4]

The other main marker for Category 1 items, along with black plastic and manual fragments, was fragments of the primary suitcase's fabric-lined cardboard partition. Hayes acknowledged that there was nothing to distinguish fragments of fabric lining that originated from the inner surface of the suitcase's shell from those originating from the partition. Furthermore, there was nothing to indicate that some of the fragments that were attributed to the partition contained any cardboard, which meant they may have well have originated from the shell lining. If that was the case, then, logically, they should have been regarded as no different to fragments of suitcase shell, which were, of course, a marker for Category 2 items. Keen also pointed out – as had Campbell – that some of Hayes's Category 1 items failed the Category 1 criteria, either because they contained no bomb fragments, or because they contained fragments of suitcase shell. In attempting to explain such anomalies, Hayes said that in each case he'd made a 'balanced judgement, dependent on the extent of the disruption'.[5] The answer did not explain why, for example, the cardigan was included in Category 1 and items that displayed far more blast damage were in Category 2.

Hayes also admitted under cross-examination that neither the black plastic fragments nor the circuit-board fragment PT/35b had been tested for explosive residues, and that he had concluded that they were involved in the explosion on the basis of their appearance alone. He added that the additional work required would not have been justified and that the chances of finding such residues were 'vanishingly small'.[6] Keen quizzed Hayes on his examination notes and in particular his failure to produce a sketch of PT/35b and the renumbering of the five subsequent pages.* Hayes was initially unable to explain the renumbering,[7] but, during re-examination by Campbell, suggested that it was because he had only numbered the pages after completing the notes and must have inadvertently used 51 twice.[8]

Keen also significantly undermined the Crown's claim that the primary suitcase was in the second layer of luggage within container AVE4041. He did so initially by mounting a robust challenge to the highly technical evidence concerning the stand-off distance given by experts from the AAIB and RAE.[9]†

Hayes confirmed that his examination suggested that the largest primary suitcase fragment, PI/911, was resting against the container's base. This claim was a notable omission from the joint report, which instead suggested that small fragments of foamed blue plastic material on PI/911's surface indicated that it had been touching a blue American Tourister case belonging to passenger Patricia Coyle. During his evidence in chief, Hayes told Campbell that the damage indicated that it had been lying on a relatively immoveable surface. Although he had initially believed that surface to be the base, he was satisfied that it was in fact a suitcase.[10] When asked by Keen why he did not record this view in his notes, he could only reply, 'I'm afraid I'm unable to offer an explanation. I can only imagine I was pressing on with the examination and where I may have had that thought in mind, chose, for no obvious reason to me now, not to put it to paper.'[11]

If Hayes was right, it stood to reason that there was at least a 50 per cent chance that the case lying on the base, underneath the primary suitcase, was the American Tourister; indeed, under cross-examination Hayes suggested that it was.[12] This left the Crown with a problem, because that case had arrived at Frankfurt on PA103A.[13] Since the entire base of AVE4041 was covered with luggage before

---

* See Chapter 8.
† The RAE had by then been subsumed within RARDE's successor organisation, the Defence Evaluation Research Agency. For further details of Keen's challenge, see Appendix 2.

its arrival, the only way it could have been in the bottom layer was if one of the cases originally placed there was moved. This supported the defence's suggestion that the primary suitcase may have been the brown hard-sided case seen by John Bedford lying on the base.

Keen also challenged Hayes on the Heathrow check-in bag PH/137, within which two metal fragments of the primary suitcase had been found. The joint report claimed that the two blackened holes in the bag were not bomb damage and that the two fragments appeared to have been placed there by hand rather than blasted in by the explosion.[14] Keen reminded Hayes that the draft joint report, produced in November 1990, described the bag as 'lightly explosion-damaged'.[15] Hayes admitted that he had not carried out any further examinations of the bag between producing the draft and signing off on the final report, and could not explain the change of view.[16] Feraday was given a similarly rough ride by Keen about the bag. He said he was unable to convince himself that it was explosively damaged, but acknowledged that the cuts might be penetration holes.[17]

His examination notes were also subjected to critical scrutiny. When cross-referenced with the Dexstar log, they indicated that he had examined items on dates when, according to the log, they were not at RARDE. In one instance the examination appeared to have occurred ten months after the item had been destroyed by the police and, in another, four months after it had been returned to the owner's relatives.[18]

There was further embarrassing cross-examination concerning the Toshiba radio-cassette player that housed the bomb. According to the joint forensic report, the device was a black RT-SF16. Keen read to Feraday the memo he'd written to SIO John Orr on 3 February 1989, in which he expressed himself 'completely satisfied' that the device was a white Toshiba RT8016 or RT8026.* Feraday admitted that, with hindsight, his language was 'probably a little bit strong'. He explained that he had been influenced by the presence among the Toshiba circuit-board fragments, AG/145, of some white plastic fragments. It was only after writing the memo that he had realised they appeared to come from a white area within the radio.[19] In fact there was only one very small fragment of white plastic found within

* See Chapter 8.

AG/145 and one similarly sized piece of off-white plastic. Given that it also contained a very small piece of black plastic, there was no obvious forensic reason for originally choosing a white device over a black one.[20] Furthermore, the joint report did not attribute the white fragments to the radio's interior and nothing in the other disclosed RARDE paperwork justified Feraday's claim.

Keen also challenged Feraday on how AG/145 had found its way into the small aluminium plate AG/117, which was originally riveted to the outside of AVE4041. He replied, 'I've long ago given up trying to predict exactly where particles will fly,' and agreed with Keen that the fragments must have somehow exited the container then forced their way behind the plate.[21] If an explosion could be so unpredictable then it was surely impossible to determine where the primary suitcase was positioned and what it contained.

The next of the major witnesses was Edwin Bollier. Unusually, the Crown and defence each sought to undermine his credibility while relying upon parts of his evidence. For the Crown it was essential to demonstrate that he had supplied 20 MST-13 timers to Libya. Bollier had confirmed this in 1990, but had thrown a spanner in the works three years later when he said he had also supplied at least two of the timers to the East German Stasi. Crown Counsel Alan Turnbull QC drew attention to the fact that his revelations about the Stasi timers had coincided with substantial expenses payments from the defendants' former Libyan lawyer Ibrahim Legwell.

The defence's best hope was to demonstrate that the Lockerbie fragment might have originated from one of the Stasi timers. Bollier insisted that it did, but also maintained that those timers contained grey/brown prototype boards, made by Mebo's technician Ulrich Lumpert, rather than the green ones used in the Libyan timers, which had been made for Mebo by its supplier Thüring. To further complicate matters, he now insisted that there were two circuit-board fragments; the one he was originally shown, he insisted, came from one of Lumpert's prototype boards, and the one shown to the Court was part of a green one. In the absence of any evidence to support this claim of cover-up, his testimony was more of a hindrance than a help to the defence. Fortunately for the defence he

232

was contradicted by Lumpert, who testified that he built the Stasi devices using the green Thüring boards.[22] In contrast to the Crown, the defence suggested to Bollier that his true loyalty had always lain with the Stasi and that he had only revealed the supply of timers to the Stasi when he learned that his former handlers had been interviewed by the BKA. David Burns QC suggested that his letter to the CIA, which implicated Libya, was written after the encounter in East Berlin, in January 1989, with the Stasi officers, one of whom referred to the Olympus timers that Bollier had taken to Libya the previous month.* Bollier denied it, and also refuted Burns's suggestion that the Stasi officer had actually referred to MST-13 devices, rather than Olympus ones. He repeated that he had in fact written the letter under the instruction of a mysterious intelligence agent who had appeared at Mebo's offices on the morning of 30 December 1988. He said the man ordered him to use a Spanish typewriter and had warned that, if he failed to write the letter, he would 'have to suffer the consequences'.[23] Burns accused Bollier of concocting the story and suggested he had written the letter to cover up for the Stasi and squeeze money out of the CIA.[24]

Keen's cross-examination ridiculed Bollier, repeatedly referring to him as 'a legitimate Swiss businessman' and suggesting the mystery intelligence agent story was straight out of the film *The Third Man*.[25] He concluded by asking, 'At the beginning of this investigation you were still a collaborator of the Ministry of State Security, you became drawn in to a web of cunning and deceit and lies, in which you are still enmeshed, Mr Bollier. Is that not the case?'[26] Bollier denied it but left the witness stand humiliated.

Three of Bollier's former Stasi handlers, 'Wenzel', 'Gerber' and 'Arnold' were called by the Crown. Wenzel was the most important, as it was he who had received timers from Bollier. He said there were around ten to twelve in total of at least two different types. He could not say for sure that they included MST-13s, but when shown a photograph of the decade-wheel switches that were used in MST-13s he said one or two of the devices had them.[27] He claimed he kept the timers as 'demonstration items', and that following the fall of the Berlin Wall in 1989 he destroyed them.[28] These claims did not ring

* See Chapter 4.

true; it would be understandable if he had destroyed terrorist devices and top secret files, but why bother with one or two timers, which, on their own, were entirely innocuous? Could it be that Wenzel knew very well that one of the timers had been used in a terrorist device? If so, then there would be all the more reason to destroy the other, or at least to pretend that he had.

During cross-examination Burns reminded Wenzel he had admitted to the BKA that, while working for the Stasi, he had built various IEDs for use outside East Germany, including a car bomb. He later became secretary to the head of Stasi's Department 22, which, as Burns pointed out, was subsequently revealed to have supplied various anti-Western terrorist groups, including the Red Army Faction and the Carlos Weinrich group. Wenzel did not deny making the bombs, but claimed he was unaware that the Department supported such groups until the Stasi's archives were made public after German reunification.[29] As for the fate of the MST-13s, he admitted that his superiors had access to the equipment store and that he could not be sure which of the various timers he had destroyed.[30] Under cross-examination by Keen, Wenzel acknowledged that Bollier had told him the timers he supplied contained circuit boards produced for Mebo by a small company in Zurich.[31] This was further vital confirmation that the Stasi timers incorporated green Thüring boards, rather than Lumpert's grey/brown prototypes.

Far less contentious than the supply of timers was the supply of Toshiba RT-SF16 radio-cassette players. Toshiba section manager Yoshihiro Miura confirmed to Campbell that 20,000 of the machines were sold to the Electronics General Company of Libya in November 1988 and that between October 1988 and March 1989 almost 76 per cent of sales were to Libya.[32] Campbell did not ask about the three years prior to October 1988, doubtless because he knew that over that period only 8,000 were sold to Libya, which was just 11 per cent of global sales, with 63,000 sold elsewhere.[33]

Tony Gauci entered the witness box on 11 July 2000. *(It was the first time that I had ever set eyes on the man who was to become central to my fate.)* Surprisingly, given his centrality to the case, his evidence lasted only a few hours. Although he had given his police statements in English, he opted to give his evidence in Maltese. If his understanding of English was not sufficient to testify in the language, it cast further doubt on the statements' reliability.

His examination in chief was remarkable for the number of occasions on which his testimony was helpful to the Crown case, when compared to his statements. He was originally certain that the clothes-buyer was at least 50 years old, at least six feet tall and well-built. Although he told Alastair Campbell QC that the man was 'under 60', he added, 'I don't have experience on height or age'.[34] He also now claimed that the man was 'below six feet', adding, 'I am not an expert on these things'. Gauci didn't need to be a good judge of age to know that the man was older than him and that Abdelbaset was considerably younger; moreover, it was ridiculous to claim that, as a clothes-shop proprietor, he lacked experience in judging people's sizes. He had told the police that he could not specify the date of the purchase, but was sure it was before the Christmas lights had been erected outside on Tower Road. However, he told Campbell that it was around a fortnight before Christmas and that the lights were being erected.[35] This made it far easier for the Crown to assert that the date was 7 December, when Abdelbaset was in Malta, rather than the previously most likely date, 23 November, when he was not. However, it contradicted his police statement of 10 September 1990, in which he said that the purchase took place in November,[36] and his defence precognition statement, in which he suggested that the date was 29 November.[37]

Campbell read Gauci's statement of 15 February 1991 and showed him the photospread that he had seen that day. The shop-keeper agreed that on that occasion he had picked out Abdelbaset's photograph. He was then asked about the *Focus* magazine article and confirmed that when he showed it to Inspector Scicluna he had told Scicluna that the photograph of Abdelbaset looked liked the clothes-buyer. Then came the trial's most farcical moment. Campbell asked Gauci to look around the courtroom to see if he could see the man who bought the clothing. He was hardly likely to look anywhere other than the dock, where, of course, he had a choice of just two. Pointing there, he said, 'He is the man on this side, he resembles him a lot.' When asked to which of the two he was referring, he said,

235

'Not the dark one . . . the one next to him,' meaning Abdelbaset.[38] This process, known as dock identification, is banned in most other Western countries for the obvious reason that a suspect's presence in the dock is highly prejudicial to an objective identification.* It was rendered all the more ridiculous by the fact that he had just been shown two photographs of Abdelbaset, the second of which identified him as one of the accused. Furthermore, by distinguishing Abdelbaset from the darker Lamin, he had strayed further from his original description of the purchaser as dark-skinned.

Gauci repeated the claim from his precognition statement that he had carried the clothes up the road to the man's taxi and that, as the man left, his brother Paul arrived.[39] This, of course, contradicted his police statements and was not supported by any of Paul's statements. The Crown did not call Paul to give evidence, perhaps realising that he might have undermined Tony's account. Abdelbaset's team opted not to call him because he might 'fill in the gaps' in Tony's evidence. They were particularly concerned that, according to DC John Crawford's statement of 14 December 1989, Paul had agreed that 7 December was the more likely date.[40†]

Bill Taylor's cross-examination of Gauci began by establishing that his memory of events would have been fresher at the time he first spoke to the police than it was currently.[41] When taken through his first and later police statements, he agreed that he had described the man as around 50. He also acknowledged that, when he picked out Abdelbaset's photo on 15 February 1991, he had said that the man was ten or more years older.[42]

It was apparent from some of Gauci's answers that the customer had mysteriously shrunk. When Taylor reminded him that in his first

---

* A number of other witnesses made dock identifications, among them Bollier's Mebo partner Erwin Meister. Under cross-examination he acknowledged that, prior to giving evidence, he had been given an important prompt: 'I knew that he was here, and I was told that he was sitting over there, so it wasn't really so difficult to identify him.' Asked if someone had told him where Abdelbaset would be sitting, he replied, 'When I arrived here, I was shown this room, and I was told who was sitting here . . . I think it was a lady who brought me here first. She showed me this room from the outside. She showed me the court.'
† See Chapter 5.

statement he had described the man as 'six foot or more in height', he claimed, falsely, 'I always said six foot, not more than six feet.'[43] It was put to him that in the same statement he had said that the 42-inch size jacket that the man bought was too small for him. In response, he stated, for the first time, that the jacket had an Italian-style waist, which he said 'were a bit tighter on the waist – not like the English; they used to be looser.'[44] Gauci had never before suggested that the jacket had this type of waist; however, the claim was rather undermined by his subsequent assertion that Harris tweed jackets were looser than the Italian style. It had, perhaps, slipped his mind that the jacket he had described selling was tweed and had the very English brand name of 'Anglia'.

Taylor read to Gauci sections of his statements in which he had said that, at the time of the incident, the Christmas lights were not up. He responded, 'I remember that they were already starting to put up the Christmas decorations', but went on to confuse the date of purchase with occasions on which the police had come to pick him up from the shop.[45]

Having got Gauci to confirm that the purchase had taken place 'midweek', Taylor attempted to define the term. He asked: 'Would another way of approaching it be this: that midweek entails being separate from the weekend; in other words, the shop would be open the day before and the day after? And that would give me a clue to what you mean.' Gauci replied, 'That's it. Exactly.'[46] Taylor did not ask Gauci directly whether the shop was open on the day after the purchase. Had he confirmed that it was, it would have ruled out 7 December, because 8 December was the public holiday of the Feast of the Immaculate Conception. The defence feared that, had the question been put directly, Gauci might have replied that the shop was closed, in which case 7 December was all but proven.[47] However, Gauci had never mentioned this in any of his 19 previous statements; therefore, had he done so now, he could have been robustly cross-examined on the omission.

The reluctance to tackle Gauci head-on was apparent throughout Taylor's cross-examination. It meant that key elements of his Crown evidence went unchallenged, in particular his claims that Abdelbaset resembled the purchaser, even though he described him as 'not the dark one'; that his brother Paul had arrived as the man left the shop; and that the purchase took place around a fortnight before Christmas about the time the lights were being put up. It also meant that the Court was unaware of numerous contradictions and anomalies within his police statements, for example, the fact that he originally was adamant that he did not sell the man shirts, but two years after the event changed his mind; that his descriptions of some of the items changed radically; and that he had never previously seen the customer, but later said he thought he may have visited the shop in 1987. Taylor also opted not to challenge Gauci's nonsensical claim that he had no experience of judging people's size and age. Neither did he enquire how often he had been exposed to media images of Abdelbaset prior to picking him out at the ID parade and in the dock. In particular, there was no questioning about the *Focus* magazine article, which, in addition to including Abdelbaset's photo, could have alerted Gauci to the weaknesses in the Crown case – weaknesses that his Crown evidence went some way to repairing. Had all this ammunition been deployed, then Gauci's credibility might have been destroyed, but, as it was, it remained largely intact.

Richard Keen's cross-examination was brief. He began by quizzing Gauci about the language in which he had conversed with the customer and about why his first statement of 1 September 1989 was not signed until the following day, but the answers he received were typically vague. More importantly, Keen then asked about the *Sunday Times* article, shown to him by his brother, which included a photograph of Mohamed Abu Talb. Crucially, Gauci confirmed that Talb 'resembles [the customer] a lot'.[48]

At the end of that day's proceedings I met with my legal team and told them that I was unhappy about Taylor's cross-examination. One of the team then told me not to worry, as Gauci came over as 'dodgy' and the judges would not believe him. The optimism proved to be misplaced. I have no doubt the defence tactics were the product of a lot of careful thought, but neither do I doubt that they backfired.

The Libyan supergrass Majid Giaka was due to give evidence in August 2000, but, in the event, his testimony was delayed by an extraordinary wrangle over the telex cables in which his CIA handlers described their meetings. It proved to be one of the most disgraceful episodes in the Crown Office's recent history.

Twenty-five of the cables were originally disclosed to the defence, all of which were heavily redacted. During November 1999 the defence conducted precognition interviews in relation to the cables with CIA agents with the assumed names Johnson, Stauton, Capp and McNair. Stauton stated that the defence had all the cables that existed, not merely a selection.[49]

The defence naturally wanted to know who was responsible for the redactions and what information had been blanked out. In January 2000, Procurator Fiscal Norman McFadyen wrote to confirm that the redactions had been carried out by the CIA in consultation with attorneys from the US Department of Justice. He said the Crown had not seen the unedited cables and that the redacted material was either irrelevant or potentially damaging to US national security.[50] The CIA then provided new copies of the cables in which the redactions were described using very general terms such as 'Operational details', 'Electronic addressing' and 'Administrative marking'.

On 21 August 2000, during a meeting on an entirely different subject, Alastair Campbell revealed to David Burns and John Beckett that McFadyen and Alan Turnbull QC had seen the unedited cables during a secret meeting at the US Embassy in The Hague on 1 June. Turnbull confirmed that he had seen the cables with a view to establishing that the Crown had met its legal duty to disclose all relevant material to the defence.

The following day Bill Taylor raised the issue with the Court. Describing it as 'a matter of some considerable importance', he submitted that without access to the complete cables the defendants would be denied their right to a fair trial, adding, 'I emphatically do not accept that what lies behind the blanked-out sections is of no interest to a cross-examiner . . . Further, I challenge the right of the Crown to determine for the Defence what is or is not of relevance to the Defence case.' He urged the Court to ask the Crown to obtain the complete copies from the CIA.[51]

In an unusual move, the Lord Advocate, Colin Boyd QC, attended the Court to respond to the submissions in person. He confirmed that McFadyen and Turnbull had seen what he described as 'largely unredacted cables', and assured the Court: 'it was clear from the context that they had no bearing at all on the cables themselves . . . While they may have been of significance to the Central Intelligence Agency, they had no significance whatsoever to the case.' He explained that the purpose of the exercise was to consider whether the blanked out passages might reflect on Giaka's credibility or otherwise undermine the Crown case. A further consideration was whether those sections might contain information that might be relevant to the special defence of incrimination. He said that on all of those matters Turnbull had concluded 'that there was nothing within the cables which bore on the defence case, either by undermining the Crown case or by advancing a positive case which was being made or may be made, having regard to the special case.' Lord MacLean asked Boyd if there was any reason why the defence should not be shown the complete cables. He replied: 'Well, my Lord, that is not a matter for me. I do not have control over these documents. They are in the control of the United States, and they are not here. So, I do not have authority to allow access to documents which are not documents which are under my control, or indeed in my jurisdiction.' He then stated categorically, 'there is nothing within these documents which relates to Lockerbie or the bombing of Pan Am 103 which could in any way impinge on the credibility of Mr Majid on these matters.'[52]

The reason the Lord Advocate had no control over the documents was that, at the CIA's insistence, McFadyen had signed a non-disclosure agreement, which read: 'I understand that the US government is providing me access to US national security information solely for the purpose of determining whether it contains any information which is exculpatory to the defendants in the case of the Lord Advocate v Abdelbaset Ali Mohmed Al Megrahi and Al Amin Khalifa Fhimah. Furthermore, I agree not to use this US national security information for lead purposes in furtherance of the Crown's case without the consent of the proper US [Government] official.'[53] The Crown had effectively, and secretly, ceded to the CIA the right to determine what information should, or should not, be disclosed in a Scottish court.

On 25 August the Crown handed over less redacted versions of the cables. The newly revealed passages included crucial information about Giaka, including that he had requested sham surgery to avoid national service, that he had admitted to being a shirker who tended to dodge JSO assignments and that he had claimed to be a relative of Libya's former monarch, King Idris. The passages also revealed that his handlers harboured grave doubts about the value of his intelligence and that by the end of August 1989 they were considering ceasing all financial support unless he could demonstrate his worth by the end of the year. Further sections referred to meetings between Giaka and his handlers that were not covered by the disclosed cables.[54]

Richard Keen QC told the Court it was 'abundantly clear' that much of the newly uncovered information was highly relevant to the defence and added, 'I frankly find it inconceivable that it could have been thought otherwise . . . Some of the material which is now disclosed goes to the very heart of material aspects of this case, not just to issues of credibility and reliability, but beyond.'[55] Put less elegantly, the Lord Advocate had seriously misled the Court.

Watching from the public gallery was a group of FBI agents, among them Hal Hendershot, who, along with Philip Reid, had interviewed Giaka when he fled Malta in July 1991. As a Crown witness who was yet to give evidence, his presence in court was highly irregular. Advocate Depute Campbell later told the Court that, although it was 'a matter for regret', the agents only entered the court in the late afternoon of 25 August and therefore only observed the procedural discussions concerning the Giaka cables. He explained: 'the rules to which they are used in the United States of America are that witnesses are not permitted to come into court during the testimony of other witnesses, but may be permitted to come into court during procedural matters.' However, this begged the questions: how did they know the procedural hearing was taking place? And why did neither Crown nor court officials stop them? Campbell could say only: 'I don't really know how they came to be in court. They should have been better shepherded, I suppose . . . I think anybody in the building would know it was a procedural hearing that day.'[56]

On 29 August Keen petitioned the Court for letters of request to be sent the US authorities, under the terms of a 1986 mutual legal assistance treaty, seeking all documents relevant to Giaka. He pointed out that foreign states could not assert any kind of privilege over UK court proceedings; furthermore, under the treaty's terms, the United States government was obliged to hand over any relevant documents requested by the Crown.[57] The judges rejected the motion and again requested the Crown to use its best endeavours to obtain further information from the CIA. After a three-week adjournment, the Lord Advocate informed the Court that, following the review exercise, he was handing over 36 further redacted cables to the defence.[58] So much for CIA officer Stauton's claim that the 25 original cables were all that existed.

Once again, the newly disclosed details were highly relevant to the defence case. Among other things, they demonstrated that Giaka was specifically asked about Lockerbie, but was unable to provide any information, and that the CIA concluded that the bombing 'may be a non-subject with his colleagues'. A number of the cables made further references to Giaka's requests for sham surgery and some betrayed the CIA's increasing impatience with what one described as his 'demanding nature'. Another revealed that Giaka lied to his handlers about returning to Libya to seek a job and that they eventually considered him to be 'at best . . . a cooperative contact'.[59]

In view of the CIA's concealing of evidence helpful to the defence, Taylor requested that the Agency be urged to hand over, not only the Giaka cables, but all the information it held about Lockerbie. He argued: 'It is perfectly obvious, in our submission, that the Lord Advocate is not master in his own house. It's obvious that he can only disclose to the Defence material of which he is in possession. And it's equally plain that those who have been determining relevancy outside the law of Scotland have made fatal errors of judgement in important areas of direct relevance to this trial, and to its fairness.'[60]

The defence again petitioned the Court for letters of request to be sent the US authorities, but were again denied. To this day it is not known what information lies behind the redactions and what other important documents are buried in the CIA's files.

Nevertheless, there was sufficient in the new material to demonstrate that one of the Crown's key witnesses was a money-grabbing fantasist. When Giaka finally took to the witness stand on 26 September 2000 it was as a lamb to the slaughter. Campbell did his best to rescue the situation during his Crown evidence, but Taylor and Keen's cross-examinations were appropriately brutal. As Taylor systematically exposed the Libyan's deceptions, he noted that the witness kept turning to the US Department of Justice officials seated with the Crown team, as if seeking their help. 'You needn't look at the Crown benches,' Taylor warned, 'You'll not get any assistance there, Mr Giaka.'[61] Keen asked Giaka how he knew Libya's leader was a mason. When he refused to give a straight answer Keen repeated the question five times, until he answered, 'I knew that from a person, but I cannot divulge the name of that person. The person is in Libya, and for security considerations, I cannot mention the name of that person.' Keen suggested that he write the name on a piece of paper and pass it to the judges, but following a Crown objection, the judges declined the proposal. Keen resumed by asking how he had discovered that Foreign Minister Bishari and Maltese President de Marco were also masons, and in each case Giaka claimed to have forgotten.[62] The final exchange verged on cruelty:

Q. While you've been in America, Mr Giaka, have you managed to dip into any of the gems of American literature, such as the short-story writers like James Thurber?

A. I have had – read some books, but not all authors.

Q. Have you encountered someone called Mitty, first name Walter?

A. I do not recall.

Q. No further questions, My Lords.[63]

Giaka had been destroyed, but the episode left a very nasty taste. The CIA and the Department of Justice had suppressed evidence that had a direct bearing upon his credibility and, by extension, the fairness of the trial. Subsequently the head of Scotland's prosecution service and two of his most senior officers, whether deliberately or not, had contrived to withhold that evidence from the defence and in the process the Lord Advocate seriously misled the Court. Had a witness acted in this way, he or she might have been subjected to a criminal investigation, yet all those involved remained untouched and the matter was barely reported by the media.

In attempting to prove the Maltese suitcase theory, the Crown relied principally on the bomb-damaged Maltese clothes and the documents from Frankfurt Airport, which supposedly indicated the transfer of a bag from Air Malta flight KM180 to PA103A. Various witnesses were called to explain the Frankfurt baggage system, Pan Am's loading procedures and the related paperwork.

The Crown's case required the KIK computer printout to be cross-referenced with the worksheet for coding station 206. The printout showed that at 13.07 an unaccounted-for bag was coded in to the baggage transit system at station 206, and the worksheet indicated that between 13.04 and 13.10 or 13.16 the coders Mehmet Candar and Yassar Koca were dealing with bags from KM180. Candar gave evidence, but, strangely, the Crown did not call Koca, even though it was he who had actually completed the worksheet.

The Crown was reliant on the accuracy of the timings recorded on the documents. During cross-examination by Jack Davidson QC, Candar, the deputy head of baggage-handling Joachim Koscha and interline writer* Andreas Schreiner all testified that employees based the timings on their own wristwatches and unsynchronised clocks.[64] The defence also adduced evidence that, using the same cross-referencing technique, it was possible to demonstrate that an unaccounted-for bag from Lufthansa flight LH1071 from Warsaw had been loaded onto PA103A.[65]

Davidson's cross-examination of Koscha considered the evidence relating to the four wagonloads of baggage that had been unloaded from Lufthansa flight LH669 from Damascus, one and a half of which were not accounted for on the corresponding coding-station worksheets. It also addressed the smoking suitcase, which appeared to have been reported at coding station 207 at around the time that LH669 bags were being processed there.[66] Given that bags from KM180 were being processed at the next-door station 206 at almost exactly the same time, it raised the possibility that some of the 'missing' LH669 luggage was transferred to station 206, and coded in

---

* Interline writers were responsible for recording the number of wagonloads of baggage and the flight number of all the incoming transfer baggage. They then allocated the wagons to individual coding stations. See also Appendix 3.

Wrecked cockpit of Pan Am 103, Maid of the Seas *(© Newsquest (Herald & Times). Licensor www.scran.ac.uk).*

Luggage container AVN7511. It was next to the luggage container holding the bomb which destroyed Pan Am 103.

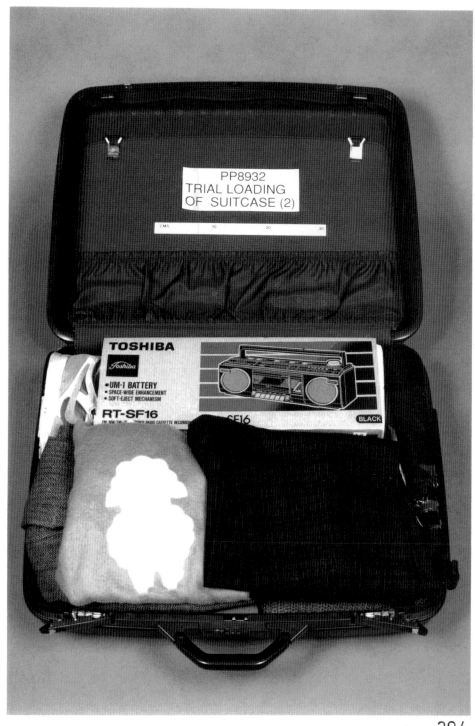

394

How the primary suitcase may have been loaded, according to the RARDE forensic experts.

PP8932 PR/105(part) Control Sample Toshiba RT–SF 16

Toshiba RT-SF16 radio-cassette player.

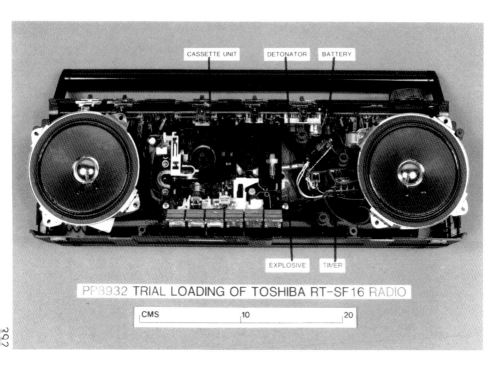

| CASSETTE UNIT | DETONATOR | BATTERY |

EXPLOSIVE TIMER

PP8932 TRIAL LOADING OF TOSHIBA RT–SF16 RADIO

Mock-up radio-cassette bomb.

MST-13 timer

33L

(Left) Circuit-board fragment PT/35B. (Right) PT/35B matched to control sample

Abdelbaset's student identity card

The photospread shown to Tony Gauci, more than two years after Lockerbie,
when he picked out Abdelbaset's photo (right of middle row).

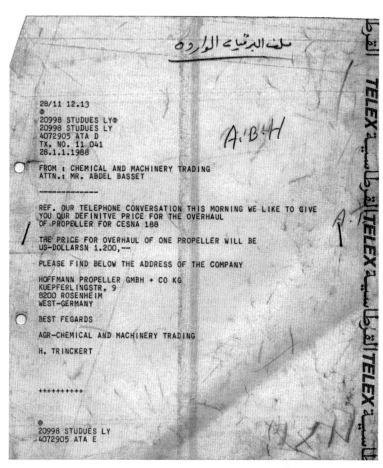

ملف البرقيات الواردة

28/11 12.13
⊕
20998 STUDUES LY⊕
20998 STUDUES LY
4072905 ATA D
TX. NO. 11 041
28.1.1.1988

A.B.H

FROM : CHEMICAL AND MACHINERY TRADING
ATTN.: MR. ABDEL BASSET

REF. OUR TELEPHONE CONVERSATION THIS MORNING WE LIKE TO GIVE
YOU OUR DEFINITVE PRICE FOR THE OVERHAUL
OF PROPELLER FOR CESNA 188

THE PRICE FOR OVERHAUL OF ONE PROPELLER WILL BE
US-DOLLARSN 1.200,--

PLEASE FIND BELOW THE ADDRESS OF THE COMPANY

HOFFMANN PROPELLER GMBH + CO KG
KUEPFERLINGSTR. 9
8200 ROSENHEIM
WEST-GERMANY

BEST FEGARDS

AGR-CHEMICAL AND MACHINERY TRADING

H. TRINCKERT

++++++++++

⊕
20998 STUDUES LY
4072905 ATA E

0414072905+

4072905 ATA D
ZCZC
TRIPOLI IN   30/1/1988   21/20
TO:- CHEMICAC MARKETING
FROM:- ABH COMPANY
ATTN MR. H. TRINCKERT.
REF TO YOUR TLX NO. 01.073
DATED 25.01.88 CONCERNING
THE VISIT OF YOUR ENG. FOR
THE COMPUTER PLS INFORM
EXPECTED DATE OF HIS TRIP
TO MEET AND ASSIST ALSO
VISA WILL BE PROVIDED UPON
HIS ARRIVAL.
ALSO YOUR KINDLY REQUESTED
TO INFORM IF YOURSELF READY
TO MEET PEOPLE OF SOAP
COMPANY AND THE ENGINEERS
OF AGRICULTURE MATERIAC.
BEST RGDS.
BASET.
COL/TLX NO .01.073
DATED 25.01.88
NNNN
⊕

*Telexes sent to and from Abdelbaset when he was a partner in the Libyan
company ABH. It was allegedly a JSO front, but he insists it was a legitimate
trading company.*

$4,000,000

REWARD

Diplomatic Security Service

On 12/21/88, Pan Am Flight 103 from London to New York exploded over Lockerbie, Scotland killing all 259 on board and 11 more people on the ground. A massive investigation over the next three years culminated in the indictments of two suspects, who are both Libyan nationals and intelligence officers.

Abdel Basset Ali Al-Megrahi, one of the two suspects, is believed to be in Libya. The Libyan Government, against which the United Nations has invoked resolutions and sanctions, has been unwilling to turn Al-Megrahi over to the United Kingdom or United States for trial.

The United States Department of State and the U.S. airline industry are offering a reward of up to $4,000,000 for information leading to the apprehension and prosecution of Al-Megrahi. The U.S. Government also can provide for the protection of identity and the possibility of relocation for persons and their families furnishing such information. If you have information about Al-Megrahi or the Pan Am 103 bombing, contact authorities or the nearest U.S. Embassy or consulate. In the United States, call your local office of the Federal Bureau of Investigation or 1-800-HEROES-1, or write to:

HEROES
Post Office Box 96781
Washington, D.C. 20090-6781
U.S.A.

ABDEL BASSET ALI AL-MEGRAHI

DESCRIPTION

Date of birth:	April 1, 1952
Place of birth:	Tripoli, Libya
Height:	Approximately 5'8"
Weight:	Approximately 190 lbs
Hair:	Black curly, clean shaven
Eyes:	Dark brown
Complexion:	Light brown
Sex:	Male
Nationality:	Libyan
Occupation:	Formerly Chief of Airline Security, Libyan Árab Airlines, in Malta
Aliases:	Abd Al Basset Al Megrahi, Abdelbaset Ali Mohmed Al Megrahi, Mr. Baset, Ahmed Khalifa Abdusamad

Program developed and funded by Air Line Pilots Association and Air Transport Association in coordination with U.S. Department of State

US government reward poster.

DISCRIPTION:- *a was an old ugr.*
I would describe this man as
follows.

He was about 6' foot or more in height.
He had a 'big chest' and a large
head. He was well built but he
was not fat or with a big stomach.
His hair was very 'Black'. . . . .

56 Malta found. He then
walked out to stop with the
'Umberella' which he opened up as
it was raining. 	 	 	 	

Extracts from Tony Gauci's first statement to police on 13 September 1989, ten months after the events he describes.

Radio Ship MEBO II

Studio 3

Edwin Bollier in the early 1970s, when his company Mebo sold its pirate radio ship to the Libyan government.

5. ◼◼◼◼ CAVEAT ON COOPERATION: DURING COURSE OF DISCUSSIONS ◼◼◼◼◼◼◼◼◼ BECAME SOMEWHAT DEFENSIVE, AND CLARIFIED HIS CONDITIONS FOR COOPERATING ◼◼◼◼◼◼◼◼◼◼◼◼ STATED THAT HE NEVER INTENDED TO BECOME A "SPY ◼◼◼◼◼◼◼ AND THAT HE DESPISED SPYS, AND THAT WAS WHY HE WANTED ◼◼◼◼◼◼◼◼◼ ESO. ◼◼ STATED CLEARLY, AND WITH EMOTION, THAT HE WILL ONLY REPORT ON TERRORIST-RELATED INTENTIONS AND ACTIVITIES OF THE ESO AND THAT HE WILL NEVER REPORT ON ROUTINE GOVERNMENT OR MILITARY DEVELOPMENTS. ◼◼ STATED THAT HIS INTENTIONS HAVE BEEN CLEAR FROM THE BEGINNING AND HE WAS NEVER GOING TO CHANGE.

5. P/1'S CAVEAT ON COOPERATION: DURING COURSE OF DISCUSSIONS ON ◼◼◼◼◼◼ P/1 BECAME SOMEWHAT DEFENSIVE, AND CLARIFIED HIS CONDITIONS FOR COOPERATING WITH ◼◼◼◼◼◼ P/1 STATED THAT HE NEVER INTENDED TO BECOME A "SPY" FOR ◼◼◼◼◼ AND THAT HE DESPISED SPYS, AND THAT WAS WHY HE WANTED OUT OF THE ESO. P/1 STATED CLEARLY, AND WITH EMOTION, THAT HE WILL ONLY REPORT ON TERRORIST-RELATED INTENTIONS AND ACTIVITIES OF THE ESO AND THAT HE WILL NEVER REPORT ON ROUTINE GOVERNMENT OR MILITARY DEVELOPMENTS. P/1 STATED THAT HIS INTENTIONS HAVE BEEN CLEAR FROM THE BEGINNING AND HE WAS NEVER GOING TO CHANGE.

6. ASSESSMENT: IT IS CLEAR THAT P/1 WILL NEVER BE THE PENE-TRATION OF THE ESO THAT WE HAD ANTICIPATED. P/1 IS NOW OUT OF THE ESO AND HAS NO INTENTION TO ATTEMPT TO REGAIN DIRECT ACCESS. UNFORTUNATELY, IT APPEARS THAT OUR ASSISTING HIM IN SCAM SURGERY ON HIS ARM TO AVOID MILITARY SERVICE HAS HAD THE REVERSE RESULT THAT WE HAD INTENDED. IT HAS ALSO ALLOWED HIM TO AVOID FURTHER SERVICE WITH THE ESO, P/1'S TRUE INTENTION FROM THE BEGINNING. P/1 HAS NEVER BEEN A TRUE STAFF MEMBER OF THE ESO AND AS HE STATED AT THIS MEETING, HE WAS COOPTED WITH WORKING WITH THE ESO AND HE NOW WANTS NOTHING TO DO WITH THEM OR THEIR ACTIVITIES. P/1 WOULD PREFER TO

Extracts of one of the CIA cables concerning the key Crown witness Majid Giaka. At the top is the version originally provided to Abdelbaset's defence team and below it the version that was eventually disclosed, in which vital information asbout Giaka is revealed.

Hafez Dalkamoni, the leader of the PFLP-GC's West German cell.

PFLP-GC bomb-maker Marwan Khreesat.

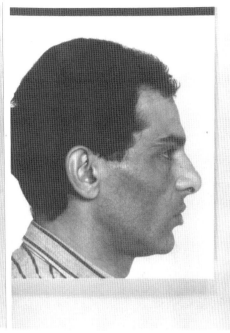

Mohamed Abu Talb, the Swedish-based terrorist with links to both the PFLP-GC's West German cell and Malta.

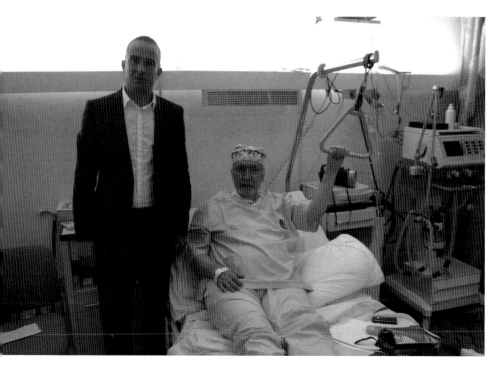

Abdelbaset and John Ashton.

Abdelbaset with Nelson Mandela.

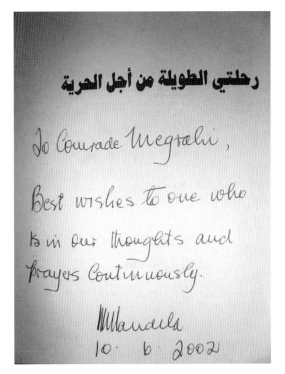

رحلتي الطويلة من أجل الحرية

To Comrade Megrahi,

Best wishes to one who
is in our thoughts and
prayers Continuously.

Mandela
10. 6. 2002

Inscription written by Mandela in Abdelbaset's copy of Long Walk to Freedom

without being recorded.* The records indicated that, prior to being processed, the LH669 luggage was sent to be checked by Customs. When cross-examined by Burns, Koscha said that, prior to being sent to Customs, bags had to be reloaded into a single layer, which meant that a full wagon might be reloaded onto two or even three wagons. Although this explained why the coding-station worksheets sometimes recorded more wagonloads from certain flights than had actually been unloaded from the flights,[67] it did not explain the reverse phenomenon, which had been observed with the wagons from LH669.

A further weakness in the Crown's Frankfurt evidence was that the KM180 bag – if it ever existed – would have been X-rayed prior to loading. The X-ray operator, Kurt Maier, was too ill to attend court, so the Crown instead called FAA investigator Naomi Saunders, who had interviewed him a fortnight after the bombing. He told her he had been trained to spot plastic explosives and was vigilant for objects such as radios, tape recorders and other equipment with wires, although, for no obvious logical reason, he said that he would not be suspicious of devices that had a plug. He insisted that there were no explosives in any of the bags that he had X-rayed.[68] Although the X-ray operators' formal training was poor, Maier's supervisor, Oliver Koch, described him as a careful operator who had seen the so-called Toshiba warning that was circulated to airlines in late 1988 and was therefore aware of the need to pay particular attention to radio-cassette players.[69†]

The Crown did not lead evidence to account for how the primary suitcase might have been loaded onto KM180 at Luqa Airport. Air Malta's General Manager for ground operations, Wilfred Borg, described the airline's baggage procedures, in particular the

* See Chapter 6 and Appendix 3.
† *I was keen that Maier's claims be put to the test and asked my defence team if it would be possible to bring an X-ray machine into court in order to demonstrate to the judges what a bomb would look like when compared to innocent items. In the event, however, this did not happen. At my first appeal, in January 2002, the Lord Justice General, Lord Cullen, appeared to pick up on the question of what would be visible on an X-ray machine, asking Bill Taylor QC whether any X-ray photographs of a reconstructed Toshiba radio-cassette bomb were available to the Trial Court.*

system of physical reconciliation, which required the head loader to count the number of hold bags to ensure it matched the number checked in. He explained that the load plan and the ramp progress sheet for KM180 each recorded a total of 55 bags, which tallied with the check-in records.[70] Taken together, these facts appeared to rule out the possibility that there was a rogue bag on the flight; however, Borg acknowledged to Alan Turnbull QC that human error may have allowed one to slip through. He also accepted it was possible for an insider to subvert the system, but added, 'It's the level of difficulty of achieving that possibility. One can also rob a bank.'[71]

The Heathrow evidence largely focused on the loading of AVE4041. The most substantial problem for the Crown was loader John Bedford's recollection of a brown hard-sided suitcase lying on the base of the container well before PA103A arrived from Frankfurt. Understandably, Bedford could no longer remember the episode, but testified that his police statements were truthful.[72] If, as the Crown claimed, the primary suitcase was in the second layer of luggage, then, for the Bedford's case to have been the primary one, the luggage must have been rearranged. Bedford's colleague Terence Crabtree told the Court that this would not have been unusual.[73] Significantly, the Crown did not attempt to rule out the Bedford suitcase by linking it to a particular individual.

By contrast, they went to some lengths to exclude Khaled Jaafar as the owner of the primary suitcase. Evidence was heard that he had checked in two bags and that only two of his bags were found at the crash-site; however, as Taylor pointed out, both were small hold-alls, of a size that would normally be permitted as hand luggage.[74] PA103A passenger Yasmin Siddique confirmed that she had stood directly behind Jaafar in the passport queue at Frankfurt Airport and said she could not recall seeing him with any bags. If he had no bags at that point, then it was more likely that the two found at Lockerbie had been checked in. However, during cross-examination by Taylor, Siddique agreed that her attention was focused on Jaafar's very nervous and strange behaviour, rather than on whether he had hand luggage. She also agreed that, had she taken a transatlantic flight, she would have taken hand luggage.[75]

The Crown also called Jaafar's friend Hassan El-Salheli, with whom he'd stayed while in Dortmund. Turnbull asked him to read out a 1989 BKA statement in which he had described being present when Jaafar had packed his bags. He had claimed that there were only two small bags and had given an unusually precise description of their contents.* Taylor also revisited the BKA interviews, drawing out some of the peculiarities in his account, before putting it to him that he was 'a fairly lowly foot soldier in a fairly big operation'. He claimed not to know what Taylor meant. Keen pressed him on the role of Naim Ali Ghannam in the purchase of Jaafar's flight, the late change of booking, the collection and delivery of the ticket, and the photographs taken at Dortmund railway station on the morning of Jaafar's departure.[76]

On Monday 9 October 2000 the Lord Advocate returned to court with an important announcement. Five days earlier the Crown had received 'certain information from a foreign country, not the United States, which is relevant to the evidence in this case', and that, as a result, 'Certain inquiries were carried out at a very senior level on Friday, and the matter reviewed by me with Crown counsel and others over this weekend.' He described the matters as being of 'some complexity and considerable sensitivity', and said that they related to the special defence of incrimination. He added that it was likely, though not certain, that the information would eventually be disclosed to the defence.[77] The Court granted Boyd a motion for a seven-day adjournment while the matters were further explored. On 17 October he reported that the Crown was still not in a position to release the new evidence to the defence and sought another adjournment until 23 October.[78] On the morning of the 23rd the information was finally handed to the defence. It included a number of documents and the names of five individuals who were described as being 'presently in another European state'.[79] The Court granted the defence a further adjournment until 7 November to carry out their own inquiries.[80]

The five turned out to be relatives and associates of Mobdi Goben, the PFLP-GC member who ran the safe house in Yugoslavia which was raided in the wake of the Autumn Leaves raids. He had evaded arrest and had died in 1996. The 'European state' was

---

* See Chapter 6.

Norway, where the five, who included his wife, Miroslava, and son, Samir, had sought asylum.

The key document was a lengthy memorandum, which Goben had dictated shortly before his death. Much of it described his background in the group, the various members whom he encountered and how he had established its Yugoslavian cell. However, the latter part provided a highly detailed account of the Lockerbie plot, which was very much at odds with the Crown case. A number of those arrested in the Autumn Leaves raids were also implicated in the plot, including Hafez Dalkamoni and Abdel Fattah Ghadanfar (whose involvement obviously came to an end with their detention) and Salah Kwekes, a.k.a. Ramzi Diab. Goben said that, following the German raids, he had helped coordinate the attack from Yugoslavia. He said Marwan Khreesat was not the group's only bomb-maker and described personally smuggling a bomb from Syria, which had been designed by a man called Awad, who was based in a Palestinian refugee camp in Damascus.

Most importantly, the memorandum claimed the operation's lynchpin was PFLP-GC member Abu Elias, who had planted the bomb on an unsuspecting Khaled Jaafar. Goben reported that, according to Miroslava, Elias and Jaafar met in Belgrade in early December 1988. This contradicted the El-Salheli brothers' claim that Jaafar did not leave Dortmund between 8 November and the day of his death. The young man's American passport might have helped prove or disprove this, but, although he had it at Frankfurt Airport,[81] it was supposedly never recovered from the crash-site.

Much of the memorandum's detail tallied with facts uncovered by the BKA and with information revealed to the FBI by Khreesat. For example, both Moben and Khreesat said that they had met in Belgrade in the summer of 1988, together with Dalkamoni.* Crucially, Khreesat had also suggested that Elias was central to the group's plans, and claimed that, four days before the Autumn Leaves raids, Dalkamoni told him Elias had arrived in West Germany. He recalled Dalkamoni also saying that Elias was an expert in airline security and he believed that Dalkamoni was driving them to meet Elias when they were arrested on 26 October 1988.[82]

* Khreesat said the meeting was in September.

Goben said that Abu Elias was the *nom de guerre* of a relative of Ahmed Jibril. He did not name him, but the Crown informed the defence that there was evidence to suggest that he could be Mahmoud Almari,* a Syrian living in a particular Western country.

On 25 and 26 October 2000 Alastair Duff and Eddie MacKechnie interviewed the five new witnesses, plus one other, in an Oslo hotel. With one exception, the lawyers considered all to be disappointing. None had first-hand knowledge of the bombing, and some of the details relayed by Miroslava Goben in particular were at odds with her late husband's account. One of the six named 'Almari' as Elias and five of them confirmed that 'Almari' was a relative of PFLP-GC leader Ahmed Jibril, but did not claim that he was Abu Elias. The clearest point to emerge was that Goben hated Jibril, who had treated him very badly following his return to Syria at the end of 1988. Whatever the truth of its allegations, the memorandum was obviously an act of revenge.[83]

The only one of the six whom the lawyers considered a potential defence witness was a man who used the alias Rabbieh. He claimed to be a 20-year veteran of the PFLP-GC and to have been responsible for its military division's finances. He said Goben told him the group was responsible for Lockerbie and that he (Goben) had personally arranged the bomb. More importantly, Rabbieh said he recalled from the group's financial records that someone called Khaled Jaafar had been paid substantial sums by the group. Although he could not recall meeting him, or confirm that he was the same Khaled Jaafar, he said he had been told that this person had been duped into carrying the bomb.[84] He said, although he had met 'Almari' only once, he would be very surprised if he was Abu Elias.

The week after the Oslo interviews, the Crown informed the defence that in May 1987 'Almari' deposited $5,850 in Thomas Cook traveller's cheques into his bank account. The cheques had been bought a few days earlier by a Mr Hafez Hussein from the Société Bancaire Arabe in Limassol, Cyprus.[85] Hafez Hussein was one of the names used by Dalkamoni.[86] On 3 November the Crown wrote again to inform the defence that in December 1990 an FBI handwriting analyst had compared a photocopy of Hafez Hussein's signature with

* Mahmoud Almari is an alias used for the purposes of this book.

a photocopy of a document believed to bear Dalkamoni's signature. Although it had not been possible to make a definitive comparison, some of the common characteristics indicated they might have been written by the same person.[87]

On 31 October Duff and MacKechnie interviewed 'Almari', who attended the meeting voluntarily with his lawyer. MacKechnie noted: 'Appeared very nervous. Was evasive at times . . . Very suspicious character but there could be good reasons why he is so nervous and evasive.' 'Almari' declined to answer whether or not he was a relative of Jibril's, and also would not say whether his father was a senior member of the group. He said he could not recall receiving the traveller's cheques 13 years earlier and did not know who Hafez Hussein was. He said Dalkamoni was a well-known figure in Syria, but claimed never to have met him. He denied ever having used the name Abu Elias, or to have heard of Khaled Jaafar and Mobdi Goben. He said he returned to Syria many times in the years between 1982 and 1988. His diary and the passport of his adopted country, which was issued in 1988, indicated that he obtained a Syrian visa on 19 December 1988 and flew there, via Frankfurt, on 30 and 31 December.[88] He said he had also visited Yugoslavia and had friends there. He did not bring his Syrian passport to the meeting, but said he would look for it and get back to MacKechnie. An entry in his diary suggested he had met with two FBI agents on 15 August 1988 at their instigation.[89] He admitted meeting the FBI frequently throughout 1988, 1989 and thereafter, but in Duff and MacKechnie's view he did not adequately explain the purpose and nature of the discussions.[90]

On 1 November the defence wrote to the Crown to ask what contact US agencies might have had with 'Almari'. The following day an Assistant Procurator Fiscal provided the following very interesting reply: 'I understand that [he] was seen by the FBI during the period 1988/1989 when he was considered to be someone who may have had information to impart on a number of matters. What may be of interest to you is the fact that [he] was seen by the FBI on 23 January 1989 and was asked specifically if he had any information to impart in relation to the Lockerbie bombing. He had none but advised that he would contact the FBI if he became aware of any such information. On the same occasion, he was also provided with the identities and aliases of the suspects arrested by the BKA in the "Autumn Leaves" operation. He advised that, although a few of the family names were familiar, he did not recognise any specific individual . . . I have no information that [he] may have had any contact with any other "agency" although, on a general note, it would be highly unusual for such information to be disclosed in any event.'[91] Why had the FBI thought to ask him about Lockerbie just a month after the bombing? Was it simply because they knew – or believed – that he was related to Jibril?

On 7 November, during a closed meeting in the judges' chambers, defence counsel sought the Court's authority for letters of request to be sent to Syria, Iran, Sweden and the USA. Having heard submissions from both sides, the Court refused to grant the letters with the exception of one to Syria seeking a complete copy of the original memorandum, as a few pages were thought to be missing. On 5 December, the Court granted a defence motion to protect the anonymity of Miroslava and Samir Goben if they were called to give evidence, but, in the event, they were not.

During November and December MacKechnie made repeated requests, via the lawyer of 'Mahmoud Almari', for a copy of his Syrian passport, but to no avail. On 8 January 2001, the Lord Advocate informed the Court that the Syrian authorities had refused to cooperate with the letter of request. The defence case closed later that day without any reference being made to the Goben evidence.[92]

While the Goben saga was unfolding, 10 November 2000 saw the appearance of the only bona fide terrorist to set foot in the courtroom. Mohamed Abu Talb had been transported from the Swedish prison in which he was serving a life sentence for the 1985 Amsterdam and Copenhagen bombings. It was perhaps the only occasion in Scottish legal history on which a convicted murderer was invited by the Crown to deny his role in another murder for which he was once the prime suspect. He originally came under suspicion following his brother-in-law Mohamed Mougrabi's trip to Neuss shortly before the Autumn Leaves raids. It was then discovered that in October 1988 he had been in Cyprus at the same time as Dalkamoni and had then travelled to Malta, where, among other things, he had obtained clothes, which he took back to Sweden.

Campbell's examination of Talb did not gloss over his conviction, nor did it duck the fact that he had seen active duty with the Palestinian People's Struggle Front and had a number of false passports. The most important questioning concerned his trips to Cyprus and Malta in October 1988. He claimed the Cyprus trip was to recuperate after being stabbed in the leg, adding 'and maybe I wanted to meet some of my relatives who were in Cyprus'. He then travelled to Malta, he said, because he was hoping to make his way to his home country Egypt, via Libya, to visit his sick mother. He had wanted to travel from Cyprus to Libya, he said, but was unable to get a Libyan entry visa, so he called his friend Abdelsalem Abu Nada in Malta, who had promised to help him. He related the strange story of how, when he arrived at Rome Airport, on his way from Cyprus to Malta, he met some Libyan people who lent him money to buy an LAA ticket to fly directly to Libya. He claimed that Libyan security staff then refused to allow him on the flight, so he reverted to his original plan. Campbell showed him the Maltese entry and exit stamps on his Swedish travel document, which indicated that he arrived on 19 October 1988 and left on the 26th.

Taylor's cross-examination began with an exploration of Talb's background, largely based on what he had told the police when interviewed in May 1990. Strangely, he denied certain things that he had said then; for example, that in 1968 he had attended a six-month commando training course in Armenia. He also refused to confirm facts that he had stated in 1990, for example that in 1969 and 1970 he spent 18 months in the Soviet Union learning how to use SAM-3 rockets. He claimed that, following his move to Sweden in 1983, he ceased involvement in the Palestinian struggle. Asked how he squared this with his conviction for the 1985 bombings, he denied involvement in the attacks, adding: 'I was convicted on one charge only, a bombing in Denmark of a Jewish site, not of anything else. I was convicted even though I was not there, and I did not confess to the crime.' He also denied that in 1985 he had pressured another brother-in-law, Mahmoud Mougrabi, into travelling to Syria to learn bomb-making. He did not deny that Mahmoud made the trip, but said he had not influenced him to do so. He also denied knowing that Mahmoud had returned with $5,000 dollars, and detonators concealed in the handle of his bag.

The cross-examination raked over numerous circumstantial details, such as the terrorist conviction of his sister-in-law Rashida Mougrabi, and the fact that, on the day of the Lockerbie bombing, four people named Mougrabi flew on flight CY1364 from Cyprus to Heathrow.* Talb acknowledged that one of his aliases was Intekam, meaning 'he who takes revenge', but denied ever being known as Elias, or being involved with the PFLP-GC. He admitted that he had rented a video store from a man called Hamid al-Wani, whom the Swedish intelligence service believed was the group's commander in central Sweden, and whose brother Sadi was one of its founders. He claimed, unconvincingly, that he never discussed politics with al-Wani, or with anyone else.

Taylor asked about the phone call that he had made to Mohamed Mougrabi the day he returned from Malta. Mougrabi had not long since returned from Neuss, where he had been sent by Talb's close associate Martin Imandi – a.k.a. Imad Chabaan – to collect his brother Jehad Chaaban and their cousin Samir Ourfali. Like Dalkamoni and Khreesat, the pair had been staying in Neuss courtesy of Hashem Abassi. He said the call was purely social and denied that the two trips were connected. He admitted that he had met Mohamed's two passengers, along with Imandi, at Hamid al-Wani's café two days later, but again claimed the occasion was social.

Talb said his October 1988 stay in Cyprus was to visit a relative and old friends. When asked about Dalkamoni's overlapping presence on the island, he said, 'I was never with Dalkamoni anywhere in the world. I do not know this person.' The subsequent trip to Malta, he repeated, was because he hoped to get home to Egypt via Libya, as he had discovered that his mother was ill. Taylor reminded him that in 1990 he told the police that he visited the island to do business with his friends Abdel and Hashem Salem Abu Nada. He did not deny it, but maintained that his primary concern was to see his

---

* Also on that flight was Lockerbie victim Daniel O'Connor, who was a security officer based at the US Embassy in Cyprus and was believed to be a colleague of Major Charles McKee.

mother. The border between Libya and Egypt was at that time officially closed, but he said he would have had no problem arranging a crossing. The journey he claimed to have been planning would have involved three flights, a 250-mile boat trip and a very long drive. This seemed strange, given that a similar length boat trip could have taken him directly from Cyprus to Egypt. Talb agreed that he had told the police that he avoided this simpler journey because he feared being arrested by the Egyptian security police. In fact crossing from Libya into Egypt would have been far riskier, as the very poor relations between the countries meant the border was heavily militarised. He was vague about his efforts to get to Libya from Malta, stating: 'We paid visits to certain individuals who worked in Libya and who had connections to an airline company, people who Abdel Salem knew. I knew or contacted some people in the PLO to see if they could help me enter Libya, but unfortunately no one was able to.' He did not name the PLO people, but said Malta's Palestinian community was very small so it was 'very easy to meet all of them'. He confirmed that, while on the island, he helped out at the Miska bakery, which was part-owned by Abdelsalem, but he denied knowing the original Palestinian co-owners Alaa Shurrab, Dr Khaled Nahhal, Imad Hazzourri and Magdy Moussa. He also claimed ignorance of their successor Jamal Haider, who, according to the Swedish police, was an intelligence officer for the main PLO grouping, Fatah. Taylor pointed out that his denial was undermined by the discovery of a list of the original directors during the 1 November 1988 Swedish police raids. Taylor did not raise the fact that Hazzouri's girlfriend worked at Yorkie Clothing.

Taylor reminded Talb that his ticket home to Sweden from Malta was an open return and that the return half, which was valid until 26 November 1988, was unused. Talb insisted, 'I had no intention whatsoever of going back to Malta,' and claimed it was cheaper to buy an open return than a single ticket.* If Talb had made a further trip to Malta prior to Lockerbie, then he might well have decided to use one of his false passports, in which case the return ticket would no longer be of use.

* *From my knowledge of the airline industry at the time, I doubted very much that this was true.*

254

Keen's cross-examination began in typically confrontational style: 'Mr. Talb, on 30th October 1989, the United States government officials announced: Mohamed Abu Talb, a Palestinian being held on terrorism charges in Sweden, has admitted to investigators that between October and December 1988, he retrieved and passed to another person a bomb that had been hidden in a building in West Germany used by members of the Popular Front for the Liberation of Palestine General Command.'* Talb maintained that he had made no such confession and also denied having spat in the face of an FBI agent who attempted to interview him. The denial prompted one of the trial's most heated exchanges:

Q. Mr Talb, you are not only a murderer, you are a liar. Is that not correct?

A. I am not a liar.

Q. You are just a murderer?

A. Nor a murderer.

Q. Well, Mr Talb, you can spin a convincing tale to this court, but others have witnessed your behaviour and spoken of it, and the fact is that whether you are or are not a devout Muslim, you spat at American investigators who came to interview you. You spat in the face of one of them, Mr Talb. Are you not capable of admitting your own conduct?

A. This is not true. This is a lie. And I have witnesses who were there during that interview which I attended. And these witnesses are available.

Q. We've already heard from them, Mr Talb, and they have told us of the spitting. Are you saying that they lied about it?

A. Yes. Yes. I am telling you here that they are all liars. If they said that I spat in the face of the Americans, then they are liars.

Q. Yes. Everyone except you is a liar, Mr Talb. That's about what it amounts to, isn't it?

---

* There was no official announcement by the US government that Talb had made this admission. Rather the information was attributed to unnamed officials by the *New York Times* on 31 October 1989.

A. No, that is not so. I didn't say that.

The friction barely subsided throughout the cross-examination. When Keen attempted to again explore Talb's training in the Soviet Union he refused to answer questions. Talb was ordered to leave the court while Keen appealed to the judges to compel him to answer. In truth there was little the judges could do; as he fell under Swedish jurisdiction, it was unclear whether they had any power to punish him for contempt of court, and, even if they did, since he was already serving a life sentence, any such punishment would be meaningless. On his return to the witness box, Talb was warned by Lord Sutherland that he must answer Keen's questions. He confirmed that he understood the warning, but the subsequent exchanges were barely less rancorous.

Returning to the subject of Talb's false passports, Keen described his Crown evidence as 'a misleading mix of half-truths and omissions'. He accused him of replacing his Egyptian passport in 1980 in order to conceal the record of his movements over the previous four years. Talb denied it, claiming the original passport was accidentally washed along with his trousers. He also denied deliberately losing his Swedish travel documents in order to conceal his movements at the time of the Copenhagen, Amsterdam and Stockholm bombings.

He again claimed not to have instructed his brother-in-law Mahmoud to learn bomb-making in Syria. Keen suggested the trainer was a Lebanese or Syrian man called Abnan Abu Sultan, who was in Uppsala in the mid-1980s and had paid Talb 2,000 Swedish kronor. Talb said the Abnan Abu Sultan he knew was a Palestinian who had lived in Sweden for 30 years. He also denied that Mahmoud had returned from Syria with concealed detonators, $5,000 and instructions to bomb Jewish and American targets.

When asked about the Copenhagen attack, Talb's response was markedly different to the one he'd given Taylor. While not directly admitting his involvement, he gave the curious answer, 'I have no explanation to give. I am saying I was convicted, and I am not innocent.' He claimed he'd acted at his own initiative, rather than at the instruction of any particular group.

Keen reminded Talb of objects that were seized during the 18

May 1989 raids on his and his brother-in-law's houses, including his burnt passport, the tampered-with watches and the barometer missing its barometric mechanism. Asked about the 85,000 kronor that he had received in five instalments in 1988, he maintained that 45,000 of it comprised a bank loan. The other instalments, he said, were repayments of loans that he had made to various people, but he could not adequately explain how he had found 40,000 kronor to lend in the first place. He denied Mahmoud's claim that he had made regular trips to Cyprus to collect funds from the PPSF.

Talb admitted to making various foreign journeys with Martin Imandi, including one to Berlin. He insisted that they visited the Western part of the city, but Keen pointed out that Imandi's passport for the relevant period included numerous East German stamps. He reminded him that he had flown to Cyprus the day after the still un-solved assassination of Swedish Prime Minister Olaf Palme in Febru-ary 1986. Talb claimed to have travelled on from Cyprus to Egypt, but, as Keen pointed out, he had earlier claimed that he could not return to Egypt for fear of arrest.

The cross-examination finished with a further exploration of the October 1988 visits to Cyprus and Malta. Talb stuck to his earlier explanations. He insited that Abdelsalem was an old acquaintance from Lebanon and that he had hoped to export to Sweden clothes manufactured by his bother Hashem. Keen pointed out that Abdel-salem told the Scottish police that he had only met Talb for the first time during that visit and, whereas Talb had insisted that Abdelsa-lem collected him from the airport, Abdelsalem claimed their first encounter was a chance meeting in Valletta. Regarding the clothes, Keen asked, 'Mr Talb, do you seriously expect this court to believe that you thought in 1988 there might be a market in Sweden for T-shirts with the word "Malta" printed on the front?' Talb replied, 'Why not?' He was then asked if he was aware that Abdelsalem had told the police that Hashem was not in the clothing business. Talb said he was not, but again insisted that he had told the truth. Predict-ably, he denied Keen's acusation that, following his telephone call to Malta on 11 December 1988, the package he sent to a PO box in Malta was not, as he had claimed, five video tapes, but was rather a PFLP-GC radio-cassette bomb.

Following a short re-examination by Campbell, Talb left the witness stand and returned to Sweden.[93] The Crown produced evidence from a Swedish Ministry of Labour official that he was in Sweden on 10 November 1988[94] and it was agreed by joint minute that he attended various appointments in Uppsala on 5, 9 and 16 December, and that around six hours after the Lockerbie bombing, his sister-in-law gave birth in Uppsala.[95] This gave some support to his claim that he remained in Sweden following his return from Malta on 26 October. It was, nevertheless, difficult to escape the conclusion that Talb had something to do with Lockerbie. As well as being a known bomber, he had a number of links to the PFLP-GC, which multiplied in the run-up to the Autumn Leaves raids; his movements in October 1988 were strangely circuitous and his explanations for them incredible; he had returned from Malta with clothing; he had burned one of his passports; he had received a large sum of money that he could not properly account for; and the Swedish police raids discovered various dismantled watches and a barometer minus its barometric mechanism.

Five days after Talb's evidence, on 20 November 2000, the Crown ended its case. Keen immediately informed the judges that he would in due course be making a formal submission that his client, Lamin, had no case to answer.[96] The submission was heard eight days later. Keen argued, in essence, that the prosecution had presented insufficient evidence to justify a conviction.[97] The judges rejected the motion, saying the entries in Lamin's diary, his association with Abdelbaset, and, 'crucially', Giaka's testimony, constituted sufficient evidence to convict. However, in doing so, they made clear that they were not passing judgement on the credibility and reliability of that evidence.[98] It was clear that, unless they considered Giaka to be reliable, Lamin was almost certain to be acquitted. Since Giaka's credibility had been shattered, this seemed by far the likeliest outcome. Lamin's team therefore opted not to mount a defence.

Since we had to contend with Gauci, Bollier, the forensic evidence and the Frankfurt Airport documents, that was a risk my team couldn't countenance. The most important question facing us was whether or not I should give evidence. Although I could answer every point that the prosecution was likely to raise, some of those answers might sound suspicious to those unfamiliar with Arab culture and everyday life in Libya. For example, in the late 1980s there was nothing especially unusual in state employees developing parallel careers as small-time entrepreneurs, but those unfamiliar with the country at that time might easily be persuaded that such businesses were merely a front for the JSO. Similarly, there was nothing unusual in Libyans travelling to Malta and elsewhere to buy goods for their homes and families.

On 16 November 2000, my team met to discuss the issue. The choice facing me was far from straightforward. They considered my assertions of innocence to be 'quite convincing' and recognised that the Court would be entitled to draw an adverse inference from my silence. However, they highlighted a number of major problems that might arise were I to testify, the main one being that it would have allowed the Crown to raise issues that would otherwise not be especially damaging to my defence. These included my involvement in the company ABH, the payments into my Swiss bank account, my role at the Centre for Strategic Studies and my work on secondment to the JSO. Although there was plenty of evidence to demonstrate that I was not a JSO operative and that my job at the Centre for Strategic Studies, my business activities and movements were entirely unrelated to terrorism, it might not be believed. Furthermore the Advocate Depute was bound to exploit the lies I'd told when interviewed by ABC's Pierre Salinger. Inevitably I would also face fierce cross-examination on my use of the Abdusamad coded passport, and on why I didn't use it again after the trip in 1988. It was also feared that my relationships with Said Rashid and Ezzadin Hinshiri would be used against me, as would my knowledge and experience of airline security. At the end of their deliberations, the lawyers agreed unanimously to advise me against giving evidence and in favour of calling only 'some carefully selected defence and Crown witnesses to speak to certain specific matters'.[99]

I subsequently met with the lawyers and asked them to tell me the pros and cons of testifying. I considered them to be very finely balanced and, at the lawyers' suggestion, requested a meeting with Kamal Maghour; however, he was seriously ill and did not respond. Unable to make up my mind, I asked the lawyers for their frank

259

advice, which they gave me. I opted to accept it and subsequently signed a mandate confirming my position. With hindsight, I wish I had given evidence, although I'm not convinced that it would have altered the trial's outcome.

In the event, only three defence witnesses were called: Malta's former chief meteorologist, Major Joseph Mifsud, and FBI agents Edward Marshman and Lawrence Whittaker, both of whom had been listed as Crown witnesses.

Mifsud testified about the weather conditions on 23 November and 7 December 1988, which were critical in view of Tony Gauci's claim that it was raining when the man first left the shop. He confirmed to David Burns QC that light rain was recorded at the relevant time on 23 November and none on 7 December. The data was collected at Luqa Airport, around 5 km from the shop in Sliema. Asked whether it might have been raining in Sliema, he estimated that there was a 90 per cent probability that it would not and a 10 per cent possibility that there were 'some drops of rain'. He was also asked about 8 December 1988 and confirmed that it was a public holiday in Malta to mark the Feast of the Immaculate Conception, on which shops were closed.[100]

Marshman was asked to recount the interview that he and his FBI colleague William Chornyak conducted with Marwan Khreesat in November 1989.* This demonstrated, not only that Khreesat had made five bombs, one of which had gone missing, but, more importantly, that Abu Elias avoided arrest and was at large in Germany. It also recorded that Dalkamoni had described Elias as an airline security expert and had collected a number of flight timetables from Düsseldorf Airport, including a Pan Am one.[101] Khreesat had, of course, gone much further than this when interviewed by Alastair Duff and Eddie MacKechnie. In addition to claiming that Ahmed Jibril had given specific orders to target a Pan Am flight from Frankfurt, he recalled that Dalkamoni had a twin-speaker radio-cassette bomb, which may well have been a Toshiba. The defence had hoped to call Khreesat as a witness, but in the event he refused, so the judges remained unaware of these important revelations.

* See Chapter 3.

The final witness, Lawrence Whittaker, was asked about the occasion in September 1989 when he and DI Watson McAteer had observed a Frankfurt Airport employee input a suitcase at coding station 206, apparently without making any record of the transaction. Asked if he mentioned the incident to anyone, Whittaker said he had discussed it with McAteer and, within a day or two, the BKA. When cross-examined by Alan Turnbull, he said he could not be certain that the baggage handler had not filled out the worksheet. Asked, 'Do I take it that you would not be close enough to see whether this particular worker made an entry in a notebook?' he replied, 'It would be very likely that that could have been missed, yes.'[102] The defence team and the Court were unaware that, in an undisclosed statement, McAteer specifically stated that the handler made no note of the incident. Furthermore, contrary to what could be inferred from Whittaker's evidence in court, they questioned a Frankfurt Airport supervisor about what they had seen, who conceded that the practice was not unusual.[103]

The defence case closed at 12.45 on 8 January. All that then remained was for each side to present their final submissions.

Before beginning his submissions the following morning, Alastair Campbell informed the Court that the Crown was amending the charges against the two accused. Although done without fanfare, the changes were highly significant. Charge 1, which accused them of conspiracy, was dropped altogether, which meant that the Crown had abandoned its claims in relation to the companies ABH, Medtours and Al-Khadra, all of which it had originally claimed were JSO front companies. There was also no longer mention of Abdelbaset's travels prior to the bombing, with the exception of the two visits to Malta in December 1988. Equally significantly, the amended indictment no longer alleged that Lamin was a JSO agent. Most of these allegations had been based on the claims of Giaka. It was a strong indication that the Crown anticipated that the judges would reject his evidence.

Cambell was on his feet for a day and a half. Crucially, he reminded the Court of Wilfred Borg's testimony concerning the difficulty of getting a rogue bag onto an Air Malta flight, adding: 'whatever means was used to introduce the suitcase comprising –

261

containing the improvised explosive device, it seems clear that Mr Megrahi would not be able to achieve it alone. He would require assistance from someone in a position to render such assistance at Luqa Airport.' He submitted that the two men must therefore have acted in concert.[104]

Taylor's submissions were spread over five days and challenged every major element of the Crown case, with the exception of the forensic evidence. Although he disputed the location of the bomb and the explosive residues evidence, he accepted that the bomb was contained in a Toshiba RT-SF16 radio-cassette player, which was placed in a brown Samsonite Silhouette 4000 suitcase and surrounded by clothing that 'was probably bought in Mary's House, Malta, at some point after the 18th of November 1988'. And, while he raised doubts about the provenance of the circuit-board fragment PT/35b, he did not dispute that it originated from an MST-13 timer.

Summarising his position, he told the judges: 'I indicated there that the Crown case against the first accused has been a wholly circumstantial one. The court will, of course, be familiar with the cable analogy in our law. At a superficial glance, the cable might look strong and sure, but on closer inspection, Your Lordships may conclude that it has been revealed that the strands are mere threads; some were frayed, some break during examination, and others have turned out never to have been joined together at all. The cable made up of these strands is simply not one which will bear the weight of a guilty verdict, and I invite the court to find the first accused not guilty.'[105]

Keen's final submissions lasted little over half a day. Many of them, inevitably, were focused on the discredited Giaka. As for the diary entries about Air Malta tags, he said that, even if Lamin had supplied them to Abdelbaset, there was no evidence that he knew that they would be used as part of the bomb plot. Concluding, Keen described the Crown case as 'a largely untested chain of conjecture and assertion, incapable of establishing complicity on the part of Lamin Fhimah, let alone of eliminating reasonable doubt'.

Keen finished at around 14.30 on 18 January. The two men's fate now lay in the lap of the judges. Lord Sutherland announced that the Court would adjourn until 30 January, by which time, he said, 'we might be in a position to indicate a date upon which the verdict will be delivered'.

Shortly afterwards I met with my legal team. They said they found some of the Crown submissions strange and doubted that the judges would rely on Gauci's evidence. Although no one believed we were home and dry, they thought there was a very good chance I would be acquitted. My optimism was boosted when Lamin told me his team had assured him he would be going home. Since the Crown insisted that we must have acted in concert, if he was to be acquitted, then it followed that I would be too.

On 30 January Lord Sutherland announced that the verdict would be delivered at 11.00 the following morning. That evening the staff told us to have our bags packed ready to leave, in case of acquittal. I managed a reasonable night's sleep and in the morning prayed to God to grant us justice. Within hours our entire futures and those of our families would be decided by three complete strangers. We neverthe-less managed to keep our nerves under control and think positively.

At 11.00 precisely we were led into Court. The three judges fol-lowed moments later. The Clerk of the Court asked the judges if they had reached a verdict in respect of each of the accused. Lord Suth-erland confirmed that they had. The Clerk then asked, 'Would you give me, please, your verdict in respect of the first named accused Abdelbaset Ali Mohmed Al Megrahi.' Sutherland delivered the dev-astating one-word answer: 'Guilty'. My horror was matched only by my disbelief. There were gasps from some of the victims' relatives and one of them, Dr Jim Swire, fainted and had to be carried from the Court. Then it was Lamin's turn. This time came the words for which we had both prayed, 'Not guilty'. I turned, shook his hand and congratulated him, but his acquittal did little to ease my own devastation. The greatest torture was knowing what my family was going through. With the exception of my brothers Mohamed and Nassr, who were in court, all were in Tripoli and heard the news on television. Everyone was distraught, and Aisha and my mother both collapsed and had to be taken to hospital.

Following the verdicts I was taken to a court cell while the judges adjourned to consider my sentence. I prayed to God, telling Him:

'You have ruled on my fate and I accept your judgement, but I look forward to Your grace and generosity in granting me the hope that I shall achieve justice.'

I had a duty to my family and to the world to prove my innocence. It was clear to me that it would be a huge struggle that would have to start immediately. It would involve studying every scrap of evidence and reading every document. A new era of suffering, bitterness and pain had begun, but I knew that, with the support of my family and my strong faith in God, it was a fight I could win.

I was taken back into Court to receive my sentence. Life sentences for murder are mandatory, but the judges had discretion in setting the minimum tariff. Lord Sutherland announced that I should serve a minimum of 20 years and explained that they had taken into account my age – I was 49 – and the fact that I was a father of five who would be serving his sentence in a foreign country. Given that I had supposedly killed 270 people, the tariff was extraordinarily lenient. Had they expressed their reasonable doubt about my guilt in the sentence, rather than the verdict?

Later that day the judges published an 80-page judgment, in which they set out their reasoning. It was an astonishing document. The penultimate paragraph summarised their deliberations: 'We are aware that in relation to certain aspects of the case there are a number of uncertainties and qualifications. We are also aware that there is a danger that by selecting parts of the evidence which seem to fit together and ignoring parts which might not fit, it is possible to read into a mass of conflicting evidence a pattern or conclusion which is not really justified. However, having considered the whole evidence in the case, including the uncertainties and qualifications, and the submissions of counsel, we are satisfied that the evidence as to the purchase of clothing in Malta, the presence of that clothing in the primary suitcase, the transmission of an item of baggage from Malta to London, the identification of the first accused (albeit not absolute), his movements under a false name at or around the material time, and the other background circumstances such as his association with Mr Bollier and with members of the JSO or Libyan military who purchased MST-13 timers, does fit together to form a real and convincing pattern.'

The judgment failed to address the glaring question of how Abdelbaset could be guilty when, according to the Crown, he would have been unable to put the bomb on flight KM180 without Lamin's help; in other words they were either both guilty or both not guilty – there was no third way. The judges had found Abdelbaset guilty, but not guilty as charged by the Crown; they had, in effect, amended the already amended indictment to fit the case they made in the judgment, which was not that made by the Crown. In his report on the trial, UN Observer Professor Hans Köchler noted: 'This is totally incomprehensible for any rational observer when one considers that the indictment in its very essence was based on the joint action of the two accused in Malta.'

The illogicality of the verdicts was, however, as nothing compared to the judgment's more detailed reasoning. In UK courts guilt must be proved beyond reasonable doubt. Time and again during the trial the defence had knocked holes through the prosecution evidence, yet time and again the judges reversed the burden of proof and repaired the holes by drawing inferences based upon equally shaky inferences, rather than solid evidence.

The most shocking instances related to the evidence of the clothes purchase. The judgment described Tony Gauci's identification evidence as 'a highly important element in this case'. It acknowledged that there were 'undoubtedly problems' with the evidence, before navigating them in the following remarkable passage:

'What did appear to us to be clear was that Mr Gauci applied his mind carefully to the problem of identification whenever he was shown photographs, and did not just pick someone out at random. Unlike many witnesses who express confidence in their identification when there is little justification for it, he was always careful to express any reservations he had and gave reasons why he thought that there was a resemblance. There are situations where a careful witness who will not commit himself beyond saying that there is a close resemblance can be regarded as more reliable and convincing in his identification than a witness who maintains that his identification is 100% certain. From his general demeanour and his approach to the difficult problem of identification, we formed the view that when he picked out the first accused at the identification parade and in Court, he was doing so not just because it was comparatively easy to do so but because he genuinely felt that he was correct in picking him out as having a close resemblance to the purchaser, and we did regard him as a careful witness who would not commit himself to an absolutely positive identification when a substantial period had elapsed. We accept of course that he never made what could be described as an absolutely positive identification, but having regard to the lapse of time it would have been surprising if he had been able to do so. We have also not overlooked the difficulties in relation to his description of height and age. We are nevertheless satisfied that his identification so far as it went of the first accused as the purchaser was reliable.'

The judgment failed to elaborate upon the 'situations' in which a witness such as Gauci might be regarded as 'more reliable and convincing' than someone who made a less equivocal identification, but the most obvious such situation was one in which the reputation of the police and Crown Office were at stake. While the judges may not have overlooked the difficulties in relation to height and age, they had clearly chosen to set them aside, as they knew very well that the man Gauci had described was around 50 years old and six feet tall, whereas Abdelbaset was 36 and 5 ft 8 inches. They also knew very well that Gauci's identification of Abdelbaset was not originally one of 'close resemblance', but was of someone 'ten years or more' younger than the clothes buyer. As experienced judges, they should have known that the ID parade and dock identification were almost worthless. However, they did not need judicial experience to know that, as the keeper of a clothes shop, Gauci was better equipped than most to estimate accurately someone's size.

Still more remarkable was their approach to the date of the clothes purchase. In preferring 7 December over 23 November, they relied on Gauci's claim, which he had never before made, that the sale occurred around a fortnight before Christmas, and on his rather confused recollection of the Christmas lights. Since Gauci had always maintained that it was raining lightly when the man first left the shop, the meteorological evidence provided a far more reliable indicator of the date. The judgment acknowledged that there was 'no doubt that the weather on 23 November would be wholly consistent with a light shower between 6.30pm and 7.00pm,' but added: 'The possibility that there was a brief light shower on 7 December is not however ruled out by the evidence of Major Mifsud.' What Mifsud had in fact said was that no rain had been recorded at the monitoring station on 7 December, but that there was – possibly – a 10 per cent chance of some drops falling 5 km away in Sliema. In other words a 90 per cent chance that an event *did not* occur did not give rise, in their minds, to reasonable doubt that it *did* occur. Against such Alice in Wonderland logic, Abdelbaset never stood a chance.

Regarding the Feast of the Immaculate Conception, the judges said: 'We are unimpressed by the suggestion that because Thursday 8 December was a public holiday, Mr Gauci should have been able to fix the date by reference to that. Even if there was some validity in that suggestion, it loses any value when it was never put to him for his comments.' This further illustrated their tendency to diminish evidence favourable to the defence, but also underlined the perils of not cross-examining Gauci on the fine detail of his police statements.

While they accepted that the complete absence of evidence of how the primary suitcase was placed on flight KM180 was 'a major difficulty for the Crown case', the judges considered the Frankfurt Airport documents and the blast-damaged Maltese clothes were sufficient evidence that the case was on that flight. They acknowledged that the timings recorded on the documents were not infallible, but added, 'the suspect case was recorded as being coded in the middle of the time attributed to baggage from KM180, so that the possible significance of such errors is reduced.'

The judgment raised other weaknesses in the Frankfurt evidence, only to brush them aside. For example, it accepted that an unaccounted-for bag from flight LH1071 from Warsaw was likely to have been loaded onto PA103A and that the informal work practices among the baggage handlers might have resulted in bags being coded into the system without being recorded. It noted that FBI agent Whittaker may have witnessed this happening, but that he could not be certain that no record was made.

In considering the unaccounted-for one-and-a-half wagonloads of baggage from flight LH669 from Damascus, the judgment significantly distorted the trial evidence. Taylor had submitted that this

267

'missing' baggage might have been coded in at station 206, without being recorded, at the same time that the bags from KM180 were being processed. If that were the case, the unattributed bag coded in at 13.07 could have originated from LH669, rather than KM180. While it did not dispute the evidence, the judgment observed: 'The witness Joachim Koscha, however, referred to notes in the records which indicated that wagons of luggage from that flight had been taken to Customs, as happened from time to time, and gave evidence that wagons taken to Customs might be reloaded in different ways, which might account for the discrepancy.' In fact Koscha never stated that the repacking of wagons for Customs might result in fewer wagonloads being sent from Customs to the coding stations than had been unloaded from a flight. Rather, he said that wagons arriving from flights might be repacked *before* being sent to Customs and that this tended to result in *more*, rather than fewer, wagons going to Customs.

Taylor had also submitted that a bomb would, in all probability, have been detected prior to being loaded onto PA103A by X-ray operator Kurt Maier, who, in statements to the FAA, said he had taught himself to distinguish various types of electrical equipment, and could spot explosives by their appearance. In dismissing the submission, the judges again effectively reversed the burden of proof, stating: 'Neither statement directly dealt with the question whether, and if so how, Mr Maier would detect explosives hidden in a radio-cassette player. What he said was that the approach in dealing with electrical equipment was to see whether it presented a normal appearance, for example whether it had a plug. Other evidence, however, particularly that given by the witness Oliver Koch, Alert's trainee manager at the time, shows that the standard of training given to Alert employees was poor. That was also the view of the FAA investigators who visited Frankfurt in 1989. Mr Maier's description of what he looked for does not suggest that he would necessarily have claimed to be able to detect explosives hidden in a radio-cassette player. There was no expert evidence as to the ease or difficulty of detecting such hidden devices.' It was for the Crown to prove that the bomb was likely to evade detection, not for the defence to prove the opposite.

The judgment took a similar approach to the evidence concerning the brown hard-sided suitcase seen in container AVE4041 by Heathrow loader John Bedford. It acknowledged that the case 'could fit the forensic description of the primary suitcase' and described Bedford as 'a clear and impressive witness'. It also accepted that, if the bags had been rearranged, the case might have been placed in the second layer of luggage, but added: 'if there was such a rearrangement, the suitcase described by Mr Bedford might have been placed at some more remote corner of the container, and while the forensic evidence dealt with all the items recovered which showed direct explosive damage, twenty-five in total, there were many other items of baggage found which were not dealt with in detail in the evidence in the case.' It was for the Crown, not the defence, to account for all those other items of baggage and, more generally, it was for the Crown to demonstrate convincingly that the Bedford suitcase did not contain the bomb. The Maltese clothes were not a reliable basis for ruling out the Bedford suitcase and neither did they prove that the primary suitcase had travelled on KM180. In the absence of such proof, it was possible that the primary case had travelled directly from Luqa to Heathrow, or that the bombers had used Maltese clothes in order to lay a false trail to Malta and its neighbour Libya.

The one major plank of the Crown case to be rejected was, unsurprisingly, Majid Giaka. The judges made clear that they considered him neither credible nor reliable. Without Giaka there was no case against Lamin, and, as the judgment accepted, if there was no case against Lamin, then his diaries could not be used as evidence against Abdelbaset.

The rejection of Giaka raised the question: what would have happened if the judges had accepted the Lord Advocate's misleading assurance that nothing in the CIA cables bore upon Giaka's credibility? The obvious answer was that Lamin might also have been convicted, in which case the diaries would have become a further strand in Abdelbaset's false conviction.

Despite finding Giaka neither credible nor reliable, the judges accepted his 'description of the organisation of the JSO and the personnel involved there'. On this slender basis they concluded that Abdelbaset was a JSO officer 'occupying posts of fairly high rank', one of which was head of airline security. Based on this inference they further inferred that he would have been 'aware at least in general terms of the nature of security precautions at airports from or to which LAA operated'.[106] In the absence of any supporting evidence, there was no justification for cherry-picking elements of Giaka's account.

In his damning report on the trial, UN Observer Professor Köchler wrote: 'A general pattern of the trial consisted in the fact that virtually all people presented by the prosecution as key witnesses were proven to lack credibility to a very high extent, in certain cases even having openly lied to the Court. Particularly as regards Mr Bollier and Mr Giaka, there were so many inconsistencies in their statements and open contradictions to statements of other witnesses that the resulting confusion was much greater than any clarification that may have been obtained from parts of their statements. Their credibility as such was shaken. It seems highly arbitrary and irrational to choose only parts of their statements for the formulation of a verdict that requires certainty "beyond any reasonable doubt." The air of international power politics is present in the whole verdict of the panel of judges. In spite of the many reservations in the Opinion of the Court explaining the verdict itself, the guilty verdict in the case of the first accused is particularly incomprehensible in view of the admission by the judges themselves that the identification of the first accused by the Maltese shop owner was "not absolute" (formulation in Par. 89 of the Opinion) and that there was a "mass of conflicting evidence".' Köchler concluded, to his 'great dismay', that the trial, 'seen in its entirety, was not fair and was not conducted in an objective manner. Indeed, there are many more questions and doubts at the end of the trial than there were at its beginning. The trial has effectively created more confusion than clarity and no rational observer can make any statement on the complex subject matter "beyond any reasonable doubt."'[107]

Apart from all its strange logic, the judgment contained a significant factual error. It was contained in Paragraph 52 and concerned the two MST-13 timers retrieved from Togo in 1986 and the one confiscated in Senegal in February 1988. The relevant passage read: 'The timer recovered in Togo which, as we have said, was one of two, was considered by the witness Richard Sherrow to be identical to one which was discovered in Dakar, Senegal, on 20 February 1988 within a briefcase found on board a passenger aircraft which had arrived at

270

the airport there from Cotonou in Benin. It was recovered in October 1999 by C. I. Williamson from the French Ministry of Justice in Paris but was not examined forensically.'[108] This was simply wrong, as the timer handed to Williamson was one of the two Togo timers. The fate of the Senegal timer was unknown; there was no evidence that it had been destroyed along with the other arms recovered on 20 February, or that it had been passed back to the Libyans from whom it was allegedly seized. It could therefore not be ruled out that during the ten months before Lockerbie an MST-13 timer was at large, which may have been used by those who bombed PA103.

The Bar-L 12

The Court's verdicts meant that, after nearly two years of enforced companionship, Lamin and I were finally to be separated. After receiving my sentence, I pleaded with the Prison Governor, Ian Bannatyne, for permission to see my friend before he was freed. He kindly agreed and we were allowed a few minutes together. It was a very sad occasion, as I was going to miss him terribly. I asked him to visit my mother in Tripoli and assure her that God was with us and would help me achieve justice. Shortly afterwards Lamin walked out of HMP Zeist to return to his home, family and country,* while I returned to my cell to become acquainted with my new role as Britain's worst mass murderer.

At around 17.00 I was visited by Alastair Duff, Bill Taylor, David Burns and Kamal Maghour. All were shocked by the verdict. Taylor was especially angered by the judgment and reported that John Beckett was also.

Naturally, I wished to overturn my conviction. Under the legislation that established the trial, if I chose to attend the appeal, it had to be heard in the same court.[1] This, of course, meant remaining in

---

* Lamin received a hero's welcome on his return to Tripoli, but, following the Libyan revolution, he claimed in an interview with the Swedish newspaper, *Expressen*, that Gadafy's government had abandoned him: 'Gadafy made a show of my arrival. We didn't say anything to each other. He welcomed me and nothing more. After that I stopped hearing from them.' He complained: 'I lost my travel agency in Malta. I had a farm that I was forced to sell in order to provide for myself and my family. I haven't received any compensation from the regime. The only thing they did after welcoming me was confiscating my passport. I don't know why, they claimed that when the sentence against al-Megrahi would be repealed by them, I had to be here to testify.' He described the fall of Gadafy as a 'blessed moment' adding 'I was never part of the regime. I am an ordinary citizen, who was connected to a crime I had nothing to do with and I don't know who made that connection.'

*Kamp Zeist. Within a day of the verdicts most of the media and many
of the Court staff had gone, and the place returned to its empty calm.
The population of HMP Zeist having halved, I was left with only the
guards for company.*

*The first days alone were hell. I was so agitated by the unjust ver-
dict that the prison nursing team decided to put me on sleeping pills.
It was a huge relief to be visited by my family for the first time. I tried
to be positive, reassuring them that I would mount a strong appeal
and would be back home in within months, but they no doubt recalled similar reassurances before I left for Holland two years earlier.*

*Apart from their occasional visits, my only respite was meetings
with my legal team and a variety of officials and well-wishers. These
included a number of UN observers, the ambassadors of Egypt, Jordan, Sudan, Morocco, Algeria, Tunisia and Palestine, the Chairman
of the International Judges Association, the Chairman of Arab Lawyers Association and a number of other prominent Arab lawyers. All
were baffled by the guilty verdict and many considered that it was
politically motivated. I was also privileged to receive a visit from
the famous Syrian actress Miss Raghda. She gave me a gift of a silver
ring, on which the opening chapter of the* Holy Koran, *the Sura Al
Fatiha, had been inscribed.*

*Shortly after my conviction my family were visited by Nelson
Mandela, who had by then retired as President of South Africa. Having played a key role in persuading the UK and US governments to
accept a neutral venue trial, he was deeply concerned by my conviction. That he should take the trouble to demonstrate his solidarity
meant a lot to them. A few weeks later he flew to the Netherlands
to attend the wedding of Prince Constantijn, the youngest son of the
Dutch monarch Queen Beatrix. On landing he told the South African Ambassador, Priscilla Jana, that he wished to meet me. When a
protocol officer advised him that this would not be appropriate, he
insisted that the Ambassador visit me instead, which she duly did. To
my surprise, she passed on Mandela's mobile phone number, and said
he'd like me to call between 9.00 and 9.15 the following morning. I
rang at around 9.10 and, as good as his word, Mandela answered. I
thanked him warmly for his support. He said that my thanks were
not necessary, as Libya had been a great friend to South Africa. I*

*asked him to pray for a fair appeal and for the judges to avoid specu-
lating as their trial court colleagues had done. He said he would and
promised to visit me. The conversation lasted only a couple of minutes, but was a huge boost to my morale.*

*Eventually I managed to adapt to my new situation and cope with
my distress and bitterness, but eight months into my sentence my relative composure was shattered. On 11 September 2001 I watched my
TV in horror as aircraft were shown crashing into the World Trade
Center. As the tragedy unfolded, like so many others, I broke down in
tears. It was not only the victims' suffering that affected me, but also
the knowledge that Muslim people, and Arabs in particular, would
pay the price for the hijackers' insane acts. I knew I was likely to be
one of the collateral casualties in the newly declared War on Terror,
as it would require exceptionally brave judges to overturn what was,
at that point, the West's most important terrorist conviction.*

*I had the option of replacing my Scottish legal team, but chose to
retain them. Although I had serious concerns about certain aspects
of my defence, in particular Bill Taylor's cross-examination of Tony
Gauci, I didn't doubt their commitment to my cause. Equally importantly, I was keen for the appeal to begin as soon as possible; if I
appointed a new team they would need many months to familiarise
themselves with the case.*

*Shortly after the trial finished our Libyan lawyer Kamal Maghour
died. He was very ill throughout the trial, but continued his work to
the end. Also a renowned writer of fiction, he was a true gentleman
and his death was a sad loss for Libya as well as his family. In his
place, Dr Ibrahim Legwell, who had represented us prior to the trial,
was reappointed. He assembled at great expense what he termed a
parallel defence team. It was largely comprised of renowned international jurists, who were asked to provide opinions on various aspects
of the case and the Trial Court judgment. Although universally critical
of the verdict, the opinions were of little other than academic interest.*

As preparations for the appeal progressed, two remarkable developments came out of the blue. The first arrived in September 2001
courtesy of the *Daily Mirror*. A front-page story revealed that on
the night before the disaster, someone had broken through the doors

leading from the check-in area of Heathrow Terminal 3 to the baggage build-up area, where PA103's checked-in luggage was stacked into containers prior to loading. The source of the story was retired Heathrow security officer Raymond Manly, who had discovered the break-in. He said the intruders had broken the hefty padlock that usually secured the doors.[2] Although the container AVE4041 was not supposed to contain Heathrow check-in baggage, shortly before 5 p.m. on the 21st the loader John Bedford had left it in the baggage build-up area before going off duty[3] and it had remained there for approximately 45 minutes until PA103A arrived from Frankfurt. Manly gave a statement to the police at the time, but, incredibly, it was never disclosed to the defence. The *Mirror* article appeared on 11 September and momentarily caused a sensation, but within hours was forgotten amid the horrors of that day.

The second surprise development occurred less than a month before the appeal commenced. On 28 December 2001, at the request of one of the parallel team, legal investigator George Thomson visited Tony Gauci's Mary's House shop while holidaying in Malta. On hearing Thomson's accent, Gauci asked if he was from Scotland. When he confirmed that he was, Gauci volunteered that he had been there around five times and would be going again soon. Thomson asked if he had friends or relatives in Scotland, and he replied that he had friends in 'Scotland Yard'. Although Scotland Yard is a colloquial term for the Metropolitan Police, it was clear that he meant the Scottish police. He said these friends had taken him salmon-fishing and, without prompting, went on to explain that he was a very important witness in a terrorist case and that the police had to look after him 'very good' to keep the man in jail. He explained that the man was due to appeal shortly, which was why he was being taken to Scotland. When Thomson asked, 'Are you looked after OK?' he replied, 'They have to, they want this man to stay in jail.' He said that when he was in Scotland he was moved a number of times, staying only two days in any one place. He mentioned hotels in Glasgow, Perth and Inverness.[4]

Thomson returned to the shop the following day, this time tape-recording the conversation. Gauci again referred to his trips to Scotland, saying that he was accompanied at all times by police officers.

He said he was taken to a fish farm, a bird sanctuary and to Lockerbie, where he was shown memorials to the bombing victims. He seemed to suggest that on one occasion he was accompanied by his brother Paul and three other siblings. From his description, it was clear that one visit coincided with the UK foot-and-mouth disease outbreak, which occurred during the first half of 2001, shortly after Abdelbaset was convicted.[5]

The appeal hearing opened on 23 January 2002, just under a year after the trial. The bench comprised Scotland's chief judge, The Lord Justice-General Lord Cullen and Lords Kirkwood, Osborne, Mac-fadyen and Nimmo Smith.

The case had two main strands: the first was an essentially legal argument that, in reaching their verdict, the judges had, in effect, misdirected themselves; and the second was the new Heathrow evidence. Notably, it was not submitted, as many observers had, that the trial verdict was unreasonable and that there was insufficient evidence to sustain the conviction. The first strand took up most of the hearing and consisted of a very lengthy submission by Taylor and equally detailed responses from Advocate Depute Alastair Campbell QC.

As the legal arguments ground on, further interesting developments were unfolding elsewhere. On 27 January the *Mail on Sunday* published a lengthy article based on Thomson's investigation. Two days later Alastair Duff wrote to the Crown to request details of the number, nature and duration of Gauci's visits to Scotland and whether there was any truth in the allegation that he had received 'treats' while there. He also asked whether Gauci had been taken to Lockerbie on his first trip to Scotland.[6] Replying the following day, Procurator Fiscal Norman McFadyen explained that, as there were concerns for Gauci's safety, he could not elaborate upon the arrangements made to ensure his protection. He stated that, prior to giving evidence, the brothers' only visit to Scotland was in order to be precognosced; they stayed for two days and at no point were they taken to Lockerbie. He was not prepared to discuss any of the arrangements made after Gauci gave evidence, but said he had been assured that the shopkeeper at no time received gifts.[7]

Another significant discovery relating to Gauci occurred as the appeal was under way. Alastair Duff instructed Maltese solicitor Dr Gianella Curran to investigate once again the date on which the Christmas lights were erected and illuminated in Tower Road in 1988. She established that the Maltese electricity company, Enemalta, routinely supplied temporary meters to monitor the power consumed by public illuminations around the island.[8] Fortunately, the company had retained the records for meter installations in 1988 and was able to identify the staff involved. Duff travelled to Malta to take statements from these witnesses and from James Busuttil, the shopkeeper who had organised the Tower Road lights that year. The witnesses explained that temporary meter applications could only be submitted once the lights themselves had been erected, as the meter fitters had to test the installations.[9] Busuttil submitted an application on 29 November and the meter was fitted the following day. He said that in 1988 the Tower Road lights were erected over two nights and, while he could not provide specific dates, he said it was most likely only a day or so before 30 November. He recalled that the lights were officially switched on that year by the Tourism Minister Michael Refalo.[10] The Minister's diary revealed that he had done so on 6 December.[11]

The Trial Court had accepted that the clothes purchase had occurred around the time the lights were being erected. The new information suggested the date was no later than 29 November, which was over a week before Abdelbaset was on the island. This tallied precisely with Gauci's recollection in his defence precognition statement, prior to the trial, that the purchase had occurred on 29 November, and was also consistent with his police statements.

David Burns QC and John Beckett were asked to consider whether the evidence should be introduced at the appeal. While both recognised that it was capable of undermining the trial judgment, both were concerned that it might have the opposite effect. Gauci's testimony was confused, and at one stage he had said the lights were on when the purchase occurred. He also claimed the incident occurred around a fortnight before Christmas. They were especially concerned that the Appeal Court might view the latest information as confirming those positions and justifying the Trial Court's choice of 7 December.[12]

While Duff was in Malta, more evidence emerged that the bombing was the work of the PFLP-GC and Iran. The source was Robert Baer, a retired CIA Middle East specialist who was involved in the Lockerbie investigation, whose memoir, *See No Evil: The True Story of a Ground Soldier in the CIA's War on Terrorism* was published in late January 2002. It confirmed that the CIA established, within days of the shoot-down of Iran Air flight 655 in July 1988, that Hafez Dalkamoni and a fellow PFLP-GC member, known as 'Nabil', met members of the Iranian intelligence service, the Pasadaran. The Iranian instructions were, according to Baer, 'crystal clear: Blow up an American airplane – in the air in order to kill as many people as possible.' He claimed that Dalkamoni was one of 'a small group of Islamic fundamentalists in the General Command who looked to Iran for inspiration', and had been vetted by the Iranians to determine whether he was 'a true believer who could be counted on to keep his mouth shut if caught'. The book further alleged: 'At Iran's direction, Dalkamoni organised two separate attacks on US military trains in West Germany, one on August 31, 1987, and the other on April 26, 1988. No one was killed, but Dalkamoni had shown he was prepared to take risks and follow orders.' Baer claimed that the CIA established with 'a fair amount of certainty' that 'Nabil' was Nabil Makhzumi, a.k.a. Abu Abid, a Farsi speaker who was, at the time, Dalkamoni's assistant. He was described as the PFLP-GC's main contact with the Pasadaran and was said to have a Pasadaran case officer called Feridoun Mehdi-Nezhad, who had visited Frankfurt in July 1988.

Dalkamoni was arrested two months before Lockerbie, but, as Baer pointed out, 'that didn't exclude the possibility that the operation had been handed off to one of the cell members who got away'. Crucially, he added, 'as the weeks went on, an avalanche of information began to point in that direction.' That information included a $500,000 payment to Mohamed Abu Talb on 25 April 1989 and an $11 million transfer to a PFLP-GC account at a bank in Lausanne, Switzerland only two days after Lockerbie. The $11 million was moved to another of the group's accounts at the Banque Nationale de Paris, and then to a third one at the Hungarian Trade Development Bank. Baer claimed that the Paris account number was found in Dalkamoni's possession when he was arrested in October 1988.

It was not the first time such claims had been made, but they had never before been made on the record by a member of the Western intelligence services. Furthermore, the degree of detail was compelling. The book did not contend that the payments proved Iran's and the PFLP-GC's guilt, but simply posed the questions: 'Did that and the other payments originate in Iran? Were they success fees for Pan Am 103? Certainly none of those are illogical conclusions.'

It said of Talb: 'We also knew that Talb was travelling in and out of Libya. Was he coordinating with the Libyans for Dalkamoni? Again, the logic seemed to fit.'[13] Here Baer appeared to be mistaken, as Talb's movements were accounted for from well before Dalkamoni's arrest. He claimed he had attempted to fly to Libya from Rome in October 1988, but was not permitted to board the flight. Libya did not have a close relationship with Iran and, according to some, had ceased financial support for the PFLP-GC following the 1986 American air raids.

Shortly after the book's publication, a member of the parallel legal team met Baer in Washington to see if he had further information about Lockerbie. He did. He confirmed that he was involved in the investigation from the time of the disaster until August 1991. Information was gathered from a multitude of sources, ranging from European police forces, including the Scots, intelligence services, signals intelligence and on-the-ground agents. He could not disclose anything more about the sources, but insisted they were 'as good as it gets'. He said that the Autumn Leaves arrests appeared not to disrupt the PFLP-GC's plans and that some of its members continued to have clandestine meetings in West and East Germany, Sweden and elsewhere. He added that the 'big, big centre of the investigation' in its initial stages, was Abu Elias. He could not remember Elias's real name, but recalled that he was based in Sweden and was an associate of Talb. Like Khreesat, he claimed Elias was an airline security expert. Another of those to enter the frame shared a family name with 'Mahmoud Almari', the Syrian interviewed by Alastair Duff and Eddie MacKechnie on 31 October 2000.

He said the CIA established that Talb was an Iranian agent and that he and Dalkamoni were officially recognised by Iran as heroic martyrs. He implied that there was a secret list of such people, but would not elaborate. The $500,000 payment to Talb, he said, was paid into an account numbered 560200 at the Degussa Bank in Frankfurt.

Baer volunteered that 'for me the big question is Khaled Jaafar.' He was surprised when Libya came into the frame because he was not convinced by the evidence. He recalled 'when it came round to them I shrugged my shoulders and said "I'm not in the middle of this investigation and don't have access to the files" so I just let it go.'[14]

On 13 February 2002 the Court heard the new Heathrow evidence. It was agreed by joint minute that the break-in had taken place between 22.05 on 20 December and 00.30 on the 21st. Abdelbaset's team called security officer Raymond Manly and his colleague Philip Radley, while another security officer, Geoffrey Myers, security manager Richard Harris and baggage manager Keith Willis appeared for the Crown. Manly was visibly very frail and some of his recollections contradicted those of Radley and documentary records from the time.

Taylor submitted that the new evidence supported the defence case that the primary suitcase was the brown hard-sided one seen by loader John Bedford on the base of AVE4041. He acknowledged that, having broken through the doors, the intruders would have had to conceal the bomb for many hours before placing it into the container and that this would have required an 'insider' at Heathrow. Although no such insider had been identified, neither had one at Luqa Airport. He suggested that concealing the primary suitcase would not have been difficult, especially given the ongoing building works at Terminal 3. Even without concealment, it might not have attracted attention in such a busy terminal; furthermore, there was evidence at trial that individual bags were occasionally carried around by staff. If the primary suitcase was the one seen by Bedford, Taylor argued that it would not necessarily have required an interline tag as Bedford had said that the handles were facing inwards, which would have concealed the tag's absence. In any event, he pointed out, according to the uncontested evidence of Radley, the tags were not always kept secure, and, he argued, the conspirators could have stolen one in advance. He submitted that, if they had a tag, they could have left the case on the conveyor belt outside the interline shed, which was not guarded. Had this happened, the bag would have been X-rayed by Sulkash Kamboj; however, he had told the police he was not aware of the Toshiba warning, so would not have known to be alert for radio-cassette players.[15]

Crown counsel Alan Turnbull QC submitted that the evidence of Myers, Harris and Willis indicated that the door was almost certainly broken open by airport employees on the airside trying to avoid a circuitous route back to the landside. A number of staff had complained about having to take this long route and there was evidence of previous damage to locks and doors. The general tenor of the airport authority's response, he said, suggested they did not regard the incident as especially serious. It was widely known among staff that a person with appropriate identification could pass from landside to airside during working hours without being searched. Turnbull argued that it would therefore have been illogical for terrorists to draw attention to their actions by breaking in. He pointed out that, had an IED been infiltrated overnight, the bombers would have reduced the risk of detection if they had targeted one of Pan Am's earlier New York flights, which departed at 11.00 and 13.00. Taking the case hundreds of yards to the interline shed was, he said, nonsensical, especially as it would have been X-rayed. It would have been far easier to leave it in the baggage build-up area where the Heathrow check-in luggage was stored, and which the broken doors led directly to. Turnbull also reminded the Court that the Frankfurt Airport documents and the Maltese clothes suggested the bomb had been infiltrated at Luqa.

The hearing closed on 14 February. Exactly a month later Lord Cullen announced that the appeal had been refused.

The judges described the new Heathrow evidence as credible and reliable, and did not accept that the doors must have been broken by staff trying to get landside. However, they concurred with most of the Crown's other submissions. In dismissing Taylor's position, they observed: '[It] seems to us that if the additional evidence merely demonstrates one way in which infiltration might have taken place, without linking one of the Bedford suitcases to that means of infiltration, it adds nothing of materiality to the evidence that was before the trial court. It does not transform a mere possibility into anything more substantial. It merely confirms that that which was regarded as a possibility was indeed a possibility. In our view the Advocate Depute was right in submitting that the additional evidence did not demonstrate any link between the break-in . . . and the Bedford suitcases.'

It has often been said by those who support Abdelbaset's conviction that the appeal judges supported the guilty verdict.* In fact they did not; indeed, their written opinion stated explicitly: 'We have not had to consider whether the verdict of guilty was one which no reasonable trial court, properly directing itself, could have returned in the light of that evidence.' [16]

As the verdict was announced I caught the look of devastation on Aisha's face and feared the impact that it would have on the children. As I returned to my cell I was terribly depressed and again prayed to God to give me the strength to continue my struggle and to ultimately grant me justice.

The appeal over, my family returned to Tripoli on a flight specially chartered by the Libyan government, which they had dearly hoped would be taking me with them. Instead I was finally to serve my sentence in Scotland. The Scottish Prison Service (SPS) and police wasted no time in arranging my transfer. Within hours of the verdict, I was told to put on what appeared to be a spacesuit and escorted to a helicopter. It was explained that it was a survival suit, in case of an emergency landing on water. Both of my hands were handcuffed to a guard and I was led on board. In the distance I could see a gaggle of photographers and TV crews vying for a view of the man they called the Lockerbie bomber.

It was the most exhausting flight of my life, and before long I felt horribly dizzy. Fortunately, we were accompanied by a doctor, who gave me some tablets. The journey took around four hours, including a 20-minute refuelling stop somewhere in the south of Scotland.

* For example, in a joint letter to the Scottish Justice Secretary, Kenny MacAskill, in August 2009, former SIO Stuart Henderson and the former head of the FBI's Lockerbie investigation, Richard Marquise, stated: 'The eight judges who have already heard the evidence including three who were able to observe each witness under direct and cross-examination came to the same conclusion the rest of us did – Mr Megrahi was guilty of murder.'

As we approached Glasgow, I could see the city spreading out into the distance, its glittering lights reminding me of a Christmas tree. We eventually landed on a playing field within the walls of HMP Barlinnie. As I walked from the helicopter, I could see and hear some of the prisoners who had gathered at their cell windows to witness my arrival. The Governor Bill MacKinlay was there to meet us, and I was driven the short distance to the prison building.

Situated around three miles east of Glasgow city centre, 'The Bar-L', as it's known locally, is by reputation Scotland's toughest jail. Opened in 1894, it was designed for around 900 inmates, but by the time of my arrival regularly held over 1,200. Tabloid newspapers reported that I would be given a rough reception by its notoriously hard inmates, but there was little chance of that, as my new home was to be a specially-built secure unit where I would be held in isolation from the rest of the prisoners and in very different conditions.

Dubbed 'Gadafy's Café', the unit was built at a cost of £250,000. The entrance area was equipped with special scanning equipment, and two of the external doors were fitted with surveillance cameras. There were three cells ready for occupation, and another two that were used by the guards as offices. There was a living room equipped with a satellite television, which could receive a number of Arabic channels, a kitchen and small dining room, which was also fitted with cameras, whose tapes were changed every three hours, plus a small bathroom and a side room in which I was able to keep my personal belongings, but was forbidden from entering.

My first days in the unit were dreadful. A doctor had to prescribe me sleeping pills and I was kept under observation by the guards. There was an automatic alarm system, which emitted nerve-shattering rings every 20 minutes. I complained repeatedly to the Governor, telling him that sleep deprivation amounted to torture and, following an intervention by the Libyan Embassy, it was adjusted to activate hourly.

While the living conditions were otherwise relatively good, I was officially the UK's worst mass murderer, which meant that my visitors had to endure laborious security checks. Some of these proved to be useless. The day after my arrival, Aisha and my brother-in-law tried to visit me, but Aisha was refused entry because a swab taken on her hand gave a false reading for explosives. The following day *they visited again. This time Aisha was allowed in, but my brother-in-law was barred because his swab registered positive for drugs, even though he had never touched them in his life. I complained, and soon after it was decided to abandon the system. I was taken to these early visits in handcuffs, which was degrading for me and upsetting for my family. I again complained to the Governor, explaining to him that it was causing my children unnecessary distress, and eventually the procedure stopped. It was to the Governor's and the SPS's great credit that they responded positively to this and my other pleas for humane treatment.*

During the first few days I was also visited by the Libyan Consul General, Rafiq al-Zwai, who informed me that arrangements were under way, under the provisions of the agreement between the British government and the UN, to establish a Libyan Consulate in Glasgow to look after my personal affairs and those of my family. It was reassuring to know that my government had not abandoned me.

I tried to make the best of my new circumstances. I obeyed all the prison's rules and, as at Kamp Zeist, observed everyday courtesies, such as greeting everyone and saying please and thank you. The officers respected me for it and, on the whole, once they got to know me, were friendly and highly professional. There was one exception, who called me a 'stinking Libyan', but his colleagues made clear to me their embarrassment at his behaviour.

On a few occasions a couple of them invited me to play three-a-side football in one of the prison's sports halls. They made up the numbers with 'pass men', meaning inmates who'd earned the privilege of freer movement around the prison. During one match I accidentally fouled an officer, who responded by calling me 'a dirty Libyan'. The others chastised him, and I decided to complain to a Deputy Governor. Everyone was interviewed, but no one could recall hearing the remark.

In November 2003, I awoke to find that secretly-taken photographs of me and my cell were splashed across the News of the World *under the headline: 'Insult to the Dead – Convicted Lockerbie Bomber in Luxurious Prison Paradise'. Since cameras were not* allowed in the unit, this was an important breach of security. By studying the detail of the pictures I was able to narrow down the date they were taken to a two-week period. The paper reported that the person who took them had left the prison service.[17] Piecing together these and other snippets of information, I soon worked out who he was. The police were called in and I reported my suspicions, but the man was never caught. I asked his best friend, who was a particularly good man, what he thought had motivated the betrayal, but he remained tight-lipped, clearly uncomfortable about the episode. Shortly before I returned to Libya the culprit wrote me a nice letter, saying he was pleased I was going home, so I guess he had a guilty conscience. The episode made me rather paranoid. If someone was prepared to take a camera into my cell to make a quick buck, how easy would it be for someone more malign to smuggle poison into my food?

One of the few consolations during my first year in Barlinnie was regular family visits. Shortly after my transfer they moved to a house in Newton Mearns, a middle-class southern suburb of Glasgow. In many ways their life was more difficult than mine. Within the first few weeks the house was pelted with eggs three times. During their first Christmas there Aisha sent cards to 17 of the neighbours, but 14 were sent back to her and she received none in return.

Our two middle sons, Mohamed and Ali, were enrolled in a local state school, which thankfully was far more accepting. They soon made friends and under their influence became avid Celtic fans, although Mohamed later changed his allegiance to Rangers, a defection that would be unthinkable to native Glaswegians.

During this period my daughter Ghada, our eldest child, became engaged. I was delighted that she had found a good man, but it was very upsetting not to be able to play my full role as a father. Everyone did their best to include me in the process. Her fiancé's parents visited me in prison and we discussed the plans and agreed on a wedding day. The Governor kindly allowed the final part of the marriage formalities to take place in the prison. The Imam of the Glasgow Mosque was good enough to lead the ceremony, which was attended by a handful of close relatives. I was elated to see Ghada so happy and I prayed to God that I would witness my four sons happily married, and live among my grandchildren as a free man.

The family had a 12-month visitors' visa. In late February 2003, as the year came to an end, the Home Office notified Aisha that it would not be automatically renewed. She and the children were given just 48 hours to leave the country and were told that they must reapply from Tripoli. To compound our anxiety, the Home Office stipulated that, if they were to get another visa, they would not be allowed to use any state facilities, which meant the children could not return to their school. The Libyan Consulate tried to find them a private school, but all refused on security grounds.

I decided it was best not to challenge the decision and recommended to Aisha that she take the three youngest children back to Tripoli and return only during school holidays. Our daughter Ghada stayed with her husband, who was studying at Glasgow's Caledonian University, and so too did our eldest son Khaled, who was also at the University.

Before leaving, the family came to visit for what we knew would be the last time in many months. One of the boys asked me, 'Dad, why do they hate us so much?' I didn't want the children to grow up embittered, so I reassured them, 'They don't hate us, it's just the rules.'

The family were later given a six-month tourist visa, which they were able to renew a few times. They usually came for two months in the summer and two weeks in the winter. Saying goodbye at the end of each stay was agonising. It is a further tribute to the prison officers' decency that they saw my suffering and did their best to console me.

The stresses of prison life began to take their toll on my health. One day I felt a sharp stomach pain and later began vomiting continuously, eventually bringing up blood. The prison doctor referred me to Glasgow Royal Infirmary for an endoscopy and treatment. I was transferred amid a pantomime of over-the-top security measures, which made me feel still more stressed and unwell.

In August 2003 I suffered another blow, as the Libyan government wrote to the UN Security Council to formally accept the Trial Court's verdict and agree to pay compensation of $2.7 billion to the Lockerbie victims' families. I was visited by Consul General Mr al-Zwai, who explained that the government was simply complying *with manifestly unjust UN Security Council resolutions in order to be free of sanctions and fully rejoin the international community. The government stated publicly that the move was driven by political expediency, and continued to insist that neither it, nor I, were involved in the bombing. Nevertheless, in the eyes of many, the settlement was an admission of guilt.*

My setbacks were counterbalanced by the support offered by a number of highly respected public figures. Three months after my transfer to Barlinnie, Nelson Mandela kept his promise to visit me. That the world's most respected statesman should again take the trouble to demonstrate his solidarity gave me a great lift. We chatted for some time, mainly about the unjust guilty verdict. Having spent 27 years imprisoned on Robben Island, the agonies of prison life were etched into his soul. He asked me about my living conditions, the standard of my food and my bed, clearly aware of the huge importance of those things to a prisoner's wellbeing. Before he left I introduced him again to my family, who thanked him and presented him with a bouquet of flowers. I was allowed to take photographs of him in the reception area and he signed my Arabic version of his book Long Walk to Freedom, *which describes his prison years. In it he wrote: 'To Comrade Megrahi, Best wishes to one who is in our thoughts and prayers continuously. Mandela.'*

Following the meeting he held a press conference, in which he declared: 'Megrahi is all alone. He has nobody he can talk to. It is a psychological persecution that a man must stay for the length of his long sentence all alone.' He called for me to be transferred to a prison in a Muslim country close to Libya, such as Morocco, Tunisia or Egypt. He pointed out that doubts persisted about my conviction and that the trial process had been criticised by the Organisation of African Unity.[18]

Not all my visitors were so welcome. On 29 August 2002, following a routine legal visit, the prison officers told me that I had further guests, whom I was required to see immediately. I was very surprised, as I was supposed to be notified of and approve every meeting. I said I didn't want to meet anyone without warning, but was told I had no choice. On entering the visiting room I came face to face with two

287

members of the prosecution team. * *I told them that I had no desire to see them without my lawyer present. They replied that this would not be necessary, as the meeting was confidential. They said that, as I had been convicted, I should tell them who had given me the instructions to carry out the bombing and who had helped me to get the bomb on the plane at Luqa Airport.*

At the time I was awaiting a court hearing to set my life-sentence tariff. Although the judges had recommended a minimum of 20 years, human rights legislation had since been introduced requiring courts to set precise tariffs for life-sentence prisoners, rather than simply make recommendations. The two men made it clear that, if I cooperated, I could expect a more lenient tariff. I made it equally clear that I was innocent and, in any case, would never speak to them without my lawyer present. Appalled that I was being leant on in this way, I called a prison officer and told him the meeting was over.

The officials had warned they would return and, sure enough, on 13 September, they did. I again made it clear that I wouldn't see them without my lawyer present. At this point the more senior of the two angrily warned me that I would regret my decision at the sentencing hearing.

The hearing took place on 24 November 2003. The judges announced that my tariff was to be extended from 20 to 27 years. Explaining the decision, Lord Sutherland said: 'Quite clearly this was a wicked act carried out in the full knowledge that the plan, if successful, would result in the slaughter of many entirely innocent persons. It would be difficult to consider a worse case of murder.'[19] Of course, he was quite right, it would be difficult to consider a worse case of murder, yet murderers convicted of killing fewer people had received 30-year tariffs. He said they'd taken into account my age and the fact that I was serving my sentence in a foreign country. However, they had cited precisely these factors in justifying their original recommendation. Why, then, had they increased the tariff by seven years? Could it be that they had been told that I refused to admit my guilt?

* In response to a Freedom of Information request by John Ashton, the Crown Office refused to disclose the names of the two individuals, but confirmed the dates of their visits.

288

Had I lied like Majid Giaka I would almost certainly have been dealt with more leniently.

Before renewing my fight for justice I had to decide whether to re-tain the same legal team. A few days after the appeal verdict, the team visited me in Barlinnie. I told them frankly that I was unhappy with Bill Taylor's cross-examination of Tony Gauci. Taylor said that, if I wished to pursue a further appeal on the grounds of defective representation by the legal team, they would have to step down. Shortly afterwards I met with Alastair Duff. I told him I believed I was in prison because of the defence's handling of Gauci and that I wished to replace the entire team. It was a tough decision, as he was a good man, who was strongly devoted to my cause, and we'd built a solid personal rapport, but I had to put my quest for justice before sentiment.

In Duff's place I appointed Eddie MacKechnie, primarily be-cause, having successfully represented Lamin, he was familiar with the case. Suave and charming, the 51-year-old golf lover was not the typical criminal appeal lawyer, and, although he felt strongly that I'd been wrongly convicted, did not immediately jump at the invitation. As he'd by then left McGrigor Donald, on accepting the instruction, he set up his own firm, MacKechnie & Associates.

The only legal avenue open to Abdelbaset was to have the convic-tion reviewed by the Scottish Criminal Cases Review Commission (SCCRC), the statutory body established in 1999 to consider alleged miscarriages of justice. A small team set about the groundwork for the SCCRC application, initially working out of offices in Glasgow's St Vincent Street, and later Park Circus. MacKechnie appointed two new advocates to advise on and shape the application. The more senior, Maggie Scott QC, was widely regarded as the leading Scottish criminal appeal counsel of her generation. She came to prominence fighting so-called Anderson appeals, named after a 1996 case that es-tablished the principle that an appeal may be fought on the grounds of defective preparation or presentation by the appellant's original defence team. At Scott's recommendation, MacKechnie appointed as her junior Jamie Gilchrist, a meticulous criminal trial specialist who later also became a QC. Scott and Gilchrist were asked to consider, among other things, whether the Gauci cross-examination and other aspects of Abdelbaset's original defence fell within the Anderson judgment's definition of defective representation. They concluded that they did.

In November 2002, a member of MacKechnie's team noticed an intriguing anomaly concerning Tony Gauci's police statements. Every statement taken by the police was supposed to be logged on the Home Office Large Major Enquiry System computer, known as HOLMES. The system designated each statement by its own unique reference number, comprising an 'S' prefix (the 'S' standing for statement) and a number that was unique to the witness. In Gauci's case the number was 4677. If witnesses gave more than one statement, the subsequent ones were given an alphabetical suffix, which reflected the order in which they were added to the system, rather than the order in which they were produced. Thus, Gauci's first statement was S4677, the next one added was S4677A, and the fifth one S4677D. The team member noticed that the last Gauci statement was S4677U. Given that U is the 21st letter of the alphabet, there should have been 22 statements, yet the Crown had disclosed only 20. On further checking, it was apparent that those with the suffixes J and S were missing. With only a few exceptions, the alphabetical sequence of the statements reflected the chronological order in which Gauci had given them. Given that S4677I and S4677K were respectively dated 4 and 2 October 1989, it was likely that S4677J had been produced at around the same time. The date of S4677S was more difficult to pinpoint, as the preceding statement, S4677R, described the crucial occasion on 15 February 1991 when he picked out Abdelbaset's photograph as resembling the purchaser, and S4677T was dated 4 November 1991.[20]

In early 2003 MacKechnie's team was joined by the investigator George Thomson. Not long after, one of his Scottish police contacts introduced him to a retired detective who had worked on the Lockerbie inquiry and was said to be unhappy with certain aspects of it. The officer, who became known as 'the Golfer', indicated his willingness to talk, on condition of anonymity. Over a series of meetings with MacKechnie and Thomson, he made a number of allegations about the police investigation, the most serious being that certain clothing fragments had been planted in order to reinforce the link to Gauci's Mary's House shop.

MacKechnie presented Abdelbaset's 400-page SCCRC application in September 2003. Produced by Scott and Gilchrist, it submitted, in essence, that Abdelbaset had been denied a fair trial. In addition to arguing defective representation, it contended that the trial verdict was unreasonable and that there had been abuses of process in a number of areas, including interference with the recovery of evidence and irregularities surrounding the circuit-board fragment PT/35b. It also invited the Commission to consider the missing Gauci statements and a number of areas of fresh evidence, including the alleged inducements received by Gauci, and the revelations by Robert Baer and the Golfer.

It was clear that the SCCRC's review would last at least a year. In the meantime, MacKechnie & Associates continued their investigations. Thomson revisited the Maltese clothing evidence and, in doing so, noticed a number of potentially significant anomalies, which appeared to tally with claims the Golfer had made about the brown-checked Yorkie trousers and the babygro. Thomson independently uncovered a still more intriguing inconsistency in relation to PI/995, the piece of grey shirt collar from which PT/35b was supposedly extracted by RARDE's Dr Thomas Hayes on 12 May 1989. Hayes and Feraday's joint forensic report stated that photograph 116 of the report depicted PI/995 prior to its dissection by Hayes. Thomson found other records indicating that, if the report was correct, then the dissection must have taken place months after 12 May 1989.* He detailed his findings in a series of reports, which MacKechnie sent as further submissions to the SCCRC during 2004.

Since three of the reports repeated the Golfer's allegations, the Commission wished to interview him. After some wrangling over the terms, he agreed, again on condition of anonymity. His accounts were erratic, often inconsistent and sometimes contradictory, and on one occasion he called the Commission from a bar when clearly drunk. During one of the interviews he revealed that he had 'worked' at MacKechnie & Associates' office. In the Commission's view, this involvement with the company 'went beyond that normally expected

* This anomaly is explained in more detail in Chapter 8.

of a witness'.[21]* There was little doubt that these episodes soured the Commission's view of MacKechnie's further submissions and may have cost his team a good deal of credibility.

In early 2005 I was told that I was to be transferred from the Barlinnie unit to an open wing of HMP Gateside in Greenock. Although this meant I was to be officially downgraded from Category A, I was very concerned by the news, fearing that I would be in grave danger from other prisoners. The governors of both prisons did their best to reassure me. The Gateside Governor, Derek McGill, took the trouble to meet me three times to address my concerns. He told me that I would be moving to a wing called Chrisswell House, which was populated exclusively by long-term prisoners – many of them lifers. He explained that they were all nearing the end of their tariffs and would be very unlikely to jeopardise their chance of parole by attacking me. He'd met with the prisoners and, although some initially objected to being locked up with a supposed terrorist, he'd assured them that I was a model prisoner and not the monster they imagined.

The transfer took place in February 2005. On the morning of the move I was up early to gather my belongings and say goodbye to the guards. Almost all of them had proved to be thoroughly decent people, and highly courteous and professional in their manner. In my three years in Barlinnie, only two had ever been unpleasant and disrespectful. There were three in particular whom I would miss, 'Big John', 'Little John' and Alistair. The governors of the two prisons kindly agreed that Big John and Alistair would accompany me to Greenock and remain in Chrisswell House for a week to help everyone acclimatise.

At 6.10 a van arrived take me the 20 miles or so to my new home. I had been in prison for five years, but had never before been among convicted prisoners. The transfer was covered by the press, and the next day I received 27 letters, 24 of which were from well-wishers. However, the move was overshadowed by the death the same day of my father-in-law, al-Haj Ali. I was very distressed when I heard the news, as we were exceptionally close and I regarded him almost as a

---

* *I was not aware of this arrangement, which would no doubt have destroyed his value as a witness in any future appeal.*

second father. I also knew how devastating his passing would be for Aisha and the children.

Chrisswell House had four sections, separated from each other by metal doors, with each able to house 15 men in single cells. I was originally supposed to spend my first few nights in isolation elsewhere in the prison, but the cell was very cold, so after the first night it was agreed that I could be transferred to the unit. My new cell was tiny, containing only a bed, a small, wall-mounted table and a wardrobe, but it was better than the isolation cell.

For the first few days the other prisoners were wary of me, but none were openly hostile. After that their suspicions subsided, and I began to have proper conversations with a number of them. Conditions in the unit were pretty good. We all had our own cell and key, so could move around the section as we chose. It was clean and well-decorated, and we kept it in good condition. Each section had a snooker table, and a soft seating area, but there were only two toilets and two bathrooms, which meant we often had to queue. Outside the unit there were two Astroturf pitches, which we were free to use outside patrol periods.

We received our meals in the cafeteria adjacent to the kitchen, and bags of fruit and cereal were available. Each week we were provided with a menu and allowed choose our meals for the following week, and we had a microwave for cooking items bought from the canteen. As a Muslim, my options were limited, although the SPS provided halal meat daily. My meals were often prepared by a Sikh man called Singh, who worked in the prison kitchen and was probably my best friend among the inmates. I liked his cooking, because, like me, he was from a culinary culture rich in spices. Eventually, with the Governor's permission, a member of the Libyan consular staff taught him to cook some Libyan dishes.

In contrast to Barlinnie and Zeist, during the holy month of Ramadan I was allowed to receive my fast-breaking meals from outside the prison.* The families of the Libyan Consul General in Glagow, Abdulrahman Swessi, the Consulate's Financial Controller, Abdullah Grede, and the Administration Officer, Ali Abjed, kindly prepared the food and brought it to the prison. It was thoroughly checked

* During Ramadan Muslims are expected to fast during daylight hours.

then handed to me in time to eat after sunset. There was always more than I could possibly eat, so I would share it with the other men in C Section, who seemed to enjoy their introduction to Libyan cuisine.

During the day most of the unit's residents were employed in the prison or on community work placements. For security reasons these options were not open to me. One day a week I attended the education centre, but the teaching on offer was very limited. I wanted to do a master's degree in climatology, but this wasn't feasible, as it would have required access to the internet. Generally, though, the security measures were more relaxed and flexible than at Barlinnie.

The Glasgow Consulate gave me around £500 a month, which I mainly used for phone calls, snacks from the canteen and the occasional luxury item, which we were allowed to order through the Argos catalogue. Had I chosen to, I could have spent the money less wisely, as, to my amazement, it was frequently easy to get hold of drugs. Even in Chrisswell, where men tended to be on their best behaviour, I'd say around 95 per cent of men took drugs at one time or another. The habitual users were far easier to deal with when high and best avoided when none were available. The SPS ran a strict random drug-testing regime, under which offenders were automatically downgraded, which meant a loss of privileges, and temporary transfer to another prison. Sadly, this was barely a deterrent to many, and some prisoners were transferred out more than once, only to return a few months later. While I was in Gateside one man travelled this merry-go-round at least three times. I have never touched drugs in my life and the officers knew it, so I was probably the only prisoner in the place never to undergo testing.

We were free to make as many telephone calls as we liked, using cards that we topped up with credit. On entering a PIN number the phones gave a read-out of the available credit. One day I discovered that my credit had gone down by £5 since my last call. I suspected that someone had stolen my PIN number and reported what had happened to the staff. They quickly established that rogue calls had been charged to my account, which were traced to friends and relatives of a fellow inmate, ironically someone with whom I got on well. As punishment he was downgraded and transferred out of Chrisswell House for a while.

During 2005 a spate of press articles appeared that cast doubt on my conviction. The Consulate provided me with daily updates of the coverage, and supplied hard copy of the most important articles, which helped me win over many of the Chrisswell inmates. I also showed them extracts of my case papers, which further persuaded them that there was something very wrong with my conviction. As one of them said, 'Why are you in here? You shouldn't be!'

The officers were also supportive, a genuinely nice bunch of people who did whatever they could to help me and my family. As in Barlinnie, I was always courteous and respectful towards them, which soon prompted one to comment, 'You're different, we've never had one like you!' I built a good rapport with all the officers and we'd have a lot of fun bantering about Celtic and Rangers and other footballing matters.

They were especially helpful during family visits. The visiting room was only around eight feet square and was separated from the adjacent one by a thin wall with frosted-glass panels. Since they were unable to run around, my young sons could be quite noisy. On one occasion a lawyer meeting his client next door banged on the window and asked us to be quiet. From then on the officers would do their best to divert prisoners and their lawyers to rooms further down the corridor, so the adjacent one remained empty. The visits were supposed to be time-limited, but the staff almost always allowed us a little leeway, as they knew we wouldn't take liberties.

I continued to be visited by important well-wishers, including UN Observers. It was important for me and my family to know that we remained in the thoughts of the international community and that our own government was doing all it could to help me achieve justice.

One of my most cherished visitors was Dr Jim Swire. Ever since losing his daughter Flora, a day short of her 24th birthday, he has fought to uncover the truth about Lockerbie and in doing so he had become a reluctant figurehead for the British victims' relatives. He attended every day of my trial, by the end of which he strongly believed in my innocence and that the truth about the bombing remained concealed. His visit, in September 2005, was prompted by rumours then circulating that I might be repatriated to Libya to serve my sentence. It was the first time that I had met one of the bereaved. He wanted to know whether, if I were to return, I would wish SCCRC to continue its review. I reassured him that I would. I liked him very much; he had an impressive grasp of the case and was a man of faith, who only wanted the truth.

Another esteemed visitor was Dr Swire's close ally, the Labour MP and former Father of the House of Commons,* Tam Dalyell. He had maintained a close interest in Lockerbie ever since he was privately approached by a corncerned police officer on New Year's Eve 1988, and over the years had asked dozens of Parliamentary questions on the subject. An old-fashioned gentleman, he expressed his sincere apologies for the failure of the Scottish legal system and promised to continue highlighting the injustice I'd suffered.

The visitor who best understood my plight was Paddy Joe Hill. As one of the 'Birmingham Six', he'd spent 17 years wrongly imprisoned for the 1974 IRA Birmingham pub bombings, which claimed 21 lives. The case was based primarily on the men's apparent confessions and on forensic tests, which supposedly established that they'd handled explosives. In 1991, at their third attempt, the men were freed on appeal after the tests were discredited and key passages of the statements were proved to have been fabricated. Freedom had not proved easy; within a few years he'd spent his compensation money and he was continually tormented by the UK government's failure to apologise for the Six's ordeal. He channelled his anger into helping fellow victims of injustice, and in 2001 co-founded the Miscarriage of Justice Organisation (MOJO) to campaign on behalf of those wrongly convicted.

Hill knew better than anyone the innate reluctance of the criminal justice system to right its wrongs. Following their first unsuccessful appeal, the Six attempted to press charges against West Midlands Police. The case eventually reached the High Court, where it was rejected by a panel of three judges led by England's most senior civil judge, the Master of the Rolls, Lord Denning. In one of the most notorious judgments of recent times, he opined: 'Just consider the course of events if their [the Six's] action were to proceed to trial . . . If the six men failed it would mean that much time and money and worry

---

* Father of the House is a title given to the longest serving MP. Dalyell was first elected in 1962 and served until 2005.

would have been expended by many people to no good purpose. If they won, it would mean that the police were guilty of perjury; that they were guilty of violence and threats; that the confessions were involuntary and improperly admitted in evidence; and that the convictions were erroneous. That would mean that the Home Secretary would have either to recommend that they be pardoned or to remit the case to the Court of Appeal. That was such an appalling vista that every sensible person would say, "It cannot be right that these actions should go any further."' By the time I was convicted 21 years later, no judge would dare to so nakedly place the reputation of the justice system before the interests of justice, but the common ancestry of judicial myopia was all too obvious.

Another visitor familiar with the unique stresses endured by the wrongly imprisoned was the retired Governor of HMP Zeist, Ian Bannatyne. I'd got to know him well during my time there and greatly respected his decency and professionalism. We had got on at a personal level, sharing, among other things, a love of Italian food. Although professional etiquette had prevented him from discussing the case, he'd taken a keen interest in it and was in court most days. Freed from those constraints, he told me frankly that, in his view, had I faced a jury trial I would have been acquitted.

The letters also kept coming. On average I received one a day, and on some days three or four. At least 99 per cent were supportive and I was very cheered by their warmth and kindness. Many people enclosed photos of themselves and their families, and some even sent me money to buy stamps and telephone credits. At first I tried to reply to everyone, but eventually I became too enmeshed in my case to spare the time.

The Church of Scotland wrote to me enclosing a letter to Tony Blair, urging him to allow me to return to Libya. I also had a staunch ally in Father Pat Keegans, Lockerbie's Catholic parish priest at the time of the bombing. Perhaps the most interesting letter of support I received was anonymous. Written on high-quality paper, the contents and phrasing strongly suggested to me that the author was a figure of some importance, who couldn't be seen to support my cause publicly.

The kind words were always uplifting, but I also had to cope with further bereavements, among them those of my beloved uncles Gaith and Ali. Worst of all was the sudden death of my nephew Faris in a car accident. My grief was always magnified by the anguish of being unable to help and comfort their immediate families.

By the time I was moved to Greenock I had been waiting almost a year and a half for the SCCRC to complete its review of my case. The Commission refused to be drawn on when it would issue its decision, but, reading between the lines, it was clear that they had some way to go. In the meantime, I was becoming increasingly unhappy with my solicitor Eddie MacKechnie, and in summer 2005, in the presence of Maggie Scott, made it clear that I was considering replacing him. I subsequently contacted Scott, via the Libyan Consulate, to tell her that I wished to dispense with MacKechnie and retain her and Jamie Gilchrist as counsel. Professional rules limited what she could say. She advised me that I would have to sack the entire legal team and discuss my choice of counsel with whomever I chose to replace MacKechnie.

In the event MacKechnie resigned in August, citing a potential conflict of interest.

Having taken soundings from respected legal sources, I appointed in his place Tony Kelly, a young solicitor whose small practice, Taylor & Kelly, was based in the Lanarkshire former steel town of Coatbridge. The contrast with his predecessor could not have been sharper: whereas MacKechnie was from a commercial civil law background, Kelly had made his name in the unglamorous, and poorly-paid, field of prisoners' rights. His spartan office, above a branch of the Airdrie Savings Bank, was a far cry from MacKechnie's premises in Glasgow's exclusive Park Circus, and he preferred a seat at Celtic's Parkhead stadium to the golf courses of Ayrshire and Portugal. He had won a series of landmark human rights cases, most notably against the Scottish Executive over the degrading practice of 'slopping out'. This had made him unpopular with the tabloid press, whose attitude to his clients, as he jokingly put it, boiled down to 'they're not human and they don't have rights'.

Kelly brought a fresh pair of eyes to the case and immediately impressed me wih his determination to review every area. Getting to grips with the evidence presented a huge challenge, as by this time the *case papers ran to hundreds of lever-arch files and thousands of electronic documents. Fortunately he was able to call on the knowledge of the advocates Maggie Scott and Jamie Gilchrist, and investigator George Thomson, all of whom I had insisted should be reinstructed.*

However, the task was too great for the four of them alone, so the team was gradually expanded. Two highly able junior advocates, Shelagh McCall and Martin Richardson, were instructed to work alongside Scott and Gilchrist. Kelly also drafted in additional solicitors, John Scott (later named Scottish Criminal Lawyer of the Year), and Taylor & Kelly associates Laura Morton and Jennifer Blair. At my request the team was joined by researcher John Ashton, who had worked briefly for MacKechnie. The vital job of organising and locating paperwork fell to recent law graduates Paul Scullion and Aileen Wright.

An obvious area of priority for Kelly was Tony Gauci's identification evidence. Two months after he took on the case, further doubt was cast on that evidence from a most unlikely source. In an interview published on 23 October 2005, the former Lord Advocate, Lord Fraser of Carmyllie, told the *Sunday Times*: 'Gauci was not quite the full shilling. I think even his family would say [he] was an apple short of a picnic. He was quite a tricky guy, I don't think he was deliberately lying but if you asked him the same question three times he would just get irritated and refuse to answer ... You do have to worry, he's a slightly simple chap, are you putting words in his mouth even if you don't intend to?' The comment was all the more astonishing because Fraser was the Lord Advocate responsible for the original indictments in 1991. The point was not lost on Bill Taylor QC, who told the newspaper: 'A man who has a public office, who is prosecuting in the criminal courts in Scotland, has got a duty to put forward evidence based upon people he considers to be reliable. He was prepared to advance Gauci as a witness and, if he had these misgivings about him, they should have surfaced at the time. The fact that he is now coming out many years later after my former client has been in prison for nearly four and a half years is nothing short of disgraceful.'[22]

Although remarkable, Fraser's comments were, for Kelly, a distraction. He was keen to explore the factors that undermined the reliability of Gauci's identification evidence and the subconscious influences that might have led him to pick Abdelbaset out of the photospread and ID parade. In doing so he accumulated a small library of academic papers that demonstrated the fallibility of eyewitness identification.

Some of the factors undermining Gauci's reliability were obvious and had been canvassed at trial, in particular the extraordinary length of time between the event and the crucial photoshow. Others were less obvious: for example, the fact that the man he identified was of a different race. It was also clear that Gauci had been exposed to an array of influences that could have steered him in Abdelbaset's direction. Again, some, like his exposure to media images, were obvious and had been raised by the previous team. Among the less obvious was the presence during the photoshow of police officers who knew which of the photos was of the suspect. Academic studies have demonstrated that even those acting in good faith can unintentionally give signals that might influence a witness. For this reason, recognised good practice requires photoshows and ID parades to be conducted by officers unconnected with the investigation.

The original defence team had considered instructing experts in eyewitness evidence, but concluded that their opinions would be inadmissible and would, in any case, simply reiterate what the judges already knew.[23] In Maggie Scott's view, the judges had not demonstrated an awareness of the factors that could have impacted on the identification. On the one hand, they had taken into account matters that were either irrelevant or inaccurate, such as the supposed reliability of his recall of the clothing, and, on the other, they had failed to take into account relevant risk factors in the identification procedures. And, while she agreed that Scots law would not admit expert opinions on the credibility or reliability of any particular witness, there was a strong case that the defence could, and should, have led expert evidence on the risk factors and on the general pitfalls of identification evidence.

Kelly instructed some of the world's leading authorities on the subject, among them Professor Steve Clark of the University of California, Riverside, Professor David Canter, Director of Liverpool University's Centre for Investigative Psychology, and Professor Tim Valentine of Goldsmith's College, London.

The other main area requiring expert investigation was forensics. To look afresh at the findings of the RARDE scientists Dr Thomas Hayes and Allen Feraday, Kelly engaged Dr Roger King of Coventry-based firm Key Forensic Services. Trained in bomb-scene investigation and a veteran of a number of major terrorist bombing cases, he had previously spent 25 years with the Home Office's Forensic Science Service (FSS). Kelly gave him all the material available at the trial, including the scientists' joint report and their examination notes. His review was, necessarily, slow-going, but would eventually produce some very significant conclusions.

When Kelly took over the case, he anticipated that the SCCRC would deliver its findings within a few months, but a year later he was still waiting. The delay was due in part to the Commission's decision to interview dozens of witnesses, among them Abdelbaset's original solicitor Alastair Duff, and advocates Bill Taylor QC and John Beckett. Since the trial Duff had ceased criminal defence work, having been appointed a Sheriff. Beckett became a QC in 2005 and since 2003 had been a full-time Advocate Depute. By the time of the interview he had succeeded Alan Turnbull QC as Scotland's Principal Advocate Depute, and the following month became Solicitor General.[24]

As they were intended, primarily, to explore the issue of alleged defective representation, the interviews concentrated largely on their approach to Gauci's evidence. While Duff and Beckett each said that the responsibility for Gauci's cross-examination lay ultimately with Taylor, neither disagreed with his light touch approach. Taylor confirmed that the decision to avoid a head-on challenge was a tactical one, as the defence team perceived him to be a volatile witness requiring careful handling.[26] Beckett said the cross-examination 'required one to tiptoe through a minefield', adding, 'it is easy now for the applicant to say that things should have been done differently. However, there was much information out there that could have been very damaging to his defence . . . Giaka had not yet been called. We did not know that Fhimah would be acquitted, or that the evidence relating to the diary would be ruled inadmissible in the case against the applicant.' More generally, he observed: 'I feel that the Commission's process involves a lot of hindsight. It is easy to query decisions once

301

you know what evidence was accepted and what was not accepted. It was a very difficult thing to deal with at the time.'[26]

While Abdelbaset waited for the SCCRC review to conclude, one of the trial judges, Lord MacLean, made an extraordinary public statement. Clearly stung by the widespread criticism of his guilty verdict, he told *The Scotsman* newspaper, 'I have no doubt, on the evidence we heard, that the judgments we made and the verdicts we reached were correct.' It was highly unusual for a judge to comment publicly on a case over which he had presided, especially as he knew very well that the SCCRC had yet to reach a decision on the case. He said he expected the Commission would grant a further appeal, commenting: 'They can't be working for two years without producing something with which to go to the court.' He added, 'But it depends upon what the bases are for a fresh appeal, but I wouldn't have a problem with that.'[27] As events proved, the Commission did not share MacLean's faith in the judges' power of reasoning.

The Truth Emerges 13

In June 2007 the SCCRC's Senior Legal Officer, Robin Johnston, notified Tony Kelly that, after almost four years, the Commission had completed its review and would reveal its findings on 28 June. Although my team were hopeful of a second appeal, bitter experience held my optimism in check. A public announcement was to be made at midday on the 28th, but Johnston agreed to deliver the Commission's report – known as the Statement of Reasons – to Kelly's home at 7.00. He even went to the trouble of a dry run the night before to be sure of finding the right address. Though he obviously knew the decision that evening, he gave nothing away to Kelly.

He duly arrived promptly the following morning, handed over two copies of the Statement, and broke the news that my application had been successful – I had been granted a second appeal.

The Statement ran to 820 pages, and was supported by 13 volumes of appendices. It identified six grounds for referring the case back to the Appeal Court – in other words, six reasons why I might have suffered a miscarriage of justice. There was too much for Kelly to read there and then, so Johnston summarised the conclusions over a cup of tea. If he'd imagined Kelly would be happy, he was mistaken. Although obviously relieved by the decision, Kelly was dismayed at some of the findings and the narrow scope of the Commission's investigation. What both men had hoped would be a relaxed chat soon became a heated discussion and, by the time Johnston left an hour later, each was fairly disheartened.

By 8.30 Kelly had arrived at Gateside prison, bringing with him a copy of the Statement of Reasons and the appendices. As he entered the officers looked at him expectantly, and one commented that he could tell what the decision was, but Kelly didn't rise to the bait. He somehow carried the three boxes of appendices to the meeting room, then waited for me to arrive.

As I entered the room I noticed he was carrying a CD-rom. I immediately knew I had won, as Johnston had said that successful applicants were given their statements of reasons on a CD, whereas unsuccessful ones received only a hard copy. As Kelly confirmed the news, we hugged for the first time since I'd known him. I was elated, but he made clear his disappointment at the Commission's findings and warned that we now faced a far bigger fight than he'd hoped.

The most significant of the SCCRC's six grounds was that the trial court's judgment was unreasonable; specifically, there was no reasonable basis for concluding that the clothes purchase date was 7 December. Had it been a jury trial, the finding would have been unremarkable, but the judgement had, of course, been delivered by three of Scotland's most senior judges.

In concluding that the purchase must have taken place on a Wednesday, they had, in the Commission's view, 'ignored the many passages in Mr Gauci's evidence (and the terms of his statement of 10 September 1990) in which he made it clear that he was unable to remember the day or date of the purchase'. Regarding the choice of Wednesday 7 December, rather than 23 November, it stated what most rational observers already knew, namely, that 'Although the weather evidence did not necessarily exclude 7 December as the date of purchase, in any choice between that date and 23 November it strongly favoured the latter . . . In the absence of a reasonable foundation for the date of purchase accepted by the Trial Court, and bearing in mind the problems with Mr Gauci's identification of the applicant, the Commission is of the view that no reasonable Trial Court could have drawn the inference that the applicant was the purchaser.' Then came the *coup de grâce*: 'Based on these conclusions the Commission is of the view that the verdict in the case is at least arguably one which no reasonable court, properly directed, could have returned.'[1] The words 'properly directed' clearly implied that the judges may have misdirected themselves, which, given their seniority, was extraordinary.

But, while this finding was very welcome, Kelly was bitterly disappointed that the Commission had upheld only one of the six 'unreasonable verdict' grounds in the original application. The most

important of these concerned the judges' treatment of the identification evidence. The Statement noted, quite correctly, the extraordinary
length of time between the purchase and the ID parade and dock
identifications. In its view, this 'cast significant doubt' on the reliability of the identification. As for the supposed identification of Abdelbaset's photo on 15 February 1991, this 'was one of resemblance only
and was qualified and equivocal . . . It was also made two years after
the event and was undermined by Mr Gauci's initial description of the
purchaser, particularly his height and age.'[2] Given these observations,
how could the Commission have regarded as reasonable the Court's
finding that Abdelbaset was the purchaser?

A further disappointment was its rejection of the submission that
the trial defence had been defective, in particular Bill Taylor QC's
cross-examination of Gauci. With one exception, the Commission
also rejected the written submissions made by Eddie MacKechnie
subsequent to lodging the original application.

The exception also related to the purchase date and, in particular,
the Christmas decorations in Tower Road, where the shop was located. At trial Gauci said the purchase had taken place 'about a fortnight before Christmas', and was at 'about the time when the Christmas lights would be going up'. MacKechnie had submitted that the
new evidence concerning the Christmas lights, which was obtained
by Alastair Duff and the Maltese lawyers during the first appeal, cast
doubt upon 7 December as the purchase date. The key element of that
evidence was the diary entry of Tourism Minister Dr Michael Refalo,
which indicated that he switched on the lights on 6 December. The
defence team did not present this evidence at the appeal because they
felt that it would bolster Gauci's initial trial evidence that the lights
'were on already' at the time of the purchase.[3] However, he later told
the Court, 'I believe they were putting up the lights',[4] and in his police statements Gauci had said that the lights were not up. Moreover,
the judges accepted that the date was likely to have been around the
time the lights were being put up. The Commission noted that, 'if the
purchase was "about the time when the lights would be going up"
then in terms of Dr Refalo's diary the date is unlikely to have been 7
December 1988, as by that time the lights were illuminated . . . it follows that Dr Refalo's account is capable of undermining the court's

conclusion that the applicant was the purchaser.'[5] It was therefore, in its view, 'reasonable to conclude that had the police recovered Dr Refalo's diary during the course of those enquiries it would have cast significant doubt upon the prevailing view at that time that 7 December 1988 was the "probable" date of purchase.'[6]

The Commission barely disguised its irritation at the other written submissions. It had clearly spent a great deal of time investigating each one in detail, only to dismiss them all. It also wholly rejected the Golfer's allegations that the police had covered up and fabricated evidence. Having interviewed him three times, it found 'a vast array of inconsistencies' within his various accounts, which gave rise to 'serious misgivings' as to his credibility and reliability.[7]

Fortunately, the Commission had unearthed new evidence that provided the four other grounds of referral. One of these also concerned the clothes purchase date. When interviewed by the defence prior to the trial, Gauci said he thought it was 29 November. When asked why, he could say only, 'all I can say is that is what I think'.[8] When the inquiry team checked his Crown precognition statements they discovered there was a good reason for the date sticking in his memory, which was that he had had a row with his girlfriend.[9] The Commission observed that the statement 'might have played a useful part in the preparation and presentation of the defence case,' and concluded, 'by withholding this information the Crown deprived the defence of the opportunity to take such steps as it might have deemed necessary. Given the importance which the Trial Court attached to the date of purchase in drawing the inference that the applicant was the purchaser the Commission is unable to say that such measures might not have affected the verdict.'[10]

The third ground for referral concerned Gauci's exposure to articles about the case featuring Abdelbaset's photograph, in particular the one from *Focus* magazine. At trial it was accepted that he was shown the article by a neighbour in late 1998 or early 1999, and that he subsequently showed it to Superintendent Godfrey Scicluna, and pointed to the photograph, saying, 'That's him.' The SCCRC uncovered a statement by another Maltese officer, Sergeant Mario Busuttil, which revealed that Gauci did not hand the article to Scicluna until 9 April 1999, just four days before the identity parade at Kamp Zeist.

In other words, the Commission pointed out, 'whereas the evidence at trial perhaps gives the impression that the magazine was in Mr Gauci's possession only fleetingly, in terms of Sergeant Busuttil's statement the period seems to have been of the order of four months. During that time Mr Gauci appears to have kept the magazine at his home where he would have been free to view the contents of the article, including the applicant's photograph, as and when he wished. Critically, Mr Gauci's possession of the magazine, and therefore his potential exposure to the applicant's photograph, came to an end, not months before the identification parade as the evidence at trial perhaps tends to convey, but on 9 April 1999, a matter of only four days.'[11]

The Commission also uncovered a confidential police report, which demonstrated that Gauci had been exposed to more photos of Abdelbaset. Dated 20 March 1999, it discussed the difficulties caused by the increasing media coverage of the case and contained the following passage: 'On 28 February 1999 the Malta local language newspaper It Torca (The Torch) published a two page spread on pages 16 and 17 in which a photograph of the two accused appeared along with other photo montages of the various scenes at Lockerbie. Just after this appeared a local (thought to be a shopkeeper) (unidentified at present) came into Mary's House shop and showed Tony Gauci the article. The following week a further two page spread in the same newspaper was published which concluded the article begun the previous week, this was similar to the first with photographs supporting the main article. Needless to say the publication of this article had a profound effect on both of the brothers, it is more likely that Paul would be more worried than Tony as he can probably grasp the potential threat to his and his brother's safety.'[12]

When the Commission subsequently interviewed Gauci, he said that people came into his shop 'every day' with newspaper cuttings and he had also seen news items on TV that featured Abdelbaset's image.[13] More importantly, Paul Gauci told the Commission that he collected articles about the case as they were published and had kept them at home before the trial. He said 'there was practically an article every week' as well as programmes on the BBC, and that he would summarise their contents to Tony.[14] In the Commission's view, 'there was a substantial risk that the applicant would be instantly

307

recognisable to Mr Gauci, not from any genuine memory of the purchaser, but rather as a result of his exposure to photographs of the applicant in the media and, in particular, to the one he saw only four days previously.'[15]

Gauci told the Commission he did not believe the photos had influenced his ability to identify the clothes-buyer, indeed, in contrast to his earlier partial identifications, he was now confident that Abdelbaset was '100 per cent the right person'.[16] However, the Commission considered it unlikely that he could have put the photos out of his mind entirely at the ID parade, adding, 'In any event his assurances in this connection do not lessen the risk that his identification was influenced by such factors. This is not to suggest that Mr Gauci was seeking at interview to hide the possibility that his identification of the applicant was unreliable, simply that he himself may not be fully aware of the extent to which his identification evidence was affected by what he had seen in the media.'[17] Once again, the Commission considered that the newly uncovered documents should have been disclosed to the defence, as they were likely to have been 'of real importance in undermining the Crown case'.[18]

The fourth and final of the Gauci grounds for appeal was the most sensational, as it concerned the discussion of reward payments to him and his brother. The Commission discovered an extract from DCI Harry Bell's diary that suggested the issue was first raised less than a month after the police first met the brothers. Dated 28 September 1989, the entry concerned a conversation that Bell had that day with FBI agent Chris Murray. It stated that Murray 'had the authority to arrange unlimited money for Tony Gauci and relocation is available. Murray states that he could arrange $10,000 immediately.' It added, 'Murray was advised that no facilities are to be used without Bell's knowledge and consultation with the Maltese authorities.'[19] The US government's rewards and witness protection programmes were originally intended to provide an incentive to informants in organised crime cases, yet here was the FBI suggesting they might apply to a straightforward witness of fact, whose evidence had been willingly volunteered.

The Commission was unable to establish whether the FBI made the offer to Gauci; however, it confirmed that Tony had first expressed an interest in a reward prior to picking out Abdelbaset's photograph on 15 February 1991. This was revealed in a memo produced six days later by Bell for Superintendent James Gilchrist. Headed 'Security of Witness Anthony Gauci, Malta' it discussed measures that might be taken to safeguard Gauci's safety, should news of the partial identification leak out. The last paragraph revealed: 'During recent meetings with Tony he has expressed an interest in receiving money. It would appear that he is aware of the US reward monies which have been reported in the press.' It continued, 'If a monetary offer was made to Gauci this may well change his view and allow him to consider a witness protection programme as a serious avenue.'[20] In a further memo, dated 14 June 1991, Bell wrote: 'I have had no personal contact with the witness Anthony Gauci since he made the "Partial Identification of Abdel Baset".'[21] In other words, the 'recent meetings' referred to in the earlier memo must have occurred on or before 15 February.

In 1999, with the trial looming, the police again considered witness protection measures. The results of the assessment were contained in a confidential report dated 10 June 1999. It described Gauci as being 'somewhat frustrated that he will not be compensated in any financial way for his contribution to the case', but added that great care had been taken never to offer him inducements to give evidence. It emphasised that Tony Gauci was a 'humble man who leads a very simple life which is firmly built on a strong sense of honesty and decency'. Its assessment of Paul, however, was rather different: 'It is apparent from speaking to him for any length of time that he has a clear desire to gain financial benefit from the position he and his brother are in relative to the case. As a consequence he exaggerates his own importance as a witness and clearly inflates the fears that he and his brother have. He is anxious to establish what advantage he can gain from the Scottish police. Although demanding, Paul Gauci remains an asset to the case but will continue to explore any means he can to identify where financial advantage can be gained. However, if this area is explored in court with this witness however [sic] he will also strongly refute that he has been advantaged.'[22] Following the appraisal, the brothers were included in the Strathclyde Police's witness protection programme.[23]

The police assessment was subsequently echoed privately by the Crown Office. In a note at the end of Tony's Crown precognition statement, a Procurator Fiscal wrote: 'He [Mr Gauci] has never at any stage sought to benefit from his involvement. His brother, whilst not openly seeking any reward, has been more alive to the possibility of obtaining substantive assistance from the police which, in accordance with good practice, has been restricted to matters ensuring their immediate safety.'[24]

Eighteen months later, as the trial drew to a close, the police again reviewed the question of rewards. In a report entitled 'Impact Assessment Anthony and Paul Gauci', produced in January 2001, an unidentified officer once more insisted that, 'The issue of financial remuneration has not previously been discussed in detail with the witnesses and no promises exist.' However, an earlier section of the report noted that, according to Paul, the publicity surrounding their involvement in the case 'has had an adverse impact on the turnover of the shop'. It also described how the brothers and their seven siblings had yet to resolve 'a number of issues relating to the disposal of the family home and other related financial matters surrounding the estate', which had arisen since the death of their father. Tony and Paul had 'delayed the resolution of these issues until the case has been concluded'. The report noted, 'This course of action has caused friction within the family group and whilst Paul considers that it was a prudent measure to await the outcome of the trial, it has impacted on the complex situation regarding the family finances.' The clear implication of all this is that Tony and Paul had delayed the resolution of the family financial issues in the expectation that they would receive a reward; indeed, the report went on, 'It is considered that the witnesses may harbour some expectation of their situation being recognised.' Although at pains to point out that 'whilst proceedings were still "live" they displayed a clear understanding that such matters could not be explored', it then argued that it was 'vital that they continue to perceive that their position is recognised and they continue to receive the respect that their conduct has earned'. The next paragraph was the most remarkable: 'It is considered that the implementation of the foregoing recommendations will ensure that when the inevitable reflections and media examinations take place in future years the

THE TRUTH EMERGES

witnesses who are the subject of this report will maintain their current position and not seek to make adverse comment regarding any perceived lack of recognition of their position. Nor is it anticipated they would ever seek to highlight any remuneration received.'[25] The message seemed clear: if the Gaucis were paid, they would not say anything that might embarrass the police or Crown.

A further undated document, headed 'Anthony and Paul Gauci Reward/Compensation Payments', which was clearly written after the trial, was adamant that rewards had never been discussed prior to the trial's end. It added, 'The motivation of both witnesses has never at any stage been financial, as can be seen from their refusal of money from the media. They have received no financial gain from the Scottish police; as a result, their integrity as witnesses remains intact. This has been the priority from the outset.' On the subject of Tony, it said, 'The very fact that the witness was not motivated by financial gain and as a result his integrity as a crucial witness was maintained, reinforces the need to ensure that at this stage his contribution and more importantly the manner of his contribution is recognised.' These claims were, no doubt unintentionally, undermined by the memo's observations concerning Paul. It noted that, although he did not give evidence, 'it should never be overlooked that his major contribution has been maintaining the resolve of his brother. Although younger, Paul has taken on the role of his father (died 7 years ago) with regard to family affairs. His influence over Anthony has been considerable (It is considered critical that the contribution of Paul is recognised in order to preserve their relationship and prevent any difficulties arising in the future).'[26] 'Paul's 'considerable' influence over Tony was especially significant, given what the 10 June 1999 memo described as his 'clear desire to gain financial benefit'.

A week after the trial verdict, Detective Chief Superintendent Tom McCulloch, who was by then Senior Investigating Officer, wrote to the US Embassy in The Hague to nominate Tony for a reward. The letter reported that 'Following the conviction of Megrahi the witness Gauci was visited by two men at his shop in Sliema and invited to travel to Tripoli for a "meeting with Government officials and members of the Defence Team". He was also informed that he "would not return home empty handed" but would be "handsomely rewarded".

311

As expected, Gauci refused the invitation but this incident is perhaps evidence of his continued vulnerability.'* Having reminded the Embassy that the judges considered Gauci to be 'a major factor' in the case, McCulloch concluded, 'I therefore feel that he is a worthy nominee for the Reward Programme and ask for your assistance in forwarding this nomination to the Department responsible for administering the Programme.'[27]

It seems that McCulloch did not follow up the matter until over a year later, after Abdelbaset's unsuccessful appeal. In a letter to the Deputy Chief of the US Department of Justice's Terrorism & Violent Crime Section,† dated 19 April 2002, he wrote, 'Following our very positive meeting on 9 April 2002, I am writing to confirm the submission by Dumfries and Galloway Constabulary for payment of a reward to Anthony and Paul Gauci . . . I was particularly satisfied that the meeting acknowledged the significant role of Paul Gauci and recognised the need to reward him separately from his brother. At the meeting on 9 April, I proposed that US 2 million dollars should be paid to Anthony Gauci and US 1 million dollars to his brother Paul. These figures were based on my understanding that US 2 million dollars was the maximum payable to a single individual by the Rewards Programme. However, following further informal discussions I was encouraged to learn that those responsible for making the final decision retain a large degree of flexibility to increase this figure. Given the exceptional circumstances of this case which involved the destruction of a United States aircraft with the loss of 270 innocent lives and the subsequent conviction of a Libyan Intelligence Agent for this crime, I would invite those charged with approving the reward to ensure that the payments made to Anthony and Paul Gauci properly reflect not only the importance of their evidence, but also their integrity and courage.' McCulloch said that, at the request of a US official, he had consulted with the Crown Office about the reward

* This approach took place without the knowledge or consent of Abdelbaset's defence team. In a memo of 27 January 2002, an unidentified police officer stated that one of the two men who approached Gauci was Maltese and the other Sicilian.
† The Deputy Chief's name was redacted in the copy of the letter obtained by the SCCRC.

application. He reported, 'The prosecution in Scotland cannot become involved in such an application. It would therefore be improper for the Crown Office to offer a view on the application, although they fully recognise the importance of the evidence of Tony and Paul Gauci to the case.' So, the Crown Office was not allowed to seek a reward, but apparently had no intention of preventing the police from doing so. The letter ended, 'it would be helpful if a decision on this matter could be reached in a very short timescale, and I would be grateful if this application could be processed expeditiously.' It was never denied that Tony and Paul received at least $2 million and $1 million respectively.[28]

When interviewed by the Commission, Tony disputed the contents of Bell's memo of 21 February 1991 and denied ever asking for money. He said he'd never been offered a reward prior to giving evidence and only recalled his brother raising the subject after the trial.[29] Paul also maintained that the police had never made an offer, but said it was well known from the press that a reward was available and that he had insisted on being paid once the appeal was over. Asked about the Bell memo, he said he was not present at the meetings to which it referred;[30] however, Bell told the Commission that the meetings would have involved Paul and that Paul was pushing for a reward to compensate for the difficulties caused to the family. Bell said he would always 'clamp down' on any discussion of the issue and was also adamant that there had been no discussion of rewards with Tony on 15 February 1991, when he picked out Abdelbaset's photo. When asked whether FBI agent Chris Murray had ever met with Gauci to discuss a reward, Bell replied, 'I cannot say that he did not do so'. He also revealed that FBI agent John Hosinski had met Tony alone on 2 October 1989, but said he seriously doubted that money had been discussed at that meeting and was insistent that the $10,000 offer had never been put to Tony.[31]

In evaluating the newly uncovered evidence, the Commission noted that, whether consciously or not, Gauci's trial evidence had veered away from his original description of the clothes purchaser in a way that was helpful to the Crown. Whereas he was originally certain that the man was around 50 years old and six foot or more in height, he told the Court 'I think he was below six feet. I'm not an expert on these things, I can't say'[32] and 'I don't have experience on height and age'.[33] The Commission also pointed out that the *Focus* magazine article highlighted the fact that Abdelbaset was much younger and smaller than the man he had originally described.[34] Gauci confirmed to the Commission that someone had read him this passage, so he must have been alert to the problems that his evidence might cause the Crown.[35]

The Commission should, perhaps, also have pointed out that Gauci's trial evidence was much more helpful to the Crown than his police statements on the matter of the date of purchase. Whereas he had consistently told the police that the purchase took place in November or December and that the Christmas lights were not up, he had told the Court that it was around a fortnight before Christmas and that the lights were either on, or being put up.

The Commission concluded, 'In referring the case on this ground the Commission is conscious of the potential impact of its decision upon Mr Gauci who may well have given entirely credible evidence notwithstanding an alleged interest in financial payment. On the other hand there are sound reasons to believe that the information in question would have been used by the defence as a means of challenging his credibility. Such a challenge may well have been justified, and in the Commission's view was capable of affecting the course of the evidence and the eventual outcome of the trial.'[36]

The last of the Commission's grounds of referral was set out in Chapter 25 of the Statement of Reasons. It was certainly the strangest of the six. It concerned two secret intelligence documents, supplied by another country, which members of the Commission's inquiry team had been allowed to view at Dumfries police station in September 2006. They were forbidden from copying them, and, although they were allowed to take notes, they had to leave them in the police's possession. On 27 April 2007 the Crown Office confirmed to the Commission that they had carefully considered whether or not the documents required to be disclosed to the defence and had concluded that they did not. They also acknowledged that neither they, nor the police, had investigated the information they contained. In March 2007 the Commission sought the consent of the Crown Office and police to include the documents with the Statement of

Reasons, but the Crown Office said it required the approval of the country that had supplied them.

The Statement of Reasons gave only two clues to the documents' contents. The first was an extract from the Crown's 27 April 2007 letter, which read, 'it has never been the Crown's position in this case that the MST-13 timers were not supplied by the Libyan intelligence services to any other party or that only the Libyan intelligence services were in possession of the timers.' The second came in paragraph 25.6 of the Statement, which read, 'In the Commission's view the Crown's decision not to disclose one of the documents to the defence indicates that a miscarriage of justice may have occurred in applicant's case. In reaching this decision the Commission has taken into account paragraphs 49, 73 and 74 of the Trial Court's judgment.'[37] Since paragraphs 49, 73 and 74 all referred to MST-13 timers and the PFLP-GC, it seemed certain that the documents also did.

In addition to the six grounds of referral, the Statement of Reasons considered all the matters raised in Abdelbaset's original application, among them the missing Gauci statements S4677J and S4677S. The Commission established that both statements were held on the HOLMES computer, along with a third undisclosed one, S4677V. S4677J and S4677V contained only Gauci's name and the words 'Registered in error'. The Commission raised the issue with retired SIO Superintendent Thomas Gordon, who identified two likely causes. The first was the sheer volume of material faced by the staff who typed the statements into the system. The second arose from the fact that many statements were faxed, which sometimes made them difficult for the typists to read. They would therefore sometimes wait for the original versions to be delivered before typing them up. As a consequence, those responsible for indexing the statements would be able to see that a statement had been registered, but would not be able to see its text. According to Gordon, in such circumstances the indexers sometimes mistakenly assumed that the original was the first version received, when in fact a faxed copy had already been registered. As a result, a single statement might be recorded on the system in duplicate, one of which would be marked as 'Registered in error' once the mistake had been detected. He reported that, as of 4 October 1991, 39 statements had been erroneously registered in this way.

S4677S was more surprising. It was dated 8 October 1991, but related to 6 December 1989, when Gauci was shown a selection of 12 photographs, including one of Mohamed Abu Talb. It was written in the first person under Gauci's name and confirmed that he had viewed the photos and was unable to identify any of them as the clothes purchaser, but a note at the end stated: 'Statement submitted by DS Byrne as continuity for final report, no statement having been submitted from Gauci. Gauci has not been re-interviewed for this additional statement.' So, the police had written a statement for Gauci without his knowledge. Despite establishing that the original version of the statement was sent to the Crown, along with Gauci's other statements, prior to the trial,[38] the SCCRC apparently did not seek access to it. The Commission concluded that, since the defence was aware of the events reported in the statement, its non-disclosure was of no consequence.[39]

The SCCRC's most significant additional Gauci discovery concerned his statement of 26 September 1989, in which he had described someone he believed to be the 'same man' visiting the shop the previous day. The Commission uncovered a report by DCI Bell, which described a meeting with Gauci a week later. It contained the following passage: 'He (Tony) now states that he can only be 50% sure that it was the same "Man" in the shop on Monday 25 September 89. The question now is with an apparent ability to recall in detail events of November and possibly December 1988 coupled with his recollection of the "Shooting trip" several years ago Tony can only be 50% sure of a week old sighting. DCI Bell pointed out that Tony was still under pressure from his father and brother Paul not to give information.'[40] As the Commission pointed out, if Tony was only 50 per cent certain of a sighting he had made seven days earlier, then it called into question the one he had made of the purchaser ten months earlier, and, more importantly, his subsequent partial identifications of Abdelbaset.[41]

The Commission also discovered that just a week after giving his first statement, Gauci was shown a photo line-up by Inspector Godfrey Scicluna of the Maltese Police. The information was contained in a fax sent to the Joint Intelligence Group, which acted as liaison between the Scottish police and the intelligence services. Scicluna had shown the photos because he thought that Gauci's description of the purchaser matched someone he knew. It made clear that he had acted against Bell's wishes.

Gauci did not pick out the photo of Scicluna's suspect, or any of the others; however, according to the fax, 'he said that the suspect had a hairstyle identical to No 2 (afro-style) and the facial features of No 20.'[42] The Crown Office claimed it had no record of the fax, but when the Commission's team checked the MI5 file containing the fax, they discovered a note indicating that Crown officials had viewed the file in March 2000.[43] Although the Commission was concerned that the episode was not recorded in a police statement, it did not believe that the non-disclosure had compromised Abdelbaset's right to a fair trial.[44] However, the reference to the afro hair was highly significant, because, when coupled with Gauci's original description of the suspect as 'dark', it was a fairly strong indication that the man was black or mixed race.

During the course of its inquiries the Commission obtained various 'diaries' that Bell had written during the police investigation in Malta. Rather surprisingly, he did not use a notebook while on the island. He said that he kept the diaries 'simply as a personal guide for me as to the state of the inquiry'; however, they were considered important enough to be handed over to the Lockerbie Incident Control Centre and typed up. Since they were the only contemporaneous record of the Malta investigation, the diaries were potentially of great importance. Unfortunately the appendices to the Statement of Reasons contained only small extracts of the typed versions, which were clearly dictated summaries, rather than verbatim copies of the handwritten originals.[45] The diaries did not commence until 11 September, twelve days after Bell's arrival in Malta, and the handwritten originals covering the periods 11 to 19 September and 25 September to 24 October 1989 were missing. Bell insisted that these missing sections were not significant, even though Gauci gave ten of his nineteen police statements during those periods.[46] Abdelbaset's legal team sought disclosure of both the remaining originals and complete copies of the typed summaries, but to no avail. Short, heavily redacted extracts of the originals, covering only 24 days, were finally disclosed in 2009. The typed versions, which were disclosed simultaneously, ran from 11 September 1989 until 30 January 1992, but most of the entries were blanked out. Less redacted extracts of both versions were subsequently disclosed; nevertheless, 20 years on, most of what the officer in charge of the Malta investigation wrote about that investigation during its crucial stages remains unknown.

The Commission unearthed potentially significant information about the MST-13 timers found in West Africa. Two timers were recovered from Togo in 1986, but it had been impossible to prove that they were connected to the supposedly Libyan-backed coup plot. The Senegal timer had never been traced and records obtained from the Senegalese government in 1990 suggested it was not among the items destroyed by the army in September 1989.* When interviewed in January 1991, the official in charge of the operation, Jean Collin, claimed not to know what had happened to the timer.[47] Among the documents disclosed to the Commission was a previously confidential memo, produced by SIO Stuart Henderson the month after Collin's interview, which provided a lengthy overview of the investigation and set out a series of directives. As the following passage made clear, the West African investigations were a causing considerable concern: 'After the recent interview of Jean Baptiste Collin, it is now more clear than ever that the circumstances surrounding the recovery of the "unboxed MST 13 timer" allegedly in Togo and the "boxed MST 13 timer" in Senegal, must be clarified beyond doubt. The whole essence of the "MST 13 TIMERS" is the sole manufacture by the MEBO company in world terms and the explicit distribution to the Libyan ESO. Unless we can consolidate the precise number of timers manufactured and especially the number of MST 13 circuit-boards manufactured to fit the "boxed timers" and confirm the fact that they were distributed, solely to the Libyans, then we have serious problems with our direct evidence.'[48]

A confidential police note, produced at the time of Collin's interview, demonstrated that Collin knew far more about the Senegal timer than he was prepared to say on the record. Apparently written

* See Chapter 4.

318

by DI William Williamson, it stated: 'There is no doubt in the minds of the investigating officers that the witness Jean Collin has much more information on this matter but chooses not to disclose it. In the course of his interview he stated angrily that he did not think the presence of American FBI personnel was proper* and inferred that the Americans knew the whole story. That [two named individuals], Americans were in Senegal at the time and were given all information.' Crucially, the notes went on to record that Collin said the timer had been given to 'an intelligence agency'.[49] The Commission established that the 'two named individuals' were the CIA agents who gave evidence at trial under the assumed names Kenneth Steiner and Warren Clemens.[50] Both had described examining the timer, but neither said that they had taken it from Senegal. The Commission also discovered a note in Bell's diary, which suggested that Collin was interviewed in America in December 1990, two months before the Scottish police saw him.[51] Details of that interview have never been disclosed.

The Commission was unable to explore these matters further with Collin, as he had died before the trial. It found no evidence that the timer had been given to an intelligence agency, but had clearly not raised the issue with either of the foreign agencies most involved in the Senegal episode, the DGSE and the CIA. It instead referred to an MI5 memo, dated 18 April 1991, which reported that, according to the latest intelligence reports, the timer may have been handed back to Libya.[52] Certain witnesses, including Steiner and Williamson,[53] also believed that to be the case. Whereas Williamson simply had a hunch, Steiner's belief, expressed in his Crown precognition, was based on remarks by Collin's successor André Sonko.[54] Given that the Senegalese government believed that Libya was plotting an attack on its soil, the idea that it would meekly hand back any of the items seized in February 1988 was quite bizarre. Indeed Collin, who, unlike Sonko, had overseen the operation, had described the suggestion as 'straight out of a serialised novel!'[55] Henderson's memo suggested the police believed the French knew more than they were saying. Among the action points listed at the end were: 'Further enquiries necessary with the French Authorities to develop the unboxed

---

* FBI agents were present during the interview.

MST 13 timer in possession of Mr Calisti and who obtained the boxed MST 13 timer in Senegal.'[56]

The SCCRC was apparently unaware that another MI5 document it unearthed may have supported Collin's claim that the timer was given to an intelligence agency. The memo, dated 29 August 1990, referred to an electronic component, known as the PX503Z, which was made by a company called CML. It added: 'Incidentally, PX503Z was first marketed by CML in June 1984. The Chad equipment was recovered in September 1984. The Nymph crystal used in the Senegal timer was first marketed in June 1986 and the timer, as you know, was recovered in September 19868 – exactly the same timescale, but two years apart. It is the opinion of our experts that the appearance of components in operational devices so soon after initial marketing is very unusual and may suggest a similar procurement route.'[57]

The author may have confused the Senegal timer with those recovered from Togo in September 1986, which was the date originally cited in the memo. However, the 1986 had been changed by hand to 1988, which is the year in which the Senegal timer was recovered (although it was in February, rather than September). If the memo was referring to the Senegal timer, it begged the question, how did the author know that it contained a Nymph crystal? According to both Steiner and Clemens, they were unable to examine the timer's interior components, because the Senegalese objected to them dismantling it.[58]

Even if the memo was referring to one of the Togo timers, the revelation that the crystal used in the timer was not marketed until June 1986 was potentially highly significant, because all 20 timers supplied to Libya were built in 1985. If any were made after 1985, it strongly suggested that Mebo had made further timers, or that someone else was making identical ones. The likelihood of that someone else being Libya was minute, as the country had no electronics manufacturing capacity, hence its reliance on companies like Mebo. It was equally unlikely that Mebo had sold further timers to Libya. Bollier had been quite open about supplying the original 20 devices and about the Libyans' unsuccessful order for 40 more in December 1988. There was therefore no reason for him to conceal the supply of additional ones.

The Togo and Senegal stories were always highly irregular, and the new information lent weight to the suspicion the timers had been planted in order to implicate Libya in armed subversion. More importantly, it illustrated that Henderson's insistence on clarifying the stories 'beyond doubt' was in vain, and that there remained 'serious problems with our direct evidence'.

The SCCRC investigated the claims of former CIA agent Robert Baer. While finding no reason to doubt his credibility, they noted that, as he openly acknowledged, his information was all secondhand. The inquiry team was allowed access to MI5 files concerning the alleged $11 million payment to the PFLP-GC on 23 December 1988. The Statement of Reasons noted: 'The materials show that while initial reports suggested that $11m may have been deposited in a PFLP-GC account on 23 December 1988 it was later revealed that the payment was in fact one of $10m made in June 1987. According to the materials examined by the Commission the source of the payment was not established.' In the Commission's view this information refuted Baer's claim, but it was hard to see how the CIA could have confused a payment of $11 million with one of $10 million made 18 months earlier.

The team also examined the claim that $500,000 was paid to Mohamed Abu Talb on 25 April 1989 via an account numbered 560200 at the Degussa Bank in Frankfurt. They were given access to two files held by the Dumfries and Galloway police which indicated that $500,000 was indeed transferred to that account on that date and that the payment was made from an account at the Indosuez Bank. One of the documents suggested that account 560200 was almost certainly also at the Indosuez rather than the Degussa Bank. Four days earlier the same amount had been transferred to the Indosuez bank account by two individuals, one of whom was called Zaki, which was allegedly the name of the PFLP-GC's treasurer. The police informed the Commission that no link had been found between Talb and account 560200. The team subsequently examined another MI5 file, which it considered relevant to the matter. The Commission sought MI5's consent to reveal its contents, but it refused, claiming it originated from a sensitive source and that disclosure might therefore present a risk to national security. However, the Statement of Reasons made clear that

the Commission 'saw nothing in the materials viewed by it to suggest that Talb had access to an account numbered 560200 held at the
Degussa Bank or any other bank.'[59] Unfortunately the Commission
did not see fit to explore the matter further with any of the relevant
foreign governments.

Amid the welter of detail in the Statement of Reasons, it was easy to
lose sight of one central and shocking fact: the Crown had withheld
a mass of evidence that would have helped Abdelbaset's defence at
trial. This was not only morally wrong, but was also in defiance of
their legal obligation to disclose all evidence that might weaken the
prosecution case. Yet, ten years on from the trial, no one had been
held to account for this scandalous failure.

Tony Kelly's team was, of course, very relieved by the SCCRC's
decision, and by the disclosure of so much important new evidence
about Gauci, but they were disturbed that key areas had been left
untouched. For example, although the inquiry team, in response to
Eddie MacKechnie's written submissions, thoroughly investigated
the provenance of important debris items, such as the grey Slalom
shirt, the Yorkie checked trousers and the Toshiba manual, it did not
undertake a wholesale review of the forensic evidence. The evidence
relating to Luqa, Frankfurt and Heathrow airports remained untouched and, with the exception of Lamin and Baer, they interviewed
no one outside the UK and Malta. Most notably they failed to make
inquiries with the US authorities about the discussion and payment
of rewards to the Gauci brothers.

Furthermore, there were other newly uncovered documents
whose significance had apparently been overlooked. For example,
the police report of 10 June 1999 on the Gauci brothers said that
Tony had given a total of 23 statements and had been visited by
the police probably in excess of 50 times.[60] Only 19 of Tony's statements were disclosed to the defence, so, if the document was to be
believed, four statements and details of over 30 meetings were never
disclosed.

The Statement of Reasons also failed to comment on a notable
change in Gauci's account of his brother's movements. In his initial
statements he made no mention of Paul arriving at the shop, but at

trial he claimed that Paul arrived just as the man left the shop and that 'I told my brother to keep an eye on the shop till I took the stuff to the taxi.'[61] However, in his interview with the Commission he said, 'Paul definitely left the shop when the man came in. The man came in and Paul went out.' He later added, 'Paul took the clothing bought by the Libyan man to the taxi across the road . . . When Paul was going in the man was leaving. Paul accompanied him to the taxi with the clothing. . . . I recall that Paul took the clothes bought by the Libyan to his taxi. When Paul was entering the shop, the Libyan was leaving. Paul accompanied the man to the taxi with the clothing.'[62] Paul was not asked directly about this claim during his interview with the Commission, but made no mention of seeing the customer and confirmed that he could not recall the day in question.[63] If true, Tony's new account was very important, because it meant that Paul would have got a good look at the man, in which case he might have been able to corroborate Tony's description when he was first interviewed by the police. However, the account was far more likely to be yet another product of Tony's malfunctioning memory.

Another classified memo directly contradicted Dr Thomas Hayes's trial testimony that no explosive residue tests were conducted on the circuit-board fragments PT/35b and AG/145.[64] Since the fragments supposedly originated respectively from the bomb's timer and the Toshiba radio-cassette player those items were central to the forensic case. The memo, dated 3 April 1990, reported that both items were in fact tested for explosive traces and found to be negative.*[65]

Further important forensic information was contained in a Crown precognition statement by Hayes's RARDE colleague Allen Feraday. He revealed that he had been unable to rule out one of the debris items, PI/1588, as being part of a barometric trigger. Given that the PFLP-GC bombs found in Neuss were barometric, this was potentially significant. He said it did not match any of the barometric devices that he examined,[66] yet he made no reference to those inquiries in the joint forensic report.

More remarkably, in a later statement Feraday expressed unease about the categorisation system, which the report used to distinguish

* See Chapter 8.

primary suitcase clothing from other garments. He commented: 'Tom Hayes established the criteria and I did not feel comfortable using them . . . The more precise the criteria, the greater the number of items which will fall on the borderline . . . It is so difficult to be precise about such classifications. I would not have adopted such strict criteria for the clothing.'[67] The clothing categorisation system was central to the Crown's forensic case. If Feraday was unhappy with it, why did he put his signature to the joint forensic report?

There was another significant forensic development. As part of the review, the Commission wished to conduct fingerprint tests on the two largest umbrella fragments, PI/449 and PK/206. They sought an opinion from the FSS on the merits of such tests and asked the Dumfries and Galloway police to liaise with the FSS to arrange the handover of the items. However, as work was due to commence, the police advised the Commission that the Crown Office would instead be instructing the FSS and would relay the results to the Commission. Although concerned that its independence would be undermined, the Commission did not seek to block the Crown Office. The two items were submitted to the Forensic Science Service (FSS) along with several others, including PT/57a, which comprised two pieces of black plastic from the umbrella's handle, and PT/23, which was the primary suitcase locking mechanism. If the Crown case was correct, these were the two items most likely to bear Abdelbaset's fingerprint.

The FSS raised the possibility of conducting DNA analysis of the items. In November 2006 the Crown Office handed over five reports by the FSS on their various tests. According to these, there were no identifiable fingerprints on any of the fragments; however, an incomplete low copy number (LCN) DNA result was obtained from the two PT/57a fragments. The FSS concluded, 'There was sufficient information still remaining within the result to determine that the profile did not match Abdelbaset Ali Mohamed [sic] Al Megrahi and that the DNA could not therefore have originated from him.'[68]

For the purposes of comparison, the Crown Office subsequently arranged for DNA samples to be taken from all the people who were known to have handled the fragments, including Hayes and Feraday. In June 2007 the FSS produced a further report, which indicated that all but one of the components of the LCN profile were present in Feraday's DNA profile. The remaining one could have originated from a source other than Feraday, but was unsuitable for interpretation purposes, as it was very common throughout the general population.[69]

If the DNA recovered from the fragments was indeed Feraday's, it was likely that the items had somehow become contaminated at RARDE. It was unclear whether he and Hayes used gloves when examining items; however, one photograph of PT/35b in their joint report showed it resting on a bare fingertip, which suggested that someone at RARDE was unconcerned by the possibility of DNA or fingerprint contamination.[70]

The limited scope of the SCCRC's Statement of Reasons increased the burden on Abdelbaset's legal team. Fortunately, many months earlier, Tony Kelly had instigated separate reviews of the case's key strands, including Tony Gauci, the evidence from the three airports, forensics, and the case against the alternative suspects.

Kelly had instructed a number of psychologists to examine Gauci's evidence, including Professors Tim Valentine, Steve Clark and David Canter. Valentine considered both the shopkeeper's recollection of the clothing sale and his partial identification of Abdelbaset. Regarding the recollection, he explained, 'Research demonstrates that memory distortion due to misleading post-event information and social influence can provide a plausible account for the changes in the witness's memory.' Noting that the frequent changes to Gauci's account often occurred after he had been exposed to such factors, he added, 'The conditions under which the testimony was obtained are those that have been found to increase the effect of memory distortion. First, the original memory would have been relatively weak because it was an event of relatively low salience recalled after a long delay. Second, repeated questioning was extended over a very long period of time. These factors provide the opportunity for misattribution of the source of recollection and the feelings of familiarity of items and events.' Taking these matters into account, Valentine concluded that Gauci's first statement was likely to be the most accurate, as that was the point at which he had been exposed to the least post-event information and social influence. This was crucial, because in the first statement Gauci had described the purchaser as at least six feet tall, well-built and dark-skinned.

Although Gauci's choice of Abdelbaset's photo on 15 February 1991 provided some evidence of identification, Valentine pinpointed important features that would have undermined both the procedure's sensitivity and its fairness. The obvious one, of course, was the more than two-year delay between the event and the identification. Valentine highlighted five others. The first was that the photo line-up was not conducted 'blind'. Four police officers were present, all of whom knew the identity of the suspect and would have been motivated to obtain a positive outcome. Despite their best intentions not to influence Gauci, they may have unconsciously provided verbal or non-verbal clues, which could have influenced his behaviour. The second was that there were discrepancies between the statements of those present and their subsequent interviews by the SCCRC, which demonstrated that there was considerable discussion before Gauci's statement was taken. In Valentine's view, this would not have occurred had the procedure been conducted blind. The third was that Gauci initially rejected all twelve photos in the line-up, but was instructed by DCI Bell to look again. Valentine considered this to be a biased instruction, which may have influenced the witness to pick out a photo, rather than once more to reject them all. The fourth was that Abdelbaset's photograph was of a grainy quality that was different from the others and therefore stood out. Finally, he pointed out that there was evidence that Gauci had confused the picture with one of Mohamed Abu Talb, whom he had previously identified from a press article about Lockerbie.

Regarding the identification parade, Valentine said the obvious dissimilarities between Abdelbaset and the stand-ins rendered the procedure 'highly biased'. He added that Gauci's exposure to photographs of the Libyan further compromised the integrity of both the parade and the dock identification. He considered that these factors generated 'a serious risk of mistaken identity'. In his view Gauci's most impressive identification evidence related to the man who entered his shop in September 1989, whom he also described as around 50 years old, six feet tall, well-built and dark-skinned.[71]

Professor Clark independently arrived at similar conclusions to

Valentine. Summarising them, he wrote, 'Is it possible that Mr Gauci could have correctly identified the man who came into his store 27 months before? Yes, it is possible, but the research suggests that such an outcome would be extremely unusual. Is it possible that Mr Gauci could have navigated his way through the many interviews and the outside sources of information (which may or may not be reliable), and steadied himself against the suggestive questions and influences to make an accurate identification that was the product of his independent recollection? Yes, it is possible, but again, based on the scientific research, it is an outcome that would be extremely unusual. By contrast, the combination of a faded, and perhaps overworked, memory, and the numerous sources of outside information, influence, and suggestiveness, define precisely the conditions which research and past wrongful convictions show to be the cause of mistaken identifications.'[72]

Prior to completing his report Clark inspected the original photospreads that were shown to Gauci.* He was accompanied by Kelly, who took detailed notes and precisely measured the photos. The examination uncovered some interesting anomalies: for example, one of the line-ups shown to Gauci on 14 September 1989 had ten photographs, whereas the version shown at trial had only nine.[73] Most interesting were the photos that Gauci was shown on 15 February 1991, which, of course, included the one of Abdelbaset. All twelve of the original photos had been rephotographed for the photospread. Eight of the twelve originals were passport size, i.e. around 4 by 5 cm, but the four provided by the FBI, including Abdelbaset's, were around 10 by 15 cm. The eight small ones had all been blown up to roughly 10 by 12 cm and the four larger ones had been reduced to around the same size. Abdelbaset's photograph also appeared noticeably different to the other 11. In addition to the poor quality and the white lines and dots, which were visible on the scanned version, Kelly's measurements confirmed that it was considerably smaller than the other 11. Whereas their widths ranged from 10 to 10.3 cm and their heights from 10 to 12.1 cm, with eight over 11 cm, Abdel-

* Until Clark's inspection the legal team only had access to scanned copies of the photo line-ups. During Abdelbaset's second appeal the Crown initially attempted to block access to the originals – see Appendix 4.

baset's was only 8.7 cm wide by 9.6 cm tall. In other words it was at least 1.3 cm narrower than all the others, at least 0.4 cm shorter, and more than 1.4 cm shorter than eight of the twelve. The card on which the photos were mounted was twice as wide as all the other photospreads and, unlike all the others, there were large spaces between the photos.* These features may have caused Gauci subconsciously to recognise that there was something different about this particular selection. This would have been reinforced by Bell's prompt to ignore any age differences.[74]

All the officers who were in the room on 15 February 1991 knew which of the photos was of their prime suspect. Professor Canter conducted research to evaluate the potential influence of their presence upon Gauci. Using the same twelve photographs, two interviewers were selected, each of whom was told to ask a random selection of people to pick a culprit from the twelve. Both interviewers were briefed to say or do nothing that might betray who they believed the culprit to be. Interviewer A was told that photograph number 8 was the culprit and interviewer B was told nothing. Of the 20 people interviewed by B, none selected photo 8, but of the 36 interviewed by A, 15 chose it. The results were consistent with many similar research studies and numerous criminal cases in which eyewitness identifications had later proved to be false.[75]

Three further developments challenged Gauci's identification evidence. The first was a statement by Inspector Scicluna, which gave a significantly different account of the 15 February 1991 photoshow to those of Bell and Gauci himself (which was written by Bell). According to those two, when Gauci stated that all twelve men were too young, Bell asked him to look again and try to allow for any age difference;[76] however, according to Scicluna, Bell gave Gauci a more precise steer, telling him the man could be ten to fifteen years older.[77] Given that Abdelbaset was in his early to mid thirties in the photo,

---

* The Crown Office granted permission for me to view the photospread in prison. I noticed that in the bottom left-hand corner, clearly visible under the clear plastic sheet that had been attached to protect the photos, was the handwritten number '8'. Given that my photo was number eight, if the number was there when Gauci viewed the photospread, it may have influenced his choice.

by adding fifteen years, he would have been almost the age Gauci had described.

There was also a discrepancy between the accounts of Gauci's reference to the *Sunday Times* article featuring a photo of Talb. Bell's statement never touched on the subject,[78] and Gauci's only mentioned it in passing in the following paragraph at the end of the statement: 'I can only say that of all the photographs I have been shown this photograph No. 8 (EIGHT) is the only one really similar to the man who bought the clothing if he was a bit older other than the one my brother showed me.'[79] The words 'other than the one my brother showed me' had clearly been squeezed in. When the subject was raised with Bell at trial, he explained, 'the statement was read out to Mr Gauci, who signed the statement. Inspector Scicluna, who was present with me at the time, made reference to the photograph that Mr Gauci's brother had shown him, in the presence of the witness, and I included that reference because of that and inserted it there.'[80] However, according to Scicluna, it was Gauci who raised the issue and he did so before picking out Abdelbaset's photo. He specifically recalled Gauci saying to him in Maltese, 'Bring me that newspaper. He is similar.'[81] When asked about the discrepancy by the SCCRC's inquiry team, Bell and Scicluna each stuck firmly to his own version of events.[82]

The second development concerned a witness from the north-east of England called David Wright. In November 1989 he contacted the police after seeing on TV that a pair of trousers bought from Mary's House were thought to have been in the bomb suitcase. He knew the shop well, because he had holidayed in Sliema in 1987, 1988 and 1989 and got to know Gauci through their mutual interest in racing pigeons. He was particularly keen to speak to the police, because he believed he had witnessed an episode that might have a direct bearing on their investigation. While in the shop in late November 1988 he saw two Arab-looking men standing in the entrance looking at plastic rain macs. When he pointed the men out to his friend, Gauci said 'Libyan pigs'. Shortly afterwards the two men entered the shop. As far as Wright could recall, one bought two pairs of trousers, including a dark pair, six pairs of boxer shorts, six pairs of socks, two vests and some ladies' stockings. He thought the other bought a pair of light brown trousers, two pairs of boxer shorts and six pairs

329

of socks, and that they both bought macs and possibly other items. The men were in the shop for about half an hour, during which time no one else entered. He described both as smartly dressed. One was in his mid-thirties, around 5ft 9in tall with quite dark skin, and the other around 50, 5ft 5in, stocky and with greyish hair. They spoke in English and were quite friendly, saying they were in Malta for a conference and were staying at the Holiday Inn. They settled their bill in US dollars and Gauci put their purchases in a plastic bag. Wright never saw the men in the shop again, but three months later he saw a BBC TV news item that featured a Libyan government spokesman discussing alleged chemical weapons production. He was sure the man was one of those he'd seen in the shop. On returning to the shop in October 1989, he told Gauci about the news item, but Gauci seemed not to remember the men.[83]

The statement suggested, not only that Gauci was biased against Libyans, but also that his long-term memory of fairly routine transactions was poor. Arguably the event Gauci described was less routine than the one Wright witnessed, in that the man seemed not to care what he bought. However, Professor Valentine explained that, when recalling the sale, Gauci was likely to experience interference from the memory of other sales. He added: 'This effect is likely to be particularly significant because he was recalling the event after a long delay. Recall of everyday events is difficult. Many details will be forgotten and similar details from other occasions may come to mind. Therefore, the task is likely to lead to confusion between details of other sales to different customers.'[84] The sale that Wright witnessed bore striking similarities to the one Gauci had described: it occurred at the same time of year; there were no other customers in the shop at the time; the men were Libyan but spoke English; they were well-dressed; one was around fifty and the other was dark-skinned; they bought a wide variety of clothing including a light and a dark pair of trousers; they paid with cash; and they were staying at the Holiday Inn. The sale could therefore easily have been subject to the confusion that Valentine described.

The third potentially important development was the discovery of two additional copies of the artist's impression, produced by FBI artist George Noble, under Gauci's instruction, on 13 September 1989.

One was held in the BKA files, which were disclosed to the defence prior to the trial, and the second was contained in files belonging to the Maltese police, to which Kelly gained access in August 2007. Both were at least second-generation photocopies, but the version to which Gauci had attested in court was also a copy and it remained unclear what had happened to Noble's original.

Intriguingly, both the BKA and Maltese copies were considerably darker than the Court version.[85] The man depicted appeared to be black or mixed race, which was significant when coupled with Gauci's original description of the customer as 'dark'. The relative darkness did not appear to be due to photocopying, as the background was not significantly darker. Rather, it seemed that the version from which they were copied had many more dark hatching lines on the skin than were obvious on the court version. Kelly instructed specialist image analysis company, BSB Forensic, to examine the various versions. Its subsequent report concurred that the relative darkness of the BKA and Maltese versions appeared not to be purely the result of copying and that they may have been early-generation copies of the original. If that was the case, BSB could not conclusively account for the disparity, but offered three feasible explanations. The first was that the BKA and Maltese versions were good-quality copies that strongly resembled the original; the second was that they, or a copy from which they were generated, had been manually or digitally darkened; and the third was that they were late-generation copies and that their backgrounds had been digitally cleaned.[86] The second and third possibilities seemed most unlikely, as there would be no point in anyone darkening or cleaning up a copy. But, if the first explanation was correct, why was the version shown in Court so much lighter?

In re-evaluating the airports evidence, Kelly's team concentrated mainly on Luqa and Heathrow. The Trial Court accepted that the bomb travelled from Luqa, via Frankfurt, but noted that the failure to account for the primary suitcase's placement on KM180 constituted a 'major difficulty' for the Crown.[87] At trial Air Malta's General Manager for ground operations, Wilfred Borg, had described the airline's strict system of physical reconciliation. This required the head loader to count the number of hold bags to ensure it matched the number checked in. The Court also heard that both the load plan and the ramp progress sheet recorded a total of 55 bags, which tallied with the check-in records.[88] However, when Alan Turnbull QC put it to Borg that the system could be foiled by human error or a corrupt insider, he accepted that either was, in theory, possible.[89] Naturally, Alastair Campbell QC emphasised this concession during his final submissions[90] and it was subsequently highlighted by the judges.[91] Since the bomber was very unlikely to have relied on the remote possibility of human error, Campbell argued that an insider must have subverted the system. That person, he submitted, was Lamin. However, Lamin was, of course, acquitted, which begged the question, who was the inside man? The only theoretical alternative was raised during the following exchange between Turnbull and Borg:

Q. You see, I am trying to just check off how difficult such things might be. And can I ask you to think of this, and I simply give it just as an example, to ascertain the measure of impossibility. If, for instance, a head loader . . . was prepared, deliberately prepared not to count a particular bag, would that circumvent the check?

A. Of course it would.

Q. So that's just an example of the sort of thing that could be possible?

A. Yes.[92]

Since he was not present when KM180 was loaded, Borg was unable to confirm first-hand that neither human error, nor a corrupt head loader, had allowed through a rogue bag. The only two people who could were the head loader himself, Michael Darmanin, and the ramp dispatcher, Gerry Camilleri. In their police statements both witnesses were adamant that the number of bags loaded exactly matched the number checked in. Darmanin, who was ultimately responsible for the loading, was certain that an extra bag could not have slipped through.[93] There was not a shred of evidence that either witness was in any way corrupt.

The Crown had a duty to present all the available and relevant evidence, yet neither Darmanin nor Camilleri was called to give evidence. Abdelbaset's draft grounds of appeal described their accounts as 'highly material and directly relevant'. It submitted that their absence was one of the many factors that had rendered the trial unfair, and that there was no good reason for either side's failure to call them.[94]

The Appeal Court invited Abdelbaset's original team to respond to the complaint of defective representation. In response, David Burns QC confirmed that he had been responsible for the decision not to call the witnesses, along with Lamin's counsel Jack Davidson QC. He said that Borg's evidence was 'sufficient to demonstrate that an unaccompanied bag had not been ingested into that flight [KM180] or at least to raise a substantial doubt as to whether that occurred', and considered that aspects of Darmanin's statements might undermine Borg's testimony. In particular, he gave differing accounts of the number of times he had carried out a physical reconciliation of baggage owing to the load sheet and ramp progress sheet totals not matching. He also acknowledged that colleagues had occasionally forged his signature on a ramp progress sheet.[95] In Burns's view, Darmanin would have been bound to accept that no airport is absolutely secure and that human error is always possible. Turning to Camilleri, Burns felt that his police statements may also have caused the defence difficulties, in particular, his acknowledgement that Luqa security was not perfect.[96]

Burns's arguments did not sway Abdelbaset's appeal team to amend the grounds of appeal.[97]

Kelly's review of the Heathrow evidence focused on the brown, hard-sided suitcase seen by loader John Bedford in container AVE4041, prior to the arrival of the Frankfurt feeder flight PA103A. At trial, Bill Taylor QC submitted that the explosion could have occurred in exactly that position, rather than, as the Crown claimed, in the second layer. Even if the Crown was right, any subsequent rearrangement of the luggage might have placed the Bedford case in the second layer. The judges had accepted Taylor's submissions, and described Bedford as a 'clear and impressive witness',[98] but had added, 'if there was such a rearrangement, the suitcase described by Mr Bedford might have been placed at some more remote corner of the container, and while the forensic evidence dealt with all the items recovered which showed direct explosive damage, twenty-five in total, there were many other items of baggage found which were not dealt with in detail in the evidence in the case.'[99]

Kelly's team uncovered evidence that, had it been heard at trial, might have denied the judges these get-outs. It was contained within two schedules compiled by Detective Constable Derek Henderson. The first itemised all the luggage that could, in theory, have been loaded into AVE4041[100] and the second detailed the arrival times and numbers of bags of each Heathrow interline passenger.[101] If the Bedford bag was not the primary suitcase, then, since he saw it before the arrival of PA103A, it must have been legitimate Heathrow interline luggage. Henderson established that there were 14 such items. Of those, only six were likely to have been in AVE4041 before the PA103A luggage was added.* Although Bedford and his fellow loaders could not recall exactly how many bags they'd seen in the container up until then, they all recalled that its entire floor was covered. When Bedford and loaders Amarjit Singh Sidhu and Tarlochan Singh Sahota reconstructed what they had witnessed for the police, using an identical container, each required seven or eight luggage items to cover the floor.[102] All three placed five or six suitcases upright in a row at the back and laid the remaining two flat at the front. If there were seven or eight bags in AVE4041 prior to the arrival of PA103A, and only six were there legitimately, then at least one must have been rogue.

By checking the surviving bags and the descriptions provided by the victims' relatives, Henderson established the colour and type of all the legitimate Heathrow interline bags. None were brown, hard-sided suitcases.[103] In other words, regardless of the number of interline bags, if Bedford's recollection of such a case was correct, it could not have been in the container legitimately, which meant it was almost certainly the primary case.

Was it possible that Bedford had seen one of Major Charles McKee's dark-grey, hard-sided suitcases and was simply mistaken

* See Chapter 6.

about the colour? According to Bedford, the supposedly brown case was one of two that were placed in AVE4041 while he was away for his tea break between approximately 16.15 and 16.40. McKee's flight arrived at Heathrow at 14.34,[104] so his cases should have been delivered to the container well before Bedford went on his break. The two bags most likely to have arrived during the tea break belonged to passenger Michael Bernstein, whose flight touched down at 15.15,[105] but neither of those was a suitcase or hard-sided.[106]

Although the first of Henderson's schedules was disclosed early on during the trial preparations, neither document featured on the Crown's final list of productions for the trial itself. The Crown indicated to the defence that they would seek to account for all the potential AVE4041 luggage. This would enable them to demonstrate, by a process of exclusion, that the primary suitcase could not have belonged to a passenger and must have arrived on PA103A.[107] However, in the event, no such case was advanced, perhaps because the schedules rendered it impossible to link the Bedford suitcase to a passenger.

Abdelbaset's draft grounds of appeal claimed that the absence of the Henderson schedules from the trial constituted 'a material irregularity'. It continued, 'The system broke down to the extent that material evidence supporting the defence was not properly presented and the appellant was denied a fair trial.'[108]

John Beckett responded with a detailed justification of the defence team's approach. In his view, had they pursued the Heathrow interline evidence any further, they risked undermining their efforts to implicate the Bedford suitcase, as it would have enabled the Crown to explore some of the inconsistencies between the loaders' statements. This may have persuaded the judges that Bedford was not, after all, a 'clear and impressive witness'. In his police statements Bedford said there were eight or nine cases in the container. Beckett argued that, if only six bags were there legitimately, the defence had to explain two or three rogue bags, rather than just one, and that the obvious explanation was that Bedford was mistaken about the numbers. He also pointed out that, according to defence forensic expert Gordon McMillen, one of the interline bags that Henderson had excluded from AVE4041 was in fact in

335

the container.* McMillen also believed that the Heathrow originating bag, PH/137, was in AVE4041. In Beckett's view, this both undermined the reliability of the Henderson schedules and made it more difficult for either side to run an exclusion case. A further difficulty was that Bedford had said the brown case was one of two similar ones placed in the container while he was away. Given that no remains of the second case were found, the Crown might easily have argued that the brown case was as likely to have been lost as to have been the primary one. He recalled that the defence team had considered running an exclusion case. In doing so they noted that the two Bedford suitcases may in fact have been Charles McKee's dark grey ones. This possibility was strengthened by the loader Sidhu's original recollection that the two cases lying flat were black. Beckett could also not exclude the possibility that an unaccompanied brown Samsonite case, belonging to Pan Am Captain John Hubbard, had found its way into AVE4041 prior to the arrival of PA103A, as there was no conclusive evidence that it was on that flight.[109]†

As with David Burns's response, Beckett's views did not persuade Abdelbaset's appeal team to amend their criticisms of the defence and Crown in the later draft of grounds of appeal.[110]

In looking again at the alternative suspects, the lawyers pieced together previously unheard evidence linking the Lebanese-American

---

*The bag in question was a fabric suitcase belonging to Heathrow interline passenger Joseph Curry. It was recovered from the crash site in five pieces, which led McMillen to conclude that it had been burst apart and was therefore likely to have been in AVE4041. However, although its inner pouch had a small area of blackening, none of the outer surfaces were blackened and the RARDE joint report stated that neither it, nor a second suitcase belonging to Curry, showed signs of explosive involvement. Curry's incoming flight arrived at Heathrow at 16.25, which, according to Henderson's investigation, was too late for the two cases to have been loaded into AVE4041. He was certain that the cases were among five late-arriving Heathrow interline bags that were loaded into hold 5.3B of PA103.

† If Hubbard's suitcase did not arrive at Heathrow on PA103A, then there must have been an extra unaccounted-for suitcase on that flight, which may well have been loaded onto PA103. For further details of the Hubbard suitcase, see Appendix 3.

passenger Khaled Jaafar to groups with the means or intention to carry out the attack. Among the most significant was the statement by Rabbieh, the former PFLP-GC member who had fled to Norway. In it he had claimed that someone called Khaled Jaafar was on the group's payroll and, although he could not confirm that it was the same person, he later learned that that person had unwittingly carried the Lockerbie bomb.[111]

There was also evidence linking Jaafar's Dortmund associate Hussein Ali Allam to the PFLP-GC. Allam, who was reportedly a member of Amal, was a cousin of Jaafar's hosts Hassan and Souheil El-Salheli and accompanied him to Dortmund railway station on the day of the bombing. Although he had an apartment in the same block as the El-Salhelis in Dortmund, his registered address was the refugee hostel in Pfullingen. Among the other residents there was a man called Majed Abbas, whose name and telephone number was found in the possession of Bassam Radi, a.k.a. Abu Ahmed, a Hamburg-based PFLP-GC member who was arrested during Operation Autumn Leaves.[112] Radi's telephone number was one of only two stored in the digital watch of the group's West German cell leader, Hafez Dalkamoni. The other belonged to Mobdi Goben.[113] The BKA observed Dalkamoni meeting Radi in the town of Giessen, north of Frankfurt, shortly before the Autumn Leaves raids[114] and, on arresting Radi, they discovered in his car a key for the PFLP-GC arsenal at 28 Sandweg in Frankfurt.[115] Abbas and Radi each said they were involved in the secondhand car trade and Abbas denied knowing Radi.[116] None of the disclosed BKA material suggested that Radi was asked about Abbas.

A further possible car-trade connection was Ahmad al-Ahmad, a Syrian who was also arrested in the Autumn Leaves raids. It was al-Ahmad who supplied the green Ford Taunus that Dalkamoni was driving when arrested.[117] Allam said he had got to know someone of that name through Hassan El-Salheli,[118] but there was no record of the BKA asking El-Salheli about al-Ahmad. Al-Ahmad appeared to know the name El-Salheli, but denied recognising Hassan's photograph.[119] This potential link was strengthened by a man called Moussa Abou-Tannoura, who had introduced Al-Ahmad to the car's original owner Zouheir Kassem around September 1988. He told

337

the BKA that on that occasion al-Ahmad was accompanied by a friend called 'Gassan' or 'Hassan'. It was not clear from the interview whether Abou-Tannoura was shown a photograph of El-Salheli.[120] It appeared that the BKA ceased to investigate al-Ahmad on discovering that he was alibied for the day of the bombing.

Another of Jaafar's associates, Naim Ali Ghannam, was linked to the PFLP-GC through a telephone number. He and a Berlin-based member, Adnan Younis, who was an associate of Bassam Radi, each had the same number in their address books. Ghannam had it listed under the name Abu Samara and Younis under the name Dawdin or Dudin.[121] Ghannam accepted that they might be the same person and claimed they had met in a refugee camp in Berlin in 1979 but had not spoken since.[122] Younis initially denied knowing Dudin, but subsequently admitted to knowing him vaguely.[123]

Abdelbaset's draft grounds of appeal argued that the trial should have heard the evidence linking Khaled Jaafar to the PFLP-GC and radical Shia groups, and that, in its absence, the judges received a 'distorted and incomplete picture'.[124] The grounds also contended that the defence should have introduced the evidence indicating that the Autumn Leaves raids did not destroy the PFLP-GC's terrorist capability. Evidence from the BKA files and elsewhere suggested a standard *modus operandi* procedure for terrorist groups was to introduce the individuals intended to execute the attack only shortly beforehand. A number of PFLP-GC witnesses, including Khreesat and Mobdi Goben, suggested that group member Abu Elias was at large in Yugoslavia and West Germany after the raids, and the Goben memorandum suggested that he oversaw the Lockerbie operation.

The grounds further argued that the defence should have introduced evidence relating to the Frankfurt-based group member Salah Kwekes, a.k.a Ramzi Diab. The BKA observed him meeting other members, including Dalkamoni, on 18 and 24 October 1988. He was arrested, but released the following day, despite maintaining the blatant lie that he did not meet Dalkamoni on the 24th.[125] His flatmates, Angelika Berner and German Hoch, told the BKA that he left the flat suddenly on 28 October, saying he was travelling to Vienna, and taking with him a radio-cassette player. Berner was sure that the device was a twin-speaker model and Hoch was sure that it was not.[126]

According to the Goben memorandum, in November Kwekes travelled to Yugoslavia and met with two other group members, Goben himself and Martin Kadorah, who was also Frankfurt-based. The memorandum indicated that Kwekes had smuggled a radio-cassette bomb into Germany, via Greece, which he did not have on his arrival in Yugoslavia.[127] If true, this bomb did not match the description of any of the five bombs made by Marwan Khreesat in Neuss, so must have been a sixth device.[128] It was possibly the twin-speaker model that, according to Khreesat's defence precognition, he had seen in Dalkamoni's car.[129] The grounds also argued that the Goben memorandum itself should have been introduced as evidence, as should the testimony of Goben's son Samir and wife Miroslava.[130]

The task of responding again fell to John Beckett. He maintained that the defence team had considered all the evidence highlighted in the grounds of appeal. Regarding the alleged failure to incriminate Jaafar and his associates, he noted that Rabbieh could not confirm that the Jaafar allegedly on the PFLP-GC's payroll was the same man who died at Lockerbie.

In his view the Goben memorandum contained no admissible evidence relating to Jaafar and, even if it had, he did not believe it would have been accepted by the Trial Court. An additional difficulty, he said, was that Miroslava Goben alleged that Jaafar had been given the device in Frankfurt, whereas the memorandum claimed it had been secreted in his luggage in Yugoslavia. Furthermore, there was no evidence to support the memorandum's claims that Jaafar had been in Yugoslavia. Even if he had been, Beckett regarded it as untenable that, over the subsequent weeks, Jaafar failed to notice that his luggage contained a radio-cassette player.

Regarding the information linking Hussein Ali Allam to Bassam Radi, Beckett stated, 'I find it hard to see what value can be said to attach to this information.' On the subject of Allam's and Hassan El-Salheli's connections to Dalkamoni's car supplier Ahmad al-Ahmad, he pointed out that the BKA found no evidence to connect al-Ahmad to the bombing. The evidence linking Jaafar and his associates to extremist Shia groups, in Beckett's view, was undermined by the evidence that he had two bags, both of which were apparently checked in and found intact at the crash site. He added,

'There is something of a leap from possibly being sympathetic or having possible connections to people who may have been sympathetic with the aims of Lebanese factions to being connected to an entirely different organisation.'

Summarising the Jaafar evidence, Beckett stated, 'I do not agree that there was any failure to investigate and consider the position relating to Khaled Jaafar. There was no evidence that any of Jaafar's associates placed a bomb in his luggage. There was no evidence that he was involved in introducing the IED on to the aeroplane and a body of evidence suggesting to the satisfaction of the court that he did not. I doubt very much that this material would have had any impact on a jury. In my view, there is no prospect of it having had any impact on experienced judges. Had attempts been made to lead all the material proposed, I see little prospect that the terms of paragraph 75 [of the Trial Court judgment] would have been different, and none that the verdict would have been different.'

Beckett did not accept that Berner and Hoch's evidence supported the existence of a sixth bomb, adding, 'there was no realistic basis for asking the court to accept that Diab was seen to have a radio similar to that which contained the bomb on Pan Am 103, let alone that it contained an IED.'

He pointed out that there was no evidence that the PFLP-GC had an MST-13 timer. He therefore did not believe that the judges would have been swayed by evidence of the group's continuing capacity following the Autumn Leaves raids. A further problem, he said, was that the type of bombs made by Khreesat would almost certainly have exploded on the Frankfurt to Heathrow flight.

Addressing another aspect of terrorist methodology, Beckett argued, 'If it be the case that PFLP-GC cells would not know of the intended target and that instructions would be issued at the last moment, the fact that the group in Frankfurt had, *inter alia*, a Pan Am timetable would lose any significance it might otherwise have had.'

Evidence regarding Abu Elias had been adduced by the defence during the examination of the FBI's Edward Marshman. In Beckett's view, that evidence would have been undermined if – as the grounds of appeal contended it should – it had been supplemented by Dalkamoni's BKA interview, because the interview contradicted a number of Khreesat's key claims, in particular that Elias had travelled to Europe and that he was an explosives specialist.

Beckett maintained that the decision not to lead evidence relating to the Goben memorandum was taken after a great deal of consideration. He suggested that, aside from problems of admissibility, there were substantial pitfalls for the defence in leading the evidence. Of particular concern was that Abdelbaset visited Yugoslavia on his way back from Czechoslovakia in October 1988, shortly before the Autumn Leaves raids, and that Lamin was there for a week shortly after. Given that the visits occurred when, according to Goben, the PFLP-GC was plotting in Yugoslavia, it was feared the Crown might suggest the two Libyans were part of that plot. Goben also described how in the spring or summer of 1988 the group's leader, Ahmed Jibril, had introduced him to a Libyan Military Attaché in Yugoslavia.

Beckett pointed out that the SCCRC had investigated the claim of defective representation and found it to be baseless. He added: 'A difference of view between the counsel acting at the trial who did not know what the outcome would be; who sought to use the material to best effect as they saw it; and who sought to shield the appellant from evidence linking the PFLP-GC and Libya, and the views apparently now held by counsel who represent a convicted client, who now has nothing to lose in putting this material before the court, does not demonstrate that the appellant's defence was not "properly" presented.'[131]

The final major area of Tony Kelly's review was forensics, in particular the joint report of RARDE's Dr Thomas Hayes and Allen Feraday, which was a cornerstone of the Crown case. The initial impression of Kelly's forensic expert, Dr Roger King, was that the report was thorough and comprehensive, but on closer reading he developed a number of concerns, which were amplified when he scrutinised the scientists' examination notes and their SCCRC interviews.

The production of full, contemporaneous examination notes is a bedrock of forensic science. King noticed that many of Hayes's notes contained non-contemporaneous additions and amendments by both him and Feraday. There was nothing wrong with this per se;

what concerned King was that, contrary to internationally accepted guidelines, they were almost all unsigned and undated.

A further concern was that neither scientist was an expert in fibre comparison, yet their report repeatedly asserted that fragments of clothing matched both each other and control samples, which the police had sourced in Malta. King was also disquieted by the joint report's failure to refer to the comparative work undertaken by Feraday in order to establish whether the unidentified item PI/1588 was part of a barometric device.

King's most significant observations concerned the clothing categorisation system, which the scientists used to distinguish primary suitcase garments from other clothing. Category 1 clothes – i.e. those most likely to have been in the primary suitcase – were supposedly found to contain IED fragments, without fragments of suitcase shell, and Category 2 clothes – which were thought most likely to have been in the surrounding cases – contained either no fragments at all, or fragments including shell. The theory underpinning the system, although not spelled out in the joint report, was that the explosion would have blown fragments of the bomb, the shell of the primary suitcase and other nearby luggage outwards, away from the device. All clothing close to the bomb could potentially trap these fragments, but, since no suitcase shells lay between the primary suitcase clothes and the device, those clothes should, in theory, have been free of shell fragments.

His investigation of the system was conducted in three stages: firstly, he closely analysed the key documentary evidence, namely the joint report, the scientists' corresponding notes and the reports of the explosive tests conducted in the United States in 1989; secondly, he conducted a similar explosive test; and, thirdly, he examined the Lockerbie clothing fragments.*

His immediate observation during the first stage was that the categorisation system appeared to lack any scientific basis. In particular the US test reports contained only brief descriptions of the tests, and contained no analysis of the results and no detailed conclusions. Having completed the analysis, he was concerned that the categorisation system had not been applied consistently; in other words, some

* King's findings on the clothing categorisation system are described in more detail in Appendix 2.

Category 1 garments met the Category 2 criteria and vice versa. Had it been applied rigorously, then six of the thirteen Category 1 items should have been reclassified as Category 2, and two of the Category 2 garments shifted to Category 1.

More importantly, the system was, in King's view, illogical, because the markers for Category 1 included not only the bomb itself and the radio-cassette manual, but also fragments of the primary suitcase's cardboard partition. If the partition had been positioned between the bomb and the primary suitcase clothes, this would have been understandable, but RARDE's own photographs of a trial loading of an identical suitcase, with an identical bomb and similar clothes, suggested this was highly unlikely. It would have been more logical to designate the partition fragments as markers for Category 2 garments. The scientists also appeared to have overlooked the presence within some Category 1 items of fragments of the primary suitcases's fabric lining. There was no logical reason for not also regarding these a marker for Category 2. If the system was adjusted in line with these criticisms, then a further six Category 1 garments should have been reclassified as Category 2. So, if the categorisation system had been applied consistently and logically, twelve of the thirteen Category 1 items would move to Category 2.[132]

King's own explosive test confirmed that it was impossible to distinguish primary suitcase from other clothing on the basis of the fragments found within them.[133] So too did his examination of the Lockerbie debris. This included an analysis of some of the black plastic fragments, which the RARDE scientists suggested had originated from the radio-cassette player's casing. Remarkably, of the nine that he tested, only one matched the casing. This meant that garments that supposedly held bomb fragments may actually have held something else entirely. It was another substantial nail in the categorisation system's already firmly secured coffin.

Since it was impossible to establish with certainty which of the Lockerbie clothes were in the primary case, King instead attempted to assess which might have been close to the bomb. On the basis of their explosive damage, he established that there were 39 such garments in addition to Hayes and Feraday's 13 Category 1 items.[134] So, in total there were 54 garments that, on a forensic basis, could not be ruled out of the primary suitcase, 45 of which were not linked to Mary's House. Furthermore, the joint report detailed thirteen small, unidentified, heavily blast-damaged items, any one of which might have originated from objects originally in the primary suitcase.[135]

Some of the additional 45 garments could be ruled out of the primary suitcase because there was non-forensic evidence linking them to the surrounding luggage, such as name-tags and family photographs. However, nothing in the disclosed police material indicated exactly how many such garments there were. On the orders of SIO Henderson, DC Callum Entwistle produced 'a report detailing the recovery, origins and ownership of all explosive damaged clothing',[136] but its findings were never revealed.

The logical basis of the categorisation system had gone unchallenged at trial and it was never put to Hayes that, if the system had been applied more logically and thoroughly, then 12 of the 13 supposed primary suitcase garments failed the Category 1 criteria. Although Richard Keen suggested in cross-examination that the system had not been applied consistently to certain clothing fragments, Bill Taylor did not raise the matter during his final submissions. No doubt the limited scope of the challenge reflected the defence's FSANI experts' satisfaction with the RARDE categorisation system.[137]

Abdelbaset's draft grounds of appeal contended that this approach produced 'a serious risk of a miscarriage of justice'. It contrasted the 'silence at trial' with the 'positive and searching challenge' presented by King, which, it said, was 'likely to have had a material bearing upon the critical forensic issues at trial, from raising a doubt over whether any of the expert opinions are reliable to whether proof of important and specific forensic links is open to doubt . . . most importantly as to whether the clothing from Malta was in the primary suitcase.' It concluded, 'On any view this evidence would have had a material impact on the determination of this chapter of evidence. Absent of this challenge the appellant did not receive a fair trial.'[138]

The grounds of appeal also addressed the Crown's failure to disclose the precognition statement by Feraday in which he cast doubt on the clothing categorisation system. It argued that the statement was 'obviously material and fell to be disclosed . . . At the least it undermined his own credibility – in signing a joint report which he did not agree with; at best it completely undermined the Hayes system and in so doing breaks the crucial link between the clothing and the IED and hence between the appellant and the offence.'[139]

It once again fell to John Beckett QC to respond to the criticism of the defence team's approach. He disagreed that they had failed to investigate the Crown's forensic case and said the FSANI experts were credible and highly experienced. He pointed out that, even if the clothing categorisation system had been discredited, the fact remained that a number of heavily blast-damaged garments could be linked to Tony Gauci's shop. He believed it would have been too much of a coincidence if those clothes had been within luggage adjacent to the primary suitcase, rather than in the suitcase itself.[140]

Beckett's opinion again did not convince Abdelbaset's appeal team to alter the corresponding grounds of appeal.[141]

A Death Sentence $\quad$ 14

I had won the right to a second appeal, but any hope of a swift end to my nightmare was slowly strangled. What should have been a simple route to the Appeal Court became littered with obstacles, most of which were placed there by the Crown. I had always dreamed of achieving justice and freedom, but, as a consequence of these delays, I was eventually forced to choose between the two.

An initial problem – not of the Crown's making – was the selection of five judges to hear the case. Scotland's pool of senior judges is very small. Eight had been used up by the trial and first appeal, and a ninth, Lord Turnbull, was one of the Advocates Depute who prosecuted the case. Eventually it was decided that the presiding judge would be the Lord Justice General Lord Hamilton, sitting with Lords Kingarth, Eassie, Wheatley and Lady Paton. Ronnie Clancy QC was appointed leading Crown counsel, with juniors Nick Gardiner and Douglas Ross. The Crown Office team was headed by Procurator Fiscal Lindsey Miller.

From the outset, almost every attempt by Abdelbaset's team to progress the appeal was hampered by the Crown, if not by legal blocking tactics, then by seeking extra preparation time. There were two main blocking tactics,* the first of which was to attempt to restrict the scope of the appeal. Abdelbaset's grounds of appeal encompassed the forensic evidence, Luqa and Heathrow airports, the special defence of incrimination and defective representation. Although he was within his legal rights to advance such broad grounds, the Crown fought a pointless ten-month battle to reduce their scope to the six identified by the SCCRC. The Court eventually rejected the Crown's submissions, but by then both sides had needlessly expended masses of time and energy.

* A fuller account of the delays is provided in Appendix 4.

The second tactic was to attempt to block access to vital evidence. In order properly to fight the case, Abdelbaset's team needed to analyse material held by the Crown, police and various other agencies, most notably RARDE. Time and again the team sought access to this evidence, only to find themselves impeded. Once again the Crown's efforts failed, but only after numerous court hearings and many wasted months.

The only issue on which the appeal team was successfully thwarted concerned the two undisclosed intelligence documents referred to in Chapter 25 of the SCCRC's Statement of Reasons. The Crown confirmed that the documents had been provided to the UK government by a foreign government.[1] It did not object to the documents' disclosure, but the UK government did, making its objection known through Advocate General, Lord Davidson of Glen Clova QC.* He informed the Court that Foreign Secretary David Miliband was likely to issue a Public Interest Immunity (PII) certificate to prevent disclosure.[2] Miliband subsequently issued the certificate, on the grounds that the documents' release could damage relations with the government in question. The Advocate General further exacerbated the delays by insisting on reviewing every witness statement that, in the Crown's view, might raise issues of PII.

After a series of court hearings the judges agreed to initiate a procedure, used in English terrorism cases, requiring the appointment of a security vetted so-called Special Counsel to assess the Chapter 25 documents and report to the Court. Under this system, Abdelbaset's team were denied access to the documents so were unable to address the Court, either to challenge the claim of PII, or to insist upon disclosure. Worse still, once the Special Counsel had seen the documents, there could be no communication with him. The team would therefore instead have to rely upon his having a complete understanding of the material's possible relevance. In the event, Abdelbaset returned to Libya before the procedure was finalised, so the content of those vital documents remained unknown.

The wranglings over the scope of the appeal and access to evidence entailed numerous procedural hearings, at least one of which

* The Advocate General represents the UK government's interests in Scottish legal affairs.

was closed,* and even more court rulings and orders. Ultimately every issue contested by the Crown was resolved in Abdelbaset's favour. Had they refrained from using public money to fight battles they had no chance of winning, his appeal could have got under way by mid-2008, but in the event it did not start until almost a year later.

Commenting on the delays at the end of October 2008, the Scottish law professor Robert Black QC† wrote on his blog: 'More than thirteen months have passed since the first procedural hearing in the new appeal was held. More than ten months have passed since the appellant's full written grounds of appeal were lodged with the court. Why has no date yet been fixed for the hearing of the appeal? Why does it now seem impossible that the appeal can be heard and a judgment delivered by the twentieth anniversary of the disaster on 21 December 2008? The answer is simple: because the Crown, in the person of the Lord Advocate, and the United Kingdom Government, in the person of the Advocate General for Scotland, have been resorting to every delaying tactic in the book (and where a particular obstructionist wheeze is not in the book, have been asking the court to rewrite the book to insert it).'[3]

Black might have added that the Court itself shared culpability for the continuing delays. Rather than taking the initiative to set out a clear framework for the management of the case, including deadlines, the judges instead ordered the appeal team to issue proposals, and invited responses from the Crown and Advocate General.[4] Despite the best efforts of Abdelbaset's team, the judges seemed more inclined to deal with the various procedural issues in sequence, rather than in parallel. To compound matters, there were often intervals of a few months between hearings.

It was decided that, owing to its size and complexity, the appeal itself should be heard in stages. The first, which considered appeal grounds 1 and 2, ran from the end of April 2009 until mid-May.

---

* There were 13 procedural hearings in all, some of which related to practical issues of case management.

† Following Abdelbaset's conviction, Professor Black entered into an agreement with Abdelbaset's Libyan lawyer, Ibrahim Legwell, that he would be paid for future legal advice on avenues of appeal. In the event the only sum paid to him barely covered his expenses.

Since these grounds alleged that the guilty verdict was both unreasonable and based on insufficient evidence, they did not touch upon any of the important new evidence. It nevertheless left the judges with a very uncomfortable choice: to justify a patently unreasonable verdict, or to rule that the three fellow High Court judges had made a catastrophic error. Fortunately for them, events would conspire to rid them of that responsibility.

Two months after the hearing, Lord Hamilton announced that Lord Wheatley had unexpectedly undergone heart surgery and was not expected to recover until the autumn, so a decision on grounds 1 and 2 would be delayed until at least then. Two days later they decided that, owing to the pressure of other court business and Lord Wheatley's illness, the next stage of the appeal, on grounds 3.1 to 3.3, would be delayed until 2 November 2009. Since these grounds concerned Tony Gauci, the hearings would have aired the sensational documents concerning the payment of rewards. This was bound to cause the police and Crown considerable embarrassment, as they would be obliged to explain why the information was previously withheld. However, in the event, they would be spared that difficulty, because away from the courtroom a three-way game of diplomatic chess was about to bring the appeal to a halt.

On 29 May 2007, in one of his last acts as Prime Minister Tony Blair travelled to Libya for talks with Colonel Gadafy. Following the two-hour meeting, he told the press, 'I'd just like to say how positive and constructive the meeting with leader Gadafy has been. The relationship between Britain and Libya has been completely transformed in these last few years. We now have very strong co-operation on counter-terrorism and defence.'[5] However, it appeared that the main purpose of the meeting was not counter-terrorism or defence, but to seal a $900 million deal between the British oil company BP and the Libya Investment Corporation. Described by BP as its 'biggest exploration commitment', it was the company's first venture in Libya since the oil industry was nationalised in 1974.[6]

Behind the scenes another, far more controversial document was signed, this one between the two governments. It comprised a memorandum of understanding on various issues of bilateral legal cooperation, including, crucially, the transfer of prisoners between the two countries. In essence, it paved the way to a treaty allowing Libyan prisoners held in the UK to be transferred to Libyan prisons and vice versa.

Although Abdelbaset was not referred to in the memorandum, it was obvious that the deal was all about him, and reflected his government's unstinting commitment to get him home. There were, however, two major catches. The first was that, prior to the trial, the British government had assured the US government and the UN that, if convicted, the men would serve their sentences in Scotland.[7] The second was that, under Scottish devolution, any decisions on Abdelbaset's transfer would rest with the Scottish Justice Secretary, rather than with the UK Home Secretary. This might not have been a problem had the Labour Party held power in Scotland, but, just three weeks before the deal was signed, they lost the 2007 Parliamentary election to the Scottish National Party.

Unfortunately, the UK government did not tell their Scottish counterparts about the memorandum until a few days after it was signed. It handed the new Scottish First Minister, Alex Salmond, an opportunity to pick his first major fight with Westminster. On 7 June, he made an emergency statement to the Scottish Parliament in which he condemned the lack of consultation over the matter as 'clearly unacceptable', and gave a reminder of the assurances to the UN. He made clear that 'decisions on any individual case will continue to be made following the due process of Scots law'.[8]

The prisoner transfer treaty took almost 18 months to ratify. By then my life had been turned upside down.

During the summer of 2008 I began to feel unwell and noticed that there was blood in my stools. I called a prominent Libyan physician Dr Ibrahim al-Sherif and described my symptoms. He advised me that I should have blood tests done as soon as possible, including one for Prostate Specific Antigen (PSA), a protein produced by the prostate gland, which, when raised, can be an indication of prostate cancer. The normal range of results is between 0 and 6.5. Mine was 363. Soon afterwards I received an MRI scan at Inverclyde Royal Hospital. The results were horrifying. I had advanced prostate can-

cer. I was told that my primary tumour had a Gleason score of 9 out of 10, indicating that it was highly aggressive.* Worse still, the disease had spread to other parts of my body, including my bones. My condition was, in short, terminal. The SPS sought a second opinion from a consultant clinical oncologist, who confirmed my prognosis. He could not predict my life expectancy and said much would depend on how I responded to hormone therapy.

I was terribly traumatised. Although my time was limited, I was determined that my appeal should continue regardless of whether I'd live to see it succeed. My immediate priority, however, was to get out of prison. In October 2008 I applied to the Court to be released on bail pending the appeal's outcome. At a hearing on 6 November, Maggie Scott QC described my case as 'both unusual and compelling' and reminded the Court that the appeal was substantial. She detailed both my terrible physical condition and my intense psychological suffering, which was exacerbated by my isolation from my family and culture. She gave assurances that I would live with my family in Glasgow and emphasised that I was a low-supervision prisoner who was not considered a 'flight risk'. Unsurprisingly, the Crown opposed the application, with Ronnie Clancy QC arguing that the 'incomprehensible gravity' of the crime should outweigh the humanitarian considerations.

On 14 November my application was refused. In a remarkably harsh ruling, the judges said, 'While the disease from which the appellant suffers is incurable and may cause his death, he is not at present suffering material pain or disability. The full services of the National Health Service are available to him, notwithstanding he is in custody.' It added that there appeared to be no immediate prospect of serious deterioration in my condition, and continued, 'If he responds well to the course of palliative treatment which he has now started, his life expectancy may be in years.'9

I did not respond well to the treatment. Although my PSA reading dropped in October 2008, it rose again in December and continued rising during 2009. It's well known that stress plays a major role in cancer, and I'm certain that the stress of being wrongly convicted had made me ill and that the bail refusal hastened my decline.

* The Gleason score is based upon an assessment of the types of cells contained within the tumour and allows it to be graded on a scale of 1 to 10, with 10 being the most serious.

Three days after the decision, the prisoner transfer treaty was signed by the UK and Libyan governments. It meant that I, or my government, could apply for me to be transferred under the Repatriation of Prisoners Act 1984. However, the Act contained the following terrible caveat: 'The [Trial Court's] judgment is final and no other criminal proceedings relating to the offence or any other offence committed by the prisoner are pending in the transferring State.'[10] In other words, in order to obtain a transfer I had to abandon my appeal. It left me with an appalling choice: to die in prison in the hope of being cleared posthumously, or to die at home still bearing the weight of my conviction. For my family's sake I decided I must choose the latter, and on 23 March 2009 I signed a provisional undertaking to abandon the appeal.

The treaty was not fully ratified until 29 April 2009. During the previous few weeks senior civil servants quietly encouraged the Libyan government to apply for my transfer as soon as ratification took place. With my approval, an application was submitted by Libya's Minister of European Affairs, Abdulati al-Obedi, on 5 May.

The decision rested with the Scottish Justice Secretary Kenny Mac-Askill. The treaty allowed him 90 days to deliberate, which could be extended if necessary. MacAskill was in a very difficult position. If he were to refuse the application and leave me to die in prison, he would not only appear monstrously callous, but would also run the risk of the appeal bringing the Scottish criminal justice system into massive disrepute. However, granting it would breach the assurances given to the US government and the UN prior to the trial. It would be a tacit endorsement of an arrangement that had been foisted upon Scotland by Westminster.

There was, though, a third way, which avoided the problems of granting the application. Under the Prisoners and Criminal Proceedings (Scotland) Act 1993, MacAskill had the power to release me on licence on compassionate grounds. SPS guidance issued in 2005 recommended that compassionate release should be considered for inmates whose life expectancy was three months or less. When I was initially diagnosed, it was thought that I might live much longer, but my steady deterioration during 2009 meant three months was now a realistic prognosis. A few weeks after receiving the transfer application, the same Scottish civil servants advised their Libyan counterparts that I should apply for compassionate release. This solution held two great advantages over the prisoner transfer option: firstly, I would be allowed home to my family, rather than placed in a Libyan prison; and, secondly, under the 1993 Act, I was not required to abandon my appeal.

I submitted an application to MacAskill on 24 July. The final paragraph read: 'I am a family man: first and foremost I am a son, husband, father and grandfather. I have been separated from my family as a result of what I consider to be an unjust conviction. I have tried to bear that with a degree of equanimity and dignity. I have refrained from recourse to publicity in respect of my plight despite my burning belief about the injustice that I have suffered. There have been considerable delays in the process to challenge my conviction. Through my legal advisors I have voiced my concern about that to the Court in a measured way. I have never publicly taken a stance which would seek to impugn your nation and its system of justice. I have behaved with respect to the due legal process which I am subject to. It is with the same respect that I make application to you to enable me to return to my country and my family with what is left of my life, as a son, husband, father and grandfather.'[11]

MacAskill announced that he would consider the two applications together and, to assist his deliberations, invited representations from interested parties, including the Lockerbie victims' relatives and the Libyan and US governments. In accordance with normal procedure, comments were sought from the Greenock Prison Governor, Malcolm McLennan, and the prison's social work and medical staff. All stated that I was suitable for release. McLennan wrote, 'His manner and demeanour are exemplary' and confirmed that I'd never presented any security or control issues.[12] The Scottish Parole Board also unanimously recommended that I was suitable for release.[13]

On 3 August I was examined by two consultant urologists and two consultant oncologists. The subsequent report by the SPS's Director of Health and Care, Dr Andrew Fraser, stated: 'Reviewing the total picture, the concluding specialist view is that, in the absence of a good response to treatment, survival could be in the order of "months" and, *no longer "many months". Whether or not prognosis is more or less than 3 months, no specialist "would be willing to say".' Three months was, nevertheless, thought to be a reasonable estimate.*[14]

Three days later MacAskill visited me in Greenock Prison. It was a controversial decision, which drew much criticism from the media and the relatives of the American victims. I reiterated what I'd said in my application and again emphasised my innocence. He was courteous throughout and gave the impression of being strong-minded yet gentle. Prior to the meeting I'd obtained a copy of his book Building a Nation, as I wanted to know more about his political views. He was no doubt surprised when I asked him to sign it, but he agreed to do so. I promised him jokingly that I would not run off and tell the media.

On 10 August, MacAskill and his senior civil servants met a delegation of Libyan officials, including Minister al-Obedi, the Libyan Supreme Court Judge Azzam Eddeeb, and the London Chargé d'Affaires Omar Jelban. By this time I was desperate. The 90-day limit for considering the prisoner transfer application had passed and, although I had some vocal public supporters, MacAskill was coming under considerable pressure to reject both applications. After the meeting the Libyan delegation came to the prison to visit me. Obedi said that, towards the end of the meeting, MacAskill had asked to speak to him in private. Once the others had withdrawn, he stated that MacAskill gave him to understand that it would be easier to grant compassionate release if I dropped my appeal. He said he was not demanding that I do so, but the message seemed to me to be clear. I was legally entitled to continue the appeal, but I could not risk doing so. It meant abandoning my quest for justice. *

Next day, with huge reluctance and sadness, I broke the news to Tony Kelly that I was dropping the appeal. He was utterly shocked and reiterated that I had a legal right to continue, but my mind was made up. He dejectedly drove to Edinburgh for what was supposed to be a routine meeting with counsel and broke the news to them.

---

* On 6 August 2009, four days before the Libyans met MacAskill, the *Herald* reported: 'Technically he could continue his appeal [if granted compassionate release], but there is a growing expectation that he would be encouraged to first drop legal proceedings.' The source of this information was not stated, but it seems likely that it was someone within the justice department.

By a horrible irony Abdelbaset's decision coincided with the destruction of the last major plank of the Crown case.

For all the case's weaknesses, one fact seemed unassailable; the circuit-board fragment PT/35b appeared to originate from a Mebo MST-13 timer. At trial there was no challenge to Allen Feraday's assertion that it had been 'conclusively established that the fragment materials and tracking pattern are similar in all respects to the area around the connection pad for the output relay of the "MST-13" timer'.[15] Feraday was adamant that 'the same pattern of tracks will not occur on any other electronic product, only the "Mebo" brand "MST-13" type timers.'[16]

The only person to dispute the Crown case was Mebo's Edwin Bollier. He continued to insist that the fragment he was initially shown did not originate from one of the green, professionally manufactured boards, which Mebo had ordered from its supplier Thuring, and which everyone agreed were used in the 20 timers sold to Libya. Rather, he claimed, it was from one of the greyish-brown prototype boards, made by Mebo technician Ulrich Lumpert and used in the two MST-13s that were supplied to the East German security service, the Stasi. Lumpert, on the other hand, testified that the Stasi timers had contained the Thüring boards.

Bollier appeared to believe that his claim demonstrated Abdelbaset's innocence, but in fact it undermined his defence. There was no doubting that the fragment that was shown to the Court, and depicted in numerous photographs in the forensic report, was green and not one of Lumpert's prototypes. Bill Taylor QC submitted on Abdelbaset's behalf that the fragment could have originated from one of the Stasi timers and, in doing so, argued that Lumpert's evidence should be preferred over Bollier's.

There seemed little hope that the timer fragment evidence could be challenged during the second appeal. Tony Kelly nevertheless requested his team to review all the relevant paperwork. It was clear from this that Feraday's assertion that PT/35b was 'similar in all respects' to the MST-13 circuit boards was supported by a good deal of evidence. The expert analyses conducted on the fragment during the first half of 1990 had enabled the police to build a comprehensive profile of all its constituent elements. Its basic laminate was a standard 9-ply glass fibre, its circuitry comprised a layer of copper 35 microns thick, coated with a thin layer of pure tin, and its reverse side was coated with solder mask.

Two years later, the police returned to the same experts, and asked them to conduct similar analyses of a Thüring-manufactured MST-13 circuit board, DP/347a. Thüring had in fact made two variations of the board, one of which was solder-masked on both sides and the other, like PT/35b, on the reverse side only. The police were careful to select the control sample from among the latter type.

Most of the tests conducted on DP/347a gave near identical results to PT/35b; however, Kelly's team noticed one potentially significant disparity. It concerned the metallic coating of the boards' copper circuitry. Such coatings are applied to all commercially manufactured circuit boards in order to enable components to be attached. The two scientists tasked with comparing the coatings were Dr Rosemary Wilkinson, a metallurgist at Strathclyde University, and Dr David Johnson, a materials scientist from the University of Manchester Institute of Science and Technology. Each independently established that, whereas PT/35b's coating was pure tin, DP/347a's appeared to be an alloy of tin and lead.

Wilkinson and Johnson each speculated that the difference may have been due to the heat of the explosion causing a change in PT/35b's coating.[17] Wilkinson pointed out in her police statement that lead has a low boiling point, and suggested that the fragment's original coating was, like DP/347a's, a tin/lead alloy and that the heat had caused the lead to boil off. However, she advised that 'this hypothesis should be tested by experiment.'[18]

There was nothing in the Crown paperwork to suggest that the police had taken Wilkinson's suggestion any further. What of the defence team? Had they noticed the disparity in the coatings and, if so, had they explored the issue?

There is no doubt that they were aware of the issue. A few weeks before the trial commenced, David Burns QC sent a memo to one of the solicitors, Alex Prentice, requesting that he send Dr Wilkinson's statement to the defence forensic expert, Gordon McMillen. Burns wrote: 'Could Gordon tell us whether he agrees with what is said in the statement and whether the differences in PT/35 and DP/347(a) are of any significance. Can these differences be explained by the explosion? Is the only way to verify this "by experiment"? If so what experiment? If this is not his field, can he tell us who to go to?'[19] A week later McMillen wrote back, confirming that he had read Wilkinson's statement, but added that its contents were 'somewhat beyond my experience and that of my colleagues in our Metallurgy department'.[20]

Shortly before sending Wilkinson's statement to Gordon Mc-Millen, the defence instructed the forensic metallurgy firm Capcis. Although its experts concentrated, in the main, upon the evidence relating to the break-up of the aircraft and the location of the explosion, after the trial had opened, one of its experts, Dr Dennis Ryder, was invited to comment on Dr Wilkinson's statement. Rather than examining her theory that the explosion had caused a change in the metallic content of PT/35b, he instead considered the more basic question of whether the fragment had been involved in an explosion in the first place. He subsequently reported that 'there is nothing in Dr Wilkinson's work to indicate that [PT/35b] had ever been in the proximity of an explosion.'[21] While dramatic, his conclusion proved to be a red herring. He was not called to give evidence, perhaps because both Feraday and McMillen were in no doubt that the fragment had been involved in an explosion. Since both those experts had far more experience of explosive forensics than Ryder, the defence team may have concluded – no doubt correctly – that the Court would prefer their evidence over Ryder's.

So, Johnson and Wilkinson's hypothesis remained untested. Moreover, the defence team seemed satisfied that the fragment originated from one of the green, Thüring-manufactured boards. All of the timers that Mebo supplied to Libya contained this type of board, some with solder mask on both sides and some on one side only. Although the Mebo technician Ulrich Lumpert had testified that the Stasi timers contained similar boards, he later swore an affidavit in which he said he had been mistaken. He now agreed with his former boss Edwin Bollier that he had in fact fitted the Stasi timers with greyish-brown prototype boards, which he had himself made. Clearly, if Lumpert and Bollier were right, then PT/35b could not have originated from a Stasi device.

It was, nevertheless, undeniably the fact that the fragment's circuitry appeared to be coated with pure tin, while that of DP/347a appeared to be coated with a tin/lead alloy. A simpler potential explanation than that offered by Dr Johnson and Dr Wilkinson was that some of the circuit boards made by Thüring were coated with pure tin and the others with a tin/lead alloy. Remarkably, it seemed that no one had pursued this issue with Thüring, and in particular with the man responsible for the manufacture of the MST-13 boards, the company's production manager, Urs Bonfadelli. He was jointly interviewed by the defence and Crown in March 2000, and three months later gave evidence at Abdelbaset's trial. On each occasion he confirmed that he had handled the order and provided a fairly detailed account of the manufacturing process, but neither side asked him directly whether the circuitry was coated with pure tin, a tin/lead alloy, or whether boards of both types were produced.[22]

The SCCRC also failed to ask the question, despite having taken almost four years to investigate the case. It produced a 53-page supplementary report on PT/35b, but this was little more than a comprehensive chronology of the police investigation of the fragment. Although it noted the discrepancy highlighted by Dr Johnson and Dr Wilkinson, it accepted their untested hypothesis that this was due to the fragment having been involved in an explosion, and concluded that the issue 'does not appear significant'. As for Bonfadelli, the report noted: 'Urs Bonfadelli, an employee of Thüring, who made the MST-13 circuit boards, stated that the tracking was to be in tin, he did not mention lead. This is consistent with the tracks having been coated in pure tin.' It was true that in his pre-trial interview Bonfadelli had referred to the circuitry as being 'tin-plated' and at trial he said 'the trackings were in tin.'[23] However, the Commission, and, it seemed, everyone else, had missed one very important point: within the electronics industry 'tin' can mean both pure tin, and tin/lead alloy.

On 23 October 2008, at just after 7 p.m., a member of Kelly's team finally put the crucial question to Bonfadelli: was the circuitry of the MST-13 boards coated with pure tin or a tin/lead alloy? His answer was clear and devastating: all were coated with an alloy of 70 per cent tin and 30 per cent lead. There could be no mistaking this, he said, as Thüring only ever made circuit boards in this way. The use of pure tin required a completely different production process, which the company had never used.[24] It was immediately apparent what this meant; if PT/35b's coating had not been changed by the explosion, then it could not have been made by Thuring and therefore could not have been from one of the 20 timers supplied to Libya. Neither could it have been from one of the prototype boards, which, if Bollier and Lumpert were to be believed, had been used in the Stasi timers.

Kelly's priority was to establish whether or not the heat of the explosion could change the coating from tin/lead alloy to tin. To help answer the question, he instructed two independent experts. The first, Dr Chris McArdle, had over 25 years' experience in the electronics industry, much of which he had spent designing circuit boards, and had latterly been a UK Government advisor on microelectronics and nanotechnology. The second, Dr Jess Cawley, was a metallurgist of over 35 years experience, and a former senior lecturer at Sheffield Hallam University, who now worked as a consultant to the engineering industry. Each was sent the reports of the various Crown experts and all the available photographs of PT/35b.

McArdle immediately observed something that he considered to be highly significant; the blob of solder, which occupied the upper end of the fragment's '1' shaped relay pad, appeared to bear the imprint of a piece of wire. He concurred with the Crown experts that this indicated that an electronic component had once been attached. But, more importantly, he said it was an indication that the solder had never been hot enough to melt; had it done so it would have flowed across the pad, and the wire imprint would have disappeared. Electronic solder, like the coating used in Thüring's production process, is a tin/lead alloy. If it had not become hot enough to melt, McArdle pointed out, then there was no way that it would have been hot enough for the lead to have evaporated away. And, if it had not evaporated away from the solder, then, in theory, it could not have evaporated away from the circuitry's coating. Cawley agreed, pointing out that, although plastic explosives of the type used in the Lockerbie bomb produce a flash of intense heat, lead, like most metals, requires a far longer exposure to high temperature before it would melt, let alone evaporate.

It was important to test the two experts' provisional conclusions. Between them they devised a series of experiments, which involved exposing a replica Thüring MST-13 board to extreme heat. McArdle had a number of boards made using Thüring's original circuit diagram, some of which had their circuitry coated with tin/lead and the others with pure tin. He then applied a blob of solder to a number of the boards in the same position as that on PT/35b. Each type of board was analysed using a scanning electron microscope in order to confirm the metallic content of the coating. Next, Cawley placed some of those with the solder blobs into a laboratory furnace and timed how long it took for the blobs to melt – the answer was about four seconds. Given this melting, it stood to reason that those boards had been exposed to more heat than PT/35b.

Cawley repeated the exercise with some of the tin/lead coated boards with no solder blobs. Finally, these boards were again analysed using the scanning electron microscope to see whether the heat had changed the tin/lead coating to pure tin. The results, Cawley concluded, were clear; no such change had occurred.[25] McArdle's conclusion was equally clear: 'The PT/35b fragment was originally manufactured with a pure tin coating . . . This would suggest that this fragment is not consistent with any of the PCBs recovered from Mebo.' In other words, the fragment did not originate from a Thüring circuit board and therefore could not have been part of one of the 20 timers sold to Libya. Its green colour meant that it could not have been from one of Ulrich Lumpert's prototype boards either.

McArdle noted that the tin on PT/35b was very thin. This suggested that the board may well have been made using a process called immersion tin, which is more commonly used in DIY type production, rather than commercial manufacture.

In addition to analysing PT/35b's metallic content, McArdle was asked by Kelly to comment upon Feraday's claim at trial that the fragment's circuit pattern 'will not occur on any other electronic product, only the "MEBO" brand "MST-13" type timers'. Having reviewed all the evidence and analysed both the fragment and the control sample board DP/347a, McArdle's view was that the assertion was not entirely correct. He pointed out that the fragment had only a few distinctive features and that, while these were undoubtedly similar to the MST-13 boards, those boards were just one version of billions of circuit boards made worldwide for all manner of applications. He could not exclude the possibility of the same configuration occurring in another product. Neither could he rule out that Mebo, or some other entity, had incorporated the relevant section of the MST-13 layout into the design of a subsequent board, or, indeed, that the section derived from a layout of an earlier product.[26]

Feraday had, of course, also claimed – wrongly – that PT/35b's materials, as well as its circuit pattern, were 'similar in all respects' to the control sample board. At first glance it appeared that his mistake was born of ignorance, as the reports of Dr Johnson and Dr Wilkinson, which highlighted the difference between the two items' lead content, were not produced until a few months after he completed the RARDE forensic report. However, some of the RARDE papers disclosed by the Crown, shortly before Abdelbaset dropped his appeal, cast the omission in a less charitable light. The documents contained data from metallurgical tests conducted on PT/35b and DP/347a, each of which was accompanied by a handwritten notation by Feraday. In one he reported that the coating of PT/35b's tracks 'is of <u>pure tin</u>' and in the other he noted that the coating of DP/347a's tracks 'is of [approximately] 70/30 Sn/Pb'. (Sn and Pb are, respectively, the chemical symbols for tin and lead.) The note speculated that DP/347a's tin/lead coating may have been applied on top of a layer of pure tin, but no evidence was produced to support this. Both notes were initialled by Feraday and dated 1 August 1991.[27] Here, then, was proof that four months before completing the forensic report in December 1991, he knew that there was a significant difference between the metallic content of PT/35b and the control sample DP/347a. Why then had his report claimed that the items were 'similar in all respects'?

Had these documents been disclosed to the defence team, they would have provided the basis for a vigorous cross-examination of Feraday. Arguably, though, even without the documents, the lawyers had sufficient information to uncover the truth about PT/35b, if only they had asked the right questions of their expert metallurgists and Thüring's Urs Bonfadelli. Sadly, they instead accepted that PT/35b originated from exactly the type of circuit board that was used in the

20 Libyan timers. Taken together, the evidence of Bonfadelli, McArdle and Cawley proved beyond any doubt that it did not.

The strongest remaining element of the case against Abdelbaset was destroyed and with it the case against his country. But it was all too late.

The day after I decided to abandon my appeal Tony Kelly notified the Court. Later that day, the BBC reported that I was to be released on compassionate grounds.[28] Intriguingly, the story's unnamed source was in Westminster, rather than Edinburgh. The Scottish government denied the story, claiming that MacAskill was still deliberating. On 14 August Kelly formally announced my decision. The following day it was reported that the US Secretary of State Hillary Clinton had personally called MacAskill to convey the US government's view that I should be kept in prison.[29] In a TV interview four days later she said it was 'absolutely wrong' for me to be released.[30] On 19 August the Scottish government indicated that MacAskill would reveal his decision the following day.

Shortly after 12 noon on 20 August, he announced that he was granting me compassionate release. He concluded a lengthy statement with the following words: 'In Scotland, we are a people who pride ourselves on our humanity. It is viewed as a defining characteristic of Scotland and the Scottish people. The perpetration of an atrocity and outrage cannot and should not be a basis for losing sight of who we are, the values we seek to uphold, and the faith and beliefs by which we seek to live. Mr Al-Megrahi did not show his victims any comfort or compassion. They were not allowed to return to the bosom of their families to see out their lives, let alone their dying days. No compassion was shown by him to them. But, that alone is not a reason for us to deny compassion to him and his family in his final days.'[31] MacAskill knew very well that I had a great deal of compassion for the victims, and it would be very surprising if, as a former lawyer, he did not have reservations about my conviction.

The decision provoked a carnival of political point-scoring, which kept the issue at the top of the news agenda for over a fortnight. The controversy was entirely founded on the assumption that I was the Lockerbie bomber. Very little of the media and political comment acknowledged that I had had an appeal pending and that the SCCRC considered the original verdict was 'at least arguably one which no reasonable court, properly directed, could have returned'.[32]

But what really mattered, of course, was that I was going home. Shortly after the announcement I was summoned to the office of Chrisswell House's Hall Manager, where Deputy Governor Martin McDonald broke the good news. The enormity of the relief that I experienced is impossible to describe. For 18 years I had been the victim of politics; now, finally, I was its beneficiary.

I returned to my cell for the last time, packed my bags and tidied up. Sadly, the other prisoners were locked in their cells as a security precaution, so I was unable to say goodbye. I was taken to a small room in the prison reception area, from where I called Aisha in Tripoli. She had already heard the news on television. I was joined by a Scottish Justice Ministry official who showed me the licence that officially granted my release. Once I'd read its terms and conditions he took it back from me, explaining that, for security reasons, it would not be handed over until we reached the aircraft. Tony Kelly also arrived and we chatted together for a couple of hours while we waited for the necessary formalities to be completed. Eventually I was searched one final time, along with my baggage. A prison van was waiting to take me to Glasgow Airport. Before getting in I was given a white tracksuit to put on, together with a bulletproof vest. When I objected to the vest, I was told politely but firmly to comply, again for security reasons. Kelly wanted to accompany me in the van, but was refused permission, so we hugged and said our farewells. Like the rest of the legal team, he dearly wished to clear my name in court, but understood that my freedom came first.

At around 14.40 the van trundled out of the prison gates under armed police escort and drove the 18 miles to the airport. I had left prison, but remained behind bars until the very end. I was accompanied by two Greenock officers, neither of whom was from Chrisswell House, but whom I nevertheless knew reasonably well. Friendly and helpful, they exemplified the prison's high professional standards.

At the airport an aircraft belonging to the Libyan commercial carrier Afriqiyah was waiting on the tarmac. I said goodbye to the officers and to McDonald and gave them my sincere thanks for their *warm and humane treatment over the previous four years. I then slowly mounted the stairs to the aircraft door, shielding my face against the long lenses of the press photographers.*

As I entered the plane I was met by Colonel Gadafy's son, Saif al-Islam al-Gadafy, whose diplomacy had sown the seeds for my release. We embraced and I thanked him sincerely for all his efforts. I was then reunited with my eldest son Khaled, who had flown out from Tripoli. Words cannot express the elation I felt seeing him for the first time in ten years as a free man. He broke down in tears of joy as he found me sitting beside him. I greeted all those on board in turn, offering particular thanks to Dr Ibrahim al-Sherif, the esteemed Libyan doctor who had visited me in prison.

Once the greetings were over, we settled into our seats and taxied down the runway. Within a few minutes the aircraft's wheels were leaving the ground and I was leaving Scotland. It was ten years, four months and 15 days since I had surrendered to its justice system. The route south took us close to Lockerbie, the town in whose tragedy I had become so enmeshed.

I spent most of the journey talking to Khaled. The flight lasted four hours and twenty minutes, but it seemed like no time. By the time we approached Tripoli it was dark. I looked through the window at the beautiful Roz al-Bahr – Bride of the Sea – as locals call the city. Everywhere there were decorative lights to celebrate the Fortieth Anniversary of the Al-Fateh Revolution on 1 September.

We touched down at Mitiga Airport, not far from the city centre, rather than at Tripoli International Airport. Owing to the crowd who had come to greet me, we had to remain on board the aircraft for 40 minutes. Some of the well-wishers had brought with them Scottish Saltire flags, which they waved enthusiastically as I emerged from the plane. The celebration was portrayed in the Western media as an official welcome, but it was no such thing, and most of those present were either friends or members of my tribe and extended family. The flags reflected their genuine gratitude to the Scottish government, for a decision they regarded as just and brave.*

* A confidential cable from the US Embassy in Tripoli, published by Wikileaks, undermined the US and UK governments' claims that Abdelbaset's

(note continued opposite)

My son-in-law was waiting at the airport to drive us home and had brought with him my three other sons, Mohamed, Ali and Motasem. A couple of years earlier the family had moved to a new house. It was strange walking into the place that I called home, yet which was completely unfamiliar. Aisha had organised a reception for friends, neighbours and family. As I walked in she greeted me, and I was finally reunited with my parents. It was so incredible to see them all again, that I had to ask one of the children to slap my face to ensure I wasn't dreaming.

The joy and happiness surrounding me caused my aches and pains to melt away. Eventually, though, my exhaustion caught up with me and I was left alone to rest.

(note continued)
reception was a gross state-orchestrated pageant. It acknowledged that the crowd assembled at the airport numbered only around 100, and that only one Libyan TV channel broadcast the event. An Associated Press reporter told the embassy that the international press corps was held on a bus for more than three hours and not allowed access to the tarmac to cover the return. Moreover, he reported 'that he observed the Libyan Government hastily removing "thousands" of people who had gathered to welcome Megrahi while the Libyan Government kept the plane closed and waiting on the tarmac for a more subdued welcome scene.'

The Real Story of Lockerbie   15

There are two real stories of Lockerbie: one is the story of Abdelbaset's conviction, the other that of the bombing.

It is only possible to write with authority about the conviction. Even here much remains unknown. It is, for example, far from certain that the encounter described by Tony Gauci ever occurred. He certainly believed that it did, but he did not describe it until nine months later, and it is now known that a purchase with a number of similar features occurred around the same time. It is possible that, in attempting to recall what had happened, he subconsciously conflated two or more events.

Even if there was an event along the lines he described, his recollection was clearly erratic, with important details changing radically between his statements, sometimes following unintentional prompting by the police. His trial evidence also diverged from his earlier accounts, yet the judges were satisfied he was reliable.

In concluding that the purchase date was 7 December, they relied on his claim that the encounter was around a fortnight before Christmas. Since he was never specific about the date and had never before suggested it was a fortnight before Christmas, the validity of that conclusion was, to say the least, questionable.

A proper assessment of the date should have considered four factors: Paul Gauci's absence from the shop, the Christmas decorations in Tower Road, the public holiday on 8 December and the weather. It was clear from Paul's statements that he probably watched football on both 7 December and 23 November,[1] but he told Abdelbaset's lawyers that he was often away from the shop for other reasons.[2] His absence was therefore not a reliable indicator of the date. Tony's first and clearest reference to the Christmas lights was on 19 September 1989, when he said the purchase occurred before they were up.[3] The evidence gathered in 2002 proved they were erected, at the latest, on 29 November, which obviously ruled out 7 December. Gauci never suggested it was anything other than a normal weekday and never made reference to the public holiday on the following day, which again counted against 7 December.

The weather was the most reliable clue of the four. Gauci had a clear and consistent memory of the man buying an umbrella as he left the shop, because there was a light rain shower. The meteorological data for 23 November was entirely consistent with light rain at the relevant time, and indicated that there was no rain on 7 December. There was a theoretical and estimated 10 per cent chance that it rained in Sliema on 7 December, but it would have amounted only to 'some drops', so would not have warranted the purchase of an umbrella. In short, the date in question was almost certainly not 7 December.

Even if it was, the conviction was also reliant upon Gauci's identification evidence. By the time he picked out Abdelbaset's photograph on 15 February 1991, well over two years had passed. He did so only after being advised to ignore any age difference and, contrary to accepted best practice, all the officers in the room were aware of the suspect's identity.[4] The ID parade and the dock identification were farcical, not least because of the media coverage of Abdelbaset during the previous years, some of which, it later emerged, was kept by Paul.[5] At least one of these articles outlined weaknesses in Gauci's identification evidence,[6] which his trial evidence went some way towards patching over. In particular, he claimed, 'I don't have experience on height or age' and that the man was 'below six feet'.[7]

It is also now known that the subject of rewards was raised within a month of his first statement, when FBI agent Chris Murray told DCI Harry Bell that he had authority to arrange 'unlimited money' for Gauci and 'could arrange $10,000 immediately'.[8] It is not known whether the FBI put the offer directly to Gauci, but documents uncovered by the SCCRC indicate that he expressed an interest in rewards to the police prior to picking out Abdelbaset's photo.[9] Furthermore, regardless of Bell's subsequent efforts to quash discussion of rewards, Gauci was strongly under the influence of his brother, who had 'a clear desire to gain financial benefit'.[10] The exact rewards paid by the US Department of Justice are not clear, but the figures of $2 million to Tony and $1 million to Paul were discussed. It is clear that the police pushed for more and that the Crown Office raised no objections to the payments.[11]

Even if Gauci was entirely reliable and unaffected by the prospect of a reward, the fact remains that the man he described was six feet tall, broadly built and around 50 years old. It is inconceivable that he could have mistaken someone eight years younger than himself for someone around six years older. It is also hard to believe that, as a clothes seller, he was not a good judge of size and could not distinguish a man of 5ft 8in from one four inches taller. If there ever was a single clothes purchaser, it is perfectly clear that it was not Abdelbaset.

Although the police found blast-damaged garments traceable to Mary's House, the work of Dr Roger King demonstrated that RARDE's clothing categorisation system was fundamentally flawed and that it was therefore impossible to say with certainty whether those clothes were in the primary suitcase. In total there were 54 garments that could not be excluded from the suitcase on forensic grounds, only nine of which could be linked to Mary's House.[12] It has never been demonstrated that all of the remaining 45 could be attributed to the owners of other luggage.

Regardless of these problems, the presence of Maltese clothes in the primary suitcase was far from proof that the bomb originated in Malta, less still that it was carried on KM180. There was no evidence that the bomb was loaded at Luqa Airport; indeed, the evidence of dispatcher Gerald Camilleri and loader Michael Darmanin appeared to rule it out.[13]

The Frankfurt documents fell far short of proving that the unknown bag B8849 came from KM180 and that it was transferred to PA103A. There were a number of credible alternative explanations for B8849. In particular, the evidence of FBI agent Lawrence Whittaker and Detective Inspector Watson McAteer suggested that someone could have approached coding station 206 with a single suitcase and entered it into the system, without making a record or being noticed. Indeed, McAteer's corresponding statement, which remained undisclosed until 2009, suggested this practice was not unusual.[14]

None of the disclosed evidence demonstrated that every bag found at the crash-site could be ruled out as B8849.

Frankfurt and Heathrow airports were both much larger than Luqa and far easier for bombers to penetrate inconspicuously; furthermore each offered a clear alternative to the Crown's Luqa theory. The Frankfurt scenario involved the duping of Khaled Jaafar into carrying the bomb. He checked in two items at the airport, shortly after which he seemed to be 'very agitated and nervous'.[15] The only two bags of his found at the crash-site were hand luggage-sized, had no check-in labels attached and contained travel documents. It would have been unusual for anyone making a transatlantic journey not to take at least one cabin bag. We now know that some of Jaafar's Dortmund associates were linked circumstantially to people arrested during the Autumn Leaves raids. He was also implicated by two PFLP-GC members, one of whom, Mobdi Goben, confessed to being a central figure in the plot.[16]

The Heathrow scenario centred on the brown, hard-sided suitcase seen by loader John Bedford in the luggage container AVE4041. DC Derek Henderson's analysis demonstrated that none of the container's legitimate luggage was of that type.[17] The fact that the bomb was ideally positioned to destroy the plane and was unlikely to have been fatal in most other positions, suggested either that the bombers got very lucky, or that it was deliberately placed at Heathrow. There was a clear window of opportunity to have repositioned the Bedford case, or added another, prior to the arrival of PA103A when the container was standing in the baggage build-up area for approximately 45 minutes.

The only other major plank in the Crown case was the circuit board fragment PT/35b. As the head of the FBI investigation, Richard Marquise, put it, without it 'I don't think we would ever have had an indictment.'[18] There is no doubt that its circuitry had a similar pattern to the boards used in the MST-13 timers and that 20 such timers were supplied to Libya, but it's now clear that the fragment did not originate from one of those devices.

What, then, is left of the case against me?
The apparent impossibility of the bomb being placed on KM180 means my visit to Malta on 20 and 21 December 1988

using the Abdusamad coded passport is irrelevant. Setting that aside, I used the passport on that occasion for innocent and relatively trivial reasons. It was originally intended to assist me with sanctions-busting on behalf of LAA. Had I chosen to, I could have entered Malta without filling out an embarkation card or showing the passport. I never used the passport again, but neither did I destroy it; indeed, I kept it safe for over a decade before surrendering it willingly to the Crown. Similarly, the Libyan passport authority preserved, then handed over, the corresponding paperwork. Only then was the Crown able to prove that I was Abdusamad.[19]

I've never denied lying to Pierre Salinger about the Malta trip and my association with Mebo. I didn't expect to be questioned on those matters and, when put on the spot, tried to conceal anything that might be used against Libya. It was very unwise of me and brought me much greater trouble.

The only remaining thread to the conviction is my connection to the JSO. Here the judges relied on the evidence of Majid Giaka, which was perverse, given their rejection of his other claims. My only JSO role was the 12-month secondment as LAA's acting head of airline security. I do not deny that some of my friends and relatives occupied senior positions within the JSO, but that makes me neither a senior JSO officer nor a terrorist.

If I was a terrorist, then I was an exceptionally stupid one. I entered Malta on 7 December using my own passport and stayed at the Holiday Inn in my own name. Had it been a Libyan state-sponsored operation, I would surely have been ordered to stay at one of Malta's Libyan-owned hotels or at Lamin's flat. On the same day I ostentatiously bought clothes, rather than discreetly in a large store. Terrorists generally compartmentalise their operations, yet I am supposed to have returned to Malta two weeks later to somehow plant the bomb at Luqa Airport. Rather than flying there by LAA and bypassing immigration and passport control, I took an Air Malta flight. Had I been planning a bomb attack, I would surely then have lain low, but instead Lamin took me to meet a local man, Vincent Vassallo, whom I'd never before met. I then went to see a carpet-seller, who again was a new acquaintance, and finally checked into the same hotel as previously, thereby inviting staff to notice my use of two passports within a fortnight. The following morning I enacted the final stage of the plot at Luqa Airport, a place where my face was known to some of the local staff and which has tighter security procedures than most. I chose to use a distinctive timing device, which, as far as the JSO would have been aware, was made exclusively for Libya. The alleged seizure of one of these devices from two Libyans in Senegal, ten months earlier, meant they were traceable to Libya. I also left the labels in the clothes, enabling the police to link them to Malta and even to Mary's House. The cunning genius that I showed in getting the bomb onto KM180 was more than outweighed by the stupidity of sending it on a three-legged journey, during which the plot might easily have been derailed by seasonal delays and X-ray inspection at Frankfurt.

How then did Libya and Abdelbaset come to be in the frame for the bombing? During the 1980s, the Reagan government consistently blamed Libya for terrorist attacks committed by others. It would be unsurprising if that tradition was continued by the successor administration of George Bush Snr.

The first inkling that Libya was being framed came within days of the bombing, when, for reasons that remain unclear, Edwin Bollier tipped off the CIA. Whether the CIA at that stage were aware of their tipster's identity is also unclear. They claim not to have been,[20] but, given their role in concealing information about Giaka, that denial is hardly reassuring. The Western intelligence services had known since the early 1970s that Bollier was supplying sensitive Western equipment to the Stasi. He was reporting back to the Swiss police, and it is unlikely that the CIA and BND would have tolerated his activities unless he was also helping them. Assuming he was, then it is very likely that the CIA was well aware of Abdelbaset's connection to Mebo. Even if it was not, thanks to Giaka, the Agency knew about Abdelbaset before Lockerbie and, according to the FBI's Richard Marquise, he was also monitored by another US intelligence agency, most likely the NSA. Giaka also told the CIA, prior to Lockerbie, that Abdelbaset's friend Said Rashid worked for Libya's General Electronics Company, which prosecutors would later allege was the likely source of the radio-cassette player that contained the bomb.*

The *La Belle* nightclub bombing story suggests that some of the Western intelligence services may have been prepared to concoct evidence and use agents provocateurs to lay a false trail to Libya.[21] The CIA knew well before Lockerbie that Bollier had supplied MST-13 timers to Libya, and it had possessed one since 1986.[22] That timer was supposedly among weapons seized in Togo following a coup attempt, but here too the story was not all that it seemed. The BATF agent Richard Sherrow, who in good faith took it back to the United States, believed it 'had been handled and manipulated by unknown parties';[23] moreover, the Togolese President and senior army officers suggested the timers seized were of a very different type. It is quite possible that the MST-13s were planted in order to implicate Libya in the coup attempt.

The Senegal timer story is also highly suspect. The device was supposedly part of an arms cache seized from two Libyans and their Senegalese accomplice. However, the accomplice was later revealed to be a Senegalese government informant. The DGSE was involved in the operation and the CIA was tipped off in advance of the arrests.[24] There was no reliable evidence to link the Libyans to the cache and the charges against them were eventually dropped. Again, it is possible the weapons were planted. More importantly, Senegalese army records suggested the timer was not destroyed along with the other weapons[25] and the official in charge of the operation, Jean Collin, strongly hinted that it ended up in American hands.[26]

Against this background, it is a remarkable and suspicious coincidence that a fragment of an MST-13 circuit-board should turn up among the Lockerbie debris, and more remarkable still that it should be discovered within a garment that could be neatly linked to Malta. The story of the fragment's recovery and identification remains riddled with anomalies, which may or may not have an

* Interestingly, the CIA cable in which Rashid's relationship with the company was reported was not among those originally disclosed. This raised the possibility that the Agency was reluctant to reveal its foreknowledge of the company.

innocent explanation. It is also now clear that the CIA identified it
as part of an MST-13 and pointed the investigators towards Mebo.

If the fragment and the Maltese clothes were not planted after
the bombing, then, together with the attention-seeking behaviour of
Gauci's 'Libyan' customer, they suggest the bombers were looking to
implicate Libya. While it's impossible to prove such a conspiracy, it
can now be proven that the Lockerbie fragment PT/35b did not originate from one of the timers supplied to Libya. Who exactly made it?
We may never know.

Once the groundwork was laid, it was, perhaps, inevitable that
Abdelbaset's association with Mebo, his presence in Malta and his
background in airline security would bring him to the police's attention. Once in the frame he was shoehorned into Gauci's description
of the clothes purchaser. His use of the coded passport and lies to
Salinger helped seal his fate, and Giaka became the rancid icing on
the prosecutors' cake.

What then is the real story of the bombing? Again, we may never
know.

What seems certain is that some within the Iranian government
were determined to avenge the shoot-down of Iran Air flight 655 and
hired the PFLP-GC to do their dirty work. Marwan Khreesat built at
least five bombs designed to blow up aircraft, at least one of which
was built into a Toshiba radio-cassette player. One of his radio-cassette
bombs went missing and may have been smuggled out of Germany by
Salah Kwekes, a.k.a. Ramzi Diab. Khreesat denied using twin-speaker
models, such as the RT-SF16, but said he had seen one in the back of
Dalkamoni's car.[27] According to Mobdi Goben, who led the PFLP-
GC's Yugoslavian operation, Khreesat was not the group's only bomb-
maker and he (Goben) took a bomb from Syria to Yugoslavia.

Although the Autumn Leaves raids took out Khreesat, Dalkamoni and Ghadanfar, most of the group's European network was left
intact and the key operative Abu Elias remained under the radar. According to Goben[28] and the CIA's Robert Baer,[29] Elias was central to
the plot post-Autumn Leaves and, according to Khreesat, he arrived
in West Germany shortly before the raids.[30] The group's continuing
capacity and intent was indicated by the remarkable terrorist alert

received by the US State Department's Office of Diplomatic Security on 2 December 1988, which gave warning of an imminent attack on a Pan Am target in Europe by Palestinian rejectionists.[31]

Exactly how the group executed the bombing remains unclear. They were certainly linked to Malta via Abu Talb, and it is possible that he took a bomb there; however, it is unlikely he would have taken that risk, especially given the difficulties that his unknown accomplices would have faced in subverting Luqa Airport security. It seems more likely that his presence in Malta was related to the supposed primary suitcase clothing.

It would have been simpler for the bombers to dupe Frankfurt passenger Khaled Jaafar than to smuggle a bomb on to flight KM180. According to RARDE's Allen Feraday, it would have been possible to construct a barometric bomb that would not have exploded on the Frankfurt to Heathrow flight.[32] There is no suggestion that Jaafar was a suicide bomber, though his demeanour at Frankfurt Airport suggested he was very nervous about something.

It is possible that the bombers used Jaafar as a decoy, and instead introduced the primary suitcase at Heathrow. That might explain both the Bedford suitcase and the bomb's apparently optimal location within AVE4041. Furthermore, the interval of 38 minutes between take-off and the explosion tallied with the settings of one of Khreesat's bombs.[33]

Why conceal the truth about Iranian and PFLP-GC involvement in the attack? Iran and the group's other main backer, Syria, were far trickier enemies for the US government than Libya, not least because of their influence over many of the region's fervently anti-Western armed groups. Despite its public hostility to Iran, the United States was more reliant on Iran's oil than Libya's, and Iran needed the oil revenues. While it was waging its secret campaign against Libya, US NSC secretly armed Iran, which was then at war with Iraq, in return for help in releasing American hostages held in Lebanon. When the war ended, shortly before Lockerbie, the Reagan administration was looking to stabilise relations with Tehran.

It is possible that the Americans had more to conceal, in particular that the bombers had penetrated an illegal CIA drugs-for-hostages operation, which allowed Lebanese producers to ship heroin to the

United States. Advocates of this scenario have claimed Khaled Jaafar was a drug mule and was conned into carrying the bomb. A number of investigations have suggested that Major Charles McKee learned of the operation and, concerned that it would jeopardise his own hostage rescue efforts, was returning to the United States to blow the whistle.[34] This might explain the official denial of the drug finds at Lockerbie and some of the odd events at the crash-site, including the arrival of American officials within two hours of the crash and the removal and replacement of McKee's suitcase. It would also explain the extraordinary official reaction to David Johnston's radio news item linking the bombing to McKee.

A yet more horrifying scenario, first outlined in Juval Aviv's Interfor Report, is that the CIA people and other intelligence services were aware that PA103 would be targeted and allowed it to happen. It is claimed that elements within the CIA wished to neutralise the threat of McKee. In 1993 the British tycoon Tiny Rowland was told by a senior South African official that a government entourage, including Foreign Minister Pik Botha, was scheduled to fly on PA103, but was instead booked onto an earlier flight. According to Rowland, the official told him that the change of plan followed a warning from a source that 'could not be ignored', although he would not say who.[35] There is no suggestion that Botha and his party knew of the bombers' plans, but, if Rowland was correct, someone obviously did.* This might well explain the government campaigns against Aviv and the Rowland-backed documentary *The Maltese Double Cross*.

Though it might seem unthinkable that anyone would allow a plane crash to happen, the fact that the PFLP-GC was preparing to attack at least five flights may have prompted a gruesomely pragmatic reckoning: better allow Iran to get even than risk a far greater loss of life.

* In 1994 Botha's Private Secretary told Reuters: 'We . . . got to London an hour early and the embassy got us on an earlier flight. When we got to JFK airport a contemporary of mine said, "Thank God you weren't on 103. It crashed over Lockerbie."' However, in a subsequent Parliamentary answer, the South African Justice Minister, Dullah Omar, said: 'Shortly before finalising their booking arrangements for Pan Am flight 103 to New York, they learned of an earlier flight from London to New York, namely Pan Am Flight 101.'

It is not my intention to blame others for the bombing, but merely to point out that there is a wealth of evidence – much of which remained hidden from my trial – to support alternative versions of the bomb plot. However, I often wonder who is to blame for my ordeal. I doubt we'll ever know who framed me and my country. The police cannot be blamed for following leads that fell into their laps. Together with the Crown, they stitched together a flimsy case based around a merce-nary double agent, a highly unreliable identification, a hopeless CIA informant, some highly equivocal documents and overstated forensic conclusions, but, again, they were only doing their jobs. They can be criticised for their handling of Gauci, which, while no doubt con-ducted in good faith, may have subconsciously led him in my direc-tion. Harder to forgive was the Crown's blatant breach of their legal obligation to disclose all the evidence that would have undermined the case against me.

As for Gauci himself, he was aware that a substantial reward was on offer and was under the influence of his sharper brother, who had the reward firmly in his sights. Prior to the trial he read an article that highlighted the holes in the Crown's case and his trial evidence went some way towards filling them. He was, nevertheless, a simple man who, without wishing it, found himself the key witness in a massive international investigation.

As I near the end of my life, I wish to say the following to him directly. I swear to God that I was never in your shop and never saw you in my life until we were in court. While you and your brother received a huge reward, your wrongful incrimination of me brought great suffering to my family and my country. I therefore ask you one question: do you feel any pangs of remorse? I wish to make clear that I forgive you. One day we shall both meet our God and I hope He is as forgiving. I have nothing to fear from Him.

I find it harder to forgive those who failed to reveal that reward payments had been repeatedly discussed, since they must have known that the information was relevant to my defence. I also cannot forgive those responsible for comprehensively misleading the Court over the Giaka cables.

Allen Feraday knew that PT/35b was not 'similar in all respects' to the control sample Thüring circuit board, yet failed to mention this in the report that he produced jointly with Thomas Hayes. Again, I find this hard to excuse.

My defence team worked tirelessly and with my best interests at heart, but the decision not to challenge Gauci head-on during cross-examination backfired badly and their apparent acceptance that PT/35b was from a Thüring board may also have cost me dear.

However, the ultimate responsibility for the guilty verdict lies with Lords Sutherland, Coulsfield and MacLean. Thirty years ago Lord Denning rejected an appeal by the Birmingham Six on the grounds that their victory would present 'such an appalling vista that every sensible person would say, "It cannot be right that these actions should go any further".' There were no police beatings or false confessions in my case, neither were there such naked judicial assertions. Nevertheless, an acquittal would have brought numerous powerful institutions into very serious disrepute. It would have meant that the largest criminal inquiry in British and American history had snared the wrong people; it would mean that the gaping holes in the police investigation and the Crown case would be open to public scrutiny; it would mean that the UN Security Council had passed resolutions on a false basis, which had resulted in years of suffering for the Libyan people; and it would be an acknowledgement that the real bombers remained untouched. In short it would have presented a vista so appalling that the judges, consciously or not, were unwilling to contemplate it.

It is ironic that three of Scotland's best legal minds believed me to be guilty, yet the ordinary Scots who got to know me believed I was innocent. To them, and to all the others who have shown me kindness over the past decade, I offer my heartfelt thanks.

Many of those who lost relatives at Lockerbie believe me to be guilty and were appalled by my release. I've no wish to add to their pain and can say only that I am an innocent man, and ask that they consider all the facts in this book, many of which will be new to them. To British relatives who are seeking a public inquiry into the bombing, I give my wholehearted support and shall do all I can to support their efforts.

Almost certainly I will die with the weight of my conviction still on my shoulders. My conscience, however, will be clear, and until my last breath I shall pray that the real stories of Lockerbie will one day be known to all.

The Police Statements of Tony Gauci

Tony Gauci made 19 police statements, an extraordinarily high number for any witness.* Some were wide-ranging, others just a few lines long, and only two – the seventeenth and the nineteenth – concerned Abdelbaset. Together they reveal a man with an unremarkable constellation of excusable human frailties: uncertainty, suggestibility, eagerness to please and, above all, inconsistency. Ironically, the matter on which he was most consistent – the description of the clothes-purchaser – was the one most problematic for the Crown.

The clothes-purchaser
When first interviewed by the police, on 1 September 1989, although ten months after the event, Gauci was able to give a clear physical description of the purchaser:

> 'He was about 6' or more in height. He had a big chest and a large head. He was well built but he was not fat or with a big stomach. His hair was very black . . . He was clean shaven with no facial hair. He had dark coloured skin . . . I would say that the jacket was too small for him, although it was a 42 inch size, that is British inches.'[1]

On 13 September 1989 he helped to produce two images of the suspect: the first a photofit assembled by two BKA officers, and the second an artist's impression drawn by the FBI's George Noble. They appear on page 380.

In his corresponding statement, Gauci commented:

> 'The photograph on the screen was as similar looking to the man I saw as I think I could get. The hair and forehead are

* A police report of 10 June 1999 said that Tony had given a total of 23 statements – see Chapter 13.

*The photofit image (left) and the artist's impression (right) produced on 13
September 1989 from Tony Gauci's description.*

similar. The man's eyes were a bit bigger than that in the
photofit and his eyebrows may have been a slight bit longer.
The nose, mouth, shape of face and thickness of neck were
all similar to the man. I think the man I described would be
about size 16½" or 17" collar.'

Crucially, for the first time he gave details of the man's age:

'He was about 50 years of age and I think the age of the man
in the photofit is between 45 and 50 years which is just about
right.'[2]

The artist's impression looked rather different. Above right was
the version shown to the court, as Crown production 427. Gauci's
statement said:

'With a few minor alterations to the age of the man and to the
style of the hair, I was able to say that the artist impression
was a very close resemblance to the man I saw in my shop.'[3]

380

It is not clear whether he meant that the man he saw was younger or older; however, the drawing suggests that, unlike Abdelbaset, whose hair was thinning and receding, the man had a full head of hair. It may well have been afro-type, which tallies with Gauci's original description of the man as dark-skinned. The original version of the drawing was never disclosed; however, the following copies (see below), discovered by Tony Kelly's team in the BKA and Maltese police files, suggested that it might have been darker than the court version.

The darkness of these images appeared not to be an artefact of photocopying or faxing; indeed, the analysis of the images by BSB Forensic all but ruled that out.[4] Rather, it appeared that many more of the fine, dark hatching lines were visible, which suggested that the original drawing was indeed notably darker. Assuming that it accurately reflected Gauci's memory, this again ruled out the light-skinned Abdelbaset.

Gauci gave a third significant statement on 13 September. He had remembered that around three months earlier he'd seen someone resembling the customer at Tony's Bar on the Strand in Sliema.

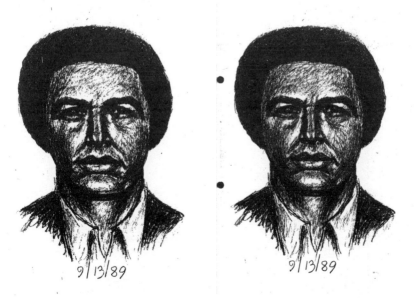

Copies of the artist's impression discovered by Tony Kelly's team in the BKA and Maltese archives.

Although he could not be sure that it was the man, he described him as 'very similar' and repeated that he was around 50 years old.[5]

The following day the police showed Gauci two photospreads, one of which showed ten men and the other nine. He picked out the following photograph and commented:

'This photograph is similar to the man who bought the clothing. The man in the photograph I identified is too young to be the man who bought the clothing. If the man in the photograph was older by about 20 years he would look like the man who bought the clothing. I signed the front of the photograph of the man I identified as similar. I also signed the 2 cards containing the photographs I was shown. I have been asked in what way the photograph is similar to the man who bought the clothing. The photograph looks like the man's features at the eyes, nose, mouth and shape of face. The hair of the customer was similar but shorter to that in the photograph.'[6]

The man in question was 33-year-old Mohamed Salem.[7] Even if the photo was a few years old, if he appeared 20 years younger than the man, then the man must have been around 50.

Less than a fortnight later, on 26 September 1989, Gauci told the police he believed the customer had visited the shop the previous day.

The description was consistent with his earlier statements:

'This man had the same hair style, black hair, no hair on his face, dark skin. He was around 6 foot or just under that in height. He was about 50 years of age. He was broad built, not fat, and I would say he had a 36" waist.'[8]

Given that the encounter was still fresh in his memory, this was likely to be the most reliable of Gauci's accounts.

The description was relayed to, among others, Inspector Alphonse Cauci of the Maltese police, who believed it matched a Libyan journalist called Mohamed Zomiat, who had been based in Malta.[9] Significantly Zomiat was dark-skinned, had afro hair[10] and would have been 46 at the time of the purchase.[11] His photograph was included among twelve shown to Gauci the following day, but Gauci said none resembled the customer.* He picked out one man as having the same hair, but said he was too young to be the purchaser.[12] Since this man, who was called Shukri, was the same age as Zomiat,[13] the observation was consistent with the man being around 50.

On 2 October he was shown a video freeze frame of Mohamed Abu Talb from a BBC *Panorama* programme about Lockerbie. He described the picture as 'similar' to the clothes-buyer, adding:

'I noted that the eyebrows upwards on the photograph are the same although the hairstyle of the man that came in to the shop was more full and rounded and did not recede at the temples. The face in the photograph is also thinner than the person who came in to the shop.'[14]

The statement reinforced the earlier assertions that the man was well-built and had a full head of hair. Five months later, on 5 March 1990, Gauci told the police that, a week earlier, his brother Paul had shown him a *Sunday Times* article from 5 November 1989 featuring

* Gauci's statement concerning this photoshow is dated 26 September 1989, but it is clear from other evidence that the date is mistaken and that he was actually shown the photos the following day.

a photograph of Abu Talb. He couldn't be certain that Talb was the clothes-purchaser, but stated:

> 'All I can say about the photograph printed in the newspaper is that I think the man looks the same as the one who bought the clothing.' [15]

It was notable that in both statements Gauci failed to comment on Talb's age, even though, at the time of the incident, he was only 34 and therefore patently far younger than the purchaser. In both instances it must have been clear to Gauci that Talb was a suspect. This may subconsciously have influenced him to note a similarity, which, in reality, did not exist.

On 31 August 1990 he was shown two more photospreads, which each depicted 12 men. Although he was, once again, unable to make a positive identification, he picked out the following photo as being 'similar in the shape of the face and style of hair.'

The face suggested a heavy build and, although the hair was not afro-style, it was nevertheless very thick and not receding at the temples. He picked out the three men on the following page as being 'of the correct age of the man'. All three appeared to be at least in their forties.

On 10 September he was shown more photos, but failed to pick any out. He confirmed his earlier descriptions of the man, reiterating that he was about 50, although he again said that the *Sunday Times* photograph of Abu Talb was 'similar'.[16]

The 'identification' of Abdelbaset

It has frequently been claimed that, prior to Abdelbaset's trial, Gauci identified him as the clothes-buyer, but in fact he merely suggested on two occasions that there was a resemblance. The first was, of course, on 15 February 1991, when he picked Abdelbaset's photograph from a spread of 12. He described the photograph, which was numbered 8, only as 'similar', adding:

> 'The man in the photograph No. 8 is in my opinion in his thirty years (30 years). He would perhaps have to look about 10 years or more older and he would look like the man who bought the clothes . . . I can only say that of all the photographs I have been shown this photograph No. 8 is the only one really similar to the man who bought the clothing if he was a bit older other than the one my brother showed me.'

Earlier he had clearly stated that all 12 appeared younger than the man. Crucially, he only made the selection having been asked by DCI Bell to look again and allow for any age difference, a direction not given during the previous photoshows.[17] According to Inspector Godfrey Scicluna, Bell gave a more exact cue, telling Gauci that the man could be ten to fifteen years older than the people in the photographs.[18] Bell denied this, but, even if Scicluna was wrong,

Gauci had received a hefty steer. To make matters worse, the officers present knew which photo was of Abdelbaset, so may inadvertently have influenced his choice.

Of course, not only was Abdelbaset only 36 at the time of the purchase, he was also 5ft 8in tall, slender, light-skinned and had thinning, receding hair. In other words, he was clearly not the 50-year-old, 6-foot, well-built, hirsute, dark-skinned customer whom Gauci had described.

The second partial identification, made during the identity parade at Kamp Zeist on 13 April 1999, was described in his final statement, as follows:

> 'I was asked if I saw the man who had been in my shop. I said I wasn't sure, but the one who looked most like him was No. 5 . . . I'm not 100% sure, it has been 10 years, and I want to be as fair as possible.'[19]*

This again fell well short of a positive identification. Notably, he no longer insisted that Abdelbaset was younger than the customer. This was perhaps because Abdelbaset was by then 47, and therefore much closer in age to the customer. In any case, the procedure was ludicrous; eleven years had passed since the clothes-purchase, and for the previous seven-and-a-half Abdelbaset's image had appeared repeatedly in media articles, some of which had been collected by Paul Gauci. To compound the absurdity, none of the parade's stand-ins looked anything like Abdelbaset, and all bar one were significantly younger.

Further sightings of the customer

On this subject, Gauci was rather more erratic. In his first statement he was clear that the man 'has not been in the shop before or since',[20] but twelve days later he remembered the sighting of a similar man three months earlier at Tony's Bar. Five months later, he recovered another memory, telling the police that a Libyan resembling the man

---

* According to the police identity parade report, his exact words were: 'Not exactly the man I saw in the shop ten years ago. I saw him, but the man who look a little bit like exactly is the number five.'

had been in the shop in May or June 1987 and had bought blankets. Gauci admitted that 'I have not mentioned this before because I did not remember it.'[21]

On 26 September 1989 he gave the dramatic statement detailing how, the previous day, the suspect, or someone very much like him, had been in the shop. The police later learned that Abdelbaset was in Malta between 21 and 24 September. A police officer's note at the bottom of the statement read:

'When initially seen, this witness referred to the visit to the shop and sale of the dresses as having occurred on 21st or 22nd September, 1989. When his statement was noted he referred to this having taken place on 25th September and was not questioned about the date change. Evidence outlined in section 38 of the final report* indicated that the accused Megrahi arrived in Malta on 21 September and left on 24 September. It may therefore be that Gauci is confused as to the date of the incident. An action has been raised to have him re-interviewed.'[22]

The re-interview took place over two years after the incident, on 4 November 1991. The resulting statement contained this unusual passage:

'I have been advised that when I was interviewed on the morning of Tuesday 26 September, 1989 within my shop, I had at that time stated that the Man had come into my shop on the Thursday (21 September, 1989) or the Friday (22 September, 1989) and purchased the children's dresses. I have also been advised that when I met Mr. Bell and Mr. Scicluna that evening I had stated that the Man had come into the shop on the Monday (25 September, 1989). I have been asked if I can clarify this and if I can explain why I appear to have mixed up the days. At this time I can not explain this. I can only say that

* The 'final report' is the police report to the Crown Office, which set out the evidence against the two Libyans and the basis on which they were indicted for the bombing.

I had problems with my father and brother at that time, they did not want me to speak to you anymore and I may have got things mixed up. I cannot explain this now.'[23]

If nothing else, this indicated the frailty of Gauci's memory.

The date

Gauci's memory of the purchase date was also problematic. In his original statement of 1 September 1989, he could recall only that it was 'during the winter in 1988'. There were, however, several other clues: it was 'midweek'; his brother Paul 'had gone home to watch a football match on television'; and 'it was raining' as the man first left the shop. The next mention was on 13 September, when he referred to the 'man who had bought clothing from my shop in December 1988'.[24] In the following day's statement, December had changed to 'November or December'.[25] And in the next statement, of 19 September, he gave a more precise clue:

'At Christmas time we put up the decorations about 15 days before Christmas, the decorations were not up when the man bought the clothing.'[26]

His statement of 2 October 1989 referred to the person who had 'entered my shop in November and December 1988'.[27] The use of 'and' rather than 'or' was curious and remained unexplained. By 31 January 1990 he had reverted to December,[28] but by 21 February it was once again November or December,[29] which he repeated on 5 March.[30]

On 10 September 1990, Gauci gave one of his longest and most important statements. Before beginning, DCI Bell explained that one of the purposes of the interview was 'to go over the statements he had previously made'. Bell then 'went over each aspect of [the] statements and asked him questions to clarify a number of points'.[31] Although Gauci's statement again referred to 'November/December' and 'November and December', it contained this important passage:

'I have been asked to again try and pinpoint the day and date that I sold the man the clothing. I can only say it was a

388

weekday, there were no Christmas decorations up as I have already said, and I believe it was at the end of November.'[32]

On 21 February 1990 he revisited the subject of the rain shower, recalling:

'When he returned to the shop . . . the umbrella was down because it had almost stopped raining and it was just drops coming down.'[33]

On 5 March he confirmed that 'at that time it was raining',[34] and on 10 September he further elaborated:

'Just before the man left the shop there was a light shower of rain just beginning. The umbrellas were hanging from the mirrors in the shop and the man actually looked at them and that is how I came to sell him one. He opened it up as he left the shop . . . There was very little rain on the ground, no running water, just damp.'

Taken together the statements strongly suggested that the date was not 7 December 1988, but, when coupled with the meteorological and Christmas lights evidence, they all but ruled it out.

The clothing

Gauci's recollection of the clothing he had sold portrayed him at his most suggestible and erratic. Nowhere was this more apparent than in relation to the supposed sale of two Slalom-brand shirts, one of which was grey and the other pin-striped. The grey one was especially significant, because a fragment of a similar shirt, PI/995, supposedly housed the crucial timer fragment, PT/35b.

The problem for the police, however, was that in his original account Gauci never described selling a shirt.[35] In January 1990 they began investigating the circuit board in earnest, and on the 30th they showed him another section of the shirt, PK/1978. He instantly recognised it as a type sold in Mary's House and also confirmed that a piece of blue and white pinstriped material, PH/999, matched other Slalom shirts stocked. However, he added, unequivocally, 'I am sure that I did not sell him a shirt . . . That man didn't buy any shirts for sure.'[36]

When DCI Bell went over his earlier statements for the key review statement of 10 September 1990, Gauci performed a remarkable volte-face:

'About three weeks ago I was cleaning boxes out in the shop and I remember that they had contained a 'SLALOM' shirt and a blue and white light denim (texture) material shirt. I know that I sold you shirts like these and I now remember that the man who bought the clothing also bought a 'SLALOM' shirt and a blue and white striped shirt.'

Had a criminal suspect offered such an explanation for a dramatic U-turn, the police might well have rolled their eyes in disbelief. Interestingly, the original handwritten version of Gauci's statement, which Abdelbaset's lawyers obtained from the Maltese police many years later, said the man bought 'a beige SLALOM shirt'.[37] If true, the shirt did not match the remains found at Lockerbie; however, the word beige was later crossed out and initialled by a police officer.[38]

In his original statement, Gauci calculated the total bill for the clothes as 76.50 Maltese pounds, adding, 'I am sure that I gave him £4 change. I could have given him the 50 cents off the bill.'[39] To confuse matters, on 30 January 1990 he said:

'I have also remembered that the man who bought all the stuff spent 77 Maltese pounds (142.59p), he gave me 8 × 10 [Maltese pound] notes and I gave him 3 [Maltese pounds] change. I think I said it was only 56 LM before.'

The sale of the shirts would, of course, have increased the bill. He recalled that one of them cost 5.25 Maltese pounds and the other 3.75 or 5.25, which would bring the total to 86.00 or 87.50.

There were other U-turns, most notably concerning the cardigan. In his first statement, he said that the man 'also bought a tartan cardigan, a large size, we do not have any left but it had colours red/black. I cannot recall exactly.'[40]

On 13 September 1989 he elaborated:

'It was a two colour cardigan with big imitation leather, brown coloured buttons. I think six buttons. I think my brother Paul got the cardigan from a shop in Paola in Malta. I cannot remember the shop name.'

On 19 September Bell and DC John Crawford visited the shop to investigate further. According to Crawford:

'About 12.50, whilst in the shop premises, I saw a blue coloured woollen cardigan which was, in all respects, except colour, identical to a brown coloured cardigan which I had viewed at RARDE and which was blast damaged.'

Gauci gave them the blue cardigan and Crawford established that both it and the Lockerbie cardigan had been supplied by a local manufacturer: Eagle Knitwear Notabile Road, Mriehel, Malta.[41] Crawford's sharp-eyed detective work prompted Gauci to alter his account radically:

'I have already mentioned about the man coming into the shop and buying various articles. One of them he bought was a cardigan, different from the one I have already described but was a beige or maybe darker colour. It is the same as the one which you now have (DC92 – no longer a production) except that it is not blue. It is exactly the same as this blue one (DC92) with the same buttons.'[42]

A week later the police showed him photographs of the Lockerbie cardigan, PI/594, which he agreed was 'the same as the one I sold to the man'.[43] However, on 30 January 1990, he said the one sold was one of three that he had bought from a retired police officer from Msida, who had in turn obtained them from a supplier in Paola called Hammet Brothers. He added, 'they were Italian make with big checks'.[44]

More than a year later, on 15 February 1991 – the day he picked out Abdelbaset's photo – Crawford took him aside and went over the cardigan story once more. In the corresponding statement, Crawford reported that Gauci 'now realises that the Puccini cardigan was bought from Eagle Knitwear and not from this ex-policeman';[45] however, no statement was taken from Gauci to confirm this claim.

There were also fluctuations in his description of the babygro and the jacket. He originally said the babygro had a white sheep's face motif on the front.[46] Bell then showed him one obtained from the Lockerbie babygro's manufacturer, which had a whole lamb's body on the front. Gauci said it was different to the one sold, which, he continued to insist, had only a sheep's head.[47] Three weeks later, however, he accepted that 'the lamb motif on the front were probably all the same style.'[48]

When first visited by the police, he gave them a jacket like the one in question, but a few months later, on 21 February 1990, the police informed him that it did not match the fragments found at Lockerbie. Having been shown the fragments, he discovered there was a matching one in stock, which he gave to the police.[49]

Gauci maintained throughout his statements that he sold three pairs of pyjamas, yet only one set of that particular type was recovered at Lockerbie. The other two might have been lost within the crash-site, but, if that were the case, they were the only garments he described not to be recovered.*

The customer's departure

In his first statement Gauci said that, when the customer left the shop for the second time, he carried the parcels and turned left up the street towards a parked taxi. Gauci went back into the shop, so did not see the man get into the taxi, but assumed it was waiting for him.[50]

On 21 February 1990, he described the man's initial departure and return, and elaborated on his second departure:

> 'He left the shop having made the purchases and turned right down Tower Road ... When he returned to the shop he came from the same direction ... After he had collected the parcels the man left the shop carrying them in both hands with the

---

* When interviewed by the Crown prior to Abdelbaset's trial, Gauci said he had sold only two pairs of pyjamas.

umbrella still down. He walked towards the Mercedes taxi which was parked about 20 yards from the shop. I did not see him get into it. He had told me that he had a taxi waiting and I assumed this was it.'[51]

On 5 March the police asked him to go over the events once more. This time he gave a rather different account:

'I now remember that when the man left my shop he walked downhill in Tower Road towards the seafront . . .
  About fifteen minutes later I was standing near the shop front when I saw a white Mercedes taxi driving up Tower Road. I could see that the man who had bought the clothing was seated in the front passenger seat of the taxi. I went back inside the shop, but before I did so I saw the taxi pull into the kerb on the same side of the road as my shop about 20 yards up the street, where I have shown you. I then saw the man get out of the front passenger seat and start walking towards my shop. I went to get his parcels and he came into the shop.
  I handed over the two parcels and the man left the shop walking back up the road to the taxi. He put both parcels on the back seat of the taxi before climbing back into the front passenger seat. The taxi then drove off up Tower Road.
  I have been asked why I have not mentioned this before and I can only say that I did not think you asked me directly about it. I have been thinking about the man and I remember this now.'[52]

So, Gauci was now saying that he saw the man arrive and depart in a taxi. He attempted a further clarification on 10 September 1990:

'I made up the clothing that the man had bought into two parcels which I wrapped. In my original statement I said that I next saw the man when he returned to the shop but subsequently I said that I had seen him sitting in the front seat of the taxi which was driven up Tower Road. What happened was I went to the front of the shop and was looking out and saw the taxi being driven up the street. As it passed my shop I recognised that the front seat passenger was the same man who had bought the clothing. I saw the taxi stop on the corner, where I pointed out to the officer (top of Tower Road) and I went back into the shop to collect the parcels. The man came down to the shop and I met him in the hallway. I asked him if I could carry the parcels to his car and he said he had a taxi. The man then walked up to the taxi, put the parcels on the back seat and he got into the front beside the driver.'[53]

These fluctuating accounts provided further confirmation of Gauci's erratic memory. The only major points of consistency were that the man walked alone to the taxi carrying the parcels and that throughout no one else was present.

Conclusion

The most remarkable aspect of Gauci's police statements is how little they supported his evidence at trial. Most obviously, in telling the court that Abdelbaset 'resembles him a lot' and was 'not the dark one', he defied all his earlier descriptions of the customer. His claim to Crown counsel that 'I don't have experience on height or age' not only flew in the face of common sense, but also overlooked his previous precise assessments of the man's age and size. The crucial assertion that the incident occurred around a fortnight before Christmas, when the Christmas lights were being erected, flatly contradicted the statements. So too did his claims that he carried the parcels for the man and that, as the man was leaving, his brother Paul arrived.

Appendix 2
The Primary Suitcase: the
Forensic Evidence

In their joint report, the RARDE scientists Dr Thomas Hayes and Allen Feraday set out a number of key findings regarding the primary suitcase. It was, they said, a Samsonite-brand, 26-inch, antique copper Silhouette 4000 model; it contained a radio-cassette bomb incorporating between 350 and 450 grams of plastic explosive; it was not resting against the floor of container AVE4041; and it contained at least 13 garments, including an umbrella.

The make and model of the suitcase had little bearing on the prosecution case, but the interrelated conclusions concerning the explosive's size and position strengthened the Crown's claim that it arrived at Heathrow on PA103A from Frankfurt, and was not the hard-sided case seen earlier on the floor of AVE4041 by Heathrow loader John Bedford. More important still was the primary case's supposed contents, as nine of the thirteen items had been positively identified by Tony Gauci.

The amount and location of the explosive

According to the joint report, the centre of the explosion was 25 to 30 cm* above the base of AVE4041 and it was overhanging the angled section by around 5 cm. The distance from the aircraft's outer skin, known as the stand-off distance, it claimed, was around 64 cm. This meant the primary suitcase must have been in one of the two positions shown on page 396.[1]

At trial the defence argued that there was a third possible position, in which the case was in the bottom layer with one end pushed slightly upwards against the container's sloping overhang, as in the following photograph (p. 397).[2]

---

* The joint report in fact gave two estimates. The first, in section 2.3, was 25 to 28 cm, and the second, in the conclusions section, was 28 to 30 cm.

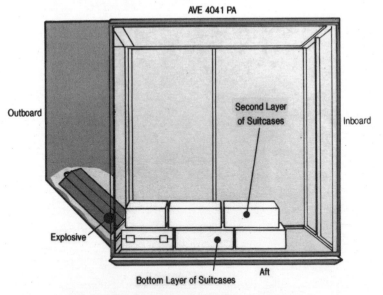

FIRST POSTULATED POSITION OF THE IED WITHIN THE CARGO CONTAINER

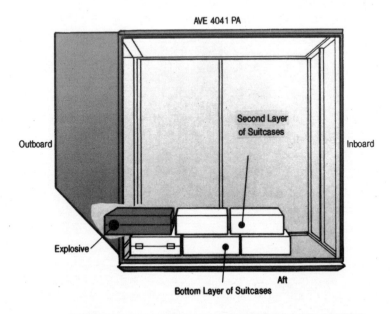

SECOND POSTULATED POSITION OF THE IED WITHIN THE CARGO CONTAINER

Third possible position of the primary suitcase.

The RARDE conclusions were bolstered by the AAIB's crash report and two reports by the Royal Aerospace Establishment (RAE) in Farnborough, the first from 1990 and the second from 1999. All agreed that the stand-off distance was approximately 24 or 25 inches (around 62 to 64 cm). The AAIB's report calculated the distance from the container's base to be around 10 inches (25.5 cm) and the RAE's estimate of 450g of explosive was also within the joint report's range.[3]*

The supporting evidence comprised three strands: firstly, the observed damage to AVE4041 and its neighbouring fibreglass container AVN7511; secondly, the explosive tests conducted in the US in April and July 1989; and, thirdly, the highly technical findings of the AAIB and RAE experts.†

* The AAIB report and the first RAE report did not consider the amount of explosive, and neither RAE report considered the vertical distance between the centre of the explosion and the container's base.

† The Royal Aeronautical Establishment was later subsumed within RARDE's successor organisation, the Defence Evaluation and Research Agency (DERA).

The observed damage

The AAIB and RARDE experts believed their conclusions were supported by the pattern of explosive pitting, cratering and sooting on the recovered pieces of AVE4041. While prevalent on the surfaces and struts from the lower part of the angled section, these markings were relatively absent from the base section. The experts also considered that the dish-shaped indentation on the base suggested that a suitcase in the bottom layer had been forced downwards by an explosion above it. However, neither phenomenon was conclusive. The area of base section most likely to have been explosively marked was never found; furthermore, the extent of such markings might have been significantly curtailed by the primary suitcase clothing.

A further influential factor was the damage observed on AVN7511. There was an area of blackening roughly adjacent to the explosion, within which was a small hole around 10 inches (25.5 cm) above the container's base. At first glance this provided strong support for the AAIB and RARDE conclusion that the explosion occurred a similar

The blast-damaged luggage container AVN7511.

distance from AVE4041's base. However, the fibres surrounding the hole had not been burned or melted;[4] furthermore, as this AAIB photo illustrates, it lay at one end of a horizontal band of damage to the fibreglass laminate.[5] Together these factors suggested that the damage occurred when the horizontal metal bar securing the bottom of AVE4041's curtain was blasted against AVN7511.

At trial the AAIB's lead investigator, Peter Claiden, accepted it was possible that the primary suitcase was in the third position.[6] It was notable that the Crown did not suggest that the damage to the primary suitcase ruled out that position.[7] This was perhaps because, according to Hayes's notes, he initially believed it had been resting on the base of AVE4041. When examining the largest fragment of the suitcase's shell, PI/911, he noted it was 'compressed and fractured in a manner suggesting it was in contact with the luggage pallet's base and subjected to explosive forces from above'.[8] However, this important claim was absent from the joint report's subsequent description of the fragment.[9]

The US tests

Of the nine tests, only numbers 1 to 7 were of any use in determining the bomb's location, as tests 8 and 9 did not use luggage-filled containers. Tests 1 to 5 were conducted at US Naval Explosive Ordnance Disposal Technology Center at Indian Head, Maryland, in April 1989, while 6 and 7 took place at the FAA's Headquarters in Atlantic City, New Jersey, in July 1989. In each of the tests the primary suitcase was put into an aluminium luggage container, which was then filled with luggage and placed next to a similarly-sized fibreglass container. This mimicked the position of container AVE4041 and its fibreglass neighbour AVN7511. Tests 1 to 5 were conducted on the ground, with the containers resting on a wooden test frame, and tests 6 and 7 utilised a fuselage section of a DC10 aircraft. In all the tests the bomb was contained within a Toshiba RT-8016 radio-cassette player.* Varying amounts of plastic explosive were used, with tests 1 to 5 respectively using 435g, 360g, 680g, 400g and 460g of explosive, and tests 6 and 7 680g and 570g. The only disclosed reports on the tests were brief

* The RT-8016 model was almost identical to the RT-SF16 model, which supposedly housed the Lockerbie bomb.

descriptive ones on each by Feraday, and two lengthier summaries by DCI Harry Bell.

The purpose of tests 1 to 5, according to Bell's first report, was 'to estimate the amount and location of the explosive used on PA103 by comparing the damage of test luggage containers to the actual damage'.[10]

His second report, on tests 6 to 9, explained that 6 and 7 were instigated by the FAA's Walter Korsgaard, and that Feraday was only present as an observer. Although their primary purpose was similar to the first five,* it appeared that Feraday harboured substantial reservations, which were expressed in the following caveats:

'9.2.1 The section of aircraft, namely a McDonnell Douglas DC10 was the wrong type in that it was not of the "747" aircraft structure or design. The basic diameter of a "DC10" is smaller than a "747". The floor arrangement of structural beams are different. The basic strength of a "DC10" is less than a "747".

9.3 Containers

9.3.1 The Pan Am containers of the type used on "747" aircraft would not fit into the cargo hold section of the "D.C. 10" two abreast as normally fitted in the 747 aircraft. To accommodate this the aluminium container housing the I.E.D. suitcase was installed in the normal position as located in P.A.103 at Position 14L. However the adjacent container on the inboard side at position 14R had to be positioned at a 90 degree angle and merely rested against the IED container . . .

9.3.2 The containers surrounding the IED container had been used in previous test explosions and may have had structural faults as a result, therefore a full evaluation of test explosion damage could not be made in respect of tests 6 and 7.

9.4 Cargo Floor of D.C.10

9.4.1 The floor of the cargo hold of the section of DC10 aircraft was missing and a section of expanded laminate was

---

* Bell's second report described the primary purpose as 'to "duplicate" as near as possible, damage to the aluminium baggage container.'

utilized. This resulted in the floor area being raised at the outboard side causing the I.E.D. container to rest at an angle, therefore the container was not in the correct position in relation to the floor beams of the D.C.10.'[11]

According to Bell's first report, Test 5 – which used 460g of explosive – came closest to replicating the damage observed on AVE4041. It also stated that tests 1 to 5 indicated 'that the explosive device was located in a suitcase in the second layer of baggage from the floor of the container'. However, in only one of the seven tests, Test 4, was the primary suitcase positioned anywhere other than the second layer. Furthermore, the same report noted in relation to Test 4 that, 'Due to an uncontrollable fire caused by the detonation, results were not easily recordable as during previous tests', in other words, no meaningful conclusion could be drawn from it.

Bell's first report stated that 'the explosive charge weight was in all probability of the order of 454 to 680 grams (1 to 1.5 pounds).'[12] However, without explanation the joint report revised the figure downwards to 350 to 450 grams.[13] The RARDE material disclosed in October 2009 revealed that Korsgaard believed the amount to be 680g and was keen to conduct further tests on an actual 747 aircraft. A draft version of Bell's report stated that Korsgaard had:

'approached the Lockerbie Representatives namely Detective Chief Inspector Bell and Detective Inspector Gilmour and asked if Lockerbie Enquiry would support his intended request to his supervisors for a further test explosion using an actual "747" aircraft.'

It continued:

'[Korsgaard] pointed out that A.A.I.B. were interested in such a test. However if Lockerbie* did not show interest he could have some problems convincing his supervisors of the need in his view to carry out such a test. It was clearly pointed out

* 'Lockerbie' is a reference to the Lockerbie Incident Control Centre (LICC), which ran the police investigation.

to Mr Korsgaard that the Lockerbie enquiry could see no further justification in such a test and therefore could not support his view. He was asked what benefits could be gained on behalf of the Lockerbie enquiry following such a test. He could give no reason other than to state that he was of the opinion that the explosive charge weight was in excess of 1½ lbs [680g].'[14]

So, the criminal investigators were not prepared to back further experiments that were intended to more accurately mimic the Lockerbie explosion, and which might undermine their conclusion about the amount of explosive used.

In a handwritten internal memo, dated 8 August 1989, Feraday set out his opposition to Korsgaard's request. He said the proposed tests were 'unnecessary and ill advised and, as such should be discouraged', adding:

'I do urge you in the stongest possible terms that Korsgaard be stopped from carrying out any further tests in connection with the Lockerbie investigation.'

Feraday believed the five tests conducted at Indian Head in April had proved valuable in determining the amount and position of the explosive, but in his view Korsgaard appeared to have taken 'virtually no cognizance' of them. He warned that further tests:

'could readily be misconstrued by any defence counsel as implying some doubts concerning the results of the earlier trials, and as such could be destructively exploited by counsel . . . It would be foolish and detrimental to the case to allow any errant defence laywer to gain succour from any future explosions tests designed purely to enhance an opinion as to the charge weight against all previous test results and the scientific findings to date.'[15]

The joint report did not reveal that the FAA's lead investigator harboured serious reservations about its conclusions and, since the relevant paperwork was never disclosed to Abdelbaset's defence team, the matter was not raised at trial.

Although Korsgaard did not get his way, a RARDE photographic job register, disclosed to the SCCRC, indicated that a further test was conducted, apparently in the UK. An entry stated that, at Feraday's request, a photographer took four rolls of film of 'Test 10' on 3 March 1990, and two more rolls on 14 March.[16] Some of these photos were among the RARDE material disclosed in October 2009. They indicated that, like tests 1 to 7, a full luggage-container was used, but, unlike those, the primary suitcase was placed against the overhanging angled surface. As there was no report on the tests, its results remain unknown.

The technical findings

The AAIB and RAE investigations involved complex analytical modelling. At trial, the expert witnesses were vigorously challenged on their calculations by Richard Keen QC. The AAIB's Christopher Protheroe admitted that the AAIB report contained a significant error, which, if rectified, would reduce the stand-off distance from 25 inches (64 cm) to just 12 inches (31 cm).[17] Professor Christopher Peel, who led the RAE investigation, conceded that the second RAE report failed to make clear that it used a different causal analysis than the first one. More importantly, he acknowledged that there was 'a strong element of judgement' in his estimation of a 24-inch (62 cm) stand-off distance and that it might have been anything from 20 to 28 inches.[18]

A further reason to distrust the 24-inch figure was that the modelling assumed the bomb contained C4 plastic explosive rather than – as the Crown asserted – Semtex. This was significant, because, as Peel's colleague Dr Ian Cullis confirmed, C4 is around 10 per cent more powerful than Semtex.[19] It was therefore reasonable to assume that, in order to create the same observable damage to the fuselage's skin, the stand-off distance for Semtex would be less than that for C4. This gave further credence to the defence's suggestion that the primary suitcase was in the bottom layer of luggage.

Arguably that suggestion was lent weight by the following diagram from the AAIB report, headed 'Likely lateral and vertical position of the IED'.[20]

Likely lateral and vertical position of the IED

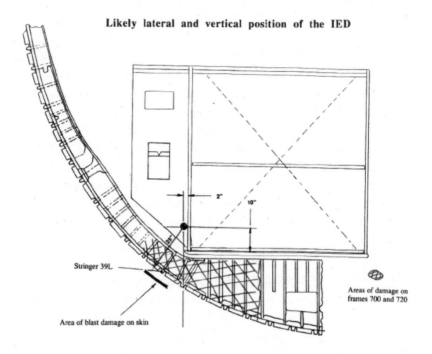

Stringer 39L

Areas of damage on frames 700 and 720

Area of blast damage on skin

The downward-pointing arrow indicated the shortest distance between the centre of the explosion and the aircraft's skin. The point at which the arrow met the skin was not, as one might expect, in the centre of the section marked 'Area of blast damage on skin', but rather at its upper edge. As the following diagram illustrates, if the centre of the explosion was lowered down the same vertical axis until the stand-off distance was 20 inches, a similar arrow would meet the skin in the middle of the damaged area.

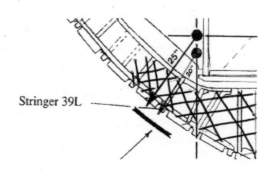

Stringer 39L

The clothing

The joint report suggested it was possible to distinguish the contents of the primary suitcase from those of the surrounding luggage. The items most likely to have been in the primary suitcase were designated Category 1 on the basis that they contained fragments of the IED, but no fragments of suitcase shell. Of the thirteen Category 1 items, the following nine appeared to fit Tony Gauci's description of the items he'd sold: two pairs of Yorkie trousers, one dark-brown checked and the other light-brown herringbone; two Slalom shirts, one grey, the other pinstriped; one pair of Panwear pyjamas; a blue babygro; a brown herringbone tweed jacket; a light-brown Puccini cardigan; and an umbrella. Two further garments, a white T-shirt and a dark-blue sweatshirt or jumper, were a possible match for items stocked at Mary's House. The last two, a training shoe and a piece of light-blue cloth, could not be linked to the shop. The Category 2 items, which the report suggested were probably from the surrounding luggage, were said to contain either no fragments or ones that included suitcase shell.[21]*

The findings relied substantially on the nine US explosive tests, and on the clothing analysis conducted by Dr Thomas Hayes. The report implied that the tests provided the experimental basis for the categorisation system, but, when closely analysed, that basis appeared to be very slender.

A preliminary draft of Bell's report on the April 1989 tests stated:

'It was assessed by Mr Feraday that an on-site supervisual [sic] examination would indicate that there would be some confusion between blast damaged clothing from the IED suitcase and the contents of adjacent suitcases. It was found that the time factor between each test explosion was insufficient to allow a detailed search to be made in an attempt to recover such clothing for future forensic examination. It was agreed that the five tests could only provide a comparison of the explosive damage to the floor of the baggage container and an estimate of the amount of the explosive charge.'

* See Chapter 8.

In other words, none of the five tests was any use in identifying the primary suitcase clothing. The passage did not appear in the final version of Bell's report. The draft went on to explain that the tests planned for July 1989, which came to be numbered 6 to 9, would be 'structured to allow the recovery of articles of clothing from the IED suitcases in order that detailed forensic comparisons could then be considered in respect of such clothing'.[22]

Tests 6 and 7 took place at Jersey City, and 8 and 9 at Indian Head. The main objective of 8 and 9 was described as:

'To facilitate a full recovery of all of the IED suitcase, the radio and the content, post explosion. This would permit a complete assessment to be made of the recovered "debris", and to establish what parts of the IED suitcase and content it was possible to recover and identify. These recoveries would permit the Forensic Scientists to make comparisons with the items recovered after the fatal crash of Pan Am 103, at Lockerbie.'[23]

Unlike the first seven tests, 8 and 9 used only a primary suitcase, which, rather than being placed in a luggage container, was suspended inside a 9 ft tall, 6 in thick steel cylinder, the top of which was covered with a steel sheet weighed down with sandbags. In the absence of other luggage there was no secondary clothing with which to compare the clothes from the primary suitcase. The container's shape and strength meant the explosive dynamics were likely to have been rather different to those experienced in a flimsy aluminium luggage container. Furthermore, the cylinder was filled with foam to prevent fire.[24] Taken together, these factors undermined the value of comparing the clothing debris with that found at Lockerbie.

So, only tests 6 and 7 enabled the scientists to establish whether it was possible to make a forensic distinction between primary and secondary clothing. However, both tests were done at the initiative of the FAA, with the RARDE representative, Feraday, taking no active role. According to Bell's second report, a study of the primary and secondary debris showed 'transference of the case and content from one to the other. It clearly showed that there was a lot of impregnation of one material into another. Pieces of radio, packing etc., were embedded onto pieces of suitcase and clothing.'

The report confirmed that Feraday took large amounts of debris back to RARDE as control samples for comparison purposes. He also took 'certain other' samples from the IEDs in Tests 6 and 7 to Lockerbie to assist officers in the identification of the IED or surrounding cases. According to Feraday's reports, following both he closely examined the debris in order to 'determine what parts of the IED radio-cassette, together with the suitcase and its contents in which it was contained could be recovered. Also to study the cross fertilisation from the IED suitcase into the adjoining baggage.'

However, the disclosed RARDE material neither detailed those examinations, nor contained any kind of scientific analysis to support the clothing categorisation system.

Even if the debris was examined in detail, it was clear from Bell's and Feraday's reports that the test conditions were radically different to those of the Lockerbie explosion. Among the differences was the amount of explosive used. According to the RARDE joint report, the Lockerbie bomb contained 350 to 450 grams; however, Test 6 used 680 grams and Test 7 570 grams. Furthermore, the secondary luggage items used in both tests had also been used in the April tests, when they were saturated to prevent fires, and, according to Bell, remained saturated.[25] This could have affected the extent and nature of the damage to the clothes, including the degree to which IED and suitcase fragments became embedded within them. There were fires following both tests, which were kept under control by further saturation.[26] This might have dislodged some of the embedded fragments and transferred them elsewhere.

The most rigorous analysis of the clothing categorisation system was conducted by Dr Roger King, the forensic scientist instructed in preparation for Abdelbaset's second appeal. His first observation about the system was that it did not appear to have any experimental scientific basis. The brief test reports, in his view, did not constitute proper scientific studies, leading him to conclude that: 'The absence of any such experimental data to support the classification scheme means that no valid basis has been demonstrated for its use in case-work.'

He pointed out that, even if there was such data, tests conducted on the ground were of limited value in predicting what would happen when an explosion occurs at 31,000 feet, giving rise to a catastrophic decompression in strong winds. The method of debris-collection at the crash-site may also have affected the distribution of IED and suitcase fragments. Owing to the scale of the disaster, the police were forced to abandon the standard rules of evidence-gathering and instead allowed items of debris to be collected together in large plastic sacks. King considered that, as a consequence:

'Any explosion material that was loosely associated with a fragment of clothing might then have been transferred to other clothing or debris in the bags, or may have been lost when items were re-packaged.'

He noted that, if the categorisation system was rigorously applied to the thirteen Category 1 items, then six of them would be reclassified as Category 2, namely the light-brown Yorkie trousers, the umbrella, the Puccini cardigan, the sweatshirt, the training shoe and the light-blue material. Similarly, two of the Category 2 garments would be reclassified as Category 1.[27]

For the purposes of the categorisation system, the joint report defined IED fragments as '(i) a radio-cassette recorder, (ii) the radio-cassette recorder owner's instruction manual and (iii) the brown fabric-lined cardboard partition from within the primary suitcase.'[28] (i) and (ii) were perfectly logical, but why were fragments of the suitcase partition classified as part of the bomb, when plainly they were not? A possible answer was that, in contrast to the suitcase shells, the partition could have been positioned between the bomb and some of the primary suitcase clothes. However, photographs elsewhere in the joint report demonstrated that this would be impossible if the suitcase also contained a Toshiba RT-SF16 radio-cassette player. That being the case, King observed, pieces of the partition should have been regarded as suitcase fragments (i.e. as markers for Category 2 clothing), rather than as part of the bomb. The categorisation system made no mention of the primary suitcase shell's fabric lining. King considered that, logically, lining fragments should also be considered as Category 2 markers.

408

If the system was amended in line with these observations, then a further six Category 1 items would have been reclassified as Category 2, namely the dark-brown checked Yorkie trousers, both Slalom shirts, the tweed jacket, the babygro and the pyjamas. So, overall, if the system was more logical and applied consistently, then 12 of the report's 13 Category 1 items would shift to Category 2.

In King's opinion, the logical basis for the categorisation system was further undermined by Feraday's statement to the Trial Court that he had 'long ago given up on trying to predict exactly where particles will fly'.[29] He also noted that Feraday had revealed in his Crown precognition statement that he harboured doubts about the classification system.[30] If that was his view when preparing the report, then, in King's view, the system should not have been included.[31]

In the absence of any experimental data from the 1989 explosive tests, King undertook his own test, at a firing range in Lincolnshire, with the help of explosives expert Dr John Wyatt of the security consultancy SDS Group.* Wyatt constructed an IED using 400 grams of plastic explosives fitted within a Toshiba radio-cassette player. A piece of electronic circuit board was placed next to the explosive to simulate the timer's circuit board and the device was placed in a cardboard box, along with a paper booklet to simulate the instruction manual. The IED was then packed into a hard-sided suitcase, along with clothing and an umbrella similar to the joint report's Category 1 items. The suitcase was placed in an aluminium luggage container, like AVE4041, along with other luggage, and positioned so the bomb was in exactly the position suggested by the joint report.

Following the explosion, all the debris was collected and analysed by King. He discovered that every primary suitcase garment survived, at least in part. So too did small pieces of the radio-cassette player, circuit board, paper and cardboard box.† On examining the primary

---

* Wyatt was an expert witness in the successful appeals of Hassan Assali and John Berry, see Chapter 8.

† A BBC *Newsnight* programme, broadcast on 6 January 2010, claimed that no fragments of circuit board survived the test explosion. This false assertion was based on an interview with Dr Wyatt, who, unlike Dr King, did not analyse the debris and was therefore not aware that circuit-board, plastic, paper and cardboard fragments were recovered. On the day of the broadcast Tony Kelly emailed the editor of *Newsnight* to inform him that

suitcase clothing, he found that much of it contained fragments of the IED, cardboard box and paper. However, some also contained fragments of the suitcase, which, if the joint report's criteria were applied, would have ruled them out of Category 1. And, while much of the clothing from the surrounding cases met the Category 2 criteria, some met those of Category 1. To complicate matters, he was unable to identify much of the material embedded in the clothing, which made definitive categorisation, using the joint report's criteria, all but impossible. He concluded:

'Taken together these findings show that the criteria used to classify clothing in the FEL Report have limited value in distinguishing between the test items that were in the IED suitcase at detonation and the test items that were in the surrounding suitcases. Overall, the effect of using the criteria from the FEL Report was to assign more of the test items to the IED suitcase than were originally present.'[32]

As a final stage of his investigation, King examined key items of Lockerbie debris, including the explosively damaged clothing and a representative sample of nine black plastic fragments, which Hayes had recovered from the clothing. Having completed the examinations, he reported that he had 'found no reliable indicators that could conclusively identify which [clothing] fragments originally came from the IED suitcase'.[33] The conclusion was bolstered by his analysis of the plastic fragments. The joint report claimed that these had originated from the casing of the radio-cassette player and were therefore key markers of Category 1 items. However, having subjected them to standard infrared spectroscopy, King determined that eight of the nine did not match the casing.[34] 'In other words,' he stated:

(note continued)
the programme was based on misinformation, but the BBC went ahead with the broadcast. *Newsnight*'s claim was repeated by freelance journalist Marcello Mega in the *Mail on Sunday* on 5 September 2010. His article went further, stating, falsely, that this book would also claim that no circuit-board fragments survived the test.

'I could not be sure whether the black plastic fragments had come from another part of the radio that I was not able to test, or the suitcase shell, or some other unidentified item that might have been close to the IED.'

Since he could not determine which clothes had been in the primary suitcase, he could say only that some were likely to have been near to the bomb and others might have been. Significantly, he identified 17 Category 2 garments that were likely to have been and a further 24 that might have been.[35]

There was little doubt that blast-damaged Maltese clothes were found at the crash-site, and that those clothes were not linked to anyone known to have luggage on the flight. However, not only was there no reliable scientific method of determining which clothes were in the primary suitcase, but the investigators never did, and never could, fully account for all the clothes that were on the flight. It has never been revealed how many of the other blast-damaged clothes were unidentified, and we will never know how many items were destroyed by the blast or lost amid the 750-square-mile crash-site. In such circumstances, it was impossible to assert that the Maltese clothes were, beyond reasonable doubt, in the primary suitcase.

The Crown's claim that the bomb originated in Malta relied on the paperwork from Frankfurt Airport. The key documents were the KIK computer printout for PA103A and the worksheet for coding station 206, which had been filled out by operators Yassar Koca and Mehmet Candar. The Court was satisfied that these demonstrated the transfer of a suitcase from Air Malta flight KM180 to PA103A, but, in reality, they fell far short of proof.

The printout indicated that 111 items of luggage were sent via the airport's baggage transit system to PA103A. Of these, 86 had been checked in at the airport and 25 were transferred from other flights. Neither the bags' owners nor the transferring flights were documented; rather the paperwork was a mass of digits, which recorded the times and locations at which bags entered and exited the luggage system. There were two types of entry point: the Pan Am check-in counters, and the coding stations, through which bags from incoming flights were processed. By cross-referencing the printout with Pan Am's check-in records, it was possible to establish, with a reasonable degree of accuracy, the ownership of all the check-in bags listed on the printout.

The 25 transfer bags were more of a challenge. Under the airport's standard procedures, transfer luggage was unloaded from the incoming flights and placed into wagons, which were taken to one of two reception areas, Halle Mitte and V3. On arrival there, the number of wagons and the flight number were noted by the so-called interline writer, who then allocated the wagons to individual coding stations within the reception areas. At the stations the bags were unloaded and entered individually into the system by the station operators, also known as coders. This involved checking the label of each bag, then entering a code into the computer, which corresponded with the departure gate of its outgoing flight.

The coders were required to document on their worksheets the originating flight of each wagonload and the time at which it was processed. Thus, by cross-referencing the times recorded on the printout with the worksheets it was, in theory, possible to establish the originating flight of each bag on the printout. However, the BKA's Inspector Jürgen Fuhl discovered that 11 of the 25 bags were coded in during a two-minute period when, according to the coding station's corresponding worksheet, no transfer bags were being processed. He concluded that they were most likely so-called re-booked bags, meaning they were either lost, or had arrived on incoming flights too late to make their intended connections. Such bags were diverted to the airline's lost and found department, which would then allocate them new flights. Provided there was sufficient time, the bags would then be taken to a coding point where they would be processed like normal transfer bags, except that they would not be recorded on the worksheet.

All 14 remaining bags could be linked to incoming flights. Of those, five had arrived on Lufthansa flight LH1452 from Vienna and belonged to Lockerbie victims Patricia Coyle and Karen Noonan, and three, belonging to fellow victim Thomas Walker, arrived on Lufthansa LH631 from Kuwait. The other six were not accompanied by passengers on PA103A: two of these arrived on Air India Flight AI465 from Delhi and belonged to a man called Adolph Weinacker; one, belonging to a Susan Costa, was on Al Italia AZ422 from Rome, and one, belonging to a Mr Wagenfuhrer, came on PA643 from Berlin. The final two unaccompanied bags were unidentified. One appeared to have arrived on Lufthansa flight LH1071 from Warsaw and was coded in at station HM3 at 15.44. The other, numbered on the printout as B8849, appeared to be from Air Malta flight KM180 and was coded in at coding station 206 at 13.07.[1] When coupled with the Maltese clothing debris, this convinced the police that B8849 was the primary suitcase.

However, the computer printout demonstrated only that bags were sent to Gate 44. There was no proof that they were actually loaded on to either PA103A, or PA103. Furthermore, the theory was dependent upon the accuracy of the airport workers' time-keeping. All worksheets were filled in by hand, with the coders relying either on their watches or airport clocks. Although the computer timings were automated, the time was reset each day by the system's operators, who were also reliant on clocks and watches. Furthermore, it was established that small fluctuations in the electrical power supply could cause the recorded time to vary by a few minutes.[2]

The Frankfurt baggage system was exhaustively scrutinised in 1992 by Denis Phipps and Nan McCreadie, the aviation security experts instructed by Air Malta's lawyers in the legal action against the Granada TV documentary *Why Lockerbie?* * They established that the worksheets were filled out only for the purpose of billing the airlines and that charges were calculated according to the number of wagonloads processed, rather than the time taken. It was therefore not imperative for the coders to record the time with pinpoint accuracy. Phipps reported: 'I gained the distinct impression that completion of the worksheet was a casual process in which accuracy was not a priority.' The worksheet entry immediately preceding the one for KM180 illustrated the coders' fallibility. It stated that between 12.57 and 13.03 they were processing bags from flight LH1498; however, Phipps established that, although there was a flight LH1489, there was no LH1498.[3]

The pair noted that, according to baggage workers, it took the operators approximately seven seconds to process each bag. The 29 items of interline luggage from KM180 should therefore have taken coders Koca and Candar around three and a half minutes to process, but their worksheet recorded that it took at least six minutes; indeed, it may have been twelve minutes, as it was unclear from Koca's handwriting whether the end time was 13.10 or 13.16. (The BKA's inspector Jürgen Fuhl appeared to favour the latter, as his investigative report stated, 'The coders from 206 had recorded in the worksheet the input of one truck of baggage from flight KM180 from 13.04 to 13.16 hours (the end of the input time could also be 13.10 hours).')[4]

In common with other coders, Koca and Candar recorded half-full wagons on the worksheets as '½'. Since the wagons could hold around 40 bags, it is possible that they would have recorded one con-

---

* Both had previously been employed in the security department of British Airways, Phipps as its head. He was also a former Chair of the International Air Transport Association (IATA)'s Security Advisory Committee.

taining 29 as half. It may be that their time-recording was not wholly accurate, or that they were especially slow, but another possibility was that the wagon had been topped up with luggage from other flights.[5]

Phipps and McCreadie also established that it was possible to enter a bag into the luggage system without the transaction being recorded, either by adding it to a wagonload, or by processing it individually at a coding station. The latter scenario was observed at coding station 206 on 22 September 1989 by Detective Inspector Watson McAteer and FBI agent Lawrence Whittaker. McAteer's corresponding statement described watching two operators process a wagonload of luggage as normal, then walk away, leaving the station 'completely unattended, with the computer switched on and operable'. It continued:

> 'Within the space of one minute, I observed a V3 worker carry a single suitcase from a batch located some fifty yards from gate 206 to that particular gate. This worker entered gate 206 coding booth and after keying details into the computer sent the single piece of luggage into the system. This operation was started and completed in less than fifteen seconds with no entry being made on the work sheet which was still in situ within the gate.'

Through Whittaker, McAteer questioned an FAG supervisor called Zimmerman about what they had observed and he 'reluctantly agreed that such a practice was not unusual'. McAteer concluded:

> 'Bearing in mind that KM180's luggage input was the last entry recorded on the work sheet, by Koca, and the relatively short time taken to input a single piece of luggage into the system, it is feasible that items attributed to KM180 from Gate 206 on 21.12.88, may well have been input after that aircraft's luggage had been disposed of.'[6]

The interline writers' records also cast doubt upon the reliability of the coding station worksheets. The records documented every wagonload of baggage to arrive at the V3 area, including the time of the arrival and the number of the bags' originating flight. When compared with the coding station worksheets it was apparent that more wagons had arrived in V3 than were recorded on the worksheets. The most glaring example concerned Lufthansa flight LH669 from Damascus. The interline writer recorded that four wagons of luggage from the flight arrived in V3 between 12.30 and 12.37.[7] However, the worksheets recorded only the processing of two and a half wagonloads, one and a half of which were done at coding station 202 between 12.58 and 13.07 and one at station 207 between 13.03 and 13.09.[8] These times coincided almost exactly with when the KM180 bags were being processed at station 206, which was next to 207. It raised the possibility that the 'missing' one and a half wagonloads, or at least part of them, were coded in at station 206 without being noted.

Intriguingly, the airport's incident log for 21 December recorded that at 13.01 smoke was seen coming from a suitcase in V3. The person who reported it was noted as 'Graf'.[9] The worksheet for coding station 207 recorded that, at the time of the incident, it was being manned by an employee called Axel Graf, which strongly suggests that the smoking suitcase was discovered at that station.[10] If so, the incident is likely to have delayed the processing of the LH669 luggage, so it's possible that Koca and Candar lent a hand by transferring it to their own station.

Frankfurt was one of Europe's largest airports so, unlike Luqa, anyone with a security pass could move around anonymously. The loadmaster in charge of PA103A's luggage, Roland O'Neill, told the BKA:

> 'I would not notice if an unauthorised person was to add another piece of baggage to the normal baggage that was standing ready for loading. This would in fact be no problem because a large number of people are working in the area of the aircraft . . . In my opinion it would be possible from my knowledge of the working practices for an airport worker to open a piece of baggage when it is unsupervised and place something in it. There is no one hundred per cent check which would stop this. In my opinion it would be no problem for

one of the workers in this area to put a piece of luggage on board an aircraft. No check is made of the bag that I bring to work when I enter airside. The only thing that is checked is my identification card to make sure that I am allowed airside.'[11]

Among the items almost certainly loaded onto PA103A was one belonging to a Pan Am pilot called John Hubbard. On the morning of 21 December he arranged for two cases to be sent from Berlin Tegel Airport to his home city of Seattle, while he piloted a Pan Am flight to Karachi. They were fitted with so-called rush tags, which airlines used to get unaccompanied bags to their destination as quickly as possible. They were probably originally routed to travel on PA637 to Frankfurt, PA107 to Heathrow and PA123 to Seattle;[12] however, one of the cases was found at Lockerbie. This was probably owing to a 40-minute delay to PA637, which meant the luggage arrived too late to be transferred to PA107. The case was therefore likely to have been among the 11 bags that, according to Inspector Jürgen Fuhl, were rebooked on to PA103A.[13] It was not clear why it was subsequently loaded onto PA103 to New York. According to Hubbard, there were no direct flights at that time from New York to Seattle, although he acknowledged that the Heathrow baggage loaders may not have been aware of that.[14]

Intriguingly, his cases were both brown, hard-sided Samsonites. It has been speculated that both were supposed to be loaded on to PA103A in Frankfurt and that the bombers switched one of them for the primary suitcase. If that were so, it might explain why only one ended up on PA103. However, the bombers could not have known in advance that two such suitcases would be diverted to PA103A.

Setting aside this theory, the fact that Hubbard's two suitcases ended up on different flights illustrated the difficulty of planning or predicting the movement of unaccompanied luggage. Such difficulties would have made it impossible for Abdelbaset and Lamin to guarantee that a suitcase sent from Malta would reach PA103.

And that was not the only problem. If they had attached Air Malta tags to the case and marked it for onward transit to New York, Pan Am's Frankfurt staff would have treated it as interline baggage. Interline was the term for bags transferred from other airlines, while those transferred from the same airline were known as on-line.* Crucially, the regulations stipulated that all interline baggage should be X-rayed prior to loading. Likewise with online rush-tag baggage, even those bearing a security stamp, with the exception of those stamped at Frankfurt Airport's pressure chamber.[15]

The luggage to be X-rayed was separated out by Pan Am loader Kilinc Tuzcu and X-rayed by security officer Kurt Maier. The analyses conducted by the Scottish police and the BKA's Inspector Fuhl managed to trace the ownership of 11 legitimate interline items loaded at Frankfurt.[16] Five of these belonged to Patricia Coyle and Karen Noonan, three to Thomas Walker, two to Adolph Weinacker and one to Susan Costa.† Maier's records indicated that he X-rayed 13 items.[17] So, what were the two extra bags? Could they have been the two unidentified bags from Air Malta flight KM180 and Lufthansa flight LH1071? Unfortunately for the Crown, there was no way of telling.

One of the reasons was that Tuzcu and Maier were unsure of the procedures for online rush-tag baggage. Tuzcu initially said he was unaware of the X-ray requirement and that those bearing a security check stamp would generally not be X-rayed. However, he said that they sometimes were, although he did not say why,[18] and, to add confusion, in his Crown precognition statement he said they always would be.[19] Maier was not sure about the procedures,[20] but his job was simply to X-ray the bags, rather than check their tags.

When interviewed by the FAA two and a half weeks after Lockerbie, Tuzcu said there were two rush-tagged bags among those he sent for X-ray.[21] If true, it is likely that one was Susan Costa's interline bag.‡ If the primary suitcase arrived unaccompanied on flight KM180, then it should have been the second one; however, there were other credible possibilities. Among the most likely were that it was one of Hubbard's cases, or the bag from LH1071.

There may have been more or fewer rush-tagged items than Tuzcu recalled. If he sent all the rush-tagged bags for X-ray, then they were

* Confusingly, transfer bags are sometimes referred to generically as interline.
† Neither Weinacker nor Costa accompanied their cases.
‡ Weinacker's bag was almost certainly not rush-tagged, as he was meant to fly on PA103A but changed his plans at the last minute.

likely to have included all 11 re-booked items noted by Inspector Fuhl. This would mean that Maier X-rayed at least 22 bags, rather than the thirteen that he noted. Even if there were just 13, Maier's record did not tally with the police investigation. Whereas he logged ten suitcases, two travel bags and one box,[22] police records indicated that, of the eleven legitimate bags that should have been X-rayed, only five were suitcases, while four were holdalls.[23]

Whatever the true number of bags X-rayed, if the Crown case was correct, the unaccompanied bag from KM180 must have been among them and Maier must have missed it. When FAA inspectors reviewed Pan Am's Frankfurt security procedures in 1989, they were unimpressed by the standard of the X-ray operators' training. Furthermore, the machine used by Maier had a black and white display screen, making explosives fairly difficult to distinguish. The Toshiba and Helsinki warnings had been circulated to staff, and Maier knew that he should be vigilant for radio-cassette players and other electrical devices. Although he told the FAA that sight of a plug would satisfy him that a device was safe, he was confident that he could spot explosives.[24] However, Maier's competency was beside the point, as terrorists intent on bombing Pan Am 103 were unlikely to have risked X-ray detection and therefore would not have used an unaccompanied interline bag.

Abdelbaset was granted his second appeal by the SCCRC on 28 June 2007, and his draft grounds of appeal were submitted to the Court on 21 December 2007. Yet, by the time he returned home 20 months later, only the first stage of the appeal had been heard. There were a number of reasons for the delays, among them inefficient use of court time and the Advocate General's insistence on checking any material that might raise issues of Public Interest Immunity (PII) prior to its disclosure. However, the greatest responsibility lay with the Crown, in particular its twin efforts to reduce the scope of the appeal and block access to evidence.

The day before the grounds were submitted, Crown counsel, Ronnie Clancy QC, informed the Court that the Crown would seek to restrict their scope to the six grounds identified by the SCCRC. It was a surprising move, as under Scots law, once the SCCRC had referred a case for appeal, the appellant could argue any relevant grounds that he wished.* The judges nevertheless agreed that there should be a hearing specifically to consider the issue. That did not take place until six months later, and the judges deferred their ruling on the matter until October 2008. Although they comprehensively rejected the Crown's submissions, ten months had by then elapsed and huge amounts of the appeal lawyers' energy had been wasted.

In order properly to prepare the forensic grounds of appeal, the lawyers required Dr Roger King to examine many of the Crown label productions presented at trial, in particular the clothing debris. Under normal circumstances such access would be routine; indeed on 13 July 2007 the Crown Office wrote to Tony Kelly confirming that all the items had been preserved and could be made available for examination.[1] The following month the Crown Office wrote again to advise Kelly that the productions were held by the Dumfries and Galloway Police and that he should liaise with the force to arrange access.[2] Kelly

* The law has since changed.

did so, and on 6 November the police agreed to make the items available in Dumfries.[3] However, three weeks later they wrote again to say they had been informed by Crown Office that releasing the items required the Court's permission.[4] Kelly served the Court with a full and detailed petition for authority to release the items.[5] To his surprise, the Court wrote back to say that its authority was not in fact required. At the procedural hearing of 20 December, Maggie Scott QC described the difficulties accessing the material, and explained that the Crown was seeking confirmation that the items were related to a particular ground of appeal. She submitted that this was not an appropriate test for whether they should be released. In response, Clancy confirmed that the Crown was seeking to block access until the Court decided the scope of the appeal.

On 20 February 2008 the Crown lodged its formal answers to the petition. The document was riddled with factual inaccuracies and significantly distorted the appellant's position. It argued, in essence, that King's examinations should not proceed because the SCCRC, and the FSANI experts instructed by the original defence team, had each investigated much of the Crown's forensic case and judged it to be sound.[6] In fact, as the Crown well knew, the SCCRC did not review the forensic evidence, but rather investigated the provenance of five specific items,* and, with the exception of a handwriting expert, who examined Dr Thomas Hayes's notes, did not instruct any forensic experts. Moreover, neither the SCCRC not FSANI touched upon King's most important area of concern, namely the flaws in the clothing categorisation system. The Crown said the new forensic claims raised in the grounds of appeal should be investigated by the SCCRC. This was bizarre and unprecedented, because, once the SCCRC had referred the case to the Appeal Court, it had no further statutory role.

The matter dragged on for a further six months until a hearing in August 2008, when the Court agreed in principle that access to the forensic items should be granted.† It was another significant victory for Abdelbaset's team, but the unnecessary battle had taken over a year.

---

* The five items were the grey Slalom shirt, the Yorkie checked trousers, the babygro, the circuit board fragment PT/35b and the Toshiba manual.

† The items were subsequently examined by Dr King. The results of the examinations are summarised in Appendix 2.

Kelly also sought access to the photo line-ups shown to Tony Gauci. He had the electronically scanned versions used at trial, but wanted the originals to be examined by the eyewitness evidence expert, Professor Steve Clark. Again the Crown refused to grant automatic access, again Abdelbaset's team had to petition the Court and again a hearing was convened to consider the matter, this one on 16 July 2008. Scott once more submitted that there was no legal basis for objecting to the release of evidence that had been presented at trial. The Crown was unable to respond, as Clancy was on holiday, so the Court held the matter over until a more general hearing scheduled for 20 August. At that hearing Clancy dropped the Crown's objection and the Court ordered the photospreads to be delivered for inspection.* Another victory for Abdelbaset, but another pointless six-month delay.

The appeal team's attempts to access previously undisclosed paperwork proved even more tortuous. Among the papers required were the two intelligence documents which were the focus of Chapter 25 of the SCCRC's Statement of Reasons. In early July 2007 Kelly wrote to the Crown Office to establish the steps being taken to determine whether the documents could be disclosed. The following month they wrote back confirming that the documents had been provided to the UK government by a foreign government, whose permission had been sought to include them in the Statement of Reasons. The letter added that, in light of the SCCRC's decision, the Crown had asked for the request to be given the highest priority, but no response had been forthcoming.

Kelly lodged another petition with the Court. There followed almost two years of legal wrangling with numerous exchanges of correspondence and Court hearings. Although the Crown did not object to the disclosure request, the UK government did. Arguing on its behalf at the hearing of 20 December 2007, the Advocate General, Lord Davidson of Glen Clova QC, informed the Court that a PII certificate was likely to be issued to prevent the documents' disclosure. Scott argued that the Court should not accept the Advocate General's plea of PII when no such plea was being made by the Crown. The Court did not agree, and subsequently Foreign

* The results of the inspection are described in Chapter 13.

Secretary David Miliband issued a PII certificate, which asserted that the disclosure might damage relations with the government in question.

Further hearings were held. In June 2008 the judges saw the documents for themselves and arranged a hearing for 19 August, from which Abdelbaset's counsel were excluded, to hear the UK government's objections. Eventually it was agreed to adopt a procedure similar to the system used in England for assessing intelligence information in terrorist cases. Under this procedure the appeal team would not be allowed sight of the documents and instead a security-vetted Advocate, known as Special Counsel, would be appointed to assess the documents and make representations on the appellant's behalf. The obvious flaw with this procedure was that it relied on the Special Counsel having a complete understanding of the documents' possible relevance, yet simultaneously ensured that, owing to the prohibition on him from betraying its contents, Abdelbaset's lawyers could not determine its relevance and could therefore not ensure that he was appropriately briefed. Since the Court was now in uncharted legal waters, at least for Scotland, numerous additional procedural details required agreement. Eventually the Court appointed David Johnston QC as Special Counsel, who was one of those suggested by the appeal team, but, by the time Abdelbaset returned to Libya, the procedures were still far from being finalised, let alone the matter of disclosure being settled. To this day the documents' contents remain unknown.

In April 2008, Kelly wrote to the Crown with a lengthy schedule of undisclosed documents that he wished to see, most of which related to Tony Gauci.[7] Almost six weeks later the Crown wrote back to say, among other things, that the documents disclosed should be restricted to the SCCRC's six grounds of referral.[8] In October the team issued another formal petition to the Court. In addition to the documents in the original schedule, it sought disclosure of all the statements made by every Crown's witness and details of all their criminal convictions.[9] By this time the Crown had failed in its attempts to reduce the scope of the appeal, so had no legal excuse for withholding the documents. The Crown Office indicated their willingness to cooperate, but the process remained glacial. In December 2008 the Crown handed over 7,000 police statements, many previously undisclosed.[10]

However, when Kelly's team cross-referenced them with the accompanying schedule, they discovered that around 400 were missing.[11] Having initially claimed that they had disclosed all relevant material and possessed nothing else, the Crown later admitted that the 'Crown estate' had not been fully searched, and argued that such an exercise was too great to be expected. More statements and documents were released over the following months, but the disclosure appeared to be piecemeal, apparently because neither Crown nor police knew exactly what material existed. Eventually a team of six people spent seven weeks sifting 47 cabinets, safes and all available electronic data,[12] but even then not all the requested material had been uncovered. This begged the question, why did the Crown not commence the search immediately after the SCCRC granted Abdelbaset's second appeal in June 2007? An additional complicating factor was that the Office of the Solicitor to the Advocate General (OSAG) insisted on having sight of any material that, in the Crown's opinion, might raise PII issues, prior to its disclosure. Furthermore, since it was likely that some of the material was held by other countries, the Crown would have had to seek permission from the relevant authorities within those countries, in particular the US Department of Justice.

At a meeting on 27 January 2009, the head of the Crown Office team, Lindsey Miller, said she understood that, owing to the way the Maltese authorities had insisted that inquiries were carried out, no reports were prepared by FBI agents regarding their contact with Gauci. On 30 January 2009 she wrote to Kelly to confirm that the Crown Office held no reports by the FBI agents who were in Malta and that the US Department of Justice had informed her that only three such reports were prepared, all by the same agent, Keith Bolcar.[13] Gauci was by far the most important witness in the case, and FBI agents were in Malta for long periods and were present when he gave many of his statements. It was therefore difficult to believe that the FBI did not hold further relevant information, and given the Department of Justice's role in the concealment of the Giaka cables, Kelly's team took all its claims with a sizeable pinch of salt.

In November 2008, Kelly petitioned the Court for disclosure of documents held by RARDE's successor organisation, the Defence Science and Technology Laboratory (DSTL), including some referred to in the SCCRC's Statement of Reasons.[14] At a meeting with the Crown Office on 29 January 2009, Kelly requested that they check with RARDE whether it held the materials requested.[15] The Crown Office indicated their general willingness to cooperate, but once again there were lengthy delays. On 22 May they informed Kelly that DSTL had confirmed that the requested information did not exist.[16] Three days later they wrote again to say that DSTL did in fact hold papers, but believed them to be copies of the documents discussed at trial. The papers would nevertheless be reviewed to see if there was anything relevant to the request.[17] On 15 June the Crown Office confirmed that Kelly could have access to the material, subject to its being reviewed by OSAG.[18] On 24 June they informed Kelly that the material had been reviewed by Crown Office staff and police officers on 4 June and the 'vast majority' of it was found to be documents that were disclosed at trial. They added that the material was currently being reviewed 'by representatives of Her Majesty's Government',[19] which presumably meant members of one of the intelligence services.

In early July the Crown Office sent a handful of previously undisclosed forensic documents, from the police and DSTL, some of which proved to be highly significant.* At the end of the month, Kelly was finally allowed to visit DSTL to view the RARDE material. There were eight boxes of it. While much of it had, indeed, been previously disclosed, many documents had not, including, once again, some of great significance. It was not until October 2009, two months after Abdelbaset's return to Libya, that copies of the material were handed over.

---

* Some of these documents are referred to in Chapters 8 and 14.

Afterword

As I was completing this book Libya erupted in protest against Colonel Gadafy's brutal and sclerotic 42-year dictatorship. The following
month a coalition of countries, led by the UK and France, began air-
strikes against Gadafy's forces. Within no time, and without a clear
UN mandate, the military mission metamorphosed from humanitarian military intervention into regime change. After six months Gadafy
was toppled and the rebel National Transitional Council (NTC) was
in power.

The stated aim of the intervention was to prevent a massacre of
the rebels, but it seemed likely that the real intention was to back
the winners in a civil war in which more than three per cent of the
world's oil reserves were at stake. The humanitarian justification
sounded hollow when contrasted with the same governments' hands-
off approach to Bahrain – where the Saudi-backed government forces
never looked likely to be toppled by the anti-government protesters
– and oil-light, strategically sensitive Syria, where the Assad regime
has been slaughtering rebels with impunity for almost 12 months.

I have had no contact with Abdelbaset since the start of the conflict. No doubt he would have seen the irony in western governments
claiming to stand against the collective punishment of the Libyan
people, given that they inflicted 12 years of collective punishment on
the same people by driving through UN sanctions, based on evidence
that they knew, or should have known, was at best shaky and at
worst concocted. Oppressing Libyans is fine, you see, when it is done
by 'civilized' regimes.

Given the fragile moral pretext for the intervention, it was inevitable that Lockerbie would become a propaganda tool. The first senior
western politician to exploit it was Republican former presidential
candidate Senator John McCain. After visiting the rebel capital of
Benghazi he told his fellow countrymen who were squeamish about
the military action, 'The blood of Americans is on [Gadafy's] hands
because he was responsible for Pan Am 103.' Shortly afterwards, under pressure from the Foreign Office, the NTC invited to Benghazi
the British lawyer, Jason McCue, who represents IRA and Lockerbie
victims. The aim of the visit was to gather evidence that Gadafy had

ordered the bombing and to secure 'an apology from the Libyan people' for Lockerbie and for supplying explosives used by the IRA.*

Two months later, with public support for the war waning, President Barack Obama attempted to justify why Libya was being singled out for enforced regime change by telling a White House press conference: 'Gadafy, prior to Osama bin Laden, was responsible for more American deaths than just about anybody on the planet.'[1] He did not refer to Lockerbie directly, but everyone understood what he meant. Following Abdelbaset's appearance at a pro-Gadafy rally on 26 July, British Foreign Secretary William Hague joined in, taking the opportunity to launch a further swipe at the Scottish government for releasing Abdelbaset.[2] The NTC's London PR company, Bell-Pottinger, played its part, circulating a claim by a leading cancer specialist that the compassionate release decision was based on flawed medical advice.[3] In August the NTC's newly appointed representative in London, Guma El-Gamaty, said Megrahi's release had sent the 'wrong signal', and handed Gadafy 'a political and diplomatic victory'.[†4]

Earlier in July it was reported that President Obama had asked Libya's rebel leaders to capture Abdelbaset and hand him over to US special forces so he could be sent to 'face justice' in the US. Senior US politicians and commentators lined up to demand his extradition,

* McCue's visit did not go entirely smoothly. While the head of the NTC, Mustafa Abdel Jalil, signed an apology for the role of the Gadafy regime in the Lockerbie bombing and IRA attacks, other NTC members were clearly unhappy. They claimed that the issue only arose because it was pressed on them by the British government, and pointed out that most Libyans did not consider themselves responsible for Gadafy's actions. The *Guardian* reported: '[NTC] officials said that they regarded McCue as working with a team of British diplomats in Benghazi, led by the UK's ambassador to Rome, Christopher Prentice. Prentice has declined to talk to the press. A council spokesman, Essam Gheriani, said that Jalil had had little choice but to sign as part of the rebel administration's attempts to win diplomatic recognition and gain access to desperately needed funds frozen overseas.'

† El-Gamaty stopped short of claiming that Abdelbaset was involved in the bombing, telling *Scotland on Sunday*: 'I think if [Abdelbaset and Lamin] are implicated they are a very, very small fish in the chain. The people higher up are the real culprits. The Moussa Koussas of this world and Gaddafi himself.'

most notably Republican presidential hopeful Mitt Romney. Someone should perhaps have reminded them that such a move would be, not only inhumane, but also contrary to US law* – not that legality has always been a prerequisite of US foreign policy.

A far more likely consequence of the Libyan revolution for Abdelbaset is that he will be subjected to a new level of disinformation. On 22 February 2011, with the uprising in full spate, I posed a rhetorical question on Professor Robert Black's Lockerbie blog: 'What's the betting that, sometime in the next few weeks, the following happens: 1) In the burned out ruins of a Libyan government building, someone finds definitive documentary "proof" that Libya and Megrahi were responsible for Lockerbie; and/or 2) A Libyan official reveals, "we did it".' I pointed out that the official case was now so thin that only such concoctions could save it (although it had previously crossed my mind that a Scottish prisoner might one day claim 'Megrahi confessed to me' – another hallmark of paper-thin cases).

Within 24 hours my prediction had come true, as the country's newly defected Justice Minister, and soon to be head of the NTC, Mustafa Abdel Jalil, told the Swedish newspaper *Expressen*, 'I have

---

* Article vi, clause 2 of the US Constitution obliges the US government to abide by the all the treaties to which it is a signatory. The government signed the treaty that established the UN and, as a permanent member of the UN Security Council, which was set up by that same treaty, co-sponsored a mandatory Security Council resolution that the Lockerbie trial process would be governed by Scots law. Abdelbaset was convicted in a trial in which US government lawyers were part of the prosecution team and remains convicted under Scots law, so could therefore not legally be tried again for the same offence. Romney and others argued that their government was no longer bound by the agreement as the Scottish government's release of Abdelbaset had rendered it void. The claim rested on the fact that the US-UK letter that set out the agreement, which was approved by the Security Council resolution, stated that, if convicted, the two accused 'will serve their sentence in the United Kingdom', which, in practice, meant Scotland. However, the compassionate release decision did not breach that condition because Abdelbaset served all of the sentence that Scots law required him to serve. While it was true that the judges set a 27-year tariff, as justice minister acting under legislation enacted by the sovereign UK parliament, MacAskill was legally and constitutionally entitled to apply the general law relating to compassionate release, to which every prison sentence imposed by a Scottish court is subject.

proof that Gaddafi gave the order on Lockerbie.'[5] In the following weeks more senior defectors implicated their former leader in the bombing, most notably the ex-Interior Minister Abdel Fattah Younes* and the ex-Ambassador to the UN, Abdul Rahman al-Shalgham. So too, according to media reports, did the ex-Foreign Minister and former intelligence chief Moussa Koussa.

When subjected to even the slightest scrutiny, the defectors' claims fell apart. At the time of writing, the most detailed ones have been made by Jalil in an interview with the *Sunday Times*. As former Justice Minister he was probably well aware that the case against Abdelbaset was beyond repair. This was perhaps why he told the newspaper that Abdelbaset 'was not the man who carried out the planning and execution of the bombing, but he was "nevertheless involved in facilitating things for those who did".' Any credibility that this lent his account was destroyed by his claim, in the same interview, that Abdelbaset had blackmailed Gadafy into securing his release from prison by threatening to expose the dictator's role in the bombing, and had 'vowed to exact "revenge"' unless his demand was met.[6] The notion that Abdelbaset held any power over Gadafy was ludicrous. As his response to the uprising illustrated, the Colonel would not tolerate challenges to his authority. Abdelbaset was reliant on Gadafy's government to fund his appeal and to shelter his family in Tripoli, so would have been insane to attempt blackmail. Setting that aside, even if Gadafy had been guilty of the bombing, what possible jeopardy was there for him, in those pre-revolutionary days, if Abdelbaset implicated Libya? In the eyes of the international community the country was already guilty, it had suffered sanctions and had paid compensation to get them lifted. Nothing that Abdelbaset might say could change this, and a confession would harm only himself. And if his sole aim was to achieve freedom, why would he have bothered to dedicate so much of his remaining life to cooperating with this book?

Nine months on, Jalil is yet to reveal publicly his 'proof'. The closest he came was during an interview with BBC *Newsnight*, broadcast on – perhaps appropriately – 1 April. When asked about the evidence of Gadafy's involvement in the bombing, he 'revealed'

---

* Younes was killed in July 2011, reportedly by rebel forces who mistrusted him.

that the dictator had supported Abdelbaset and paid for his legal case. This was not even a revelation, let alone evidence. Was it the best he could do?

The ex-interior minister, Younes, described by the BBC when they interviewed him as 'the man considered by many to have been Colonel Gaddafi's number two', was less explicit than Jalil. Asked by the BBC's John Simpson if Gadafy had personally ordered the bombing, he replied, 'There is no doubt about it, nothing happens without Gadafy's agreement. I'm certain this was a national governmental decision.'[7] Simpson claimed in an online article that Younes 'maintains that Col Gaddafi was personally responsible for the decision to blow up the Pan Am flight',[8] yet in the broadcast section of the interview he appeared to be expressing a firm belief, rather than certain knowledge. This was rather odd, because he had been close to Gadafy for 47 years and was supposedly his number two, so, if Gadafy *had* ordered the bombing, he must have known all about it.

It was harder for the other two senior defectors, Shalgam and Koussa, to implicate Gadafy and Abdelbaset in the bombing, because both had previously publicly denied Libyan involvement.[9] When questioned by the Arabic newspaper *al-Hayat*, Shalgam was vague, claiming: 'The Lockerbie bombing was a complex and tangled operation . . . There was talk at the time of the roles played by states and organisations. Libyan security played a part but I believe it was not a strictly Libyan operation.'

Koussa's story was the most mysterious yet the most illuminating of them all. Reportedly the head of Libyan intelligence for 16 years, he had been one of the most notorious and feared members of Gadafy's inner circle – the 'black box' of the regime, according to Shalgham.[10] He first gained notoriety in 1980, when, as head of Libya's London embassy, he told *The Times*: 'The revolutionary committees have decided last night to kill two more [Libyan dissidents] in the United Kingdom. I approve of this.'[11] Although expelled from the UK two days later, his name was frequently linked to the shooting of WPC Yvonne Fletcher outside the embassy four years later.

Shortly after his arrival in the UK at the end of March 2011, a London-based Libyan acquaintance, Noman Benotman, who claimed to have helped coordinate the defection, said that Koussa

431

would be willing to open up to the British authorities about Libya's involvement in Lockerbie.[12] Benotman's role was itself interesting. A former leader of the anti-Gadafy islamist terrorist organisation the Libyan Islamic Fighting Group, he had renounced violent extremism and become a leading figure in the counter-radicalisation think-tank Quilliam.[13] He remained opposed to Gadafy yet was friendly with one of the most powerful and feared members of the Gadafy regime, who had once attempted to have him extradited to Libya.

Koussa was debriefed at an MI6 safe house and, a few days later, was interviewed about Lockerbie by the Scottish police.[14] He was then allowed to leave the country and his assets were unfrozen. He is now living in a luxury hotel in Qatar, whose government has been the most supportive of the Libyan rebels among the Arab states, but the NTC continues to regard him with extreme suspicion.[15] Prime Minister David Cameron insisted that Koussa had not been offered immunity from prosecution,[16] while behind the scenes Whitehall spinners were busy downplaying his role in terrorism. A 'senior government source' briefed the *Daily Telegraph* that Koussa was not in London at the time of the murder of WPC Yvonne Fletcher (as if that cleared him of responsibility) and added 'seeing him as the mastermind behind Lockerbie doesn't make any sense in terms of his career. He might, however, possess some useful information about such cases.'[17]

The glaring problem here was that for years sources in Whitehall and Washington had been privately briefing the media that Koussa was Libya's terrorist-in-chief* and the probable mastermind of Lockerbie. The day after his defection, the CIA's Vincent Cannistraro, who had previously worked on the US government's covert campaign to unseat Gadafy, part of which involved spreading disinformation, told CBS news: 'Moussa Koussa was personally responsible

---

* A US State Department briefing paper entitled *Libya's Continuing Responsibility for Terrorism*, issued in 1991 to coincide with the indictments against Abdelbaset and Lamin, claimed that Koussa was the head of the Libyan Anti-Imperialism Centre, which 'is used by the Libyan government to support terrorist networks and thus plays an important role in Qadhafi's terrorism strategy.' It stated that the Centre's mission was 'to identify and recruit revolutionaries for ideological and military training in Libya,' adding, 'During their training at AIC camps, individuals are selected for advanced training, including weapons and explosives, and indoctrination.'

for the actual organization of [Lockerbie].' It was, in short, inconceivable that the Libyan government could be guilty of the bombing
and Koussa be innocent. If, as we had been led to believe, Libya was
guilty, then asking for his help to find those responsible for Lockerbie
was like seeking the help of Radovan Karadzic or Ratko Mladic in
finding those responsible for the Srebrenica massacre.

So why wasn't Koussa arrested? There were two obvious explanations and one less so. The first was that, in its desperation to overthrow Gadafy, the UK government was prepared to make a pact with
the most notorious devil in his inner circle. The second was that the
government was well aware that neither he nor Gadafy had anything
to do with Lockerbie and that he had simply called their bluff. The
less obvious explanation, which does not preclude the other two,
was that Koussa was a long-time MI6 asset. Former foreign secretary
Jack Straw confirmed in a BBC Radio 4 interview that Koussa had
been 'a key figure' in the 2003 negotiations with the Libyan government over weapons of mass destruction. Straw then went further:
when it was put to him that Koussa had had 'exceedingly close contacts at a very sensitive level with – what shall we call them for the
sake of argument? – "British officials" for the best part of a decade',
he answered, 'Yes, if not more.'[18] The *Daily Telegraph* went further
still, stating: 'As head of Libya external intelligence, Mr Koussa was
an MI6 asset for almost two decades.'[19] If true, this was not only
breathtaking, but might also account for much of the disinformation
surrounding the case. Even if it were not true, the affair exposed the
ugly reality of the government's approach to Lockerbie.

By the second anniversary of his return home, Abdelbaset was
still clinging to life. The fact that he was bedridden and in great pain
did little to mute the conspiracy theorists, who claimed that he was
never as ill as the Scottish government had stated. In early October
he gave a brief interview to Reuters TV. According to Reuters, he told
them that his role in the bombing had been exaggerated.[20] This was
widely reported as being a partial confession, but the word he had
used, 'ichtira', means invented or concocted, rather than exaggerated.

Still shoddier journalism was to come, most notably an ITV
Tonight programme, broadcast in January 2012, which followed
the British Lockerbie relative Dr Jim Swire to Tripoli as he tried to

uncover information about the bombing. The programme's denoue-
ment was an interview with Ashur Shamis, described as an adviser to
the Prime Minister, who told Swire there was no doubt that Gadafy
was personally involved in the planning and execution of the bombing. He added: 'Regardless of what Megrahi did or did not do, that
[sic] is a small fish. He is an employee of Libyan security, there is
no doubt about it – of external security – and if he was told to do
something he would have done it.' Swire could be sure of Gadafy's
involvement, he said, because 'He paid all this money to cover up
himself . . . If he had no role, he wouldn't have paid a penny, he
wouldn't have paid a penny.' [21]

This was, of course, nonsense: the Gadafy regime had paid compensation to the Lockerbie victims, reluctantly, because it was the
only way to rid the country of harsh UN sanctions. Had the pro-
gramme-makers checked Shamis's background, they would have discovered that he had not lived in Libya since 1973 and therefore had
no first-hand knowledge of the inner workings of the Gadafy regime.
In 1981 he was one of the founders of the CIA-backed National
Front for the Salvation of Libya, and in 1985, at the height of the US
government's covert campaign against the Gadafy regime, became
chair of its National Congress.[22]

The programme claimed that Swire 'is now persuaded that
Gadafy was probably behind his daughter's murder.' In fact, as he
subsequently told the *Times,* he found Shamis unconvincing. He explained: 'I found Tripoli percolated with the desire to pin everything
imaginable under the sun on the defunct Gaddafi regime, because the
people are so delighted to have got rid of him . . . Mr Shamis certainly
believes al-Megrahi was guilty. I tried to make plain that if you look
at the evidence that it is not at all likely.'[23]

Thankfully, not all the influential voices in the new Libya are
as badly informed as Shamis. The first interim justice minister, Mohamed al-Alagi, a former head of Libya's human rights association
who was involved in Abdelbaset's case, has stated publicly that Abdelbaset is innocent and should not be extradited to the US.[24]

The NTC's leader, Jalil, has yet to reveal his 'proof' of Gadafy's involvement in the bombing, but it may yet appear: maybe a document
in a burned-out building; maybe files on a government computer;

maybe a 'confession' by one of the Lockerbie masterminds – indeed I would not be surprised to read that Abdelbaset has made a full deathbed confession. The case has been littered with phony evidence; we should expect more. It won't alter the fact that the prosecution case is destroyed and, more importantly, that Abdelbaset is innocent.

John Ashton, January 2012.

Notes on the Text

1 The World's Most Wanted Man

1. Alan Topp trial evidence, 3 May 2000, trial transcript pp.83 to 126.
2. DC John Crawford interviewed in the STV documentary *The Lockerbie Bomber: Sent Home to Die*, broadcast 9 August 2010.
3. US State Department spokesman Richard Boucher, 14 November 1991.
4. US and UK Governments' joint declaration A/46/827 S/23308, 27 November 1991.
5. International Court of Justice Application, 3 March 1992.

2 Before the Nightmare

1. *Sunday Times*, 17 November 1991.
2. US State Department Fact Sheet, *Additional Information on the Bombing of Pan Am Flight 103*, 15 November 1991.
3. Chemical Marketing telex to Abdelbaset, 27 January 1988.
4. Telex from Trinckert to Abdelbaset, 19 July 1987.
5. Telex to Badri Hassan from Homac Aviation Ltd, 13 October 1988.
6. Abdelmajid Arebi defence precognition statement, 24 January 2000.
7. 'Sea of Lies', *Newsweek* article, 13 July 1992.
8. *Washington Post*, 23 April 1990.
9. Cooley, John, *Payback: America's Long War in the Middle East*. New York: Brassey's, 1992.
10. USAF Military Airlift Command warning, 5 July 1988.
11. German Chief Federal Prosecutor's press announcement re the release of Marwan Khreesat, 19 May 1989, police reference D/5198.
12. BKA memo, 13 February 1989.
13. BKA inventory of items seized from 28 Sandweg, Frankfurt, police reference DW/198, Crown Production 1672.
14. BKA photos of 28 Sandweg, police reference DW/166, Crown Production 1637.
15. BKA report: *Terrorist activities of the Popular Front for the Liberation of Palestine, General Command, in the Federal Republic of Germany*, 27 October 1988.
16. Translation of Dalkamoni passport in BKA memo, 3 March 1989.
17. FBI FD302, report of interview of Marwan Khreesat.
18. Abdel Fattah Ghadanfar BKA interview, 26 October 1988.
19. Martin Kadorah BKA interview, 8 December 1988.
20. BKA letter to Frankfurt Public Prosecutor, 17 March 1989.
21. Judicial interview of Kadorah, 6 July 1989.

22. Hafez Dalkamoni BKA interview, 13 January 1989.
23. Khreesat BKA interview, 27 October 1988, police reference D4748.
24. Emerson, Steven and Duffy, Brian, *The Fall of Pan Am 103*. USA: Putnam, 1990.
25. Judgment of Judge Christian Rinne, Federal Court, Karlsruhe, 10 November 1988.
26. Note of Khreesat interview by Pierre Salinger.
27. Emerson and Duffy, *The Fall of Pan Am 103*.
28. *New York Times*, 28 August 1988.
29. Jim Berwick statement S620G.
30. Report of the President's Commission on Aviation Security and Terrorism, pub. US Government Printing Office, 1990.
31. ABC Television interview, 30 November 1989.
32. DIA Terrorism Intelligence Branch Defence Intelligence Terrorism Summary, 1 December 1988.
33. US State Department Office of Diplomatic Security departmental digest, 2 December 1988.
34. *The Guardian*, 29 July 1995.

3 Pan Am 103

1. David Connel trial evidence, 8 May 2000, trial transcript pp.667–670; Alisdair Campbell Crown precognition statement, 26 January 1999.
2. Photographs of labels of items PSI/1 a.k.a. PF/544 a.k.a. AG/151 and PSI/4 a.k.a. PF/547 a.k.a. AG/152 contained in photo album police reference AZ/17, Crown Production 81.
3. LPS form 1, police reference DP/28, Crown Production 288.
4. Report by Dr John Douse, police reference PT/84, Crown Production 1496.
5. AAIB report 2/90, police reference AZ/45, Crown Production 138.
6. DI Donald MacNeil defence precognition statement.
7. Owen Schneider statement S3825A.
8. Samsonite export sales data, police reference DC/27, Crown Production 167.
9. Hashem Abassi BKA interview, 25 April 1989, police reference D4129.
10. Report by DCS Patrick Connor for SIO John Orr, 5 June 1989.
11. BKA inventory of items seized from 28 Sandweg, Frankfurt, police reference DW198, Crown Production 1672; BKA photos of 28 Sandweg, police reference DW166, Crown Production 1637.
12. Peter Claiden statement S903A.
13. RARDE joint forensic report, section 6.

14. RARDE joint forensic report, photograph 269.
15. Hashem Abassi interview, 14 April 1989, police reference D/4039.
16. Rainer Gobel statement S5811.
17. BKA inventory of items seized from 28 Sandweg, Frankfurt, police reference DW/198, Crown Production 1672.
18. Gobel report, 26 May 1989, police reference CS/279, Crown Production 1712.
19. Allen Feraday fax to Bell, 23 June 1989.
20. Cooley, *Payback*; Emerson and Duffy, *The Fall of Pan Am 103*.
21. *Quick Magazine* (West Germany), May 1989.
22. *Sunday Times*, 26 March 1989.
23. *The Times*, 12 September 1989.
24. Mohamed Mougrabi SAPO interview, 12 November 1988.
25. Jamila Mougrabi diary, police reference DC/1757, Crown Production 1252.
26. Swedish National Laboratory of Forensic Science report 5 July 1989; SAPO reports 4 July 1989 and 24 August 1989.
27. Abu Talb Crown precognition statement, 21 September 1999.
28. Scottish police summary of Mohamed Abu Talb investigations, 9 January 1991, police reference D6921.
29. Abu Talb SAPO interview, 1 November 1988, police reference D5438.
30. Abu Talb police interview, 3 to 5 April 1990, police reference D6023.
31. Abu Talb Scottish police interview, 3 April 1990, police reference D6023.
32. Mahmoud Mougrabi statement S5050.
33. *Daily Mail*, 17 March 1989.
34. Scottish police summary of Talb investigations, 9 January 1991, police reference D6921.
35. *The Sun*, 17 March 1989.
36. *Today*, 17 March 1989.
37. *Washington Post*, 28 July 2004.
38. *Washington Post*, 11 January 1990.
39. Interview with Martin Cadman in *The Maltese Double Cross* documentary.
40. John Ashton non-attributable interview with Scottish mountain rescue team members, 26 November 2001.
41. British High Commission in Canberra, Australia, press release 16 May 1995.
42. John Ashton non-attributable interview with Scottish mountain rescue team members, 26 November 2001.
43. John Ashton non-attributable interviews with members of mountain rescue teams.

44. John Ashton interview with David Thomson.
45. Written answer by Scottish Office Minister Lord James Douglas-Hamilton, 6 March 1995.
46. John Ashton non-attributable interviews with police officer.
47. John Ashton non-attributable interview with search volunteer.
48. Emerson and Duffy, *The Fall of Pan Am 103*; *Private Eye*, 8 May 1992.
49. John Ashton non-attributable interview with witness.
50. Tony Lloyd MP, Minister of State, Foreign and Commonwealth Office, House of Commons debate 11 June 1997.
51. Tam Dalyell interview, *The Maltese Double Cross* documentary.
52. John Ashton interview with Scottish mountain rescue team members, 28 November 2001.
53. John Ashton interview with non-attributable military helicopter crew member.
54. John Ashton non-attributable interviews with search volunteers.
55. John Ashton non-attributable interview with search team leader.
56. John Ashton non-attributable interview with military helicopter crew member.
57. Innes Graham interview, *The Maltese Double Cross* documentary.
58. John Ashton non-attributable interview with search volunteer.
59. John Ashton non-attributable interview with police officer.
60. Johnston, David, *Lockerbie: The Real Story*. London: Bloomsbury, 1989.
61. John Ashton non-attributable interview with police officer.
62. PC Duncan Smith statement S1177; PC Calum Weir statement S1286E.
63. DI William Williamson SCCRC interview, 2 April 2007.
64. DCI Jack Baird Crown precognition statement.
65. David Johnston interview, *The Maltese Double Cross* documentary.
66. SCCRC Statement of Reasons, paragraphs 12.41 to 12.61.

4 The Double Agent

1. CIA telex cable, 13 December 1990.
2. Note of meeting between Alastair Duff and Edwin Bollier, 14 July 1999.
3. Edwin Bollier letter to CIA, January 1989, police reference DP/162, Crown Production 323.
4. Richard Marquise Crown precognition statement, 10 December 1999.
5. Harris, Paul, *More Thrills than Skills: Adventures in Journalism, War and Terrorism*. Glasgow: Kennedy & Boyd, 2009.
6. Dexstar log for PI/995, police reference AZ61, Crown Production 114.
7. LPS form 305, police reference DP/28, Crown Production 288.
8. Hayes notes, police reference PT/90, Crown Production 1497.

9. Hayes notes, 12 May 1989, police reference PT/90-E51, Crown Production 1497.

10. Allen Feraday memo to DI William Williamson, 15 September 1989, police reference DP/137, Crown Production 333.

11. Polaroid photographs accompanying Feraday memo to Williamson, 15 September 1989, police reference DP/138, Crown Production 334.

12. Williamson statement S872BS.

13. Williamson statement S872BS.

14. Williamson statement S872BS.

15. Williamson statement S872BS.

16. James 'Tom' Thurman Crown precognition statement, 11 January 2000.

17. Richard Sherrow FBI FD302 statement, police reference D6518.

18. Williamson statement S872CK.

19. SIO Stuart Henderson statement S4710J.

20. Photographs of Senegal timer, police reference DE/51, Crown Production 272.

21. Henderson statement S4710J.

22. Edwin Bollier and Ulrich Lumpert police interviews, police reference CS/136, Crown Production 1527.

23. Thüring order form, 13 August 1985, police reference DP/473, Crown Production 402.

24. Thüring delivery note, 16 August 1985, police reference DP/159, Crown Production 319.

25. Thüring delivery note, 5 November 1985, police reference DP/407, Crown Production 400.

26. Bollier Police interview, 14 January 1991, police reference CS/135, Crown Production 1531.

27. Bollier Police interview, 14 January 1991, police reference CS/135, Crown Production 1531.

28. Bollier Police interview, 14 January 1991, police reference CS/135, Crown Production 1531.

29. Bollier Police interview, 25 March 1991, police reference DP/264, Crown Production 1533.

30. Bollier Police interview, 25 March 1991 , police reference DP/264, Crown Production 1533.

31. Sherrow FBI FD302 statement, police reference D6518.

32. Williamson statement, S872CK.

33. Craig Bates defence precognition statement, 16 March 2000.

34. DS Peter Avent statement S5388AW; DI Watson McAteer statement S3743Q.

35. Avent statement S5388AW; McAteer statement S3743Q.

36. McAteer statement S3743Q.

37. Avent statement S5388AW.

38. Bates defence precognition statement, 16 March 2000.

39. *Washington Post*, 5 October 1986.

40. Reuters report in *New York Times*, 12 August 1986.

41. Woodward, Bob, *Veil: The Secret Wars of the CIA*. New York: Simon & Schuster, 1987.

42. John Orkin Crown precognition statement, 10 January 2000.

43. Orkin report 85SP002, police reference DE52, Crown Production 284.

44. Bollier interview by BKA, 9 September 1992, police reference CS148, Crown Production 1535.

45. Kenneth Steiner Crown precognition statement, 6 June 2000

46. Steiner Crown precognition statement, 15 September 1999.

47. Translation of Jean Collin interview, police reference DM137, Crown Production 1589.

48. Steiner Crown precognition statements, 15 September 1999.

49. Mohamed El-Marzouk police interviews, police reference DP/76, Crown Production 256; Mansour El-Saber police interviews, police reference DP/75, Crown Production 256.

50. Custody photo, police reference DC1670, Crown Production 262; Custody photo, police reference DC1671, Crown Production 263.

51. Joint minute number 5, 8 June 2000, Trial transcript pp.2905 to 2907.

52. Trial Court Opinion, paragraph 52.

53. Williamson statement S872AN; DS Michael Langford-Johnson statement S1983BR.

54. Order of destruction, 17 January 1989, police reference DP/78, Crown Production 258.

55. Record of destruction, 8 September 1989, police reference DP/77, Crown Production 258.

56. Translation of Collin interview, 15 January 1991, police reference DM137, Crown Production 1589.

57. DCS James Gilchrist Crown precognition statement, 14 December 1999.

58. Henderson Crown precognition statement, 29 February 2000.

59. Crown letter to defence solicitors, 23 April 2000.

60. Henderson Crown precognition statement, 29 February 2000.

61. Marquise Crown precognition, 12 December 1999.

62. Bollier FBI interview, 11 to 15 February 1991, police reference CS84, Crown Production 1532.

63. Bollier police interview, 25 March 1991, police reference DP/264, Crown Production 1533.

64. Henderson Crown precognition statement, 29 February 2000.

65. FBI FD302 report on Bollier interview 11 to 15 February 1991, police reference CS/84, Crown Production 1532.

66. Marquise Crown precognition statement, 10 December 1999.
67. Bollier interview by Swiss Federal Police, 17 December 1990, police reference CS/147, Crown Production 1529.
68. Marquise Crown precognition statement, 10 December 1999.
69. Bollier letter to CIA, January 1989, police reference DP/162, Crown Production 323.
70. FBI FD302 report on Bollier interview 11 to 15 February 1991, police reference CS/84, Crown Production 1532.
71. Bollier letter to Ezzadin Hinshiri, 6 February 1991, police reference DP/184, Crown Production 291.
72. Bollier interview by BKA, 5 October 1993, police reference CS/262, Crown Production 1537.
73. Lumpert interview by BKA, 7 October 1993, police reference CS/154, Crown Production 1577.
74. Bollier interview by BKA, 24 March 1994, police reference CS/145, Crown Production 1543.
75. Bollier interview by Swiss Federal Police, 26 January 1994, police reference CS/146, Crown Production 1541.
76. Bollier interview by Swiss Federal Police, 26 January 1994, police reference CS/146, Crown Production 1541.
77. Bollier interview by BKA, 24 March 1994, police reference CS/145, Crown Production 1543.
78. Bollier interview by Swiss Federal Police, 26 January 1994, police reference CS/146, Crown Production 1541.
79. Bollier trial evidence, 22 June 2000, trial transcript pp.4080 to 4081.
80. Bollier interview by BKA, 6 October 1993, police reference CS/264, Crown Production 1539.
81. Bollier interview by BKA, 25 July 1995, police reference CS/266, Crown Production 1549.
82. Bollier interview by BKA, 9 September 1992, police reference CS/148, Crown Production 1535.
83. Steiner BKA interview, 25 July 1991.
84. Arnold BKA interview, 9 December 1991.
85. Gerber BKA interview, 9 March 1992.
86. Gardener BKA interview, 22 September 1999.
87. Gerber BKA interview, 22 September 1999.
88. Gerber BKA interview, 23 November 1992.

5 The Shopkeeper

1. Dexstar log, police reference AZ/61, Crown Production 114.
2. Dr Thomas Hayes notes, 22 May 1989, police reference PT/90, Crown Production 1497.

3. DI George Brown statement S4458B.
4. Paul Gauci Big Ben Ltd statement S4692.
5. Hayes notes, 14 March 1989, police reference PT/90, Crown Production 1497.
6. DCI Harry Bell statement S2632C.
7. Tony Gauci statement S4677.
8. Paul Gauci statement S4680.
9. Tony Gauci statement S4677B.
10. Tony Gauci statement S4677D.
11. Tony Gauci statement S4677C.
12. Tony Gauci statement S4677E.
13. Tony Gauci statement S4677F.
14. Police document *Summary of Swedish Investigations*, 9 January 1991, police reference D6921.
15. Mohamed Abu Talb police interview, 3 to 5 April 1990, police reference D6023.
16. Abdelsalem Abu Nada statement, 9 July 1990.
17. Abu Talb police interview, 3 to 5 April 1990, police reference D6023.
18. DC Alexander Smith statement S606H.
19. Abu Talb police interview, 3 to 5 April 1990, police reference D6023.
20. Schedule of clothing confiscated from Abu Talb's house, prepared by DC Callum Entwistle.
21. Police document *Summary of Swedish Investigations*, 9 January 1991, police reference D6921.
22. Jamila Mougrabi statement S5080B; Wafa Toska interview, 29 November 1989, police reference D5376.
23. Tony Gauci statement S4677K.
24. Bell statement S2632E.
25. Dr Drago Dragavac Crown precognition statement.
26. Paul Gauci statement S4689D.
27. DC John Crawford statement S609V.
28. Hayes notes, various dates, police reference PT/90, Crown Production 1497.
29. Tony Gauci statement S4677K. Tony Gauci statement S4677M.
30. RARDE joint forensic report section 5.
31. *Il-Helsien*, 20 October 1989.
32. *Sunday Times*, 3 December 1989.
33. David Wright statement S5114; Associated Press, 1 December 1989.
34. *Sunday Times*, 29 October 1989.
35. Tony Gauci statement S4677L.
36. Tony Gauci statement S4677P.
37. Tony Gauci statement S4677Q.
38. Bell statement S2632AR.

39. Crawford, John, *A Detective's Tale*. Canada: Trafford, 2002.
40. Tony Gauci statement S4677R.
41. Crawford, *A Detective's Tale*.
42. Bell statement S2632AR.
43. Crawford, *A Detective's Tale*.
44. Tony Gauci statement S4677.
45. Tony Gauci statement S4677L.
46. Tony Gauci statement S4677.
47. Tony Gauci statement S4677A.
48. Tony Gauci statement S4677.
49. Tony Gauci statement S4677N; Tony Gauci statement S4677O.
50. DC Graham Cairns statement S23AC.
51. Bell Diary extract, 21 February 1990.
52. Tony Gauci statement S4677F.
53. Tony Gauci statement S4677T.
54. Crawford, *A Detective's Tale*.
55. Crawford statement S609V.
56. RAI TV schedules, referred to in joint minute during Lockerbie trial, 11 July 2000, trial transcript pp.4830 to 4832.
57. Paul Gauci statement S4680.
58. Paul Gauci statement S4680.
59. Paul Gauci statement S4680D.
60. Crawford statement S609V.
61. Tony Gauci statement S4677.
62. Tony Gauci statements S4677A, B, D, E, K, N, and O.
63. Tony Gauci statement S4677Q.
64. Tony Gauci statement S4677A.
65. Tony Gauci statement S4677Q.
66. Major Joseph Mifsud letter to Maltese police, 14 September 1989.
67. Rainfall totals for November 1988 in Malta, police reference DC/1620, Crown Production 446.
68. Rainfall totals for December 1988 in Malta, police reference DC/1617, Crown Production 443.
69. Daily weather summaries, 17 November to 21 December 1988, attached to letter from Major Josph Mifsud to Maltese police, 14 September 1989.
70. Undated notes by Crawford recovered from BKA investigative files.
71. Tabulated hourly rainfall figures for Luqa, November and December 1988; Maltese Met Office monthly returns for November 1988, police reference DC/1616, Crown Production 442. Maltese Met Office monthly returns for December 1988, police reference DC/1621, Crown Production 447.
72. Scottish Home and Health Department Guidelines on the Conduct of Identification Parades, May 1982.

73. Bell statement S2632AR.
74. Manifest for Swissair flight 649, police reference DC/1652, Crown Production 1037.

6 The Suitcase

1. Heathrow central terminal plan, police reference PZ/161, Crown Production 1108.
2. John Bedford statement S1548A; Amarjit Sidhu statement S967G; Tarlochan Sahota statement S2139.
3. AAIB report 2/90, police reference AZ/45, Crown Production 138; RAE report April 1990, police reference AZ/37, Crown Production 186; RAE report October 1999, police reference PT/93, Crown Production 187.
4. Bogomira Erac precognition interview 31 August 1999.
5. KIK computer printout, police reference DW/135, Crown Production 1060.
6. Coding station 206 worksheet, police reference DW/136, Crown Production 1061.
7. Report by Jürgen Fuhl, 2 July 1990.
8. Roland O'Neill statement S3003C
9. Marquise, Richard, *Scotbom: Evidence and the Lockerbie Investigations. New York: Algora, 2006.*
10. Holiday Inn registration card, police reference DC/972, Crown Production 723.
11. Doreen Caruana trial evidence, 29 June 2000, trial transcript p.4671.
12. Vincent Vassallo's diary, police reference DC/1149, Crown Production 531.
13. Abdelbaset Shukri defence precognition statement; Abdusalam El-Ghawi defence precognition statements.
14. Lamin Fhimah defence precognition statement.
15. Saviour Fenech, Director of Civil Aviation, Malta, statement, 26 April 1990.
16. Benjamin Demps letter to Saviour Fenech, 31 August 1987.
17. Ramp progress sheet, police reference DC/625, Crown Production 939; Load plan, police reference DC/626, Crown Production 940.
18. Gerald Camilleri statement S4910.
19. Michael Darmanin statement S5019A.
20. FAA report of Kurt Maier interview, 5 January 1989, police reference CS/320, Crown Production 1791.
21. Report by Denis Phipps in the case of Air Malta v Granada Television, 29 March 1993.
22. DI Watson McAteer statement S3743A.

23. Frankfurt Airport incident log, police reference DW/29, Crown Production 1077.
24. DC Derek Henderson statement S452AH; DS James Russell statement S942AI.
25. Blum, William, *Killing Hope: US Military and CIA Interventions since World War II*, Monroe: Commo Courage Press, 2004.
26. Bedford statement S1548.
27. Bedford statement S1548A.
28. Bedford statement S1548.
29. Sulkash Kamboj trial evidence, 25 August 2000, trial transcript p.6407.
30. Bedford statement S1548.
31. Heathrow air traffic control flight arrivals log, police reference PZ/415, Crown Production 236.
32. DC Derek Henderson, evidence to the Lockerbie Fatal Accident Inquiry, Day 27.
33. Bedford statements S1548, S1548A, S1548D and S1548F.
34. Kamboj statement S1963; Sidhu statement S967G; Sahota statement S2139.
35. Photographs of trial loading, PZ/336, Crown Production 1114.
36. Photographs of trial loadings police reference PZ/345, Crown Production 1228.
37. Terence Crabtree trial evidence, 24 August 2000, trial transcript p.6305 to 6306.
38. Bedford trial evidence, 25 August 2000, trial transcript p.6473 to 6474.
39. Joint Minute Number 15, 5 December 2000, trial transcript p.9305 to 9306.
40. Peter Walker trial evidence, 24 August 2000, trial transcript p.6272 to 6273.
41. Defence Forensic report by Gordon McMillen, Forensic Science Service of Northern Ireland, 20 April 2000.
42. AAIB report 2/90, police reference AZ/45, Crown Production 138.
43. *Washington Times*, 30 December 1988; *Daily Express*, 31 December 1988.
44. *Sunday Times*, 16 April 16th 1989.
45. FBI FD302 report of interview of Nazir Jaafar.
46. FBI FD302 report of interview of relative of Khaled Jaafar.
47. Jaafar relative interview, *The Maltese Double Cross* documentary.
48. Yasmin Siddique statement S3135B.
49. Nazir Jaafar interview, *Mail on Sunday*, 1 January 1989.
50. BKA memo, 21 April 1989, BKA investigative file VI-7.
51. Pan Am leaflet found in luggage of Khaled Jaafar, police reference PD1043, Crown Production 197.

52. List of Jaafar baggage contents attached to memo from FBI West German Legal Attaché David Barham to BKA, 7 April 1989.
53. LPS forms 329 and 330, police references DP/28 and DP/28, Crown Production 288.
54. Allen Feraday examination notes, 29 March 1990, police reference PT/91, Crown Production 1498.
55. Henderson statement S452CC.
56. DI William Williamson SCCRC interview, 5 January 2006.
57. John Irving, Metropolitan Police Senior Identification Officer, statement S4587.
58. Nazir Jaafar FBI interview, 4 January 1989, police reference D2146.
59. Hassan El-Salheli BKA interview, 26 April 1989.
60. Hassan El-Salheli BKA interview, police reference D7705.
61. Abdel Salame BKA interview, 5 July 1989.
62. Hassan El-Salheli BKA interview, 26 April 1989.
63. Hassan El-Salheli trial evidence, 9 November 2000, trial transcript p.8105.
64. Ali Jadallah BKA interview, 13 June 1989, police reference S4378A.
65. Hassan El-Salheli BKA interview, 26 April 1989.
66. Ghannam BKA interview, police reference S4695.
67. Ghannam BKA interview, 25 April 1989, police reference D4093.
68. Hassan El-Salheli BKA interview, 26 April 1989.
69. Naim Ali Ghannam BKA interview, police reference S4695.
70. Bilal Dib BKA interview, 27 July 1989; Charif Makke BKA interview, 5 July 1989; Yassar Hamdan BKA interview, 2 October 1989.
71. Abdallah Morue BKA interview, police reference S4671.
72. Telephone number found among Khaled Jaafar's possessions, police reference PD/1043, Crown Production 197.
73. Khaled Graupnerspath BKA interview, police reference S4519.
74. Morue BKA interview, police reference S4671.
75. Translation of BKA memo, 15 February 1989.

7 The Fantasist

1. CIA cable, 10 August 1988, police reference DE/84, Crown Production 804.
2. CIA cable, 11 August 1988, police reference DE/85, Crown Production 805.
3. CIA cable, 15 September 1988.
4. CIA cable of 1 May 1989 reported that Giaka had been paid $1,000 per month since September 1988.

5. CIA cable, 15 September 1988.
6. CIA cable, 13 October 1988, police reference DE/90, Crown Production 810.
7. CIA cable, 7 October 1988.
8. CIA cable, 11 October 1988, police reference DE/88, Crown Production 808.
9. CIA cable, 12 October 1988.
10. CIA cable, 11 November 1988, police reference DE/91, Crown Production 811.
11. CIA cable, 10 November 1988.
12. CIA cable, 19 January 1989, police reference DE/97, Crown Production 817.
13. CIA cable, 20 January 1989, police reference DE/99, Crown Production 819.
14. CIA cable, 23 January 1989, police reference DE/102, Crown Production 822.
15. CIA cable, 28 February 1989, police reference DE/103, Crown Production 823.
16. CIA cable, 12 April 1989, police reference DE/104, Crown Production 824.
17. CIA cable, 18 April 1989.
18. CIA cable, 10 May 1989, police reference DE/105, Crown Production 825.
19. CIA cable, 1 September 1989, police reference DE/108, Crown Production 828.
20. CIA cable, 8 September 1989.
21. CIA cable, 30 August 1989, police reference DE/107, Crown Production 827.
22. CIA cable, 6 September 1989.
23. CIA cable, 17 October 1989.
24. CIA cable, 26 October 1989.
25. CIA cable, 18 November 1989.
26. CIA cable, 15 December 1989; CIA cable, 18 December 1989.
27. CIA cable, 14 February 1990.
28. CIA cable, 13 June 1990.
29. CIA cable, 12 December 1990.
30. CIA cable, 10 July 1991.
31. CIA cable, 11 July 1991.
32. CIA cable, 13 July 1991.
33. Report of FBI interview, 14 July 1991, police reference DE/121, Crown Production 1486.
34. DCI Harry Bell statement S2632BV.
35. Report of FBI interviews, 8 August 1991.

36. FBI interviews, 27 July to 1 August 1991, police reference DE120, Crown Production 1485.
37. Marquise, *Scotbom*.
38. Majid Giaka police statement, 2 and 3 August 1991, police reference DP/394, Crown Production 856.
39. Marquise, *Scotbom*.
40. Bell statement S2632BV.
41. Lamin Fhimah defence precognition statement; Lamin Fhimah diary, police reference DC1148, Crown Production 517.
42. *The Herald*, 12 November 2006.
43. Marquise defence precognition statement.
44. Marquise, *Scotbom*.
45. *USA Today*, 16 October 1990.
46. Associated Press, 2 May 1990.
47. Associated Press, 16 October 1990.

8 The Experts

1. R v Ward [1993] 1 WLR 619, 96 Cr App Rep 1.
2. May Inquiry interim and final reports.
3. Allen Feraday evidence to the IRA Gibraltar shootings inquest, 1988.
4. Dr Michael Scott report on the McNamee case.
5. Appeal judgment in the case of Gilbert McNamee, 17 December 1998.
6. Allen Feraday trial evidence in the case of R v Berry.
7. Report by Dr John Wyatt for the appeal of John Berry.
8. Appeal judgment in the case of John Berry, 28 September 1993.
9. Allen Feraday trial evidence in the case of R v Assali.
10. Report by Michael Moyes in the case of Hassan Assali.
11. CCRC Statement of Reasons in the case of Hassan Assali.
12. Confidential memo cited in BBC Scotland *Frontline* documentary *Silence over Lockerbie*.
13. Hal Hendershot defence precognition statement.
14. FBI memo, 8 May 1989.
15. Dr Thomas Hayes examination notes, police reference PT/90, Crown Production 1497.
16. RARDE joint forensic report section 6.2.2.
17. David Keyes letter to BKA, 17 July 1989.
18. Hayes examination notes, police reference PT/90, Crown Production 1497.
19. DCS James Gilchrist letter to Feraday, 19 February 1990.
20. Hayes examination notes, police reference PT/90, Crown Production 1497.

21. John Irving, Metropolitan Police Senior Identification Officer, statement S4587.
22. Memorandum from DC Brian McManus to DS Robert Goulding, 3 April 1990.
23. Fax from Feraday to Gilchrist, 9 April 1991.
24. Henderson letter to Marshall, 11 November 1991.
25. Henderson letter to Hayes and Feraday, 12 March 1990.
26. Entwistle SCCRC interview, 24 June 2005.
27. Paul Boyle, New England Laminates statement S5577.
28. Allan Worroll statement S5586.
29. Correspondence between Feraday and Henderson, 8 July 1991, police reference M2736.
30. Report by Dr John Douse, police reference PT/84, Crown Production 1496.
31. RARDE joint forensic report, Section 2.3.
32. Report by DCI Bell on April 1989 explosive tests 1 to 5 at Indian Head, police reference D4198.
33. Hayes notes 26 January 1989, police reference PT/90, Crown Production 1497.
34. Defence Forensic report by Gordon McMillen, Forensic Science Service of Northern Ireland, 20 April 2000.
35. Memorandum by DC McManus, 18 August 1989.
36. Hayes and Feraday draft forensic report, 15 November 1990, police reference PT/90, Crown Production 1497.
37. RARDE joint forensic report section 4.3.1.
38. Feraday memo, 8 August 1989.
39. RARDE joint forensic report, Section 5, and photos 158 and 197.
40. Hayes notes, police reference PT/90, Crown Production 1497.
41. Miura Crown Precognition statement; Toshiba sales figures.
42. Feraday memo to Orr, 3 February 1989.
43. Phillips statement S3492B.
44. Entwistle statement S450F.
45. Hayes notes, police reference PT/90, Crown Production 1497.
46. RARDE joint forensic report section 6.
47. Gilchrist trial evidence, 9 May 2000, trial transcript pp.107 to 112.
48. Hayes notes, 12 May 1989, police reference PT/90, Crown Production 1497.
49. Hayes trial evidence, 7 June 2000, trial transcript pp.2871 to 2872.
50. Report by K. Hughes, Document Evidence Ltd, 1 July 2009.
51. Hayes notes, 12 May 1989, police reference PT/90, Crown Production 1497.
52. Hayes notes, 12 May 1989, police reference PT/90, Crown Production 1497.

451

53. Feraday Crown precognition statement, 30 March 2000.
54. Feraday interview with the Scottish Criminal Cases Review Commission, 7 March 2006.
55. RARDE joint forensic report section 5.1.3.
56. Hayes trial evidence, 6 June 2000, trial transcript p.2484.
57. Hayes notes, 12 May 1989, police reference PT/90, Crown Production 1497.
58. LPS form 305, police reference DP/28, Crown Production 288.
59. Feraday interview with the Scottish Criminal Cases Review Commission, 7 March 2006.
60. Williamson statement S872BS.
61. Feraday memo to Williamson, 15 September 1989, police reference DP/137, Crown Production 333.
62. Feraday Crown precognition statement, 2 December 1999.
63. Hayes trial evidence, 7 June 2000, trial transcript pp.2681 to 2684.
64. Entwistle memo, 3 April 1990, police reference D8925.
65. Williamson statement S872BS.
66. Marquise, *Scotbom*.
67. Translation of Helge Tepp memo from BKA files.
68. Commission Rogatoire to the Swiss Central Authority from the US Department of Justice, 18 October 1990.
69. Marquise, *Scotbom*.
70. Henderson statement S4710J; Marquise Crown precognition statement, 10 December 1999.
71. Thurman Crown precognition statement, 11 January 2000.
72. *Tegenlicht: Lockerbie Revisited*, Dutch TV documentary 2009.
73. Henderson statement S4710J.
74. Feraday Crown precogntion statement, 2 December 1999.
75. Williamson Crown precognition statement, 17 November 1999.
76. Orkin Crown precognition statement, 10 January 2000.
77. Orkin Crown precognition statement, 10 January 2000.
78. Orkin Crown precognition statement, 15 September 1999.
79. Orkin Crown precognition statement, 10 January 2000.
80. Stuart Henderson statement S4710J.
81. Orkin Crown precognition statement, 10 January 2000.
82. Thurman Grand Jury testimony, 9 October 1991, police reference number CS93, Crown Production 1743.
83. Thurman Crown precognition statement, 11 January 2000.
84. Hayes examination notes pages 42 and 42a, police reference PT/90, Crown Production 1497.
85. Entwistle statement S450U (handwritten version).
86. DI George Brown statement S4458G.

87. Bell statement S2632C (original version); Armstrong statement S2667H (original version).
88. Entwistle SCCRC interview, 24 June 2005; Brown SCCRC interview, 26 September 2005.
89. Hayes SCCRC interview, 8 March 2006.
90. Hayes letter to Marshall, 13 September 1990.
91. Hayes letter to Marshall, 23 August 1990.
92. Hayes SCCRC interview, 8 March 2006.
93. Feraday SCCRC interview, 7 March 2006; Feraday examination notes, police reference PT/91, Crown Production 1498.
94. BKA memo 24 April 1989.
95. Hayes SCCRC interview, 6 March 2006.
96. Notebook of DC William Grant, police reference AZ/68, Crown Production 124.
97. DC James Barclay statement S453B.
98. Barclay trial evidence, 8 May 2000, trial transcript p.690.
99. BKA photos of Khreesat barometric bomb, police reference DW/189, Crown Production 1668.
100. LPS form 1, police reference DP/28, Crown Production 288.
101. Dexstar log for item PF/546.
102. Dexstar log for item PH/930.
103. LPS forms, police reference DP/28, Crown Production 288.
104. Feraday examination notes, 29 March 1990, police reference PT/91, Crown Production 1498.
105. LPS forms, police reference DP/28, Crown Production 288.
106. LPS forms, police reference DP/28, Crown Production 288.
107. Crown Office letter to Taylor & Kelly Solicitors, 1 September 2008.

9 Target Libya

1. Woodward, *Veil*.
2. Melvin Goodman interview in *The Power of Nightmares*, BBC documentary series, Episode 1, broadcast 20 October 2004.
3. Sterling, Claire, *The Terror Network*. New York: Holt, Rinehart and Winston, 1981.
4. Martin, David and Walcott, John, *Best Laid Plans: The Inside Story of America's War against Terrorism*. New York: Harper & Row, 1988.
5. Perry, Mark, *Eclipse: The Last Days of the CIA*. New York: William Morrow & Co., 1992.
6. Yallop, David, *To the Ends of the Earth: The Hunt for the Jackal*. London: Jonathan Cape, 1993.
7. 'Target Qaddafi', Seymour Hersh, *New York Times Magazine*, 22 February 1987.

8. Woodward, *Veil*; Martin and Walcott, *Best Laid Plans*.
9. Martin and Walcott, *Best Laid Plans*.
10. Woodward, *Veil*.
11. Yallop, *To the Ends of the Earth*.
12. Woodward, *Veil*.
13. Martin and Walcott, *Best Laid Plans*.
14. Yallop, *To the Ends of the Earth*.
15. 'Target Qaddafi', *New York Times Magazine*, 22 February 1987.
16. BBC online, 2 December 1997.
17. BBC online, 13 November 2001.
18. Stasi papers contained within BKA Lockerbie investigation files; ZDF *Frontal* documentary, 25 August 1998; 'The La Belle Disco Bombing: Ten Years Later', John Goetz, article in *Covert Action Quarterly*, number 56, spring 1996.
19. Ostrovsky, Victor, *The Other Side of Deception*. New York: Harper Collins, 1994.
20. Channel 4 *Dispatches* two-part documentary, *Murder in St James's*, 1997.
21. Andrew, Christopher, *Defence of the Realm: The Authorized History of MI5*. London: Allen Lane, 2009.
22. *Washington Post*, 5 October 1986.
23. *Washington Post*, 2 October 1986.
24. Martin and Walcott, *Best Laid Plans*.
25. Vincent Cannnistraro evidence in the trial of Oliver North, April 1989; *Final Report of the Independent Counsel for Iran/Contra Matters*, 4 August 1993; Cannistraro Federal Grand Jury testimony in the case of Duane Clarridge, August 1991.
26. Biography provided to the Senate Democratic Policy Committee Hearing: *National Security Implications of Disclosing the Identity of an Intelligence Operative*, 24 October 2003.
27. Cannistraro interview for American Radio Works documentary *Shadow over Lockerbie*.
28. Marquise, *Scotbom*.
29. *Washington Post*, 21 November 1990.
30. *New York Times*, 10 October 1990.
31. *Washington Post*, 21 November 1990.
32. *Independent*, 19 December 1990.
33. Reuters, 3 June 1991.
34. *New York Times*, 21 November 1990.
35. Cohen, Daniel and Cohen, Susan, *Pan Am 103: The Bombing, the Betrayals and a Bereaved Family's Search for Justice*. New York: New American Library, 2000.
36. *The Interfor Report*.
37. *Observer*, 25 November 1989; CNN report, 21 December 1990; CBS

60 Minutes, 20 December 1992; *New York Magazine*, 31 August 1992; *Washington Journalism Review*, September 1992.
38. Gerald Shargel deposition.
39. Jacobo Finkielstain video deposition.
40. Tam Dalyell MP, interview with author; Todd Leventhal, letter to Tam Dalyell MP, 28 April 1995.
41. Letter from Michael O'Brien, US Embassy, London, to UK press with enclosures, 9 May 1995; press release with enclosures issued by Scottish Crown Office, 10 May 1995.
42. Press release with enclosures issued by British High Commission, Canberra, 16 May 1995.
43. Fax from First Secretary (Information and Internal), British High Commission, Canberra to Foreign and Commonwealth Office, Drugs, International Crime and Terrorism Department, 25 May 1995.
44. *Guardian*, 13 May 1995.
45. FBI memo cited in motion to dismiss criminal charges against Juval Aviv.
46. *Wall Street Journal*, 18 December 1995.
47. Martin Kenney affidavit for Aviv fraud case.

10 HMP Zeist

1. Identity parade report police reference DN/33, Crown Production 1324.
2. Scottish Home and Health Department Guidelines on the Conduct of Identification Parades, May 1982.
3. Mario Busuttil defence precognition statement.
4. Police video of identity parade.
5. Busuttil statement, S5725.
6. *Focus* magazine article, Police Reference DC/1626, Crown Production 451.
7. Marquise, *Scotbom*.
8. Letter from Lord Advocate Andrew Hardie QC to Sir Teddy Taylor MP, 21 December 1999.
9. FSANI letter to Alastair Duff, 10 December 1999.
10. AAIB report on examination of baggage container, police reference AZ/11, Crown Production 137.
11. RARDE joint forensic report, Sections 2.2.1 and 10.2; AAIB report 2/90, police reference AZ/45, Crown Production 138.
12. Note of defence meeting with FSANI experts, 20 December 1999.
13. Note of defence meeting with Gordon McMillen, 3 February 2000.
14. Memo by Paul Phillips, 9 March 2000.
15. Note of defence team meeting, 7 March 2000.
16. Defence forensic report by McMillen, 20 April 2000.

17. Letter from MacKechnie to Eversheds, 27 March 2000.
18. MacKechnie letter to Professor Salim al-Hassani, 27 March 2000.
19. Report by Professor al-Hassani and Stephen Burley of Capcis, 10 April 2000; Note of defence meeting with Capcis experts, 17 May 2000.
20. John Beckett QC SCCRC interview, 14 August 2006.
21. Tony Gauci statement S4677T.
22. Tony Gauci defence precognition statement.
23. Tony Gauci statement, 14 September 1989, S4677E.
24. Paul Gauci defence precognition statement.
25. DC John Crawford statement S609V.
26. Paul Gauci defence precognition statement.
27. Vincent Vassallo defence precognition statement.
28. Marwan Khreesat defence precognition statement.
29. Notice under the terms of Section 67 of the Criminal Procedure (Scotland) Act 1995, 26 November 1999.
30. Section 67 notice, 29 April 2000.
31. Memo by Fiscal Depute Mirian Watson, 1 July 2000, police reference D12017.
32. *Sunday Times*, 20 December 2009.

11 Trial and Error

1. Report of UN Observer Professor Hans Köchler, 3 February 2001.
2. Dr Thomas Hayes trial evidence, 6 June 2000, trial transcript p.2473.
3. Hayes trial evidence, 6 June 2000, trial transcript p.2537.
4. Hayes trial evidence, 6 June 2000, trial transcript p.2708.
5. Hayes trial evidence, 6 June 2000, trial transcript p.2737.
6. Hayes trial evidence, 6 June 2000, trial transcript p.2627.
7. Hayes trial evidence, 6 June 2000, trial transcript pp.2577 to 2597.
8. Hayes trial evidence, 7 June 2000, trial transcript p.2781.
9. Professor Christopher Peel trial evidence, 2 June 2000, trial transcript pp.1912 to 2064; Dr Ian Cullis trial evidence, 31 May 2000, trial transcript p.1696 to 1722; Christopher Protheroe trial evidence, 25 May 2000, trial transcript pp.1297 to 1336.
10. Hayes trial evidence, 6 June 2000, trial transcript pp.2343 to 2344.
11. Hayes trial evidence, 6 June 2000, trial transcript p.2627.
12. Hayes trial evidence, 6 June 2000, trial transcript pp.2631 to 2633.
13. AVE4041 baggage schedule by DC Derek Henderson, police reference DP/515.
14. RARDE joint forensic report section 4.3.1.
15. RARDE draft joint report, 15 November 1990, contained within Hayes's examination notes, police reference PT/90, Crown Production 1497.
16. Hayes trial evidence, 7 June 2000, trial transcript pp.2646 to 2662.

17. Allen Feraday trial evidence, 15 June 2000, trial transcript pp.3329 to 3336.
18. Feraday trial evidence, 15 June 2000, trial transcript pp.3316 to 3325.
19. Feraday trial evidence, 15 June 2000, trial transcript pp.3360 to 3364.
20. RARDE joint forensic report section 6.2.1.
21. Feraday trial evidence, 15 June 2000, trial transcript pp.3337 to 3339.
22. Lumpert trial evidence, 28 June 2000, trial transcript p.4434.
23. Bollier trial evidence, 22 June 2000, trial transcript pp.4079 to 4082.
24. Bollier trial evidence, 22 June 2000, trial transcript pp.4196 to 4198.
25. Bollier trial evidence, 23 June 2000, trial transcript p.4245.
26. Bollier trial evidence, 23 June 2000, trial transcript p.4267.
27. Wenzel trial evidence, 27 June 2000, trial transcript pp.4302 to 4303.
28. Wenzel trial evidence, 27 June 2000, trial transcript pp.4347 to 4348.
29. Wenzel trial evidence, 27 June 2000, trial transcript pp.4363 to 4369.
30. Wenzel trial evidence, 27 June 2000, trial transcript pp.4371 to 4373.
31. Wenzel trial evidence, 27 June 2000, trial transcript pp.4377 to 4379.
32. Miura trial evidence, 18 July 2000, trial transcript pp.5416 to 5418.
33. Miura Crown precognition statement.
34. Tony Gauci trial evidence, 11 July 2000, trial transcript p.4753.
35. Tony Gauci trial evidence, 11 July 2000, trial transcript pp.4739 to 4741.
36. Tony Gauci statement S4677Q.
37. Tony Gauci defence precognition statement.
38. Tony Gauci trial evidence, 11 July 2000, trial transcript pp.4774 to 4778.
39. Tony Gauci trial evidence, 11 July 2000, trial transcript p.4779.
40. John Beckett QC SCCRC interview, 14 August 2006.
41. Tony Gauci trial evidence, 11 July 2000, trial transcript p.4782.
42. Tony Gauci trial evidence, 11 July 2000, trial transcript pp.4797 to 4813.
43. Tony Gauci trial evidence, 11 July 2000, trial transcript p.4789.
44. Tony Gauci trial evidence, 11 July 2000, trial transcript p.4791.
45. Tony Gauci trial evidence, 11 July 2000, trial transcript p.4803.
46. Tony Gauci trial evidence, 11 July 2000, trial transcript p.4821.
47. John Beckett QC SCCRC interview, 14 August 2006; Alastair Duff SCCRC interview, 29 September 2006; Bill Taylor QC SCCRC interview, 6 October 2006.
48. Tony Gauci trial evidence, 11 July 2000, trial transcript pp.4823 to 4829.
49. Stauton defence precognition statement.
50. Norman McFadyen letter to Eddie MacKechnie, 2 January 2000.
51. Bill Taylor QC, 22 August 2000, trial transcript pp.6087 to 6091.

52. The Lord Advocate Colin Boyd QC, 22 August 2000, trial transcript pp.6093 to 6101.
53. Non-disclosure agreement, June 2000.
54. Partially unredacted CIA cables, 25 August 2000 version, Crown Productions 804 to 828.
55. Richard Keen QC, 25 August 2000, trial transcript p.6522.
56. Alastair Campbell QC, 28 September 2000, trial transcript pp.7104 to 7107.
57. Keen, 29 August 2000, trial transcript pp.6596 to 6610.
58. The Lord Advocate, 21 September 2000, trial transcript pp.6695 to 6700.
59. CIA cables released by Crown, 20 and 21 September 2000.
60. Taylor, 21 September 2000, trial transcript p.6723.
61. Majid Giaka trial evidence, 26 September 2000, trial transcript p.6880.
62. Giaka trial evidence, 27 September 2000, trial transcript pp.6979 to 6986.
63. Giaka trial evidence, 28 September 2000, trial transcript p.7059.
64. Joachim Koscha trial evidence, 20 July 2000, trial transcript p.5684; Andreas Schreiner trial evidence, 20 July 2000, trial transcript p.5722; Mehmet Candar trial evidence, 20 July 2000, trial transcript p.5775.
65. Gunther Kasteleiner trial evidence, 21 July 2000, trial transcript p.5828; Schreiner trial evidence, 20 July 2000, trial transcript pp.5743 to 5744; Joint Minute Number 10, 27 July 2000, trial transcript p.6042.
66. Koscha trial evidence, 20 July 2000, trial transcript pp.5654 to 5690.
67. Koscha trial evidence, 20 July 2000, trial transcript pp.5694 to 5705.
68. Naomi Saunders trial evidence, 25 July 2000, trial transcript pp.5999 to 6019.
69. Oliver Koch trial evidence, 25 July 2000, trial transcript pp.5928 to 5944.
70. Wilfred Borg trial evidence, 14 July 2000, trial transcript pp.5106 to 5108.
71. Borg trial evidence, 14 July 2000, trial transcript p.5039.
72. John Bedford trial evidence, 25 August 2000, trial transcript pp.6461 to 6465.
73. Terence Crabtree trial evidence, 24 August 2000, trial transcript pp.6304 to 6306.
74. Taylor final submissions, 29 January 2001, trial transcript pp.9768 to 9770.
75. Yasmin Siddique trial evidence, 10 November 2000, trial transcript pp.8190 to 8205.
76. Hassan El-Salheli trial evidence, 8 and 9 November 2000, trial transcript pp.7994 to 8165.

77. The Lord Advocate, 9 October 2000, trial transcript pp.7765 to 7766.
78. The Lord Advocate, 17 October 2000, trial transcript pp.7862 to 7864.
79. Trial transcript, 23 October 2000, pp.7886 to 7889.
80. Trial transcript, 31 October 2000, p.7914.
81. Yasmin Siddique trial evidence, 10 November 2000, trial transcript p.8193.
82. FBI FD302 report of interview with Marwan Khreesat.
83. Defence precognition statements of Miroslava Goben and four other PFLP-GC witnesses, 25 and 26 October 2000.
84. Rabbieh defence precognition statement.
85. Letter from Crown Office to defence team, 31 October 2000.
86. BKA report, 11 November 1988, police reference CS/207, Crown Production 1677.
87. Letter from Crown Office to defence team, 4 November 2000.
88. Defence notes on Almari diary and adopted country passport.
89. Note of meeting by Eddie MacKechnie.
90. Draft declaration by Eddie MacKechnie, 13 December 2000.
91. Letter from Crown Office to defence team, 2 November 2000.
92. Trial transcript, 8 January 2001, pp.9327 to 9365.
93. Mohamed Abu Talb trial evidence, 10, 14 and 15 November 2000, trial transcript pp.8220 to 8549.
94. Gunilla Bluhn trial evidence, 15 November 2000, trial transcript pp.8550 to 8554.
95. Joint Minute Number 11, 27 July 2000, trial transcript pp.6043 to 6049.
96. Richard Keen QC, 20 November 2000, trial transcript p.8975.
97. Richard Keen QC, 28 November 2000, trial transcript pp.9006 to 9107.
98. Trial transcript, 29 November 2000, pp.9148 to 9149.
99. Defence team position document, 16 November 2000.
100. Major Joseph Mifsud trial evidence, 5 December 2000, trial transcript pp.9187 to 9231.
101. Edward Marshman trial evidence, 8 January 2001, trial transcript pp.9240 to 9304.
102. Lawrence Whittaker trial evidence, 5 December 2000, trial transcript pp.9329 to 9435.
103. McAteer statement S3743A.
104. Alastair Campbell QC final submissions, 10 January 2001, trial transcript p.9504.
105. Bill Taylor QC final submissions, 11, 12, 16, 17 and 18 January 2001, trial transcript pp.9534 to 10136.
106. Trial Court judgment, 31 January 2001.

107. Report of UN Observer Professor Hans Köchler, 3 February 2001.
108. Trial Court judgment, 31 January 2001.

12 The Bar-L

1. The High Court of Justiciary (Proceedings in the Netherlands) (United Nations) Order 1998, para. 14.
2. *Daily Mirror*, 11 September 2001.
3. Bedford trial evidence, 25 August 2000, trial transcript pp.6473 to 6474.
4. George Thomson, undated statement.
5. Transcript of conversation between Thomson and Tony Gauci, 29 December 2001.
6. Letter by Alastair Duff to Norman McFadyen, 29 January 2002.
7. Letter by McFadyen to Duff, 30 January 2002.
8. Dr Gianella Curran precognition statement, 23 January 2002.
9. Tarcisio Mifsud precognition statement, 28 January 2002; Charles Tabone precognition statement, 28 January 2002.
10. James Busuttil precognition statement, 28 January 2002.
11. Duff memo, 28 January 2002.
12. Note by Davd Burns QC, 1 February 2002; note by John Beckett, 1 February 2002.
13. Baer, Robert, *See No Evil: The True Story of a Ground Soldier in the CIA's War on Terrorism*. New York: Crown, 2002.
14. Note of meetings with Baer, 9 and 10 February 2002.
15. Sulkash Kamboj statement S1963D.
16. Appeal Court judgment, 14 March 2002.
17. *News of the World*, 16 November 2003.
18. *The Herald*, 11 June 2002.
19. High Court of Justiciary, sentencing judgment 24 November 2003.
20. John Ashton memo to Eddie MacKechnie, 9 November 2002.
21. SCCRC Statement of Reasons, Chapter 5.
22. *Sunday Times*, 23 October 2005.
23. Beckett SCCRC interview, 14 August 2006.
24. Beckett biography, Faculty of Advocates website.
25. Bill Taylor QC SCCRC interview, 6 October 2006.
26. Beckett SCCRC interview, 14 August 2006.
27. *The Scotsman*, 31 January 2006.

13 The Truth Emerges

1. SCCRC Statement of Reasons, para. 18.204.
2. SCCRC Statement of Reasons, para. 21.90.

3. Tony Gauci trial evidence, 11 July 2000, trial transcript p.4739.
4. Gauci trial evidence, 11 July 2000, trial transcript p.4740.
5. SCCRC Statement of Reasons, para. 24.66.
6. SCCRC Statement of Reasons, para. 24.68.
7. SCCRC press release, 28 June 2007.
8. Gauci defence precognition statement, 8 October 1999.
9. Gauci Crown precognition statement, 25 August 1999.
10. SCCRC Statement of Reasons, para. 24.108.
11. SCCRC Statement of Reasons, para. 22.64
12. SCCRC Statement of Reasons, para. 22.31.
13. Tony Gauci SCCRC interview, 2 and 3 August 2006.
14. Paul Gauci SCCRC interview, 2 and 3 August 2006.
15. SCCRC Statement of Reasons, para. 22.67.
16. Tony Gauci SCCRC interview, 2 and 3 August 2006.
17. SCCRC Statement of Reasons, para. 22.73.
18. SCCRC Statement of Reasons, para. 22.84.
19. DCI Harry Bell diary extract, 28 September 1989.
20. Bell memo to DCS James Gilchrist, 21 February 1991.
21. Bell memo to Gilchrist, 14 June 1991.
22. Strathclyde police report, 10 June 1999.
23. SCCRC Statement of Reasons, para. 17.12.
24. Tony Gauci Crown precognition statement, 18 March and 25 August 1999.
25. Impact Assessment Anthony Gauci Paul Gauci, 12 January 2001.
26. Anthony and Paul Gauci Reward/Compensation Payments, undated report.
27. SIO Thomas McCulloch letter to US Embassy in The Hague, 7 February 2001.
28. SIO McCulloch letter to US Department of Justice, 19 April 2002.
29. Tony Gauci SCCRC interview, 2 and 3 August 2006.
30. Paul Gauci SCCRC interview, 2 and 3 August 2006.
31. DCI Bell SCCRC interview, 25 and 26 July 2006.
32. Tony Gauci trial evidence, 11 July 2000, trial transcript p.4752.
33. Gauci trial evidence, 11 July 2000, trial transcript p.4753.
34. SCCRC Statement of Reasons, para. 23.59.
35. Tony Gauci SCCRC interview, 2 and 3 August 2006.
36. SCCRC Statement of Reasons, para. 23.64.
37. SCCRC Statement of Reasons, para. 25.1 to 25.8.
38. Police action A11783 log print obtained by SCCRC.
39. SCCRC Statement of Reasons, para. 17.34 to 17.59.
40. SCCRC Statement of Reasons, para. 26.14.
41. SCCRC Statement of Reasons, para. 26.18.
42. SCCRC Statement of Reasons, para. 26.20.

43. SCCRC Statement of Reasons, para. 26.22.
44. SCCRC Statement of Reasons, para. 26.25.
45. SCCRC Statement of Reasons: Chapter 8, appendix 26; Chapter 11, appendix 19; Chapter 23, appendices 3, 4 and 5.
46. Bell SCCRC interview, 25 to 26 July 2006.
47. Translation of Jean Collin interview, 15 January 1991, police reference DM/137, Crown Production 1589.
48. Memo from SIO Stuart Henderson to all LICC staff, 25 February 1991, police reference D7351.
49. SCCRC Statement of Reasons, para. 8.112 and 8.113.
50. SCCRC Statement of Reasons, para. 8.117.
51. SCCRC Statement of Reasons, para. 8.119.
52. SCCRC Statement of Reasons, para. 8.123.
53. DI William Williamson SCCRC interview, 13 April 2006.
54. Kenneth Steiner Crown precognition statement, 6 June 2000.
55. Translation of Collin interview, 15 January 1991, police reference DM/137, Crown Production 1589.
56. Memo from SIO Henderson to all LICC staff, 25 February 1991, police reference D7351.
57. Classified fax to Joint Intelligence Group, 29 August 1990.
58. SCCRC Statement of Reasons, Chapter 15.
59. Steiner Crown precognition statement, 6 June 2000; Clemens Crown precognition statement, 10 January 2000.
60. Strathclyde police report, 10 June 1999.
61. Tony Gauci trial evidence, 11 July 2000, trial transcript p.4779.
62. Tony Gauci SCCRC interview, 2 and 3 August 2006.
63. Paul Gauci SCCRC interview, 2 and 3 August 2006.
64. Dr Thomas Hayes trial evidence, 7 June 2000, trial transcript pp.2681 to 2684.
65. Memo by DC Callum Entwistle, 3 April 1990 police reference D8925.
66. Allen Feraday Crown precognition statement, 2 December 1999.
67. Feraday Crown precognition statement, 30 March 2000.
68. Report by FSS scientist John Lowe, 18 October 2006.
69. SCCRC Statement of Reasons, paras. 4.51 to 4.56.
70. RARDE joint forensic report, photograph 330.
71. Report by Professor Tim Valentine, 19 December 2008.
72. Report by Professor Steve Clark, 18 December 2008.
73. Photospread 14 September 1989, police reference DC/114, Crown Production 426, Tony Gauci trial 11 July 2000, trial transcript p.4758.
74. Tony Kelly notes of inspection of photospreads, 17 and 18 September 2008.
75. Report of Professor David Canter, November 2006.

76. Tony Gauci statement S4677R; Bell statement S2632AR.
77. Supt. Godfrey Scicluna statement S5262D.
78. Bell statement S2632AR.
79. Tony Gauci statement S4677R.
80. Bell trial evidence, 12 July 2000, trial transcript p.4883.
81. Scicluna statement S5262D.
82. Bell SCCRC interview, 25 and 26 July 2006; Scicluna SCCRC interview, 1 December 2004.
83. David Wright statement S5114.
84. Report by Professor Valentine, 19 December 2008.
85. Tony Gauci trial evidence, 11 July 2000, trial transcript p.4754.
86. Report by BSB Forensic, February 2009.
87. Trial Court Opinion, para. 39.
88. Ramp progress sheet, police reference DC/625, Crown Production 939; Load plan, police reference DC/626, Crown Production 940.
89. Wilfred Borg trial evidence, 14 July 2000, trial transcript p.5039.
90. Crown final submission, 11 January 2001, trial transcript pp.9503 to 9504.
91. Trial Court Opinion, para. 38.
92. Borg trial evidence, 14 July 2000, trial transcript p.5039.
93. Gerald Camilleri statement, S4910; Darmanin statement S5019A.
94. Draft grounds of appeal, 12 December 2008, section 3.4.1.
95. Michael Darmanin statement S5019B.
96. Camilleri statement S4910; David Burns QC, response to Appeal Court, 16 March 2009.
97. Draft grounds of appeal, 31 July 2009, section 3.4.1.
98. Trial Court Opinion, para. 23.
99. Trial Court Opinion, para. 25.
100. AVE4041 baggage schedule by DC Derek Henderson, police reference DP/515.
101. 'Interline Passengers London Heathrow', schedule prepared by DC Henderson.
102. Photographs of trial loading, police reference PZ/336, Crown Production 1114; photographs of trial loadings, police reference PZ/345, Crown Production 1228.
103. AVE4041 baggage schedule by DC Henderson, police reference DP/515.
104. Heathrow air traffic control flight arrivals log, police reference PZ415, Crown Production 236.
105. 'Interline Passengers London Heathrow', schedule prepared by DC Henderson.
106. AVE4041 baggage schedule by DC Henderson, police reference DP/515.

107. Note of meeting between John Beckett and Procurator Fiscal Depute Alyson Forbes, 8 October 1999.
108. Draft grounds of appeal, 12 December 2008, section 3.4.2.
109. Beckett, response to Appeal Court, 15 March 2009.
110. Draft grounds of appeal, 31 July 2009, section 3.4.2.
111. Rabbieh defence precognition statement.
112. Radi BKA interview, 16 August 1989.
113. BKA memo, 14 June 1989.
114. German Federal Prosecutor's indictment of Hafez Dalkamoni and Abdel Fattah Ghadanfar, 19 January 1990.
115. BKA memo, 10 November 1988.
116. Bassam Radi judicial interview, 22 November 1990; Majed Abbas BKA interview, 25 April 1989.
117. Ahmad al-Ahmad BKA interview, 24 January 1990.
118. Hussein Ali Allam BKA interview, 31 May 1989.
119. Al-Ahmad BKA interview, 25 April 1989.
120. Moussa Abou-Tannoura BKA interview, 23 May 1989.
121. BKA memo, 27 July 1989.
122. Naim Ali Ghannam BKA interviews, 30 June 1989 and 23 August 1989.
123. Younis BKA interview, 14 August 1989.
124. Draft grounds of appeal, 12 December 1988, section 4.1.1.
125. Ramzi Diab BKA interview, 27 October 1988.
126. Angelika Berner judicial interview, 24 January 1990; German Hoch BKA interview, 8 May 1989.
127. Goben memorandum.
128. Draft grounds of appeal, 12 December 1988, section 4.1.2.
129. Marwan Khreesat defence precognition statement.
130. Draft grounds of appeal, 12 December 1988, section 4.1.3.
131. Beckett, response to Appeal Court, 15 March 2009.
132. Report by Dr Roger King, December 2007.
133. Report by Dr Roger King, 2 July 2008.
134. RARDE joint forensic report, section 8.
135. Report by Dr Roger King, 2 July 2008.
136. Entwistle statement, S450X.
137. FSANI letter to defence team, 10 December 1999.
138. Draft grounds of appeal, 12 December 2008, section 3.5.2.
139. Draft grounds of appeal, 12 December 2008, section 3.5.1.
140. Beckett, response to Appeal Court, 15 March 2009.
141. Draft grounds of appeal, 31 July 2009, section 3.5.2.

14 A Death Sentence

1. Crown Office letter to Taylor and Kelly.

2. Advocate General submission to High Court of Justiciary, 20 December 2007.
3. Posting by Professor Robert Black QC on lockerbiecase.blogspot.com, 26 October 2008.
4. High Court interlocutor, 15 October 2008.
5. BBC TV News, 29 May 2007.
6. BBC News website, 29 May 2007.
7. Acting Permanent Representatives of the UK and US, joint letter to the UN Secretary General, 24 August 1998.
8. First Minister emergency statement to the Scottish Parliament, 7 June 2007.
9. Judgment 14 November 2008.
10. *Treaty between the Government of the United Kingdom of Great Britain and Northern Ireland and the Great Socialist People's Libyan Arab Jamahiriya on the Transfer of Prisoners*, 17 November 2008.
11. Letter of application for compassionate release, 24 July 2009.
12. Report by Governor Malcolm McLennan for Scottish Executive in response to application for compassionate release, 5 August 2009.
13. Scottish Parole Board response to compassionate release application.
14. Report by Dr Andrew Fraser in response to compassionate release application, 10 August 2009.
15. RARDE joint forensic report, section 7.2.1; Feraday trial evidence, 13 June 2000, trial transcript p.3172.
16. RARDE joint forensic report, section 7.1.1; Feraday trial evidence, 13 June 2000, trial transcript p.3139.
17. Report by Dr David Johnson, 6 March 1992, police reference DP/510.
18. Dr Rosemary Wilkinson, statement S5579A.
19. Memo by David Burns QC to Alex Prentice, 30 March 2000.
20. Letter from Gordon McMillen to Alastair Duff, 7 April 2000.
21. Dr Dennis Ryder fax to McGrigor Donald solicitors, 31 May 2009.
22. Urs Bonfadelli precognition statement, 30 March 2000; Urs Bonfadelli trial evidence, 16 June 2000, trial transcript pp.3402 to 3443.
23. Urs Bonfadelli trial evidence, 16 June 2000, trial transcript page 3413.
24. Note of John Ashton telephone conversation with Urs Bonfadelli, 23 October 2008; Urs Bonfadelli affidavit, 1 April 2009.
25. Report of Dr Jess Cawley, 11 May 2009.
26. Report of Dr Chris McArdle.
27. RARDE documents PT/82 and PT/88.
28. BBC News, 12 August 2009.
29. *The Herald*, 15 August 2009.
30. BBC News website, 19 August 2009.

31. SCCRC Statement of Reasons, section 18.204.
32. Statement by Justice Secretary Kenny MacAskill, 20 August 2009.

15 The Real Story of Lockerbie

1. Paul Gauci statement S4689D.
2. Paul Gauci defence precognition statement.
3. Tony Gauci statement S4677A.
4. Tony Gauci statement S4677R.
5. Paul Gauci SCCRC interview, 2 and 3 August 2006.
6. Tony Gauci SCCRC interview, 2 and 3 August 2006.
7. Tony Gauci trial evidence, 11 July 2000, trial transcript p.4753.
8. DCI Harry Bell diary extract, 28 September 1989.
9. Bell memo to DCS James Gilchrist, 21 February 1991; DCI Bell memo to Deputy SIO Gilchrist, 14 June 1991.
10. Strathclyde police report, 10 June 1999.
11. SIO Thomas McCulloch letter to US Department of Justice, 19 April 2002.
12. Report by Dr Roger King, 31 July 2009.
13. Gerald Camilleri statement S4910; Michael Darmanin statement S5019A.
14. DI Watson McAteer statement S3743A.
15. Yasmin Siddique statement S3135B.
16. Goben memorandum; Rabbieh defence precognition statement.
17. AVE4041 baggage schedule by DC Henderson, police reference DP/515.
18. *Tegenlicht: Lockerbie Revisited*, Dutch TV documentary 2009.
19. Marquise, *Scotbom*.
20. Declassified CIA cable, 13 December 1990.
21. 'Target Qaddafi', Seymour Hersh, *New York Times Magazine*, 22 February 1987; Stasi papers contained within BKA Lockerbie investigation files; ZDF *Frontal* documentary, 25 August 1998.
22. John Orkin Crown precognition statement, 10 January 2000; Orkin Crown precognition statement, 15 September 1999.
23. Richard Sherrow FBI FD302 statement, police reference D6518.
24. Kenneth Steiner Crown precognition statement, 15 September 1999.
25. Record of destruction, 8 September 1989, police reference DP/77, Crown Production 258.
26. SCCRC Statement of Reasons, para. 8.112 and 8.113.
27. Marwan Khreesat defence precognition statement, 22 June 2000.
28. Goben memorandum.
29. Baer, *See No Evil*.
30. FBI FD302 report of interview with Marwan Khreesat.

31. US State Department's Office of Diplomatic Security security digest, 2 December 1988.
32. Allen Feraday fax to Bell, 23 June 1989.
33. Gobel report, 26 May 1989, police reference CS/279, Crown Production 1712.
34. *The Interfor Report*; *The Maltese Double Cross* documentary; 'The Untold Story of Pan Am 103', *Time* magazine, 27 April 1992.
35. Tiny Rowland statement, 14 August 1994.

Appendix 1: The Police Statements of Tony Gauci

1. Tony Gauci statement S4677.
2. Tony Gauci statement S4677B.
3. Tony Gauci statement S4677D.
4. Report by BSB Forensic, February 2009.
5. Tony Gauci statement S4677C.
6. Tony Gauci statement S4677E.
7. DCI Harry Bell statement S2632AS.
8. Tony Gauci statement S4677F.
9. Bell diary extract, 26 September 1989.
10. Photospread, police reference DC/156, Crown Production 431.
11. BKA memo, 5 January 1990.
12. Tony Gauci statement S4677H.
13. Photospread, police reference DC/156, Crown Production 431.
14. Tony Gauci statement S4677K.
15. Tony Gauci statement S4677O.
16. Tony Gauci statement S4677Q.
17. Tony Gauci statement S4677R.
18. Supt. Godfrey Scicluna statement S5262D.
19. Tony Gauci statement S4677U.
20. Tony Gauci statement S4677.
21. Tony Gauci statement S4677N.
22. Tony Gauci statement S4677F.
23. Tony Gauci statement S4677T.
24. Tony Gauci statement S4677D.
25. Tony Gauci statement S4677E.
26. Tony Gauci statement S4677A.
27. Tony Gauci statement S4677K.
28. Tony Gauci statement S4677M.
29. Tony Gauci statement S4677N.
30. Tony Gauci statement S4677O.
31. DCI Bell statement S2632AE.
32. Tony Gauci statement S4677Q.

33. Tony Gauci statement S4677N.
34. Tony Gauci statement S4677O.
35. Tony Gauci statement S4677.
36. Tony Gauci statement S4677L.
37. Tony Gauci statement S4677Q, original version obtained from Maltese police.
38. Tony Gauci statement S4677Q.
39. Tony Gauci statement S4677.
40. Tony Gauci statement S4677.
41. DC John Crawford statement S609H.
42. Tony Gauci statement S4677A.
43. Tony Gauci statement S4677A.
44. Tony Gauci statement S4677L.
45. Crawford statement S609BF.
46. Tony Gauci statement S4677.
47. Tony Gauci statement S4677C.
48. Tony Gauci statement S4677I.
49. Tony Gauci statement S4677N.
50. Tony Gauci statement S4677.
51. Tony Gauci statement S4677N.
52. Tony Gauci statement S4677O.
53. Tony Gauci statement S4677Q.

Appendix 2: The Primary Suitcase: the Forensic Evidence

1. RARDE joint forensic report, photographs 40 and 41.
2. Photo of trial loading of luggage container, police reference PZ/345, Crown Production 1228.
3. AAIB report 2/90, police reference AZ/45, Crown Production 138; RAE report April 1990, police reference AZ/37, Crown Production 186; RAE report October 1999, police reference PT/93, Crown Production 187.
4. Peter Claiden trial evidence, 30 May 2000, trial transcript p.1601.
5. Photograph from AAIB report 2/90, police reference AZ/45, Crown Production 138.
6. Claiden trial evidence, 30 May 2000, trial transcript pp.1590 to 1591.
7. Crown final submissions by Alastair Campbell QC, 9 January 2001, trial transcript pp.9381 to 9384.
8. Dr Thomas Hayes notes, 26 January 1989, police reference PT/90, Crown Production 1497.
9. RARDE joint forensic report section 4.1.2.
10. Report by DCI Harry Bell on April 1989 explosive tests 1 to 5 at Indian Head, police reference D4198.

11. Report by Bell on July 1989 explosive tests, police reference DP23.
12. Report by Bell on April 1989 explosive tests 1 to 5 at Indian Head, police reference D4198.
13. RARDE joint forensic report, Section 10.2.
14. Draft report by Bell on explosive tests.
15. Allen Feraday memo, 8 August 1989.
16. RARDE photographic log book job register.
17. Christopher Protheroe trial evidence, 25 May 2000, trial transcript p.1302.
18. Professor Christopher Peel trial evidence, 2 June 2000, trial transcript pp.2143 to 2144 and p.2105.
19. Dr Ian Cullis trial evidence, 31 May 2000, trial transcript p.1718.
20. AAIB report 2/90, police reference AZ/45, Crown Production 138.
21. RARDE joint forensic report, Section 5.
22. Draft report by Bell on April 1989 explosive tests 1 to 5 at Indian Head.
23. Report by Bell on July 1989 explosive tests 6 to 9, police reference DP/23.
24. Reports by Feraday on explosive tests 8 and 9 in July 1989 at Indian Head.
25. Report by Bell on July 1989 explosive tests 6 to 9, police reference DP/23.
26. Reports by Feraday on explosive tests 6 and 7 in July 1989 at Atlantic City.
27. Report by Dr Roger King, December 2007.
28. RARDE joint forensic report section 5.
29. Feraday trial evidence, 15 June 2000, trial transcript p.3339.
30. Feraday Crown precognition statement, 30 March 2000.
31. Dr Roger King report, December 2007.
32. King report, 2 July 2008.
33. King report, 2 July 2008.
34. King report, September 2009.
35. King report, 31 July 2009.

Appendix 3: The Frankfurt Documents

1. Report by Jürgen Fuhl, 2 July 1990.
2. Ralf Schaefer BKA statement, 9 March 1999, and deposition in Pan Am civil trial, 17 January 1992.
3. Report by Denis Phipps in the case of Air Malta v Granada Television, 29 March 1993.
4. Report by Jürgen Fuhl, 2 July 1990.
5. Phipps report in the case of Air Malta v Granada Television, 29 March 1993.
6. DI Watson McAteer statement S3743A.

7. Interline writer's record, sheet 164, police reference DW128, Crown Production 1092.
8. Coding station worksheets, police reference DW136, Crown Production 1061.
9. Frankfurt Airport incident log, police reference DW29, Crown Production 1077.
10. Coding station 207 worksheet, police reference DW136, Crown Production 1061.
11. Roland O'Neill statement S3003.
12. Pan Am claim baggage claim form questionnaire completed by John Hubbard, police reference DG/24, Crown Production 1105.
13. Fuhl report, 2 July 1990.
14. Hubbard statement S3028A.
15. Pan Am operations bulletin 17 July 1988, police reference DG/25, Crown Production 1058.
16. AVE4041 baggage schedule by DC Derek Henderson, police reference DP/515; Fuhl report, 2 July 1990.
17. X-ray duty report by Kurt Maier, police reference DW/26, Crown Production 1076.
18. Kilinc Tuzcu BKA interview, police reference S2583G.
19. Tuzcu Crown precognition statement.
20. Maier FAA interview 5 January 1989, police reference CS/320, Crown Production 1791; deposition in Pan Am civil trial 1 November 1989.
21. FAA report of Tuzcu interview, 6 January 1989.
22. X-ray duty report by Maier.
23. AVE4041 baggage schedule by DC Henderson, police reference DP/515.
24. FAA report of Kurt Maier interview, 5 January 1989.

Appendix 4: Justice Delayed

1. Crown Office letter to Taylor and Kelly, 13 July 2007.
2. Crown Office letter to Taylor and Kelly, 21 August 2007.
3. Dumfries and Galloway Police letter to Taylor and Kelly, 6 November 2009.
4. Dumfries and Galloway Police letter to Taylor and Kelly, 26 November 2009.
5. Taylor and Kelly letter to High Court of Justiciary, 3 December 2007.
6. Crown answers to petition for access to forensic materials, 20 February 2009.
7. Taylor and Kelly letter to Crown Office, 11 April 2008.
8. Crown Office letter to Taylor and Kelly, 23 May 2008.
9. Petition and specification, 23 October 2008.
10. Crown Office letter to Taylor and Kelly, 12 December 2008.

11. Taylor and Kelly letter to Crown Office, 20 January 2009.
12. Crown Office letter to Taylor and Kelly, 8 June 2009.
13. Crown Office letter to Taylor and Kelly 30 January 2009.
14. Petition and specification, 25 November 2008.
15. Note of meeting, 27 January 2009.
16. Crown Office letter to Taylor and Kelly, 22 May 2009.
17. Crown Office letter to Taylor and Kelly, 25 May 2009.
18. Crown Office letter to Taylor and Kelly, 15 June 2009.
19. Crown Office letter to Taylor and Kelly, 24 June 2009.

Afterword

1. White House press conference, 29 June 2011.
2. *Daily Telegraph*, 27 July 2011.
3. Bell-Pottinger email to journalists, with subject line 'Al-Megrahi Prostate Cancer Comment', 27 July 2011.
4. *Scotland on Sunday*, 14 August 2011.
5. Translated extract of *Expressen* article on Aljazeera English website, 23 February 2011.
6. *Sunday Times*, 27 February 2011.
7. Text accompanying Younes statement, BBC News website, 25 February 2011; BBC interview with General Abdel Fattah Younes Al-Abidi, BBC News website, 25 February 2011.
8. Article by John Simpson, BBC News website, 25 February 2011.
9. *The Times*, 5 September 2009; *english.peopledaily.com.cn/200402/25/ eng20040225_135801.shtml*.
10. *Al-Arabiya*, 18 April 2011.
11. *Daily Telegraph*, 30 March 2011.
12. *The Herald*, 2 April 2011.
13. *quilliamfoundation.org/noman-benotman*.
14. *The Herald*, 1 April 2011 and 8 April 2011.
15. *Daily Telegraph*, 27 June 2011.
16. *Daily Telegraph*, 31 March 2011.
17. *Daily Telegraph*, 2 April 2011
18. Jack Straw interview, BBC Radio 4 Today programme, 31 March 2011.
19. *Daily Telegraph*, 30 March 2011.
20. Reuters TV report 3 October 2011; Reuters online article 3 October 2011.
21. ITV Tonight programme, broadcast 19 January 2012.
22. Ashur Shamis interview, *Spotlight on Terror*, vol. 3, issue 3, 24 March 2005.
23. *The Times*, 20 January 2012.
24. *The Times*, 29 August 2011.

Glossary and Abbreviations

AAIB. Air Accidents Investigation Branch, an agency of the UK Government's Department for Transport, responsible for investigating aviation accidents in the UK.

ABH. Aviation Business Holdings, the company established by Abdelbaset's associate Badri Hassan, in which Abdelbaset became a partner. It rented office space in Zurich from Mebo.

Advocate. The Scottish equivalent of an English barrister or US trial lawyer.

Advocate Depute. Senior Crown advocate, responsible for presenting the prosecution evidence in High Court cases.

ANO. The Abu Nidal Organisation, more formally known as the Fatah Revolutionary Council, a Palestinian rejectionist group established by Sabri Khalil al-Banna, whose *nom de guerre* was Abu Nidal.

Autumn Leaves. The BKA operation against the PFLP-GC, which resulted in the arrests of Hafez Dalkamoni, Marwan Khreesat, Abdel Ghadanfar and others on 26 October 1988. Known as *Herbstlaub* in German.

BATF. The Bureau of Alcohol, Tobacco, Firearms and Explosives, a US Federal law enforcement agency, whose responsibilities include investigation and prevention of the illegal use of firearms and explosives.

BKA. Bundeskriminalamt, the German federal police, equivalent to the US FBI.

BND. Bundesnachrichtendienst, the German foreign intelligence service.

CIA. The Central Intelligence Agency, the US Government's main civilian foreign intelligence agency.

Crown. The formal name for the prosecution side in UK criminal cases.

Crown Office. The Scottish Government's criminal prosecution service. Its full title is the Crown Office and Procurator Fiscal Service.

DERA. The Defence Evaluation and Research Agency. One of RARDE's and the RAE's successor organisations.

DGSE. Direction Générale de la Sécurité Extérieure, the French foreign intelligence service.

DSTL. Defence Science and Technology Laboratory, DERA's successor organisation.

ESO. The External Security Organisation, the JSO's external section.

FAA. The Federal Aviation Administration, the US Government agency responsible for civilian aviation.

FAG. Flughafen Frankfurt/Main AG, the company that ran Frankfurt Airport.

FBI. The Federal Bureau of Investigation, the United States' main criminal investigation agency.

FSANI. The Forensic Science Agency of Northern Ireland, an agency of the Northern Irish Government, which was instructed by the defence in the Lockerbie trial.

IED. Improvised explosive device, a homemade bomb.

JSO. The Jamahiriya Security Organisation, Libya's intelligence and security service.

KIK. The computer controlling Frankfurt Airport's automated baggage transit system.

KM180. Air Malta flight from Malta to Frankfurt on the morning of the Lockerbie bombing. Abdelbaset and Lamin Fhimah were alleged to have placed the primary suitcase on this flight after labelling it for New York via PA103.

LAA. Libyan Arab Airlines, Libya's flag carrier.

LICC. The Lockerbie Incident Control Centre, the headquarters of the Scottish police investigation.

Lord Advocate. Scotland's head prosecutor, who is also a Scottish Government minister. Various people held this post during the Lockerbie investigation and trial. The Lord Advocate responsible for the indictments of Abdelbaset and Lamin Fhimah was Lord Fraser of Carmyllie, and the one responsible for their trial Colin Boyd QC.

Mary's House. Clothes shop run by Tony and Paul Gauci in Sliema, Malta, from which the primary suitcase clothing was supposedly bought.

Mebo. The company that made MST-13 timers and supplied them to Libya. Its name derives from the first two letters of the surnames of its founding partners, Erwin Meister and Edwin Bollier.

Medtours. Malta-based travel agency run by Lamin Fhimah and Vincent Vassallo.

MI5. The UK's domestic intelligence service, formally known as the Security Service.

MI6. The UK's foreign intelligence service, formally known as Secret Intelligence Service.

MST-13. Type of electronic timing device, allegedly used in the Lockerbie bomb. They were supposedly produced exclusively for Libya by Mebo.

NSA. The National Security Agency, the US Government's signals intelligence – or electronic eavesdropping – agency.

NSC. The National Security Council, a White House body which advises and assists the US President on national security and foreign policy matters, and the Federal intelligence agencies.

PA103. Pan Am flight 103 from Heathrow to New York and Detroit, which crashed at Lockerbie. The aircraft was a Boeing 747 Clipper, *Maid of the Seas.*

PA103A. PA103's feeder flight from Frankfurt to Heathrow. The aircraft was a Boeing 727.

PFLP-GC. The Popular Front for the Liberation of Palestine – General Command, a rejectionist Palestinian splinter group founded by Ahmed Jibril.

PPSF. Palestinian Popular Struggle Front, another Palestinian rejectionist group, of which Mohamed Abu Talb was a member.

Primary suitcase. The suitcase that contained the Lockerbie bomb.

Procurator Fiscal. Public prosecutor employed by the Crown Office.

PT/35b. Crucial fragment of circuit board, found among the

Lockerbie debris, which supposedly originated from an MST-13 timer.

RAE. The Royal Aircraft Establishment, a Ministry of Defence research agency, which, like the AAIB, was based at Farnborough. It subsequently merged with RARDE to form the Defence Research Establishment, which became the Defence Evaluation and Research Agency and eventually the DSTL.

RARDE. Royal Armaments Research and Development Establishment, a Ministry of Defence body, whose forensics explosives laboratory led the Lockerbie forensic investigation. It was respectively superseded by the Defence Research Establishment, DERA and DSTL.

SAPO. Säkerhetspolisen, the Swedish security police.

SCCRC. The Scottish Criminal Cases Review Commission, the statutory body with responsibility for investigating alleged miscarriages of justice in Scotland, which has the power to refer cases back to the Court of Appeal.

SIO. Senior Investigating Officer. The senior Scottish police officer in charge of major criminal investigations. A number of officers occupied the post of Lockerbie SIO.

SPS. The Scottish Prisons Service.

Stasi. Nickname for the Staatssicherheit, the East German state security service.

People Mentioned in the Text

Abu Elias. Assumed name of PFLP-GC member who evaded arrest during the Autumn Leaves raids. His identity remains unknown.

Abu Talb, Mohamed. Member of the Palestinian Popular Struggle Front, based in Uppsala, Sweden, who was one of the original prime suspects in the Lockerbie case.

Beckett, John. Junior defence counsel for Abdelbaset at his trial and first appeal.

Bell, DCI Harry. Scottish police officer who led the investigation in Malta.

Bollier, Edwin. Partner, along with Erwin Meister, in the Swiss electronics company Mebo, who supplied 20 MST-13 timers to Libya.

Burns QC, David. Defence counsel for Abdelbaset at his trial and first appeal.

Campbell QC, Alastair. The senior Advocate Depute who led the Crown case at the Lockerbie trial.

Dalkamoni, Hafez Kassem. Leader of the PFLP-GC's West German cell. Arrested during the Autumn Leaves raids and subsequently convicted of terrorist offences.

Duff, Alastair. Abdelbaset's original Scottish solicitor, who represented him until 2002.

Feraday, Allen. RARDE forensic expert who, together with Dr Thomas Hayes, was responsible for most of the Lockerbie forensic investigation.

Fhimah, Lamin. Abdelbaset's co-accused, formerly LAA Station Manager in Malta, and co-owner, with Vincent Vassallo, of the Medtours travel agency.

Gauci, Paul. Brother of Tony Gauci.

Gauci, Tony. Shopkeeper of the Mary's House boutique in Sliema, Malta. The Crown's most important witness, he allegedly sold the clothes that ended up in the primary suitcase.

Ghadanfar, Abdel. Senior member of the PFLP-GC's West German cell, he was arrested during the Autumn Leaves raids and was subsequently convicted, with Dalkamoni, of terrorist offences.

Giaka, Majid. Another key Crown witness, he was LAA's Deputy Station Manager in Malta. He became a CIA informant a few months before Lockerbie.

Goben, Mobdi. PFLP-GC member who ran the group's Yugoslavian cell. He evaded arrest following the Autumn Leaves raids and fled to Syria.

Hayes, Dr Thomas. RARDE forensic expert, who, together with Allen Feraday, was responsible for most of the Crown's forensic case.

Henderson, Detective Chief Superintendent Stuart. SIO for most of the key stages of the Lockerbie investigation.

Jaafar, Khaled. Lebanese-American victim of PA103, who flew to Heathrow from Frankfurt on PA103A.

Jibril, Ahmed. Leader of the PFLP-GC.

Keen QC, Richard. Lead defence counsel for Lamin Fhimah.

Kelly, Tony. Solicitor who represented Abdelbaset from 2005.

Khreesat, Marwan. PFLP-GC bomb-maker, who constructed barometric bombs in the West German town of Neuss. He was arrested in the Autumn Leaves raids and released shortly afterwards.

MacKechnie, Eddie. Originally Lamin Fhimah's solicitor. Represented Abdelbaset from 2002 to 2005.

Marquise, Richard. Headed the FBI's Lockerbie investigation.

Orkin, John. Assumed name of CIA technical analyst who first linked PT/35b to the MST-13 timer recovered from Togo by Richard Sherrow.

Scott QC, Maggie. Lead counsel for Abdelbaset at his second appeal.

Sherrow, Richard. BATF agent who investigated the allegedly Libyan-backed coup plot in Togo in September 1986. He returned to the United States with an MST-13 timer, which was supposedly among the arms confiscated from the plotters.

Steiner, Kenneth. Assumed name of CIA agent who gained access to the MST-13 timer allegedly seized from two Libyans in Senegal in February 1988.

Taylor QC, Bill. Lead defence counsel for Abdelbaset at his trial and first appeal.

Thurman, James 'Tom'. The lead FBI forensic examiner assigned to the Lockerbie investigation.

Turnbull QC, Alan. Advocate Depute who, together with Alastair Campbell, presented the Crown case at the Lockerbie trial.

Vassallo, Vincent. Lamin Fhimah's Maltese business partner in the travel agency Medtours.

Index

Note: Arabic names. In accordance with normal convention, Arabic personal names prefixed with al- or el- have been indexed under the main part of the surname, e.g. Abdelbaset al-Megrahi is indexed under Megrahi. However, corporate bodies and places have been indexed under the prefix, e.g. El Al airlines is under El.

Abassi, Ahmed 41, 42, 48
Abassi, Hashem 30, 41-44, 48, 253
Abbas, Majed 337
ABC Television 10, 53, 94, 178, 193, 259
Abdusamad, Ahmed Khalifa (alias of Abdelbaset al-Megrahi) 6, 8, 10, 11, 23, 109-111, 113, 212, 259, 370
Abernethy, Lord 214
ABH (Libyan company) 6, 7, 10, 20-25, 59, 60, 68, 211, 213, 259, 261
Abjed, Ali 293
Abou-Tannoura, Moussa 337, 338
Abu Abid (alias of Nabil Makhzumi) 278
Abu Achmed 61, 77
Abu Ahmed (alias of Bassam Radi) 337
Abu Elias 45, 46, 60, 104, 221, 248-250, 253, 260, 279, 338, 340, 341, 373
Abu Fouad (alias of Mobdi Goben) 33, 44
Abu Hassan 50
Abu Jaber, Mahmoud 184
Abu Jaber, Mohamed 184
Abu Nada, Abdelsalem 89, 80, 225, 252, 253
Abu Nada, Hashem Salem 89, 90, 225, 253

Abu Nidal Organisation (ANO, aka Fatah Revolutionary Council) 35, 61, 77, 90, 115, 179, 254
Abu Sultan, Abnan 256
Abu Talb, Mohamed 47-50, 88-92, 94, 96, 211, 225, 238, 251, 252, 254-256, 258, 278-280, 316, 321, 322, 326, 329, 383, 384, 385
    convicted for 1985 bombings 252, 256
Achille Lauro, hijacking of 179
Aero Leasing and Sales 22
African Airlines 20
African National Congress 197
Afriqiyah Airline 363
Ahmad, Ahmad al- 337-339
Air Accidents Investigations Branch (AAIB) 39, 40, 106, 121, 150, 159, 216, 217, 230, 397-399, 401, 403
Air Egypt 115, 179
Air France 32
Air India Flight AI465 413
Air Malta 5, 8, 83, 108, 110, 111, 114, 116, 117, 227, 245, 261, 262, 331, 370, 414, 417
    Flight KM180 5-8, 108, 109, 113, 116-119, 227, 244-246, 265, 267, 269, 331-333, 368, 369, 371, 374, 412-416, 418, 419

Al-Azziziya Barracks, Tripoli 182
Al-Burkan terrorist group 185, 186
Al Kabir Hotel, Tripoli 60
Al-Hayat newspaper 431
Al-Khadra travel agency 26, 213, 261
Alagi, Mohamed Al- 434
Albright, Madeleine 199
Alert company 268
Ali, Al Haj and Salma 15, 292, 293
Alitalia Flight AZ422 413
Allam, Hussein Ali 125, 126, 337, 339
Almari, Mahmoud 249-251, 279
Amal (Lebanese Shia faction) 18, 122, 126, 337
Amayiri, Mahmoud 184
Amsterdam bombings, 1985 88, 251, 252, 256
Anderson, Jack 53
Andrew, Professor Christopher 186, 187
Annan, Kofi 199, 225
Arab Drilling and Workover Company 102
Arab Lawyers Association 273
Arab League 30
Arafat, Yasser 61
Arebi, Abdelmajid 20, 25-27, 133, 213
Armstrong, Morag 214
Armstrong, DS William 85, 169
Arnold (codename for Stasi handler) 81, 233
Ashek, Mustafa El- 183
Ash-Shirra (Lebanese magazine) 164
Ashton, John 299
Ashur, Mohamed 183
Ashur, Nassr 6, 68, 69, 131
Assad, President (Syria) 189, 427
Assaf, Adnan 126, 127
Assaf, Ali Nasri 126, 127

Assali, Hassan 147, 409
Assih, Colonel 70
Associated Press 365
Austria Airlines, bomb attack on 31
Autumn Leaves operation (Herbst-laub) 31, 36, 37, 42, 44, 45, 49, 88, 89, 104, 124, 127, 171, 189, 210, 222, 247, 248, 251, 258, 279, 337, 338, 340, 341, 369, 373
Avent, Peter 70, 71
Aviation Business Holding Co – see ABH
Aviv, Juval 190-195, 375
Awad 248

Baer, Robert 278, 279, 291, 321, 322, 373
Baird, DCI Jack 57
Balfour, Gordon 210
Bandar, Prince – see Sultan
Bannatyne, Ian 208, 272, 297
Banque Nationale de Paris 278
Barclay, DC James 171
Barlinnie Prison, Glasgow 283-289, 292-295
    'Gadafy's Cafe' unit 283
Bates, Craig 70, 71
BBC Arabic Service 4
BBC Newsnight 409, 430
BBC Panorama 91, 383
BBC Radio 4 433
BBC TV news 94, 330
Beckett, John 200, 209, 210, 239, 272, 277, 335, 336, 339-341, 345
Bedford, John 105, 119-122, 216, 231, 246, 269, 275, 280, 281, 301, 333-336, 369, 374, 395
Bekaa Valley, Lebanon 47, 122, 179
Bell, DCI Harry 43, 46, 85, 93, 95-98, 101, 105, 106, 160, 169,

220, 308, 313, 316, 317, 319, 326, 328, 329, 367, 385, 387, 388, 390, 391, 400, 401, 405-407
Bell-Pottinger PR company 428
Ben Rabha, Mohamed 27
Benghazi, Libya 8, 71, 174
Benin 271
Benotman, Noman 431, 432
Berlin Wall, fall of 82, 233
Berner, Angelika 338, 340
Bernstein, Michael 335
Berry, John 146, 147, 409
Berwick, Jim 35
Biehl, Dana 225
Big Ben (Maltese company) 84
Bin Laden, Osama 428
Birmingham Six 296, 377
Bishari, Ibrahim 10, 11, 18, 61, 140, 243
BKA 29, 31-34, 41-46, 48, 49, 79, 81, 84, 87, 107, 108, 126, 148, 164, 171, 210, 222, 233, 234, 247, 248, 251, 261, 331, 337-339, 379, 381, 413, 414, 418, 429
Black, Professor Robert, QC 197, 348
Blair, Jennifer 299
Blair, Tony 198, 297, 349
Blue Band Motors, Lockerbie 39
BND 29, 30, 34, 81, 371
Bolcar, Keith 424
Bollier, Edwin 7, 22, 59-62, 66-69, 72, 73, 75-82, 95, 96, 227, 232, 233, 258, 264, 270, 320, 355, 357, 359, 371, 372
BomBeat radio-cassette players – *see under* Toshiba
Bonfadelli, Urs 358, 362
Borg, Gaetana 90
Borg, Wilfred 245, 246, 261, 331-333

Botha, Pik 375
Boyd, Colin, QC (Lord Advocate) 214, 239, 240, 247, 251, 269, 348
BP oil company 349
Brennan, John 195
British Airways 32, 121, 414
British Transport Police 38, 57
Brown, DI George 84, 168, 169
BSB Forensic 331, 381
Bundesamt fur Verfassungsschutz 181
Bundeskriminalamt (West German Police) – *see* BKA
Bundesnachrichtendienst (West German Intelligence Service) – *see* BND
Bureau of Alcohol, Tobacco and Firearms (BATF) 65, 70, 71, 167, 372
Burley, Stephen 218
Burns, David, QC 215, 233, 234, 239, 245, 260, 272, 277, 333, 336, 356
Bush, George Jnr (US President) 178
Bush, George Snr (US President) 28, 29, 53, 54, 177, 189, 371
Busuttil, James 277
Busuttil, Sgt Mario 206, 207, 306, 307
Byrne, DS 316

Cadman, Martin 53, 54
Calisti, Mr 320
Calleja, Alexander 85
Cameron, David 432
Cameron, John Taylor, QC – *see* Lord Coulsfield
Camilleri, Gerald 116, 332, 333, 368
Camilleri, Tony 113
Campbell, Alastair, QC 214, 227-

230, 234, 235, 239, 241, 242, 252, 258, 261, 276, 332
Campbell, PC Alistair 38
Candar, Mehmet 244, 412, 414, 416
Cannistraro, Vincent 178, 185, 187-191, 432
Canter, Prof David 300, 325, 328
Capcis 217, 357
Capital Radio 62
Capp (alias of CIA agent) 239
Carlson, Commander David 28
Carmon, Yigal 191
Carruthers Farm 38, 56, 171
Carter, Jimmy (US President) 175
Caruana, Doreen 112
Casey, William 71, 175-178
Cauci, Insp Alphonse 383
Cawley, Dr Jess 359, 360, 362
Central Intelligence Agency – see CIA
Centre for Strategic Studies, Tripoli 18, 19, 22, 211, 259
Chabaan, Imad (alias of Martin Imandi) 48, 253
Chabaan, Jehad 48, 253
Chabaan, Ziad 48
Chad 26, 72, 73, 83, 166, 320
    war with Libya 26, 72, 73, 83
Chanaa, Ali 182, 183
Chanaa, Verana 182
Channel 4 TV Dispatches 185, 186, 192
Channon, Paul 52, 53
Checkpoint Charlie, Berlin 183
Chemical Marketing Company 24, 25
Chornyak, William 44, 45, 260
Chraidi, Yassir 182-184
Chrisswell House – see Greenock Prison
Church of Scotland 297
CIA 24, 34, 56, 60-62, 65, 66,

71-73, 75-77, 80, 81, 128, 129, 132-137, 140-142, 165, 167, 175, 177, 178, 183, 184, 188, 190, 191, 233, 238, 240, 242, 269, 278, 319, 321, 371-373, 375, 376, 432, 434
    offering Gaucis a reward 308-313
    Office of Soviet Affairs 175
    relationship with Majid Giaka 128-142
    searching crash wreckage 56
City of Poros (ship) 35
Claiden, Peter 42, 159-161, 399
Clancy, Ronnie, QC 346, 351, 420, 421, 422
Clark, Professor Steve 300, 325-327, 422
Clemens, Warren 66, 319, 320
Clinton, Bill (US President) 198, 199
Clinton, Hillary 362
CML company 320
Cohen, Daniel and Susan 189
Cohen, Thoedora 190
Collin, Jean Baptiste 73-75, 318-320, 372
compensation for Lockerbie victims 285, 434
Conlon, Gerard 144
Connel, PC David 38
Connor, DSupt Pat 42
Cook, Robin 198
Copenhagen bombings, 1985 88, 91, 251, 252, 256
Costa, Susan 413, 418
Coulsfield, Lord (formerly John Taylor Cameron) 214, 225, 377
Coyle, Patricia 230, 413, 418
Crabtree, Terence 246
Crawford, DC John 93, 95, 96, 98, 100, 101, 219, 220, 236, 391, 392

Credit Suisse bank 21, 27, 223
Criminal Cases Review Commission (CCRC) 147
Crowe, Admiral William 29
Cullen, Lord 245, 276, 281
Cullis, Dr Ian 403
Curran, Dr Gianella 277
Curry, Joseph 336
Cyprus Air flight CY1364 253

Daily Express 122
Daily Mirror 274, 275
Daily Telegraph 432, 433
Dalgleish, DCI Michael 58
Dalkamoni, Hafez Kassem 30-33, 41-45, 48, 60, 88, 89, 171, 221, 222, 248-251, 253, 260, 278, 279, 337-339, 373
Dalyell, Tam 55, 192, 296
Darmanin, Michael 116, 332, 333, 368
Davidson, Jack, QC 215, 244, 333
Davidson, Lord, of Glen Clova 347, 422
Dazza, Mohamed 20, 25, 50, 51
De Marco, Guido (President of Malta) 140, 243
Defence Evaluation and Research Agency (DERA) 397
Defence Intelligence Agency (DIA) 36, 56
Defence Science and Technology Laboratory 424, 425
Degussa Bank 280, 321, 322
Demps, Benjamin 115
Denning, Lord 296, 377
Dexstar store, Lockerbie 39, 43, 55, 63, 64, 160, 162, 163, 172, 231
DGSE (French Intelligence Service) 72-74, 319, 372
Diab, Ramzi (alias of Salah Kwekes) 44, 248, 338, 340, 373

Dib, Bilal 126
Douse, Dr John 152
Drug Enforcement Administration (DEA) 192
Duff, Alastair 12, 200, 201, 204-206, 215, 221, 249, 250, 260, 276-279, 289, 301, 305
Dumfries and Galloway Police 38, 57, 58, 163, 173, 205, 212, 312, 317, 321, 324, 420
   Joint Intelligence Group (JIG) 58, 317
Düsseldorf Airport 260

Eagle Knitwear 101, 391, 392
Early Call operation 178
Eassie, Lord 346
East German Intelligence Service – *see* Stasi
Eddeeb, Judge Azzam 354
Eid, festival of 51
El Al airline 31, 49, 191
   bomb attacks on 31, 49
El Dorado Canyon (US operation) 174
Elias, Abu – *see* Abu Elias
Elletson, Anthony 186
Elliot, Walter 144
Elliott, Ingrid 210
Enemalta energy company 277
Entwistle, DC Callum 150, 160, 164, 168, 169, 344
Erac, Bogomira 107
ESO (Libyan external intelligence agency) 132, 134, 137, 138, 318
Eter, Musbah 182
European Convention of Human Rights 213
Eversheds lawyers 200, 210, 215
explosive tests 105, 120, 121, 154-156, 228, 342, 343, 397, 399, 402, 403, 405, 406, 409
Expressen newspaper 272, 429

Eyadema, Gnassingbe (President of Togo) 65, 70

Fatah Revolutionary Council – *see* Abu Nidal Organisation
FBI 8, 44, 47, 66, 70, 72, 76-78, 87, 95, 105, 109, 122, 139-142, 147-149, 151, 152, 166, 188, 191, 193, 194, 241, 248-251, 267, 282, 308, 313, 319, 327, 330, 340, 367-369, 371, 379, 424
  Quantico Academy 76
Feast of the Immaculate Conception 220, 237, 260, 267
Federal Aviation Authority (FAA) 34-36, 105, 115, 117, 154, 156, 245, 268, 399, 400, 402, 406, 419
Federal Bureau of Investigation – *see* FBI
Federal Deposit Insurance Corporation (FDIC) 192
Feraday, Allen 43, 46, 63-65, 93, 105, 143, 145-147, 149-152, 154-156, 159, 160, 162-164, 166, 167, 170, 172, 215, 227, 231, 232, 291, 301, 323-325, 341-343, 355, 357, 360, 361, 374, 376, 395, 400, 402, 403, 405, 407, 409
Ferranti company 151
Ferrie, Gordon 165
Fhimah, Lamin 3, 5-7, 10, 16, 17, 26, 28, 51, 60, 79, 83, 102, 109, 110-115, 130-133, 138-141, 159, 196, 199, 200, 202-204, 208-211, 213, 215, 227, 236, 240, 258, 261, 262-264, 269, 272, 289, 301, 322, 332, 333, 341, 370, 417, 432
  charged with murder 213
  found not guilty 263, 264
  return to Libya 272

Finkelstein, Jacobo 192
Fletcher, WPC Yvonne, killing of 185, 186, 431, 432
Flower/Rose operation 178
Focus magazine 235, 238, 306, 314
foot-and-mouth disease 276
Forensic Science Agency of Northern Ireland (FSANI) 215, 216, 344, 345, 421
Forensic Science Service (FSS) 301, 324
Fortier, Donald 178, 180
Frankfurt Airport 5-7, 45, 46, 85, 104, 106-108, 116, 117, 119-123, 125, 227, 244-246, 248, 258, 261, 267, 268, 275, 281, 322, 331, 340, 368, 369, 371, 374, 395, 412, 414-419
Frankfurt Airport Company Ltd (FAG) 107, 117, 118, 415
Fraser, Dr Andrew 353
Fraser, Lord, of Carmyllie (Lord Advocate of Scotland) 58, 165, 299
Freedom of Information Act 192, 194
French Intelligence Service – *see* DGSE
French Ministry of Justice 271
Frendo, Alfred 92
Fuhl, Inspector Jürgen 107, 108, 413, 414, 418, 419
Fulton, Ian 215

Gadafy, Colonel Muammar 18, 21, 30, 61, 71, 77, 140, 174-178, 182-188, 197, 199, 272, 349, 364, 427-435
  assassination attempt on 182
  overthrow of regime 427-435
  planning terrorist campaign 177
  seizing power 175, 176
'Gadafy's Cafe', Barlinnie 284

Gamary, Guma el- 428
Gannon, Matthew 56
Garadat, Yassan 35
Gardener (codename for Stasi handler) 81
Gardiner, Nick 346
Gates, Robert 178, 179
Gateside Prison – *see* Greenock Prison
Gauci, Edward 85, 86, 316
Gauci, Paul 86, 87, 92, 93, 96, 98, 99, 156, 219, 220, 236, 238, 276, 309-313, 316, 322, 323, 366-369, 376, 383, 386, 388, 391, 394
    TV football evidence 92, 93, 98, 99, 219, 366, 388
Gauci, Tony 6, 7, 28, 85-103, 104, 108, 143, 156, 159, 162, 163, 168, 204-207, 210, 218-220, 227, 234-238, 260, 263, 265-267, 274-277, 289-291, 299, 300, 304-317, 322, 323, 325-331, 345, 349, 366-369, 373, 376, 377, 379-394, 395, 405, 422-424
    giving evidence at trial 234-238
    identifying Megrahi photo 95, 96-102, 206, 265, 266, 290, 299, 300, 305, 308, 326, 379-394
    discussions of reward for information 220, 308-313, 367, 376
    police statements 379-394
General Electric Company 193
General Electronics Company of Libya 5, 132, 159, 234, 371
George, Dr Alan 215
Gerber (codename for Stasi handler) 81, 233
Gerwel, Jakes 202
Ghadanfar, Abdel Fattah 31-33, 248, 373
Ghannam, Naim Ali 125, 126, 247, 338
Ghawi, Abdusalam El- 115
Gheriani, Essam 428
Ghorbanifar, Manucher 177
Giahour, Ali El- 186, 187
Giaka, Majid 8, 18, 96, 128-142, 227, 238, 240-243, 258, 261, 262, 269, 270, 289, 370, 371, 376
    evidence discredited 242, 243
    incriminating Megrahi 128-131, 139
    requesting fake surgery 133, 134, 241
Gilchrist, Detective Chief Superintendant James 75, 149, 150, 309
Gilchrist, Jamie 289-291, 298, 299
Gilchrist, DC Thomas 63, 161
Gilmour, DI 401
Glasgow Caledonian University 286
Glasgow Royal Infirmary 286
Gobel, Rainer 46
Goben, Miroslava 248, 249, 251, 339
Goben, Mobdi (aka Abu Fouad) 33, 44, 247-251, 337-339, 341, 369, 373
Godman, Dr Norman 54
'Golfer, The' (alias for police officer) 290, 291, 306
Goodman, Melvin 175
Gordon, Superintendant Thomas 315
Gousha, Samir 48
Graf, Axel 118, 416
Graham, Innes 56, 57
Granada TV 117, 414
Grant, DC William 171
Graupnerspath, Khaled 126

Grech, Assistant Commissioner George 97
Grede, Abdullah 293
Greenock Prison (HMP Gateside) 292-299, 303, 353, 354, 363
Chrisswell House 292, 295, 363
Guardian newspaper 192, 428
Guildford Four 144, 170
Gulf of Sidra 180

Habbash, George 30
Habre, Hissen (President of Chad) 72
Hague, William 428
Haider, Jamal 90, 254
Haig, Alexander 175, 176, 178
Hajj pilgrimage to Mecca 28
Hamdan, Yassar 126
Hamilton, Lord 346, 349
Hammet Brothers 391
Hannushi, Captain Ali 16, 17
Hardie, Andrew, QC 212, 214
Harris, Lillian 176
Harris, Paul 62, 72, 80
Harris, Richard 280, 281
Hassan, Badri 6, 7, 14, 16, 20-22, 25, 52, 59, 68
Hassani, Prof Salim Al- 218
Hayes, Dr Thomas 40, 43, 63, 83, 93, 143-145, 148, 149, 151, 154, 159-164, 168-172, 215, 227-231, 291, 301, 323-325, 341, 343, 344, 377, 395, 405, 421
Haynes, DC Stephen 163
Hazzouri, Imad 90, 254
Heathrow Airport, London 1, 2, 5, 7, 39, 46, 104, 108, 116, 117, 119, 121, 122, 151, 154, 210, 217, 231, 246, 253, 269, 275, 276, 280, 322, 331, 333-336, 340, 346, 369, 374, 395, 417
Hein, Hilmar 185, 186
Hellane company 84

Hendershot, Hal 77, 139, 148, 241
Henderson, DC Derek 119, 334-336, 369
Henderson, Detective Superintendant Stuart (SIO) 64, 65, 75, 96, 140, 150, 151, 164-167, 282, 318, 319, 321, 344
Herbstlaub – *see* Autumn Leaves
Hersh, Seymour 182
Hezbollah 30, 122, 123, 126, 127
Hideiry, Dr Hamid al- 203
Higgs, Douglas 143-145
Hijazi (Lebanese businessman) 52, 223
Hill, Paddy Joe 296
Hill, Paul 144
Hilton Hotel, Malta 97
Hinshiri, Ezzadin 6, 21, 22, 52, 60, 66-69, 78, 128, 130, 259
Hoch, German 338, 340
Holiday Inn, Sliema, Malta 102, 112, 114, 330, 370
HOLMES police computer 169, 212, 213, 290, 315
Horton, Gwendoline 160
Hosenball, Mark 122
Hosinski, John 313
House of Commons Scottish Affairs Committee 224
Hubbard, Captain John 336, 417
Human Rights Act 1998 213
Hungarian Trade Development Bank 278
Hussein, Hafez (alias of Hafez Dalkamoni) 249, 250
Hussein, Saddam 189

Iberia airline 32
Flight 888 45
ID Inquiries 215
Idris I, King of Libya 174, 175, 241
Il-Helsien newspaper 94

Imandi, Martin (aka Imad Chabaan) 48-50, 253, 257
Independent newspaper 189
Indosuez Bank 321
Intekam (alias of Abu Talb) 253
Interfor intelligence firm 190, 192, 375
Internal Revenue Service 194
International Air Transport Association (IATA) 17, 414
International Court of Justice 9, 198
International Criminal Court 21
International Judges Association 273
International Society for the Reform of Criminal Law 214
Inverclyde Royal Hospital 350
IRA bombings 143-145, 427, 428
Iran Revolution, 1979 30
Iran Air 28
    Flight 655 28, 31, 47, 60, 189, 278, 373
Iran-Contra affair 177, 188
Iranian intelligence service – *see* Pasadaran
Iranian Revolutionary Guards 30
Iraq invading Kuwait 189
Islam, Saif al- (son of Colonel Gadafy) 21
Israeli Intelligence Service – *see* Mossad
ITV *Tonight* programme 433
Ivory Coast 73

Jaafar, Khaled 55, 122-127, 190, 191, 246, 247, 249, 250, 279, 337-340, 369, 374, 375
Jaafar, Nazir 122, 124, 125
Jackmann, Lothar 183
Jadallah, Ali 125
Jalil, Mustafa Abdel 428-431, 434
Jamahiriya Security Organisation (Libyan Intelligence Service) – *see* JSO
Jelban, Omar 354
JFK Airport, New York 1, 2, 375
Jibril, Ahmed 30, 44, 47, 61, 77, 79, 123, 190, 221, 249-251, 260, 341
Johnson (alias of CIA agent) 239
Johnson, Dr David 356-358, 361, 423
Johnston, David 57, 58, 375
Johnston, Robin 303, 304
Jordanian Intelligence Service – *see* Mukhabarat
JSO (Libyan Intelligence Service) 3, 5, 6, 9, 10, 17-19, 21, 22, 25, 59, 60, 67, 68, 114, 128, 129, 131-137, 174, 183, 211, 213, 241, 259, 261, 264, 370, 371

Kadar, Samir 35
Kadorah, Martin 33, 339
Kamboj, Sulkash 120, 281
Kamp Zeist 201-271, 273, 284, 293, 297, 306, 386
Kassem, Zouheir 337
Keegans, Fr Pat 298
Keen, Richard, QC 209, 217, 226, 228-234, 238, 241, 243, 247, 255, 256, 258, 262, 344, 403
Kelly, Tony 298-301, 303, 304, 322, 327, 331, 333, 334, 341, 354-356, 358-360, 362, 363, 381, 409, 420-425
Kelly, William 35, 36
Kenney, Martin 195
Key Forensic Services 301
Keyes, David 148, 149
KGB (Soviet intelligence service) 128, 184
Khamenei, President Ali 29
Khreesat, Marwan 31-34, 41-46, 48, 53, 60, 63, 88, 104, 159, 171,

221, 223, 248, 253, 260, 279,
338-341, 373, 374
KIK computer baggage system 107,
117, 244, 412
King, Dr Roger 301, 341-344, 368,
407-410, 420, 421
Kingarth, Lord 346
Kirao, Mohamed al- 203
Kirkwood, Lord 276
Klinghoffer, Leon 179
Koca, Yassar 244, 412, 414-416
Koch, Oliver 245, 268
Kochler, Prof Hans 225, 226, 265,
270
Korsgaard, Walter 105, 154, 400-
403
Koscha, Joachim 244, 245, 268
Koussa, Moussa 428, 430, 431, 433
Kuwait invaded by Iraq 189
Kwekes, Salah (aka Ramzi Diab)
44, 248, 338, 339, 373

La Belle nightclub bomb attack,
Berlin 21, 181, 182, 185, 372
Lafico company 114
Lake, Jonathan 214
Langford-Johnson, DS Michael 74
Lariviere, Ronald 57
Lebanese Civil War 126
Lebanese Movement of the Disin-
herited 18
Legwell, Dr Ibrahim 9, 10, 12, 79,
200, 232, 274, 348
Leuenberger, Commissioner 73
Leventhal, Todd 192, 193
L'Express newspaper 74, 188
Libya
discovery of oil 174
Gadafy coup 175
gaining independence 174
history of 174, 175
overthrow of Gadafy regime
427-435

relations with USA 4, 83, 175-
180, 187, 374
UN sanctions against 196, 427
US air-raids on 8, 27, 52, 95,
131, 140, 180-182, 185
US trade sanctions 83
war with Chad 26, 72, 73, 83
Libya Investment Corporation 349
Libyan Anti-Imperialism Centre
432
Libyan Arab Airlines (LAA) 3, 5-8,
11, 14, 15, 17-19, 21, 22, 27, 51,
68, 83, 102, 109, 111-114, 128-
131, 133-135, 138, 139, 141,
200, 211, 227, 270, 370
Flight LN147 109, 113
Libyan Arab Foreign Investment
Company (Lafico) 24
Libyan Commercial Marine Or-
ganisation 13
Libyan Consulate, Glasgow 284,
293, 294, 298
Libyan Cultural Centre 95
Libyan Embassies
East Berlin 181
London 185, 431
Madrid 223
Libyan Intelligence Services – see
ESO and JSO
Libyan Islamic Fighting Group 432
Libyan National Oil Company 102
Libyan National Soap Company 25
Libyan National Transitional Coun-
cil 427-429, 432, 434
Libyan Office of Military Security
72
Libyan People's Bureau 186
Libyan Revolutionary Committees
136, 137
Lochte, Christian 181
Lockerbie 1-5, 8, 10, 28, 34, 36,
38, 42, 43, 46, 47, 54-56, 63,
69, 76, 126, 135, 143, 148, 163,

164, 171, 188, 232, 240, 246, 253, 276, 295, 297, 317, 339, 342, 343, 353, 366, 375, 377, 383, 399, 401, 406, 407, 427-435

Incident Control Centre 317, 401

Longtown store 162, 172

Lonrho 192

Lothian and Borders Police 38, 55, 57, 149

Lufthansa 32, 244
  Flight LH631 413
  Flight LH669 118, 119, 244, 245, 267, 268, 416
  Flight LH1071 107, 244, 267, 413, 418
  Flight LH1452 413
  Flight LH1489 (or 1498) 414

luggage container AVE4041 40, 42, 60, 104-106, 108, 119-121, 143, 154, 160, 216, 217, 230, 232, 246, 268, 275, 280, 333-336, 369, 374, 395-399, 401, 409

luggage container AVN7511 398

Lumpert, Ulrich 66-68, 79, 232, 233, 355, 357, 359, 360

Luqa Airport, Malta 6, 83, 90, 100, 108, 111, 115, 117, 135, 137-139, 141, 179, 227, 245, 260, 262, 269, 280, 281, 288, 322, 331, 333, 346, 368-371, 374, 416

MacAskill, Kenny 282, 350, 352-354, 362, 429

Macfadyen, Lord 276

MacKechnie, Eddie 160, 209, 210, 217, 221, 249-251, 260, 279, 289-292, 298, 305, 322

MacKechnie & Associates 289, 291

MacKinlay, Bill 283, 284

Maclean, Lord Ranald, QC 214, 225, 240, 302, 377

Macleod, DS 41

Macleod, Murdo 209

MacNeil, DI Donald 41

Maghour, Kamal 9, 10, 200, 221, 226, 259, 272, 274

Maguire Seven 144, 170

Mahayoun, Samra 35

Mahmoud, Imad 183

Maid of the Seas (aircraft) 1, 105

Maier, Kurt 117, 245, 268, 418, 419

Mail on Sunday newspaper 276, 410

Makhzumi, Nabil (aka Abu Abid) 278

Makke, Charif 126

Maltese Civil Aviation Authority 99

Mandela, Nelson 197, 198, 273, 287

Manly, Raymond 275, 280

Marine Broadcasting Offences Act 1967 62

Marquise, Richard 76, 77, 109, 140, 142, 164, 165, 188, 282, 369, 371

Marshall, Dr Maurice 150, 170

Marshman, Edward 44, 45, 260, 340

Mary's House clothes shop 6, 7, 28, 85, 91, 93, 94, 97, 99, 100, 102, 163, 228, 262, 275, 291, 307, 329, 344, 368, 371, 389, 405

Marzouk, Mohamed El- 66, 73, 74

Masoud, Abougela 140

May, Sir John 144, 145

McArdle, Dr Chris 359, 360, 362

McAteer, DI Watson 70, 71, 117, 118, 261, 368, 415

McCain, Senator John 427
McCall, Shelagh 299
McColm, DC Thomas 63, 161
McCourts (legal firm) 12, 209, 215
McCreadie, Nan 117, 414, 415
McCue, Jason 427, 428
McCulloch, Det Chief Supt Thomas (SIO) 204, 311, 312
McDonald, Martin 363
McFadyen, Norman 214, 239, 240, 276
McGill, Derek 292
McGrigor Donald (legal firm) 209, 210, 289
McKee, Major Charles 56-58, 120, 191, 253, 334-336, 375
McLennan, Malcolm 353
McManus, DC Brian 163
McMillen, Gordon 215-217, 335, 336, 356, 357
McNair (alias for CIA agent) 239
McNamee, Gilbert 'Danny' 145, 146
Mebo (Swiss company) 5-7, 10, 11, 22, 59, 60, 66-68, 72, 75, 78-81, 93, 95, 165-167, 210, 211, 215, 216, 227, 232-234, 236, 320, 355, 357, 360, 361, 370, 371, 373
Mebo II (radio ship) 61, 62
Mecca 28, 111
Medtours 6, 8, 26, 102, 111, 130, 140, 211, 213, 261
Mega, Marcello 410
Megrahi, Abdelbaset al-
  abandoning appeal 352, 354
  application for compassionate release 352-354, 362
  charged with Lockerbie murders 4, 9, 213
  childhood 13
  diagnosed with cancer 350, 351
  employment at Centre for Strategic Studies 18-20, 22, 259
  employment with LAA 11, 14-16, 68
  found guilty 263, 264
  identified by Tony Gauci 95, 96, 98, 100-102, 218, 219, 305, 308, 326, 379-394
  incriminated by Majid Giaka 128-131, 133, 139, 140
  indictments issued against 196
  involvement with ABH 20-25, 59, 60, 211, 259
  involvement with car importing 52, 223
  involvement with Paris-Dakar rally 19, 25, 50, 51, 110, 111, 113, 211
  marriage to Aisha 15, 16, 23
  opening of trial against 222, 223, 225
  presence in Czechoslovakia 26, 27, 109, 110, 133, 211
  presence in Malta 16, 27, 28, 83, 84, 95, 98, 102, 109-115, 131, 133, 139-141, 211, 212, 219, 227, 235, 261, 370, 371, 373, 387
  relationship with Edwin Bollier 59, 60, 69, 79
  relationship with family 4, 15, 23, 110, 196, 197, 200-202, 207, 284, 297, 298
  relationship with Lamin Fhimah 16, 17, 26, 28, 51, 79, 83, 84, 110-115, 131, 204, 208, 209, 272
  relationship with prison officers 208, 284-287, 292, 294, 295, 297
  return to Libya 363-365
  seconded to JSO 17

Swiss bank account 21, 27, 223, 259

time in Barlinnie Prison 283-289, 292

time in Kamp Zeist Prison 201-271

time in Greenock Prison 292-299, 350-354

use of Abdusamad passport 6, 8, 10, 11, 23, 109, 110, 113, 212, 259, 370

Megrahi, Aisha 4, 11, 15, 16, 23, 24, 110, 196, 197, 200, 201, 207, 263, 282-286, 293, 363, 365

Megrahi, Ali (son of Abdelbaset) 196, 201, 207, 285, 365

Megrahi, Ali (uncle of Abdelbaset) 298

Megrahi, Faris 298

Megrahi, Gaith 297

Megrahi, Ghada 15, 196, 197, 201, 202, 285, 286

Megrahi, Khaled 15, 27, 196, 197, 201, 202, 286, 364

Megrahi, Mohamed (brother of Abdelbaset) 203, 263

Megrahi, Mohamed (son of Abdelbaset) 196, 201, 285, 365

Megrahi, Motasem Billah 200, 202, 207, 365

Megrahi, Nassr 263

Megrahi, Zeinab 15

Mehdi-Nezhad, Feridoun 278

Mehedwi, Fawzi 89

Meister, Erwin 22, 59, 61, 62, 66, 77, 78, 80, 236

Meneme, Colonel 70

Mercieca, Joseph 113

Metropolitan Police 122, 124, 149, 275

Anti-terrorist Branch 122

Meyer, Manfred 185, 186

MI5 (UK domestic intelligence service) 75, 187, 317, 319-321

MI6 (UK foreign intelligence service) 62, 72, 75, 80, 432, 433

Mifsud, Major Joseph 99, 260, 267

Miliband, David 347, 423

Miller, Lindsey 346, 424

Ministry of Defence 38, 39

Miscarriage of Justice Organisation (MOJO) 296

Miska bakery 90, 254

Miura, Yoshihiro 234

Mohamed, Mahmoud 48-50

Mohtashemi, Ali Akbar 47

Montreal Convention 1971 8, 9, 198

Morton, Elaine 187

Morton, Laura 299

Mossad (Israeli Intelligence Service) 30, 47, 184, 190, 191, 193, 194

Motorola 72

Mougrabi, Dalal 48

Mougrabi, Jamila (wife of Abu Talb) 48, 49, 91

Mougrabi, Mahmoud 252, 253, 256, 257

Mougrabi, Mohamed 48-50, 88, 91, 251, 253

Mougrabi, Mustafa 49

Mougrabi, Rashida 48, 253

Moussa, Madgy 90, 254

Moyes, Michael 147

MST-13 timers 7, 65-70, 73, 78, 79, 93, 97, 104, 143, 149, 151, 166, 167, 216, 227, 232, 234, 262, 264, 270, 271, 315, 318, 320, 340, 355, 356, 358, 360, 361, 369, 372, 373

Mukhabarat (Jordanian Intelligence Service) 34

Murray, Chris 308, 313, 367

Murray, Dr Gerard 215
Murtagh, Brian 225, 226
Myers, Geoffrey 280, 281

Nagler, Helmut 185, 186
Nahhal, Khaled 90, 254
Nasser, Gamal (President of Egypt) 175
National Congress 434
National Front for the Salvation of Libya 434
National Security Agency (NSA) 47, 109, 180, 182, 371
National Security Council (NSC) 178-180, 185, 374
National Transitional Council (NTC) 427-429, 432, 434
Network International 215
Neuss, Germany 30-32, 34, 41, 42, 45, 88, 221, 251, 253, 323, 339
New England Laminates 151
New York Times 188, 255
Newcastleton Forest 57
News of the World newspaper 284
Niasse, Ahmed Khalifa 66, 73, 74
Nicaragua 177
Niger 164
Nimmo Smith, Lord 276
9/11 bombings 274
Noble, George 87, 217, 330, 331, 379
Noonan, Karen 413, 418
North, Colonel Oliver 177, 180, 185, 187
Northwest Orient Airline 49

Obama, Barack (US President) 178, 428
Obedi, Abdulati al- 352, 354
O'Brien, Kerry 192
O'Connor, Daniel 253
Office of the Solicitor to the Advocate General 424, 425

Omar, Dullah 375
O'Neill, Roland 416
Organisation of African Unity (OAU) 198, 287
Orkin, John 65, 72, 166, 167
Orr, John (SIO) 43, 57, 64, 159
Osborne, Lord 276
Ostrovsky, Victor 184
Ourfali, Samir 48, 253
Owens, Edward 65, 70

Pacific Southwest Airlines 195
Palestine Liberation Organisation (PLO) 30, 36, 37, 179, 183, 184, 254
Palestinian Popular Struggle Front (PPSF) 47, 48, 50, 88, 257
Palme, Olaf, assassination of 257
Pan Am airline 1, 2, 5, 36, 45, 57, 79, 116, 119, 123, 190, 191, 194, 195, 221, 244, 260, 281, 374, 412, 417-419
Flight PA103 1, 2, 5, 7, 38-58, 61, 76, 78, 104, 108, 119, 120, 173, 240, 271, 275, 279, 340, 375, 400, 406, 413, 417, 419, 427
Flight PA103A 5, 7, 46, 47, 60, 104-108, 116, 119-121, 152, 216, 227, 230, 244, 246, 267, 268, 333-336, 368, 369, 395, 412, 413, 416-418
Flight PA107 417
Flight PA123 417
Flight PA637 417
Flight PA643 413
Panorama TV programme 91, 383
Pappalardo, Victor 22
Paris-Dakar Rally 19, 25, 50, 51, 110, 113, 211
Parkinson, Cecil 53
Pasadaran (Iranian intelligence service) 278

Paton, Lady 346
Peel, Prof Christopher 403
PFLP-GC 29-34, 36, 37, 41-44, 46, 47, 52, 54, 60, 61, 64, 88, 104, 123, 159, 183, 188-190, 211, 222, 225, 247, 248, 249, 253, 255, 257, 258, 278, 279, 315, 321, 323, 337-341, 369, 373-375
Phillips, Paul 210, 216
Phillips, Reginald 159, 160
Phipps, Denis 117, 414, 415
Poindexter, Admiral John 185, 187
Popular Front for the Liberation of Palestine – General Command – *see* PFLP-GC
Prairie Fire operation 181
Prentice, Alex 209, 356
Prentice, Christopher 428
Primark (retailer) 84
'primary suitcase' (*see also* Samsonite) 41, 94, 104-106, 108, 120, 152, 155, 156, 216, 217, 227-231, 246, 269, 280, 333, 334, 336, 342-344, 368, 374, 395-411, 417
Prisoners and Criminal Proceedings (Scotland) Act 1993 352
Protheroe, Christopher 403
Pulitzer Prize 53
PVC Plastics Ltd 84

Quilliam think-tank 432

Rabbieh (alias) 249, 337, 339
Radi, Bassam (aka Abu Ahmed) 337-339
Radio Forth 57
Radio Nordsee International (RNI) 61, 62
Radley, Philip 280
Raghda, Miss (actress) 273
RAI Television 87
Ramadan 51, 293

RARDE 38, 40, 42, 46, 63, 64, 93, 105, 108, 124, 143-152, 154-156, 159, 160, 162-164, 168- 173, 215, 216, 227, 230, 231, 291, 301, 323, 325, 336, 341, 343, 344, 347, 361, 368, 374, 391, 395, 397, 398, 401, 403, 406, 407, 424, 425
    involvement in miscarriages of justice 143-147
Rashid, Said 6, 17, 21, 128, 130-132, 140, 159, 259, 371, 372
Rath, Volker 119
Raufer, Xavier 74
Reagan, Ronald (US President) 29, 71, 174-179, 185, 187, 190, 371, 374
Red Army Faction 234
Refalo, Dr Michael 277, 305, 306
Reid, Philip 95, 139, 241
Repatriation of Prisoners Act 1984 352
Reuters 375, 433
Revell, Oliver 'Buck' 47
reward for information on Lockerbie 142, 220, 308-312, 367, 376
Richardson, Martin 299
Rinne, Judge Christian 34
Robben Island 287
Rogers, Commander William 29
Rome Airport, shootings at 179
Romney, Mitt 429
Ross, Douglas 346
Rowland, Tiny 192, 375
Royal Aeronautical Establishment (RAE) 106, 217, 230, 397, 403
Royal Armaments Research and Development Establishment – *see* RARDE
Rumney Technical College, Cardiff 13
Russell, DS James 119
Ryder, Dr Denis 218, 357

Saber, Mansour El- 66, 73, 74
Sabha (Libya) 7
Sadr, Imam Moussa al- 18
Sahota, Tarlochan 105, 120, 334
Sakerhetspolisen (Swedish Security Police) – see SAPO
Salame, Abdel 125
Salem, Abdel 264, 257
Salem, Hashem 91, 257
Salem, Mohamed 382
Salheli, Hassan El- 124-126, 246, 248, 337-339
Salheli, Souheil El- 124, 125, 248, 337
Salinger, Pierre 10-12, 259, 370
Salmond, Alex 350
Samsonite suitcases 5, 7, 10, 41, 42, 60, 94, 108, 113, 119, 120, 128, 139, 141, 216, 262, 336, 395, 417
SAPO (Swedish Security Police) 49, 90, 91
SAS (Special Air Service) 186
Saunders, Naomi 245
SBS Television, Australia 193
Scharf, Michael 141
Schneider, Owen 41
Schreiner, Andreas 244
Schwanitz, Lieutenant General Wolfgang 81, 82
Scicluna, Inspector (later Superintendant) Godfrey 95, 97, 206, 235, 306, 316, 317, 328, 329, 385, 387
Scotland Act 1998 213
Scotland on Sunday newspaper 428
Scotsman newspaper 302
Scott, John 299
Scott, Maggie, QC 289-291, 298-300, 351, 421, 422
Scott, Dr Michael 146
Scottish Criminal Cases Review Commission (SCCRC) 58, 124, 149, 150, 163, 167, 169, 223, 289, 291, 298, 301-304, 306, 316, 320-322, 325, 326, 329, 341, 346, 347, 358, 363, 367, 403, 420-425
Scottish Parole Board 353
Scottish Prison Service 208, 282, 293, 294, 296, 351-353
Scullion, Paul 299
SDS Group 409
Senegal 66-68, 70, 73-75, 166, 270, 271, 318-321, 371, 372
Senoussi, Abdullah 3, 17, 18, 21, 61, 128, 130, 132, 138
Seraj, Nun 20
Shalgham, Abdul Rahman al- 430, 431
Shamis, Ashur 434
Shargel, Gerald 192, 194
Shatta, Khaled 184
Shaugnessy, James 191
Shebani, Mustafa 102, 110, 111, 113
Sheffield Hallam University 359
Sherif, Dr Ibrahim al- 350, 364
Sherrow, Richard 65, 70, 71, 271, 372
Shukri, Abdulbaset 115
Shultz, George 180
Shurrab, Alaa 254
Siddique, Yasmin 123, 246
Sidhu, Amarjit 105, 120, 334, 336
Simpson, John 431
Slalom shirts 162, 322, 389, 390, 405, 409, 421
Société Bancaire Arabe 249
Soloranta, Mr 35
Sonko, Andre 319
SPECAT intelligence traffic 182
Special Counsel, appointment of 347
Srebrenica massacre 433
Stark, James 180, 187

Stasi (East German Intelligence Service) 62, 73, 78-82, 183, 184, 232-234, 355, 357

Stauton (alias for CIA agent) 239, 242

Steinberger, Dr 81

Steiner (codename for Stasi handler) 81

Steiner, Kenneth (alias for CIA officer) 66, 73, 74, 319, 320

Sterling, Claire 175, 176

Stethem, Robert 179

Stockholm bombings, 1985-86 88, 256

Strathclyde Police 309

Strathclyde University 356

Straw, Jack 433

Sultan, Abnan Abu 256

Sultan, Prince Bandar bin (Saudi Arabia) 197, 202

Summers, Andrea 210

Sunday Telegraph 60

Sunday Times 24, 94, 122, 223, 238, 299, 329, 383, 385, 430

Sutherland, Lord Ranald, QC 214, 215, 225, 256, 262-264, 288, 377

Swessi, Abdulrahman 293

Swire, Dr Jim 263, 295, 296, 433, 434

Swissair, bomb attack on 31

Swiss Federal Police 73, 79

Talb, Mohamed Abu – *see* Abu Talb

Taylor, Bill, QC 200, 201, 209, 225, 226, 236-239, 242, 243, 245-247, 252-254, 256, 262, 267, 272, 274, 276, 280, 281, 289, 299, 301, 305, 333, 344, 355

Taylor, Lord, of Gosforth (Lord Chief Justice) 146

Taylor, Sir Teddy 212

Taylor & Kelly (lawyers) 298, 299

Technical Threat Countermeasures Committee 166

Teesdale Mountain Rescue Team 54

Teicher, Howard 180, 187

Tepp, Helge 165

Thatcher, Margaret 53, 54, 58, 185

Thomson, David 54

Thomson, George 275, 276, 290, 291, 299

Thüring company 67, 80, 232-234, 355, 356, 358-360, 376, 377

Thurman, James 'Tom' 65, 72, 105, 147-150, 160, 165-167

Times of Malta newspaper 93, 219

Times newspaper 431, 434

Togo 65, 66, 70-74, 149, 166, 270, 271, 318, 320, 321, 372

Tony's Bar, Malta 381, 386

Topp, Alan 1

Torca, Il (newspaper) 307

Toshiba radio-cassette players 5, 32, 42-45, 60, 94, 104, 132, 148, 159, 160, 164, 171, 172, 215, 221, 222, 228, 231, 234, 245, 260, 262, 281, 322, 323, 373, 399, 408, 409, 419, 421

Toska, Wafa 91

Tourister suitcase 230

Tripoli Airport 14, 16, 115

Turnbull, Alan, QC 214, 232, 239, 240, 246, 247, 261, 281, 301, 332

Turnbull, Lord 346

Tuzcu, Kilinc 418

TWA airliner, hijacking of 179

UK Department of Transport 34

Umrah pilgrimage 111

UN Security Council 202, 286, 287, 429

    agree compensation for victims 285

resolutions against Libya 8, 141, 198, 199, 225, 377
sanctions against Libya 196, 198, 434
UNESCO 13
University of Benghazi 14, 16
University of Manchester Institute of Science and Technology (UMIST) 217, 356
University of Pennsylvania 14
US Aviation Underwriters 195
US Bureau of Alcohol, Tobacco and Firearms (BATF) 65, 70, 71, 167
US Defense Intelligence Agency (DIA) 36, 56
US Department of Justice 138, 147, 149, 165, 194, 239, 243, 312, 368, 424
US Embassies
  Cyprus 253
  Helsinki 34-37
  London 192
  Malta 128, 137
  The Hague 239, 311
  Tehran 176
US Federal Aviation Authority (FAA) 34-36
US Internal Revenue Service 194
US National Security Agency (NSA) 47, 109, 180
US Naval Explosive Ordnance Disposal Technology Center, Indian Head 105, 120, 399, 402, 406
US State Department 24, 36, 56, 141, 142, 175, 374, 432
  Office of Diplomatic Security 36, 374
US Virgin Islands 193, 194
USA
  air-raids on Libya 8, 27, 52, 71, 95, 131, 140, 180
  relations with Libya 4, 71, 175-180, 187, 374

relations with Syria 189
reward for information on Lockerbie 142, 220, 308-312, 367, 376
shooting down Iran Air flight 28, 29
USAF Military Airlift Command 29
USS Butte 139
USS Sides 28
USS Vincennes 28, 29
UTA airline 21, 164

Valentine, Professor Tim 300, 325-327, 330
Van Atta, Dale 53
Vassallo, Vincent 3, 6, 102, 110, 111, 114, 115, 138, 141, 220, 370
Vienna airport, shootings at 179
Vietnam War 176

Wagenfuhrer, Mr 413
Walker, Gavin 210
Walker, Thomas 413, 418
Wall Street Journal 187, 194
Walla, Colonel 70, 71
Wallace, Ben 224
Wani, Hamid al- 253
War on Terror 274
Ward, Judith 143, 144, 155
Washington Post 53
Washington Times 122
Watergate 53, 179
Watson, Miriam 223
Weinacker, Adolph 413, 418
Weinberger, Caspar 178
Weinrich, Carlos 234
Wenzel (codename for Stasi handler) 81, 233, 234
West Midlands Police 296
Wheatley, Lord 346, 349
Whitehurst, Fred 147

Whittaker, Lawrence 260, 261, 267, 368, 415
Wilkinson, Dr Rosemary 356-358, 361
Williamson, DI William 57, 63-65, 74, 124, 151, 163, 166, 167, 271, 319
Willis, Keith 280, 281
Wilson, Inspector Brian 205
Wilson, Harold 62
Woodward, Bob 179, 187
World Trade Center, bombing of 274
Worroll, Allan 151
Wright, Aileen 299
Wright, David 329, 330
Wyatt, Dr John 146, 409

Yorkie Clothing 85, 86, 89, 90, 93, 168, 169, 227, 228, 254, 291, 322, 405, 408, 409, 421
Younes, Abdel Fattah 430, 431
Younis, Adnan 338

Zadma, Abdusalam 9
Zaki 321
Zatout, Rageb 185, 186
Zomiat, Mohamed 383
Zurich Airport 21, 27
Zwai, Mohamed al- 197, 199, 209
Zwai, Rafiq al- 284, 286